An Introduction

to Ukrainian History

Other works by the same author:

The Economic Factors in the Growth of Russia, Philosophical Library, New York, 1957
Old Ukraine, Its Socio-Economic History prior to 1781, Florham Park Press, Madison, New Jersey, 1963
The Ukrainian Economy, Schevchenko Scientific Society, New York, 1965
An Introduction to Russian History, Philosophical Library, New York, 1967
Ukraine and the European Turmoil, 1917-1919, Schevchenko Scientific Society and the Ukrainian Scientific-Historical Library, New York-Scranton, 1973, (co-authored with M. Stachiv and P. Stercho), 2 volumes
Philosophy in Economic Thought, Florham Park Press, Madison, N.J., 1972, (co-authored with V. Mott)
A History of the Russian Empire, Volume I, *Grand-ducal Vladimir and Moscow*, Philosophical Library, New York, 1973
On the Historical Beginnings of Eastern Slavic Europe, Readings, Shevchenko Scientific Society, New York, 1976, ed. by the author
Philosophical Foundations of Economic Doctrines, Florham Park Press, Florham Park, N.J., 1977 (co-authored with V. Mott), third edition 1981, second edition 1978
An Introduction to Ukrainian History, Vol. I, *Ancient and Kievan-Galician Ukraine-Rus'*, Philosophical Library, New York, 1981

AN INTRODUCTION TO UKRAINIAN HISTORY

Volume II

*The Lithuanian-Rus' Commonwealth,
the Polish Domination and the Cossack-Hetman State*

by Nicholas L. Fr.-Chirovsky
Seton Hall University

Philosophical Library
New York

Chirovsky, Nicholas L., 1919-
  The Lithuanian-Rus' commonwealth, the Polish domination, and the Cossack-Hetman state.

  (An introduction to Ukrainian history / Nicholas L. Chirovsky; v. 2)
  Bibliography: p. 381
  Includes index.
  1. Ukraine—History—1350-1800. I. Title. II. Series:
Chirovsky, Nicholas L., 1919-   . An introduction to Ukrainian history; v. 2.
DK 508.A3C48 vol. 2 [DK508.755] 947'.71048 82-12255
ISBN 0-8022-2407-5

Copyright, 1984, by Philosophical Library, Inc.
200 West 57th Street, New York, N.Y. 10019

All rights reserved

Manufactured in the United States of America

To all those heroic Dissidents who gave their lives defending human rights and the right of all nationalities, submerged by the Soviet Union, to have freedom and national independence.

Map — Ukraine. A Dutch Map, 17th Century

TABLE OF CONTENTS

List of Illustrations — xiii

Preface — xv

Acknowledgments — xix

Part One. *The Lithuanian-Rus' Commonwealth and the Polish Domination*

Chapter One: The formation and growth of the Lithuanian-Rus' Commonwealth — 1
The beginnings of Lithuanian political organization — The decline of the Golden Horde — The absorption of Ukrainian-Rus'ian lands by Lithuania — The struggle against Polish domination — The Polish supremacy — The rise of Cossacks.

Chapter Two: The political structure and the government of the Lithuanian- Rus' Commonwealth — 37
The constitution and the law — The Grand Prince and the territorial princes — The Council of Nobles and the Plenary Parliament — The central and local administration — The judiciary — The military.

Chapter Three: The spiritual and cultural life of Lithuanian-Rus' society — 58
The status of the Orthodox Church and Roman Catholicism — The Church Union of Berest — Education — Literature — Architecture — Painting and carving — Music and theatre — Other arts.

Chapter Four: The social structure of Ukrainian society during the Lithuanian-Polish era — 89
Ethnic and social changes — Social classes — Nobility and clergy — Peasantry — Townspeople — Foreigners — The feudal order — The Cossacks as a social class.

Chapter Five: Extractive industries of the European frontiers — 113
Economic growth — Hunting and fishing — Cattle raising — Agriculture — Mining.

Chapter Six: Industrial growth — 130
    Towns — Trades and crafts — Food-processing, the textile and the leather industries — Paper manufacturing and the printing industry.

Chapter Seven: Commercial process — 145
    Domestic trade — Foreign trade — The trade routes and the import and export items — Finance.

Part Two. *The Ukrainian Cossack-Hetman State*

Chapter Eight: The formation of the Cossack-Hetman State and its political fortunes — 169
    On the eve of the Khmelnytsky Uprising — The National Revolution and building of the Cossack-Hetman State — Political developments and the Agreement of Pereyaslav — From Khmelnytsky to Mazepa — Hetman Ivan Mazepa and the war for liberation — The Hetman state after Mazepa — The Territory of the Zaporozhe Host — The Haidamaky movement — The Russian political take-over.

Chapter Nine: The political structure and the government of the Cossack- Hetman State — 226
    The constitution and the law — The Hetman — The General Council — The Council of Seniors — The central administration — The local administration — The judiciary — The military.

Chapter Ten: The spiritual and cultural life of the Cossack- Hetman era — 252
    The status of the Churches — Education and the sciences — Literature — Architecture — Painting and carving — Music and theatre — Other arts.

Chapter Eleven: The social structure of the Ukrainian Cossack- Hetman society — 288
    Ethnic and social changes — The Cossacks — Nobility and clergy — Peasantry — Townspeople — Foreigners — Eastern and southern frontiers — The colonization of the borderlands.

Chapter Twelve: Growth of the national economy: extractive industries   311
The national economy of Ukraine — Agriculture — Hunting, fishing and cattle-raising — Mining.

Chapter Thirteen: Trades and industries   331
Mercantilism in Ukraine — The city and its economy — Trades and crafts — Textile and leather production — Metallurgy and arms — Chemical industries — Glass and ceramics — Paper industry.

Chapter Fourteen: Commerce and finance   357
Transportation and communication — Domestic commerce — Foreign trade, its development and composition — Foreign trade policies — Money and credit— Public finance.

Bibliography.   381
Index of names.   391

LIST OF ILLUSTRATIONS

	Page
Map — Ukraine, 17th Century	ii & iii
Map — Ukraine. A Dutch Map, 17th Century	viii
Map — Ukraine, 18th Century	xiv
Map — West and North Ukraine, 17th Century	xx & xxi

	Facing Page
Castle in Kamianets-Podilsky (14th Century)	36
Slavic-Greek grammar, Lviv (1591)	88
Koriatko's building in Lviv (16th Century)	88
Hetman Dmytro Baida-Vyshnevetsky (1550-1563)	89
Hetman Petro Konashevych-Sahaidachny (1614-1622)	89
Metropolitan Petro Mohyla (1632-1647)	170
Hetman Bohdan Khmelnytsky (1648-1657)	170
Hetman Ivan Samoilovych (1672-1687)	170
Hetman Petro Doroshenko (1665-1676)	170
Hetman Ivan Mazepa (1687-1709)	171
Hetman Kyrylo Rozumovsky (1750-1764)	171
Holy Trinity Church, erected by the Cossacks in Novoselytsia, 1773-1778	252
Wooden church towers from the 17th and 18th centuries	253
Wooden church in Matkiv, Boykivshchyna (1838)	253
Sahaidachny captures Kaffa	304
Fortress of Kodak	304
Cossacks at sea	305
A Cossack chayka	305
Ostrozhsky's castle at Stare Selo (16th Century)	316
Fortress of Bilhorod (15th Century)	317

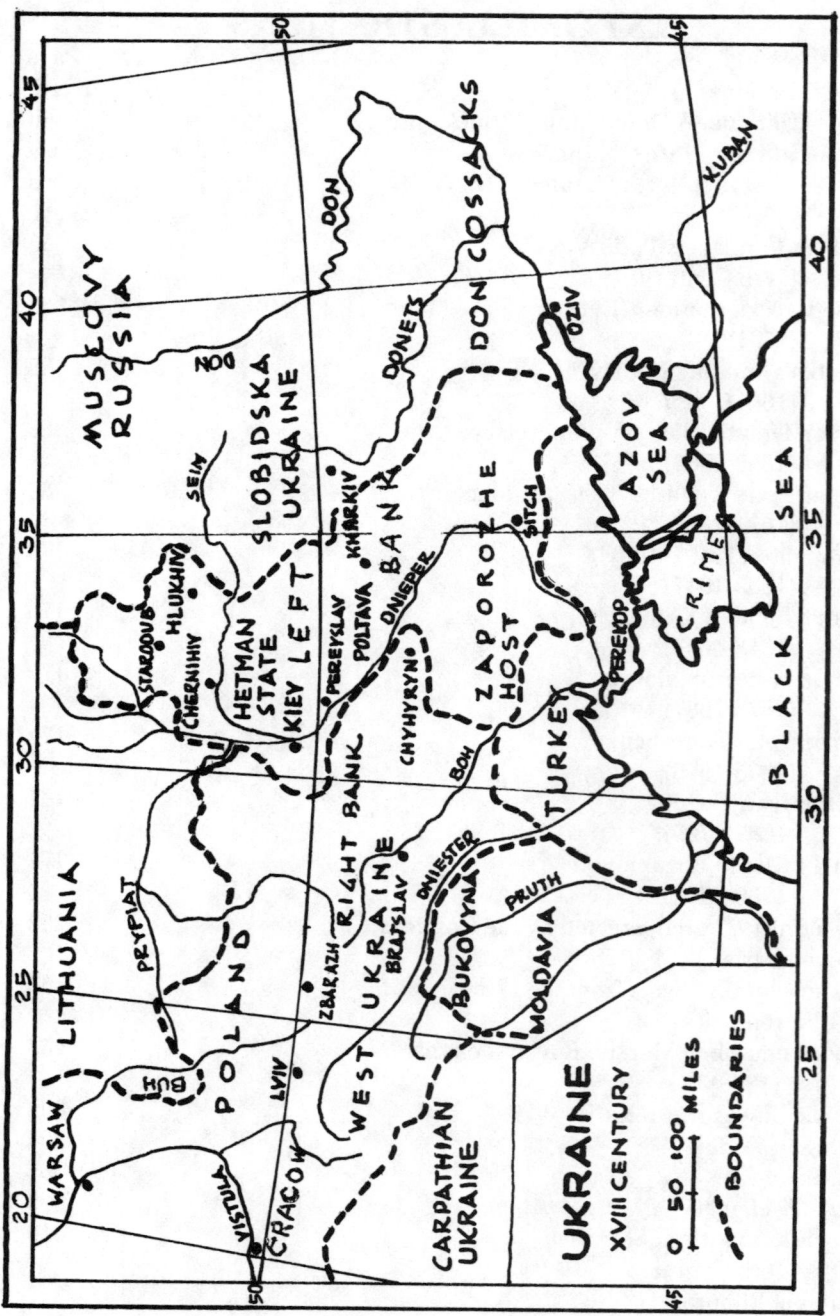

Map — Ukraine, 18th Century

PREFACE

Three years ago the first volume of the *Introduction to Ukrainian History,* covering the Ancient and Kievan-Galician eras of the Ukrainian past, was published, and then favorably received as a college textbook. Now, the author gives the English speaking student and the English speaking interested public the second volume of the work, covering the Lithuanian-Rus'ian (Ukrainian), Polish and Cossack-Hetman eras. The Lithuanian-Rus'ian era, especially in its earlier stage, presents a time of free and nationally favorable development of the Ukrainian nation, followed by the period of Polish domination and oppression. This Polish political, social, economic and religious oppression of the Ukrainian people provoked a powerful National Revolution under Bohdan Khmelnytsky's leadership, a national and religious liberation and the formation of the independent Ukrainian, Cossack-Hetman State in 1648-1649.

Meanwhile, the military might and the imperialist drive of Muscovy-Russia began to exert itself in a very aggressive way and to gravely affect the political fortunes of Ukraine, especially after the notorious Battle of Poltava in 1709. By 1781-1783 the last vestiges of Ukrainian political autonomy were liquidated by the Tsars, and Ukraine was incorporated into the Russian Empire, becoming one of the early victims of the ruthless imperial growth which suppressed numerous peoples and nationalities by an incessant course of violent aggressions and invasions, culminating in the second half of the twentieth century by the suppressions in Hungary, Czechoslovakia, Afghanistan and Poland. The Tsarist and the Soviet regimes have done all this in the name of the growth of "Mother Russia."

This second volume follows the same format of presentation as the first one. It consists of two parts. The first part discusses the Lithuanian-Rus'ian and the Polish times, while the second one covers the events of the Ukrainian national Cossack-Hetman State. Each part covers various aspects of the national life of the Ukrainians in the following respective order: political developments, governmental structure, spiritual and cultural life, social structure and economic process. Much attention has been paid to that aspect of the economic life, as in the first volume, since it actually reveals how the people lived and earned their living.

The almost five hundred years of the Ukrainian past covered in this volume can be more richly and reliably related than its ancient and medieval history. This time an historian does not need to rely heavily on geology, archeology and comparative historical studies and other related disciplines, since this historical period contributes rich and comprehensive written source material for his use and disposition. Of course, he has to use caution and discretion, since in many cases the older the written sources are the more subjective and partial they tend to be. Also, statistical material is scarce for these times. However, considering such limitations, historical studies of this era of the Ukrainian past rest on a more reliable foundation than studies of the ancient period. The secondary sources, general historical works, monographic writings and related materials, are also more numerous and comprehensive.

As far as the primary source materials are concerned, they are available in Ukrainian, Polish, Russian and other languages, such as Swedish, German, French and Turkish. There are collections of old laws and codifications of laws, such as *Metryka Velikoho Kniazhestva Litovskoho*, the official collection of documents and records of the Grand Principality of Lithuania; the *Litovskyi Statut*, the codification of the Lithuanian-Rus'ian laws, in all of its three versions; and the *Acts of the Union of Berest*, the document reconstructed, written down in old Rus'ian or Latin. In order to reflect the developments in the Cossack-Hetman State, in particular in the fields of constitutional, legal and political thought, one can successfully use Orlyk's constitution, *Konstytutsia prav i volnostei Zaporozhskoho voiska* of 1710, and *Prava, po kotorym sudytsia Malorossiiskii narod* of 1743, while *Generalni slidstva o majetnostiakh* of 1729-1731 is an invaluable source of primary information on the economic and social history of Ukraine. *Akta grodzkie i ziemskie*, a collection of documents and records of the territorial government of old Poland, and *Zródla dziejowe*, documented materials from the Polish, Lithuanian and Ukrainian history of a secondary source nature, largely in the Polish interpretation, can also be very useful when caution and discretion are constantly applied.

Primary sources pertaining to Ukrainian history and published in Russia include among others, *Akty yugo-zapadnoi Rossii* and *Akty otnosiashchiesia k istorii yuzhnoi i zapadnoi Rossii*, in many volumes that contain documents and records of the past of great value toward researching the political, social and economic developments. *Polneoie sobranie zakonov Rossiiskoi Imperii*, a full collection of laws of the Russian Empire, may serve as another source of primary material for Ukrainian history, but with limitations. First of all, only relatively few acts refer directly to Ukraine, the majority of them being largely Russian legislation and administrative regulations. Secondly, it must be borne in mind that some legal acts pertaining to Ukraine were simply forged by the Russian official circles to fit Ukraine's legal and political status more effectively into the framework of the Russian imperial plans for the future. One flagrant example of Russian forgery is the official text of the purported original Agreement of Pereyaslav of 1654 in the *Polnoie sobranie*. By the original agreement, the Muscovite Tsar Aleksei solemnly promised not to violate any autonomy, rights and liberties and financial independence of the Ukrainian State, while in 1781-83, Ukraine and all its provinces were unceremoniously incorporated into the Empire. The Russian ruling circles had to find some kind of justification for such an unorthodox action.

An historian again must be very careful with the use of those Russian published source materials. It must be underscored here that several times libraries have been burned in various places in Ukraine, and a few years ago in Kiev again, during which invaluable archives, records and source materials embarrassing for Russian political plans and projects, were destroyed.

In addition, the records of numerous Russian Tsarist and Soviet government agencies, such as *Little Russian Prikaz* and the *Sacred Chancellory*, may supply substantial source materials for the study of Ukrainian history from the seventeenth century on, only if carefully evaluated.

Still another category of the primary sources are various chronicles from the Lithuanian and Cossack eras, recording the events of these respective times such as the *Supraslsky litopys'* or *Kratkoie opysanie Malorossii* and several other works of that kind, including the *Litovsko-rus'ky litopys;* while *Istoria Rusiv*, for example, reflects the development of political thought in Ukraine in the late Cossack era. A series of diaries have also been preserved for the use of an historian. Yet, we should guard ourselves from the partiality and subjectivity of the respective authors and compilers.

From among the pragmatic and secondary history works, however well documented, an historian writing a new work on the Ukrainian past should rely heavily on Hrushevsky's celebrated *Istoria Ukrainy-Rusy*, a ten volume work covering the period of history to the Hadiach Agreement of 1658, Vernadsky's *History of Russia*, early volumes, Bobrzynsky's *Dzieje Polski w zarysie*, Kluchevsky's *History of Russia*, all of which deal with the Ukrainian past, and from among the more recent publications, such as Doroshenko's *Narys istorii Ukrainy* and Polonska-Vasylenko's *Istoria Ukrainy*, which conclude with the First World War.

The rich historical sources therefore, enable an historian to give a true picture of the Ukrainian past between the fourteenth and eighteenth centuries, to contribute effectively to the understanding of the contemporary reader of times long gone by in Eastern Europe, and to help him understand contemporary developments in that part of the world.

The third volume of this *Introduction to Ukrainian History* is scheduled to follow in two or three years. It will cover the developments of the nineteenth and twentieth centuries in Ukraine, and it shall adhere to the same pattern of presentation of historical material as the preceding two volumes have.

Nicholas L. Fr.-Chirovsky

Maplewood, N.J., 1982

ACKNOWLEDGMENTS

The author wishes to express his deep appreciation and to make his grateful acknowledgments to Prof. Vasyl Luciw, Ph.D., of Pennsylvania State College; Prof. Vincent Mott, Ph.D., and Prof. Jack Stukas, Ph.D., both of Seton Hall University, for their valuable suggestions toward improving the quality of this second volume of the *Introduction to Ukrainian History* as a possible textbook for college and university students. He also thanks Mr. Lubomyr Kalynych for drawing the maps and assisting in the selection of illustrations to reflect the Ukrainian civilization and its development from the fourteenth to the eighteenth century.

Many thanks are also expressed to Mrs. Mary Pawlowsky, Prof. Stanley Strand, Prof. Alfred Kana, Prof. John Deehan of Seton Hall University, Mrs. Gloria Kana, and the author's own son, John M. Chirovsky for their able assistance in editing the volume. A great appreciation from the author was also earned by Mesdames Blanchard Friedman, Joan Driver and Dolores Condon for their tireless typing, retyping and making photostatic copies of the manuscript to make it fit for typesetting. God bless all these kindly people.

Nicholas L. Fr.-Chirovsky

Maplewood, N.J., 1982

PART ONE

The Lithuanian-Rus' Commonwealth and the Polish Domination.

CHAPTER ONE

THE FORMATION AND GROWTH
OF THE LITHUANIAN-RUS' COMMONWEALTH

The beginnings of Lithuanian political organization — The decline of the Golden Horde — The absorption of Ukrainian-Rus'ian lands by Lithuania — The struggle against Polish domination — The Polish supremacy — The rise of the Cossacks

The Beginnings of Lithuanian Political Organization. The Lithuanian tribes, a branch of the Indo-European ethnic family, in the eleventh century, at the dawn of their recorded history, were settled on the eastern shores of the Baltic Sea in the territory which stretched from the Vistula River in the west and the West Dvina River in the north-east. There were several Lithuanian tribes; the Prussians lived between the mouth of the Vistula and the mouth of the Nieman Rivers; the Yatvingians — between the Nieman and the upper Buh Rivers; the Lithuanians-proper — on the shores of the Nieman's right tributaries; the Zhmudians — north of the Nieman; further north — the Korsians or Kuronians; the Semgalians — on the left shores of the West Dvina; and the Letts or Latvians — on its right littorals.

For a long time all those tribes lived their separate lives under conditions of poverty and economic primitivism. They were pagans directed in their religious life by a strong and influential class of pagan priests who were called the *Kunigai*. Some of these tribes, especially the Yatvingians, were rather aggressive, and, anticipating rich booty, frequently assaulted neighboring lands. The old Rus'ian chronicle recorded under the date 983 the military expedition of Prince Volodymyr the Great against the Yatvingians. From that date until 1203, there were some twelve recorded Rus'ian wars against the Lithuanians at various times. The same was going on on the other Lithuanian borders, both western and southern ones.[1]

The political situation of the Lithuanians changed substantially later on, to their disadvantage. The so-called Livonian Knights established themselves in Livonia or Latvia in 1202, having subjugated the Letts or Latvians living there, and subsequently the Teutonic Knights established themselves in Prussia, having been brought there by a Polish prince, Konrad of Masovia, in 1230. These two German military orders, under the pretext of converting the Lithuanians to Christianity, proceeded with a harsh conquest of that land by sword, fire, plunder and extinction. These developments forced the Lithuanians to unite politically in order to present an effective opposition against the German assaults.

Then, the chronicles referred to a "Great King," not mentioned by name, who supposedly by the end of the twelfth century had initiated the unification of Lithuania. His two sons, Mendog and Dovsprunk, continued their father's work of unification in a rather ruthless way; some tribal or local princes were eliminated, others expelled from the country, while still others loyally accepted Mendog's rule. In 1230-1240 Mendog was already the recognized leader and ruler of Lithuania, and he not only spread his authority over many Lithuanian lands, but also over some Byeloruthenian regions. Mendog's aggressiveness and energy irked Prince Danylo of Galicia, who attempted to organize a coalition against Mendog with Masovia and some Lithuanian tribes, and was able to restrain him. Certain territories were then given back to Danylo by a treaty. Shortly thereafter, however, a conflict erupted again which resulted in Mendog capturing additional Byeloruthenian territories, including an onslaught on Smolensk. His nephew, Tovtovil, reigned for two years in Polotsk, between 1258-1260. Shortly before his death, Mendog seriously considered a military expedition on Chernihiv, to add that principality to his possessions. Mendog's death in 1263 unleashed in Lithuania a period of political turmoil. At first Prince Voishelk, Mendog's son, assumed supreme authority, but he gave up the throne and entered a monastery, entrusting the rule of Lithuania to Prince Shvarno, a son of Danylo of Galicia and Volhinia. Shvarno was then killed by a Prince Lev out of vengeance, and Troiden became the grand prince of Lithuania. Troiden was hostile toward the Ukrainian princes, in particular, the Galician-Volhinian branch, and the Ukrainians. During his reign, 1270-1280, a continuous chain of additional Ukrainian and Byeloruthenian territories were added to Lithuania. The Polotsk and Vitebsk principalities, and the Byeloruthenian lands of the Krivichians and Dregovichians, also parts of the Ukrainian Derevlianian land, had to accept Lithuanian supremacy.[2]

Historical sources give very scant information about the Lithuanian constitutional process for the subsequent decade or two, except that additional Ukrainian lands were absorbed by the Grand Principality of Lithuania and the Lithuanian princes replaced the Ukrainian-Rus'ian ones on various princely thrones.

In the early 1290's a new dynasty assumed supreme authority in Lithuania in the person of King Putuver, but the new era of Lithuanian political growth actually began during the reign of Putuver's son, Gedymin, who soon began to use the title of "King of Lithuania and Rus' ." He ruled from 1316 to 1341, and always stressed that he was the heir of the Rus' princes, meanwhile extending his royal authority over northern Kievan lands and some other Ukrainian provinces. Subsequently, Gedymin's son, Prince Lubart, was elected Prince of Galicia and Volhinia after the violent death of Yurii-Boleslav, the last prince of the principality. It obviously was a success for Gedymin, since the incident indirectly extended his influence over more Ukrainian territories.

Of course, as discussed previously in the first volume, because of a Polish-Hungarian intrigue, Lubart did not establish himself in Galicia. It was a great political mistake of the Galician *boyars* that they did not support Lubart's quest for the Galician principality. As a result of that mistake, it became a rather easy prey for Polish aggression, which was disastrous in the long run. A series of wars followed with Poland and Hungary and some allies on the one side, and Lithuanian princes, Lubart and Keistut, and some others, with the Volhinians and Galicians, on the other. Not only the Ukrainian *boyars*, but also the townspeople and peasants participated, defending themselves against the onslaught of the "Latinians," since the Lithuanians were then largely Orthodox. Lubart himself was Orthodox, hence less objectionable for Ukrainians. It was unfortunate for Galicia that at that time the Lithuanian princes were more interested in *snatching* from nominal Mongol domination the eastern and south-eastern Ukrainian territories which willingly joined the Lithuanian Commonwealth, whenever the opportunity simply rendered itself, rather than conduct costly wars with Poland and Hungary. An agreement between Casimir of Poland and the Lithuanian princes brought them some kind of a compromise, but not for the Ukrainians. The areas of political influence were divided; Poland retained Galicia, Kholm and Belz, while most of Volhinia remained under Lithuanian supremacy. But this arrangement was very unstable, and continually changed. Casimir's death in 1370 unleashed another war in which the Lithuanian princes wrenched from Poland whatever parts of Volhinia that Poland occupied.³

Meanwhile, Olgierd ascended to the grand princely throne of Lithuania and Rus', and proceeded most energetically with the expansion of the Commonwealth, with splendid results. The reasons for Olgierd's success were the following: First, he was a very able, almost ingenious ruler. Secondly, the Golden Horde, which dominated almost all of Eastern Europe, ran into grave turmoil and began to disintegrate. Thirdly, the Ukrainian lands and territories willingly tended to join the Lithuanian-Rus' Commonwealth, which was speedily accepting the Ukrainian Orthodox faith, culture, language, and social, legal and political institutions.⁴

The Decline of the Golden Horde. The gradual and progressive disintegration of the Horde was, probably, the leading reason for Lithuanian success. Khan Batu's intention to keep a close check on East Europe was motivated by his desire to secure for his state high tax revenues and a supply of auxiliary armed forces on a regular basis. On his return from the Central European campaign, he established the Khanate of Kiptchak or the state of the Golden Horde with its capital of the new city of Sarai on the banks of the lower Volga River.⁵ Batu died in 1255 and was succeeded by Sartak, who, in his father's time, was already a co-ruler of sorts. He died a year later, and Ulagchi, Batu's other son, became the third Khan of the Golden Horde, but again only for a short, two-year period, for he died in 1258.

Meanwhile, Great Khan Mongka, residing in Mongolia, being involved in his Chinese campaigns, imposed new burdens on the East European, "vassal" lands, including Ukraine. He needed more troops and more money. As a result, a permanent Mongol administration was introduced by dividing Eastern Europe into military districts and a new census for tax collection and recruiting soldiers and artisans was taken. The Mongol tribute was efficiently and systematically collected everywhere, contributing to the impoverishment of Rus' and her people.

After Ulagchi's death, Berk, Batu's brother assumed the authority of the Khan of the Golden Horde. Because he was more preoccupied with internal conflicts in the entire Mongol empire and developments in the Near East, he paid less attention to the European East. Since Berk was already a Mohammedan, it gave him a reason for an involvement in the Islamic affairs in Asia Minor and for his misunderstanding with Hulagu, the Khan of the Mongols in Persia. He also became involved in the Mongol civil war between Kublay and Arik-Buka, which strained his relations with the Great Khan Kublay.

Consequently these developments brought a slight relaxation in the Mongol grip over Ukraine.

Khan Berk died in Tiflis in 1266 during one of his Near East campaigns, and was succeeded by Batu's grandson, Mangu-Temir, having been elected by the regional council of Mongols, the *kuriltay*, and confirmed by Great Khan Kublay in Mongolia. Mangu-Temir pursued a benevolent policy toward all East European vassal lands. He eased the tax collections and exempted the Orthodox Church in most cases from the census, taxation and military service, making the "church people" a kind of privileged group by his special *yarlik*. As a result, Mangu-Temir succeeded in obtaining the loyalty of the North-Eastern princes in particular, and the appreciative attitude of the Church. On his demise, his brother, Tuda-Mangu, became the Khan. However, Nogay, cousin of the two former Khans, an able warrior and statesman who previously acted as ruler of the lower Danube region, became so powerful that in fact a dual authority of Tuda-Mangu and Nogay prevailed in the Golden Horde. Shortly thereafter Nogay's power was actually greater than that of the official Khan, Tuda-Mangu. Relations between these two became badly strained, and some East-European princes and autonomous communities tried to play one against the other to their own advantage in order to strengthen their political positions.

Eventually, Tuda-Mangu was forced to abdicate in favor of Tele-Buga, his nephew, and Nogay's loyal associate in the latter's Hungarian exploits. Relations between Nogay and Tele-Buga also began rapidly to deteriorate, and since Tele-Buga's wars in the Caucasian areas were not successful, his prestige swiftly declined. Nogay was only too glad to get rid of his embarrassing co-ruler, and he soon perfidiously arrested Tele-Buga and handed him over to his rival, Tokhta, Mangu-Temir's son, another contender for the Khan's authority. Tokhta immediately ordered the execution of Tele-Buga and his associates, and he became the Khan of the Golden Horde, by Nogay's grace, in 1291.

Tokhta, however, did not intend to be a mere tool in Nogay's hands. He acted very independently in political areas in order to make himself known as the suzerain, and in a mammoth punitive action he mercilessly looted and burned Vladimir, Tver and Moscow, for their attempt to associate themselves with Nogay. Finally, the rivalry between Tokhta and Nogay resulted in a civil war in the Golden Horde, which ended in Nogay's downfall and death in 1300. Tokhta's reign presented an era of the restoration of unity, order and power in the Horde. He was followed in 1313 by Khan Uzbek, his nephew, as the Khan, who distinguished himself in many political-military projects including the Galician-Volhinian and Lithuanian affairs. In this connection he undertook a few punitive raids against stubborn vassal princes and territories.

Uzbek, who died in 1341, was succeeded by his son, Tinibeg, for a period of one year, and in 1342, by Janibeg, the latter's brother, who seized power and ruled until 1357. No doubt, all these developments were not an indication of growing power and prestige, but rather of a declining control of the Mongol suzerain over the vassal Ukrainian principalities and territories, which enjoyed a rising degree of freedom. This, on the other hand, especially the short reigns of the Khans who quickly succeeded each other and the Golden Horde's internal strifes, enabled Grand Prince Gedymin to proceed with his plans of annexing additional Ukrainian and Byeloruthenian regions, and to continue to expand his Lithuanian-Rus' Commonwealth, as already described. However, the process of disintegration of the Golden Horde began during the second half of the fourteenth century, in 1357, when Khan Janibeg was murdered by his son Berdibeg, who wished to ascend to the throne. The era of the "Great Trouble" in the Horde featured bloody struggles among Janibeg's three sons, Berdibeg, Kulpa and Nevruz, during which they killed each other. The prestige of the Juchi ruling clan, descending from one of the sons of Genghis Khan Temudzhin, slipped to a record low.[6] Power in the Golden Horde was then captured by Mamai, who was not a member of the Juchi clan and therefore his authority was not generally recognized. The growing weakness of the Horde was revealed in the battle on the Kulikovo plain in September 1360, where Dimitrii, Grand Prince of Moscow, badly defeated Mamai's cohorts.

Subsequently, chaos in the Golden Horde continued and deepened. One Khan quickly replaced another while various regions of the Horde sought more autonomy and freedom, especially those with ethnically alien populations. At that very time, Grand Prince Olgierd of Lithuania-Rus' completed the construction of his huge Commonwealth, largely at the expense of the dwindling Mongol might. The two major landmarks of subsequent developments in the Golden Horde were the victory of Khan Tokhmatish, from the Juchi clan, over Mamai, and then of the Great Khan Tamerlane over Tokhmatish in 1395.

Tamerlane began to build his empire in 1360 after he became the ruler of his native city of Kesh, in Central Asia. He subsequently conquered Samarkand and became Khan. In his attempt to conquer Kazakhstan, he antagonized the Golden Horde, since Kazakhstan was considered a traditional region of the Juchi clan or Juchi *ulus*. Tamerlane supported Tokhmatish in his quest for Sarai against Mamai and the other Khans, Urus-Khan and Timur-Melik. After establishing himself in Sarai, Tokhmatish became one of the mightiest rulers of his time, desiring to consolidate the Golden Horde anew. He acted accordingly, but in 1386 an open conflict erupted between Tokhmatish and Tamerlane, which had already been brewing for several years. Thereafter, for years the two Mongol Khans waged bloody wars against each other in Caucasia, the Volga-Caspian steppes and Central Asia. Finally, Tokhmatish was completely routed by Tamerlane in two decisive battles; one on the banks of the Kondurcha River, in the Middle Volga region, in 1391 and the other in the Terek River valley, in Caucasia, in 1395. Thereafter Tokhmatish gave only sporadic resistance, while Tamerlane proceeded with the vicious plunder of the territories of the Golden Horde.

Tamerlane's wars against the Golden Horde dealt it a severe blow. Its political prestige was ruined and its foreign commerce, the basis of its economic prosperity, was gravely damaged. It soon became a vassal of Tamerlane's Khanate, and was subjected to shattering civil wars and foreign interventions. Khan Edigey tried desperately to save the Horde, but this was in vain. Its days were over.

The complete disintegration of the Horde followed in the middle of the fifteenth century, when in 1445 the Khanate of Kazan on the Middle Volga separated itself from Sarai, and a few years later, in 1449, the Crimean Tartars founded their own Khanate, independent of the crumbling Golden Horde. In 1502, the Crimean Tartars completely defeated the Golden Horde, but from the very time of the establishment of the Crimean Khanate a new era of the Tartar impact on the history of Ukraine began.[7]

The Absorption of Ukrainian-Rus' Lands by Lithuania. It was, therefore, no wonder that Grand Prince Olgierd, a ruler of grand stature, immediately recognized the political mission for which he was destined by history. He knew that he had to follow the political blueprint, outlined by his father, to complete the construction of the Lithuanian-Rus' Commonwealth against the background of the disintegrating Golden Horde. Lithuania was a country thoroughly Ukrainianized culturally and spiritually, but led by the Lithuanian Gedymin dynasty, where three ethnic communities, the Lithuanians, Ukrainians and Byeloruthenians were to live together. The social-political essence of the Commonwealth was a few decades later, so accurately expressed by a monk in the following way: "Our Christian Rus' Commonwealth, the Lithuanian Grand Principality."[8]

Grand Prince Olgierd reigned from 1341 to 1377. Almost from the very beginning of his rule, the main direction of his international policies was aiming south and south-east, mainly towards the vast Ukrainian territories, which had been partly nominally and partly factually under Mongol domination for one hundred years beforehand. However, Olgierd's plans to dominate the self-governing communities of Novgorod the Great and Pskov in the north did not succeed. Perhaps, he was not so deeply interested in these projects.

In the 1350's, as it was pointed out, serious political troubles developed in the Golden Horde, and partially because of it some conflicts among the Ukrainian princes evolved. Olgierd immediately seized the opportunity, and extended his supremacy over a major part of the Chernihiv land and its major towns, like Chernihiv, Briansk, Novhorod Siversky, Starodub, Trubchevsk and others. Here he placed his relatives on the local princely thrones in most cases, while the territories further east were allowed to retain their old princes of the Rurik dynasty under Lithuanian suzerainity. In the 1360's Olgierd succeeded in dominating the ancient city of Kiev, which was the traditional capital of Rus', and the Kievan land, and subsequently also the Pereyaslav territory. Especially important was the expansion of the political influence of the Grand Principality of Lithuania and Rus' into the Chernihivian and Siverianian regions which immediately produced a confrontation and rivalry with the growing Muscovite principality, which also soon began to aspire to gather under its authority former Rus' territories. At first, the Lithuanian-Rus' Commonwealth seemed to be winning the contest as Polonska-Vasylenko and other historians remarked.[9]

Since the invasion of Batu's cohorts, Kiev remained under Mongol supremacy, the prince of which from the Ruryk dynasty ruled there by the Tartar *yarlik*, or Khan's authorization. For example, in 1246-47, Prince Alexander Nevskii whose political allegiance was to the Vladimirian north, had temporarily received the Mongol *yarlik* on Kiev, but he was not interested in Ukrainian affairs and confined his interests to the Vladimirian-Muscovite North. At first, after the Muscovite princes were able to overcome to some extent the Mongol threat in the fourteenth century, they were again eager to resume the old Suzdalian-Vladimirian aggression southward, against Ukraine, under various dynastic and pseudo-political pretexts. Perhaps, at times, Kiev had no prince, and governed itself "democratically" under Mongol protection.

In the middle of the fourteenth century, Prince Fedir ruled in Kiev by Sarai's grace. Olgierd removed Fedir and appointed his own son, Volodymyr, prince of Kiev. The Tartars were badly irked by Olgierd's unilateral and arbitrary action and undertook a military expedition to assist

8

their vassal. But, Olgierd routed them completely in the battle on the banks of the *Syni Vody*, the Snyvod River, and forced their retreat. As a result, also in Kiev, a prince of the Gedymin dynasty, Volodymyr, replaced a prince of the ancient Ruryk dynasty, Fedir, on a permanent basis. A change of dynasty was taking place throughout the Lithuanian-Rus' Commonwealth. It was also another important result of the decisive battle on the Snyvod River. The river was on the borders of Kiev, Volhinia and Ponyzzia, soon to be called, Podillia, the southern region of Ukraine. This opened the door to further southern expansion plans by Vilna, the capital of the Lithuania-Rus' Commonwealth, a newly established city by Gedymin beautified by many pagan temples and Orthodox and Catholic churches, reflecting the spiritual and cultural mosaics of the young and growing power.

The Podillian regions eliminated the princely authorities of their local princes immediately after the Mongol invasion, and proceeded with the organization of local and regional life on the basis of self-governing communities, directly subject to the Mongol supremacy, and loosely governed by Sarai's agents. It has already been pointed out in connection with the coverage of Danylo's reign in Ukraine, that this monarch was very hostile toward these self-governing communities which were generally referred to in Podillia as "Tartar people," a kind of anarchism during that period. Danylo and other allied princes undertook several military expeditions to suppress these communities, with not much success. It must be accepted that for some one hundred and twenty years the social-political process of the Podillian population proceded in the framework of these communities under conditions of social, economic and cultural primitivism. These communities were led by the so-called *otamany* who were a type of intermediary between the tribute paying population and the Mongol suzerain.

After having defeated the Tartars, Grand Prince Olgierd appointed princes for Podillian regions; his nephews, Yurii, Oleksander and Konstantyn, sons of Prince Koriat of Novhorod Lytovsky, were each given a separate region as a vassal and confederated principality. The huge commonwealth was growing. The records of that time asserted that these Lithuanian princes, who were already thoroughly Ukrainianized, knew very well how to cooperate with the people's "otamans" and their self-governing communities; how to defend them against the Tartar chicanes and the continuing attempts of the Tartar agents to collect tribute. In order to put the anti-Mongol defense on a more permanent basis, these princes constructed towns and fortresses, such as Bakota, Smotrych and Kamianets.[10] Also in this way a permanent grip of the Lithuanian-Rus' Commonwealth over the newly acquired Ukrainian territories became politically established.

Rather unfortunate was the political fate of Volhinia at the time of the formation of the Lithuanian-Rus' Commonwealth. One of the largest and most powerful Ukrainian principalities during the twelfth and fourteenth centuries, Volhinia was well populated and economically wealthy, and of considerable political influence; thus it soon became an object of continuous strife and warfare. Everybody wanted to have at least a piece of that rich principality.

The Poles and the Hungarians tried to disregard the will of the Volhinian people to live their own political life under Prince Lubart. In 1352, as a consequence of the struggle for the Galician-Volhinian inheritance after Yurii-Boleslav and Polish Casimir's war expeditions, the Volhinian land was divided into several political units; Yurii, Narymunt's son received the provinces of Belz and Kholm; Keistut — Berest; Olgierd — Kobryn; while Lubart retained only eastern Volhinia. All these princes were of the Gedymin house, of course, but Lubart, Casimir's main rival, was seriously weakened when his share was reduced again in 1366 when the so-called "eternal peace" gave the Volodymyr land to Oleksander, Koriat's son, as a vassal of the Polish king. As has already been discussed, Casimir's death again unleashed a war for the Galician-Volhinian inheritance. Finally the death of Ludvig of Hungary, the heir to the Polish throne at that time, enabled Lubart to reestablish himself on most of the Volhinian territories, to which he was rightfully entitled. This occurred after 1382.

Since that time, Lubart's Volhinia, while being within the framework of the Lithuanian-Rus' Commonwealth, occupied a singular, separate and independent political position as an entity of a strict Ukrainian national character in itself. Lubart cared for his principality; he aided its cultural, social and economic development; he constructed towns, fortresses and churches.[11] Meanwhile, the Lithuanian-Rus' Commonwealth reached the very height of its development, headed by Olgierd, who lived in peace with his brothers, Kiestut and Lubart, and consulted them in important state matters. Olgierd also extended the domination of his Commonwealth on additional Byeloruthenian lands, including the lands of Polotsk and Vitebsk. To strengthen the dynastic ties, he subsequently married Maria, the princess of Vitebsk.

Polonska-Vasylenko asserted that at the end of Olgierd's reign, the Ukrainian and Byeloruthenian ethnic stocks constituted nine-tenths of the total population of the Commonwealth, while the upper class of the Lithuanian population was thoroughly Rus'ianized.[12] Olgierd and his co-rulers, various princes, realized the situation very well, and in order not to antagonize the people of the Commonwealth, who were used to traditional ways of life, they repeatedly underscored in their decrees that "their old customs will not be changed, nor will new ones be introduced." And these princes were actually very loyal in this respect. Even the constitutional principle of the princely order was not altered; in most cases the only alteration made was the replacement of the princes of the Ruryk dynasty by the princes of the Gedymin dynasty. Meanwhile, the Ukrainian and Byeloruthenian *boyars* voluntarily entered into the military and administrative services of the new dynasty, which, naturally was considered their own — Lithuanian-Rus'ian. Ukrainian culture and civilization, as asserted before, thoroughly penetrated the whole Lithuanian-Rus' Commonwealth; the military organization, the system of constructing castles and fortresses, defense walls and ditches, the country's administrative system, economy and business, the official language and terminology, and the entire social and legal life, were rooted in the old Ukrainian-Rus'ian origins. The book of law, the *Rus'ka Pravda*, was the source of legal inspiration for the whole Commonwealth. The princes of the Gedymin dynasty, for these reasons, felt themselves to be a part of the Ukrainianized-Rus'ianized Commonwealth and considered their mission to be one of gathering all the Ukrainian and Byeloruthenian lands under their scepter and to preserve their unity and integrity. Truly, the Lithuanian-Rus' Commonwealth was a serious historical attempt to restore the old splendor of the Kievan-Rus' empire under new conditions and in cooperation with the Lithuanian people after the terrible experience and short domination of the Mongol invasion. The sudden termination of this historical process, much to the disadvantage of the Ukrainian people, was manifest in the unfortunate Polish-Lithuanian political union which was to immediately follow.

This unfortunate development was brought about by the following forces: First, the genius of Grand Prince Olgierd tailored the Commonwealth partially to his personality. Secondly, Olgierd decided to give Yagiello, his son from a second marriage, the grand princely and senior position in the state thus omitting older sons. This gave rise to some grave political complications and a feeling of dissatisfaction and embitterment after Olgierd's death. Thirdly, the Lithuanian-Rus' Commonwealth was not a monolithic and centralized state, but rather a federation of semi-independent principalities, ruled by princes of the Gedymin and Ruryk dynasties. Therefore the presence of any kind of internal trouble could develop into a serious political complication, because the Commonwealth was also greatly differentiated ethnically. However this was not a major problem, since the three ethnic components, the Lithuanians, Ukrainians and Byeloruthenians, lived in harmony. In this respect, the Lithuanian-Rus' Commonwealth certainly resembled the early stages of the Kievan-Rus' realm.

At the death of Grand Prince Olgierd, Kiestut ruled in Berest, Lubart — in Volhinia, Narymunt — in Turiv and Pinsk, Volodymyr — in Kiev and Pereyaslav, Korybut — in Chernihiv; and the Koriat brothers — in Podillia.

Apparently Prince Kiestut was favored as the heir to the grand-princely throne by the conservative circles of the Commonwealth, while Yagiello began to fight for his assumed right to succeed his father. Prolonged dynastic warfares were waged, from which Yagiello emerged a dubious victor. Though Kiestut was defeated, imprisoned and strangled on Yagiello's order, his son, Prince Vitovt, escaped from prison and went to the Teutonic order to seek protection and assistance against his murderous uncle. Yagiello then fought against other members of his princely clan, who did not want to submit to his controversial grand-princely authority. Andrei of Polotsk, the oldest among the Olgierd sons, allied himself with Pskov and later with Moscow, in order to resist Yagiello and to regain the authority of the Grand Prince for himself, which he thought was denied him unjustly. Subsequently, he conspired also with the Teutonic order against Yagiello's "usurpation." Nevertheless, he was finally defeated, and kept in prison for many years. Prince Dymytrii of Briansk, another one of Yagiello's half-brothers also joined the Muscovites. For a long time there was no peace in the Lithuanian-Rus' Commonwealth.

The Struggle Against Polish Domination. The political situation of Yagiello continued to be most difficult. Internally, he still faced a strong opposition and could not quell it for a number of years. His authority was challenged. Externally, he was threatened by the hostile Teutons, Poland and the growing power of the Muscovite principality, which from its very political beginnings exhibited aggressive imperialism towards all neighboring lands, and especially the Byeloruthenian and Ukrainian-Rus' commonwealth.

Poland also had at that time her own share of problems. A large number of the Polish nobility objected to the original plan of a Hungarian-Polish union, as developed by King Ludvig. The Poles also objected to Maria's ascendence to the Polish throne because she was immediately proclaimed the Queen of Hungary following Ludvig's death, and this might have strengthened the undesirable union, and because her fiance, Prince Sigismund, was disliked in Poland. Other contenders for the Polish throne did not please the nobles either. Finally, the Polish nobility accepted Jadviga, Maria's younger sister, as the Queen of Poland in 1384, and developed a plan to marry Jadviga to Yagiello who was in political trouble and seemed to be a weak candidate, thus arranging a union between Poland and Lithuania. It was a much more practical solution than a union with powerful Hungary, which could prevail over Poland.

In 1385, an agreement at Krevo was negotiated between the Polish Crown and the Lithuanian-Rus' Commonwealth according to which the Commonwealth was incorporated into Poland. It was really an inconceivable act on the part of Yagiello and all other Lithuanian-Rus'ian princes, including Vitovt, who signed the convention. It was a treacherous abandonment of the sovereignty and independence of the Commonwealth.[13] It could be explained by the political desperation or insatiable ambition of Yagiello, who thought to solve all his problems by becoming a Polish king and by the other princes' complete lack of perception of what they were doing. Other articles of agreement were of a minor importance, except where Yagiello, all princes, *boyars* and all the people were to become Catholics by recanting Orthodoxy, and all lands taken by Lithuania were supposed to be revindicated to Poland. Introduction of Catholicism immediately sparked a split and hostility between the Lithuanians and the Rus'ians, who before lived in a perfect harmony in the Lithuanian-Rus' Commonwealth. The Polish nobility conceived of this long-range plan, as far as the agreement of Krevo was concerned, thereby incorporating this religious split in the Commonwealth in order to subdue both nationalities—the traditionally Orthodox Ukrainian-Rus'ians and the newly Catholic Lithuanians—in a speedier way, thus making the Polish Crown so much more powerful. This policy was continuously and with ever greater insistence pursued by the Polish ruling circles, which were steadily increasing their influence on the political, social and economic developments in the Lithuanian-Rus'ian lands. More and more favoritism was shown and extended to the Catholic Lithuanians and an ever graver and graver discrimination was applied against the Orthodox Ukrainians and Byeloruthenians in order to deepen the cleavage among them, thus encouraging jealousy, hatred and an ever stronger feeling of Catholic superiority and Orthodox inferiority. This conflict among the Lithuanians and the Ukrainians was constantly driving the former closer and closer to the Polish camp and inducing them, especially the Lithuanian nobility and gentry, to sell out their fatherland to the Poles in exchange for class privileges and favors. This ultimately pushed the Ukrainians down to the very bottom of the social-political structure of the now Polish-Lithuanian state. Finally, in the Union of Lublin of 1569, the Lithuanian nobility ceded almost all of Ukraine to Poland, proving by the act its full class egoism, which completely paralyzed its ability to think patriotically and nationally. It took some two hundred years of an often interrupted struggle of the Lithuanians to resist Polish pressure, and eventually to totally capitulate. Of course, throughout these two centuries, the Polish nobles and government circles used intrigue, intimidation, pressure and bribery to achieve their political end of the complete absorption of Lithuania, Ukraine and Byeloruthnia.

In the wake of the Krevo agreement, Jadviga had to divorce her first husband under different pressures (even that of the Polish Catholic ecclesiastic circles) and to marry Yagiello, who was then crowned a king, although for a long time he was not considered by the Poles a king, but rather a husband of the queen.

Queen Jadviga, who immediately assumed rule over Lithuania, caused great dismay among the Lithuanian-Rus'ian circles when she freely disposed of some of their affairs. Prince Vitovt, having realized the grave mistake of Krevo, assumed the mission of defending the independence and sovereignty of the Lithuanian-Rus' Commonwealth, championing the Lithuanian cause, but neglecting the interests of the Ukrainian nobility and people. Vitovt vacillated between alliances with the Teutonic order against Poland and conventions with Poland in order to protect the political independence of Lithuania. In the early 1390's he was fully recognized as the Grand Prince of the Commonwealth, and the Krevo agreement was for all practical reasons annulled. The high-handed demands of Jadviga, who was not considered by the Lithuanian nobles as their sovereign, pushed the Lithuanian and Rus'ian nobles to proclaim Vitovt the Lithuanian king on Salin Island in 1398.[14] The Poles had to compromise with these developments for the time being, because of Vitovt's prestige and power, resulting from the marriage of his daughter to the Muscovite Grand Prince Vasilii I, which allied him with Moscow, and also because of his securing of the support of the Teutons. They decided to wait for an opportune moment in the future.

The coronation of Vitovt was prevented by the defeat that he suffered in the battle with the Tartars on the Vorskla River in 1399, which weakened his position as the champion of Lithuanian-Rus' political independence, but did not totally destroy his power. Subsequent developments again strengthened his position.

In 1399, Queen Jadviga died and Yagiello was afraid of losing the Polish crown. Therefore, a convention was called in 1401 in Vilna to clarify the over-all political situation. Two important documents were drawn there. In the first, Grand Prince Vitovt affirmed his loyalty to Poland and promised that with his death the Grand Principality of Lithuania would be returned to Yagiello. In the second, the Lithuanian nobility guaranteed the return of the Grand Principality to Yagiello after Vitovt's death, while the election of the next king would require the consent of the Lithuanian nobility. The Vilna conventions simply underscored the personal character of the so-called Polish-Lithuanian union which was related to the person of Yagiello only and was without any real foundations. Though Polish diplomacy had attempted to give different interpretations of the Vilna documents, Vitovt insisted on his sovereign rights, referring to his recent election by the people to the dignity of the Grand Prince or even King at the Salin convention.

The sovereignty of the Lithuanian-Rus'ian Grand Principality was a realized fact due to Vitovt's personality and aggressiveness, and since the Polish national circles had to come to terms with reality over and over again no matter how unpleasant that reality was for them. As a result of this compromise, the Polish Crown and the Lithuanian principality waged a "great war" against their common and deadly enemy, the Teutonic order, which culminated in the resounding victory of the united, Polish-Lithuanian and Rus'ian-Ukrainian arms in the battle of Grunwaldt. As Antonovych pointed out, the Rus'ian-Ukrainian regiments actually decided the outcome of the battle which might have been lost without their bravery. The Order might have been fully uprooted as a result of its crushing defeat, but Prince Vitovt did not allow this to happen because he wanted to weaken the Polish position, to emphasize his authority, to preserve an ally for the future, and above all, to maintain the Lithuanian-Rus'ian sovereignty in the presence of the arrogant Polish political maneuvers.[15]

Subsequently, another convention was held between the Polish and Lithuanian ruling circles in 1413, in Horodlo, by which the Polish nobility attempted to advance the cause of Lithuanian incorporation into the Polish Crown. However, the Horodlo agreement affirmed the separate political exsistence of the Grand Principality, stating that after Vitovt's death a new Grand Prince would be elected, who, like Vitovt, would recognize the Polish king as his suzerain; and that the estates of the Grand Principality would participate in the election of the new king. Nevertheless, the Polish interests experienced great progress in Horodlo. Namely, the convention extended privileges and equal rights to the Polish nobility and only to the Lithuanian nobility of the Catholic faith, thus denying them to the Orthodox nobility, and in this way driving a deep and tragic wedge between Lithuanian Catholics and the Ukrainian Orthodox. This vicious Polish maneuver advanced the Polish cause by means of religious turmoil and hatred within the Commonwealth. It was an unforgivable error on Vitovt's part to allow this to happen, and to not have taken proper care of the interests of the Orthodox people, who actually constituted a majority in his state. From Horodlo on, religious and national discrimination became a constitutionally established policy in the Lithuanian-Rus'ian Commonwealth. It spelled trouble for the future.

At the end of his life and reign, Vitovt finally decided to accept the crown and to become the king of a separate kingdom. Emperor Sigismund supported Vitovt in this respect, and even Yagiello agreed to it, but then retracted his consent under the pressure of the Polish nobility. The coronation, which was supposed to take place in Vilna in September of 1430, was prevented by the Polish lords who intercepted the crown. Soon afterwards Vitovt died unexpectedly and the dubious champion of Lithuanian sovereignty was gone.

Vitovt strengthened the power of the Grand Principality in order to resist Polish pressure and consequently he proceeded with the centralization of authority. He either reduced the power of the vassal princes of his clan, or eliminated them by annexing their lands directly under his own rule. The old federative constitution of the Commonwealth was quickly phased out, making room for a centralist realm. Many once vassal princes such as the families of the Chortoryisky, Chetvertynsky, Zaslavsky, Zborovsky, Vyshnyvetsky and many others, with some sovereign rights, had to submit and become a new breed of landed grand nobility without any ruling authority, faithfully serving the sovereign.

Another phase of his reign was his Tartar policy. He intervened in the internal wars of the Golden Horde, and supported Tokhmatish against Edigey and other contenders. Twice Vitovt's armed forces penetrated the Mongol steppes and went as far as the Crimean Peninsula. Assisting Tokhmatish, Vitovt greatly extended his domination over territories to the south and south-east, reaching the littorals of the Black Sea. The thankful Tokhmatish then officially gave up the "historical rights" of the Mongols to Ukraine and transferred them to the Lithuanian-Rus' realm, making Vitovt's reign over these territories legitimate, *de jure*. This led, however, to a catastrophe in the Lithuanian defeat at the battle on the Vorskla River in 1399. The defeat was resounding and very costly, and it taught Vitovt not to underestimate Mongol strength. But it did not stop him from further intervention in the internal affairs of the Mongols. He only changed tactics from military participation to diplomatic intrigues and measures. In this way Vitovt substantially contributed to the final disintegration of the Golden Horde and the formation of the Crimean Horde a few decades later. He also supported the claims of Khadji-Gerey to Crimean possessions. Subsequently, Khadji-Gerey and his son, Mengli-Gerey, affirmed Tokhmatish's old secession of the Mongol rights to Ukraine and southern Ukrainian steppes in favor of Lithuania.[16]

In order to strengthen their defense and to make his rule permanent in these areas, Grand Prince Vitovt immediately proceeded with the construction of fortresses, such as Karavul on the middle Dnieper River, Bilhorod and Chornohorod on the lower Dniester River, and Khadjibei on the banks of the Black Sea, approximately where present-day Odessa is located. Then, he settled these territories with *boyars*, who were military service bound, Tartars, Germans, and whoever was willing to go there, while throughout his vast realm he promoted colonization according to the self-government principle of the Magdeburg law system. His country was growing in wealth and power. In order to make the Ukrainian Orthodox Church independent from the Moscow Metropolitan and to not allow Moscow to confuse ecclesiastic matters in the Grand Principality of Lithuania-Rus', Vitovt took matters in his own hands, arranging for a council of the Orthodox bishops in Novhorodok and inducing them to elect their own Metropolitan against the politically motivated wishes of Moscow and Constantinople. Hryhorii Tsamblak became the Metropolitan in 1415, but was soon condemned by the Patriarch; however, nobody in Ukraine worried about this until Tsamblak died *circa* 1419. The Muscovite Metropolitan Photii was allowed by Vitovt to be the head of the Lithuanisn-Rus' Orthodox Church. It was a mistake and it proved that the Grand Prince was not greatly preoccupied with the interests of the Ukrainian and Byeloruthenian population in his realm.

Though Vitovt ardently defended the cause of the Grand Principality, he deserted the interests of the Orthodox population, the Ukrainians and Byeloruthenians in his realm, and as a Catholic who always looked for a compromise with the Polish Crown, he permitted injustice, inequality and discrimination against that population, turning the Orthodox into second or third-class subjects of the realm. The cause of the Orthodox Ukrainians and Byeloruthenians in the Commonwealth was immediately taken up by Prince Svidrigiello, the youngest brother of King Yagiello and the most colorful figure of the area. He closely aligned his personal interests, as a candidate for the grand-princely dignity, with the interests of the Ukrainians and Byeluruthenians, though he himself was a Catholic.

After his mother's death in 1392, Yagiello tried to regain the city of Vitebsk from Svidrigiello, having sent a Polish governor. Svidrigiello resisted, killed the governor and started an anti-Polish uprising, immediately recognizing the Polish threat to the Commonwealth. He did not meet with success; nevertheless, he did not submit and continued for many years to fight against both Polish attempts to penetrate and dominate Lithuania-Rus' and against those who treacherously collaborated with Polish plans, including Vitovt himself, against whom he waged a war in 1409 and by whom he was imprisoned for nine years. Prince Ostrozhsky secretly helped him to escape from prison in 1418.

In various periods of his unceasing struggle, Svidrigiello tried to ally his Catholic and Orthodox supporters' causes with those of the conservative Lithuanian circles, which opposed the union with Poland. He also allied himself with the Hungarians, the Muscovites, the Tartars, the Wallachians and the Teutonic Order. Thus, in order to preserve the independence of the Lithuanian-Rus' Commonwealth and the dominance of the Orthodox-Ukrainian and Byeloruthenian nobility, he was capable of organizing uprisings and continuing to wage wars against Yagiello, Vitovt, and later on his chief rival, Prince Sigismund.

At the time of Vitovt's death Svidrigiello ruled as a sovereign prince in the Siverian land, and then he was elected by the Lithuanian and Russian Lords as the Grand Prince and confirmed as such by King Yagiello. Yet, the Polish nobles feared his aggressive personality and developed an intrigue to stop him from assuming the office. There was also another reason for the conflict. Already during Vitovt's life time, Yagiello, following the dictation of the Polish nobles, conspired with the pro-Polish aristocrats in Volhinia and Podillia to snatch those provinces away from the Grand Principality and to annex them to the Polish Crown. Grand Prince Svidrigiello objected violently and a large-scale Polish-Lithuanian war was waged in 1431 with the Teutons, Wallachians and Tartars on the Lithuanian side. A temporary truce saved Yagiello and resulted in a compromise.

In order to defeat Svidrigiello, the Polish noblemen induced the election of Prince Sigismund, Vitovt's younger brother of a weaker personality, to the office of the Grand Prince of the Commonwealth. The Lithuanian ethnic territories were joined to Sigismund's, while the Byeloruthenian and Ukrainian ethnic territories were joined to Svidrigiello's camp. The Polish intrigue paid a handsome dividend: the Lithuanian-Rus' Commonwealth was divided into two hostile and warring parts with two hostile Grand Princes, a situation where ethnic, national and religious antagonisms could only lead to further troubles. The political organism of the Commonwealth was weakened substantially. Sigismund recognized Yagiello as his sovereign. Then an assassination attempt on Svidrigiello was organized by Sigismund and the Polish lords, but the Grand Prince luckily escaped the close call. A prolonged and very bloody war between the two contenders for the grand-princely throne resulted and lasted for three difficult years, accompanied by the burning, pillaging, ruining and impoverishing of the unhappy populace. Even Yagiello's death did not interrupt the war.

Although Svidrigiello succeeded in mobilizing a great armed force, joined again by the Teutonic and Livonian Knights, Tartars and Wallachians, he was defeated by Sigismund's forces on the Sviata River, because most of his allies arrived too late for the battle in September of 1435. The losses of Svidrigiello were too large; the number of those killed and imprisoned by Sigismund was enormous. Yet, Svidrigiello continued to resist and champion the cause of the Orthodox Ukrainians. He continued to organize the Ukrainian territories against Lithuanian and Polish aggression, including those territories under the domination of the Polish Crown, such as Galicia, Kholm and Podillia.

Eventually, Svidrigiello had to give up all hopes of retaining the grand-princely office, but he succeeded in becoming a sovereign prince of Volhinia and ruled there until his death in 1451. It was the most developed Ukrainian province, socially, culturally and economically, with a dense population. Under Svidrigiello's rule, the province lived its own separate Ukrainian national life without interference from Lithuania or Poland, since he always supported the cause of the Orthodox people, as was evident by his entire political career. Although brief, Svidrigiello's era in the national life of Ukraine, and in particular of Volhinia where he stayed longer, was very important since it was the time of their political self-assertion through uprisings and wars against the Polish and Lithuanian Catholic onslaughts. In addition, the principality of Kiev under the rule of Prince Olelko (Oleksander), Olgierd's grandson, and his son Semen, was also able to assert its national-Ukrainian character for a short period of time.[17]

At the time, when the bloody war was waged between Svidrigiello and Sigismund, an important ecclesiastic event took place which deeply affected the spiritual and cultural life of the Ukrainian people, both in the short and the long run. Namely, a strong movement toward a union between the Catholic Church of Rome and the Orthodox Church of Constantinople developed. The Ukrainian Orthodox Church under the leadershjp of Metropolitan Isydor was ready for the move. The Ferraro-Florentine Council was held between 1437 and 1439, at the end of which the act of the union was concluded.

After having defeated Svidrigiello in his bid for grand-princely authority, and after the latter withdrew to the principality of Volhinia, Grand Prince Sigismund came to a full realization of the growing inroads made by the Poles in Lithuania through colonization and the assuming of influential offices there, as well as by increasing the core of the pro-Polish nobility among the Lithuanian lords. He began to look for allies in defending Lithuanian political integrity among the Livonian Knights, Mongols and Austrians, in order to prevent the eventual over-powering and annexation of the Grand Principality by the Polish Crown. He tried to assert Lithuanian sovereignty by political declarations and diplomatic measures.[18]

He was not popular, having been rather cruel and insulting towards the nobles. His feud with Svidrigiello also made him many enemies. In 1440, he was killed by a group of aristocratic assassins, having been accused of being hostile to the nobility and friendly to the commoners. There were a few Ukrainians among the assassins, and it was possible that Svidrigiello was somehow involved in the plot. From the point of view of the Ukrainian national and political interest in the Lithuanian-Rus' Commonwealth, Sigismund must be negatively appraised. He deepened the split between the opposing camps, increased the religious and national discrimination and actually facilitated the growth of Polish inroads.

After Sigismund's death, Casimir, a younger brother of the Polish king Wladyslaw, was elected the Grand Prince of Lithuania against the will of the king and the Polish nobles. Initially, Casimir, being too young to rule, was fully under the influence of the Lithuanian noblemen and thus the independence of Lithuania was asserted. However, soon thereafter King Wladyslaw of Poland was killed in a war against the Turks, and Casimir was immediately elected the king, according to the Polish wish to unite the royal and the grand-princely dignity in one person as a step toward a more real and lasting union between Poland and Lithuania. The Lithuanian nobles objected, and demanded that Casimir either stay in Lithuania or resign as the Grand Prince. Casimir did not do either. After having moved to Cracow, the Polish capital, he began to pursue a strictly centralistic policy, continuing to use his authority as the Grand Prince to advance Polish interests in Lithuania according to the wishes of the Polish ruling circles. Not only were the Lithuanians losing during the prolonged reign of King Casimir, favoring the Polish cause, but the Orthodox Ukrainian population was also steadily forced into ever more difficult and more disadvantageous positions in all respects, religious, national, social and economic, because of the legal, administrative and social discrimination which became the official policy of the Polish-Lithuanian state at that time.

With Casimir's death in 1492, matters improved a little in favor of the Lithuanians, but not with respect to the Orthodox Ukrainian population. Oleksander, Casimir's younger brother, was elected as the Grand Prince, while Jan Olbracht was elected King. During his short reign, 1492-1506, the Lithuanian lords attempted again to assert their independence from Poland. Both political entities lived for a while in a completely separate national life.

Antagonism was on the rise; both countries refused to help each other in their separate political difficulties. The Lithuanian Council of Nobles (Lords) refused to assist the Polish Crown, which faced a threat of war with the Ottoman Empire, unless Poland agreed to create "fair and equal conditions" in the relations of both nations.

The election of Oleksander to the Polish throne in 1501 again restored the personal union between Poland and Lithuania. Although the Polish nobles had drawn the act which attempted to bring a closer federation calling for "one people, one nation, one brotherhood, common council, one head, one king and lord," the Lithuanian nobles rejected the proposal.

The degradation of the legal and social position of the Orthodox Ukrainians, having been jointly suppressed by the Polish and Lithuanian aristocratic rules, was complete. Only Catholic bishops were admitted to the Council of Nobles, while Orthodox bishops were excluded from it; high state offices were reserved for Catholics only; an Orthodox could not be a chancellor or governor, *voyevoda*, or top military commander, *hetman*. Discriminatory practices were constantly on the rise despite the fact that Grand Prince Sigismund once *de jure* granted equal rights and privileges to the Orthodox and the Catholic nobility and gentry in order to undermine Svidrigiello's political standing with the Orthodox Ukrainians and Byeloruthenians.[19] He was not trusted, but the move caused some dissension and desertion in Svidrigiello's camp. The unfair treatment and direct abuses of the Orthodox townspeople and peasantry mounted; the Orthodox felt deeply insulted. Anti-Polish and anti-Lithuanian conspiracies on religious and national grounds were increasing, and the Ukrainian and Byeloruthenian nobles were exhibiting ever greater leanings toward Orthodox Muscovy, Lithuania's deadly enemy for a century and a half already.

In Vitovt's time, Muscovy was comparatively weak and afraid of the Lithuanian-Rus' Commonwealth. In the second half of the fifteenth century the situation was entirely different. The Grand Principality of Muscovy already was a powerful state, while Lithuania was hopelessly weakened by the continuous struggle against Polish inroads and internal dissension. Ukrainian princes and nobles were going over to Moscow's camp, giving Moscow an ever greater justification to intervene in Lithuanian internal affairs under the guise of protecting the interests of the Orthodox population suffering from Catholic Polish-Lithuanian oppression. In fact, Moscow, in order to justify its growing imperialistic policies, developed the doctrine of being "the Third Rome" with the historical mission of uniting under its scepter all Orthodox peoples, in particular, the Ukrainians and Byeloruthenians. The claim was also supported by the dynastic argument that Muscovite Grand Princes, having been of the Ruryk house, were fully entitled to take over the Kievan-Rus' traditions and to restore the realm under Muscovite leadership. The argument led to the Muscovite principle of "gathering all Rus' lands" once believed in and championed by Olgierd, and perhaps by Vitovt. Unfortunately, in the second half of the fifteenth century Lithuania was too weak to maintain that claim and thus it was waging a losing battle against the growing aggressiveness of Muscovy.[20]

In 1481, there was a conspiracy of the Ukrainian-Rus'ian noblemen to separate and annex to Muscovy all lands east of the Berezyna River, *de jure* under Lithuanian sovereignty. The conspiracy was discovered and the conspirators, Princes Mykhail Olelkovych, Ivan Holshansky, Fedir Bilsky and others were punished by death; however, some Siverianian and Chernihivian princes accepted Muscovite protection and joined their territories with the Muscovite Grand Principality. This took place in the last quarter of the fifteenth century. Numerous armed border skirmishes between Lithuania and Muscovy continued.

The wars of 1492-1494 and 1500-1503 between the two contenders for the Ukrainian and Byeloruthenian inheritance gave to Muscovy enormous territorial gains, some 70 regions with 319 towns and numerous villages, including Chernihiv, Novhorod Siversky, Starodub, Putivl, Rylsk, Homel, Lubech, Briansk, Dorohobuzh, Bila, Toropets and others. The Muscovite Grand Prince Ivan III arrogantly stated to Lithuanian envoys that he considered as his fatherland all of Rus', meaning also those Rus'ian territories which were still under Lithuanian authority. A few years later, in 1519, Muscovite envoys declared in Rome that Lithuania unjustly dominated Kiev, Smolensk, Vitebsk and Polotsk, and if the Grand Prince of Moscow wanted to annex those lands, then he wanted only his own former lands and not any foreign ones.[21] It was a very convenient Muscovite maneuver to circumvent any accusation of being imperialistic. Ivan continued arrogantly and aggressively to intervene supposedly on behalf of Orthodoxy in the internal affairs of the Lithuanian-Ukrainian Grand Principality.

One must agree that Lithuania and Poland made grave mistakes in struggling between themselves about whether they should or should not constitute a political union. This led to an internal split of the ethnic, national, religious and social character of their commonwealth which weakened their resistance and helped Muscovy to grow. Three centuries later, the Russian Empire, continuing Muscovite imperialism, absorbed all of Lithuania and most of Poland and Ukraine through the partitioning of Poland.

The political aspirations of the Ukrainians were at this time manifested by two developments: the Hlynsky and Mukha uprisings against Polish and Lithuanian oppression. Prince Mykhailo Hlynsky was Catholic, a well educated and trained man of exceptional abilities, a capable military leader. He played a major political role at Grand Prince Oleksander's court and provoked the hatred of others, especially so because he supported and favored the Ukrainians and Byeloruthenians and eventually became their leader. When Oleksander died, Hlynsky was unjustly accused of his murder and of planning to seize the Lithuanian throne. His great service to Lithuania by soundly defeating the Tartars at the battle of Kletsko in 1506 was completely forgotten. An anti-Ukrainian campaign ensued. In order to defend himself and to champion the Ukrainian cause, Hlynsky with the support of the Tartars and Muscovy, began an uprising. Unfortunately neither the Ukrainian nobles nor the foreign allies significantly helped him. The Tartars did not arrive, while the Muscovites, after having achieved their ends in conquering certain Byeloruthenian towns, concluded a peace treaty with Poland. Hlynsky terminated the uprising and went to Moscow. At first he was treated favorably and with dignity, but later on Vasilii III of Muscovy failed to keep promises given to Hlynsky, in particular to grant him Smolensk as a vassal principality, from where the latter had hoped to resume his political plans. Hlynsky began negotiations with King Sigismund of Poland for his possible return and the restoration of the Polish-Lithuanian state. For this he was imprisoned in Moscow, but was later freed for family reasons. Vasilii III had married his niece, Princess Helena. At the time of Helena's regency he again rose to political prominence at the Muscovite court, but a little later he was accused by his enemies of poisoning Vasilii, the Grand Prince, and was imprisoned again and died in 1534. This marked the last attempt by the Ukrainian nobles to defend the rights of their country with Moscow's assistance.

A few years earlier, in the western corner of Ukraine, in Galicia, which for almost one hundred and eighty years suffered Polish oppressive rule and national and religious discrimination, national, social and religious uprisings began, led by Mukha, and supported by Stephan the Great, the ruler, *hospodar*, of Moldavia. The Moldavian state was Orthodox and there were vital relations between the Moldavians and the Orthodox Ukrainians of Galicia. The uprising in 1490, was participated in by all social classes; the Ukrainian *boyars*, country gentry, townspeople and peasants, and its armed force reached some 10,000 men. The insurgents soon dominated all of southern Galicia, reaching the towns of Halych and Rohatyn, and posed a real threat to Polish rule. The Poles marshalled a great army to oppose

Mukha's insurgents and finally defeated him in a battle on the Dniester River. Nevertheless, even after this misfortune, *otaman* Mukha did not give up the struggle and continued to organize anew and lead armed resistances against Polish domination in West Ukraine. Later on, there were also other attempts to rise against the Polish rule, either with Moldavian or even Turkish assistance. It must be underscored that Hlynsky's and Mukha's uprisings were nationally motivated, and represented continuing links in the never ceasing political and military struggle of the Rus'ian-Ukrainians to free themselves from Polish oppression; they were connecting Svidrigiello's struggle, somewhat ideologically, with the early Cossack uprisings and Khmelnytsky's war of liberation.[21]

The Polish Supremacy. Although *de jure* most of Ukraine was annexed by the Polish Crown immediately before the Union of Lublin in 1569 except for Galicia which was incorporated by Poland *nota bene* at the end of the fourteenth century when Polish political supremacy prevailed, the penetration of Polish political power had made enormous headway much earlier throughout all of Ukraine. Therefore, it might be safe to speak of a Polish supremacy in political, social, religious and economic respects in Ukraine since the beginning of the sixteenth century; namely, since Sigismund I, the Old, of Poland who had assumed the thrones of the Polish King and the Lithuanian Grand Prince in 1506. For 38 years he united, in his person, these two authorities and during his reign actually prepared the completion of the union with its negative aspects for the Ukrainian people in particular.

A deep dissension among various political groups was a distinct feature of this lengthy period of time. The Polish nobles pressed steadily to bring about the complete unification of two political entities; while the Lithuanian lords, who desired a specific form of unification, wanted to preserve as before a certain degree of Lithuanian sovereignty. The Ukrainian and Byeloruthenian nobility was afraid of the union and, not having recognized the danger of Muscovite imperialism, continuously exhibited pro-Muscovite political leanings. The broad masses of the population did not participate in this process, since they were legally placed in a low social and political position, and also, had no voice in, nor any knowledge of political matters.

Meanwhile, a new social-political development was taking place during the first half of the sixteenth century. The class of the landed gentry, a lower-level nobility, was growing in number and in social and political significance under the Polish Crown and in the Lithuanian Grand Principality. This new class favored the idea of a union of these two states. In the wake of the union, it expected to reduce the political influence of the grand nobility and to expand its own importance, prestige and wealth. In this way a new perspective was added to the social and political process.

King Sigismund I did not favor a complete union, and, perhaps to underscore the separate political identity of Lithuania, in 1544 he transferred grand-princely authority *de facto* to his only son, Sigismund-August, who was proclaimed *de jure* the Grand Prince. This was, as Hrushevsky and Polonska-Vasylenko pointed out, the last triumph of the Lithuanian noble separatists.[22]

Sigismund I, the Old, died in 1548, and Sigismund II August assumed the reign in both countries, ruling until 1572. In 1551, the grand nobles and the landed gentry of the Lithuanian-Ukrainian regions gathered in a *seim* (parliament), and expressed anew their anti-union feelings. The issue became very acute and sharp polemics evolved. The Polish side argued that actually the union had been an accomplished fact ever since Krevo, and it listed all the Polish lands which were supposedly annexed by Lithuania. The Lithuanian side denied these Polish arguments.

In 1558, Lithuania got involved in a prolonged and difficult Livonian war, participated in by the Livonian Knights, Muscovy, Sweden and Denmark, which hit Lithuania rather hard. The exhausted Lithuanian gentry then sent a petition to the king to carry out a union with Poland, to which the grand nobles had actually objected. The king for some time ignored the petition and matters dragged on for two years. Meanwhile, unexpectedly the gentry of the Volhinian and the Pidliashian regions, western provinces of Ukraine, again asked the king to speed up the union because the Lithuanian government did not defend them against Tartar raids, and, as a consequence of this, they would soon turn these lands into a desert. These regions suffered greatly because of the Tartar booty excursions, while the Livonian war, which increased their misery, did not interest them at all. By joining Poland, the landed gentry of these lands hoped to free themselves from the burdens of the war.

A *seim* convened in Lublin in 1569 to take care of the matter. Antagonistic feelings ran high. The Lithuanian nobles and gentry proposed a union in which there would be two separate *seimy* (parliaments) working jointly only when electing the Grand Prince and in matters concerning foreign affairs. They would have separate monetary systems, and separate top state offices held by native-born "citizens" only. The Polish side objected to the proposal. The Lithuanian delegates, counting on royal support in the controversy, left the debate with the idea of terminating the *seim* convention. However, the Polish delegates continued the deliberations, decided to annex Volhinia,

Podillia, Kiev and Pidliasha to the Polish Crown, supposedly on the basis of "Polish historical rights" to those Ukrainian lands, and to abolish all hindrances to a complete Polish-Lithuanian state union. The Lithuanian delegates returned, but their cause had meanwhile been gravely hurt. The Polish delegation, arguing in favor of the annexation of these Ukrainian provinces to the Polish Crown, listed all the possible gains from it for Poland, while the interests of the native Ukrainian population were not even mentioned.

On July 1, 1569, the Act of the Union was concluded. From now on the Polish Crown and the Lithuanian Grand Principality had to constitute one *Res Publica*, with a jointly elected King of Poland who was at the same time proclaimed the Grand Prince of Lithuania. Parliament, the *seim*, became one with one monetary system. The Polish and Lithuanian gentry received the right to unrestricted landed properties in any of the two countries. The top government offices, the state coats of arms, finances, military and administrations remained separate. The Lithuanian Grand Principality retained Ukrainian as its official language, and kept its own laws and legal system.

The Polish-Lithuanian Union in the city of Lublin had a most negative and lasting impact upon the fortunes of the Ukrainian people. It confirmed the previous direct annexation of additional Ukrainian provinces by Poland, and in this way most of Ukraine was subject to the Polish Crown, which traditionally had exhibited hostile attitudes toward the Ukrainians. Only a few Ukrainian borderlands were politically controlled by other state organizations: some parts of the Polissia region remained under Lithuania; Bukovina was under Moldavian sovereignty; Carpathian Ukraine, south of the Carpathian Mountains, was at first under Hungarian rule and after 1526, its western part was occupied by Austria and its eastern by Transylvania, *Semyhorod*. Some eastern borderlands of Ukraine, including most of the Chernihiv and Siverianian districts, were incorporated by the growing power of Moscovy. The descendents of the Chernihivian-Siverianian princes, who had come under Muscovite supremacy, initiated the famous aristrocratic families of later Muscovite Tsardom and the Russian Empire, such as Vorotynskii, Trubetskoi, Bielskii, Odoievskii and others, as asserted by Kholmsky. Some Lithuanian patriots hoped to reverse the union, but this was in vain. Lublin reduced the political and international significance of the Grand Principality almost to nothing, thus sparking a never ceasing antagonism.[23]

The Ukrainian people for the most part had been exposed to grave abuses by the ruling Polish element; ruthless religious pressure and discrimination by chauvinistic Polish Catholicism, which was more nationally than ecclesiastically minded. The Cracow, and later Warsaw governments were simply obsessed by a policy of denationalization and Polonization, by which they hoped to make Ukraine a Polish land permanently. Policies of national and religious discrimination toward the Orthodox Ukrainians became a major device in the hands of the Polish government and Church to enforce Polonization to an ever increasing degree. Later chapters in this volume will clearly illustrate the difficult conditions of life in Ukraine under Polish domination which lasted until the partitions of Poland some two hundred and twenty years later. The progress and growth of the Polish ethnic element in Ukraine immediately assumed a dominant position, and was greatly advanced by a very liberal distribution of vast land reserves among Polish noblemen, such as: Zamoiski, Tarnowski, Koniecpolski, and the Polonized family of Wisniowiecki, once the Ukrainian noble family of Vyshnyvetsky. In order to take full material advantage of the landed estates they received, where the population was sparse due to the Tartars' booty expeditions, these noblemen undertook large-scale colonization programs with Polish, German, Wallachian and other ethnic peasant elements. These settlers were attracted by being given the so-called "freedoms," exemptions from taxes and servitude labor for twenty or forty years. This irked the local Ukrainian population, which had suffered exploitation, discrimination and injustice.

The hardships of the Ukrainian people were also intensified by the political instabilities in Poland, which was constantly involved in some kind of serious war. King Stefan Batory fought against Muscovy. King Sigismund III, Vasa, waged increasing wars to acquire either the Swedish or Muscovite throne. He also embarked on a fanatical policy of discrimination against Orthodoxy and the Protestants, which seriously contributed to internal turmoil. King Wladyslaw IV, Sigismund's son, continued these warfares. Some plans were also developed to start an all-out crusade of the Christian nations against the Ottoman Empire.[24]

Polish involvement in Muscovite affairs came at the time of the Muscovite so-called "Time of Troubles." It was an opportune time for foreign intervention, since Muscovy was extremely weak and was being harassed by all kinds of political, social, and even natural misfortunes. Zigismund III and Wladyslaw IV of Poland were tempted to sieze the Tsarist throne for themselves. The material and human costs would have been enormous, and eventually all Polish plans ended in failure. In the meantime the Muscovites had overcome all their troubles, defeating Polish, Swedish and other interventions, and had elected a Muscovite, Mykhail Romanov, their Tsar in 1613, who shortly thereafter resumed Muscovite imperialistic policies. Meanwhile, Ukraine paid for all these ambitious Polish political plans and projects by hard work, human lives and great material sacrifices.

The Rise of the Cossacks. There was, however, still another dimension to the social and political life of the Ukrainian people of the period discussed. With some assistance from Grand Prince Vitovt the Crimean Horde of the Tartars was organized. Khadji-Gerey and Mengli-Gerey of the Crimean Horde remained, at first, in alliance with the Grand Principality of Lithuania-Rus', but later, Mengli-Gerey allied himself with Muscovy and accepted the protectorate of the Ottoman Empire. From that time on, for at least three hundred years, the Tartars of the Crimean Horde became the real scourge of Ukraine. It was very unfortunate for Ukraine that King Casimir allied himself with the Golden Horde, the decadent rival of the young Crimean Horde, and thus antagonized Mengli-Gerey, who was also incited against the Grand Principality of Lithuania-Rus' by Ivan III of Muscovy. In 1482, Mengli-Gerey mercilessly assaulted Ukraine, ruined the city of Kiev and devastated the country; masses of Ukrainian people were made slaves and were taken away to slave markets and sold to foreign lands. Casimir did not undertake any measures, not even diplomatic, to defend the country against Mengli-Gerey's assault, while Ivan of Muscovy thankfully rewarded him for devastating Ukraine, which was the cradle of Kievan-Rus', the inheritance of which he claimed as his assumed right.

Subsequently, in 1492-1497, the Golden and the Crimean Hordes made peace between themselves and continuously pillaged Ukraine; the Kievan, Podillian, Volhinian and Chernihivian provinces suffered the most. Material and human losses were immeasurable. In 1497, the Tartars were finally beaten by the forces of Prince Konstantyn Ostrozhsky, the Ukrainian nobleman, and a few years later (in 1505) they were defeated for the second time in the Battle of Kletsko by Prince Mykhail Hlynsky, who, as it was pointed out before, undertook an insurrection to free Ukraine from Polish-Lithuanian oppression, but did not meet with success.

The sporadic victories of Ukrainian noblemen over the Tartars did not help matters. The Polish-Lithuanian government did not undertake any worthwhile military measures to provide permanent protection of the country against the merciless Tartar looting, burning and devastating of Ukraine. The Crimean Tartars continually invaded during the spring and summer months of almost every year, using smaller or larger detachments to carry away booty and slaves from Ukraine. They were the Times of Horror, the *lykholittia* in Ukraine, which dramatically added to the misery of life under Polish national and religious discrimination and economic exploitation. In order to pacify the Tartars, Casimir and Oleksander of Poland were ready to offer them an annual tribute, instead of resisting their onslaughts by military means. The national tragedy of the Ukrainian people was not taken into account. Sporadic attempts by the Polish government to repulse the Tartar booty raids under King Wladyslaw Warnenczyk and Oleksander Olbracht failed. On the other hand, Moscow gave the Tartars money to construct fortresses against possible military retaliations by the Lithuanian government.

As a result of these unfortunate developments, a new social-military class arose: the *Cossacks*. The genesis of the Ukrainian Cossacks may perhaps be traced as far back as the early era of the Kievan realm and the early period of the Asiatic onslaught on Ukraine, and it may be associated with the military formations which fought against the Cumans and the "people under Tartar protection."[25] The term "Cossack" is, without doubt, of Turkman origin and its meaning has changed in the course of time. The name was used by the Cumans, Tartars and Turks, and not infrequently it was applied to guardsmen, warriors or adventurers. It was also used to designate light cavalry, as well as the troops used to watch and to guard the borderlands and outposts. It also identified free individuals; the freedom-loving and adventurous people without a definite occupation. The name was utilized by the Ukrainians to identify their host of freedom-fighters and it was popularized throughout the world.

On the basis of this general, historical, sociological and political background, the essentially Ukrainian Cossack phenomenon developed as a result of conditions existing in the European south-east at that time. The national and religious discrimination in Ukraine under Polish-Lithuanian rule, the growing burden of peasant serfdom, and the constant harassing of the population by the Tartar booty raids, on the one hand, and the vast availability of the wide steppes to the East and South of Ukraine where no foreign authority and no discrimination prevailed, on the other, induced the dissatisfied Ukrainian as well as some foreign ethnic elements, to penetrate the "no man's land" in the steppe regions in an attempt to escape the oppression of foreign domination, and there to lead a free although harsh life. Freedom and natural riches, the abundance of fish in the rivers and animals in the so-called "wild fields," attracted many who could not find decent living conditions in the so-called "civilized world."

At first, some individual Cossacks and later Cossack groups went into the depths of the steppes temporarily, during spring and summer months. In the autumn they would come home for the winter months. In the steppes the Cossacks led an adventurous life far from settled areas, getting more and more involved in fighting the Mongol raiders. The excursions in the steppes were called *ukhody*, and soon they began to adopt the character of pioneering. They began to settle on a permanent basis in the remote regions, where the Polish oppressive hand could not reach them. Other Cossacks settled in the townships and villages of densely populated southern Ukraine, claiming for themselves a special social standing.

In addition to the Tartar raids, the Turks also began to assault Ukraine at the end of the fifteenth century. The Cossacks, a semi-military class made war against "the infidels," the Tartars and Turks, as their "sacred duty" and "historical mission." It seems that wherever Mongol met with Arian and they clashed in a struggle for their ethnic survival, a Cossack-like formation immediately developed to resist the menace of expanding Mongol domination.[26] The Cossack class in Ukraine, in its original form, began to wither away with the gradual decline and elimination of the Mongol threat at the end of the eighteenth century. Of its past glory, only the name remained.

The Cossacks initiated the so-called armed colonization of the Ukrainian steppes, which at the end of the process were almost entirely taken away from the Tartars, and became ethnically and nationally Ukrainian. It was actually, historically speaking, a recurring revindication of traditionally Ukrainian territories, which were taken away by the recurring waves of Asiatic nomad invasions since pre-historic times.

Life in the vast steppes, the "wild fields," was extremely demanding and full of potential danger. Wild animals, vagabonds and bandits, and, of course, Tartar excursions and Tartar marauders threatened the safety and life of the Cossack pioneers, the *ukhodnyky*. As a result, they began to organize themselves into semi-military units, at times selecting their own leaders, the *otamans,* and at times acting under the command of the borderland officials and commanders. They undertook very early the defense of Ukrainian borderlands against any surprise assaults by the Tartars by maintaining distant outposts and constructing watch-towers. By fire signals they warned the Cossack units and the peaceful populace of approaching danger. Soon they shifted from defense to offense and carried out numerous expeditions and raids deep into the steppes and the territories under Tartar domination and Turk sovereignty. S. Poloz, O. Dashkevych, S. Zborovsky, I. Pidkova, B. Ruzhynsky, and of course, D. Baida-Vyshnyvetsky, some of them of noble descent, were several of the famous Cossack leaders, or *otamans,* at the early stage of the Cossack organizational process.

Already in 1492, the Khan of the Crimean Tartars complained at the Polish royal court of the Cossacks, who supposedly were Polish citizens. From that time on, the complaints continued as Cossack aggressiveness grew. The Polish court vacillated in its Cossack policy. The kings advised the Cossacks to leave the Tartars alone because Cossack warfares aggrevated Polish-Tartar-Turk relationships, which at times in later decades almost caused open wars among these nations. On the other side, however, at times Polish officials were advised to organize Cossack detachments and assault the Tartars. For example, in 1520, S. Poloz was authorized by the government to gather together and hire the Cossacks for warfare against the Mongols.[27]

Prince Dmytro Baida-Vyshnyvetsky began to unify separate Cossack units into one effective organization in the 1540's and initiated a construction of a Cossack fortress on Khortytsia Island, beyond the Dnieper cataracts. He planned to develop the Cossacks into a strong political and military force, and for this reason asked the Lithuanian government to assist him with people and arms. The government was afraid to anger the Tartars, and refused, with the usual advice: leave the Mongols alone. The Turks and Tartars, fully conscious of the Cossack threat, meanwhile beleaguered the fortress, besieged the *Sitch*, on Khortytsia. Vyshnyvetsky retreated to the city of Cherkasy and upon asking Moscow for assistance, was given money and land grants. However, a joint Ukrainian-Muscovite military expedition against the Tartars did not bring any concrete gains. On being asked by Moscow, Vyshnyvetsky fought in the Caucasian Mountains against the Chercasians, and subsequently returned to Ukraine. Vyshnyvetsky's Cossack formations were also taking part in the Livonian war on the side of the Polish king against the Muscovites. While attempting to acquire the Moldavian throne, Vyshnyvetsky, the founder of the Cossack Host, was captured by the Turks and executed in 1563.[28]

The Cossack movement continued to grow after Baida-Vyshnyvetsky's tragic death, praised in folk songs and poetry. The Cossacks established themselves permanently on the islands of the Dnieper River, where they formed an imposing organizational and military center. Since the 1580's it was generally referred to as the *Sitch*. The Ukrainian Cossacks began to be called the *Sitchovyky* or *Zaporozhe* Cossacks, from beyond the cataracts. Cossack assaults against the Tartars and Turks constantly grew in number and force, causing more and more complaints by Istanbul and Bakhchisaray at the Polish court, substantially contributing to the straining of Polish-Tartar-Turkish relations. The Turks and the Tartars considered the Cossacks subjects of the Polish Crown, while the *Sitch* Cossacks regarded themsleves as an autonomous community, which soon began to develop its own foreign relations and policies towards Moscow, the Ottoman Empire, the German Empire, Moldavia, Wallachia and other lands. In the 1570's for example, the Cossack host, under the leadership of the *otamans,* Pidkova, Shakh and others, aggressively intervened in Moldavian domestic affairs. Moldavia was a vassal of the Ottoman Empire, and Cossack intervention there angered Istanbul even more. This further strained Polish-Turkish relations. During one of such Cossack escapades in Moldavia, *otaman* Pidkova was captured, imprisoned by the Poles and executed in the city of Lviv. But this did not stop the Cossacks from involving themselves in Moldavian affairs for the next twenty years. At the end of the sixteenth century, the Cossack Host became a very important component in the strategic plan of the German emperor and the Holy See to organize an all-out Christian crusade against the Turks. An alliance was suggested to the Cossacks, and an imperial envoy, Eric Lassota, was sent to the *Sitch* to negotiate with them as an autonomous political entity.

In connection with these developments, *otaman* S. Nalyvaiko and *Hetman* H. Loboda undertook large-scale warfare against the Moldavian *hospodar* (ruler), defeated him and forced him to sever his vassal relationship to the Ottoman Empire and accept vassalage to the Emperor. Together with the Moldavians they then waged a war against the Turks.

Being afraid of political complications, which could have resulted from the bold Cossack undertakings, the Polish-Lithuanian *Res Publica's* royal court succeeded in involving Cossack troops in the Livonian war against the Muscovites, diverting their attention from Turkish and Moldavian affairs. In 1572, King Sigismund-August advised his top military commanders to register three hundred Cossacks for government services in defending the border castles and districts against the Tartars. The number of the so-called *registered* Cossacks was ridiculously small; the majority of the Cossacks continued to spend part of their time in the *Sitch*, others in the townships and villages, living by hunting, fishing and farming. King Stefan Batory increased the number of the *registered* Cossacks to 500 and finally, to 1000. The town of Terekhtemyriv, where a hospital was established for them,[29] became the organizational center of the registered Cossacks.

In the *Sitch*, beyond the Dnieper cataracts, similar to a military camp or a fortress, the active mass of the Cossacks centered their lives around military preparedness. The Cossacks came from all walks of life; nobility, gentry, townspeople and peasants. Although mainly Ukrainians, there were numerous representatives of many nationalities: Poles, Serbs, Moldavians,

Wallachians, Lithuanians, and others. However, in the *Sitch* an absolute equality of all Cossacks prevailed; there was no national or social discrimination, although the Orthodox religion was predominant. Women and children were not allowed to live or stay in the *Sitch*; it definitely was a military base and its strict discipline could not be threatened by any form of family life. During times of peace, many Cossacks left the *Sitch* and went to their settlements and villages, either in the steppes or the southern towns or villages of Ukraine where they lived their family life. They reported to the *Sitch* whenever called on to do so or when an emergency arose. Outside the *Sitch*, the social differentiation of the Cossacks began and progressed. Already in the second half of the sixteenth century there were two groups of Cossacks; the wealthy Cossack "aristocrats," small in number, and the majority of the Cossack commoners who were poor or of moderate means, the *holota* or *siroma*.

In the *Sitch*, all Cossacks gathered for the Council, which elected the officers, the *hetman*, the supreme military leader; the *koshovyi*, the commander of the *Sitch*; the commanders of divisions, the *kurinni*; the *oboznyi*, the *osauly*, the *pysar*, the chief of the office, the judges, and other minor officials. The *Sitch* provided a military training school for young males looking for a military career. Each new recruit coming to the *Sitch* was placed under the care of an older Cossack who was responsible for his training.

The Cossacks fought on land and sea. The overland military expeditions were carried out by the Cossacks as cavalry, on horseback, while other battles were fought on foot, as infantry. Military tactics had been learned from the Tartars. For naval expeditions they used large boats, called *chaiky*, with a complement of 50 to 70 men, equipped with cannons. Sea-going vessels were utilized for naval operations in the Black Sea to assault the Tartar and Turk sea-ports and their towns and cities on the seashores, from where masses of war prisoners and slaves captured by the Mongols during their raids in Ukraine, were freed.[30]

After the notorious Union of Lublin in 1569, when Polish terror substantially increased, the first stage of Cossack struggles in defense of Ukraine, the struggle against the Mongols and Turks, was coming slowly to an end. In the second stage, struggles against Polish oppression began and culiminated in the establishment of an independent national Ukrainian state, the Cossack-Hetman State, in 1648. It was the third national-political assertion of the Ukrainian-Rus'ians; the first being the state of the Antes, and the second being the Kievan-Galician realm.

1. T. Chase, *The Story of Lithuania*, New York, 1946, initial chapters: J. Stukas, *Awakening Lithuania*, Madison, N.J., 1966, pp. 1-8; N,. Polonska-Vasylenko, *Istoria Ukrainy*, Munich, 1972, Vol. I. pp. 305-310.

2. M. Hrushevsky, *Istoria Ukrainy-Rusy*, New York, 1955, Vol. IV, pp. 9-11.

3. *Ibid.*, Vol. IV, pp. 110-114, 448-449, 457.

4. M. Lubavskii, *Oblasnoie dielenie i miestnoie upravlenie V. Kn. Litovskavo*, Moscow, 1893, p. 36; also, Hrushevsky, *op. cit.*, Vol. IV, pp. 94-99; S. Kutrzeba, *Historya ustroju Polski*, Vol. II, *Litwa*, Lwow, 1914, pp. 70-72.

5. N. Fr.-Chirovsky, *A History of the Russian Empire*, New York, 1973, Vol. I, pp. 167-173; G. Vernadsky and M. Karpovich, *A History of Russia*, Vol. III, *The Mongols and Russia*, New Haven, 1953; on the fortunes of the Golden Horde.

6. Chirovsky, *op. cit.*, Vol. I, p. 171.

7. V. Smirnov, *Krimskoie Khanstvo pod vierkhovenstvom Ottomanskoi Porty*, St. Petersburg, 1887.

8. *Moskovski chtenia*, 1883, Vol. I, p. 2; the terminology of Yerodiakon Yakim; N. Fr.-Chirovsky, *Old Ukraine, Its Socio-Economic History prior to 1781*, Madison, N.J., 1963, p. 133.

9. Polonska-Vasylenko, *op. cit.*, Vol. I, p. 310; Hrushevsky, *op. cit.*, Vol. IV, pp. 66-78, 450-456.

10. The expansion of Lithuanian domination; J. Wolf, *Rod Gedyminow*, Cracow, 1886; the same, *Kniaziowie litewski-ruscy*, Warsaw, 1895; Chase, *op. cit.*, first chapters; Polonska-Vasylenko, *op. cit.*, Vol. I, pp. 310-311.

11. I. Levkovych, *Narys istorii Volynskoi zemli*, Winnipeg, 1953, pp. 82-86.

12. Polonska-Vasylenko, *op. cit.*, Vol. I, p. 312; also, Lubavskii, *op. cit., loc. cit.*; Hrushevsky, *op. cit.*, Vol. IV. pp. 94-99.

13. O. Halecki, *History of Poland*, New York, 1943. pp. 65-85; Kutrzeba, *op. cit.* Vol. II, pp. 25-35; Hrushevsky, *op. cit.* Vol. IV, pp. 128-129, 132-133.

14. D. Doroshenko, *Narys istorii Ukrainy*, Munich, 1966, Vol. I, pp. 105-106; Polonska-Vasylenko, *op. cit.*, Vol. I, p. 317.

15. V. Antonovych, *Ocherk istorii Velikavo Kniazhestva Litovskavo*, Kiev, 1885, p. 160; Doroshenko, *loc. cit.*; Halecki, *op. cit.*, pp. 77-78.

16. Hrushevsky, *op. cit.*, Vol. IV, pp. 84-88, 457-462; Smirnov, *op. cit.*, p. 240, *Acta Tomiciana*, I, app. 9.

17. Svidrigiello; M. Holubets, *Velyka istoria Ukrainy*, Lviv, 1935, pp. 348-352; Hrushevsky, *op. cit.*, Vol. IV, pp. 184-202; Hrushevsky appraised Svidrigiello very negatively (p. 198).

18. Hrushevsky, *op. cit.*, Vol. IV, pp. 227-228.

19. Polonska-Vasylenko, *op. cit.*, Vol. I, pp. 326-327.

20. O. Ohloblyn, *Moskovska teoria III Rymu v XVI-XVII st*, Munich, 1951, in particular, p. 28; V. Hryshko, *Istorychno-pravne pidgruntia teorii III Rymu*, Munich, 1953, pp. 36, 40, and 44; an older Russian interpretation of the theory; V. Malinin, "Starets Yelizarova monastyria Filofeia i yevo poslania" *Istorichesko-literaturnie issledovanie*, Kiev, 1901; the newer interpretation; N. Ulianov, "Kompleks Filofeia," *Novyi zhurnal*, New York, 1956, No. XLV, pp. 253-256; The first Rome became Catholic and fell; Constantinople, the second Rome, fell, because of similar reasons. It indulged itself in the papal union. Moscow, the third Rome, has taken over the leadership of true Orthodox Christianity and has remained faithful. It shall stand forever; briefly, Chirovsky, *A History of the Russian Empire*, Vol. I, pp. 239-243.

21. Hlynsky and Mukha: Hrushevsky, *op. cit.*, Vol. IV, pp. 281-291, and Vol. VI, pp. 243, 270-272; *Monumenta Poloniae Historica*, "Rocznik Jana z Targowiska", 1386-1491, pp. 239-240; also an interesting essay in a manuscript form: V. Lutsiv, *Anty-polske povstannia Otamana Mukhy v 1490-1492*, Penn-State University; Mukha was apparently of a noble descent and not a peasant, Lutsiv implied, since otherwise he would not have succeeded in marshalling a considerable gentry following during the uprising. Also, as a peasant he could not have been well known by the neighborhood ruling courts; Holubets, *op. cit.*, pp. 356-360; also, I. Kholmsky, *Istoria Ukrainy*, New York, 1971, pp. pp. 128-129.

22. Hrushevsky, *op. cit.*, Vol. IV, pp. 346-351; Polonska-Vasylenko, *op. cit.*, p. 341; M. Dovnar-Zapolsky, *Polsko-Litovskaia unia*, Moscow, 1897.

23. Kholmsky, *op. cit.*, p. 129-130.

24. The Muscovite episode; Chirovsky, *op. cit.*, Vol. I, pp. 327-348; The plans of a crusade; E. Barvinsky, "Prychynky do istorii znosyn tsisaria Rudolfa II i papy Klymenta VIII z kozakamy v 1593-94 rokakh", *Zapysky Naukovoho Tovarystva imeny Shevchenka*, Lviv, 1895, Vol. X; Polonska-Vasylenko, *op. cit.*, Vol. I, 364; W. Ferguson and G. Bruun, *A Survey of European Civilization*, Boston, 1958, p. 285.

25. M. Andrusiak, *Istoria kozachchyny*, Munich, 1946; N. Polonska-Vasylenko, "The Kozaks", *Ukraine, A Concise Encyclopedia*, Toronto, 1963, Vol. I, pp. 629-632; G. Stockl, *Die Entstehung des Kozakentums*, Munich, 1953.

26. D. Yevarnitskii, *Istoria zaporozhskikh kozakov*, St. Petersburg, 1895, Vols. I-II and M. Lubavskii, "Nachalnaia istoria malorusskavo Kozachestva", in *Zhurnal ministerstva narodnavo prosvieshchenia*, 1895, Vol. III; all works include an attempt to analyze the beginnings of the Cossack social-political phenomenon.

27. Andrusiak, *op. cit.*, p. 8.

28. V. Lutsiv, "Kniaz Dymtro Vyshnevetskyi-Baida, Tvorets i providnyk kozatskoho ordenu-Zaporozkoi Sichi", *I slava i hordist"*, Penn-State College, Slavia Library, 1979, pp. 38-49; M. Hrushevsky, "Baida-Vyshnevetsky v poezii i istorii", *Zapysky Ukrainskoho Naukovoho Tovarystva*, Kiev, 1909, Vol. III.

29. I. Krypiakevych, "Kozachchyna i Batorievi volnosti", *Zherela do istorii Ukrainy-Rusy*, Lviv, 1908 Vol. VIII; A. Jablonovski, "Kozaczyzna a legitymizm, dwie legendy polityczno-historyczne Ukrainy; batoryanska i baturynska", *Ateneum*, 1895, Vol. II; Polonska-Vasylenko, *Istoria Ukrainy*, Vol. I, p. 363; Andrusiak, *op. cit.*, pp. 11-12.

30. On Cossack organization and warfares; Doroshenko, *op. cit.*, Vol. I, pp. 151-161; Hrushevsky, *Istoria Ukrainy-Rusy*, Vol. VII; the beginnings and the assaults against the Tartars and Turks; pp. 66-127.

Castle in Kamianets-Podilsky
(14th Century)

CHAPTER TWO

THE POLITICAL STRUCTURE AND THE GOVERNMENT OF THE LITHUANIAN-RUS' COMMONWEALTH

The constitution and the law — The Grand Prince and the territorial princes — The Council of Nobles and the Plenary Parliament — The central and local administration — The judiciary — The military

The Constitution and the Law. The constitutional structure of the Lithuanian-Rus' Commonwealth developed gradually and organically from the ancient Lithuanian family and clan organization and through the tribal way of life, with a substantial admixture of old Kievan-Rus' constitutional elements. The chieftains of the clans or tribes were very early called "princes", or *kunigai* or *rikai*, in Lithuanian. These princes at the end of the twelfth century were undertaking joint military projects and jointly negotiating peace treaties. According to Kutrzeba, they elected their leaders to accomplish certain military objectives. Most likely from this temporary institution, Mendog succeeded by applying force and diplomacy in developing the permanent authority of the Grand Prince. Other clan or tribal princes, *kunigai*, soon recognized his grand-princely rule, probably, not without opposition.[1] According to tradition, also, the grand-princely authority received a family perspective, which became a constitutional principle after Gedymin and his dynasty occupied the Lithuanian throne.

As a result, under the original constitution of the Lithuanian state, after it was unified and united under the grand-princely authority as a Gedymin, dynasty-owned, federation of semi-autonomous lands, individual princes ruled their individual lands or principalities directly and in a somewhat absolutist manner, having fully recognized the suzerainty of the Grand Duke and having been bound to him by obedience, loyalty, duty to the council and military assistance. The similarity of this family-based, federative state to the constitution of the Kievan realm before Yaroslav the Wise, cannot be denied.[2]

Essentially three evolutionary stages can be identified in the development of Lithuania. First, the Lithuanian federative state before Olgierd, largely restricted to ethnic Lithuanian territory and with a dominating Lithuanian character. Second, the Lithuanian-Rus' Commonwealth, in which the Ukrainian ethnic element and the Ukrainian territories overwhelmingly prevailed over the Lithuanian ones. And third, the Polish-Lithuanian *Res Publica*, *Rzeczpospolita*, in the framework of which Polish national and political elements prevailed immediately before and after the Union of Lublin. In this third stage Lithuania practically lost her independent political existence. As far as constitutional and political developments in Lithuania after the Union of Lublin were concerned, they were of almost no consequence for Ukraine. From that event Ukraine was largely under the Polish Crown, and only her small northern areas were still under Lithuanian supremacy. Moreover, essentially Polish constitutional developments cannot be comprehensively discussed in the framework of Ukrainian history, since they were foreign and occupational, and introduced into Ukraine by a foreign power, the Polish Crown, and against the will of the majority of Ukrainian people.

The entire constitutional structure of the early Lithuanian federative state was solely based on customs and traditions, having been related to the principles and beliefs of the past, while practical needs nurtured its subsequent evolution. Nothing had been written down in any form of positive legislation. Since the time of Gedymin the constitutional-political institutions of Lithuania were subject to continuous and intense changes, at first under the impact of Ukrainian-Rus'ian constitutional and legal concepts, and later on, by Polish ones, as the Polish-Lithuanian union was getting closer. Meanwhile, official and written legislative acts began to modify or to replace traditional political forms, originally based only on customs and common law. This process, introduced by positive legislation, was started during the latter period of the Lithuanian-Rus' Commonwealth, and continued on a large scale in the Polish-Lithuanian *Res Publica*, *Rzeczpopolita*.

The state structure of old Lithuania was built in a pyramidic and semifeudal pattern. At the top of the structure was the Grand Prince, to whom the territorial and semi-autonomous princes were subject. They in turn had power over the lesser princes and grand *boyars*. To the latter, the country *boyardom* were respectively subject, and to them in turn the peasants and townspeople were subordinated both socially and economically. In fact, the *boyars* had a traditional "monopoly" over the government and administration of the country. Individual lands or principalities were represented by "the Princes, *boyars*, townspeople and all the land" before the Grand Prince, with whom at times special arrangements were arrived at by agreements, called the *riady*. Some territories in the Commonwealth either enjoyed special political status on the basis of an old tradition going far back to the era of the Kievan realm, like the lands of Vitebsk and Polotsk, or received special landed privileges at a later date through positive legislation, like the lands of Volhinia and Kiev at the beginning of the sixteenth century. These landed privileges of the later date, enacted under Polish legislative influence, granted the country gentry, the *shlakhta*, a politically, socially and economically favored status in the given province or territory.

According to medieval criteria the Lithuanian-Rus' society, as other European lands of that time, was a *par excellence* class or estate society. The individuals received their social and legal status only through being members of a specific class, and then the classes were built into the constitution of the society and state, the rights, privileges and responsibilities of which were based on customs, tradition and unwritten common law in the course of the early period of history. Beginning with the fifteenth century, the legal framework of each stratum had been minutely completed by various forms of positive legislation, i.e., international agreements, codes of laws, decrees of grants, privilege decrees or landed legislation, referring largely to the country gentry and the townspeople of the Magdeburg law.

At first, the sovereign princes of the Gedymin and Ruryk house began to lose their privileged position during Vitovt's centralist drive. Vitovt, as has been pointed out, proceeded with the elimination of the semi-sovereign status of individual lands, trying to build a strong centralist realm of Lithuania-Rus' in order to resist Polish pressure. Several strong princes were removed from their principalities by force; others ran over to Moscow or Hungary as a protest to Vitovt's attempt to end the federative form of the Commonwealth; while still others submitted to Vitovt, giving up their sovereign position, and becoming princes of service and thus initiating a new class of grand nobles.[3] That stratum of the grand nobility at first enjoyed a highly influential and privileged status in Lithuania, but soon it lost that position because of Polish-originated pressure toward the egalitarianism of all nobility, the grand nobles, *boyars,* and the landed gentry, the *shlakhta.* This, of course, enormously raised the social and political status of the *shlakhta,* the nobility of the lower order. As the social-political position of the landed gentry became more and more favorable in the Commonwealth, the over-all plight of other strata, the townspeople and the peasants in particular, became worse and more intolerable. The *shlakhta* tried by *fas* and *nefas* to exploit its upper-hand status in the country to the fullest extent by taking advantage of and discriminating against other classes.[4]

The constitution of the Lithuanian-Rus' state was not only based on the social inequality of various classes, but later on under the influence of Polish public law, it admitted a *de jure* and *de facto* national and religious discrimination of Orthodox Ukrainians and Byeloruthenians within the legal framework of each individual estate and showed a drastic favoritism toward the Catholic Poles and Lithuanians.

Over-all, the Lithuanian-Rus' Commonwealth, originally of a federative character but fully sovereign politically, experienced during the second half of the fourteenth and the first half of the fifteenth century a structural change toward centralism, while the semi-sovereign territorial princes were being eliminated. On the other hand, however, as a result of various union treaties with Poland, in Krevo, Vilna, Horodlo and Lublin the political sovereignty of Lithuania was somewhat *de jure,* but *de facto* disappearing while Ukraine had become a part of the Polish Crown in 1569.

The legislative process began in Lithuania with customs and tradition developing gradually into principles of common law at first highly respected and referred to by the judiciary and administration as "the old laws and traditions." With the gradual annexation of ever more and wider Ukrainian territories by the Lithuanian Grand Princes and with the formation of the Lithuanian-Rus' Commonwealth, an intense acceptance of the old Rus'ian laws including the *Rus'ka Pravda,* was taking place throughout the entire realm. The legal development of the Kievan realm had reached a much higher level than was the case in Lithuania. As a result, the rulers, having respected Ukrainian juridical principles and institutions by the assertion that they do not change "the old and do not introduce anything new" in the newly dominated Ukrainian lands, in their own judiciary and administration they applied to an ever greater extent the superior Ukrainian-Rus'ian law throughout the entire Commonwealth. Subsequently, positive legislation by the legislative bodies of the Lithuanian-Rus' state, the Grand Princes, the

Council of Nobles, and the Parliament, the *seim*, further developed, complimented or altered the constitutional and legal framework of the Commonwealth. There were essentially four sources of law which complemented and implemented that framework from the fourteenth to the sixteenth century: the international agreements, the codes of laws, the decrees of privileges and the territorial (or landed) laws.

The international agreements were negotiated by Lithuania at various times with the Galician-Volhinian princes, the Livonian and Teutonic orders, Novgorod, Pskov, Muscovy and Poland. Those treaties directly or indirectly affected the constitutional and legal process in the country. Of course, the most important, which markedly influenced the constitution and the international position of the Commonwealth, were the treaties with Poland. The Treaty of Krevo, in 1385 established a union between Lithuania and Poland. The Treaty of Vilna, 1401, was largely a mutual defense agreement between the two countries. The Treaty of Horodlo, 1413, reestablished the union on a somewhat stronger basis, while the Treaty of Lublin, 1569, introduced *de jure* a real union between Poland and Lithuania, which in its *de facto* perspective meant the beginning of the complete absorption of the latter by the former. Polish historians, however, gave a substantially different interpretation of the treaties, insisting on the earlier and much closer unification of the two countries.[5]

Two codes of laws, *Sudebnyk Velykoho Kniazia Kazymyra, the Code of Grand Prince Casimir*, and *Lytovskyi Statut, The Lithuanian Statute*, were the two codifications of laws in the Commonwealth. The *Sudebnyk* was adopted by the provincial *seim* in Vilna in 1468. It regulated, among other matters, property rights, property boundaries, armed group assaults, the *naizdy*, stealing of slaves, petty thefts and gentry judiciary over the peasant serfs. The code represented a rather unsatisfactory mixture of old Ukrainian legal concepts and principles with new legal ideas. The influence of the *Rus'ka Pravda* can easily be detected. On the other hand, it was poorly organized, lumping together private, criminal and procedural laws, full of loopholes and incomplete in any respect.

The social and political rise of the landed gentry, the *shlakhta*, in Poland and in Lithuania brought forth the enactment of the *Lithuanian Statute*, aiming at the abolition of the dominant position of the grand nobility and at the introduction of equality for all the nobility, princes, grandees and the common landed gentry. The preparatory work on the *Statute* began in 1522, and the code was enacted in 1529. This first version aspired to abolish common law and to replace it fully by its own positive and written legal principles and concepts. The *Statute* supposedly created one noble class, within which all members of the gentry were equal. However, the first version did not carry the egalitarian principle of the gentry to its fullest extent. It left some privileges to the grand nobles and respected some peasant rights. Therefore a second version of the codification was prepared and enacted in 1568, which extended the rights of the gentry and restricted those of the peasantry, laying solid foundations for peasant serfdom and bondage. The *shlakhta* was still not satisfied. Consequently a third version of the *Statute* was adopted in 1589. It became a staunch guardian of class privileges for the landed gentry, having made of it a uniform stratum, equal from within, but favored by Polish-Lithuanian society, fully ignoring the peasants as a class who were directly subject only to the noble master, with no rights of the state to interfere. The legal status of the clergy and townspeople was scarcely referred to in the *Lytovskyi Statut*, having been strictly a codified law of one class, the nobility, the bearer of all public and private rights.[6]

The first version of the *Statute* was codified by the grand-princely chancellery in its entirety, while the second version was prompted by the Volhinian gentry. Yet, it was only partially ratified. After the Union of Lublin it became apparent that the second version was not adequate for the needs of the country's judiciary and administration, and immediately a special commission was set up to prepare a new and third version of the code. The version was based on the first one, but revised and expanded, and it was adopted by the plenary *seim* of 1589. The third version of the *Statute* became a binding power, valid for all Lithuania and also the Ukrainian lands which were recently annexed by the Polish Crown. It was written in the Ukrainian language, for a long time the official tongue of the Lithuanian-Rus' Commonwealth, and one can still detect in it legal concepts of the old *Rus'ka Pravda* from the Kievan era.

The third version of the *Lithuanian Statute* completed the legal unification process for all separate lands and provinces of Lithuania, including Ukraine, where the code was the official law until the first quarter of the nineteenth century. Although it was a legal codification for one cohesive, egalitarian and highly favored social class of the nobility, it proved to be, according to juridical criteria, a superior codification in comparison with contemporary European ones.[7]

Townspeople, to some extent, enjoyed a separate legal position. Many towns and townships were granted the privilege of self-government under

Magdeburg law. Numerous private collections and translations of Magdeburg law circulated in Lithuania and Ukraine, and because principal and procedural matters were well regulated by that law, naturally it experienced a wide reception throughout these two countries, as well as in Poland which implemented its common law and positive codifications. The granting of self-government privileges under Magdeburg law, included exemption from the general laws of the country, from its general administration and judiciary, also exemption from certain taxes. It specified the right of townspeople under Magdeburg law to own real estate.

The *Decrees of Privileges*, the *privileini hramoty*, issued in great numbers in Ukrainian, Latin or German from the end of the fourteenth to the middle of the sixteenth century, constituted a component of the third source of laws in the Lithuanian-Rus' Commonwealth. Chubaty asserted that these decrees were for that period the most important source of law and legislative activity of the grand-princely court.[8] They referred either to individual persons, social classes, individual communities or ethnic groups, such as the Ukrainians, Jews, Armenians, Wallachians or Germans.

The *Decrees of Privileges* in the long-run, suspended the binding power of the common law of the land and led ultimately to the positive codification of legislation on a class basis. They can be roughly divided into three categories: the privileges of grants, the *darchi hramoty*, privileges in the narrower sense of the term and the protective decrees, the *okhoronni hramoty*. The first category granted the rights to landed estates, on church tithes, on inheritance, affirmed sales of real estate, or granted specific rights, i.e., using a flag of particular colors or a specific seal.

The privileges in the narrower sense of the term were typically of a private character, and they were therefore, referred to as *private privileges*. They granted to persons and communities immunities from the state judiciary, administration or taxation. Individual towns or regions received such privileges in case of elemental emergencies, such as plagues, war destruction or droughts, which freed them from regular taxation or other responsibilities to the state. Ethnic communities, in particular the Jews and Armenians, gained by such privileges the right to self government. Privileges given to the class of the landed gentry had, in the long-run, the most lasting effect since they initiated its development into one, highly privileged social class. They were patterned after Polish legislative practice and led to the large-scale reception of Polish law in the Lithuanian-Rus' Commonwealth. Some of them were discriminatory, granting special rights to the Catholic *boyars* and *shlakhta*, while others, like those promulgated by Grand Prince Casimir in 1437, extended class privileges to all the nobility, no matter of what ethnic or religious background, granting to the nobles freedom from taxation and broad administrative and judicial power over the peasant serfs. The privilege of 1492 limited the absolutist authority of the Grand Prince; matters of foreign policy and legislation were partially transferred to the Council of Nobles. The *protective decrees* were issued to safeguard the "ancient" rights of the people of certain localities.

The *Territorial Laws* or landed legislation, the *zemski ustavy*, were comprised of the constitutional charters of individual lands or provinces and were designed to protect their traditional rights, were issued by the grand-princely court. They regulated the legal relationship of a given territory to the Commonwealth as a whole, particularly the state when some constitutional changes were taking place, i.e., ousting a semi-sovereign prince and replacing him by a grand-princely vice-roy during a drive for state centralism or as a result of dynastic warfare.[9] Thirteen such *Territorial Laws* were preserved: for the lands of Lutsk, Volhinia, Kiev, Vitebsk, Smolensk, and Polotsk. "They were issued to pacify a popular anxiety," said Chubaty.

This was the legal picture of the Lithuanian-Rus' Commonwealth.

The Grand Prince and the Territorial Princes. The grand-princely authority or office was created by Mendog. It remained on a permanent basis, even when the Gedymin clan, another dynasty, assumed supreme rule in Lithuania. Initially, the Grand Prince considered the Lithuanian Grand Principality the property of his family, which he, as the family head, could freely dispose of. He could give to any of his sons territory to rule and to maintain, whether it was an original Lithuanian province or newly-conquered territory. He could freely determine the size and borders of such territory with no reference to any traditional frontiers. At the time of his death, he could transfer the grand-princely authority to the son whom he considered most capable for the supreme office. Other princes owed obedience, loyalty, council and assistance, including military assistance in case of war. In some cases, the Grand Prince and a given territorial prince ruled certain regions jointly.

Initially, the Grand Prince had the position of an absolute ruler, having been chief legislator, supreme justice, and chief commander of the military forces. He was responsible for diplomatic relations, proclaiming wars and negotiating treaties. He headed the country's administration; at times jointly with other princes of the dynasty he made important decisions, especially in allocating territories to individual members of the family or in matters of war and peace. At times, the Grand Prince made special arrangements with some other prince, like Olgierd did with Keistut, or Yagiello with Vitovt, granting him more authority and loyalty than to other members of the dynasty.[10] These were rather more personal than constitutional and legal arrangements.

The Grand Prince ruled his own territory directly and with full authority, while over the territories of other princes of his clan he had only an indirect authority, and only indirect power over the population which was directly subject to its own territorial and semi-sovereign prince. Of course, with the centralistic drive initiated by Vitovt and the consequent elimination of most semi-autonomous princes, the Grand Prince acquired direct authority over ever wider areas of the Commonwealth and their populations. However, a new development was soon set in motion, namely the drive toward limiting the grand-princely power. The Council of Nobles was gadually introduced in the second half of the fifteenth century. At first it had only an advisory responsibility to the Grand Prince. Nevertheless, the *privileini hramoty*, decrees of privileges, granted to the nobles in 1492 and 1506, made the participation of the Council of Nobles mandatory in legislation, office appointments, diplomacy and in matters of war and peace. This severely limited grand-princely authority. Also, the matter of succession was changed. The Grand Prince became an electoral office after 1440. After having been elected by the nobles, at times against the will of his father, the new Grand Prince was solemnly proclaimed as such, negotiated certain agreements with the nobility, the *riady*, and took an oath of office according to tradition. Crowning no longer took place. Later, the Grand Prince was jointly elected by the Polish and Lithuanian nobility after the Union of Lublin by the *seim valny*, the Plenary Parliament.

In the sixteenth century, the Council of Nobles as a constitutional body was fully replaced by the *seim*, the parliamentary representation of the landed gentry at large. From that time on, the authority of the Grand Prince was connected with the person of the Polish King and was reduced almost to mere representation of the country with only secondary authority.

Before Mendog created the office of the Grand Prince, there were a great many tribal, or possibly even clanish "princes" who disappeared. Subsequently, only members of the Gedymin house, who absorbed the Ukrainian-Rus'ian and Byeloruthenian lands, and members of the Ruryk dynasty, were legitimate territorial princes. They had direct and unlimited power over their territories, though subject to their suzerain, the Grand Prince, to whom they owed obedience, loyalty, council and military assistance. In some lands, such as Polotsk and Vitebsk, the power of the territorial prince was limited by the *viche*, people's meeting, according to ancient tradition. Otherwise, these princes were counseled by the *boyars*, bishops and top officials, who constituted their territorial advisory body. In their principalities, the princes were legislators, supreme justices, chief administrators and military leaders. In some cases there was a right to appeal from their princely judgement to the Grand Prince. Whenever the need arose, the territorial princes gathered to counsel the Grand Prince in matters of war and peace, international relations or other important affairs, jointly waged wars and signed treaties, or carried out other joint projects.

Yagiello and Vitovt began to ignore the territorial princes in state affairs. Later, Vitovt began to eliminate the princes one by one, trying to build from a Lithuanian federation a centralist state, as has already been pointed out. Gradually, the princes who submitted to the grand-princely authority resigned their territorial sovereignty and accepted the status of grand nobles of service. They were again involved in the country's governmental apparatus as top court and provincial officers and members of the Council of Nobles.

The Council of Nobles and the Plenary Parliament. The Council of Nobles developed from the old princely advisory body, which consisted of minor princes, *boyars*, officials and townspeople. During Gedymin's reign, his princely relatives already had a decisive voice in the Council. Vitovt removed the territorial princes from his council and replaced them with princes of service, grand nobles and wealthy aristocrats. However, the decisions of the Council were not binding on the Grand Prince. First, during Casimir's time, the Council of Nobles became a legitimate state institution to share government functions with the Grand Prince, according to the privileges granted to the aristocratic class, and particularly in matters of justice, appointments of top officers to the central and provincial government, foreign affairs, mobilization, and in matters of war and peace. Subsequently, the Council again assumed these responsibilities; to a great extent carrying out matters during the absence of the Grand Prince from the capital or the country. In 1492, a legal framework was given to the Council of Nobles; its composition and competences were defined. All Catholic bishops, some territorial princes, vice-roys of large lands, a number of top central officials, chancellor, marshall, treasurer and hetman, and some provincial officials, *voyevody* and *kashtelany*, joined the Council, the composition of which was constantly changing due to the evolution of the government process. For example, the territorial princes were later eliminated, and new members admitted. In the second half of the sixteenth century the members of the Council of Nobles reached eighty persons.

This body of eighty persons was definitely too large and unwieldy to be consulted most of the time. Consequently, the Grand Prince used for this purpose an unofficial body, or a "secret council" composed of eight to ten people nominated by the plenary council, but whose composition was determined by the sovereign.[11] Even within the framework of the Council of Nobles and the "secret council" a religious and national discrimination against Orthodox Ukrainians was practiced under the influence of the chauvinist Poles. The Orthodox bishops and dignitaries, with a few minor exceptions, were not admitted to the bodies.

Under the impact of Polish developments, already prior to the Union of Lublin, the Council of Nobles began to lose its political significance, due to the concerted drive of the landed gentry to establish absolute equality among all aristocratic elements and to eliminate the privileged and elevated position of the princes and other aristocratic grandees. After the notorious union, the Plenary Parliament, *seim valny,* took over all powers of the Council of Nobles. It was a general political representation of all the landed gentry, which in 1440 assumed the prerogative of electing the Grand Prince, and subsequently limiting the authority of the latter.

The Plenary Parliament of all the gentry evolved as a result of the *Decrees of Privileges,* which freed the gentry from the obligation to pay taxes. However, in the course of the sixteenth century, Poland-Lithuania waged frequent wars, and the gentry was called on by the King and the Grand Prince to conventions, where the *shlakhta* was expected to give its consent to levy new taxes to finance the wars or to repay war debts. The conventions became a regular political institution under the name of the *seim valny,* and as such they were legalized by the second version of the *Lithuanian Statute* in 1529. It soon became the most important government body, while the King and the Grand Prince were largely reduced to the status of figure-heads. This development was Polish throughout and alien to the spirit of Ukrainian history and the Ukrainian people.

In 1564, the electoral procedure was regulated. The gentry had to elect at country conventions, the *seimiky,* its two representatives, furnish them with written instructions and send them to the *seim valny.* From the Union of Lublin, the *seim* of Lithuania merged with that of the Polish Crown. Therefore it became necessary for the Lithuanian representatives to meet at the so-called *general seimik,* normally in the town of Slonim, to deliberate before the *seim valny.* The Plenary Parliament of the Polish-Lithuanian

Commonwealth, in addition to the delegates elected by the county conventions, was attended by the members of the Council of Nobles, princes and wealthy grandees, top central officials and the provincial officials, vice-roys, *voyevody, starosty*, and many others. The composition of the *seim* fluctuated, before the Union of Lublin, as well as after it. The procedure of deliberations was not properly regulated, and was largely based on customary practice.[12]

Neither was the competence of the Parliament legally and strictly defined. Its competences largely covered the matters of taxes, problems of war and peace, election of the Grand Prince, legislation and, to some extent, even matters of administration. If the *seim* deliberated in the absence of the Grand Prince, it simply sent to him the *prozby*, or applications. The affirmative answers of the Grand Prince to the applications acquired the power of new legislation, of new laws. The *seim* could have convened in any place or town, mostly in Vilna, but at times even outside the political borders of the Grand Principality, in foreign territory. The deliberations of the Parliament lasted sometimes for many months.[13]

Central and Local Administration. It developed in the Lithuanian-Rus' Commonwealth out of very modest beginnings in the original Lithuanian principalities. As the Grand Principality was becoming an ever larger and more complex political organization, the old Ukranian-Rus'ian and later Polish institutions began to affect it more and more intensely. Its administrative system expanded impressively.

At the outset, the Lithuanian administration was quite weak, a family-based and semi-feudal order, related to land ownership from the Grand Prince down to territorial princes, the *boyars*, and the peasants. The first central office of less strict responsibilities appeared at Gedymin's court. It was referred to as the *advocatus* or *vit*. A separate official was in charge of the armed forces. Territorial administration was strictly under the control of the respective princes. The first territorial officials were appointed after the suzerainty of the territorial princes was abolished. In the regions under direct rule of the Grand Prince, vice-roys who performed administrative, judicial and military functions were introduced. Overseeing court manors and settlements were the *volosti*, the lowest level of territorial administration, managed by the *tivuny*, who also had judicial authority over the common people. The *boyars* were under the executive and judicial authority of the vice-roys, while important matters were decided by the Grand Prince himself.

In the course of time, the Lithuanian administrative scheme became more complicated. Some central offices developed at the courts of the territorial princes. These automatically became local or provincial ones after the authority of regional princes was abolished, enriching the pattern of provincial and local administration. The responsibilities of these offices constantly changed along with changes of their character. Grand Prince Vitovt, having initiated state centralism to make his country stronger in order to resist Polish pressure toward a union arrangement, with consequent political disadvantages to Lithuania-Rus', created several central offices with mixed, private-princely and public responsibilities. Their competences were not legally regulated and, consequently, their subsequent formation developed solely by custom and tradition.

The office of the chancellor, *cancelarius*, was the oldest one, and until 1579 it was in the hands of the Vilna governor, *voyevoda*. The chancellor was in charge of the grand-princely office, prepared all important letters and conducted all correspondence, prepared all decrees and other official documents. In addition, he performed functions similar to today's minister of foreign affairs and internal matters. He received foreign envoys, to some extent supervised the administrative apparatus of the state, and he was first in the Council of Nobles to advise the Grand Prince. Since 1566, the office of a vice-chancellor was created to help the chancellor, who was also assisted in the performance of his duties by a number of lay and clerical scribes who technically prepared correspondence and documents in Ukrainian, Latin, German, and for a time, Polish. At the end of the fifteenth century the official registration book of all written materials issued by the chancellory was introduced, the *Metryka Lytovska*.[14]

Later on, the marshal was the most important office at the grand-princely court. His title and responsibilities were in a flux. Eventually, he was called grand marshal, assisted by a number of court marshalls. Above all he was master of ceremonies. A cane was the symbol of his office. In addition, he managed court personnel, provided living quarters to the courtiers, foreign envoys or important personalities arriving at the court or the *seim*. He watched over peace and order during the *seim* deliberations or at court. He also assumed the function of judge in case of disturbances. At an earlier time he was also referred to as the landed marshal, the *marshalok zemskyi*.

At a rather late date during the middle of the fifteenth century the office of treasurer, the *skarbovyi*, evolved. For a long time the finances of the Grand Principality, based on the natural economy, were very loosely managed. *Skarbovyi's* name and title changed under Polish influence. He was subsequently aided by a vice-treasurer and many scribes to perform technical services. He watched over the state and grand-princely revenues and expenditures and the grand-princely jewelries. He also supervised the management of state-owned manors and economies and headed the state mint.

In principle, the Grand Prince was the chief commander of all armed forces of the country. At the end of the fifteenth century, yet another new office developed, that of the *great hetman*, who became military leader in the absence of the Grand Prince or by his authority. He was commander over all standing troops and the popular country militia force. Sometime later he was aided by another military dignitary, the *field hetman*, who commanded only the standing army but not the popular militia.

At the time of Grand Prince Casimir, several new central offices were established to cope with mounting public responsibilities. The *pidkomoryi*, cammerer, was in charge of the princely premises and dwelling units; the *pidstilnyi* and *pidchashyi* were in charge of food and drinks at the court; the *kukhar*, the chef, prepared meals. There were also officials in charge of the grand-princely stables, hunting projects, forests and the like.[15]

Provincial administration experienced great changes in the course of time. There were vice-roys and *tivuny* of ancient origin. The vice-roys resided in provincial castles, once the residences of the territorial princes, and were in charge of administration and the judiciary in their provinces. Smaller areas, the counties, were administered and provided with law and order by the *starosty*, the elders. Individual castles and manors, with their populations, as far as economic matters were concerned, were administered by the *derzhavtsi*, the holders, and *tivuny* of Kievan origin.

After the administrative scheme of the Lithuanian-Rus' Commonwealth became crystallized in the second half of the sixteenth century, the country was divided into several large regions, called *voyevidstva*, such as the Kievan, Novhorodian, Volhinian, Bratslavian and other regions in Ukraine, headed by the governors, or *voyevody*. The system was introduced according to the Polish pattern. The *voyevoda* was the military, administrative and judicial authority of his region. He nominated minor officials, supervised weights and measures, and exercised judiciary over the gentry. Later on, however, his judicial responsibilities were superceded by the introduction of other courts, in particular the territorial ones, or *zemski sudy*. *Voyevoda* who was involved in calling the popular country militia to participate in military projects, led the troops under the flag of his district, carried by the flagman, *khorunzhyi*. The *kashtelany*, the castelanians, were another Polish office of an advisory nature, without any particular responsibilities.

The *starosty*, the elders, headed individual counties and were subordinate to the governors. Their origin, as public officials, was much earlier than that of the *voyevody*. According to Kutrzeba, the latter office actually developed out of the former, although the former was subject to the authority of the latter.[16] The *elder* was the head of his county's administrative, judicial and military affairs. He announced the county *seimiky* and the calling of the militia for duty, led the militia troops under the county flag to the *voyevoda*, judged the gentry, supervised fiscal affairs, collected taxes and other payments to the state and represented the county before the state and the Grand Prince. Some of them joined the Council of Nobles.

The *horodnychi*, castle-care takers, watched over the defenses of castles and town fortifications and performed other minor functions. The *khorunzhi*, the flagmen, were responsible for an orderly calling and reported to the popular country militia. The *voiski*, the military manager, administered individual castles during military expeditions. The county marshals were also involved in affairs of the militia. All these higher and lower officials were accompanied by a score of scribes and clerks who assisted them in fulfilling their responsibilities.[17]

Having surveyed the governmental structure of the Lithuanian-Rus' Commonwealth, one must point out that similar to the Kievan realm, there was no exclusive division of powers among the legislative, executive and judicial authorities. So important for the protection of the rights of people, this division of powers came later in the wake of future developments. The Grand Prince, the Council of Nobles, the Parliament, almost all top central and territorial officials were responsible for all three or, at least two of those authorities.

The Judiciary. The Grand Prince and the respective territorial princes originally performed judiciary functions on minor service princes and *boyars* in a direct way, while the peasants were subject to the domestic justice of their aristocratic masters. In some cases an appeal was possible from the judgement of the territorial prince for the Grand Prince's reconsideration. With the abolition of most of the territorial princes, it was no longer possible for the Grand Prince to attend and judge all cases. The grand-princely central and local officials began progressively to take over the judiciary functions, especially the vice-roys and elders, the *starosty*.

The Grand Prince was the supreme justice, the source of law. Like the Kievan princes once did, he travelled throughout the country and personally judged the cases. He soon began to call at his will assessors from among the members of the Council of Nobles to assist him in matters of meting out justice. The number and the composition of the college of assessors had little bearing on the gravity of the case. At times the Grand Prince postponed the hearings and decisions and waited for more assessors to arrive and participate. Their functions, however, were only advisory. The Grand Prince alone was the judge. Proceedings were conducted according to customary law in the given territory.

The chancellor and vice-chancellor as well as the marshals aided him by studying the documentation, interrogating witnesses and relating the facts and findings to the sovereign.

The jurisdiction of the grand-princely court was twofold; it presided directly over the service princes, the members of the Council of Nobles, the *boyars* and later on, the grand nobles, the central officials, the foreigners and those who were not under county jurisdiction, like the *starosty* and *vovevody*. It presided also over the public law cases; i.e., ascertaining the social status of the nobility, state revenue cases, crimes, such as group assaults, the *zaizdy*, false accusations, high treason and insult to the royalty, *crimen laesae majestatis*. Their jurisdiction also included appeals from the lower courts.

In order to ease the burden of the Grand Prince in judicial matters, at first the commissarian courts were created, which consisted of appointed commissars by the prince *ad hoc*, whenever the causes were to be judged on location. Later, assessorian courts, similar to the Polish juridical institution, were established. The assessors, a few noblemen from the Council of Nobles, were appointed to judge the cases at the grand-princely court or wherever the prince resided. The assessors were normally involved in hearing and judging a score of cases, at times consulting the Grand Prince. The matters which were judged without grand-princely consultation could be appealed to the sovereign. Also, in the sixteenth century, the marshalian courts were introduced, presided by one of the marshals over the assessors, or consisting of a few marshals in a collegial fashion. The Grand Prince normally referred particular cases to the assessorian and marshalian courts. There was a right to appeal sentence to the ruler in most cases.

Already in the second half of the fifteenth century the Court of Justice of the Council of Nobles began to operate in the absence of the Grand Prince, to consider cases of the *starosty* and *voyevody* and other top officials. The *Lithuanian Statute* of the first version called for that court to convene once a year. Its procedures were not well developed.

In the second half of the sixteenth century, a reform of the judiciary was carried out in Poland and Lithuania and two court tribunals were established: the Tribunal of the Crown in 1578 to hold sessions either in the cities of Lublin or Piotrków, and the Tribunal of the Grand Principality in 1581, to hold sessions in four places, Vilna, Troky, Novhorodok and Minsk. They became the supreme courts for the gentry for appeals from the territorial, *zemski*, urban, *horodski*, and cammeral, *pidkomorski*, courts of the lower order. They served as the first court against court officials who acted improperly.[18] Since those courts were established after the Union of Lublin, the Tribunal of the Crown was the appeal court for most of Ukraine, although not in Lithuania.

The lower courts experienced considerable evolution as well. The courts of elders, *starostynsky*, were the earliest, as has been mentioned. They were competent to hear cases of servitude princes, *boyars* and minor nobility, and held sessions in the towns and castles, and in the residencies of the *starosty*. With the creation of the office of the *voyevoda*, governor, these officials, subordinate to the elders, began to preside over the *starostynsky* courts, along with the *starosty*, while the *derzhavtsi*, the holders, were called to judge in business and economic matters. When the governors and elders were unable to take care of court matters, they delegated their authority to the county marshals and vice-elders, the *pidstarosty*.

In 1564, the lower or provincial courts were reformed. The governors, elders and holders resigned from their judicial authorities during the *seim* of 1564. The *Lithuanian Statute* of the second version introduced the territorial, *zemski*, and urban, *horodski*, and one year later, through an amendment, cammeral, *pidkomorski*, courts, according to the Polish pattern of the judiciary.

The territorial courts had jurisdiction over the gentry in almost all cases. The urban courts were presided over by the *voyevoda* or *starosta*. They were one-man courts, while the territorial ones were collegial and electoral. The urban courts were competent mostly in criminal cases, such as assault, rape, arson, robbery, and murder. The cammeral courts had jurisdiction over the cases involving real estate boundaries.

The towns, if not subject to the domicile judiciary of their gentry masters, had their own judiciary under Magdeburg law through the electoral jury or the town council, which extended its jurisdiction over the self-governing town population. The peasantry was in large part subject to the domicile or patrimonial jurisdiction of the gentry masters. Matters of field limits or real estate boundaries were decided by the *kopni sudy*, or mass courts, attended by the peasants and townspeople, and accepted by the gentry according to long-lasting tradition. On the basis of their self-governing privileges, the Jews and Armenians had their own ethnic courts for their nationals, organized according to customs and traditions. The appeals from their sentences were placed before the governors. At a later period, the gentry, either by lawful or unlawful means, tried to include these minorities in their patrimonial jurisdiction, by force.[19]

The Military. According to old customs and laws, all *boyars* had to render military service to the prince, and all the territorial princes, to the Grand Prince. The princes and *boyars* were expected to report for military duty, when the need arose, with a number of armed men and horses assigned to them by custom and in accord with their land grants and possessions. The clergy and women did not need to report for service. One member out of the princely or *boyar* family was enough to fulfill the military obligation. No compensations or payment was given for rendering military service.

In the course of time, the burden of military duty became very unequal, therefore in the sixteenth century several new decrees regulated the institution of the *pospolyte rushennia*, or the popular country militia formed by general conscription. At first these decrees regulated conscriptions *ad hoc*, for each war separately. The *Lithuanian Statute*, the first and the second versions, regulated them on a more permanent basis. It indicated how many armed men each prince or *boyar* had to mobilize for military service from each economic unit, the manor, house or chimney. The regulations were separate for the wealthy and the poor. For not fulfilling the military obligation or for desertion, monetary penalties or confiscation of properties were indicated. The general conscription of the country militia was put first into a registry in 1528. Princes, grand nobility, governors, castelanians, marshals and other military officials led the troops, which at the top were commanded by the *great hetman* and the *field hetman*. Of course, the chief leader of the armed forces, at least theoretically, was the Grand Prince. Towns and townspeople were part of the general mobilization effort and were assigned duties in defense of the country. Their military responsibilities were organized according to the craft and merchant guild structure.[20]

General conscription was insufficient to maintain an adequate armed force of the Grand Principality in view of the numerous wars it had to wage. As a result, the use of mercenary troops significantly grew from the fifteenth century on. They were led by the officers, called *rotmistry*, the troop masters, and commanded by the *great hetman*. However, the matter of mercenary troops was never satisfactorily solved during this period. Consequently, there was no standing armed force for the country.

The armed force consisted of the cavalry and infantry. The cavalry was armed with spears, swords and bows, and the infantry, with swords, bows and short and long axes. All used armor and shields for protection. Already in the fourteenth century gunpowder was sporadically used, and subsequently cannons fired stones. At the end of the fifteenth century iron bullets for cannons and the rifles came into use. The introduction of gunpowder completely changed techniques of war. A standing army was introduced, military training was required and the significance of castles declined.

Yet, throughout the entire Lithuanian-Rus' era castles constituted an important component of defense strategy. At first, they were of wood, but strongly built, like those in Zhytomyr, Vynnytsia, Kaniv, protected by towers, water moats and draw-bridges. Stone and brick castles and fortifications were built later, like those in Kholm, Kamianets, Lviv, Halych and Bar. The castles and fortifications were small or large, and of various forms. At times, even churches were built like fortifications.[21]

1. S. Kutrzeba, *Historya ustroju Polski, w zarysie*, Lviv, 1914, Vol. II, *Litwa*, p. 6.

2. Compare, Vol. I, of this work, chapter on constitution and government; also, D. Doroshenko, *Narys istorii Ukrainy*, Munich, 1966, Vol. I, pp. 50-53.

3. N. Polonska-Vasylenko, *Istoria Ukrainy*, Munich, 1972, Vol. I, pp. 320-321; also, M. Hrushevsky, *Istoria Ukrainy-Rusy*, New York, 1955, Vol. IV, pp 160-161.

4. Kutrzeba, *op. cit.*, Vol. II, *Litwa*, pp. 45-65, 201-205; Hrushevsky, *op. cit.*, Vol. V, pp. 27-107.

5. Kutrzeba, *loc. cit.*, pp. 24-35; the same, "Unia Litwy z Polska", *Polska i Litwa w rozwoju dziejowym*, Cracow, 1913; A. Lewicki, "Nieco o unii Litwy z Polska", *Przeglad polski*, Cracow, 1893, Vol. 110.

6. M. Chubaty, *Ohlad istorii ukrainskoho prava; Istoria dzherel ta derzhavnoho prava*, Munich, 1947, Pt, II, pp, 19-28; A. Yakovliv, "Istoria dzherel ukrainskoho prava", *Entsyklopedia ukrainoznavstva*, Munich, 1949, Vol. I, pp. 634-635; Kutrzeba, *op. cit.*, Vol. II, *Litwa*, pp. 168-172.

7. *Ibid.*, Polonska-Vasylenko, *op. cit.*, Vol. I, p. 409; R. Lashchenko, "Lytovsky Statut, yak pamiatnyk ukrainskoho prava", *Naukovyi Zbirnyk YVY*, Prague, 1923.

8. Chubaty, *op. cit.*, Vol. II, 8-28; Kutrzeba, *Istorya ustroju*, Vol. II, *Litwa*, pp. 37-45.

9. Chubaty, *op. cit.*, Vol. II, pp. 13-18.

10. Kutrzeba, *op. cit.*, Vol. II, pp. 14-15.

11. T. Leontovych, "Rada Velikikh Kniazei litovskikh," *Zhurnal ministerstva narodnavo prosveshchenia*, St. Petersburg, 1907, Bk. 9-10; I. Malinovskii, *Rada Velikavo Kniazhestva Litovskavo v sviazi c boyarskoiu dumoiu drevniei Rossii*, Tomsk, 1904, Pt. 1, Bk. 1; Tomsk, 1912, Pt. 2, Bk. 2; Polonska-Vasylenko, *op. cit.*, Vol. II, p. 349; Chubaty, *op. cit.*, Vol. II, pp. 118-131.

12. Kutrzeba, *op. cit.*, Vol. II, pp. 128-146, 208-212.

13. "The seim deliberations lasted at times for several months. They convened in different localities, in Grodno, Minsk, and so on, but most frequently in Vilna": *Ibid.*, pp. 146-147; T. Leontovych, "Viecha, seimy i seimiki v Velikom Kniazhestvi Litovskom", *Zhurnal ministerstva narodnavo prosveshchenia*, St. Petersburg, 1910, Bk. 2 and 3.

14. S. Kutrzeba, *Historia zrodel davnego prava polskiego*, Lviv-Warsaw, 1925, Vol. II, Metryka Litewska.

15. Offices in old Lithuania: Kutrzeba, *Historya ustroju*, Vol. II, *Litwa*, pp. 16-19, 113-128 and 212-215; Polonska-Vasylenko, *op. cit.*, Vol. I, pp. 350-351; Chubaty, *op. cit.*, Vol. II, pp. 131-137; L. Okinshevych, "Derzhavne pravo. Lytovsko-ruska doba", *Entsyklopedia ukrainoznavstva*, Munich, 1949, Vol. I, p. 641-642.

16. *Loc. cit.*, p. 118.

17. *Ibid.*, pp. 123-128.

18. *Ibid.*, pp. 216-218.

19. The judiciary: Kutrzeba, *op. cit.*, Vol. II, pp. 147-168 and 215-221; Chubaty, *op. cit.*, Vol. II, pp. 159-169; Hrushevsky, *op. cit.*, Vol. V. pp. 327-328; I. Lappo, "Podkomorskii sud v Velikomu Kniazhestve Lytovskom v kontse XVIst", *Zhurnal ministerstva narodnavo prosveshchennia*, St. Petersburg, 1899, Bk. VIII; the same "Zemskii sud v Velikom Kniazhestve Litovskom", *ibid.*, Bk. VI; the same, "Hrodskii sud v Velikom Kniazhestve Litovskom", *ibid.*, 1908, Bk. I; R. Lashchenko, "Kopni sudy na Ukraini, i ikh pokhodzhennia, kompetentsia i ustrii", *Zbirnyk Pravnychoi Komisii NTSh.*, Lviv, 1926, Vol. I-II.

20. J. Ptasnik, *Miasta i mieszczanstwo w dawnej Polsce*, Cracow, 1934, pp. 152-153; Chubaty, *op. cit.*, Vol. II. pp. 36-37, 64-65.

21. Kutrzeba, *op. cit.*, Vol. II, *Litwa,* pp. 172-187; I. Krypiakevych and B. Hnatevych, *Istoria ukrainskoho* viiska, Winnipeg, 1953, pp. 136-138, 146-157; T. Korzon, *Dzieje wojen i wojskowosci w Polsce,* Cracow, 1912; the same, "Organizacya wojskowa Litwy w okresie jagiellonskim", *Rocznik Towarzystwa Przyjaciol Nauk w Wilnie, Vilna,* 1909, Vol. II.

CHAPTER THREE

THE SPIRITUAL AND CULTURAL LIFE
OF LITHUANIAN-RUS' SOCIETY

The status of the Orthodox Church and Roman Catholicism — The Church Union of Berest — Education — Literature — Architecture — Painting and carving — Music and theatre — Other arts

The Status of the Orthodox Church and Roman Catholicism. Immediately after the Mongol invasion, the Orthodox Church in Ukraine was in a deplorable state. The Kievan Metropolitan, Cyryl, having seen ruin and destruction throughout Dnieper Ukraine, went to Galicia for a while, and later left the Ukrainian South for the North, to the Suzdalian-Vladimirian land. Near the end of his life he returned to Ukraine. His successors established themselves permanently in Vladimir and later in Moscow. From there it was rather difficult for the Metropolitans to administer the ecclesiastic affairs of Ukraine. Moreover, they soon alienated themselves from Kiev and Ukraine. Except for their unceasing ambition to continue to be called "the Metropolitans of Kiev and All-Rus'," they practically lost all interest in Ukrainian ecclesiastical affairs. The Metropolitans very early became involved in the northern dynastic and political problems and largely became the tools of both the Vladimirian, and subsequently, Muscovite imperialist projects, which by their very nature were alien to and hostile toward Ukraine.[1]

The gradual absorption of Ukrainian territories by Lithuania naturally put her Grand Princes at odds with the northern Metropolitans, who represented the political interests of the Vladimirian and Muscovite rulers. The Lithuanians did not want ecclesiastical affairs of their country to be regulated by church dignitaries residing abroad and, in particular, in a hostile land. There is a reference in the catalogue of the metropolises of the Byzantine patriarchate, that at the time of Patriarch John Hlikas, 1282-1320, the Ukrainian territory within the Lithuanian Grand Principality constituted a separate metropolitanate. However, later on, the instance was no longer mentioned.

Grand Prince Olgierd moved again to make the Orthodox Church within the political borders of his realm independent of the Metropolitan residing in Moscow. In the early 1350's, as mentioned in the first volume of this work, Metropolitan Teodoryt, of whom little is known, stayed in Kiev, but only for a short time. He was not approved by Constantinople and was forced to resign. He may have been sponsored by Olgierd. Soon, after the death of Metropolitan Theognost in Moscow, the Grand Prince sent to the Patriarch his own candidate, Roman, and requested that he be designated the Metropolitan for the Lithuanian-Rus' Commonwealth. The Muscovite candidate, Aleksei, also sought the office. The Patriarch appointed both, Roman and Aleksei, the "Metropolitans of Kiev and All-Rus'," assigning to Roman the jurisdiction over the Church under Lithuanian-Rus' sovereignty, and to Aleksei that over the northern eparchies, dioceses. The two metropolitans did not live in peace. Aleksei, ignoring Roman's authority, came to Kiev to underscore his jurisdiction there. Olgierd was furious. He ordered the imprisonment of Aleksei, who saved himself by fleeing to Moscow.

After Metropolitan Roman's death, the Muscovites tried again to recapture the Ukrainian Orthodox Church in the Commonwealth under the jurisdiction of their Aleksei. Olgierd, having threatened the Patriarch with the introduction of Roman Catholicism to all eparchies under his authority in case of a refusal to consecrate a separate Metropolitan for his realm, achieved his purpose. Cyprian became the next Metropolitan for the Orthodox people of the Lithuanian-Rus' Commonwealth. Subsequently, following Aleksei's death, after a struggle against Moscow's opposition, Metropolitan Cyprian succeeded in uniting the metropolitan jurisdiction over the Muscovite North by 1386, and later, also over the Galician territory under Polish sovereignty. The separate metropolises ceased to exist in 1401. Since 1414, even the separate eparchy of Halych did not receive a bishop, and was administered by Metropolitan's plenipotentiary.

Cyprian was really the head of the entire traditional Kievan metropolis, and as such he energetically demonstrated a tendency toward a union of the Orthodox Church with the Holy See. He even tried to gain the approval of the Patriarch of Constantinople for this idea, along the tradition of unification favored by King Danylo of Galicia and the Council of Lyon of 1274. In both cases the idea of this Church union was politically motivated and possibly for this reason unification attempts failed in both cases. However, in Lyon, during the Fourth Session of the Council, the union was officially accepted by the Byzantine emperor and his followers. The opposition immediately set forces in motion to suppress the convention. Pope Martin IV did not act positively, and the union ceased to exist after 1281. Then, Cyprian, in order to revive the idea of the union, arranged an ecclesiastic meeting in Lithuania, in 1405, where the matter of unification was deliberated. King Yagiello favored the idea, while Moscow condemned it outright. However, the Metropolitan never gave up his plan.

After Cyprian's death, Photii, a favorite of Moscow, initially took over the entire metropolis under his jurisdiction as the Metropolitan of Kiev and All-Rus', against the wishes of Grand Prince Vitovt, who favored Hryhorii Tsamblak for the high office. The few years of peace in the life of the Orthodox Church were interrupted by Photii's irresponsible conduct. In Lithuania-Rus' he levied exorbitant contributions against the churches. In 1414 he was imprisoned by the Lithuanian authorities and then expelled from the country. Vitovt, embittered against Photii, sent his candidate, Hryhorii Tsamblak, to the Patriarch and asked him to consecrate the latter for the high post in Lithuania-Rus'. A Muscovite intrigue, arranged by Photii, prevented the consecration. Subsequently Vitovt's pleas in Constantinople to appoint a separate metropolitan for his Commonwealth were fully ignored by the Patriarch. As a result, the Grand Prince called to Novhorodok a council of bishops, who elected Tsamblak the Metropolitan for Lithuania-Rus' without the Patriarch's approval. The election of Tsamblak was motivated by the precedence of a similar elevation of Klym Smolatych to this high office in 1147 and similar elections in Serbia and Bulgaria, which took place without the Patriarch's blessing.[2]

In spite of the fact that the Patriarch and Photii not only disapproved, but even anathematized him, Tsamblak headed the Orthodox Church in the Commonwealth for five years, showing a distinctly autocephalic attitude toward Constantinople. In 1418 he attended the ecumenical council in Constance. In his speech of greetings to the Pope, he made a reference to a Church union between the Orthodox and the Catholics which was desired by many and could be accomplished by the formation of a council of both Churches.[3] Although Tsamblak headed the Church in the Commonwealth too briefly to establish a tradition, this idea of the union of churches materialized two decades later. After Tsamblak's death, probably in 1419,

Photii managed to appease Vitovt and exercise his authority over the eparchies in the Commonwealth.

Meanwhile other important developments had taken place. The days of the Byzantine empire were already numbered. The Turks were about to administer a final blow against it to erase its political existence. The emperor and the patriarch were looking for ways to save Greece. A church union with Rome seemed one way of assuring some kind of Western assistance in their struggle against the Turks. In 1438, the Ecumenical Council was called to convene in Ferrara, and then transferred to Florence, to deal with, among other matters, the question of the said union.

In the meantime, Isydor, a Greek by descent, and a great proponent of the union idea, became the Metropolitan of Kiev and All-Rus'. He came to the Ferrara-Florence council, accompanied by an escort of some two hundred people, including bishops, clergy, dignitaries and laypeople. Even Avraam, the bishop of Suzdal, joined his escort, although the Muscovites were extremely hostile toward the idea of a Church union. Isydor was one of the leading participants in the council sessions. The Byzantine emperor and the Patriarch attended the gathering, which promised to be an important and successful one in the Christian world. In 1439, the Church union was concluded; the Catholic and the Orthodox churches joined again as one Christian body after an almost four hundred year old split since Patriarch Cerularius.[4] The Pope of Rome was recognized as the head of the Christian Church. Doctrinal matters, which had separated Rome and Constantinople, like "the creed of faith," some ritual questions, the issue of purgatory, the Immaculate Conception and Assumption of Holy Mary, were clarified and agreed upon. The Eastern Church retained its ritual, calendar and married clergy of the lower order.[5] Isydor, for his contributions and loyalty to the idea of the union, was made a cardinal and Apostolic legate, and was granted ecclesiastical jurisdiction over the Eastern (Uniate) and Western (Catholic) Church in the Lithuanian-Rus' Commonwealth, in particular.

However, the union was not favorably received and appreciated in the East. In Greece and the Middle East an immediate negative reaction by the conservative Orthodox circles resulted. The national pride of the Greeks was hurt. A church council held in Jerusalem condemned the union and anathematized all Uniats. The Muscovites wholeheartedly approved of this reaction.

In the Lithuanian-Rus' Commonwealth and in Poland the reaction to the Florence union also left much to be desired. In the Commonwealth it was a turbulent time. A bloody struggle between Sigismund and Svidrigiello, culminated in the assassination of the former and the election of young Casimir as Grand Prince which was an insult to and a defeat of Svidrigiello's aspirations. These political developments did not permit proper attention to be paid to the Ferraro-Florence council's religious decisions. In Poland there was a deep resentment of the union. When Isydor arrived from Rome, he was coolly received by Polish and Lithuanian official circles, since he championed the principle of a papal primate in the Christian Church, while these circles favored for the most part the supremacy of an ecumenical council over the papal office in all religious and moral matters. Furthermore, these circles were also badly irked by Isydor's jurisdiction over Catholic bishops in the Commonwealth, granted to him by the Pope. In Muscovy he was not welcome at all, since the idea of the union was traditionally abhored. On his arrival there, he was arrested twice, and only with difficulty was he able to escape and return to the Lithuanian-Rus' Commonwealth. Here he was also surprised by hostile churchmen. Maciej, the Catholic bishop of Vilna, prohibited Isydor, the Uniat Metropolitan, from saying mass and from preaching in those churches under his authority. This was outrageous and stupid. Only in Ukraine where the union might have had a chance to succeed, was Isydor warmly received. It failed, however, due to Polish intrigues. Discouraged, Isydor went to Rome.[6]

During Isydor's absence from Kiev, the ruling circles in the Commonwealth at Polish instigation, transferred the Kievan metropolis to the jurisdiction of the Muscovite Orthodox Metropolitan Yona because of their animosity to Isydor. In this way a *coup d'état* to the cause of the Church union in Ukraine was effected. This was an irresponsible move on the part of Lithuanian and Polish Catholics. Isydor resigned from the Kievan metropolitan seat on his own in 1448, and Hryhorii, a Bulgarian was appointed by the Pope to be the next Uniat metropolitan of Kiev and All-Rus'. Hryhorii later repudiated the union and was confirmed by the Patriarch of Constantinople as the Orthodox Metropolitan. In this manner the Ferrara-Florence religious council of 1439 ceased to be applied in all Ukraine.

In the course of the following decades, religious matters in Ukraine-Rus' deteriorated and moved from bad to worse for various reasons. First of all, Constantinople fell to the Turks; the Byzantine empire was gone for all time. The Patriarch of Constantinople came under the political authority of the Moslem sultan. The Patriarch traditionally followed the doctrine of "ceasaropapism"; it meant the sovereign authority of the secular ruler over ecclesiastical matters. As long as the sovereign was Orthodox, matters were not too bad. However, conditions dramatically deteriorated after the Moslem ruler took over, which gravely affected the religious affairs of the Orthodox Christians. The Patriarch's religious leadership was diminished to a considerable degree. Secondly, traditionally, the princes and *boyars* during the Kievan, Galician and Lithuanian eras, cared for and protected the churches in their respective domains; they made gifts, grants and endowments to materially help the Church. Not only had church buildings been erected by them, but the rich merchants and merchant communities had done the same. Homes for the elderly, orphanages, hospitals and many monasteries were built by people such as Prince Lubart and Prince Volodymyr, Olgierd's son, and grand nobles, such as Khodkevych, Dashkevych, Holshansky, Ostrozhsky and many others. However, there was a serious, negative side to these contributions. The princes and noblemen considered these churches and church properties their own private domain.

Utilizing their positions as church protectors, *ktytors*, they freely disposed of them by selling, leasing, renting, taxing, and collecting fees and contributions when they were utilized by other people, including the common folks and peasants. Even the bishops and parish priests became fully dependent upon these aristocratic "protectors," the *ktytors*, who installed, transferred or removed them. At times they were installed without any educational and moral qualifications and transferred or removed capriciously, without any apparent or serious reason. The kings, grand princes and princes were the first to give a scandalous bad example to others by freely disposing of eparchial (bishop) seats and other ecclesiastic dignitaries, often for money and bribes. The *boyars* and the gentry in turn did the same with the parishes and priests, monastic superiors, deacons and other members of the clergy in their landed possessions. Simony, bribery, the selling and buying of church offices and properties by unqualified, uneducated and immoral persons and other abuses became common practice.

The Orthodox Church tried to defend itself against these dreadful abuses; however, this was in vain. At first, the nobility was Orthodox, believing, and cared. Later on, as a result of Polish nationalist and Catholic pressure, that nobility gradually abandoned the Orthodox faith and Ukrainian nationality, and became progressively Polonized and Catholic. They did not care for their original faith and nationality and did many things to hurt them. This was the third factor which contributed to the rapid decline of the Orthodox faith in Ukraine. The authority to protect the churches and church institutions, inherent in the organizational structure of the Orthodox Church, the *ktytorstvo*, turned into a vicious institution, in the hands of the Polish and

Polonized Catholic nobility, and worked directly against the interests of the Orthodox faith. Not for religious reasons, but out of perhaps sheer caprice, the eparchies, (the diocesean seats), parishes, and monasteries were given by that nobility to completely unqualified, uneducated, and at times, outright illiterate, shady or even criminal characters who directly contributed to the downfall of the Orthodox Church.[7]

Let us quote a few examples of that decay. Metropolitan Yosyf III sold the Metropolitan Seat to Makarii, Bishop of Lutsk, for money. Makarii gave that seat to Stefan-Silvester, a complete illiterate. Metropolitan Yona again sold the seat to Illa Kucha, a petty nobleman. King Stefan Batory gave the Orthodox monastery in Minsk to a Catholic landowner, Stefan Dostoyevsky. Metropolitan Onysyfor Divochka was ousted for being married twice. Several times, councils of bishops censured the bigamy and illiteracy of the lower clergy and, at times, of bishops as well.

Luzhnytsky pointed out three ways in which Polish policies were destructive to the Orthodox Church in Ukraine: First, by eliminating its national-religious and traditional values; second, by disparaging and lowering its prestige among the people; and third, by artificially creating a feeling of remorse for being a member of the Orthodox Church. The spiritual vacuum, created by these measures, was expected to be filled in by Roman Catholicism, by official Polish and Catholic circles. It was, without a doubt, a sin for these circles to use their religion in ultimately achieving the political aim of Polonizing all Ukrainians.[8]

Numerous regional councils of bishops attempted to improve the over-all situation in the Church. Abuses were branded and punished and corrections were suggested, as was done by the councils at Vilna, Berest, Ternopil, Volodymyr and at other places. In the 1590's, councils were held almost every year to remedy the deplorable state of affairs, and above all, to regulate the relationship between the official Church organization and the church brotherhoods, associations of laypeople who on their own tried to prevent the complete downfall of the Orthodoxy. However, the hostile attitude of Polish circles, dominant in the country, and the lack of leadership on the part of the patriarchs of Constantinople left little hope for the future. A few visits of various patriarchs in Ukraine did not help much.

Although the church brotherhoods were traditional in Ukraine, they reached their heights and achieved the peak of their significance in the sixteenth century, having contributed greatly and in the long-run to a Ukrainian spiritual and religious revival. Polish political, social and economic pressure and discrimination did not allow any form of organized life for the

Ukrainian people at that time. Even the guilds were anti-Ukrainian. The church brotherhoods became, therefore, a natural means for the Orthodox Ukrainians to express themselves in an organized manner.

The decay of the official Church organization and of religious life permitted the well-meaning laypeople to undertake the initiative of a religious revival, when even the metropolitans, bishops and priests had failed.

At first, the scope of the brotherhood activities was narrow, having included maintenance of church buildings, their cleaning, assisting at religious services, and some social life. Later on, however, that scope was greatly expanded. The brotherhoods constructed churches and other buildings, cared for the sick, elderly, widows and orphans, defended the Church against discrimination by the courts and the administration, organized schools, opposed the noble patronage of the churches, condemned and opposed immoral and illiterate clergy, opposed Polish anti-Orthodox propaganda, and tried to influence good people to be ordained and to work for the Orthodox Church and the Ukrainian cause. Later on, when book printing was invented, the brotherhoods indulged in considerable publishing activity in order to improve the educational process and to raise the intellectual level of the clergy and the people at large. The brotherhoods in Lviv, Lutsk, Kiev and a few other cities were the most active and important. The Lviv Brotherhood of Holy Assumption was, perhaps, the oldest one, originating about 1439.

At first, the membership of the brotherhoods was comprised of townspeople, merchants and craftsmen. Later, however, the nobility of the Orthodox faith joined the organizations. In Lutsk, the majority of the members were of the nobility while in Kiev, many clergymen later joined the brotherhood. In 1616, Hetman Petro Konashevych-Sahaidachny and the entire Cossack Host became members of the Kievan Brotherhood of the Holy Transfiguration.

In 1586, the Lviv brotherhood, the most active and outstanding one, received from the Patriarch the privilege of *stavropigia*; the status of being exempt from local eparchial jurisdiction and responsible directly to the Patriarch, including the power to censure the members of the Church, and the laypeople and clergy for immoral and sinful deeds. Furthermore, the Lviv brotherhood became the central organization of its type with the authority to instruct and direct other brotherhoods throughout Ukraine, and to sponsor a religious revival of the country.[9]

The broad jurisdiction of the Lviv *stavropigia*, in particular, and the aggressive activity of the brotherhoods, in general, frequently produced conflicts among themselves and the local ecclesiastic authority, including bishops and pastors. In Lviv, the conflict was especially acute.

The Roman Catholic Church was traditionally dominant in Poland, and after the Union of Krevo, it became dominant also in the Lithuanian-Rus' Commonwealth. Catholic missionary work in Ukraine was conducted by the Dominican order as early as the thirteenth century. Soon they established their monasteries in many cities and towns in Ukraine: in Kiev, Lutsk, Bar, Brody, Buchach, Ovruch, Lviv and others. In the fourteenth century the Franciscan order established itself there; it organized a separate province with many houses, in Lviv, Horodok, Halych, Kolomyia and Sniatyn. In the fifteenth century, the Bernardinian order spread Catholicism in Galicia and Volhinia. They had good schools, in which the Orthodox youth were instructed and brought closer to Catholicism. Also many orders of Roman Catholic Sisters developed in Ukraine.

The Catholic monks and nuns were largely of Polish nationality, and concurrently with the spreading of Catholicism, they brought about the aggressive Polonization of the Ukrainian nobility and gentry, placing themselves on a higher social level and showing contempt for and discrimination against the Orthodox clergy and laity. By acting in such a way, the Polish Catholic orders and the entire Polish Catholic Church organization brought forth a hatred of the Orthodox population toward Catholicism in general. This proved to be a tragic consequence for Poles and Ukrainians as well. During the later wars of the Cossacks for Ukrainian independence, the Catholic Church and clergy became the targets of a bloody Ukrainian revenge. This hatred of Catholicism pushed the Ukrainians into the deadly embrace of Muscovite-Russian imperialism a few decades later.

King Casimir the Great, of Poland, after the temporary domination of Galicia, immediately made preparations to introduce the Roman Catholic Church organization into that territory. At the time of Prince Volodyslav Opilsky, a Latin archdiocese was established for Galicia, in 1375, with three dioceses, in Peremyshl, Kholm and Volodymyr. However, for a long time their existence was purely nominal. There were no faithful of the Latin rite there to be taken care of, and even their bishops frequently resided outside their dioceses.

King Yagiello tried by force to introduce the Latin church organization in Galicia by taking away church buildings from the Orthodox and giving them to the Roman Catholics, bishops and priests, as in the case of the Peremyshl Cathedral Church. With the progressive penetration of Polish authority and institutions in the Lithuanian-Rus' Commonwealth, the Latin church organization became a reality in Ukraine. Vitovt established a Latin diocese in the town of Kamianets Podilsky, followed by new Roman Catholic dioceses in other parts of the Commonwealth. For some unexplainable reason, Latin Church authorities were extremely hostile toward the Ferrara-Florence Church union, having largely destroyed the prospects of the unification of both Orthodox and Catholic Christianities into "one mystical body of Christ," according to the precepts of the New Testament. On the other hand, the Roman Catholic Church and the Catholic clergy and population were favored and showered with privileges, while the Orthodox were exposed to persecutions and discrimination. To the great disadvantage of the Orthodox faith was the fact that the Roman Catholic Church was at that time spiritually, intellectually and organizationally on a much higher level, making it hard for the Orthodox church to compete. In fact, it was fighting a losing battle.

The Church Union of Berest. The deplorable state of affairs in the Orthodox Church was intensified by new developments, which led to a turning point. First of all, the Reformation began to gain ground in Poland and in the Lithuanian-Rus' Commonwealth in the middle of the fifteenth century. Since young Ukrainians had studied in Bohemia, the teachings of Jan Huss began to spread in Ukraine. Subsequently, other Protestant denominations: the Anti-Trinitarists, Calvinists, Lutherans and others began at first to gain supporters in Ukraine. The Orthodox at first looked to the Protestants as their potential allies in the struggle against Catholic pressures. However, very soon they realized that their differences with the Protestant groups were much greater in the religious sphere than those with the Catholics, and after a while these Orthodox-Protestant contacts ceased. In fact, the Protestant denominations never became popular in Ukraine. Only a small group of nobles for a short time accepted Protestantism, and this lasted only about one generation. Their children returned to Catholicism or Orthodoxy. Broad masses of the population remained completely immune to Protestantism. However, the lively religious debates among the Catholics, Orthodox and Protestants proved the intellectual inferiority of Orthodox theology of that time and contributed to a further decline of the prestige of the Orthodox Church and faith.

Meanwhile, a powerful Catholic reaction against the Protestant Reformation developed. The Jesuit order proved to be the most powerful weapon. The Jesuits organized themselves as the Catholic "brain trust" of outstanding intellectual abilities, having developed scholarship, magnificent preaching and an efficient educational system. They came to the Commonwealth soon after the Union of Lublin, etablishing many schools there, including some in Ukraine, for example the towns of Yaroslav, Lviv, Kamianets, Peremyshl, Vinnytsia, Ostroh, Novhorod Siversky and some others. After defeating Protestantism in the Polish Crown and the Lithuanian-Rus' Commonwealth, the Jesuits opened a frontal attack against the Orthodox "schismatics," as Polonska-Vasylenko stated so well.[10] The children of the Orthodox nobility entered these schools in large numbers, since the Orthodox ones were no match for the former, and soon they were fully indoctrinated, became Catholic and Polish, and were fully lost to their former Church and nationality.

Polish kings openly favored the Jesuits and offered them all possible assistance which was another disadvantage for the Orthodox, who could expect only discrimination. In a political light, the Polish Jesuits developed the doctrine of a Polish-Catholic messianism to be the bulwark of Catholicism in the east; to bring Catholicism to the Orthodox and at the same time defend it against the "schism." In conclusion, the above doctrine meant converting the Orthodox to Roman Catholicism and making them at the same time Polish in order to achieve one unified state, the Polish Crown and the Lithuanian Grand Principality, with one Catholic religion.[11]

Meanwhile, another significant development took place. In 1588, Patriarch Yeremiah visited Muscovy. He was persuaded by Boris Godunov, the mighty "Lord-Protector of Muscovy," to agree to establish a Muscovite patriarchate. Bribery, trickery and coercion were used to induce Yeremiah to consent to the idea. In 1589, the Muscovite patriarchate became an accomplished fact, and Metropolitan Yov became the first patriarch.[12] Considering the traditional pressure of the Muscovite metropolitans to dominate ecclesiastically and politically in the long-run the whole of Ukraine, the creation of the patriarchate in Moscow definitely spelled danger for the independence of the Ukrainian Orthodox Church. It suggested the possibility that the submission of the Kievan metropolis to the Muscovite patriarchate might have been only a matter of time. Among the Ukrainian Orthodox hierarchy there was little sympathy to Muscovy.

The difficult situation of the Orthodox Church in Ukraine, the internal chaos, the low spiritual and intellectual level, the impact of the Reformation, the Catholic reaction, the Polish-sponsored discrimination of the Orthodox, and the formation of the Muscovite patriarchate demanded a certain radical measure to save the Ukrainian Church from a complete downfall. Against that background, the idea of a church union with the Holy See of Rome was revived in Ukraine. The debates were prolonged. Prince Constantine Ostrozhsky, one of the most powerful of noblemen in the Commonwealth at that time, submitted a plan for the unification, which was supposed to include Rome and all the Eastern patriarchates, as a solution to save the Eastern Church, under the title of "The Articles of Sokal." The Articles suggested equal rights for both Churches, the Western and the Eastern, guarantees of material possessions, correction of organizational and other inadequacies, and the development of schools and education. Ostrozhsky was initially enthusiastic and a champion of the Union.

The real beginning for the union talks was started by the Bishop of Lviv, Gedeon Balaban, who was troubled by his quarrels with the *Stavropigia*. He was joined by Dionizii, Bishop of Kholm, Cyril Terletsky, Bishop of Lutsk, Leontii, Bishop of Pinsk and Turiv, and a little later, also by the newly elevated Ipatii Potii of Volodymyr. The talks were conducted secretly, without including Prince Ostrozhsky in the scheme. Ostrozhsky felt insulted, and from that time on became an uncompromising enemy of the union idea. However, the bishops were correct, because, according to canon law, it was a matter for the ecclesiastical hierarchs to decide, not for the laity. The prince did not care to see the matter in that light. Furthermore, the hierarchs also ignored his *Articles* at the council of 1593. In fact, the split among the Orthodox with respect to the Union was visible and apparent already at the first council to consider the matter in 1590. The union plans were announced in 1594. Bishops Potii and Terletsky went to Rome to consult and receive the Pope's blessings. The Act of the Union was signed in December 1595.

The Act of the Union included the following important decisions: the Ukrainian Uniat Church retained its Eastern or Byzantine rite and the Julian calendar; it accepted and recognized the primacy of the Pope of Rome in all ecclesiastic, religious and moral matters; it retained ecclesiastic autonomy to elect, ordain and consecrate priests, bishops and metropolitans in accordance with canon law; the lower clergy retained the right to be married.[13] When on the 6th of October 1596, the Council of Berest convened to officially confirm the Union, actually two councils were held. The Uniat one included all Ukrainian bishops, except two, the Lviv and Peremyshl ones, and other clergy and representatives of the Latin Church. The Orthodox one included the Lviv and Peremyshl bishops, the representative of the Patriarch of Constantinople, Nicephor, a few foreign Orthodox bishops, and the lay membership of gentry. Although Bishop Gedeon Balaban of Lviv actually initiated the union process, for some reason he retreated and fought for the Orthodox cause. Apparently, the Orthodox council would have lacked prestige, had it not been for the presence of Prince Constantine Ostrozhsky, who changed his mind shortly before the event.

The councils deliberated for three days, the Orthodox Council rejected the Union with Rome and excluded from that Church all bishops and their followers for accepting the primacy of the Pope. In turn, the Uniat Council officially proclaimed the Union and renounced the episcopal dignity of Balaban of Lviv and Kopystensky of Peremyshl, as well as excluded from the Church all those who participated in the Orthodox *synod* or council. Since the council was held in Berest, and it was there that the Church union was officially announced, the said religious and ecclesiastic event became known as the Union of Berest.[14]

In fact, with the act of the union all of Ukraine became Uniate-Catholic. Metropolitan Mykhail Rohoza and the vast majority of bishops except two, the already named bishops, accepted the church union with Rome. The conduct of the two was fatalistic in the long-run. The union with Rome might have prevented the future association of the Ukrainian Orthodox with the Muscovite Orthodoxy on religious and political plateaus, through such developments as the Pereyaslav Treaty of 1654 and 1657, which practially introduced a political Muscovite protectorate over the Ukrainian Cossack-Hetman State, or the submission of the Ukrainian Orthodox Church to the authority of the Muscovite patriarchate in 1685-1686, or the ultimate incorporation of Ukraine into the Russian Empire in 1781-1782. A religious separation of Ukraine by the Uniate church from the Orthodox Muscovy-Russia could have been a factor in the preservation of Ukrainian independence.

The Union of Berest had, of course, some bad and some good consequences. In the short-run, the consequences of the Union were tragic; the nation was divided into two hostile religious camps fighting with each other. At times blood was shed. The Uniats argued that their move would make the Church stronger; would overcome the old inferiority complex, induced by Polish discrimination; would place it on an equal footing with all Catholics; and that it would become a more successful defense against Polonization attempts by the Polish government and Church. Furthermore, their association with Peter's Chair made them "better" Christians. In opposition, the Orthodox used the arguments that their faith was traditional and was the faith of their ancestors, that it had definitely an anti-Polish and anti-Catholic character, and that it was and would be a better and more successful bulwark against Polish assimilation, while the Uniat Church would only facilitate the Polonization process. Furthermore they believed that only the Orthodox Church was a true one and that Catholicism was a false creed. There was little doubt that the antagonism and anti-Uniat sentiments among the conservative Orthodox circles were substantially instigated by Moscow, which had different plans of its own for Ukraine. The religious fanaticism on both sides led to hatred and intolerance. In the long-run, the Union had some good aspects. The religious dialogue between the Uniats and the Orthodox, including also the Protestants, led to the organization of schools, the establishment of book publishing, the development of a living, national Ukrainian language and an over-all rise in the intellectual level of the clergy and laity, as well as the further development of literature.[15]

Education. With the revival of religious life and the Church organization, education and the maintenance of schools again became the domain of the Church according to pre-invasion tradition. The state was still too weak and too underdeveloped to assume this responsibility. Basic schools, teaching writing and reading, and more advanced ones, instructing principles of theology, literature and the Greek language, were established at the episcopal and parish churches and monasteries. Historical sources mention a school at the Krasnostav church in 1550, and a school at the Peresopnytsky monastery, which was established in 1596 by Princess Helena Chortoryisky-Hornostai. Hanna Hoiska built a school at the Pochaiv monastery and Raina Yarmolynska built one at the Zahayetsky monastery.[16] Of course, in many instances funds to establish schools came from private, aristocratic and at times urban, sources. However, at a little later date, running the educational institutions was an exclusive church or church affiliated affair, like that of the church brotherhoods.

The students in these schools were taught the alphabet, prayers, to read the *Psalmbook* and the *Letters of the Apostles*. The *Psalmbook* in many schools served as a textbook for a great many decades. In the fifteenth century a simplified form of the alphabet was developed, the so-called *skoropys*, and in the next century it came into general use, also in official and private documentation and correspondence.

In these schools, the cantors, or *diaky* according to contemporary terminology, were young people who might someday become priests but who were teachers most of the time. The nobles, who frequently made endowments and grants to the schools, often specifically reserved large amounts of money to hire qualified *diaky* as teachers. In church documents, though schools were rarely mentioned, often references were made to increases of the cantors' compensations, while pastor Oderbron asserted in 1581, that all over Ukraine there were schools affiliated with the churches. After the teaching periods were over, the parents of the students also compensated the cantors, by a pot of gruel or a *hryvna* of money.[17] Of course, the *diaky* also helped in the church and during the masses. Often, along with the parish priest, they were the only literate persons in the village or settlement.

The nobility and gentry, according to contemporary writings, like that of V. Zahorovsky, hired private cantors for their children for instruction in basic literary skills after they reached their seventh year of age. After the children of the nobility acquired some knowledge in writing and reading in Ukrainian and in religion, another, more knowledgeable cantor was employed to teach them Latin, and subsequently they were apparently sent to Jesuit or other schools to further their education.

The Reformation and Catholic reaction to Protestantism brought new types of schools to Ukraine. Both the Catholics and Protestants made a great effort to strengthen their respective positions in religious life by promoting education and schools. The Protestant schools were established in Ukraine in the towns of Dubno, Khmelnyk and other places, while Ukrainian youth attended similar institutions in Poland and Lithuania as well. The high school and college in Rakiv were particularly famous. Due to powerful Catholic reaction, on the one hand, and the ultimately unfavorable attitude of the Orthodox toward Protestantism, on the other, most of these schools did not survive for long. As a result of the Catholic counter-offensive in cultural and educational fields, numerous Jesuit high schools and colleges, with good teachers and dormitories for the students, were established all over Ukraine. After defeating Protestantism in Poland and in the Lithuanian-Rus' Grand Principality, the Jesuits concentrated their missionary work in converting the Orthodox to Catholicism; the schools were their principal missionary method. Of course, their schools and educational system, following traditional scholastic methodology, were much better than the Orthodox church schools, and consequently the Ukrainian Orthodox noble youth flocked enthusiastically to them. In the Jesuit and Protestant schools the Latin language, history, geography, cosmography and natural history were taught. However, along with a better education, the Jesuit schools, with most of the teachers Catholic and Polish, were tearing the Orthodox and Ukrainian youth away from their parental religion and nationality. Jesuit education was alien to the Ukrainian national spirit and psyche. As a result, the Ukrainian aristocratic families were becoming progressively not even Uniat but

Polish-Catholic, leaving the nation without a leading upper class; a nation of peasants only.

Prince Constantine Ostrozhsky fully understood the problem and began to organize and finance genuinely Orthodox schools in Volhinia to prepare an intelligent clergy to counteract the Catholic educational offensive. Ostrozhsky was fascinated by the idea of publishing a full text of the Holy Bible for the Orthodox as a reference source for religious polemics with the Catholics and Protestants. For this purpose, he brought to Ostroh many outstanding scholars, including Greeks and ordered them to work on the project. The complete Bible was published in 1581, marking a significant cultural event in Ukraine. From this short-range project, a long-term one was developed. In the late 1570's the Ostroh Academy, on the university level, was put into operation through the efforts of Prince Constantine Ostrozhsky who engaged most of the scholars working on the Bible as professors in the Academy. It was called "the three-lingual school," since three languages, Ukrainian-Rus'ian, Greek, and Latin, were taught. The first rector of the Academy was Herasym Smotrytsky. Among the teachers were Ukrainians, Poles and Greeks; clergymen, laymen, Orthodox, Catholics and Protestants. The Academy gave several outstanding people to Ukraine, such as Hetman Petro Konashevych-Sahaidachny and Meletii Smotrytsky, a theologian. Its over-all cultural significance for the country was rather significant in spite of its short existence. Very soon after Prince Constantine's death the Academy of Ostroh was reorganized by his granddaughter, Anna Khodkevych, into a Jesuit College.[18] Following Ostrozhsky's example the bishop of Volodymyr planned to organize a similar school in the city of Volodymyr, but this did not meet with success.

As a result of the progressive Polonization of the Ukrainian upper, noble social stratum, aristocratic sponsorship of the educational and cultural process in Ukraine came to an end and the townspeople took over this mission. In particular, the church brotherhoods took control in towns and cities. The Lviv brotherhood was, of course, setting an example in this respect. These schools definitely had an ecclesiastic character, and were of different levels. They taught Slavic and Greek languages, some mathematics, and other liberal arts courses. Several of them attempted to equate their scholastic level with that of the Jesuit institutions without much success. According to the rules of these schools, the teachers were to be pious, moral and mentally well-balanced, neither prone to be angry nor humorous, but modest. They were to be good Orthodox, not prone to heresy, responsible, required to treat all students equally whether rich or poor, and required to take care of the students in such a way that none of them would become the teachers' liability before God, their parents and the students themselves.[19] The profession of a teacher was a demanding one, but it enjoyed great social respect.

Such schools functioned in Lviv, Volodymyr, Volodava, Lutsk, Dubno, Pynsk, Mezhybozh, Peremyshl, Yaroslav, Kholm, Halych, Stryi, Rohatyn, Komarno, Mykolaiv and in many other towns. To make possible instruction in the languages, dialectics, rhetorics, philosophy, mathematics, astronomy and music, textbooks were published which were in use until the eighteenth century. Obviously, the invention of book printing advanced the publication of textbooks. The brotherhoods became greatly interested in book printing and some of them, like the Lviv *stavropigia*, also took over the sponsorship of printing.

The main purpose of the schools was the training of priests and qualified teachers, and the peak of their development came at the end of the sixteenth and the beginning of the seventeenth century. At that time the graduates of these schools spread throughout the country and exercised a great impact on the religious and national life of their Ukrainian society, especially during the period of vigorous religious polemics between the Orthodox and the Uniats. Many graduates of the schools also went abroad to the famous universities in Poland, Bohemia, Italy and Germany to continue their education. Cultural contacts with the West increased, while at home several important cultural centers developed, like in Lviv, Ostroh, Slutsk, and in the leading monasteries. In many cities there were extensive collections of books, as in the Supraslsky, Pochaivsky and Pechersky monasteries. In the meantime the famous Kievan-Mohilian Academy was established in Kiev by Metropolitan Petro Mohyla. The scholarly activities of this institution, however, belong to the next era of Ukrainian history.

Literature. The Invasion was followed by a decline in the literary activity of the people who were under stress. Following the tragedy, strictly religious-ecclesiastic writings prevailed. They attempted to explain why the tragedy occurred; the answer was: the people were not faithful and loyal to God, so this punishment followed. Metropolitan Cyprian declared that the clergy was not pious enough. He therefore promulgated new regulations for the clergy, demanding fulfillment of their responsibilities and ascetic living. The abbot of the *Percherska Lavra* monastery in Kiev, Serapion, reflected in his sermons the distress of the Invasion as Divine punishment for sins. His writings expressed in an artistic and literary way compassion for human suffering.[20]

Subsequently, South-Slavic literature from the Balkan peninsula, especially from Bulgaria where a literary revival took place in the thirteenth and fourteenth centuries, had an affect on Ukrainian culture. Metropolitan Hyhorii Tsamblak, of Bulgarian descent, worked in favor of the Church union. The South-Slavic literary and cultural trend came to Ukraine also indirectly, by way of the Athos monastic center in Greece, where many Ukrainian monks lived. From there, by their letters and sermons they influenced the spiritual and literary process of their country. In 1476, Metropolitan Mysail wrote a letter to Pope Sixtus IV to accept Ukraine under his Apostolic protection.

Important literary activity was connected with endeavors to publish in the Rus'ian-Ukrainian language a full text of the Holy Bible at the time of the Reformation and Uniat polemics. In 1581, such a Bible was published in Ostroh, as has already been pointed out, as a result of Prince Constantine's efforts and the technical help of Ivan Fedorovich. Meanwhile, the translations of the Holy Scriptures of Frants Skoryna of Polotsk were also spreading throughout all of Ukraine. They contained, however, some Protestant elements. Skoryna himself asserted that his translations were intended for the common people in their living language. The *Peresopnytska* Bible was the most outstanding example of translated literature, made from the Bulgarian tongue by Mykhailo Vasylovich in the years 1556-1561 for a better understanding of Christian doctrines by the broad classes of the population. There were no Protestant influences visible in the *Peresopnytska* version.

Two Protestant pastors, Kavechynsky and Kryshkovsky, published in a printed form the *Katechisis,* a catechism, which was the very first and the last attempt to promote Calvinism in the Rus'ian-Ukrainian language. Only a few years later, in the early 1580's, Tyapinsky, a Unitarian, also published parts of the Bible in Ukrainian. There were also other attempts to translate and publish the Holy Scriptures in their entirety or in parts, but those were not always successful. Along this religious stream, there was V. Zahorovsky's *Testament*, which instructed parents on how to raise their children; by teaching them virtues, prayers and fasting, and also how to avoid heresies.

In fact, the fifteenth and sixteenth centuries, having brought forth Humanism and the Renaissance, initiated cultural trends relating to the ancient values of the Hellenic and Roman civilizations, the Protestant Reformation and the Church Union of Berest, which largely affected the Ukrainian revival and its rise to new levels of civilization. Already at the beginning of the seventeenth century Kiev again became the cultural center of Ukraine, along with Lviv ranking second. Western spiritual and cultural streams soon penetrated literary activities. Western elements were visible in such publications as *The Heavenly Letter, Holy Mother's Dream,* and the collection

Prytochnyk of 1483, which included fragments of Western legends. Translations from the Bohemian, Polish and Latin were published, such as *About Tuadal, the Knight*, the *Story of Three Kings*, or *Oleksii's life*.[21]

Important examples of original literary works were the three editions of the *Pechersky Pateryk*, inherited from the Kievan era, but substantially enlarged in the fifteenth century. Numerous sermons and letters of clergymen, minutes of the episcopal councils, the *synody*, and writings on morality furnish evidence of the considerable literary abilities of the respective authors, as Hrushevsky points out. A special place belonged, of course, to chronicle writing, namely, to the *lytovsko-rus'ki litopysi*, the *Lithuanian-Rus'ian chronicles*. Some of them, of a quite earlier origin, reflect the gradual expansion of the Lithuanian dynasty's domination of Ukrainian-Rus'ian territories. The chronicles can be grouped into three separate classes. The collections of the first group describe the history of the Lithuanian-Rus' Commonwealth of the second half of the fourteenth and the first half of the fifteenth century. When covering relations between Yagiello and Vitovt, the chronicle takes Vitovt's side and praises him for his deeds. The second group describes the earliest times: a legendary account of Lithuanian history to Gedymin's era, followed by a story of the latter period together with a short synopsis of developments in 1575. The third group of the chronicles is made up by the collection of A. Bykhovets, which features a more lively and literary presentation. The *Lithuanian-Rus'ian chronicles* followed the Kievan tradition, and praised the Lithuanian-Rus'ian princes for whatever worthwhile deeds they accomplished for the Commonwealth. The *Supraslsky litopys*, the *Supraslsky Chronicle*, was codified from the old chronicles at the end of the fifteenth century. Then there was no Ukrainian or Lithuanian-Ukrainian sovereign who took care of national matters. Therefore the chronicler directed his work at Prince Constantine Ostrozhsky, the nobleman who protected the Orthodox Church and Rus'ian people.

The Church Union of Berest gave a mighty impetus to the growth of literary activity, which brought about a general rise in the intellectual level of society as a whole, and its upper strata in particular. The living Rus'ian-Ukrainian language developed substantially, because both sides, the Orthodox and Uniat, were involved in religious polemics and used the tongue which the broadest mass of the population could understand. These were visible positive consequences of the Chuch union in Ukraine for the future. However, they were counteracted by many long and short term negative aspects of that religious and ecclesiastic event which was of utmost significance for all concerned.

In order to defend themselves against Catholic argumentation in favor of the Union of Berest, by the end of the sixteenth century the Orthodox published a work, entitled the *Ectisis*, in which they attempted to prove the canonical righteousness of their point of view. Kryshtof Bronsky, under his literary name, Christopher Philalet, then published first in Polish and then in Ukrainian, a treatise under the title the *Apocrisis*; a superb polemical work, which came to the defense of the democratic principle in the Church; that not only the ecclesiastical hierarchy but also the laity should have a voice. The Catholic canonical principle excluded the laity from the governance of the Church. The Union of Berest included only the Church hierarchy, the metropolitan and the majority of the bishops, while the rival council of the Orthodox in Berest also included the laity.[22]

An outstanding place in religious polemical writing was occupied by Ivan Vyshensky from Sudova Vyshnia, in Galicia. He went to Greece, to the famous Orthodox monastery on the Mountain of Aphon, from where he sent letters to Ukraine in defense of Orthodox Christianity. He was a fanatical enemy of Catholicism, the Union and Western civilization, and fully condemned those Ukrainian bishops, who accepted the Union with Rome. His most outstanding treatise was the *Letter to those Bishops who ran away from the Orthodox Church*, published in 1597. This was an extremely severe criticism of the Union. His hatred of the Uniat bishops led him to a kind of religious anarchism, which asserted that it would be better for the Orthodox to pray to God without any bishops and priests, than through those who accepted the Union.

Another outstanding polemicist was Meletii Smotrytsky who published in 1610 his *Trenos* in defense of Orthodoxy. The work interpreted the doctrines of faith, expressed sorrow over the plight of the Church and deep concern over the denationalization of the Ukrainian nobility. The *Trenos*, written in a lyrical tone, with great literary skill, made such an impression on its contemporaries, that the Polish king, afraid of possible repercussions, ordered the work destroyed. However, after the murder of Josafat Kuntsevych, archbishop of Polotsk, by Orthodox fanatics in 1623, Smotrytsky undertook a journey to the Near East, and having become acquainted with conditions of the Orthodox Church there, became a Uniat Catholic himself, and wrote his *Apologetics of the Journey to the Eastern Lands* in which he acknowledged that the acceptance of the primacy of the Pope of Rome would help the Orthodox Church.[23]

Among the great number of writers and preachers who took part in the aggressive polemics on both sides, Abott Zakharii Kopystensky, who wrote the

Palinodion, or the *Book of the Defense of the Holy Catholic Apostolic Eastern Church*, ranked as a more influential one. The most important polemicist on the side of the Uniat-Catholics was Metropolitan Ipatii Potii, who wrote a letter to Prince Ostrozhsky exposing his wrong-doings and defending the Union. The Prince did not answer directly, but authorized a theologian from Ostroh to respond. The answer was a low level one. Subsequently Potii published anonymously a treatise, first in Ukrainian in 1598 and then in Polish in 1600 against the Orthodox *Apocrisis*, and then, a response to Patriarch Meletii. In 1603 he published *Apologetics of the Florentinian Council*, one of his more important works.

Another impetus to the debates, polemics and animosities, which, nevertheless had added to the intellectual growth of the society, was given by the introduction of a new Gregorian calendar, introduced by Pope Gregory XIII in 1582. It corresponded better with astronomical timing than the old one, introduced long ago by Julius Ceasar. The Orthodox generally objected to the new calander, merely because it was sponsored by the pope. The objection was so energetic, that even the Union of Berest provided that the Uniats be allowed to retain the old one. Later, of course, it created a great deal of problems, i.e., when the Roman Catholic gentry forced the Orthodox and Uniat peasantry to work in their fields on holy days according to the old calendar, thus insulting their religious feelings. Jan Latos, expelled from Cracow university for his opposition to the new calendar, went to the town of Ostroh and from there led the fight against it. Later, the Patriarch of Constantinople and an Orthodox Church council condemned the calendar. Also in this instance, literary polemics were brought forth.

Along with the chronicle writing, other secular, non-church-related literary works developed. The old *Story of Troy*, the *Story of Tristan and Isolde* and many others came from the West or the Balkan Peninsula. The *Speech of Castelanian Meleshko* was an example of literary satire which survived to recent years. Poetic literary forms began to evolve in the sixteenth century, as evidenced by the poems of Herasym Smotrytsky, while Lavrentii Zazanii in his *Grammar* (1596) formulated a theory of writing verses.[24]

From the beginning of the sixteenth century the first *dumy*, the epic folksongs praising historical events and their heroes, developed. The struggle against the Tartars, Tartar captivity, the struggle against other enemies such as the Wallachians, and subsequently, the heroic exploits of the Cossacks, were told in those epics or sagas, which vividly resembled the old *bylyny* from the glorious time of the early Kievan Empire. The terrors of the Tartar assaults in the fourteenth, fifteenth and sixteenth centuries caused the *bylyny* to be forgotten in Ukraine. However, the new form of epic songs and sagas, the *dumy*, took the place of the former.²⁵

Architecture. Designing buildings of architectural and artistic value during this era continued to be largely church-motivated. Building did, however, experience substantial evolution. Many architectural styles and forms were utilized in the Ukrainian wooden structures; the modified Byzantine churches with some elements of Western Romanesque and Gothic constructions, and Renaissance architecture.

The Mongol invasion laid waste to the magnificent architectural structures of the Kievan era. For several decades afterward, there was meager reconstruction of the churches and public buildings. The Tartars opposed and barred defense structures in Ukraine. Finally, at the end of the fourteenth century building activity again resumed. In the fifteenth and sixteenth centuries a Ukrainian national architectural style of wooden church structures evolved: prevailingly three or five frame structures, and with three or five copulas, tops. Unfortunately, almost no examples of that architecture were preserved for posterity, but similar structures from the seventeenth and eighteenth centuries have survived to recent times. It is regrettable that the current atheistic Soviet regime dismantled and destroyed some of those historic wooden structures.

Several stone church buildings of the fourteenth and sixteenth centuries have been preserved, indicating a period of transition between the modified Byzantine style and Western influences, with Romanesque and Gothic characteristics, such as the Church of the Holy Christmas in Mezheriche, in Volhinia, from the fifteenth, and the Lavrivsky monastery, in Galicia, from the sixteenth century. Romanesque and Gothic structural forms came from the West, along with the penetration of Roman Catholicism in Ukraine. The impact of the Romanesque style was rather insignificant and confined to the western regions of Ukraine, while the Gothic style achieved a greater popularity. Not only were Polish churches and monasteries constructed in that style in the cities of Lviv, Peremyshl, and others, but even some Orthodox churches were built that way or at least adopted some Gothic structural elements. Such Gothic Orthodox churches were in Nyzhankovychi, Zaluzhzha, Kodensk and Posada Rabotytska, all probably from the sixteenth century.²⁶

For defense reasons, throughout the fifteenth and sixteenth centuries many military structures were built with thick stone and brick walls and deep water ditches around them. Prince Fedir Koriatovych and several others built many such castles to defend their lands and principalities, mainly against the

Tartar booty excursions and assaults in Podillia and other border regions of Ukraine. Even some churches were constructed in this semi-defense style, such as the church-castle in Sutkivtsi from the second half of the fifteenth century, which included Gothic structural elements, the church in Sataniv and Rohatyn, and the Derman monastery. Under Western influence, the castles and palaces of the grand nobles and gentry were also built for defense, like those in Lutsk, Mezhybozh, Ostriv and other places, of which largely only ruins remain.

The Gothic architectural style was certainly popularized in Ukraine by foreign, German, Polish and Bohemian settlers, who brought the style from their predominantly Catholic homelands. This was closely related to the colonization process, as Mirthcuk pointed out. At first, these Gothic structures embodied some Byzantine architectural elements, but at the end of the fifteenth century, as the old tradition was retreating before the onslaught of new trends, the Gothic buildings became architecturally purer. Mirtchuk believed that there were numerous Gothic structures especially in Lviv, but that they were largely damaged by the great fire in 1527 and ruined by the march of time.[27]

The era of the Renaissance, having swept through Western Europe, fostered the revival of ancient and classical artistic traditions, including architectural customs which profoundly affected structural activities in Ukraine. In her western provinces in particular, churches, chapels, public buildings (city halls), castles and private palaces and residences of the nobility, church dignitaries and rich city patricians were built and decorated in the Renaissance style: in Lviv, Peremyshl, Berezhany, Starokonstantyniv, Korets, Buchach, Yaroslav, Sokal, Zamost, Lutsk, Sataniv, and other places. Lack of peace and stability in eastern Ukrainian regions were not conducive to large-scale architectural activity. This changed at a later date. In Lviv, in particular, many beautiful Renaissance buildings have been well preserved, such as the tower of the Church of the Holy Assumption, the Church itself having been built some twenty years later at the end of the sixteenth and beginning of the seventeenth century, the Chapel of the Three Wise Men, the chapel of the Boime and Campini families, Hopner's building, the Black Building, Bandinelli's building, and other Renaissance constructions in the same style around the market place and the city hall. Many private residences in that style were also preserved in other towns of Western Ukraine, as has been mentioned.

It must be emphasized that the church brotherhoods, the *bratstva*, greatly contributed to the development of Renaissance architecture in Ukraine due to their national patriotism and religious zeal. They desired to raise the spiritual, cultural and artistic level of the Orthodox Ukrainian communities. The city patricians of the Orthodox faith set the example.

The architects were at first primarily foreign: German, Italian in particular, and of Swiss descent. However, according to municipal and court records, Ukrainian architects soon mastered the art, and were able to leave an indelible imprint on the architecture of that era, such as Nychko, Luka of Priashiv, Martyn Lushnia, Ivan Kruhlyk, Ambrizii Prykhylny and many others. Luka of Priashiv renovated the city hall and built the castle of Lutsk, while Prykhylny erected the Jewish synagogue, "Golden Roza," and his own residence of Lviv.[28]

Painting and Carving. The arts of painting and carving developed along with architectural styles. The buildings were constructed in different styles and then decorated by paintings and carvings (sculptures). The art of painting reached a very high level in Ukraine in the fifteenth and sixteenth centuries, having surpassed not only Poland, Lithuania and Muscovy, but even Western Europe. The Ukrainian painters had a wide reputation and were asked to go to Poland, Muscovy, Lithuania, Moldavia and Wallachia to decorate churches, castles and palaces. These masters of the art of painting were very highly esteemed and always richly compensated for their works with horses, furs, and fur coats, and were well fed and entertained, when doing their work.

In many places in Poland, Cracow, Lublin, Sieradz, Gniezno, Sandomierz and other towns, the fresco painting of the Ukrainian artists in the Byzantine style, presenting Eastern saints, have been identified, though Catholic Poland never sympathized with the Orthodox and their creativity. The popularity of Ukrainian paintings was evidenced by their very high artistic quality. Ukrainian painting beautified churches and palaces in Vilna, Novi Troky, Moscow and other cities of East Europe, in the Kievan Byzantine tradition.

Frescos of that style, introducing elements of Gothic naturalism, were painted in Lviv, Carpathian Ukraine, and further east. At the beginning of the fifteenth century, artist Andrii became very famous and was highly appreciated. He developed his own approach and his own style, embodying realism, free composition and harmony of colors, and liberating himself from rigid Byzantic rules of painting. However, he did not fully accept Western European patterns, adopting some Italian features. *Icon* painting became generally more liberal, departing from Byzantine tradition; the faces of the saints became milder and received freer movements as opposed to Byzantine rigidity, severity of expression, unnatural solemnity and motionlessness. All these changes came about under the impact of Western art, on the one hand, in particular the Gothic style, and of local national artistry, on the other. The figures and faces received individual features, the colors became brighter, and the composition of the paintings more direct. Simplicity was coupled with artistry.[29]

In the second half of the sixteenth century Renaissance painting traditions spread in Ukraine to decorating buildings. Lviv became the center of this art. *Icons* and portraits of the princes, noblemen and city patricians were skillfully done, showing Dutch and Italian influences, while at the same time Byzantine elements were retained and Ukrainian national traits introduced. All this made Ukrainian painting highly original at that time. Like architecture, it freed itself from being exclusively church-oriented. It was highly secularized and used in decorating private homes and in painting portraits of individuals in the higher strata of society.

There were many well known local Ukrainian painters at that time, whose names were recorded and made famous. Hrushevsky furnishes a long list of such names. Some of them were wealthy, having many students and servants, but all had to struggle on their own, since Polish artists, who were artistically considerably inferior, discriminated against the Orthodox and did not admit them to the guilds of the professional painters thus denying them protection and privileges. At one time, the Orthodox artists attempted to organize a guild of their own, but it did not get proper recognition. There were also many female artist painters among the Orthodox.[30]

It has been pointed out that Byzantine culture did not include carving, but in Ukraine the art was rejuvenated after the fourteenth century by the influence of Gothic carving in stone and wood in the West. In Ukraine, the Gothic style of carving with a leaning toward naturalism evolved until the seventeenth century, and its popularity in decorating churches, chapels, palaces, residences of the nobility, and private homes spread even to the smaller towns and the countryside, where people of even modest means ornamented their dwellings with Gothic carvings.

The sixteenth century introduced the Renaissance style of carving in stone and wood, as well, which again reached a high level of artistry in Ukraine. Although carving motifs were foreign, the Ukrainian masters introduced Ukrainian national elements, since the carving art was traditional for the Rus'ians-Ukrainians. Especially artistic and famous at that time were the designs in stone on sarcophagi and tombstones in Renaissance motifs, such as those on the sarcophagus of Prince Constantine Ostrozhsky in the Kievan Pecherska Lavra, M. Herburt's tombstone in the Catholic Cathedral in Lviv, or Lahodovsky's in Univ, and many others. According to Renaissance tradition the human figures on tombstones did not show pain or suffering but rather the joy of life, while the backgrounds were decorated with floral and coat of arms designs. The whole composition indicated tranquility and balance.

Churches were decorated with wooden carvings; *icon screens*, the *ikonostasy*, placed in front of the main altars, the main altars, preacher's pulpits, and doors and door and window frames, such as in the Church of St. Paraskevia in Lviv or the Church in the town of Rohatyn. In this manner the private homes and residences of the gentry or city patricians were decorated too. Italian and German artists brought the art of Renaissance sculpturing to Ukraine. It was subsequently taken over by native Ukrainian masters of the art. In the seventeenth century carving already indicated the existence of a specific traditional school of doing this work. Plant, animal and geometric patterns were used for decorating.[31]

Music and Theatre. The dreadful time of the Mongol invasion and the first decades of Sarai's rule were definitely not conducive to the development of any art, including music and the theatre. As a result, a decline of both arts followed in Ukraine. Later, a revival came of which very little is known today. The rather impressive development of music in the sixteenth and seventeenth centuries permits one to conclude that already during the fifteenth century the resurrected art of music and singing had been gaining momentum. In the sixteenth century the folksongs, the *dumy*, praising the heroic age of the Cossack strugggles against the Tartars and the Turks, and subsequently the Poles as well, began to spread all over Ukraine. The professional *kobza* and *bandura* singers or bards, continuing the tradition of the old *bylyny* and singers-reciters of the Kievan era, travelled to village or town, castle or palace of a nobleman, or a humble hut of a commoner, performing their epic renditions, and were connected with the revival of Ukrainian national ambitions for political independence and freedom from foreign oppression. Heroic events and heroic personalities were praised; military expeditions and naval exploits of the Cossacks on the Black Sea were extolled.

A further and advanced development of this musical art followed in the next century, although during the entire period wars raged, a situation never conducive to the development of any form of cultural activity. Apparently, the case of Ukrainian folk music and songs at that time was an exception, induced by a national *risorgimento*.[32]

Church music and singing continued throughout the Invasion and the Mongol domination as a prayer and plea to God for protection and salvation. As the pressure of Polish Catholicism was growing more powerful, Orthodox church music became a form of defense of the faith and nationality. The church brotherhoods took particular care of the development of this art. Even several musical guild organizations were formed in larger towns of Ukraine. At first in the schools of the brotherhoods, four-part singing developed. Later on, the scores were written for five and eight vocal part singing in the churches. Foreign visitors to Ukraine were witness to the beautiful singing there, especially in Kiev it was more beautiful than in the West or in Moscow.[33]

The theatrical art, which sharply declined after the collapse of the Kievan realm, recovered in Ukraine at the end of the sixteenth century under the impact of the West. The Jesuits made theatre a part of their educational and missionary work; in their schools all forms of plays were performed, mostly of a religious and moral nature. The Orthodox schools and brotherhoods adopted the same technique in their religious efforts to resist the impact of Catholicism and the church union. Of course, the Uniats also followed the trend. There were five basic popular kinds of plays: the mystery plays which presented supernatural forces, blessings, and miracles, affecting human life; the passion plays, presenting the Passion and Crucifixion of Jesus Christ; the morality plays with their educational and moral content; the miracle plays presenting episodes from the lives of the miracle-working saints and martyrs; and the intermissions, the humorous scenes introduced to relax the audience. The quality of the plays continuously improved, especially with respect to the scenic decorations, imitating stars, clouds, waves, moving water vessels, and so on.

As one can surmise, the theatrical art continued during that era, as before, to serve the ideal of educating the populace, to show them the good and the noble, and to improve the lot of the poor. The string puppet shows were also popular, their contents having been also of an educational nature with interwoven satire. Puppet shows were presented in certain parts of Ukraine during Christmas time as a supplement to nativity scenes.[34]

Other Arts. Engraving developed out of medieval decoration of books with initials, miniatures, illustrations and ends. It was done at first with woodcuts, later on, with stone and iron-cuts. The city of Lviv where Lavrysh Fylypovych established a school of engraving with many students, became the center of engraving. Initially, engraving had adopted more of the style of Gothic naturalism, in which traditional Byzantine motifs were still visible.

Later on, Renaissance tradition dominated the skill with its Western influence.

The first known example of engraving in Ukraine was done in the *Apostol*. The *Letters of the Apostles* published in Lviv in 1574, embodied Renaissance elements. In particular, the image of the Apostle Luke was of outstanding artistry. All church books were ornamented with engravings of all kinds, and they were done in other centers, as well; in Ostroh, Striatyn, Krylos and Kiev. Portraits, illustrations, scenes from everyday life, historical events and images, decorated with flowers or other motifs, being influenced by Venetian, German and Dutch artistic patterns, provided the themes for engraving in that period of Ukrainian history.

Heraldry, the devising of coats of arms and the making of seals, was still another form of artistic endeavor in Ukraine in the fifteenth and sixteenth centuries. Coats of arms and seals were adopted by individual regions, cities, towns, top state and ecclesiastical dignitaries and noble families. The making of seals reached a high degree of perfection in Ukraine, and there, in contrast to Polish seals using Latin letters and initials, Cyrillic letters were used. Using the Cyrillic alphabet was for a long time considered in Ukraine as an anti-Polonization measure and a way of preserving the Ukrainian-Orthodox national identity. Latin letters came into use in Ukrainian seals and coats of arms in the latter part of the sixteenth century.

Although the coats of arms developed later on among Ukrainian noble families under Western influence, it is important to note that in Volhinia, a rich and important province in Ukrainian history, the noble clan and family insignia of the *boyar* class were known long before the introduction of Polish rule which brought with it Western coats of arms, seals and other distinctions of the nobility. In later coats of arms of the Volhinian gentry, in their shapes and designs, one could detect their ancient origin, related to Greek, Norman and even Caucasian patterns. Jablonowski, a Polish student of heraldry, has asserted that the origins of Volhinian coats of arms were much older than the Union of Horodlo, which supposedly introduced them to the Lithuanian-Rus'ian aristocracy.[35] The coats of arms of some noble families, such as the Ostrozhsky or Seniuta, or of Balaban, required a highly developed technique.[36]

Finally, jewelry-making is also a form of art. The art sharply declined during the Invasion. In Galicia, its decline was caused by Polish policies, which permitted only Catholics to be jewelers. In Peremyshl, for example, in the fifteenth century there were still Ukrainian jewelers, while a century later their number was reduced almost to zero. Only Catholic jewelers remained. The

Ukrainian masters of the art were not admitted to the respective guild. Those Ukrainians who still worked in that profession made only cheaper jewelry, from silver, bronze and copper. Ukrainian mountaineers, the *hutsuly*, were at that time developing their art of copper jewelry.

As Hrushevsky has asserted, in the fifteenth and sixteenth centuries two artistic currents met in Ukraine. One current came from the West; the Western style of jewelry making, and the other from the Orient, particularly the Ottoman Empire. Oriental jewelry became very popular among the nobility in the Lithuanian-Rus' Commonwealth; orientally ornamented weapons, saddles, and other things, made in gold, silver and with precious stones. Ukrainian jewelers combined Western and Oriental designs with the old Rus'ian ones.[37]

Ceramics as a form of art will be briefly referred to later, in the chapter on crafts and industries.

1. N. Fr.-Chirovsky, *A History of the Russian Empire*. Vol. I, *Grand-ducal Vladimir and Moscow*, New York, 1973, pp. 277-278: Yu. Fedoriv, *Istoria tserkvy v Ukraini*, Toronto, 1967, pp. 89-92, 105-112.

2. Fedoriv, *op.cit.*, p. 114: N. Polonska-Vasylenko, *Istoria Ukrainy*, Munich, 1972, Vol. I, p. 324; A. Yatsymirskii, *Grigorii Tsamblak, Ocherk yevo zhyzni i diatelnosti*, St. Petersburg, 1904.

3. M. Hrushevsky, *Istoria Ukrainy-Rusy*, New York, 1955, Vol. VI, pp. 344-345, 351, 353

4. H. Luzhnytsky, *Ukrainska tserkva mizh Skhodom i Zakhodom*. Philadelphia, 1954, pp. 179-183; Fedoriv, *op.cit.*, pp. 118-121.

5. Fedoriv, *loc. cit.*, p. 119; Luzhnytsky, *loc. cit.*

6. Luzhnytsky, *op. cit.*, pp. 181-188: I. Vlasovsky, *Narys istorii Ukrainskoi Pravoslavnoi tserkvy*, New York, 1955, Vol. I, pp. 115-116.

7. Polonska-Vasylenko, *op. cit.*, Vol. I, p. 376-386: also O. Lototsky, *Avtokefalia*, Warsaw, 1938, Vol. II. pp. 302-304.

8. Hrushevsky, *op.cit.*, Vol. V. pp. 413-417, 499-500: Luzhnytsky, *op. cit.*, pp. 160-164, 219-221.

9. On the brotherhoods: Fedoriv, *op. cit.*, pp. 140-143: N. Vasylenko. *Bratstva na Ukraini. Mynule i suchasne*, Munich. 1947; I. Ohienko. *Ukrainska tserkva*, Prague,

1942. Vol. I. pp. 189-195; Luzhnytsky. *op. cit.*, pp. 230-235; V. Lutsiv, *Tserkovni Bratstva v Ukraini*, Penn-State College, 1976.

10. Polonska-Vasylenko, *op.cit.*, Vol. I. p. 386.

11. Luzhnytsky, *op.cit.*, p. 213: E. Vinter, *Vyzantia i Rym v borotbi za Ukrainu*, Prague, 1945. pp. 56-60.

12. Fr.-Chirovsky, *op. cit.*, Vol. I. pp. 381-382.

13. The contents of the Union of Berest: *The Way*, Ukrainian Catholic Weekly, Vol. XXXX, Nos. 22-23, June 10 and 17, 1979; also, Fedoriv, *op. cit.*, pp. 157-165.

14. E. Likowski, *Unia Brzeska 1596*, Warsaw, 1907; K. Chodynicki, *Kosciol prawoslawny a Rzeczpospolita Polska*, 1370-1632, Warsaw, 1934.

15. Vinter, *op. cit.*, pp. 71-74: Vlasovsky, *op. cit.*, Vol. II. pp. 8-16; I. Kholmsky, *Istoria Ukrainy*, Munich, 1948, p. 166-167.

16. M. Vozniak, *Istoria ukrainskoi literatury*, Lviv, 1921. Vol. II. p. 94. Luzhnytsky, *op.cit.*, p. 223.

17. Polonska-Vasylenko, *op.cit.*, Vol. I. pp. 394-397.

18. Mytropolyt Ilarion, *Kniaz' Konstiantyn Ostrozhsky i yoho kulturna pratsia*, Winnipeg, 1958. pp. 46, 75, 103, 112-120; Hrushevsky, *op. cit.*, Vol. VI. pp. 479-497.

19. Hrushevsky, *op. cit.*, Vol. VI. pp. 516-521; Polonska-Vasylenko, *op.cit.*, Vol. I. pp. 398-399.

20. V. Radzykevych, *Istoria ukrainiskoi literatury*, Detroit. 1955, Vol. I. pp. 65-66; D. Chyzhevsky, *Istoria ukrainiskoi literatury*, New York, 1956, pp. 198-199.

21. Hrushevsky, *op. cit.*, Vol. VI. pp. 345-346.

22. Chyzhevsky, *op. cit.*, pp. 229-232; Radzykevych, *op. cit.*, Vol. I. pp. 83-86.

23. Fedoriv. *op. cit.*, 176-178; Radzykevych, *op. cit.*, Vol. I, pp. 85-86.

24. Chyzhevsky, *op. cit.*, pp. 243-244; Polonska-Vasylenko, *op. cit.*, Vol. I, pp. 405-406.

25. Chyzhevsky, *op. cit.*, pp. 245-246; Hrushevsky, *op. cit.*, Vol. VI, 363-368.

26. W. Sitschynsky, "Das künstlerische Schaffen in Lemberg. Das Ukrainische Lwiw". *Ukraine in Vergangenheit und Gegenwart*, Munich, 1954, No. 1-2, p. 32.

27. I. Mirtschuk. *Geschichte der Ukrainischen Kultur*, Munich, 1957, pp. 198-199; V. Yaniv, *Narys ukrainskoi kultury*, New York, 1961, pp. 42-43.

28. V. Sichynsky, "Gotyk i renesans", *Entsyklopedia ukrainoznavstsa*, Munich, 1949, Vol. I, pp. 804-815; P. Kurinnyj, "Der Rynok von Lemberg", *Ukraine in Vergangenheit and Gegenwart*, Munich, 1954, 1-2, p. 26; V. Sichynsky, *Istoria ukrainskoho mystetstva*. I, *Arkhitektura*, New York, 1956; Gotyk i renesans, pp. 57-84.

29. Yaniv. *op. cit.*, pp. 56-57; Mirtchuk. *op. cit.*, pp. 210-211; V. Sichynsky, "Malarstvo", *Entsyklopedia ukrainoznavstva*, Munich, 1949, Vol. I, pp. 825-826.

30. Hrushevsky, *op. cit.*, Vol. VI, pp. 376-377; Polonska-Vasylenko, *op. cit.*, Vol. I, pp. 416-418.

31. Mirtchuk, *op. cit.*, p. 204; Yaniv, *op. cit.*, pp. 49-50; V. Sichynsky, "Rizba", *Entsyklopedia ukrainoznavstva*. Munich, 1949 Vol. I, pp. 821-822; Hrushevsky. *op. cit.*, Vol. VI, pp. 384-385.

32. Mirtchuk, *op. cit.*, pp. 170-172; Yaniv, *op. cit.*, p. 71.

33. *Loc. cit.*

34. *Op. cit.*, pp. 77-78; Mirtschuk, *op. cit.*, pp 183-184; Radzykevych, *op. cit.*, Vol. I, pp. 105-107.

35. A. Jablonowski, "Najnowsze teorye heraldyczne", *Wisla*, Warsaw, 1891, Vol. V, the same, "W sprawie sredniowiecznej heraldyki litewsko-ruskiej", *Kwartalnik historyczny*, Lviv, 1898, Vol. 12; V. Seniutovych-Berezhnyi, "Do dzherel staroruskoi heraldyky", *Litopys Volyni*, New York, 1955, No. 2, pp. 12 and the following.

36. M. Miller, "Heraldyka". *Entsyklopedia ukrainiznavstva*, Munich, 1949, Vol. II p. 367. Polonska-Vasylenko, *op. cit.*, Vol. I, pp. 420-421.

37. Hrushevsky, *op. cit.*, Vol. VI, pp. 385-387.

Slavic-Greek grammar, Lviv
(1591)

Koriatko's building in Lviv
(16th Century)

Hetman Dmytro Baida-Vyshnevetsky
(1550-1563)

Hetman Petro
Konashevych-Sahaidachny
(1614-1622)

CHAPTER FOUR

THE SOCIAL STRUCTURE OF UKRAINIAN SOCIETY DURING THE LITHUANIAN-POLISH ERA

Ethnic and social changes — Social classes — Nobility and clergy — Peasantry — Townspeople — Foreigners — The feudal order — The Cossacks as a social class

Ethnic and Social Changes. Ethnic changes in the composition of the population of Ukraine in the course of three centuries, from the fourteenth to the seventeenth centuries, had a profound influence on the social and political development of Ukraine-Rus' and the national life of the Ukrainian-Rus'ian people. As long as Mongol domination prevailed, the process of ethnic change was insignificant, while on the other hand, the impact of Mongol rule was enormously negative. Later on, the growing grip of Polish rule and the strong Polish political, social, religious and cultural influences, which penetrated Ukraine even at the time she was still, constitutionally speaking, part of the Lithuanian-Rus' Commonwealth, deeply altered the over-all ethnic picture of the land. The Polish government planned to make its rule a lasting one, and to turn Ukraine into a colony to be exploited for centuries to come. It hoped to accomplish this by means of a growing colonization of Ukraine, the progressive and wide-spread denationalization and assimilation of the upper strata of Ukrainian society: the *boyars*, grand nobility and gentry, and the intense discrimination applied against the local Ukrainian Orthodox population. Of course, after the Union of Lublin, 1569, matters went from bad to worse. The political subjugation of Ukraine became complete and it became easier for the Polish over-lord to mold Ukrainian ethnic and social developments to fit Polish patterns.

Actually, Polish interests progressively penetrated the Ukrainian country after 1349. At first, the Galicia, Kholm, and Pidlasha districts were turned into a colony of the Polish state. Then, following the Union of Krevo, Polish ethnic elements and Polish influences spread slowly but gradually and continuously over all of Ukraine. The turning point of this development was the absorption of almost all Ukrainian territories by Poland in 1569, and the immediately succeeding Polish-Lithuanian Union of Lublin. At that time, Polish interests dominated the entire Ukrainian society, being solidly based on Polish and foreign colonists, the Polonized, grand nobility and gentry, and the Polish semi-feudal socio-political constitution.

In the course of three centuries, there were four major factors which facilitated the denationalization of the Ukrainian upper class and the growth of the foreign ethnic elements throughout all of Ukraine: the legal discrimination against Orthodox Ukrainians by the Polish-Lithuanian legislation, their social and factual discrimination, the denationalization trend among the Ukrainian aristocracy and gentry to avoid discrimination and to enjoy all the privileges of first-class citizenship, and the continuous settlement and colonization of Ukrainian eastward-moving frontiers. As a final result of these developments, only the peasantry remained Ukrainian, devoid of any political and social rights within the castes of the Polish Crown. The peasants, free since the time of the Kievan-Galician Empire, were turned under the Polish rule into serfs, deprived of any ability to protect Ukrainian social and economic interests.

After the collapse of the Kievan state, a slight influx of the Mongol (Tartar) ethnic element was introduced. This process continued at the time of the Lithuanian-Ukrainian Commonwealth. The Tartars were settled in Ukraine either as prisoners or as voluntary settlers. Tartar settlements were found all over Ukraine (Kiev, Volhinia, and Chernihiv) but they were rather small and scattered, and therefore the Tartar element was soon assimilated. The main stock of the Mongol colonists was peasants, but some Tartars were also found among the gentry. This process did not affect the socio-political evolution of the Ukrainian people to any great extent.[1]

With the growth of the Lithuanian-Rus' Commonwealth, the Lithuanian ethnic element appeared in Ukraine, mostly among the upper classes. It, too, was rapidly assimilated. In the Commonwealth, national and religious tolerance and liberalism prevailed; there was not much discrimination among the "Lithuanians" and "Ruthenians," or among the Catholics, Orthodox, and pagans, as mentioned above. Different religious affiliations were frequent at that time among the territorial princes and the noble members of the Council of the Grand Principality. Discriminatory differentiation was first introduced under Polish influence after the Union of Krevo. After 1386, the term "Lithuanian" meant the legally and socially privileged Catholics, while the term "Ruthenian" or "Rus'ians," meant the underprivileged Orthodox Ukrainians.[2]

The legal and political oppression of the Ukrainians, as the primary factor responsible for the ethnical changes in Ukraine, was first introduced in Galicia immediately after its subjugation by the Poles. All the social classes of Ukrainian society experienced oppression, discrimination, and national-religious persecution. The Ukrainian nobility and gentry were denied the full rights and privileges of their class, such as all-comprehensive real and personal property rights, a lower tax burden, and admission to the high offices of the country. This discrimination, initiated by King Casimir, was continued along the same lines by King Yagiello in his initial legislation, and by his brother, Prince Vitovt.

The privileges of the noble class were reserved for the Catholics, and the very goal of that measure was a speedy Polonization of the Ukrainian Orthodox gentry. Theoretically, the Ukrainians were granted equal rights with the Catholics by the royal decrees of 1432 and 1434, but the Orthodox were still not allowed to hold high offices. The Privileges of 1563 and 1568 granted, legally speaking, complete equality of rights to the Ukrainian-Orthodox gentry, in order to gain the Ukrainian upper class for the cause of the Polish-Lithuanian Union and for the annexation of East Ukraine by the Polish Crown. Later on, however, the decrees from the time of King Sigismund III, and King John III (Sobieski) resumed the policy of discrimination by withholding from the Ukrainian-Orthodox gentry the right to be high officers of the royal administration and members of the upper house (Senate).

A theoretical equalization in other respects was never fully borne out in practice. National and religious discrimination against the Ukrainian gentry element was even intensified in the political and social sphere after 1569, and it was then more dramatic and under more direct Polish supremacy than it had been under the Polish influenced Lithuanian rule prior to the Union and incorporation. Only the Catholic Poles were full-fledged citizens of the Polish-Lithuanian Commonwealth. The discrimination was more national than religious, and largely practiced by the courts, administrative offices, and society as a whole.

Legal equality remained a dead letter of the law until the very end of the

Polish state at the time of its partition. The fact of a national rather than a religious Polish discrimination in Ukraine became self-evident after some parts of Eastern Ukraine temporarily, and the whole of Galicia permanently (in 1700), accepted Catholicism. The Catholic Ukrainians were still discriminated against and oppressed, and for a long time were not admitted to high government offices and positions. Along with the gentry, the Orthodox higher clergy were also discriminated against and not admitted, for example, to the upper house (Senate) of the country, while the Orthodox priests, denied social prestige and government protection, were exposed to insults and persecutions.

The position of Ukrainian townspeople under Polish rule was even worse than that of the nobility. At the time of King Casimir, ghettos were established in all Galician towns and cities for the Ukrainian population, which was allowed to live only in those sections. Furthermore, Ukrainians were excluded from holding municipal offices in the larger towns. The people were thus exposed to the excesses and abuses of the local Polish-German town administration. At first, practically, and later at the time of King Sigismund III, legally, Ukrainians were not admitted to the merchant and trade guilds. They were also denied the freedom and privileges of the local government, based on the Magdeburg law.[3] Any royal or parliamentary decrees of tolerance which attempted to protect the Ukrainian town population were simply ignored by the municipal governments, and discrimination continued undisturbed in the towns. Polish oppression of the Ukrainian-Orthodox townspeople was very drastic and it was no wonder, therefore, that in the event of any Ukrainian national revolt, the towns joined it immediately. The Ukrainian peasantry was also subjected to oppression and discrimination. The Ukrainian peasants, like the Ukrainian town population, were also denied the privilege of settling in the villages, newly established on Magdeburg legal principles, with more freedom available to the peasant colonists.

The legal and social discrimination against Orthodox Ukrainians resulted in an assimilation and Polonization process, especially, as pointed out, among the Ukrainian upper class. One by one the nobles and the gentry gave up their Orthodox religion and Ukrainian nationality, and became Catholic and Polish in order to enjoy the rights and privileges of full citizenship in the Polish-Lithuanian Commonwealth. Historical documents of the times indicate a gradual but continuous replacement of Ukrainian names by Polish names on the lists of local office holders.[4] The newly Polonized upper class became a stronghold of Polish semi-feudal rule and economic exploitation of

Ukraine. Later on, in some instances, the Ukrainian clergy was also Polonized under Polish pressure, deserting its people, and using Polish, which the people did not understand, as the language of the church.

The denationalization trend among the lower classes of Ukrainian society was not so profound, but even there, the Polish ethnic element was extensively strengthened by means of large-scale colonization throughout entire Ukraine and her eastern and southern borderlands. The new settlements, villages and townlets favored Polish, German, and other foreign colonists, and discriminated against the Ukrainians. The Magdeburg colonization system was used by the Polish regime for strengthening the Polish and foreign elements and weakening the Ukrainian one. These foreigners, especially the Germans, were quickly Polonized, and soon built up in all the larger cities of Ukraine a national majority, ready to assume the local authority in order to control and to suppress the disloyal Ukrainian Orthodox population, which was reduced to a status of third or fourth-rank citizenry.

Social Classes. Under the powerful impact of the political developments of the thirteenth, fourteenth, and fifteenth centuries, such as the collapse of the Kievan Empire, foreign regimes, influx of foreign ethnic elements, and foreign cultural influences, the essentially Ukrainian social constitution of an open class system was lost. The foreign patterns aimed at a definite, rigid, and hermetically sealed class structure. The changes were rather insignificant during the relatively short Mongol rule and as long as the liberal conditions of the Lithuanian-Ukrainian constitution prevailed. The authorities of the Grand Duchy followed the principle of keeping traditions vital and introducing innovations slowly.

A rigid class structure began to evolve in Ukraine, first under Polish influence, from the time of the Krevo Union, and then under direct Polish rule, from the time of the Lublin Union. The trend originated in Galicia in the fourteenth century, and extended to the more distant Ukrainian lands much later. It reached the left-bank of Ukraine in the sixteenth century.

The four classes which crystallized under Polish influence were the gentry, the clergy, the townspeople, and the peasantry. They were rigidly separated from each other, and transition from one to another was almost impossible. No doubt, the progressive denationalization process of the upper Ukrainian class contributed considerably to the deepening of the insurmountable social cleavages among the individual classes. The gentry, the privileged upper stratum enjoying the fullness of private and constitutional rights, was dominantly Polish. Other classes, the townspeople and the peasants, were either partially or prevailingly Ukrainian, and antagonistic to the Polonized country gentry, who were marked by a feeling of superiority. Both lower strata were underprivileged. The legal and political position of the town was subject to ever increasing restrictions and limitations in the Polish state, finally concluding in the political decay of the town at the end of the sixteenth century. From the peasants, all rights were taken away, private as well as public. The entire class was relegated to the status of serfs in bondage, and placed under the patrimonial authority of their owners, the country gentry. The state had no direct relation to the peasants, who were the private property of the nobles. The legal and social position of the peasants was vastly different from the status of the fully free peasantry of the time of the Kievan Empire, a peasantry which enjoyed many rights and privileges granted by the civil public laws of that nation.

Naturally, in the course of these three centuries, some essentially Ukrainian social developments also took place. First of all, the individualistic armed adventurer and colonist appeared very early, in the Ukrainian borderlands and steppes, a refugee who, despising the foreign rule and the social inequalities and discriminations, left the more densely populated areas which were under Lithuanian-Polish controls, and settled the southern and eastern steppes. As free Cossacks, they could no longer be reached by the arm of the Polish regime and the Polish social order. In this way, the growth of a new social phenomenon, strongly military in character, began.[5]

Also, another essentially Ukrainian social trend emerged at that time, in the form of continuing traditions of equality. The so-called brotherhoods were initiated as religious and professional associations of Ukrainian townspeople. Soon they evolved into charitable and cultural organizations, owning hospitals, orphanages, and printing shops, and running schools and other educational establishments. Being at first only guild-like associations of townspeople, they subsequently developed into all-Ukrainian institutions with strong national self-assertion views, as was discussed in Chapter three.

These brotherhoods, along with the Cossack host, formed the basis of the Ukrainian national resistance and liberation movement. In the brotherhoods, class distinctions were largely ignored, and in their schools all students, regardless of their class origin, were treated equally. These essentially Ukrainian social phenomena affected the course of the country's national life as much as did the foreign developments, denationalization policies, rigid class distinctions, frictions among the nationalities and among the classes, discrimination against the Ukrainian population, exploitation of the peasants, and supression of the townspeople.

Nobility and Clergy. A separate, legally distinct, and socially separate class of nobility, or gentry, was partly crystallized in Ukraine at the beginning of the seventeenth century. In the course of the fifteenth and sixteenth centuries, within the framework of the Lithuanian-Rus' Commonwealth, while the crystallization process was in progress under Polish influences, this class was neither homogeneous nor uniform. Among the noble class, several groups of different characteristics could be identified: the princes and lords, the common gentry, the *boyars* under protection, and the underprivileged gentry, like the service men, the *minores gentes Galiciae*, and the *Skartabelat*.

The princes and lords, corresponding to the grand *boyars* of the Kievan time, were either the descendants of the Rurik and Gedimin houses, or the members of the Lithuanian Council of Lords to the Grand Prince. These noblemen possessed the most comprehensive property rights. They were directly under the jurisdiction of the Grand Prince and were exempt from the competence of the local, judicial, and administrative authorities. The princes and lords fulfilled their military duty by furnishing and equipping their own troops, which were led by them under their family flags and emblems. These privileged positions of the grand noblemen, which included princely titles and jurisdictional favoritism, were however, gradually reduced. Polish legal concepts represented the ideal of absolute equality of all the gentry. Thus, the jurisdictional exemptions were nullified in 1564, and princely and other aristocratic titles were partially prohibited.[6]

The principle of egalitarianism among the gentry, conscientiously carried out according to Polish legal and social concepts, also advanced the liquidation of the underprivileged groups of the noble class. The *boyars* under protection, and the service men, a stratum of the underprivileged nobility with limited property rights and under the patrimonial, judicial, administrative, and military authority of the lords and princes, soon disappeared, being either elevated to the status of the common gentry, or reduced to the status of the peasants.

The same thing happened to the *minores gentes Galiciae*, a temporary phenomenon in Galicia. Those *gentes* were noblemen, with terminated property rights and tax-paying, vassalage, and rigid military obligations, a class which largely disappeared at the end of the fifteenth century.

The *Skartabelat* were newly ennobled for some extraordinary deeds, but never acquired the fullness of noble privileges throughout their lifetime. But their children and grandchildren were recognized as fully privileged members of their class.[7] The later division of the gentry into the groups of the estateless, *holota*, and the poor, *khodachkovi*, was rather a factual division to differentiate among the wealthy and the non-wealthy, and a rather small segment of the class, which was later subjected to some legal restrictions.

The stock of the common gentry in Ukraine developed from the old Ukrainian grand *boyars*, vassal, immigrant nobles and other elements, who in one way or another succeeded in improving their social status. Actually, military service and the family heraldic emblem, coats of arms, were the indications of noble descent and origin. But that principle was not consistently carried out. Thus, in the sixteenth century, measures were undertaken for establishing reliable criteria for determining the aristocratic faculties. This was done first by a military census, by means of taking oaths, hearing the witnesses, and checking the original documents of ennoblement. The actual purpose of the census, however, was the obligation of military service.

In 1557, an Agricultural Reform, the *Voloka System*, was introduced in the Polish-Lithuanian Commonwealth, and it specified the land holdings of the gentry. Subsequently, the acts of the reform were used to prove one's aristocratic origin and his rightful membership in the gentry class. The upper social stratum of the gentry, crystallized and legally defined in that way, constituted the fully privileged, first class citizens. They enjoyed full personal freedom, along with the principles of *habeas corpus* and *neminen captivabimus nihil nisi jure*, and full personal and real property rights. Only the nobles could own landed estates.[8]

The common gentry was subject to the state judicial and administrative authorities, but never to any private patrimonial jurisdictions. They certainly enjoyed a higher degree of legal protection and were subject to a lesser degree of civil and criminal liability. Civil and criminal liability were always personal and individual and never collective, except in the case of high treason, while the peasants were still collectively responsible for crimes and damages. From the political aspect, every nobleman was a member of parliament, and had a voice in electing the king and the grand prince.

Among the duties of the gentry were military service and the construction of castles and fortresses. The latter duty was legally abolished in 1447. The tax burden of the noble class was negligible. The noble status was acquired either by a legitimate birth in a legal marriage, or by ennoblement. Children born out of wedlock were never noble. The noble status could be forfeited in consequence of high treason, infamy, ban, or of involvement in any mercantile activities. The last instance distinctly indicated the considerable social prejudices in Poland.

The Polish Catholic clergy constituted another privileged class in the Polish-Lithuanian society. It was a legally protected group of first class citizens, who possessed all political and civil rights, and also enjoyed some special favors through their status, like the ecclesiastic judiciary. During the Reformation, however, the Catholic clergy lost its distinctly separate court system, while retaining all other benefits of full and privileged citizenship.

The Orthodox clergy, on the other hand, were always underprivileged. The estate developed from the ancient privileged institution of the *church people* of the Kievan period, but was discriminated against in the Polish-Lithuanian Commonwealth, where another religion had a dominant position. The Orthodox metropolitans, archbishops, and bishops were not admitted to the country's senate. The legal position of the class was never definite with respect to the rights and privileges of the black and white clergy, Orthodox priests, monks, and nuns. Even the property rights of the Orthodox Church and clergy were not always respected and protected. But the fact that the clergy, both Catholic and Orthodox, constituted a class within the Polish-Lithuanian-Ukrainian society of that time, a class which was not as homogeneous as the gentry, definitely affected the socio-political development of Ukraine in general.

From the economic point of view, the gentry and clergy maintained a key position, insofar as these two classes owned all the landed properties and raw material resources of the nation. The princes and the state also owned considerable productive factors. In that capacity, the gentry and the clergy were the two most important and authoritative elements in the national income production of the agricultural economy of the Commonwealth in general, and of Ukraine in particular. In their hands was the production of food and agricultural raw materials, and domestic and foreign agricultural marketing. The agricultural and commercial interests of the gentry and clergy, and their manorial system, set the pace of the economic growth of Ukraine, and largely sponsored the colonization and development of the virgin areas of the Ukrainian steppe.

Peasantry. In the Kievan Empire, the peasants were a free class, of secondary importance. Things changed a great deal in this respect in the course of the next three centuries. At the end of the seventeenth century, the peasants in Ukraine were no longer considered a social class; they were regarded as the property of the gentry, without any personal freedom or any personal or real property rights. They had become soil-bound serfs.⁹ This sweeping change was accomplished under the impact of Western and Polish social and legal patterns. This regression from freedom to bondage was gradual and not uniform in all Ukrainian territories.

At the time of the Mongol invasion, the peasants were still a free social stratum. Even the trend toward reducing some segments of the peasantry to slavery, which was apparent in the late days of the Kievan state because of the growing powers of the *boyardom* and royalty, was considerably weakened. The Mongol suzerain favored the peasant in order to break the authority of the Ukrainian upper classes and to strengthen his own position in the newly acquired East European areas.

During the entire Lithuanian-Rus' era, a new peasant class was in the process of crystallization, destined to become a stratum of the new society. It was highly differentiated and extremely heterogeneous until the time of the Lublin Union. Slaves who were semi-free, free peasants, soil-bound peasants, manorial servants, peasants of the Ruthenian and Polish law, and the peasants of the Wallachian and German settlements constituted a variety of different peasant groups with diversified rights and obligations. At the end of the sixteenth century these differentiations largely disappeared, and the uniform class of peasant-serfs took their place.

The old Ukrainian institution of slavery withered away very early, sooner in Galicia than in the eastern Ukrainian provinces, since there the Western and Polish influences penetrated earlier, and from there gradually permeated the social constitution of Ukrainian society as a whole. Among the two strata of slaves, the manorial servants and the agricultural or farm slaves, the former were better treated. Soon, especially under the influence of Catholicism, the law began to protect the slaves, giving them legal protection against willful abuses by their masters and reducing the number of sources of slavery. In the fifteenth century, mixed marriage and indebtedness no longer resulted in permanent slavery, and only birth, crime, and imprisonment made a man unfree. The *Lithuanian Statute*, the code by which the Commonwealth tried its civil and criminal cases, in its third codification, replaced the term "slave" with the term "manorial servant," and gave him some limited property rights.¹⁰

The Agricultural Reform of 1557, *Voloka system*, liquidated the institution of slavery altogether, and made all slaves common peasants. As a matter of fact, soil-bound peasants existed already in the fourteenth century. This group probably developed from the half-free and slaves. Being subject to the patrimonial authority of the lord, they had no direct relation to the state, paid no taxes, and did no military service, nor did they bear any other public obligations. They could be transferred by their masters from one place to another, always, however, being bound to do soil service.

During the Agricultural Reform, the soil-bound peasants received a smaller land allotment, about ten acres to work on, while the free peasants received up to thirty acres but were otherwise equal to the common peasantry. The *Lithuanian Statute*, in the early codification, was also familiar with the small social stratum of the half-free, whose legal position was the temporary limitation of freedom on the basis of a voluntary contract between the free and the master-to-be. This was a cultural lag from the old institution of the *zakupy*, in the era of the Kievan Empire. Usually a free peasant sold himself into a half-free relationship, expressly reserving his right to get back his freedom after certain contractual conditions had been fulfilled. The *Lithuanian Statute* imposed various obligations upon the master, as the code of *Rus'ka Pravda* did, to take care of the half-free. In the sixteenth century, the institution dissolved into a general serfdom of the peasantry.

The common peasantry, once a class of free farm people with full personal and property rights, had been progressively restricted in its social and legal standing. By 1457, a partial soil bondage was introduced into the Polish-Lithuanian realm and its Ukrainian possessions. The peasants were prohibited from leaving the soil, the village, and their noble masters, without providing a substitute. The third codification of the *Lithuanian Statute* introduced complete bondage. This development was directly caused by economic motives.

Poland began at that time to participate extensively in foreign trade by means of heavy grain exports. The business was quite a profitable one, and the gentry were extremely interested in taking full advantage of it. Cheap labor provided by soil-bound serfs was very effective in reducing costs. Thus, the all-potent gentry pressed heavily to establish bondage. Initially, of course, the peasant still had full and hereditary ownership rights on his real estate and personal holdings. He could sell and buy, or acquire by occupation of "no man's land," the wooded and steppe areas not under cultivation. The first codification of the above mentioned *Lithuanian Statute* substantially limited the peasant alienation rights, but did not otherwise abolish the scope of his property. At that time, if a new master purchased a village, he acquired the peasant taxes and service obligations, but not property title in the peasant land holdings.

The Agricultural Reform of 1557, *Voloka system*, however, liquidated peasant property rights in real estate, leaving them but a semi-tenant right of use. The privilege of land-property was exclusively reserved for the gentry and clergy. Subsequently the peasants' service obligations were also increased and multiplied. In the sixteenth century, according to the Act of Torun in 1519 and the Act of Bydgoshch in 1520, the peasants had to work for the lords one day of the week. In the seventeenth century, things turned from bad to worse, after the gentry received unlimited authority over the serfs, and began to fix service obligations and material contributions arbitrarily. The service days were increased to 200 and 300 yearly, and by the eighteenth century, the serfs had to labor for the lord six days of the week. Only nights and holidays were left to them to work on their own small farms. The peasant could be sold with or without the land, his family could be separated, and the entire peasantry was subordinated exclusively to the patrimonial authority of the nobleman. Practically speaking, he did not own anything any more.[11] State and government were no longer interested in the peasants, who had now become fixed capital, property of the noble proprietors.

In the fifteenth century, the peasants still had a certain autonomy in the management of their own communal affairs. The oldest form of village autonomy was the Ruthenian system, in which the administration and judiciary were in the hands of the village *tivun* or *otaman* and the village eldest. This system followed the remote tradition of the old Kievan *verv* and village administration. The villages of the Polish law were also similarly governed. The novelty in the Lithuanian-Polish era was the plurality of the villages of the Magdeburg (German) law, and the Wallachian villages where the most autonomy was granted to the peasant communities, while the patrimonial authority of the nobles was largely excluded. A Ukrainian, however, could not be the founder of a Magdeburg village. The Wallachian system, most popular in Galicia, extended over large areas, including several village communities under one land leader, the *krainik*. But at the end of the sixteenth century, all these forms of village autonomy largely disappeared, and the noble lord assumed all the powers, including patrimonial judiciary and supreme administration. The gentry acquired these powers either by purchase or by usurpation, and from that time on they appointed all village officials. Political and public rights were no longer granted to the peasantry.

Serfdom and bondage of the entire peasantry were the most negative developments in the socio-economic constitution of Ukraine. They were of foreign origin and completely alien to the Ukrainian mind, so that they distorted any harmonious social growth. Furthermore, as the main labor and production force, the peasants were turned into property, without any enthusiasm, ambition, or initiative. There were no incentives to labor under such a social system. Therefore agricultural productivity was greatly hampered, and the result was primitivism and a low standard of living for the village population.¹²

Townspeople. The socio-political and economic position of the Ukrainian town and the town population also took a violent turn for the worse during the third period, the Lithuanian-Polish era, because of the predominance of the gentry, and the discrimination of the other social classes. First of all, the destructive impact of the Mongol invasion affected the Ukrainian towns most adversely. Some of the towns were thoroughly plundered and ruined by the Tartars. The rather slow economic recovery made the social position of the townspeople vulnerable and unfit to face unfavorable new developments. The town in the Kievan era, as Chubaty said, was the commercial and cultural center of a region. The town population was not crystallized and separate, isolated from the countryside and the peasantry.¹³ This favored the economic growth of the Kievan-Galician town, which, of course, was not a town in the modern sense. The late Galician period, and the Lithuanian and Polish rules introduced the Magdeburg legal system of municipal organization. The towns were in this way made completely separate self-governing units, isolated from the countryside, and socially differentiated from the peasantry, since the townspeople were essentially free and the peasants almost free. "The original idea of the Magdeburg municipal autonomous administration was to increase the freedom of the town, and to facilitate its commercial growth." But the essentially Polish developments, sacrificing almost everything for the social elevation of the upper classes, fully distorted the initial idea of the Magdeburg system. As a matter of fact, the introduction of the Magdeburg municipal organization did not help the Ukrainian town in the long run, but rather accelerated its political and economic decline.

In some cases the ancient municipal self-government with people's meetings prevailed until the sixteenth century. Economically, the towns were relatively prosperous. In the sixteenth century, however, before the Magdeburg system was ever fully established, municipal self-government was in most cases overthrown by the nobles and municipal autonomy was almost liquidated. Its subjugation either to the aristocratic patrimonial jurisdiction or to the authority of the local agencies of the central government of the Polish-Lithuanian Commonwealth became almost complete.

Of course, the townspeople were always personally free and enjoyed private property rights and freedom of economic initiative even while their political rights were greatly reduced. On the other hand, the city population, with the sole exception of Lviv, was denied the right to own landed properties. At first, the bailiffs and the municipal council under the Magdeburg privilege had extensive authority. Especially the bailiffs, the founders of the Magdeburg type of city, had a far-reaching competence in municipal affairs, and they functioned as middlemen between the townspeople and their noble masters. Subsequently, however, the noblemen, taking advantage of the loopholes in German law, abolished the office of bailiff either by buying the right out or by suppressing it and putting themselves at the head of the city administration, thereby reducing the municipal autonomy.[14]

The city council, built according to aristocratic principles from the upper bracket of the townspeople, maintained some authority. In the sixteenth century, even the city proletariat in some instances acquired some influence in municipal affairs. But at the end of the seventeenth century, municipal self-government was almost fully liquidated, and the towns were either delivered to the mercy of patrimonial lords, or included in the framework of the over-all administrative structure of the country. Ptasnik said that the cities had retained their autonomy as long as they had had certain economic power, but with the decline of the latter, their autonomy also faded away. It seems, however, that things developed differently. The liquidation of municipal autonomy and the introduction of an enormous tax burden on the townspeople produced a decline in the economic (commercial) significance of the Ukrainian town.

The internal social and economic life of the town was based on the guild organization. At first, craft guilds were introduced and then merchant guilds gained some popularity. Both groups of professional organizations began to regulate city affairs and city life. The guilds were not only associations of an economic (commerce and trade) character, but they soon developed into units of administration, welfare, and military defense. Usually, certain parts of the city walls and specific city gates were assigned to individual guilds for defense in an emergency. Orphanages, hospitals, homes for the aged, funeral homes, and relief programs were the interests of the guilds.[15] It was mentioned that the guilds frequently discriminated against the Orthodox population of the Ukrainian town. Hence the Orthodox Ukrainians organized, especially in West Ukraine, their own guilds with a similar scope of activities, to which were added the defense of their religion and nationality, and sponsorship of the development of Ukrainian culture.[16]

Foreigners. From the most ancient times, various ethnic groups inhabited the Ukrainian country, in towns and villages. However, only the Germans, Armenians, and Jews enjoyed a special, privileged social and legal position in the Lithuanian-Polish era, while all other national minority groups were directly subordinated to the general legal and administrative system of the Commonwealth.

The social position of the Tartars (Mongols) was briefly discussed in another connection, since once they were almost the ruling class in Ukraine, subsequently changing the ethnical composition of the Ukrainian population. At the time of the Polish supremacy in Ukraine, the Tartars were discriminated against slightly; they could not hold public office, their property rights were restricted, and unlike other foreigners, they rendered military services. Eventually, the Mongol ethnic element was amalgamated and became Ukrainian.

The Germans settled in Ukraine under the German (Magdeburg) law, and their privileged position withered away along with the general decay of the town. The Wallachians brought to Galicia and Podillia their colonization system, which was liquidated by the general introduction of serfdom.

The Armenians lived in Ukraine, particularly in Galicia, from the time of the Kievan era, and always enjoyed extensive self-government. After the Polish conquest of Galicia, King Casimir the Great attempted to subordinate the Armenian group to Polish law and administration, but he failed. Thus, the later Polish rulers fully acknowledged the autonomous position of the Armenians, restricting them, however, and not according them citizenship with respect to rights of inheritance and real estate holdings, and withholding from them the prerogative of participating in the Commonwealth's political and public affairs. These limitations resulted in a denationalization trend among the Armenian people, who desired to be fully privileged citizens; they accepted Polish nationality, became Roman Catholic, voluntarily subjected themselves to the common municipal administration, and in numerous cases even attempted to acquire nobility. Hence, in 1561, a decree, inspired by Armenian leaders, was issued by the Polish government for the purpose of preventing further denationalization and for preserving the identity of the Armenian nationality.[17]

As an autonomous ethnic group, the Armenians governed themselves by separate laws, like the *Datastanagirk Mechitara Gosza*, the old Armenian legal code originating in Asia Minor about 1041, the *Armenian Statute* of 1519, issued by King Sigismund of Poland, the court decisions of the Armenian judiciary, and the ancient traditions of that national group. The *Atean*, Council of the Eldest, existing already in the Kievan era, was the supreme authority with administrative, judicial, and religious competence.[18]

At this time the Jews were the largest and most important ethnic group in Ukraine. They had lived there from time immemorial, in *ghettos* in the towns, and individually or in small groups in the villages. They were regarded by Polish law as *servi camerae*, a group directly subordinated to the King and Grand Prince. As such, they paid a separate tax, the capitation. In

1495, King Oleksander of Poland banned all Jews and confiscated all their belongings. But in 1505, the decree was repealed, and the Jewish people were fully restored to all their rights.

The Jews as a separate national group enjoyed the special protection of the law, in many instances equal to that given to the gentry and noblemen. They governed themselves by special royal decrees, called Jewish Privileges, eventually codified in 1669. The *Kahal* was the local, self-governing authority of the Jewish community, with extensive competence, including the representation of the national group, building and maintenance of schools, and handling of matters pertaining to welfare, the lower judiciary, and religion. In the seventeenth century, Jewish parliaments were inaugurated, one for Poland and one for Lithuania. These later merged into one parliamentary body of that national minority for the entire territory of the Commonwealth, to act as an intermediary between the Jewish people and the Polish government.[19]

The Polish and Ukrainian townspeople, the Germans, Armenians, and Jews became pillars of trade and commerce in Ukraine. Crafts were performed largely by Ukrainians and Poles, while mercantile activities on the local, interprovincial, and international level were prevailingly concentrated in the hands of the Germans, Jews, and Armenians. The Jewish people especially acquired a very important financial and commercial position in the Lithuanian-Rus' state because of their exceptional abilities in these fields.[20]

The Ukrainians had a very rich mercantile tradition since the ancient era and the Kievan-Galician period, and considerable commercial abilities. During the Polish domination foreign ethnic elements added substantially to trade and commerce. Nevertheless, the unbearable political and social pressure of the gentry upon the town, townspeople, and national minorities did not permit trade and commerce to attain a significant position in the over-all production of the national income of the Commonwealth in general, and of Ukraine, in particular.

The Feudal Order. The socio-political constitution of the Lithuanian-Rus' state progressively absorbed some elements of Western feudalism under increasing contact with the West. Some Lithuanian princes, like Vitovt, or aristocratic land grandees, like the Radivils, energetically attempted to introduce the feudal order in their domains. Consequently, along with the advancing Lithuanian rule, the old quasi-feudal institutions of Ukraine, the remnants of Kievan supremacy, were made to resemble more closely the feudal patterns of the West. In Galicia, during the early period of the Polish regime, some feudal institutions were inaugurated to secure the defense of the borderland. There, precarious land grants of a temporary character were given to the *shlakhta*, nobles of the Polish legal type, who accepted some kind of vassalage and the obligation of military and defense services. The institutions of the "boyar under protection" and of the "service men," of a later period, were a direct reminiscence of the old feudal-vassal relationship.

Thus, on the basis of those historical data, like Vitovt's attempts to introduce feudalism, the feudal system in some possessions of the Radivil family, the precarious land holdings in Galicia in the fourteenth century, and the *boyars* under protection in the sixteenth century, some historians like Lubavskii, Lyashchenko, and others again, primarily the Marxists, believed and argued that feudalism really prevailed in the Lithuanian-Rus' state and the Polish-Lithuanian Commonwealth.

On the other hand, Vladimirskii-Budanov, Chubaty, and a number of other Russian and Ukrainian historians of that particular era, totally rejected such a view. They granted that there existed in the Lithuanian-Rus' era some similarities and tendencies to feudal characteristics, but they said that these trends soon disappeared. To be more specific, the trends toward feudalism and precarious land-holdings were soon superceded by the Polish socio-economic constitution based upon the full individual property rights of the gentry class to its latifundia, which were cultivated through a system of widespread serfdom and bondage of the peasants.[21]

Lyashchenko, a Marxist historian, himself admitted that "Feudal dispersion in Lithuania had thus not progressed as far as in Muscovy." The economic system of Ukraine under Polish domination turned out to be for the most part essentially Polish, resulting from the essentially Polish socio-political developments, where the gentry held all rights. In the eighteenth century, the Polish system eventually caused the collapse and partition of the kingdom. Chubaty rightly said that the legal terminology of that period in Ukraine, including *feudum*, *allodicum*, and *vassale*, did not prove the prevalence of the feudal order, but merely a confusion of nomenclature used by the officials trained along West European patterns. Essentially, the question as to whether Ukraine was feudal in the Lithuanian-Polish era of her history is a matter of defining the term "feudalism."[22]

The Cossacks as a Social Class. The Cossack phenomenon was *par excellence* a social development of a spontaneous character. A spontaneous drive among all classes of population to go into the depth of the steppes, the "wild fields," was produced on the one hand by the hardships suffered by the Ukrainian people under the discriminatory policies of the Polish-Lithuanian regime, and the ever increasing restrictions on personal freedoms of the lower classes of the society in particular, constantly threatened by the danger of the Tartar raids and assaults. On the other hand, it was inspired by the dangerous but free life of the Cossack, where the hand of the oppressive regime could not reach him, where a "sweet revenge" on the Tartar assailant would come true in the vast and limitless steppes. No human power could stop this drive. The official measures of the Lithuanian and Polish governments to limit the growth of the Cossack movement in the course of over a century were simply futile and ineffective. The drive to go into the steppes and taste the free life of a Cossack was so strong that the grand-princely and royal officials and military commanders who were supposed to uphold the official policy of the government to stop the movement, underhandedly joined the Cossacks, disappearing in the steppes for a while, and then reappearing in their offices after some time.

To avoid punishment for such a "lawless" conduct, they usually kept silent about their steppes exploits, the *ukhody*. However, their sporadic joining of the Cossacks greatly boosted and facilitated the growth of the whole social phenomenon, having received in that way a kind of semi-approval to exist and to aspire to become a special class of people in the Ukrainian borderlands; a separate class of military people, free of any social and economic restrictions but liable for the defense of the country against the onslaught of the "infidels."

When roaming in the depths of the steppes, constantly fighting the Tartars, and pioneering the future conquest of the "wild fields" for civilization, the Cossacks lived a primitive and simple life by hunting and fishing and using the bountiful gifts of nature, such as wild honey, fruits and vegetables. Of course, the booty acquired from fighting and defeating the "infidels" provided a substantial portion for the Cossack in making a living. After coming home, the Cossacks at first immediately intermingled with their respective classes of people, either gentry or townspeople or peasantry, to avoid possible chicanery from the hands of some officials. However, a little later on, with the growing power of the whole movement, they began to claim to be a separate class of people with a separate social status. Some of them stayed in the steppes permanently as *ukhodnyky*, the pioneers, and developed fishing, hunting, cattle raising and farming ventures, but with a distinctive feeling of a class belonging. Whenever an emergency arose, all of them from all over the country reported to the *Sitch*.

The Cossack movement toward becoming a separate class was slow but it gradually crystallized while the ability of the Polish government to limit and to control it gradually weakened. The government of the Polish-Lithuanian

Commonwealth objected to the movement on two accounts. The first reason was briefly discussed in connection with political developments in the *Res Publica*. Cossack excursions to fight and defeat the Tartar assailant produced innumerable Tartar and Turk complaints at the courts in Cracow and Vilna, complicating the political and diplomatic relations beetweem Poland-Lithuania on the one hand, and the Tartars and the Ottoman Empire on the other. There was also another reason. The Lithuanian and Polish nobility and gentry desired to increase the profitability of their *latifundium* economy by enlarging the production and exportation of grain. The intense drive of the population to join the Cossacks, especially on the part of the peasantry, reduced the supply of agricultural labor in the large-scale manorial economies of the nobles, gentry and the Church. Obviously, the influential strata of the Polish-Lithuanian society tried to undertake any measure, which would secure their agricultural interests. Therefore they used their influence with the government of the Commonwealth to stop the uncontrolled Cossack movement.

For these reasons, in particular, because of unceasing Tartar and Turk complaints, the Polish-Lithuanian government continually issued circulars and decrees to limit Cossack "lawlessness" and to punish the guilty for annoying the Tartars and Turks by their over-land and sea-going war excursions. These measures remained largely dead letters of law. First, because the local government officials were not only sympathetic to the Cossacks, who provided defense of the borderlands, but, as mentioned, they themselves frequently joined them in their steppe exploits. Ostap Dashkevych, a government official, the *starosta* of the Cherkasy district, recommended to the parliament, the *seim*, in Piotrkow, in 1533, that the government organize the Cossacks as a semi-military class for defense of the eastern and south-eastern borderlands of Ukraine.[23]

Such suggestions came also from other officials. Dashkevych came forth as an outstanding Cossack leader. The third reason for the failure of the Polish-Lithuanian government to stop the growth of the Cossack movement was contained in its spontaneity and in its pervasive social, political and economic base.

Yet, many times, as in the circular of 1541, the circulars and decrees in 1545 and 1546, and throughout the forties, fifties, and eighties of the sixteenth century, demands were made by Cracow and Vilna to curb and to stop the Cossacks from harassing the Tartars and Turks, and to search for and severely punish the guilty. But this was to no avail.[24] The sultan himself a few times demanded that the Polish government suppress the Cossacks.

Nevertheless, the class of the Cossacks steadily grew, comprised of members of all classes, the grand nobility, gentry, townspeople and peasants, and representatives of various nationalities, as pointed out, including Germans, Dutch, Italians, and even the Tartars. Obviously, moving freely in the steppes, the Cossacks began to feel themselves a separate class of people, free of any social and political restrictions. Living under constant danger, the feeling of equality for all developed among them. The strong conviction of freedom in the Cossack class included the concept of personal freedom with full rights to own personal and real property, the freedom of assembly and organization, to elect freely their leaders and not to be responsible to anybody but their own freely elected leaders and officials. Furthermore, they felt free from any taxation and other material burdens imposed by the Polish-Lithuanian state. Gradually, all these concepts acquired by custom and tradition, the force of unwritten law, constituted the "Cossack liberties." At first, the government attempted to disregard and violate this customary unwritten law, but it eventually had to submit to and honor any Cossack complaints that their "liberties" were violated.[25]

The frequent involvement of the Polish-Lithuanian state in various wars and the need for defense of the Ukrainian borderlands against the Tartar onslaught finally forced Poland to change her policy toward the Cossacks in order to use their military striking power in her own interest. King Sigismund II August ordered, probably in 1572, the organization of some 300 Cossacks under the command of Yurii Yazlovetsky and paid them for services to the state. There was a kind of friendly relation between the Cossacks and King Stefan Batory, because apparently, some Cossack representation was sent to his coronation. Supposedly, in the wake of those developments, the Batory Reform was enacted, which established the legal framework for the Cossacks as a separate social class. The Reform took place, supposedly, in 1576. In the royal document, "the Cossack liberties" were affirmed, along with their exemption from regular royal administration and judiciary, no matter where the Cossacks lived, in the towns, townships or villages, placing them under the jurisdiction of their own officials, the *hetman* and the *otamans*, directly responsible to the commander-in-chief of the Polish armed forces, the *hetman koronny*. No Cossack could be put in prison without the knowledge of his own Cossack superior. Only in the case of murder and rape could a Cossack be judged in a Polish court, but again, with the knowledge of his superior. The Cossacks were free from paying taxes or doing any compulsory work for the state, their properties could not be confiscated, their inheritance rights could not be infringed.[26]

The official "register" of the Cossacks was increased to 500 and then 1,000 men, and though all those rights and "liberties" were granted to the "registered," *reyestrovi*, Cossacks, automatically with the progress of time and by unwritten law, they were extended to all Cossacks, making them now a fully legitimate class of Ukrainian society.[27] The increasing participation of the Cossacks in the Polish wars was that vehicle which made the "liberties" legally available to the entire Cossack class. Although locally the officers of the "registered" Cossacks were under control of the royal officials, they were the part of the entire Cossack community or stratum, including the Urban Cossacks, the *horodovi*, who lived in the towns and villages, but were not listed in the official register, and the Cossacks from beyond the cataracts, the *Zaporozhtsi*, living in the *Sitch* and in the steppes around the *Sitch*, their military center and military camp, who were the standard-bearers of the struggle in defense of Ukraine.[28]

Rather early, a differentiation within the class began according to economic criteria, the accumulation of wealth and landed properties. The wealthy Cossacks were able to live better and to clothe themselves better in contrast to the rather poor mass of the Cossacks, who initially actually did not pay much attention to material things. Later on, matters slowly changed, and even antagonisms developed between the wealthy Cossack aristocracy and the mass of the Cossack commoners, the *holota* or *siroma*. However, this process belongs to the next period of Ukrainian history. It became pronounced in the Ukrainian Cossack state after 1649.

1. Yu. Lypa, *Pryznachennia Ukrainy*, New York, 1953, pp. 140-145; "They (the Tartars) were those nomads who terrorized the Ukrainian country most of all. And, according to the anthropologists and ethnographers, their influence had been equal to nothing."; also, N. Chirovsky, *A History of the Russian Empire*, New York, 1973, Vol. I. p. 165.

2. The nationality problem within the Polish-Lithuanian Commonwealth: M. Hrushevsky, *Istoria Ukrainy-Rusy*, New York, 1955, Vol. VI, pp. 235-293; also, D. Doroshenko, *Narys istorii Ukrainy*, Munich, 1966, Vol. I, pp. 131-143.

3. J. Ptasnik, *Miasta i mieszczanstwo w dawnej Polsce*, Cracow, 1934, pp. 285, 332, 335, and other places; also J. Caro, *Geschichte Polens*, Gotha, 1863, "The Ruthenians seemed to have an inferior position in the public and social developments and relations of the town".

4. Ukrainian names among the gentry and the slow Polonization process: *Akta grodzkie i ziemskie*, Lviv, 1868-1935, Vol. I-XVI; Vol. VII. nos. 55, 53, 63, Vol. IX, nos. 81, 110; Vol. XIII, no. 149.

5. V. Antonovych, "Proiskhozhdenie zaporoskoho kozachestve", *Kievskaia starina*, Kiev, 1884, Vol. VIII-IX; Doroshenko, *op. cit.*, Vol. I. pp. 145-156: he supplies a survey of different theories about the beginnings of the Ukrainian Cossacks.

6. S. Kutrzeba, *Historya ustroju Polski*, Vol. I. *Korona*, Lviv, 1917, pp. 169-170; also O. Balzer, *Verfassungsgeschichte Polens*, Cracow, 1906, p. 123.

7. O. Baltzer, *Skartabelat w ustroju szlachectwa polskiego*, Cracow, 1911.

8. Kutrzeba, *op. cit.*, pp. 170-171; also M. Chubaty, *Ohlad istorii ukrainskoho prava*, Munich, 1947, Vol. II. pp. 75-78.

9. Soil bondage was introduced in 1496, while later decrees, of 1503, 1510 and 1511, only extended and enlarged its burdens: Kutrzeba, *op. cit.*, Vol. I. pp. 96-97: J. Rutkowski, *Poddanstwo wloscian w XVIIIIw. w. Polsce i niektorych krajach Europy*, Poznan, 1921, p. 21; Balzer, *Verfassungsgeschichte*, p. 123.

10. *Statut Litewski* of 1588, chapt. XII, art. 21; the limitation of the status of the half-free: Chapt. XI, arts. 7 and 9; chapt. XII, art. 7.

11. Kutrzeba, *op. cit.*, Vol. I. p. 180; Rutkowski, *op. cit.*, p. 63

12. About the low efficiency of unfree and half-free labor in general, E. Bogart and D. Kemmerer, *Economic History of the American People*, New York. 1955, pp. 386-410.

13. Chubaty, *op. cit.*, Vol. I. pp. 82-84.

14. Kutrzeba, *op. cit.*, Vol. I, pp. 102-103; J. Rutkowski, *Skup solectw w Polsce w wieku XVI*, Poznan, 1921.

15. Ptasnik, *op. cit.*, pp. 152-153, 170; various activities of the guilds: Hrushevsky, *op. cit.*, Vol. VI, pp. 111-114.

16. Religious and national discrimination: *Akta grodzkie i ziemskie*, Vol. VI Nos. 1, 145 and other. M. Holubets, *Za ukrainskyi Lviv*, Lviv, 1927; the same, *Velyka istoria Ukrainy*, Lviv, 1935, pp. 439-442; also Hrushevsky, *op. cit.*, Vol. VI, pp. 124-127.

17. O. Balzer, *Sadownictwo ormianskie w sredniowiecznym Lwowie*, Lviv, 1909; Kurtzeba, "Datastanagirk Mechitara Gosza i statut ormianski z r. 1519". *Kwartalnik historyczny*, Lviv, 1908, Vol. 22.

18. S. Kutrzeba, *Historia zrodel prawa polskiego*, Lviv-Warsaw-Cracow, 1925, Vol. II. pp. 287-297.

19. Kutrzeba, *op. cit.*, Vol. II, 297-318; the same, *Historia ustroju Polski*, Vol. II. pp. 52-53, 109-111; the same, *Sprawa zydowska w Polsce* Lviv; Hrushevsky, *op. cit.*, Vol. V. pp. 254-260, and 651-652.

20. Kutrzeba, *Historia zrodel prawa polskiego*, *loc. cit.*, pp. 297-318.

21. M. Slabchenko, *Orhanizatsia hospodarstva Ukrainy*, Part One, *Hospodarstvo Hetmanshchyny*, Odessa, 1923, pp. 8 and 16; "It seemed that the old Polish economic system was based on two elements; *latifundium* land holding and forced labor"; also, P. Lyashchenko, *History of the National Economy of Russia*, New York, 1949, pp. 259-261.

22. *Ibid.*, pp. 251-252.

23. Hrushevsky, *op. cit.*, Vol. VII, pp. 104-105; Doroshenko, *op. cit.*, Vol. I, p. 157.

24. *Zrodla dziejowe*, Vol. IV pp. 68-69, 105-107, 109-110; *Acta Stephani Bathorei*, nos. 23 and 25; also Hrushevsky, *op. cit.*, Vol. VII. pp. 150-151; N. Polonska-Vasylenko, *Istoria Ukainy*, Munich, 1972, Vol. I, pp. 361-362.

25. *Zrodla dziejowe*, Vol. VIII, no. 34; Hrushevsky, *op cit.*, Vol VII. pp. 158-160.

26. The Batory Reform gave rise to a lengthy scholarly discussion: The old Cossack chronicles narrated that King Batory carried out the reform; hired 6,000 Cossacks, organized them in six regiments, appointed for them a *hetman* and other officers, granted them some rights, and ordered them to guard the southern borders. Several historians, such as Jablonowski, Domanytsky and Krypiakevych, attempted to prove that in fact there was no official reform at that time at all; that actually, some gradual measures were undertaken to organize the Cossacks in the framework of Polish law, and that the subsequent tradition and customs affirmed and extended the legality and the over-all organizational structure of the Cossacks, the *reyestrovi, horodovi* and the *Zaporozhski* ones. There were also some historians, who firmly believed in the historical and official enactment of such a reform, which established the legality of the Cossack movement: Doroshenko, *op. cit.*, Vol. I pp. 156-158; V. Domanytsky, "Chy bula reforma Batoria?", *Yuvileinyi zbirnyk v chest Hrushevskoho*, Lviv, 1906; I. Krypiakevych, "Kozachchyna i Batorievi volnosti", *Zherela do istorii Ukrainy-Rusy*, Lviv, 1908, Vol. VIII; Hrushevsky, *op. cit.*, Vol. VIII. pp. 152-162.

27. By 1590, the Cossack rights and privileges were granted to individual Cossacks and their chieftains, as well as, to the entire class *in corpore*: Hrushevsky, *op. cit.*, Vol. VII, p. 176.

28. The beginnings of the Cossack phenomenon were interpreted by different historians in different ways. V. Antonovych related the Cossacks to the old democratic element of the Kievan *viche*. P. Kulish considered the Cossacks a steppe phenomenon. M. Vladimirskii-Budanov and M. Lubavskii attempted to relate the institution to the old Turkman colonization. Jablonowski sought the origin of the Cossacks in the Tartar colonization of the southern Kiev region by princes Olelko and Semen in the fifteenth century. Doroshenko, *op. cit.*, Vol. I, pp 149-151, supplies a brief survey of all those theories.

CHAPTER FIVE

EXTRACTIVE INDUSTRIES OF THE EUROPEAN FRONTIERS

Economic growth — Hunting and fishing — Cattle raising — Agriculture — Mining

Economic Growth. In the course of the four centuries from the collapse of the Kievan Empire to the National Revolution of 1648, the economy of Ukraine experienced many striking transitions and transformations. Although these were neither rapid nor unexpected, their impact upon all sectors of the country's economy was deep and fundamental, resulting in a seventeenth century Ukrainian economy which differed diametrically from that of the fourteenth century.

The decline of the Ukrainian economy had already begun in the second half of the twelfth century as a consequence of the continuous dynastic wars among the members of the Ruryk house. These cruel and ruthless wars decimated the population, ruined the cities and countryside, and strangled the economy. Furthermore, the continuous raids of the Cumans contributed extensively to a general decline of the eastern and southern borderlands of Ukraine. Eventually, the highly developed economy of the Kievan Empire began to decay, the population became impoverished, and only the enormous fertility of the soil prevented large-scale famines and starvation.[1] Then came the Mongol Invasion, which deepened the economic depression.

The century witnessed a general economic retardation and regression in Ukraine. Eastern and southern borderlands were depopulated, and in many sections the economy reverted to hunting, fishing, and beekeeping. Fortunately, West Ukraine (Galicia, Volhinia, and Polisia) was in a more favorable economic situation since the Ukrainian state existed there much longer and the Mongol invasion did not strike it with full fury. From there the economic recovery of the entire country began. Already in the fifteenth century, the recolonization of the abandoned eastern and southern borderlands was resumed, this time under the protection of the Lithuanian-Rus' state. The Mengli-Gerey invasion of Ukraine in 1481 interrupted this colonization but it did not halt it entirely.

In the beginning of the sixteenth century, the Western Ukrainian economy was a well developed agricultural one, with such supplementary industries as hunting and fishing. Export and import businesses existed with such Western markets as Danzig, Neurenberg, Dresden, and Regensburg. The main product of the revived economy was grain. Commercialized argiculture was just beginning, and advanced business techniques were extending over the northern parts of Right- bank Ukraine, west of the Dnieper River.

In the southern part of Right-bank Ukraine and in her entire Left-bank area at that time, backwardness and primitivism still prevailed. Hunting, fishing, trapping, beekeeping, and limited cattle-raising were the leading industries. The main products of that primitive economy were meat, fish, honey, and fur. Very little agricultural activity was undertaken there. The economic life of the borderlands in some instances returned to the ancient Slavic communal forms, in order to provide some security in that area of continuous Mongol raids and to increase efficiency through close cooperation. All of the settlements specialized collectively in certain activities; there were villages of hunters, fishers, trappers, falconers, beaver-trappers, beekeeepers, ox-herders, and other specific professions and trades. When some limited agriculture was resumed in those areas, it was also done in a communal way. Allotments of land were given to individual members of the community for cultivation for a certain specific period of time. According to Lubavskii, a primitive agricultural technique was used by the Cherkasians (Ukrainians) at that time.[2]

The progressing colonization and the recovery of the ancient Ukrainian territories made land plentiful, and at the same time, the intensity of the Tartar menace also lessened somewhat. The result was an immediate disintegration of communal forms of economy, whereupon the instinctive Ukrainian individualism took over fully. The Kievan revenue records from the sixteenth century stated that "the Cherkasians plowed their lands wherever they desired." It seems that the individual property had already prevailed there to the fullest extent, and that agriculture had already gained significance.

In the fifteenth century, however, in the deeds and contracts of sale, still more attention was paid to the forest, hunting, and fishery rights than to farm lands. Thus, in the course of a century a significant re-evaluation was accomplished. In the fifteenth century, extractive industries other than agriculture were more important economically while about a hundred years later farming had already become a leading industry.

The re-colonization of the southern and eastern steppe regions progressed rapidly because of various factors evolving in that era, such as the growing power of the Lithuanian-Ukrainian state, the penetration of the Polish sponsored institutions of serfdom and large land holdings into Ukraine, and the increasing density of population and the development of a profit-motivated money economy in the West. First of all, the rising power of the Lithuanian-Rus' Commonwealth, as mentioned above, to some extent reduced the Mongol threat and thus encouraged the incorporation of Ukraine's steppes into her economy. This first phase of the penetration of the steppes was discussed briefly in the preceding section, in connection with the development of the semi-military class of the Cossacks. The penetration began as hunting, trapping, and fishing trips undertaken in spring and summer by individuals and small groups of adventurers. Subsequently, armed colonization was intensified as the indirect result of the introduction into Ukraine of the Polish agricultural system based on serfdom and large-scale landholding by the nobility. The growing burden of bondage and serfdom for almost three centuries resulted in serfs constantly escaping to the steppe beyond the reach of the Polish government and Polish semi-feudalism. These peasant-refugees were the vanguard of waves of colonization. Extensive farming, together with hunting, fishing, and cattle-raising, were their main occupations.

The strong drive among the gentry and the lords to acquire more and more land provided still another impetus to the colonization process. Initially the nobles had received land as temporary grants for military and administrative services. But soon the precarious nature of those grants was lost under the impact of the Polish concept of complete and perpetual property rights for the gentry. This development was no doubt due to the decisive changes in the West European economies, where the density of population, having increased greatly in the sixteenth and seventeenth centuries, resulted in an early commercial Mercantilism, a profit-motivated economy. The Western markets required more food and more raw materials; the East European extractive and agricultural production, if properly organized, could supply them.

The gentry of the Polish-Lithuanian Commonwealth were quick to recognize the opportunities. Thus their appetite and demand for ever more land grew steadily. At first they developed commercial cattle-raising to export meat and hides. In some years the livestock exported to the West through the city of Peremyshl alone exceeded eighty thousand heads. With the Torun Treaty the Western markets were wide open for the Polish export business. Especially, Ukrainian grain, wood, and raw materials were in great demand abroad.

The colonization process was enormously intensified. Slabchenko said that unbelievably large sums of money were invested to acquire landed properties. Zamojski, a Polish grandee, for example, bought the Povolok district for one million and two hundred thousand guldens. Tyshkevich paid over four hundred thousand guldens for a few villages. In both of these cases enormous land resources were required to proceed with production.[3]

The growing Western demand for grain and bread, therefore, developed the great profit opportunity for the Polish gentry, who then applied all available measures, fair and foul, to enlarge their land holdings, including even spoilation of the peasant farm land, and exploitation of serf labor. As a result of these developments, small-scale peasant farming rapidly decreased and the burden of bondage swiftly increased. This caused peasants to run away in increasing numbers and drastically reduced the labor supply at a time when it was most needed.

In order to secure more labor for their instensified manorial farming, the nobles also undertook a large-scale colonization program. They established many villages, townships, and settlements under the "Magdeburg Law," granting to the settlers temporary personal freedoms and tax exemptions. Everywhere castles were built, towns founded, new villages built, old settlements reorganized, and new market places and fairs initiated. While Ukrainians remained the principal stock of the population, settlers were also attracted from Poland, Bohemia, Hungary, Germany, Wallachia, Serbia, and Muscovy. Due to immigration and a higher birth rate, the density of population increased rapidly, and new areas were populated. After a few years the new settlers usually lost their freedom and privileges under the Magdeburg Law, and were relegated to the general pattern of bondage and serfdom. This happened either in accordance with the original provisions of the colonization agreements with the bailiffs or settlers, or by direct violations of these agreements on the part of the gentry. But the new serfs began to run away into the steppes, pushing the frontiers further and further eastward and southward. This exodus gave rise to a new wave of settlements along the Magdeburg principles to replenish the labor supply in the manorial economy of the Polish-Lithuanian state, by granting freedoms and exemptions to the colonists for a number of years (10,15, or 20 years). The same process was repeated over and over again, always, however, resulting in the addition of new areas to the Ukrainian ethnical territory.

A commercialized agriculture accompanied by the advanced business techniques and social disadvantages of early capitalism became the foundation of the entire Ukrainian economy in the seventeenth century. This seems to be quite a change when it is realized that three centuries before large areas of Eastern and Southern Ukraine were deserted steppes where a primitive subsistence economy prevailed. The main credit for this positive evolution in the economy must be given to the Cossack armed colonization, for the nobles colonized only those wild fields where some degree of security and safety had already been established by the Cossacks. Later, at the end of the sixteenth and the first half of the seventeenth centuries, the Cossack uprising in its successful attempt to free Ukraine from Polish domination, also had a favorable effect on the colonization process. In order to avoid Polish reprisals, the insurgents were again compelled to migrate.

They moved far to the East, to *Slobidska* Ukraine, on the banks of the Rivers Donets and Don. There the Polish government could not reach them since those areas were theoretically under Muscovite supremacy. The Cossack refugees who established villages, or *slobody*, were fully free and had extensive lands for agriculture, cattle-raising, and hunting. For the most part, they were not troubled by the authorities. The entire *Slobidska* Ukraine later developed into a semi-military Cossack society. The colonization on a large scale of the Donets and Don area by the Ukrainians was initiated by Ostrainyn, the leader of an unsuccessful uprising against the Polish oppression in 1638.[4]

Hunting and Fishing. There is no doubt that for the entire era of the fourteenth and fifteenth centuries, hunting was still a very important and even a predominant industry in certain sections of the country, like the northern forest districts, the southern and eastern steppes, and the Carpathian mountain areas in particular. In the fifteenth century, more attention was paid in deeds and sale contracts to the description of hunting, fishing, and beekeeping areas, and the exclusive rights and privileges connected with them, than to farm land. This emphasis reflects the greater economic importance of the former occupations. The sixteenth century brought a full appreciation of farming and grain production. The civil law of that era, the *Lithuanian Statute*, in all of its three codifications, paid considerable attention to hunting, fishing, and beekeeping rights. Such violations as killing or stealing of animals on the hunting grounds of others, hunting and fishing in areas reserved for the Grand Dukes or lords, fishing without permission, damaging traps, nets, or bee-hives, damaging ownership signs and marks or territory boundaries, and similar cases were punished by monetary penalties. Thus, a violation of the hunting rights was to be compensated by a fine of twelve guldens; an illegal killing of an elk, by a fine of six guldens; of a deer or bear, three guldens; of a lynx or boar, one gulden; of a bull or auroch, twelve guldens; the same as for killing a human being.[5]

After beavers became scarce, beaver hunting in certain areas was reserved for the Grand Duke as a regal privilege, and the animals themselves were put under the legal protection of the law. In Galicia, beavers were scarce in the sixteenth century, and similarly, were protected by law. At that time two guldens were paid for a beaver skin. For the same price one could buy more than ten hundred weights of rye. In the manorial economies of the nobles, beaver preserves were established to prevent extermination of that valuable, fur bearing animal.

The forests, woods, steppes, and mountain regions of Ukraine housed enormous resources of animals in the Kievan epoch. The contemporary written reports strongly stressed this fact. Bulls, aurochs, wild horses, elks, deer, harts, stags, bears, lynxes, wolves, beavers, foxes, wild goats, rabbits, squirrels, eagles, hawks, falcons, wild ducks, geese, swans, and many other kinds of animals and birds were mentioned in the documents, chronicles, and narratives. For example, wild goats were so numerous that in winter time, when there was nothing for them to eat in the fields and woods, they came to the settlements and villages, and there thousands were killed by the peasant, thus supplying meat and skins. In the sixteenth century, however, some kinds of wild animals began to disappear, like bulls, aurochs and beavers, as mentioned above. Intensive hunting threatened to exterminate them. Accordingly, the seventeenth century nobles began to establish beaver preserves and breeding stations for bulls and aurochs. While hunting for beasts was, economically speaking, an important industry, hunting for birds remained a sport with little economic significance.

Hunting for big beasts, like bulls and bears, was usually organized by the nobles, with extensive participation of the common people as beaters and helpers. Under the system of serfdom and bondage, the peasants were obliged to be ready to hunt for the lord as many as twelve days every year. Entire villages in the hunting areas specialized in certain hunting skills, such as hunters for beavers, wolves, and bears, serving as beaters and falconers, or catching hawks and falcons and training them for future hunting undertakings of their noble lords.

The annual contributions paid by the serfs to their lord consisted of a large portion of meats, hides, and skins. This evidence indicates that the peasants also engaged in hunting on their own. The peasants set up traps and hunted, but rather for smaller beasts, like martens, rabbits, foxes, squirrels, and sometimes, wolves. Later on, their contributions in kind were replaced by one or more monetary taxes.

Beekeeping was another ancient and significant extractive industry in the Ukrainian forests and steppes, cultivated by the peasant and manorial economies. The industry was a very popular one, especially because of a very great demand for drinking honey, a favorite drink of all social classes, and because of a large demand for wax for the domestic production of candles, as well as for export. This extensive demand for honey and wax, a traditional one from prehistoric and Kievan times, made them for a long time the major components of the peasant's annual tax contributions, paid to the state or to the noble lords, who acquired that privilege in the process of the disintegration of the Polish state authority. It was simply called the "honey tax." Beekeeping rights were, as pointed out, a special concern for the legislation of the Polish-Lithuanian era, a fact that proved its relative importance. But beekeeping as such had only a secondary significance from the over-all economic point of view. It was more important in the northern regions of Ukraine than in the southern.

No less important than beekeeping but secondary to hunting was fishing. Again, certain villages, located on the banks of large rivers or close to the lakes where fish were abundant, specialized in fishing, and their peasant inhabitants were primarily fishermen. Usually, fishing rights were the exclusive property of the gentry, and the peasants received only a privilege or a permission to fish, for which they had to supply part of their catch to the manors. Naturally, during the season of Lent the demand for fish increased.

In the sixteenth century, the nobles began to dig artificial ponds to produce fish for export. Western demand for fish and an abundance of salt in Galicia made this industry profitable. Fish were produced on a large scale, salted, and exported to Germany, Poland, Lithuania, and Muscovy. In the seventeenth century, the Ukrainian fishing industry was largely a commercialized and profit-motivated export business.

Cattle Raising, chronologically speaking, preceded farming. It was highly important up to the sixteenth century. The deeds, court acts, bills, last wills, and records of various offices and agencies of that era supply ample proof of the economic significance of animal-raising, including bull-breeding, sheep-raising, and horse-raising. Dogs and birds were bred and trained for hunting purposes. Enumerating the obligations and services of the peasants to the manor and lord, for example, those documents and records name first such various service obligations as going to hunt, serving as beaters, raising horses for the manor, supplying fish, honey, chickens, ducks, cheese, butter, eggs, hogs, skins, hides, and other products of the extensive economy, and in particular, raising cattle. Oats and hay were also among the contributions of the peasant population to the manor, while wheat and rye were scarcely mentioned. The emphasis placed on services and the type of products indicated above point out the very character of the Ukrainian economy prior to the sixteenth century. Eventually, in the sixteenth century, this was replaced by new developments, including intensive agriculture.

Werdum, Beauplan, Litvin, and other foreigners who visited Ukraine in the fifteenth and sixteenth centuries, repeatedly wrote about the pasture lands, enormous herds of cattle, sheep, and goats, the rich and abundant grass resources, the strong, enduring, and speedy horses, large stallions, the swine, and the uncounted wild birds and animals in the steppe and forest regions.[6] The fact that these things impressed foreign visitors indicates their economic importance. Especially in the steppe regions, the breeding of horses developed to a great extent, although the continuous Tartar raids prevented their smooth and speedy growth. When a certain degree of pacification of the "wild fields" occurred as a result of the slow disintegration of the Crimean Khanate and the growing power of the Cossack Host, cattle and horse-raising and sheep-breeding penetrated the steppes even farther.

In the forest areas, in the Carpathian mountain, as well as in the densely populated Western sections of the country, cattle and horse-raising was widely carried on. There was ample land not required for other purposes. Raising cows, oxen, and bulls was a widely spread practice in the royal possessions, noble manors, and peasant households, in order to secure meat, hides, milk, and milk products for domestic consumption, as well as for the exportation of livestock and meat. While the importance of hunting in this respect progressively declined, meat production and exportation increased. Grey Ukrainian bulls were particularly popular in the foreign markets. The Cossacks, on the other hand, raised in the "wild fields" (beyond the Cataracts) a special breed of very strong and fertile cows.

Horse-breeding developed chiefly in the royal and manorial economies to provide for the needs of transportation and warfare. The horse was at that time unquestionably an important draft power. It was used in farming, for wagons and carriages, for horseback riding, for hunting, for providing main transportation and field work service, and for waging wars. The peasants also raised horses extensively, although on a smaller scale. In Galicia, for example, peasants were required to render their manorial services such as delivering manure to the manorial fields, bringing wood, and supplying oats and hay for the manorial herds and stallions with their horses and wagons. In some instances the peasants had to pay a "horse tax," on each horse they owned.

Several breeds of horses were known in Ukraine at that time. In particular, the so-called Tartar or Crimean horses were very popular among the Cossacks, who also raised horses on a large scale in the wide steppes beyond the Dnieper Cataracts. Beauplan said that these horses were very strong and very well trained.[7]

Sheep raising also grew in importance, especially in the mountainous areas of Galicia and in the Kholm and Belz districts. The industry was scarcely known in the Kievan era. Since the middle of the sixteenth century, numerous villages were organized according to Wallachian legal principles in these Galician and Podillian districts. Although inhabited by the Ukrainian people, these villages were called Wallachian villages. The exclusive peasant occupation in these areas was in the rearing of sheep. Hence the contributions to be paid by the peasants under the general bondage system consisted mainly of the products of sheep raising, such as wool, woolen cloth, woolen rugs, and various kinds of cheese. Hog and goat raising also took place in the Wallachian villages, and to a lesser degree in other settlements in different parts of Ukraine. Hog raising was most common in maple wood districts, where the industry could be carried on at relatively low costs.

The Wallachian system developed primarily in those areas where the soil was poor and grain farming could not be very successful. Moreover, sheep raising progressed as long as the opportunities of commercialized grain production were not yet fully realized. With the growth of modern corn farming, the Wallachian economies declined whenever any chance for the export-motivated grain farm business existed, said Hrushevsky. The growth of a grain economy brought also the burden of serfdom and soil bondage to the peasantry of the Wallachian villages, whose lot had been rather mild and easy.

Rearing falcons, hawks, and dogs for hunting, breeding chickens, ducks, geese, and swans for food and trade, raising cats for pets and catching mice, rats, and various kinds of birds, completed the picture of this phase of the Ukrainian economy in the Polish-Lithuanian period.

Agriculture. The normal agricultural economy of Ukraine in the Lithuanian-Polish period consisted, as before, of three economic sectors: grain production, vegetable gardening, and fruit raising. All three segments, and especially grain production, experienced some basic technological and organizational changes in the course of these three centuries. These three individual industries originated and developed in a certain evolutionary sequence, until they resulted in the well developed agricultural economy of the eighteenth century.

The process was completed in the next period of Ukrainian history, the Cossack-Hetman era. Thus, grain production followed cattle-raising whereas vegetable and fruit raising, as the most intensive divisions of agriculture, arrived later. Vegetable and fruit production were no doubt developed already in the Kievan era, but they neither advanced nor achieved any economic importance at that time.

As a matter of fact, farming, primarily grain production, was a leading industry in Galicia and West Volhinia by the fifteenth century. But in the rest of the Ukrainian provinces, because of the Mongol devastations, it did not acquire economic predominance until the end of the sixteenth century. Accordingly, for almost two centuries longer a primitive economy prevailed there, based on hunting, fishing, and cattle raising. The types and forms of service obligations and tax contributions of the slaves and peasant serfs of that time clearly indicated the secondary and supplementary role of farming in the country's economy.[8]

Farming itself was extremely primitive prior to the seventeenth century, designed only to supply some necessities for individual households and not for the market, although foreign travelers, like Beauplan and de Vigenere, reported the enormous and almost incredible fertility of the steppe areas which easily produced hundredfold crops without much labor and literally without any manure or fertilizer.[9] Lack of roads, poor transportation equipment, and inadequate marketing techniques, however, did not permit efficient processing and distribution of agricultural produce.

Farming, therefore, remained stagnant for a relatively long time. Agricultural prices were not uniform, food supply was inadequate, and the standard of living was rather low. The chief source of labor consisted of slaves, and they were not very productive. In the fifteenth century, farming was largely done within the framework of small private peasant estates or tenant farm holdings, duty-bound to the *boyars* and nobles, or to the Church. Oats, rye, barley, and wheat were the leading crops (in that order) until the early sixteenth century. Hrushevsky supplied the following approximate composition of farm production for the time: forty percent of all acreage was used to raise oats, thirty-five percent to grow rye, about fifteen percent for barley, and about ten for raising wheat. This pattern in farm production was derived largely from royal books and records. There are less reliable sources of information about peasant farming, but it is highly probable that the proportions were about the same. These sources indicate unquestionably the leading importance of oats and rye and the secondary position of wheat. As has been mentioned, serfs paid their taxes in their leading products, oats and rye, until the sixteenth century. All this was in direct connection with the extensive cattle and horse raising in the old Ukrainian household economy. Still, at that time, some remnants of communal farming prevailed, and the peasant estates bore some communal material burdens which were completely lost in the next century.

In the first half of the sixteenth century, some fundamental changes in the farm economy were already initiated under the impact of the new developments in Western Europe. There, the rapidly increasing population soon exhausted the natural resources, and the quasi-agricultural system had to make way for a new economic system, early commercial capitalism. It was based on industrialization, specialization, exchange, and the wide use of money. This development caused an enormous demand in the West for food and agricultural raw materials, which could be obtained in Ukraine and other agricultural areas of East Europe. Hence, the social and economic changes in Ukraine in the sixteenth and seventeenth centuries, the rise of serfdom and latifundium-manorial agriculture in particular, were due to the emergence of capitalism in Western Europe. The price of grain rapidly increased by more than a hundred percent, creating impressive profit incentives and opportunities. In 1564, for example, one *lasht* of wheat could be bought for 21.18 Polish guldens, while in 1616 the price for the same quantity of wheat increased to almost 55 guldens.[10]

Changes proceeded in various directions, completely altering the socioeconomic constitution of Ukraine. The small individual peasant farms began to disappear rapidly, being progressively absorbed, *per fas et nefas*, into the latifundial estates of the nobility and gentry, by spoilation, seizure by force, criminal abuses, royal grants to nobles for services rendered, and unjust and discriminatory legislation. Parallel to this process, the distinction between slavery and free peasantry also disappeared, replaced by a general bondage of the rural population.

In the majority of the Ukrainian provinces peasant land ownership was practically obliterated in the seventeenth century. The manorial economy prevailed universally, managed by the gentry and cultivated by the peasant serf. Serfs performed plowing, harrowing, harvesting, thrashing, cattle raising, and other farm and house work for their lords. They were tenants of small farmsteads which supplied their meager subsistance, and they were also burdened with yearly tributes to the manor. Each individual manor was managed by an administrator who was, by rule, of noble descent. He directed the work of a number of overseers, *tivunes*, and helpers. A minute account of income and expenses was maintained. A number of manorial economies, the so-called *klutch* (key of possession), was managed by an *econom*, supervising all manorial administrators. The entire noble latifundium was administered by a "commissioner-general of goods," selected from the gentry, who had full authority over all economies and manors. Individual manors, or individual pieces of land were frequently leased to poor gentry, peasant, or others, for rental payments.[11]

Thus, in the seventeenth century, commercially motivated latifundial farming was fully developed. The vast lands, however, could not be intensively cultivated because of the relative scarcity of labor. This problem instigated a progressive enslaving of the peasants and a large-scale colonization program both sponsored by the privileged class of the Polish gentry. The noble possessions were in some cases vast. The grandees, like the Vyshnyvetsky, Chortoryisky, Ostrozhsky, Potocki, and Zamoiski, owned entire provinces, tens of towns, hundreds of villages, and hundreds of thousands of peasant serfs. The Ostrozhskys, for example, owned thirty-five towns and seven hundred villages in Volhinia, Podillia, and Kiev, and derived from those possessions about ten million guldens of yearly income. The Vyshnyvetskys owned almost all of Left-Bank Ukraine, where the country gentry were their service people.[12]

Under the pressure of needs, there was progress in the form of intensive methods of cultivation and better tools. Thus, the extensive two-field system was soon replaced by the three-field system, and finally, by crop rotation. The field was now well manured, wherever it was necessary, and well plowed by the use of oxen or horses. Werdum related about the exceeding skills of the Ukrainians in plowing their soil. Neither the man, nor the ox, nor the horse stepped on the plowed section of the field, but moved within the furrows only. Plows, harrows, hoes, forks, and other farm tools were frequently furnished with iron parts to accomplish better results. Only in the less advanced areas of Ukraine was wooden equipment primarily used. Iron sickles, scythes, knives, axes, and saws were known all over, and of course, generally used in the manorial economies.

As far as the efficiency of the Ukrainian farming of that time was concerned, it must be conceded that the manorial system was a rather wasteful one. The administration of the vast latifundia was not always up to standard, and the more so because the ruthless exploitation of the serfs took away from them a great deal of enthusiasm, ambition, and zeal for work. By the same token, it required costly and considerable supervision. The peasant tenant farms were too small and too oppressed to be efficient. But the amazing fertility of the soil and the favorable climatic conditions made up for those organizational and administrative weaknesses, and produced hundredfold crops in seventeenth and eighteenth century Ukraine.

In gardening and vegetable production also, a certain progress was achieved during the Lithuanian-Polish period. New plants were introduced and more intensive and elaborate ways of gardening were used, either brought by the foreign immigrants who came into Ukraine, or learned by the Ukrainians who traveled extensively. Thus, beans, totally unknown in Kiev, became very popular. Cabbage, rare in the Kievan era, was cultivated from the sixteenth century on. Lettuce was introduced from Italy. The great variety of horticultural produce included cauliflower, parsley, carrots, celery, asparagus, spinach, turnips, parsnips, onions, garlic, cucumbers, watermelons, pumpkins, peas, hemp, and flax. Hops production was also very popular since beer was drunk throughout Ukraine.

Intensive gardening developed first in the manorial possessions, then it slowly penetrated into peasant farming. But already in the seventeenth century some vegetables and garden produce, like onions, garlic, caraway seeds, and poppy, were included in the lists of the peasants' annual compulsory contributions to the manor. This evidence certainly indicates that the peasants raised vegetables. The crops of onions, caraway, poppy, peas, hemp, flax, and hops sometimes extended over several acres of land, having really been done on a large scale. But despite some progress in gardening, this sector of the Ukrainian economy was on a rather low level, compared with the West. The same Werdum, quoted twice already, was not at all impressed by vegetable production, and remarked ironically that the Ukrainians probably were not able to afford the kind of intensive and exact work which was required in the gardening business.

Perhaps fruit production was another indication of the great changes which took place in the Ukrainian economy as a result of the Mongol invasion. Emperor Mauricius reported very extensive fruit growing in Ukraine before the Kievan era, whereas in the fifteenth century there was very little left of that industry. In those days orchards existed in Galicia, Volhinia, and

Right-bank Ukraine, where living conditions were more certain or more easily stabilized; they grew only around the castles and manors, and in towns and cities. There was no fruit raising in the villages and countryside. Of course, in the steppes and Left-bank Ukraine, where the continuous threat of Mongol raids made intensive economies impossible, no fruit was grown.

In the western districts of the country, apples, pears, and cherries were common. Plums first appeared in Ukraine in the sixteenth century. Oddly enough, grape production was relatively extensive in spite of unfavorable climatic conditions. In Galicia and Podillia, grapes were raised on the manorial and monastic estates and pressed into a great quantity of a popular wine. Local wines were produced by merchants as well, and sold under their own brand names. According to contemporary reports, the Ukrainian grapes were good, but the wine was mediocre and sour.

Mining. In the predominantly agricultural Ukraine of the Lithuanian-Polish period, mining remained an insignificant industry of secondary importance, unable to fill even the limited domestic needs of her farm economy. Not much progress was achieved by comparison with the Kievan era, in the extraction of such mineral and non-mineral resources as iron ore, nitrate, salt, and clay.

Mining iron ore was, qualitatively speaking, most important for the Ukrainian economy as a whole, although it was by far not the leading mining business from the quantitative point of view. Extraction of iron ore was achieved in various regions of Ukraine, largely in a primitive manner within the framework of manorial and monastic economies. Peasants, also, did a little iron mining and processing. Iron ore deposits and mines were scattered, just as earlier in Kievan times, throughout the northern forest areas in Galicia, Volhinia, Polisia, and the Kiev district. Moreover, the specialist miners traveled all over and looked for iron deposits. When even poor iron ore deposits were found, constructions were immediately erected, exploitation initiated and blast furnaces built and put into operation.

Iron was then processed by blacksmiths. It was used most extensively for plow shares, harrows, knives, hoes, sickels, saws, scythes, axes, carpenter and contruction tools, wagon wheels, home building, and firearms. The demand for iron was so great that the domestic supply was by no means adequate, and iron was imported from Germany and Bohemia. Poor roads and great distances considerably hampered the importation of this bulky material.[13]

With the invention of firearms, a new business came into being, the extraction of nitrate from the nitrous earth which spread throughout Ukraine. Beauplan related in his *Descriptions* that the Ukrainians had specialists in the field of saltpetre production, and that their gunpowder was very good.[14] Nitrate production also had considerable economic significance, as was evident from the numerous court suits of that time on the commercial benefits of nitrate production. Later, however, saltpetre exploitation became largely a royal monopoly, the profits of which went into the country's treasury, either directly by way of the public administration or indirectly by means of leasing the mines to private individuals. Sometimes nobles received mines as compensation for services rendered to the crown. Nitrous earth was found in many places — the Podillia, Kiev, Ochakiv, Bilhorod, and Putivl districts, and on the banks of the rivers Vorshkla, Orel, and Psiol.

As ceramics and brick production continued to develop in Ukraine in the course of the entire Lithuanian-Polish period, so the excavation of clay was another extractive industry of considerable importance. Clay was mined in various regions of Ukraine: Galicia, Podillia, Volhinia, and in Right-bank and Left-bank Ukraine as well. Extraction of clay was done in the framework of the manorial and monastic economics, as well as by the peasants for their limited use. Ceramics and brick manufacturing as industrial sectors will be treated further in the next chapter.

Quantitatively speaking, the largest mining industry in Ukraine was salt. Salt was mined largely in the southern, pre-Carpathian regions of Galicia, like the Drohobych, Stara Sil, Dolyna, and Kalush districts, and to a lesser degree, in the neighborhood of Sianik, Kuty, and Kosiv. Mining salt was also a very important industry of the regional Galician economy in the Kievan period. About 1622, news spread that salt was found in the Left-bank, Myrhorod district, but hopes for any considerable salt deposits proved to be grossly disappointing. In the eighteenth century, in the newly settled areas of *Slobidska* (Village) Ukraine, between the Donets and Don rivers, substantial salt reserves were actually found, and extensively exploited. Nesterenko indicated a considerable salt extraction in the Izium district. In fact, West Ukraine produced a surplus of salt. Hence Galician salt was widely marketed in East Ukraine, and also exported to Poland, Lithuania, and Hungary, as far as the southern districts of Transylvania. But the eastern provinces of Ukraine still had to import salt to supply their needs from the Mongol dominated northern shores of the Black Sea and Crimean Peninsula.

Contemporary sources and records afford a great deal of information: where salt was mined, how it was done, how it was processed, who owned the salt mines, where and by whom salt was sold, where it was exported, and other such details. No doubt, this great contemporary interest in the salt business most emphatically indicates its considerable economic significance at that time. Thus, wherever salt was found, wells were drilled, and big wooden wheels constructed, installed horizontally, and moved by horses or oxen to get salt or salty liquid to the surface. Then the raw material was put in large kettles for boiling out the water and dirt.[15] There were at that time, certainly, some skilled artisans who mined and processed or boiled out the salt. Their pay was relatively high, compared to the earnings of carpenters, wood workers, and field workers. A salt miner received eight *dinars* for processing a barrel of salt, while a woodcutter was given the same amount of money for a week's work. Besides, the job was held in high social esteem.

The salt mines, at first owned by the municipalities, monasteries, and the gentry, were soon turned into royal monopolies because of their great potential profit. It was indeed a very profitable business. At the Peremyshl and Drohobych mines alone, in 1570, 35,000 barrels of salt were mined, processed, and sold, resulting in a revenue of 13,000 guldens for the treasury, including tolls and duties. The monetary yields of salt mining declined in the seventeenth century when wood, so necessary for boiling the raw and liquid salt, became scarce.

1. The rarity of any major famine in Ukraine: M. Hrushevsky, *Istoria Ukrainy-Rusy*, New York, 1954, Vol. III. p. 333-338. It may be another argument against Pogodin's theory of the Ukrainian migration to the North to avoid the hardships of the Invasion. In the European North East famines were rather frequent occurances. M. Slabchenko, *Organizatsia Hospodarstva Ukrainy*, Odessa, 1923, Part I. p. 1: "Ukraine was held for a golden country, a country of fabulous riches, where it was enough to kick the earth slightly in order to open the golden deposits".

2. M. Lubavskii, "Nachalnaia istoria malorusskavo kazachestva", *Zhurnal ministerstva narodnavo prosveshchenia*, 1895, Vol. VII. p. 264.

3. Slabchenko, *op. cit.*, Part 1. pp. 2-5; also, I Krypiakevych, "Pobut", *Istoria ukrainskoi kultury*, Vol. I, Winnipeg, 1964, pp. 113-114.

4. D. Doroshenko, *Narys istorii Ukrainy*, Munich, 1966, Vol. II. pp. 7-9; also N. Polonska-Vasylenko, *Istoria Ukrainy*, Munich, 1972, Vol. I; the grandees, pp. 455-457.

5. *The Lithuanian Statute*, 1529, chapter VIII, art. 11; Hrushevsky, *op. cit.*, Vol. VI. p. 165.

6. V. Sichynsky, *Ukraine in Foreign Comments and Descriptions, from the sixth to*

the twentieth century, New York, 1953, pp. 49-50; G.V. de Beauplan, *A Description of Ukraine*, New York, 1959, pp. 448 and 473.

7. de Beauplan, *loc. cit.*, pp. 463-464, and 473; also, Krypiakevych, *op. cit.*., Vol. I. pp. 122-123; on the extractive industries, in general: Polonska-Vasylenko, *op. cit.*, Vol. I. pp. 366-368; Hrushevsky, *op. ci.*., Vol. VI. pp. 141-234.

8. Hrushevsky, *loc. cit.*, and excellent analysis of economic transitions in Ukraine, from the old extensive system to modern commercialized agriculture.

9. de Beauplan, *op. cit.*, p. 448: "The land is so fruitful, it often produces such abundance of grain, they know not what to do with it... and that they will not work but just when necessity obliges them; Sichynsky, *op. cit.*, pp. 52-53: quotation of B. de Vigenere from his *La description du Royaume de Pologne*, published in Paris in 1573: "They say, that the soil of that country is so good and so fertile, that if a plow would be left in the fields, so after two or three days it would be covered so well by a new grass, that nobody would find it."

10. A. Szelagowksi, *Pieniadz i przewrot cen w XVI i XVII wieku w Polsce*, 1902, p. 155. One *lasht* was approximately equal to twenty-five hundred- weights (centnars).

11. Polonska-Vasylenko, *op. cit.*, Vol. I, pp. 463-465.

12. P. Lyashchenko, *History of the National Economy of Russia*, New York, 1949, pp. 255-258: a brief but good description of economic developments in Ukraine in the Polish-Lithuanian era; also, Polonska-Vasylenko,*op. cit.*, Vol. I. pp. 455-459; also, some older works: A. Jablonowski, "Ziemie ruskie, Wolyn i Podole", *Zrodla dziejowe*, Warsaw, 1889, Vol. XIX; "Ukraina, Kiow-Braclaw", *ibid.*, Warsaw, 1897, Vol. II; a more recent work: I. Baranovich, *Magnatskoie khaziaistvo na yuge Volini v XVIII v.*, Moscow, 1955, pp. 105-116.

13. Iron ore deposits were scattered throughout the forest areas of Ukraine: A. Jablonowski, "Czerwona Rus' ", *Zrodla dziejowe*, Warsaw, 1888, Vol. XVIII, p. 459: throughout these areas numerous villages and townships even today are called "Ruden", "Rudnyk", or "Rudky", the names having been derived from the word "ruda", meaning "ore" in the Ukrainian language; also, Hrushevsky, *op. cit.*, Vol. VI. pp. 217-219; O. Ohloblyn, *Dumky pro Khmelnychchynu*, New York, 1957, pp. 12-14: he asserted the existence of a great number of mines in Ukraine on the eve of the Khmelnytsky insurection.

14. de Beauplan, *op. cit.*, p. 448: "They are very expert at preparing of saltpetre"; also *Zrodla dziejowe*, Vol. XVI, p. 421.

15. Compare with a more comprehensive coverage of the extractive industries in Ukraine of the fifteenth and sixteenth century: N. Fr.-Chirovsky, *Old Ukraine, Its Socio-Economic History prior to 1781*, Madison, 1963, pp. 250-282.

CHAPTER SIX

INDUSTRIAL GROWTH

Towns — Trades and crafts — Food-processing, the textile, and the leather industries — Paper manufacturing and the printing industry

Towns. In connection with the analysis of social stratification in Ukraine during the Lithuanian-Polish period, and, in particular in connection with the socio-political position of the townspeople, it was pointed out that the Ukrainian town of that time had, to a great extent, lost its significance in the framework of Ukrainian society. First of all, the legal isolation of the town from the countryside resulted from the introduction of the Magdeburg law of municipal organization; and secondly, the discriminatory system based on the social supremacy of the nobility and gentry resulted in a decline in the urban economy. The introduction of Polish ideas and institutions into Ukraine resulted in the decay of the village and the peasantry, as well as of the city and the townspeople; social segments which once flourished and preserved a social and political balance were weakened.

Now this social balance was shaken and sacrificed for the enrichment and supremacy of the gentry. Nevertheless, the town still remained a center of commerce and trade, and the townspeople were largely merchants and craftsmen. Its life concentrated around the market place, periodic annual fairs, monthly fairs, and weekly and daily trading. In the Kievan age of early commercial capitalism, the Ukrainian town exceeded the Western European city in volume of mercantile business. Now, the situation was reversed. The commercial significance of the Ukrainian town declined, and the relative importance of its commerce, in relation to other branches of the economy, fell far below the sixteenth and seventeenth century Western level.

But the commercial abilities of the Ukrainians and of some nationalized immigrants did not permit urban mercantilism to decay completely, despite these adverse social and political developments. Thus, the foreigners who occasionally visited Ukraine, as well as the official records of the time, reported the remarkable mercantile business and considerable wealth and prosperity in such cities and towns in Ukraine as Kiev, Lviv (Leopolis), Kamianets, Lutsk, Zhytomyry, Bilhorod, Starodub, Briansk, Novhorod, Chernihiv, Putivl, Kaniv, Cherkasy, Berest, Proskuriv, Pryluky, Peremyshl, Zbarazh, and others.[1] Kiev especially was mentioned as the capital of Ukraine, and as one of the wealthiest and most beautiful places in the country, despite the terrifying devastation it had suffered earlier at the hands of the Mongols. Mueller related that the magnificent ruins of the old structures of the city of Kiev stood witness to its past greatness and glory, while Litvin wrote that Kiev was a very rich place, where merchandise was displayed from Persia, Arabia, India, Syria, Muscovy, Sweden, and Norway.[2] Silk and spices were so plentiful in Kiev that they could be bought for very low prices. Precious metals and stones, perfumes, carpets, and other costly goods were brought daily to the city by the numerous caravans of native and foreign merchants. Also, Lviv (Leopolis) flourished commercially according to Lasota, although its trading and commerce were handled more by the Armenians than by the Ukrainians (Ruthenians).

Some of those Rus'ian towns were very ancient, while others were rather newly established in the course of the colonization process of the fifteenth and sixteenth centuries. The ancient towns were built very irregularly, with no planning whatsoever, and distinctly showed by their construction the different periods of their historical growth from prehistoric times. Only their newest sections, arising in the process of the Magdeburg settlement of Ukraine, exhibited some regularity and planning of structure. Kiev, Peremyshl, Novhorod, and Chernihiv, for instance, belonged to the group of old cities. Pryluky, Lubni, Myhorod, and Lviv were newly constructed and more regularly planned, with the streets usually in a gridiron pattern.

The newly erected cities and towns were constructed close to castles, in well defended places, or on commercial crossroads, as was done centuries before. Strategic and mercantile considerations were also important criteria in erecting and developing towns in the fifteenth century. Since the colonization of the Ukrainian borderlands was largely sponsored by the gentry and noblemen, these newly erected towns and villages were initialy owned by the nobles. But gradually they bought their freedom from the original owners for money, and became self-governing municipal communities. Acquiring freedom, however, did not help the city economically, because of other enormous social and political pressures from the upper classes. All political rights were denied to the town, as was pointed out above, except in a few cases as in the city of Lviv. In addition, the property rights of the townspeople in real estate were limited.

The general appearance of the town did not change much, if compared with the previous Kievan period. Usually the town was built as a square, and surrounded by strong stone walls a few yards high, and deep moats, as in ancient times. Even the construction technique did not change much, except for the planning of the city within the walls. A few strongly defended gates led into the town by drawbridges over the moats. The stone walls were designed and equipped for defense and safety to give the besieged citizens cover from the arrows and the gun fire of the attacking enemy and to enable them to fight back. High stone towers, constructed at strategic points in the city walls, served as observation posts. Individual towers were specifically assigned to individual craft and merchant guilds to be defended in an emergency or siege. Hence the towers frequently derived their names from the particular guilds which staffed them, such as the tailors' tower, the courtwriters' tower, the tanners' tower, or the carpenters' tower.[3]

In the middle of the fortified town, there was a square marketplace with the municipal building, *ratush*, and the mercantile premises. The suburbs extended outside the walls, and the later their erection, the more regular was their construction. The economic characteristics of the city, where the mercantile and manufacturing enterprises were concentrated, were based on the principles of labor and product specialization, in contrast to the villages and countryside where farming and other extractive industries developed. From there, social and legal differentiation was projected.

Trades and Crafts. Although the Ukrainian trades and crafts experienced considerable progress during the Lithuanian-Polish period and were much better developed than in the Kievan state, at the same time they were far below the levels achieved by contemporary Western European countries. As has been stressed several times, this was due mainly to the faulty and discriminatory social structure of the Commonwealth. The trades and crafts actually developed in two different ways. Such industries as forest exploitation, iron, glass, and paper production, flour milling, saw mills, breweries, and distilleries, grew simply as supplementary activities of manorial agriculture, primarily dominated and partially run by the landed gentry.

Even these industries were located in the cities and towns, usually being operated on lease by the townspeople, and prevailingly owned by the royalty and nobility as the traditional privilege of their class. The upper classes also preferred to market and distribute the products of their industries, using only local merchants as middlemen.

The noblemen enjoyed complete freedom of action and full exemption from all kinds of levies pertaining to their industrial and commercial activities. This enabled them to accumulate considerable revenues. But, being a class descended from medieval knights whose professions were military service and land cultivation, the gentry generally looked with contempt upon the trades. Trades and crafts were socially unworthy occupations according to the prejudices of that epoch. In particular, they were unworthy as occupations for noblemen. Irresponsible exploitation of resources and their depletion by a crude technology characterized the majority of trades and crafts sponsored by the Polish gentry. Only the religious orders, in their monastic system, applied a slightly more advanced technology and a slightly more rational exploitation of the forest resources in particular. In many instances, the monasteries ran model trade and craft enterprises, although they did not always enjoy the same privileged positions as the gentry estates.[4]

On the other hand, such crafts as carpentry, wheelwrighting, joinery, tannery, turnery, ironworking, goldworking, firearm production, shoemaking, tailoring, woodwork, ceramics, the building industry, weaving, spinning, fulling, leather working, baking, butchery, and other similar crafts were primarily the occupations of the commoners, as far as the needs of the countryside were concerned. Nevertheless, due to the privileges enjoyed by the gentry, and the discrimination against the town, these occupations could not grow impressively. The townspeople were burdened with all kinds of levies and taxes; they were not permitted to dispose of and market their products freely. Their trading was legally resticted, particularly when in competition with industries owned and operated by the gentry.

Information about the individual industries and industrial occupations in Ukraine, from the fourteenth to the seventeenth centuries, is to be found in the writings of Beauplan and other foreign visitors, whose accounts are also substantiated by frequent references to various crafts in the contemporary records of the courts of justice, tax collections, deeds, and other contracts and agreements. Those crafts and trades could be classified in a few groups according to their major economic characteristics, like metallurgy, the wood industry, leather processing and manufacturing, the pottery and glass industry, the textile and garment industry, and food processing. As the dark and primitive Mongol era passed slowly into oblivion, new crafts and industries were gradually introduced in order to keep pace with the growing population in the towns and countrysides. Many new skills were brought from abroad, in particular from Germany, as is clearly indicated in the nomenclature. The names of various trades and various tools at that time were simply Ukrainianized German words and terms.

Specialized crafts developed in the city, manor and village, because only specialization could cover the extensive needs of the dense population. The period of a clumsy jack-of-all-trades, whose deficient work was acceptable in the fourteenth and the first half of the fifteenth centuries, was definitely over. The real center of crafts was the town, where the guild organization regulated production and distribution. Prices, qualities, styles, and selling practices and procedures were fixed by the guilds or the municipal governments. Competition of any kind, and advertising and sales promotion were outlawed, and marketing was strictly planned and regulated, although otherwise private initiative was preserved. Then, in the seventeenth century, trades sponsored by the manorial economies gave rise to the beginning of modern industrial manufacturing and early capitalism, which crystalized in the next (Cossack-Hetman) period.

Metallurgy experienced a modest growth in the course of the fifteenth to seventeenth centuries, delayed, first of all, because rich ore deposits were discovered in Ukraine at that time. The scanty supply of domestic iron, mined and processed in the forest belt of the country, was used to a limited extent by blacksmiths to manufacture wagon wheels, saws, scythes, sickles, hammers, axes, hoes, plow shares, candlesticks, and other farm and household appliances. At times, rails for the construction of bridges and cannons were also manufactured from domestic iron. On the other hand, iron was extensively imported for such use from Austria, Bohemia, and Transylvania, since the domestic supply was inadequate. A variety of specialized metal workers were known in the town of that epoch, such as locksmiths and blacksmiths, keymakers, kettle-makers, coopers, zinc processors, knifemakers, sword and weapon-makers, bow and arrow fabricators, and all kinds of craftsmen who were employed in producing certain articles with at least some parts made from iron or other metal. The city of Lviv was the leading center of the metallurgic crafts. The swords from Lviv were especially famous.[5]

At the beginning of the fifteenth century, the production of fire-arms and gunpowder was initiated. The first cannons were manufactured in Lviv in 1343, and ten years later, according to Krypiakevich, there were shops and craftsmen everywhere who manufactured and repaired firearms. Primarily, cannons were produced which were at first short and wide. Bullets were made initially from stones, and later from lead and iron. Muskets and guns did not become popular until the second half of the sixteenth century. Concurrently with the manufacture and use of fire-arms, the production of gunpowder proceeded. Saltpetre, coal, and sulphur were used in various proportions to produce the gunpowder, praised by Beauplan for its quality.

Arms and gunpowder were manufactured by special craftsmen, usually residing in the cities. On the landed possessions of the princes and noblemen, however, there were private shops to fill the local needs of the grandees, to supply their provincial armed forces, and to equip their large-scale hunting projects. Gunpowder was also manufactured by the peasants to supply their limited needs for hunting, and of course, by the Cossacks beyond the cataracts, to support their military expeditions against the Turks, Tartars, and Poles.

A seperate branch of metallurgy was represented by goldsmithing and watch-making. The skilled goldsmiths produced jewelry from imported gold and silver for the upper classes. These craftsmen were predominantly foreigners. The first clocks were introduced into Ukraine at the beginning of the fifteenth century; in Lviv in 1404. These clocks, as a rule, were placed in municipal buildings and palaces. Skilled watchmakers manufactured and repaired clocks. In particular, the watchmakers of Peremyshl were nationally famous, and they were frequently asked to go to Lviv, Kiev, Cracow, or Warsaw to perform their excellent skills.

Woodworking was another important industry. Above all, the exploitation of the forest became very profitable in view of the growing demand for lumber and timber, and their high prices in Western Europe. The forest workers evolved into a specialized and well-paid profession. Tar and potash production also continued in this period to be by-products of the ruthless, profit-motivated forest exploitation, primarily sponsored by the gentry. Underbrush and young forests were burned into ashes, subsequently used for bleaching linen. Even the contemporaries complained about the waste of the gentry, which threatened the forest with annihilation.

In the fifteenth century, sawmills began to come into use, representing the emergence of a more modern industry. At first, the sawmills were developed in connection with flour milling, where a special mechanism was installed to do sawing.

The introduction of sawmills intensified the ruthless exploitation of the forest, especially in the mountainous western provinces. Contemporary records stated the alarming fact with horror. Finally, in the middle of the sixteenth century, legal measures were undertaken to prevent this irresponsible devastation. These measures resulted in the establishment of a government forest monopoly in the Lithuanian-Rus' Commonwealth. However, the enormous prices offered for lumber and timber throughout that century, about six hundred guldens for a *lasht* of wood, often proved too tempting in spite of the legal restrictions and prohibitions. Not only the profitable export business, but also the growing demand for potash and tar in the expanding domestic economy, contributed considerably to a wasteful exploitation of the forests. All over the wooded areas hundreds of forest workers, called *budnyky*, continued a large-scale burning of the forests for ashes or processing wood for tar. They operated either on their own account, or on the account of the nobility. Either way they contributed to a rapid depletion of the forest resources.[6]

Wood-processing industries employed a variety of specialized craftsmen, like bridge builders, fort and palace builders, home builders, church architects, sawyers, carpenters, turners, barrel makers, shingle makers, and wood carvers. Practically speaking, everything in the peasant household was wooden, from the house, wagon, and slides to primitive tools for field work, like plows and hoes, and housewares, such as spoons, bowls, and plates. All these things needed specialized craftsmanship for their production.

Construction of churches, palaces, fortifications, and homes was another leading industry. Construction, whether in stone, brick, or wood had attained advanced status by that time. The architectural styles changed occasionally. In particular, the stone constructions of Byzantine form were largely replaced by the Gothic style introduced by Western colonists, mainly the Polish and German ethnic elements who settled the cities. However, these Gothic constructions, churches, palaces, and municipal buildings, bore distinct Ukrainian characteristics. Gothic constructions prevailed only in the Western Ukrainian provinces.

Wooden constructions prevailed in the countryside and suburbs. Several architectural styles of wooden churches had already developed, among them the Boyko, Lemko, and Carpathian styles of West Ukraine, and the Podillian, Middle-Dnieper, *Sloboda*, and beyond the Cataract styles in East Ukraine. In addition, the construction of wooden fortifications was still going on throughout Ukraine during the Lithuanian-Polish period, as in the Kievan era, but its heyday was certainly over. Wooden construction of forts, churches, palaces, and municipal buildings was predominantly the work of Ukrainian-born craftsmen of great skill and artistic ability.

Building boats was a separate branch of wooden construction, of considerably advanced technique. The Cossack boats or *baidaky*, used for military expeditions on the high seas, were especially famous. They were well built, light, and speedy. In connection with boat construction, there developed the production of linen for sails, and the manufacture of tar, which was also an exportable naval material.

In direct relation to home furnishings were the pottery, ceramic, and glass industries. Pottery and ceramics were well developed, and far ahead of the levels achieved in the Kievan era, supplying crude, fine, and ornamented appliances like bowls, plates, pots, jars, chalices, vases, and tiles. These crafts were so popular that frequently entire settlements and villages were engaged exclusively in pottery and ceramics, such as Polych, Hlynski, and other places in East and West Ukraine. The craftsmanship was on a very high level. Often the product was made in very attractive colors and artistically decorated, especially vases, tiles, and plates. Artisans of these crafts enjoyed respect, good compensation, and some social privileges. In the cities they were organized on a guild basis, while in the countryside they were unorganized.

The technology of production and the quality of the produce were good and constantly improving, while fine ceramics were also subject to importation as well. The artisans were mainly Ukrainians, heavily discriminated against by the Polish government, which desired to establish less Polish-controlled interest in this field. Needless to say, these works of ceramics often reached a high level of artistry, greatly appreciated at home as well as abroad.

Glass production was very modest. During the Polish times it did not develop into a large-scale industry. Glass manufacturing was carried on primarily within the framework of the manorial economy for the household use of the grandees and gentry. Window glass, drinking glasses, and bottles were products of the industry which were never profitable. The high cost of manufacturing, due to the small-scale operations, frequently forced the manorial glass works into liquidation. The demand for glass in the cities and towns was met mainly by imports. Glass of a better quality was mainly imported from Bohemia, but it was also brought from Germany, and even from Venice.

The Food Processing, Textile, and Leather Industries. The growth in population also caused a further development of the food processing, textile, and leather industries, so as to supply the basic necessities and supplementary materials for hunting, fishing, and waging wars. In the fifteenth to seventeenth centuries, food processing was the best developed industry in Ukraine.

It included flour production, baking, the dairy industry, brewing, distilling, butchery and meat processing, and honey and wax production.

Flour milling achieved the scale of a large industry, primarily run by the gentry. Initially, it was a small and insignificant craft of hand milling for household use, performed with two grinding stones moved by human hands, and later on by horses or oxen. The first water mills of the German style came into Ukraine in the middle of the fourteenth century. The very first mention of a water mill in Ukraine was in 1339, at the time of the last Galician ruler, Yurii-Boleslav in the village of Trepche, near the city of Sianik.[7] But water mills did not become popular in Ukraine until the sixteenth century, the hand mills still being preferred by the people. In the sixteenth century, however, various types of water mills became known there, such as those which operated the entire year; the spring mills, operating only in the spring and fall when the water supply was abundant; the large mills with five or six wheels, which often connected flour milling with lumber sawing and cloth manufacturing; and finally, the small mills with only a single wheel.

As far as the ownership and management of those mills were concerned, there were, first of all, royal mills in the royal possessions, remaining under the general supervision of the royal district officials, *starosty*, and the urban mills operated by the townspeople and municipalities. Both classes of mills were organized as large-scale, commercial enterprises. On the other hand, there were countless smaller mills throughout the country, owned largely by the gentry, but operated and managed on lease by skilled millers. The monasteries also owned and operated large and small mills for their own needs as well as for profit. The leased mills in the royal, noble, and monastic possessions were of two classes, the temporary rental mills and the hereditary leased mills. The latter, being owned by the manors, royalty, or religious orders, were hereditary in the families of the millers, descending from father to son as far as their operation and management were concerned.

Around 1520, windmills also came into wide use, mostly in Volhinia and Eastern Ukraine. The windmill, however, in contrast to the water mill, remained a small-scale enterprise filling local needs exclusively.

In the cities and towns a special craft of bread bakers developed, baking bread not only for the townspeople but for the countryside population as well. Peasants regularly bought the city bread during the fairs, although the art of bread-baking had been widely known by housewives in most parts of the country since time immemorial.[8] Professional bakers were numerous in some towns, where twenty to forty bakers supplied the demand for bread.

Meat processing was in the hands of butchers, who knew how to kill, cut, process, handle, and preserve meat and meat products. The butchers, producing in their home workshops, kept their stands at the municipal fairs, and there they sold the produce of their skill.

The supply of dairy products was almost exclusively in the hands of the peasants and the manors. Milk was processed by primitive means for sour milk, sour cream, butter, buttermilk, and various kinds of cheeses. Particularly in the western mountainous areas of the country, cheese production was extensive and sometimes developed into a major export item.

The manufacture of alcoholic beverages, drinking honey, beer, wine, vodka, brandy, rye, and gin was a very important and very profitable industry. At that time Ukrainians of all social classes drank considerably, according to the reports of eyewitnesses.[9] Drinking honey (mead), a processed natural honey, was the most traditional Ukrainian beverage, consumed over the longest period of time. Although drinking honey was still widely consumed in East Ukraine in the seventeenth century, and to a lesser degree in West Ukraine, the overall economic importance of its production progressively declined, being replaced by the growing popularity of beer and vodka, *horilka*. The monasteries usually excelled in the quality of their honey.

In connection with the production of drinking honey, the wax processing industry must also be mentioned briefly. This industry had a centuries-old tradition, because it was fairly developed in the Kievan era. During the Lithuanian-Polish period, wax was produced all over the country as a by-product of bee-keeping and honey manufacturing. The city of Lviv was the wax trading center for all Ukraine. The processing and trade of wax were under strict control by the municipal government of Lviv, which protected the brand quality, particularly in the case of exports. Export wax was always furnished with the municipal seal, to guarantee the good name. Any product misrepresentation in wax trading received severe punishment, including death by hanging. In the domestic market, wax was used for candle production. Poor qualities were used to manufacture soap. Candle manufacturing was handled mainly by the church brotherhoods to supply the needs of the church. It was also locally done for lighting the households of aristocrats and public authorities.

Wine production never developed beyond the stage of household experiment. Ukrainian wine was not very good at that time.

Brewing was introduced into Ukraine by German colonists. At first it was a small retail business, but by the sixteenth century it had begun to assume the form of a large, separate industry. Since the beginning of the fifteenth century, beer enjoyed an ever wider popularity. Large breweries were as a rule located in cities and towns, and beer production and marketing were strictly regulated by the municipal governments in order to protect the reputation of the city and its brand. Transgressors and violators of the regulations and trade codes were harshly punished.

Manorial brewing, being just another facet of the agricultural economy of the country gentry and the religious orders, was frequently connected with mills and sawing. However, it never became a really large-scale industry, like the urban and royal breweries, and it was never as profitable as the mills.

In all urban, royal, manorial, and monastic brewing, the lease system prevailed, being considered more profitable than direct brewing by the municipalities, public officials, or noblemen. Skilled private brewers received exclusive lease rights to brew and sell their product. In exchange, they had to pay rents and light taxes to the state treasury.

The free brewing of the peasantry was *de facto*, albeit reluctantly, recognized by the state and gentry. The peasants brewed freely, being obliged only to pay a beer tax to the government and to make some contribution to the manor.

At the end of the seventeenth century, brewing became a large-scale industry with all the features of the growing commercialism of the times. But the small brewery establishments still prevailed. Large, factory-like breweries were somewhat rare.

At the beginning of the sixteenth century, distilling was scarcely known in Ukraine. The records of tax collections from 1508 did not mention any distilling or whiskey tax, while the records from 1545 made several references to the new industry and its receipts. Thus, vodka or *horilka* production was a new form of processing agricultural raw materials. Already, in the second half of the sixteenth century, numerous distilleries were operating throughout the country, producing thousands of guldens of annual revenue for the owners and tenants, and large tax collections for the state. The whiskey tax was primarily used at that time to cover the costs of the provincial and district governments of the Polish Crown, as the records indicated.

In contrast to drinking honey and beer production, which was freely practiced by all segments of society with little government regulation, distilling, as a new industry growing at a time when the manorial-patrimonial system was fully established, developed strictly as a monopolistic prerogative of the gentry, usually leased against certain annual rental payments to the town and village population. In its initial stage, distilling was connected with the milling business, while later it evolved into a separate industry of considerable importance. The collections of the whiskey tax clearly indicate the enormous economic and financial significance of the business.[10]

Finally, the development of the textile and leather industries was indispensable to meet the needs of the rapidly growing population. The variety of leather manufacturing consisted of tannery, shoe and boot manufacturing, saddlery and belt production, and cap and glove making. The leather crafts were concentrated primarily in the cities. But they were also widely scattered throughout the countryside, manors, and villages, in the form of domestic industries meeting local or manorial needs.

Tannery continued to grow from ancient times; shoemaking consisted of the manufacture of footwear of better quality for the upper classes; bootmaking constituted the production of crude footwear for the common people. Saddlery and belt manufacturing had a prime economic and military importance. Caps and gloves of leather and fur were indispensable because of the harsh climate.

The textile industry advanced greatly during the Lithuanian-Polish period, paving the way for the development of large-scale textile manfacturing in the following centuries. Linen from flax, hemp, wool, and woolen materials was processed for sale all over the country by special craftsmen. It was also spun and woven by individual households for domestic consumption. Women of all classes did the spinning and weaving as they had done for centuries.

Linen was most extensively used to manufacture clothing and to produce sails. Beauplan reported extensive sail manufacturing in Eastern Ukraine, developing along with the construction of large boats for fishing and transportation, and produced by the Cossacks for their military expeditions against the Turks and Tartars. Hemp and flax were also extensively processed for manufacturing cordage, ropes, threads and nets for all possible uses in shipping, hunting, fishing, and in everyday household affairs, exactly as it was done in the previous historical periods of the Ukrainian economy. The technology of production of those numerous items neither progressed nor changed.[11]

The progress in sheep-raising since the late decades of the sixteenth century brought about an expansion of wool manufacturing and processing, and a production of woolen goods by special shops and artisans. At first, the woolen cloth was woven in water mills, after the raw wool had been cleaned and dyed by specialists. Woolen textiles, carpets, rugs, covers, and clothing were used all over the country. Clothing was produced by tailors of two classes.

The silk tailors made clothing, underwear, gowns, dresses, and suits from imported silk and other fine domestic and foreign materials, for the upper classes of society. The common tailors, working with linen and woolen materials, supplied the common people. Furriers produced fur coats and fur caps for winter.

Paper Manufacturing and the Printing Industry. Paper production was initiated in Ukraine in the first half of the sixteenth century. The first paper mills were established in the cities of Lviv, in 1522, and Yaniv, in Galicia. Shortly after, the paper mills began to operate in other towns of West Ukraine like Krosno, Busk, Lutsk, and Ostroh. The mill in Lutsk began to operate in 1570; in Busk, in 1580. The mill in Ostroh was established by Prince Constantine Ostrozhsky, in his family possessions, at approximately the same time.

Paper manufacturing was associated to a great extent with the name of Valentine Kmeller, who owned and operated several small paper mills in West Ukraine. In Eastern Ukraine, the first paper mill was established by the monastery of *Petcherska Lavra*, between 1615 and 1624. Initially, these first paper mills were located in cities and run by skilled craftsmen, but soon small shops were established in the countryside by the nobles, to cover the local needs of the manors.

From the beginning, several kinds of paper were manufactured by these paper mills, and usually furnished with elaborate watermarks. Their output was small, however, and could not cover domestic needs. They were not very profitable either with only one or two exceptions such as the *Lavra* mill. Some quickly became bankrupt. Hence paper became largely an imported article. It was needed for books, for official business, and for keeping records. Its consumption constantly grew, in particular after the introduction of printing. Later on, however, the paper industry again expanded to cover the extensive paper needs.[12]

Book printing in Ukraine was initiated by Ivan Fedorovich, a Muscovite by descent. His printing business in Muscovy did not succed, and finally he had to flee from there to avoid persecution on religious grounds. Then, via Zabludiv, in Byeloruthenia, he arrived in Lviv and established his print shop, the first one in Ukraine. The first book published by him in Lviv was the *Apostol*, the *Letters of the Apostles*, 1574, ornamented with beautiful engravings in the Renaissance style. Within the next few years he published a number of books. Financially, however, his enterprise was a failure, although his outstanding initiative and idea did not die. His printshop was acquired by the Lviv Orthodox brotherhood of *Stavropighia* in 1591, which was successful in publishing many church books, school textbooks, and other books for decades to come.

Fedorovich went then to Ostroh and began there to print books under Prince Constantine Ostrozhsky's protection, including the famous Bible of Ostroh, which was mentioned before in connection with the literary activities in Ukraine. Some thirty books were printed and published in Ostroh by him, his associates and heirs. Subsequently, many printing shops were established in Ukraine. In 1619, the Kievan *Pecherska Lavra* monastery started its widely known publishing business of largely ecclesiastic and religious books. In 1639, Mykhail Slozka founded in Lviv another competing print shop, while smaller printing establishments were organized in other Galician and Volhinian towns, such as Striatyn, Krylos, Uhertsi and Univ. Books printed in Ukraine were not only used there, but were also extensively exported to Wallachia, Moldavia, Byeloruthenia, and Muscovy as well.[13]

1. V. Sichynsky, *Ukraine in Foreign Comments and Descriptions*,from the sixth to twentieth century, New York, 1953; Mueller's *Memoirs*, p. 53; Lassota's *Tagebuch*, p. 54; Horsey's *Voyages*, p. 64 and the following; G.V. de Beauplan, *A Description of Ukraine*, New York, 1959, pp. 447, 450, 454, and numerous cities named in his map of Ukraine; also, *Akta grodzkie i ziemskie*, Vols. II, Nos. 1, 5, 11; III, Nos. 18, 97; VI, No. 105 and in many other places.

2. Sichynsky, *op. cit.*, pp. 4051, 53 and other; references by Michael of Lithuania, Mueller and others.

3. J. Ptasnik, *Miasta i mieszczanstwo w dawnej Polsce*, Cracow, 1934, pp. 152-153, 170; also, I. Krypiakevych, "Pobut", *Istoria ukrainskoi kultury*, Winnipeg, 1964, Vol. I, pp. 109-111; on the towns: N. Polonska-Vasylenko, *Istoria Ukrainy*, Munich, 1972, Vol. I. pp. 368-373 and 466-468; M. Hrushevsky, *Istoria Ukrainy-Rusy*, New York, 1955, Vol. VI. pp. 1-140.

4. Hrushevsky on devastation of resources; *ibid.*, Vol. VI, pp. 183-203, 233: "... economy and industry in the hands of the gentry evolved into a stimulus for an enormous devastation of the natural resources of the land, ..."; also, M. Slabchenko, *Orhanizatsia hospodarstva Ukrainy*, Odessa, 1923, Part I. pp. 10-13.

5. Krypiakevych, *op. cit.*, Vol. I, pp. 125-126 and 129-130: "Lviv was the center of those crafts. Lviv's swordmakers with pride recalled in 1590 ... that the craftsmen from Lviv always manufactured the best arms" (p. 130).

6. *Arkhiv yugo-zapadnoi Rossii*, VII. Vol II, pp. 317, 351-352; *Zrodla dziejowe*, III. pp. 192 and 333; VII. p. 25 and many other places; a general analysis: Hrushevsky, *op. cit.*, Vol. VI pp. 184-191 and 233.

7. Krypiakevych, *op. cit.* p. 126.

8. *Ibid.*, p. 127; N. Fr.-Chirovsky, *Old Ukraine, Its Socio-Ecnomic History prior to 1781*, Madison, 1963, p. 188.

9. de Beauplan, *op. cit.*, pp. 448, 468-469.

10. The figures about tax collections in Ukraine in the first quarter of the seveneenth century; *Zrodla dziejowe*, IX, 1894-1897, pp. 275-279; V. 1887, pp. 78-79. 103-104, 107, and in other places; Hrushevsky, *op. cit.*, Vol. VI. pp. 225-235.

11. P. Lyashchenko, *History of the National Economy of Russia*, New York, 1949, pp. 248-263; Krypiakevych, *op. cit.*, Vol. I. pp. 125-131; A. Maciejowski, *Historya rzemiosl, rzemieslnikow i rzemieslniczych wyrobow w Polsce od czsow najdawniejszych az do konca XVIII w*, Warsaw, 1877; D. Doroshenko, *Narys istorii Ukrainy*, Munich, 1966, Vol. I. pp. 133-137.

12. J. Ptasnik, *Papiernie w Polsce v XVI w,* Cracow, 1920, pp. 17-20, 34-35 and other places; V. Sichynsky, *Narys z istorii ukrainskoi promyslovosty*, Lviv, 1936, pp. 6-9.

13. D. Vyrnyk, *Ukrainskaia SSR, Kratkoi istoriko-ekonomicheskii ocherk*, Moscow, 1954, p. 16; also Krypiakevych, *op. cit.*, Vol. I, pp. 164-166; on the book printing; Polonska-Vasylenko, *op. cit.*, Vol. I, pp. 401-402.

CHAPTER SEVEN

COMMERCIAL PROCESS

Domestic trade — Foreign trade — The trade routes and the import and export items — Finance

Domestic Trade. Previously when the social position of the townspeople in Ukraine during the Lithuanian-Polish era was analyzed, it was pointed out that circumstances at that time were unfavorable for the growth of trade. Under the impact of the Mongol Invasion and occupation, Ukrainian commercial life could not develop. Even later, under Lithuanian protection, frequent Mongol raids presented a serious obstacle to smooth and steady commercial activity. It would be erroneous, however, to think that in the course of the fourteenth and fifteenth centuries commercial activities faded away entirely, particularly in East Ukraine.

On the other hand, in the sixteenth and seventeenth centuries, when the threat of the Mongol raids lessened considerably, another factor evolved which hampered any substantial growth of commerce. The city, in general, was oppressed by class discrimination; its interests were sacrificed to those of the rural nobility. Chiefly as a result of this social discrimination, and particularly because of the philosophy of mercantilism, which was making itself felt in Ukraine, an extreme regimentation of trade developed, resulting in the decline of the town and its commercial activities.

First of all, the entire commercial and industrial life of the town was dominated by a rigid guild organization. The guilds of merchants and craftsmen did not accept the principle of free competition, therefore they applied to the town economy the principle of prohibition and regulation, presumably in order to do justice to the interests of both the producer and consumer.[1] The merchant guilds, like the craft guilds, were compulsory trade associations, the membership of which was restricted to individuals qualified according to birth, nationality, creed and training. The whole life of the city was strictly regulated by prescriptions, rules, codes of behavior, and inflexible class and trade customs. Needless to say, all these factors discouraged and retarded the commercial growth of the country as a whole, and of the town in particular.

Secondly, the state issued its own laws to regiment trade and commerce; monopolies were established, commercial routes prescribed, heavy taxes imposed, and free competition prohibited. These governmental restrictions were even more intense and rigid in Poland proper. The Crown granted to a few large cities in Ukraine, namely, Lviv, Lutsk, Kolomyia, and Berest, an exclusive trade monopoly, under the provisions of which no outside merchant or foreigner from another Ukrainian town could do any selling. The city of Lviv also received the "stapel right." It obligated each and every traveling merchant, whether he liked it or not, or whether there was a potential market for his product in the city or not, to stop there to display all his merchandise for sale for a few days.

These privileges were just other forms of discrimination among the towns. They scarcely facilitated trading because they hurt foreign and inter-regional trade. The stapel right was especially harmful, since it kept merchants from seeking the best markets and exploiting competitive opportunities. Detailed state regulations regimented trade in wood, oxen, including oxen trails and routes, beverages, salt, meat, and similar commerce, and in all cases imposed substantial taxes in the form of sales taxes, excise taxes, tariffs, and tolls, which were rated upon the weight, quantity, quality, and place of origin of the merchandise.

Worst of all, however, was the practice of the government in leasing certain tax collections, like bridge and road tolls and some excises, to private persons who usually abused their franchises. Those individuals who obtained such concessions demanded excessive rates and imposed additional and unauthorized charges on traveling merchant caravans and mercantile shipments. Later, even those who had never received a tax collecting franchise from the state undertook illegal collections. Eventually, almost every nobleman or owner of landed estates raised road, bridge, passage tolls, and excise taxes from any merchant and any merchandise caravan which entered their domain. This form of racketeering nearly brought an end to mercantile activity in the towns and villages, since the costs of trading spiraled while profit opportunities simultaneously declined.

To make things difficult for the merchant class, the gentry had in time received full exemption from all trade restrictions and tax burdens associated with buying and selling transactions. The privilege of exemption was affirmed several times by the parliament and king, starting with the Piotrkow ordinance of 1496.[2] It was introduced into Ukraine with her incorporation into the Polish Crown in 1568. The exemption of the nobility from almost all mercantile restrictions automatically produced unfair competition for professional merchants and urban commerce. Naturally, the town, hampered by regimentation and numerous taxes lawfully and unlawfully collected, suffered a progressive decline of profits, while from their own commercial transactions the gentry gained proportionally. Hrushevsky rightfully remarked that the gentry were the largest sellers of food, and the largest consumers of finished products. In this respect, they fully succeeded in eliminating the urban middleman, and in many instances succeeded in illicitly replacing him. According to the letter of the law, a nobleman was not allowed to indulge in the activities of a market middleman. In practice, however, this regulation was frequently neglected or avoided, and individual noblemen indulged secretly in considerable marketing, greatly damaging the mercantile interests of the town.

Several revisions of the tax and toll system were undertaken by the federal and local governments of the Crown to suppress the abusive collections. But the administration and execution of those revisions were so weak and poor that actually only good intentions remained. Trade and commerce continued to decline. In a somewhat better position were the few privileged cities which were granted some degree of tax exemption. Their mercantile activities were declared duty and toll free. In Ukraine, only Lviv, Lutsk, and Kiev enjoyed that privileged position. Lviv received the exemption in 1505, and that of Lutsk and Kiev followed. Nevertheless, this was, like another previously discussed privilege of a city trade monopoly, still an additional form of discrimination.

Although some enlightened circles of society saw the absurdity of the situation, not much could have been done, because the all-powerful gentry protected its class interest egotistically and jealously. The class interests of the nobility were the only issue there which mattered; hence, the discrimination of commerce and trade, instead of lessening, progressively increased.

Engaged in domestic commercial activities at that time were the townspeople, predominantly the foreign born, Poles, Germans, Jews, Armenians, and also Ukrainians. The Polonized gentry and the rural traveling merchants, the Chumaks, also participated. The Chumaks were an exclusively Ukrainian social phenomenon of very ancient tradition.

The two leading commercial institutions of the times were stores and fairs.

The fairs still carried the main volume of commerce; the stores and shops had a rather secondary and supplementary economic significance. Annual, semi-annual, seasonal, and monthly fairs, and weekly and daily markets were the periodic meeting places of producers, sellers, middlemen, and consumers. Produce and merchandise were always available at the fairs and markets. As a matter of fact, the fairs represented an ancient economic institution. The novelty, however, was the legal privilege of exemption from tolls and duties, granted by the royal government to the merchants and goods going to the fairs. This was the only effective measure adopted by the government to combat discrimination and abuse and to recover urban trading.

The fairs were held annually, semi-annually, or quarterly for a few days or even a few weeks around certain important holidays, as in Lviv on St. Agnes' and St. George's days; in Peremyshl on St. Peter's and Paul's day; in Sianik on Pentecost; or in Yaroslaw on St. Andrew's. Some fairs, like those in Lviv, Yaroslaw, Sniatin, and Kiev, developed into really major commercial events of a national and international reputation, where merchants from all over Ukraine, Poland, Germany, Bohemia, Wallachia, Hungary, Lithuania, Muscovy, and even Greece, met.

According to the reports of contemporaries, the Yaroslaw fairs were probably the biggest. They were the center of Ukrainian trade with the West. The volume of business done during these fairs was tremendous for the times. Bishop Piasecki related that during the fire in 1625 in Yaroslaw, the merchandise destroyed at the fairs amounted to ten million guldens.[3] Twenty to forty thousand head of cattle were regularly driven to the fairs.

Merchandise from everywhere was exchanged during the fairs; foreign manufactured goods, textiles, garments, metal articles such as knives, sickles, scythes and saws, of domestic and foreign origin; wines, raw silk and silk materials, jewelry, carpets and rugs, spices, fruits, hides, skins, boot wax, salt, grain, flour, honey, meat and meat products, arms, tools, various appliances and numerous other items.

Smaller less important fairs were held all over Ukraine on a monthly and weekly basis. There the volume of business was smaller and the variety of merchandise less manifold, primarily limited to local produce to meet everyday needs. The weekly markets were scheduled for different days in various neighboring towns and villages in order to avoid competition among themselves and to enable the merchants to attend as many commercial events as possible.

Trading was freer and less discriminatory during the fairs. For example, in Lviv, Peremyshl, and other cities, Ukrainians were allowed to trade freely, while otherwise they were either not permitted to indulge in commercial activities, or they were at least restricted in this respect.

Naturally, the guild merchants were hostile toward free trading in the fairs and markets since this competed seriously with them. Under the pretext of apparently diminishing government revenue due to free trading at the fairs, guild merchants of Lviv in particular attempted to induce the royalty and the parliament to restrict fairs and foreign merchants, or to close the national borders.

Although mercantile activities were relatively free during the fairs, there still were numerous minute state and city regulations, sometimes rational, and other times irrational in their nature. Weights, measures, qualities, and services were regulated, and sanitary measures were adopted against the sale of adulterated products. Selling meat during Lent was prohibited. Minimun quantities which could be sold were prescribed, business and sales taxes were collected, and competition was suppressed. Transgressors were severely punished. Tax rates levied against the fairs differed according to the quality, quantity, and the origin of the merchandise.

Stores and shops constituted the other form of merchandising. Theirs was a strictly regulated domestic commerce. Market places were located in midtown, close to the municipal building. There the premises were provided for the stores and shops of the so-called "wealthy" merchants, the city patricians, and the outside merchants to display their merchandise. Jewelry, carpets, wines, metal articles, spices, and other costly products were traded there. On the side streets were the stores and shops of common merchants and craftsmen, marketing cheaper commodities, primarily items for the daily use of the local consumer, like fish, meat, grain, flour, skins, furs, wax, honey, linen, and cheap textiles. Artisans usually occupied one street or one quarter of the town, where they produced and sold their own manufactured goods, like shoes, boots, materials, clothing, leather, and various tools of their specialty.

There was a strict differentiation between the wealthy merchants dealing in costly merchandise, and the common merchants who sold cheap wares. The common merchant was forbidden under penalty to trade in costly and luxurious merchandise.[4] Some merchants were wholesalers, since the law prescribed the sale of certain goods in large quantities only, such as textiles and bulky products. The evolving store system consisted actually of specialty stores and shops, partially due to commercial regimentation, which did not permit the individual merchant or artisan to carry a variety of goods on his shelves. There were, therefore, textile stores, some specializing in fine fabrics, others in crude domestic materials, shoe shops and boot shops, butcheries, bakeries, blacksmiths, goldsmiths, tailor shops, tanneries, furriers, stores selling Oriental goods, beer and whiskey taverns, wine and honey taverns, and many other specialty establishments.

Merchandise was brought from abroad or distributed throughout the country mainly by means of the traveling merchant caravans, moving in various directions along the traditional commercial routes. Usually these caravans were sponsored and financed by a group of merchants or by merchant associations and corporations, comprising fifty, sixty or more well-constructed and well-protected wagons to resist all the dangers of a long journey. Because of the uncertainty of the times, the caravans had to be armed or escorted by soldiers.

Foreign Trade. The economic life of Kievan society was greatly commercialized. In particular, it derived considerable revenues from an extensive foreign trade, which, for reasons already explained, was on the decline. Although Ukrainian foreign trade recovered to some extent during the Lithuanian-Polish era from the blow it had received from the Mongol invasion, it never reached its previous heights and its earlier significance. Too many diversified factors preconditioned this low level of the international economy of Ukraine between the fourteenth and seventeenth centuries, especially the foreign domination of the country, the growth of agricultural interests, and social prejudices. Historically speaking, the foreign trade of that era cannot be discussed indiscriminately as a uniform segment of the economy of the country, diversified only in the geographical aspect. For the period following the fourteenth and fifteenth centuries, the international trade of West Ukraine (Galicia and Volhinia) was developing in an entirely different way from that of East (Dnieper) Ukraine, and so each segment must be discussed separately. For the next hundred and fifty years, Ukrainian foreign trade may again be considered and treated as a homogeneous and uniform branch of the country's economy. These separate trends in the economic evolution of the eastern and western provinces of Ukraine for about two hundred years have already been indicated and emphasized.

Since the western provinces, Galicia, Volhinia, and West-Podillia, were not completely dominated and not so thoroughly pillaged by the Mongol Khans, their foreign commerce evolved afterwards in a more stable way. It simply continued the old traditional trends, which were subjected only to gradual changes because of the new political and social conditions. The local Ukrainian merchants continued to participate in international economic operations, although their commercial activities were progressively restricted by the hostile Polish occupational government, and were finally reduced to a minimum. At first, Halych, Peremyshl, Volodymyr, and Berest played the leading roles of centers of foreign trade from the Galician-Volhinian times. Later on, however, in the fifteenth century, the city of Lviv in Galicia, and the city of Lutsk in Volhinia, became the leading markets for the international trade of West Ukraine. At that time, the most developed and most vital commercial ties were connecting West Ukraine with the cities of Cracow in Poland, Thorn and Danzig in Prussia, Breslau, Nuremburg, and Regensburg in Germany, Prague in Bohemia, and the city of Constantinople in Greece.

The invasion had an impact on West Ukrainian foreign commerce insofar as it altered its pattern. At first, it influenced the Ukrainian-Greek exchange. This trade was soon re-established by the Ukrainians through initiating their own mercantile factories on the Black Sea shores, as in Ackerman and Oleshe.

The Polish domination of Galicia in 1349 produced discrimination against the Ukrainians, resulting in a decline of the Ukrainian element among the merchant class, in general, and in a growing participation of the foreigners — Poles, Germans, Armenians, and Greeks — in the Galician-Volhinian international commerce, in particular. Still another development disadvantageous to the commercial interests of the Ukrainian urban population was introduced in the form of Polish rule. The Polish city of Cracow was progressively successful in establishing itself as a monopolistic middleman for the entire Galician-West European trade and exchange. King Casimir actually gave the city of Cracow in 1354 this prerogative of an exclusive market, controlling the entire East-West commerce, and placing it entirely in Polish hands.

Eventually, the initially successful trade monopoly of Cracow had to acknowledge the growing commercial power of the city of Lviv, and give up its pretentions, at least to some extent. With its rise to the position of a first class commercial center in the East, Lviv soon acquired a dominant position also in distributing West European merchandise to the Southeast European lands. Then, after having received the stapel right, Lviv evolved into another commercial bottleneck for Orient-Occident trading, along with Cracow.

The growing commercial significance of Cracow and its discriminatory practices forced the Galician merchants to search for other routes leading to West European markets, and this produced a growing exchange between the West Ukrainian commercial centers, and the city of Danzig (Gdansk) in Prussia. Moreover, this was an old route which, since the thirteenth century, had enabled the products of Ukraine to reach Western lands. Since the fifteenth century, however, its significance had increased considerably. Through Danzig, and then by the Baltic Sea, Galician grain, wax, skins, lumber, and other goods often went as far as Scotland, the Netherlands, Flanders, France, Spain, England, and Germany.

Unfortunately, however, the economic rise and development of the Ukrainian town in the sixteenth and seventeenth centuries did not enrich the Ukrainian merchants, since the towns were completely overrun by foreigners. In particular, the city of Lviv was controlled exclusively by Poles and Germans; the Ukrainians were barred from participating in its commercial life. In other towns, like Lutsk, Kamianets, Sniatyn, or Berest, the discrimination was less pronounced. But native merchants were soon completely overshadowed by Polish and German merchants from Lviv.[5] Complaints about this were of no avail.

In the Eastern provinces, on the other hand, the economic evolution went in an opposite direction. Thus, as an immediate consequence of the Mongol invasion, the Ukrainian merchant engaged in international trade disappeared completely. Throughout the fourteenth and fifteenth centuries, foreign trade in East Ukraine was almost exclusively handled by foreign merchants: Armenians, Tartars, Lithuanians, Jews, Germans, Poles, Greeks, and even Italians, as the records of that period indicate.[6] Only some Chumak caravans traveled to supply the rural population of Dnieper Ukraine with foreign necessities, like salt from the Black Sea and Azov Sea shores, spices from the Orient via the Black Sea ports, and linen.

The invasion naturally resulted in a considerable increase in the Ukrainian-Oriental commercial exchange penetrating far into the hearts of Asia, the Middle East, Central Asia, and India, from whence Far Eastern merchandise was also brought. The Tartar, Armenian, Greek, and Caucasian merchants and merchant caravans were seen particularly in Kiev, which still remained the mercantile center of Ukraine. The Oriental merchandise, being available in the markets of East Ukraine, attracted Western merchants and their wares. However, this East-West exchange in Dnieper Ukraine never reached any large volume.

Until the fall of Constantinople in 1453, the Greek trade, once so important, also continued on a modest scale, being primarily another middleman for the Oriental merchandise coming to Ukraine. After 1453, this commercial sector declined and was replaced by the Turkish trade through the Black Sea ports, such as Kaffa (Theodosia), Trapesunt, and Suroge-Solday, and the Azov Sea ports, like Tana. Of course, commercial journeys were extremely risky during the time between 1350 and 1450. Mongols frequently robbed commercial caravans, exactly as in the late years of the Kievan Empire when the princes had to undertake military expeditions to stop the nomads who endangered the trade of the country.

In order to provide safety for the commercial routes, first the Lithuanian, and later the Polish authorities established heavily armed forts along these mercantile ways to protect the merchants and their caravans, at the same time they collected duties and taxes on all imports, exports, and transits. The foreign merchants, in order to evade this tax burden, were inclined to detour their caravans through the "wild fields" and the Cossack possessions, and there they frequently became prey to either Tartar or other surprise attacks. When foreign governments complained about the lack of security in those territories under nominal Lithuanian or Polish jurisdiction, they always received the same answer: their mercantile caravans bore the full responsibility for their willful actions, since they did not travel along the guarded and secured commercial routes.[7]

In the fifteenth century, during Mengli-Gerey's rule, the increasing intensity of the Mongol raids was reflected in a continuous decline of Ukrainian foreign trade in the southern sector, and, of course, in a reduction of tariff collections. On the other hand, Ukrainian commercial exchange moved northwards along the river Dnieper. Ukrainian grain and foreign transit merchandise were shipped in large quantities to the northern principality by foreign and Muscovite merchants, and to some extent, the Chumaks. The northern trade of East Ukraine went to Moscow, Novgorod the Great, Pskov, and other cities and provinces of the Grand Principality, at a gradually rising rate.

Eventually by the second half of the sixteenth century, the sectional differences in the characteristics of the foreign trade of West and East Ukraine faded away, as already explained, and from that time on the country as a whole became a rapidly growing factor in European international commerce.

The trade routes and the import and export items. International routes were gradually established, connecting Ukraine with the Western and Eastern mercantile centers. They attained an ever growing economic importance because of grain exportation which traveled a route from Kiev, through Rivne, Lutsk, Berest, Lenchyca, and Torun, to Danzig, and from there by the Baltic Sea to West European markets. Another route ran from Kiev and Lviv to Cracow in Poland and Breslau in Silesia, and then to Prague in Bohemia, and Nuremburg and Regensburg in Germany. A third customary commercial way connected Ukraine with the Baltic Sea and

Western Europe through Sandomir, Radom, and Torun, or through Lublin and Torun. The rivers San and Buh, flowing into the great Polish stream, Vistula, which ran into the Baltic, continued to be the main waterway for rafting lumber and grain destined for the West. Finally, still another route ran from Kiev, through Lutsk and Berest, to Lublin, Pozen, and Germany.

There were three main southern commercial routes. One connected the city of Lviv, through the city of Kamianets, with Wallachia, Moldavia, and the distant Balkan lands. The second ran from Kiev through Left-bank Ukraine along the river Dnieper, and through the Cossack lands beyond the cataracts to the Black Sea and Azov Sea shores, and farther, through Perekop and the Crimean Peninsula to the city of Kaffa (Theodosia), the important market for Oriental trade and to other large sea ports of the Black Sea basin. The third and less important route led southward on the right-bank of the Dnieper. The Dnieper in its lower course was used as a commercial waterway only to a very limited degree because of the difficulty of floating the goods through the cataracts.

An eastern route led from Kiev through *Slobozhanska* Ukraine, the Don-Volga basin and the city of Astrakhan, deep into Central Asia or the Caucasian lands. Two routes went to the northern Grand Duchy of Muscovy-Russia: one, as was pointed out before, along the upper course of the river Dnieper, the traditional way "from the Varangians to the Greeks" and the other from Left-bank Ukraine and *Slobozhanschyna* straight northwards.[8]

Imports entered Ukraine in large quantities, and exports increased from one decade to another during the sixteenth century because of the internal economic strength of the country. Thus, from the Orient, via Kaffa, Trapesunt, Astrakhan, Wallachia, and Moldavia, Ukraine received for her own consumption or for furthering her transit business, spices, brocades, raw silk and silk materials, jewels, carpets, rugs, gold and silver, velvet, citrus fruit, and other luxuries. From Muscovy, mainly furs and skins, then, wax and fish were imported. From Wallachia came horses, sheep and cattle. The Hungarian economy also gave Ukraine horses, and then, wax, fish, silver, wine, and to a lesser degree, oxen and sheep. From the West (Germany, Bohemia, Flanders) came textiles, metal goods, house appliances, tools, glass and glass goods, other manufactured articles, woolen materials, linen, leather goods, and arms. From Lithuania, wax, fish, and wooden products were imported.

Salt importation from the Crimean Peninsula and the shores of the Black and Azov Seas was probably the most ancient and most essential business, supplementing the domestic Galician salt production. At first, immediately after the Mongol domination of these areas, the Ukrainian salt importation from the Black Sea basin declined considerably. But it recovered very soon, and the Tartars neither limited nor discriminated against the salt export transaction, largely done by the Ukrainian Chumaks, probably because of the considerable profits involved.

From the southern Black Sea steppes, an essentially Ukrainian area but for a long time under Mongol domination, the Ukrainian economy received various products in large quantities: wax, drinking honey (mead), meat, salt pork, skins, fish, and other produce of the hunting and fishing economy. Particularly, very large quantities of fish were brought from these steppes. In the sixteenth century, the southern towns of Ukraine developed into a monopolistic market for southern honey, which, by virtue of certain legislation, was not supposed to be exported to any other parts or provinces of the Commonwealth.

The pattern of Ukrainian exportation changed considerably in the course of these three hundred years. In general, however, it indicated a continuous growth and upward trend, as far as its volume and variety were concerned. From the thirteenth until the fifteenth century a slave trade and slave export still continued, primarily to East Ukraine, in which, however, the local population did not participate to any large extent. The Mongol merchants and chiefs, the Armenians and the Greeks, taking advantage of the Mongol rule over Ukrainian territories, hunted there for slaves, and then sold them to Greece, Italy, Spain, Northern Africa, and the Near East. The Ukrainian slaves, particularly the female, were in great demand and highly priced. At the end of the seventeenth century, with the decline of the Mongol threat, slave trade also faded from Ukraine.

Grain, which had been a traditional export item for many centuries, became by the end of the sixteenth century a tremendous one in the international economic transactions of the country, exceeding in value and volume any other export of the time. The Scandanavian countries, Muscovy and Lithuania, were the oldest markets for Ukrainian grain. Then, the West European lands, like Scotland, Netherlands, Flanders, Germany, and to some extent also Spain, France, and England became its importers.[9]

It has been stressed already several times that this intense demand for grain in Western Europe due to the growing density of population, produced some fundamental, constitutional change in the social and economic life of Ukraine. First of all, the growth of serfdom and of commercialized farming resulted from it. The new trends in the Ukrainian economy actually affected all areas of the country, even the most remote and distant, and at the end of the sixteenth century literally every Ukrainian province, except Polissia, exported grain by land through Lublin, Torun, and Danzig, and by water, via the rivers Buh and Wisla. In consequence of that enormous Western demand for Ukrainian grain, its prices rose incredibly, by 100 percent or more.[10].

Cattle export was, perhaps, the second most important branch of the Ukrainian foreign trade. The large toll and tariff collections from the cattle drives and sales indicated clearly the scale and the extent of the transactions. The so-called *Urban and Territorial Acts* and certain other documents of the time extensively relate the volume of cattle and horse exportation.[11]

Cattle exportation was exclusively in the hands of the subjects of the Polish Crown, and foreigners were practically eliminated from that business. Along with cattle export, meat and meat products were also supplied by Ukraine to Western markets.

Fish exportation achieved a very considerable extent, too, since there was also a great demand for that product in the West. The noblemen and the merchant patricians constructed and maintained large artificial lakes and ponds which were very primitive in Ukraine, as compared with West European techniques, but this deficiency did not seem to affect the volume of the export business. Sturgeons were considered to be the most valuable fish, and so they were highly priced — more than twice the price of the less sought after fish, like carp and pike.

Also, the produce of the Ukrainian forest economy maintained an important position in international trading, of which wood, fur, and skins were the leading products. Of course, furs and skins were supplied by the southern steppe areas as well, but to a lesser degree. Foreign merchants from Germany and Prussia in particular, negotiated contracts with the administrators of the royal possessions and the nobles in order to secure a regular supply of wood for ship building, house construction, barrel manufacturing, and furniture production in the West. The price of wood was greatly differentiated according to its quality and purpose. Wood was transported to Danzig mainly by waterways — the rivers Buh, San, and Vistula.

Fur and skin exportation, once a leading component of Ukraine's foreign commerce, experienced a continuous decline throughout the sixteenth and seventeenth centuries. Imported primarily from Muscovy, furs and skins, martens, beavers, squirrels, sables, foxes, and muskrats, were then re-exported to European markets. Finally, wax and honey were also exported in considerable quantities. Wax especially was in great demand abroad. The Lithuanian government even planned to establish a public monopoly of wax and to secure for itself all the pecuniary benefits derived from this lucrative trade. The plan did not succeed, but large tariff levies were collected for the fisc. The wax business was under most strict control by the municipal and federal governments, in order to maintain the good name of the product in its foreign market. Hundreds of local merchants and country noblemen were exporting wax, from two to five stones of wax each.[12] Not only was domestic Ukrainian wax exported, but there was also a large transit trade of Wallachian, southern, and Muscovite wax passing through Western Ukraine to the Western European markets for production of candles and soap.

Finance. Once absorbed by the Polish-Lithuanian Commonwealth, Ukraine was incorporated into the Polish-Lithuanian monetary and fiscal system. A detailed analysis of this system has no place in the socio-economic history of the Ukrainian people since all monetary and fiscal establishments and institutions of that time in Ukraine were elements of foreign origin. The subject will be discussed only in general terms, and insofar as it affected the economic life of Ukrainian society in those days. The financial affairs in Ukraine will be treated in two parts: (1) the monetary organization, and (2) the fiscal activities of government revenue collecting and disbursements.

The monetary system of the Commonwealth was weak and poorly organized. Consequently, Ukraine had many unfortunate experiences with it. In particular, the inflation of the Lithuanian and Polish monetary units adversely affected Ukrainian economic interests. Until the fifteenth century, the basic monetary unit in the country was the "grosh," which may be translated as "penny." In order to get at least some approximate conception of the value of the grosh (penny), the following price list in the year 1580 may serve as an indication:

average daily wage for an artisan	1 penny
daily pay for an infantryman	1-1¼ pennies
daily pay for a cavalryman	2 pennies
a carp	1 penny
a sturgeon	2 pennies
a carload of wood	7½ pennies
a jar of wine	45 pennies
a hundredweight of wheat	50 pennies
a head of sugar	180 pennies[13]

Prior to the fifteenth century the "sexageneas," equivalent to 60 pennies, and "marks," equal to 48 pennies, were in circulation. But in the fifteenth century a "gulden" of 30 pennies value was generally accepted as basic currency of a higher grade in order to match it with the value of the Hungarian gulden, the most popular gold money in Poland at that time. The Polish gulden, however, soon began to suffer a decline in purchasing power and it could not be considered equal to the Hungarian unit which, on the contrary, enjoyed a consistently rising purchasing power. Thus, at the end of the fifteenth century the Polish gulden and the Hungarian "red" gulden were each worth 30 pennies, and already, in 1526, 40 pennies were paid for the Hungarian red gulden; in 1545, 50; around 1600, 58; in 1611, 70; in 1662, 180; and in 1676 about 360 pennies. During the same time, the Polish gulden was equal to only 20 pennies or less. The Polish gulden depreciated catastrophically compared to the Hungarian gulden currency unit.[14] This fact must have upset the country's economy. Not only did Polish currency circulate in Ukraine, but so did numerous other kinds of foreign money: Hungarian, German, Muscovite, Lithuanian, Italian, and even French. This profusion came as a result of increasing foreign trade and a relatively free circulation of gold and silver, which were generally identified with wealth in those days. Besides, the national governments were unable to exclude foreign monetary units from domestic markets, and to enforce at home the circulation of only national currencies.

Inflation in Europe was general between 1500 and 1640, but the depreciation in value of the Polish gulden was extraordinary. It was caused by many factors, such as enormous economic progress in the West, the increasing velocity of money circulation, malpractices in coinage, and the general trend of bad money putting good money out of the market.

Runaway inflation in the Polish-Lithuanian Commonwealth was the result. The gentry complained and the artisans and merchants were suspected of unfair money and price speculation. At first, the gentry requested the local authorities to interfere, and to regulate or fix prices. This step was taken, but with no success. So the parliament undertook to legislate prices and to stop speculation several times after 1620. According to contemporary records, merchants and artisans plainly refused to cooperate. A black market developed in which secret connections were necessary to buy goods at high prices. Accordingly, as Szelagowski said, the government had to abandon all price fixing by 1648.

On the other hand, the foreign currencies were still better, and through foreign trade this good money could be obtained and could benefit Polish subjects, gentry and townspeople. Thus, at the beginning of the sixteenth century, in order to preserve all the benefits of foreign trade and to accept good foreign coins for his own subjects, the Polish king attempted "to close the borders." This meant the surrender of all foreign commerce to Polish nationals, merchants and noblemen, and an exclusion of foreign merchants from handling the import, export, transit, shipping and retailing in the towns and countryside of the Commonwealth. Eventually, this attempt was also unsuccessful.

Credit was extensively used in Ukraine in the sixteenth and seventeenth centuries, primarily in commercial operations, and to a lesser degree, in farming and manufacturing. A simple mercantile credit, where goods were bought and sold on terms of deferred payment, was very popular. Also, lending on promissory notes and simple forms of bills of exchange, a mercantile custom brought from the West, was extensively done by rich merchants, goldsmiths, and noblemen. The credit business was in the hands of Armenians, Germans and Jews. The interest rates varied greatly. The average legal rate was about seven per cent per annum, but wherever the risk was great and the borrower either unknown or unreliable, the rate might have been 12 to 15 per cent.

The interest charges on loans to municipalities or governments were considerably higher, because their record of responsibility was usually poor. Lending money was a profitable business, even when legally done, but lending on usurious terms at an excessive and illegal rate of interest was, of course, exceedingly lucrative. These rates went as high as 100, 200, and even up to 2,000 per cent or more. The heavy penalties for usury did not stop that kind of morally objectionable business because of the great demand for capital and a scarce supply of loanable funds. In the latter period, monasteries, churches, and merchant and craft guilds also engaged in the legal loan business.

The public economy of the Commonwealth was badly organized. There was no division of the fisc, a strictly state treasury, and the private royal treasury until 1590. Because of this, confusion existed in collecting public revenues and making disbursements, with adverse effects on the country's economy. In 1590, the parliament initiated reform by assigning certain public incomes exclusively to the fisc. These included revenues from public estates, called "royalties," export and import duties, and the revenue from the government mint. The king received the revenues from public estates, called "economies," some salt mines, transportation tax collections, and income from certain monopolies, land tax collections, coronation tribute, and other minor incomes. The trend toward separation of the fisc from the royal treasury had apparently begun in the sixteenth century when in 1569 and

1590, some reforms were undertaken for this purpose. The process was completed much later.[15]

The state and royal landed estates, which had for a long time been the most important source of public revenues, were poorly administered, resulting in a need for additional taxes. Since the tax burden was borne principally by the peasantry and townspeople, additional taxes always resulted in a new hardship for the masses. Sometimes even the nobles had to pay more levies, thus the idea of reforms in the management of public property was always acute and urgent.

The landed estates, mills, sawmills, and other public possessions were administered by leases to private persons for rents and non-tax contributions, or pawned by private capitalists for money loans which were given to the king or the fisc. The supervision of the management of all such public property was in the hands of a federal official, *starosta*, who was compensated by a portion of the rental collections and certain manorial possessions which were left for his own personal use. The kings lavishly disbursed these estates among the nobles for their services to them and to the country, or pawned them excessively to get cash. This practice considerably decreased public revenues and impelled additional taxation, so despised by the gentry.

To improve the situation, the parliament intervened by restricting the royal practices of lavish grants and willful pawning of public property. In this way it sought to prevent speculation by the nobles and to halt the rapid decline of public revenue. Since 1496, and even more since 1504, the consent of parliament was required for any granting, leasing, or pawning of public possessions. In reality, however, the reforms remained a theory only, and the kings thereafter as well as before, dealt abusively with those royalties and economies.[16] This was true not only with regard to the landed possessions, but also with respect to the royal salt mines, aluminum and silver sales, and other monopolistic rights of the king or the state.

In 1547, the Lithuanian government attempted to introduce a fiscal forest monopoly, including exploitation and importation of wood, potash, tar, and ashes. A considerable public revenue and the prevention of forest devastation were expected as a result of this move. But five years later, in 1551, under the pressure of the nobles, the monopoly principle was broken, allowing the gentry to continue its forest economy freely. In 1561, an experiment was also undertaken by the Grand Principality to establish a comprehensive salt monopoly for all the provinces of the Grand Principality, but also without success.

The tax system of the Commonwealth was neither better nor worse than in

Western Europe at the same time. It was not well developed, it was uneven and discriminatory, poorly assessed and even more poorly administered. The major tax burden was borne by peasants and townspeople, while nobles were largely exempt. Until the first half of the fifteenth century, the traditional Kievan tax system prevailed, extremely out-dated of course, with all of its direct and indirect state levies. Then the Lithuanian rulers introduced some modifications, and from that time on a general tax called tribute prevailed, being paid in money and in kind. It was supposed to be a visible indication of the dependence of the subjects upon the Grand Prince of Lithuania.

Later, the tribute was transferred to the treasury collections of the individual land dukes where it remained until abolished by the Polish tax system. In addition, an annual tax, the Horde levy, was generally applied to enable the local princes to make gifts to the Khan of the Golden Horde.[17]

With the penetration of the Polish social and political order into the economic life of Ukraine, the Polish tax system introduced deep changes into the country's public economy. The process was gradual, of course. The federal government of the Commonwealth progressively lost the ordinary and direct taxes and court charges, in favor of the growing patrimonial authority of the gentry, who acquired some of those revenues. Hence the Ukrainian nobility, acquiring step-by-step the status and prerogatives of the privileged class, were freed from the general tax burden which was then confined to the townspeople and peasants. The tax exemption of the gentry, together with other Polish institutions, was introduced in Galicia in 1430, in Volhinia in 1509, in Podillia in 1507, and in Kiev in 1529.

Direct taxes, where shifting of the tax burden had not been foreseen, were divided into two classes, the ordinary and the extraordinary taxes. The ordinary taxes were an established practice throughout the centuries, and frequently they were also paid by the nobles. The land tax, the chief form of this type of levy, was initiated at the rate of two pennies per acre. However, it increased with inflation up to twenty, thirty and more pennies. The tax was paid by all classes of society, including the gentry and clergy. Also, in case of an emergency or prolonged need, some extraordinary taxes were introduced for a short period of time, and then reintroduced, if necessary. These taxes were also paid by all social strata; therefore, they could be introduced only by the parliament and with the consent of all the nobility. The king did not have the right to impose new taxes. Two forms of a station tax were levied irregularly, more from case to case, or were designed for certain specific ends, like the quarta tax. The levy, *pobor*, was the principal tax of its kind. It was in the nature of a surtax at a relatively high rate, levied over and above the regular land tax, and paid exclusively by the peasantry and never by the gentry. Its initial rate was twelve pennies per acre of land, but because of money depreciations and the growing needs of the state, the rate also increased up to one gulden. Not only landed possessions, but also water mills, sawmills, windmills, tenants, and village domestic craftsmen, had to pay the levy.

A kind of municipal equivalent of the levy was the *shos*. At first, the *shos* was really a local municipal taxation for the needs of the town, levied in accordance with the values of real estate, personal property, financial transaction, and volume of business. Since the middle of the fourteenth century, however, the federal government began to collect it, too, and the townspeople had to pay the *shos* at two levels, local, municipal and federal.

Once, in 1520, a capitation was raised from the entire population of the Commonwealth. The churches, monasteries, cloisters, and other religious communities paid the so-called *subsidium charitativum* to finance charities. The Orthodox Church, in addition to the *subsidium*, also had to pay a special tax of a discriminatory character. Then, as a remnant of the old times, the general population was obliged to render various tax-like services, such as construction of castles, bridges, forts, and highways, and transportation for the royal court and royal envoys.

In 1563, a strictly fiscal and regular tax, the quarta, was introduced as a complete innovation. The tax was collected from the royal possessions only. Practically speaking, the king had to contribute one-fourth (quarta) of his income from landed possessions to defray the costs of maintaining some standing army. In theory, all the possessors and leasees of the royal economies had to pay the quarta levy. Also, in the seventeenth century, additional "case-to-case" extraordinary and temporary taxes were adopted to defray the rising costs of maintaining the government. The nobility rarely paid these additional levies.

The indirect, shiftable taxes, in the form of excises, customs duties, sales taxes, and consumption levies, prevailed throughout the entire Polish-Lithuanian period. The nobles were largely exempt from paying the indirect taxes, and so their financial burden was borne solely by the lower classes of society. Excises and consumption taxes were levied against the sale and use of alcoholic beverages, honey, wax, textiles, groats, molasses, and many other products. Market operations were charged with some kind of business tax. Duties were imposed on exportation, importation, and transit transactions. All kinds of tolls were raised from the use of bridges, highways, or passages. Customs and toll collections were administered by special officials, called *birches*. Fees, license charges, and in particular, court charges, as the non-tax receipts, completed the picture of the public revenues of the Commonwealth.

Maintenance of the royal court, maintenance of standing armed forces, and provision for diplomatic relations with foreign powers were the three classifications of public expenditures. The costs of internal administration, education and schooling, policy protection, and charities, were not within the scope of government expenditures out of tax and non-tax receipts.[18] Therefore, the tax and non-tax receipts, from the viewpoint of the Ukrainian political and national interest, represented a direct form of economic exploitation of Ukraine by the Polish occupational regime. These collections were used to maintain the Polish government and little was spent by Warsaw to benefit the Ukrainian people either socially, culturally, or economically.

1. J. Ptasnik, *Miasta i mieszczanstwo w dawnej Polsce*, Cracow, 1934, pp. 152-170; S. Kutrzeba, *Historya ustroju Polski*, Lviv, 1917, Vol. I, *Korona*, pp. 101-109 and 174-178; O. Balzer, "Verfassungsgeschichte Polens", *Anzeiger der Akademie der Wissenschaft*, Cracow, 1906, pp. 110-112; M. Hrushevsky, *Istoria Ukrainy-Rusy*, New York, 1955, Vol. VI, p. 119: "Absence of competition had a bad effect ..."; N. Polonska-Vasylenko, *Istoria Ukrainy*, Munich, 1972, Vol. I, pp. 368-372.

2. Similar exemption of the Lithuanian-*Rus'* gentry from trade restrictions was granted by the Parliament in 1551; then, it was extended in 1553, 1559, 1563, and 1566: *Akty yugo-zapadnoi Rossii*, Vol. III, 1861, pp. 42, 62, 98, 103 and 128.

3. Bishop Piasecki, *Chronica*, published in 1645, p. 454; quoted after Hrushevsky, *op. cit.*, Vol. VI, p. 97.

4. W. Lozinski, *Patrycyat i mieszczanstwo lwowskie*, Lviv, 1892, p. 373: a reference to a case when a small merchant had to defend himself against a serious charge of having dealt in "wealthy merchandise."

5. Ptasnik, *op. cit.*, pp. 286-332, 335; M. Holubets, *Za ukrainskyi Lviv*, Lviv, 1927: a drastic national discrimination: N. Freischyn-Czyrowski, *Geschichtlicher Abriss der staatsrechtlichen Einrichtungen in Galizien*, doctoral dissertation, Graz, 1943, in the form of manuscript, pp. 82-83.

6. Hrushevsky, *op. cit.*, Vol. IV, p. 249, Vol. V, pp. 251-252, Vol. VI, p. 7.

7. *Kniga posolskaia, Metrika Velikavo Kniazhestva Litovskavo*, eds. Obolenskii and

Danilovich, 1843, pp. 26-30; also Michael of Lithuania in his *Memoirs* related about the illegal detours of the commercial caravans and the resulting troubles: Hrushevsky, *op. cit.*, Vol. VI, pp. 9-10.

8. E. Rulikowski, "Dawne drogi i szlaki na prawyn brzegu Dniepru", *Ateneum*, 1878, III-IV; S. Kutrzeba, "Handel Polski ze Wschodem", *Przeglad polski*, Cracow, 1903, Volms. 148-150; Michael of Lithuania mentioned the ancient route to the South, the so-called "Tartar route", and the "Wallachian route."

9. About grain exportation in particular: Kutrzeba, *op. cit.*; the same, "Handel Krakowa w wiekach srednich", *Rozprawy wydzialu historyczno-filozoficznego*, Akademia Umiejentnosci, 1902, Vol. 44; Polonska-Vasylenko, *op.cit.*, Vol. I, pp. 368-373: on the trading in general.

10. A. Szelagowski, *Pieniadz i przewrot cen w XVI i XVII wiekach w Polsce*, Lviv, 1902.

11. *Akta grodzkie i ziemskie*, Vol. V, pp. 319-320, 438-439; Vol. VI, No. 114; also, the report of the Horodok region for 1534-1535, from the *Warszawskie archiwum skarbu koronnego*, notations for the months of June and July: Hrushevsky, op. cit., Vol. VI, pp. 173-177.

12. Lozinski, *op. cit.*, p. 48; exportation of wax; *Akty yuzhnoi i zapadnoi* Rossii, Vol. II, Nos. 92 and 94; Hrushevsky, *loc. cit.*, pp. 171-172.

13. Szalagowski, *op. cit.*, chapters II, VII, and VIII; Hrushevsky, *loc. cit.* pp. 85-86: price comparison of two years, 1580 and 1640:

Item	1580	1640
a stone of pepper	300 pennies	1,000 pennies (groshiv)
a stone of sugar	180 "	600 "
a jar of wine	45 "	150 "
a bushel of wheat	16 "	54 "
a bale of satin material	24 "	72 "

14. *Ibid.*, p. 85.

15. S. Kutrzeba, *Historya ustroju Polski*, Lviv, 1917, Vol. I, *Korona*, pp.159-164 and 210-214; Vol. II, *Litwa*, pp. 187-192; M. Chubaty, *Ohlad istorii ukrainskoho prava*, Munich, 1947, Vol. II, pp. 152-158; Two separate treasuries became an established fact in the seventeenth century, while in 1649, Ukraine, except for her western provinces and eastern steppes, became a sovereign state.

16. Kutrzeba, *op. cit.*, Vol. I, pp. 160-161; Vol. II, pp. 181-185.

17. Ibid., Vol. II, pp. 179-180: The tribute was first called the *Tatarshchyna*, and then, the *Ordynshchyna*, from the term the Horde, or *Orda*.

18. Additional information about the Polish finances, which affected the Ukrainian people at that era: T. Lubomirski, *Trzy rozdzialy z historyi skarbowosci w Polsce, 1507-1532*, Cracow, 1868; O. Balzer, *Historya ustroju Polski*, Przeglad wykladow uniwersteckich, Lviv, 1913: respective periods of the history, on the Polish finances.

PART TWO

The Ukrainian Cossack-Hetman State

CHAPTER EIGHT

THE FORMATION OF THE COSSACK-HETMAN STATE AND ITS POLITICAL FORTUNES

On the eve of the Khmelnytsky Uprising — The National Revolution and the building of the Cossack-Hetman State — Political developments and the Agreement of Pereyaslav — From Khmelnytsky to Mazepa — Hetman Ivan Mazepa and the war for liberation — The Hetman state after Mazepa — The Territory of the Zaporozhe Host — The Haidamaky movement — The Russian political take-over

On the Eve of the Khmelnytsky Uprising. The need to defend Ukraine, particularly her borderlands, against the continuous threat of the Tartar assaults, gave rise to the initiation and growth of the Cossack social-political phenomenon. However, since the notorious Union of Lublin, the Polish domination of Ukraine was getting more and more oppressive and intolerable, diverting the Cossacks' attention away from the struggle against the Mongol threat, and focusing it gradually more and more on the necessity to defend the country against the onslaughts of the Poles, especially the Polish or Polonized noble grandees, the *krolewieta* or "little kings." These grandees acquired enormous *latifundia*, landed estates, with hundreds of villages and townships and tens of thousands of soil-bound serfs, in which they ruled like absolutist monarchs, ignoring the king, the government, and the law and order of the Polish-Lithuanian Commonwealth. They abused their power towards the peasant serfs in a most intolerable way, always, however, with the backing of the Polish government.[1] Hence, the Ukrainian people, the Cossacks, the peasants and the townspeople, identified these aristocratic grandees with the state of Poland and the Polish government, and began their struggle against Polish national and religious oppression. In this way, the second era in the Cossack wars began, which followed the first period of the struggle against the "wild fields" and the bloody and recurring Tartar onslaughts. This did not mean that after the Cossacks had assumed their warfares against Poland in defense of the rights of the Ukrainian people, the fighting against the Tartars was abandoned; on the contrary, the Cossack excursions on land and sea against the Mongols continued in the seventeenth century in spite of the prolonged Polish wars. The era of the Cossack wars against Poland for the liberation of Ukraine from foreign domination lasted over one hundred and fifty years, from the end of the sixteenth to the last quarter of the eighteenth century.

The first insurgent wave erupted in Ukraine in 1591, when Krystofor Kosynsky, a leading personality among the registered Cossacks, was antagonized by a grandee, Janusz Ostrozhsky, and started a Cossack uprising to oppose the injustices of the nobility in Ukraine. Soon the peasant masses in the Kievan, Volhinian and Podillian regions joined Kosynsky, and the uprising assumed large proportions. The Polish forces, however, defeated the insurgents near the town of Chudniv, in 1593. Krystofor Kosynsky was himself killed not long after the battle.

The second uprising was associated with the names of two famous Cossack leaders, Severyn Nalyvaiko and Hryhorii Loboda. The two Cossack *otamans* acquired fame by their military exploits in Moldavia in 1594-1595 as the allies of the German emperor. They defeated the Moldavian *hospodar*, or prince, and forced him to join the German alliance. Upon their return from the above expedition, they were caught up in a conflict between the townspeople of the Bratslav region, and *Starosta* Strus and the royal officials of this region. A spontaneous uprising of the Cossacks, townspeople and villagers of the region erupted, and it rapidly spread to the Bar region. Fighting continued until 1596. The uprising covered ever wider and wider Ukrainian areas and extended even into the Byeloruthenian districts of Sluch and Mohyliv. The insurgents were anti-Polish and anti-Catholic and thus the bloodshed was considerable. The Polish and Polonized nobility and gentry began to panic since they were too weak to stop the tidal wave of popular fury. In the Battle of Hostryi Kamin, the Polish armed forces were badly beaten by Nalyvaiko and Loboda. Nevertheless, the Cossack insurgents also suffered heavy losses and retreated over the Dnieper River to Left-bank Ukraine, expecting support from the villagers of the Poltava region. Meanwhile, however, the Polish forces under the command of Hetman Zolkiewski, caught up with the slowly-moving Ukrainian army, accompanied by households, women and children,

Metropolitan Petro Mohyla
(1632-1647)

Hetman Ivan Samoilovych
(1672-1687)

Hetman Petro Doroshenko
(1665-1676)

Hetman Bohdan Khmelnytsky
(1648-1657)

Hetman Ivan Mazepa
(1687-1709)

Hetman Kyrylo Rozumovsky
(1750-1764)

and defeated them very badly at the Battle of Solonytsia. Zolkiewski's revenge was awfully bloody. *Otaman* Loboda was killed, while *otaman* Nalyvaiko was captured by the Poles, brought to Warsaw and murdered by them amidst inhuman tortures.[2]

The defeat at Solonytsia was so resounding, that the Cossacks and other classes of the Ukrainian people remained discouraged and passive for a while, but under the surface, social-political ferment was brewing and getting stronger. The Polish government and the upper noble stratum were blinded and did not see the writing on the wall. The Polish Parliament, the *seim*, in 1597, proclaimed all Cossacks to be "the enemies of the *Rzeczpospolita*," of the Commonwealth, and ordered their extermination.[3] This only added pressure to the dormant volcano.

Two trends were evolving among the Cossacks in Ukraine at this time: the radical one, which was ready to start another violent encounter with the Polish oppressor, and the moderate one, one of appeasement with the strong opponent to prevent bloodshed and to acquire some rights by cooperation and negotiation. Under the leadership of Hetman Samiilo Kishka, 1600-1602, a partial truce prevailed, and the Polish government tempered its hostility towards the Cossacks, while the latter assumed their traditional warfares against the Tartars and led their military excursions to Moldavia and Livonia.

Meanwhile, the Muscovite "Time of Troubles," the *smutnoie vremia*, developed. The last Tsar of the Ruryk house, Fiodor, died in 1598, and the struggle for power and succession continued until 1613, occuring among Boris Godunov, Dimitrii, the First Pretender, Vasilii Shuiskii and the Second Pretender also called Dimitrii. This conflict was also accompanied by numerous uprisings and rebellions of a few more pretenders to the throne, the large-scale rebellion of the serfs and borderland Cossacks, led by Ivan Bolotnikov, and the threatening Polish intervention in Muscovite affairs, including a questionable alliance with the Swedes. At first, the Poles only interfered by supporting the Pretenders, but at the second stage of the *smutnoie vremia*, they raised their own pretensions to the Muscovite throne. Initially, Prince Wladyslaw of Poland was a candidate for that throne, then Sigismund, the Polish king, himself became a candidate, and as an ardent Roman Catholic he was absolutely unacceptable to the Orthodox Muscovites. Sigismund, being unreasonable, spoiled the chances of Wladyslaw, his son, being elected as Tsar. Finally, a national reaction of the Muscovites developed, the Poles were defeated, and in 1613, Mikhail Romanov became the new Tsar. Later on, Wladyslaw was forced to give up his pretension to the said throne.[4]

The Ukrainian Cossacks, appeased by the conciliatory Polish attitude, participated in almost all Muscovite exploits of the Polish government, giving full expression to their anti-Muscovite sentiments, meanwhile also intensifying their war activities against their archenemy, the Turks and their Ottoman Empire. In 1606, they captured the Turkish naval fortress in Bulgaria, the city of Varna; in 1614, they ruined Sinope and Trapesunt, the important Turkish naval bases on the southern shores of the Black Sea; in 1615, having completely routed the Turkish navy at the mouth of the Danube River, the Cossacks threatened the capital of the Ottoman Empire, the city of Istanbul (Constantinople); in 1616, they captured the city of Kaffa, the main slave market in the Crimean Peninsula. The leader and hero of these Cossack war exploits in the Black Sea area was Petro Konashevych-Sahaidachny, Hetman of the Zaporozhe Host. The Cossacks were again growing in power and becoming more and more independent in their actions, by taking advantage of Polish political difficulties. At this time the Polish officials complained that the Cossack element had become absolutely uncontrollable.

Petro Konashevych-Sahaidachny was an outstanding Cossack leader; he was well educated in the Ostroh Academy and of exceptional organizational and administrative abilities. Upon his arrival in the *Sitch*, Sahaidachny quickly climbed up the military hierarchic ladder to the top and was elected the Hetman of the Zaporozhe Cossack Host in 1616. He continued in that post for six years. As the top commander of the *Sitch*, the *Koshovyi*, he reorganized the loose Cossack detachments into a well disciplined, regular armed force, which was then able to take Varna, Sinope, Trapesunt, and directly threaten the capital of Istanbul, although the Polish government attempted to limit his anti-Turk warfares.

The Polish government was not successful with its measures against the Cossacks, as long as it was involved in the Muscovite skirmishes. Sahaidachny and his Cossack army of twenty thousand men delivered the Polish prince and pretender for the Muscovite crown from bad predicaments in 1618 and enabled the Poles to negotiate a favorable peace treaty at Duelino. Then, the Polish government pressed on limiting the number of registered Cossacks and on ceasing the war expeditions on the Black Sea. The Host was unhappy with the outcome of Sahaidachny's pro-Polish policies, and the Hetman was ousted and Yatsko Nerodych-Borodavka was elected to the office. Borodavka as a Hetman, did not distinguish himself by anything, while Sahaidachny's prestige and influence still prevailed in Ukraine, chiefly because of his ardent defense of the interests of the Orthodox Church and his very tactful and balanced approach to the solution of many political problems. He still remained of pro-Polish political orientation, considering the Cossack Host too weak to fight against the Polish-Lithuanian Commonwealth chiefly because he wanted to prevent unnecessary bloodshed and destruction.

When in 1620 Poland got involved in a war with the Ottoman Empire and was badly beaten in the Battle of Cecora, the king again asked the Cossacks for military assistance. Sahaidachny was again elected Hetman. As the only condition of Cossack participation in the Turkish war, Hetman Sahaidachny demanded a full and official recognition by the Polish Crown of the newly recreated organizational structure of the Orthodox Church in the Commonwealth, which suffered badly after the Union of Berest. The king agreed, although later on he never fulfilled his promise. Nevertheless, Sahaidachny and his Cossack armed forces completely routed the Turks and saved Poland in the Battle of Khotyn. However, the Hetman was wounded during the battle and soon died.[5]

Sahaidachny's era, though short, had immense significance for the political development of Ukraine. The national and political consciousness of the Cossacks was well established. The organizational and military power of the Host increased. The politically rational thinking of the Cossack leadership replaced the simple emotionalism and rebellious spirit of a once immature and heterogeneous entity. In the minds of the leading circles of Ukrainian society, the idea of a political linkage in which the Kievan princely era and the heroic wars of the Cossack Host were two periods in the development of one nation was established. Hence, in 1628, Betlen Gabor, prince of Transylvania, pointed out to Strassburger, a Swedish envoy, that the Cossacks might some day destroy Poland and create their own Commonwealth.[6]

Sahaidachny's immediate successors, Hetmans Olifer Holub and Mykhailo Doroshenko, followed his trend of political thinking and wanted to improve the political and social situation in Ukraine by cooperation and negotiation with the Polish government. Yet, the Polish government acted in the most irrational and mandacious way. Promises given to Sahaidachny were not fulfilled. Radical and warlike moods were on the rise, while the Cossack war expeditions against the Ottoman Empire continued to the great distress of Warsaw. In the late 1620's, the Cossacks in Ukraine acted as if they inhabited an independent country and largely ignored the king, the Polish *seim* and administration. Meanwhile a confrontation between the Poles and the Ukrainians took place. The Polish forces were beaten in the Battles of Kryliv and Krukiv Lake by Hetman Marko Zhmailo, in 1625. The treaty signed between the two sides was a compromise. It granted more liberties to the Cossacks but did not meet all the demands of the radical faction, and thus a new trouble was in the making.

Since the registered Cossacks were more inclined to cooperate with the Polish government, and the Zaporozhe Sitch Host was more radical in its attitude toward the Poles, a conflict developed between these two camps. In 1630, Hetman Taras Triasylo of the Zaporozhe Cossacks, undertook a punitive expedition against the registered ones, who were aided by Polish armed forces under the leadership of Stanislaw Koniecpolski, an archenemy of the Ukrainians in general. Triasylo badly defeated the Poles in the Battle of Pereyaslav. Cossack liberties were again slightly extended. The number of the registered Cossacks was increased, however, only to 8,000 men, while others were either required to accept the domination of the Polish grandees or to join the Host beyond the cataracts.

The Thirty-Year's War considerably boosted the prestige and the feeling of self-assurance of the Cossack Host, since the Cossacks were requested by each fighting side to participate in this European conflict. Then, the death of the arch-Catholic king, Sigismund, and the election *seim* of 1632, preceded by an alliance between the Orthodox and the Protestants, granted greater freedoms to the Orthodox Ukrainians in the Commonwealth. In addition, the coronation *seim* fully legalized the reestablished organization of the Orthodox Church, so ardently demanded by Petro Konashevych-Sahaidachny. The election of Wladyslaw, an old friend of the Cossacks, whom they had helped in his Muscovite and Swedish escapades, as the new king of Poland, greatly boosted the Cossack morale, along with these other new developments.

No wonder that when the Polish government established a fortress in Kodak on the Dnieper River to prevent the flight of the Ukrainians to the *Sitch*, Hetman Ivan Sulyma immediately attacked and destroyed it. Sulyma, under the threat of a bloody Polish revenge, was delivered to the Poles in expectation of some concessions. The Poles executed Sulyma and failed to meet the Cossack demands. A gathering storm was gaining in strength. The radicals were gaining an upper-hand in Ukrainian politics. The uprising of Pavlo But-Pavluk began with tremendous initial success. The registered Cossacks joined the uprising, which speedily spread on to the left and right banks of the Dnieper River. The peasantry spontaneously arose, exterminating Polish gentry and any vestige of Polish authority. Pavluk negotiated with Muscovy and the Crimean Tartars to receive their assistance for the anti-Polish uprising. Yet, he did not act fast enough.

Meanwhile, the Polish forces under the command of Mikolaj Potocki arrived in Ukraine and completely routed the Cossack army at the Battle of

Kumeiky. While Pavluk escaped, the Poles mercilessly massacred all sick and wounded and demanded the extradition of Pavluk, Dmytro Hunia and other Cossack leaders, having promised their safety. Pavluk was delivered to Potocki and executed, while Hunia escaped to the *Sitch*. The Poles pacified the country bloodily, by executing the insurgents and burning villages. Illa Karaimovych, an appointed Hetman by the Poles, could not dominate the situation. Hunia, Skydan and other radical leaders gathered in the Sitch, and in the spring of 1638 a new uprising was started under the leadership of Yatsko Ostrianyn. The uprising was initially successful; the Poles were defeated at the Battle of Holtva. But, later, on at the Battle of Lubni, Ostrianyn was beaten, and not being able to avenge himself, he left Left-bank Ukraine and went with his Cossacks and their families to *Slobidska* Ukraine, the new eastern borderland, to settle there permanently under nominal Muscovite authority. Dmytro Hunia retreated beyond the Dnieper falls, and from there he negotiated unfavorable terms of peace with the Polish government. The Polish leading circles erroneously believed that the Cossack question was finally solved and that a "golden peace" would prevail for them.[7]

The National Revolution and the Building of the Cossack-Hetman State. The National Revolution was started, carried out and accomplished, and the national Ukrainian Cossack-Hetman state was built and organized by a genius strategist, Hetman Bohdan Khmelnytsky. Khmelnytsky's name first appeared on official papers as that of a military secretary of the Cossacks in connection with the developments after Pavluk's uprising and its unhappy outcome. After Hunia's compromise with the Poles, Khmelnytsky, as a loyal subject of the Crown, then became the *sotnyk*, centurion of the Chyhyryn district. Like Sahaidachny, he was poor, yet gentry in origin. Khmelnytsky probably participated in the Cossack expedition to France in 1645-46, since he was mentioned as an able military man in a letter of the French envoy to Cardinal Mazarin.

For a long time Khmelnytsky was a moderate of pro-Polish political orientation. He participated in a Cossack mission to Warsaw to discuss with King Wladyslaw the plans of an anti-Turk coalition and war. Apparently then, after the Cossacks complained of the excesses of the Polish grandees in Ukraine, the King said that they had sabres and could afford to defend their rights. Since the king himself had many of his own problems with the arrogant and pompous nobility, the Cossacks began to think of the king as their ally in the struggle against the *krolewieta*, and felt encouraged in their opposition to the lawless rule of the Polish nobles in Ukraine. In 1647,

Khmelnytsky was still a loyal citizen, and generally respected by the Ukrainians and Poles until he was struck by a personal tragedy.

Khmelnytsky was hated by the Polish grandee family of Koniecpolski. The Koniecpolski's plotted with Czaplinski, their aid, to ruin Khmelnytsky and his popularity. Czaplinski suddenly attacked Khmelnytsky's manor and dwellings, the *khutir*, in Subotiv during the latter's absence. He destroyed it, killed his son and kidnapped his wife. The legal proceedings, because of Polish lawlessness, not only did not help Khmelnytsky, but Koniecpolski ordered his arrest and execution. Only with the assistance of his friend, Colonel Mykhailo Krychevsky, did Khmelnytsky escape from prison and take refuge at the *Sitch*.⁸

This personal tragedy and experience with "Polish justice" finally convinced Bohdan Khmelnytsky that there was no room for any more dealings and negotiations with the Poles and that the Ukrainians had to, once more, take matters into their own hands. He himself turned from a pro-Polish moderate to a radical revolutionary fighting for the national cause. He was soon elected by the Zaporozhe Cossacks in the *Sitch* as their hetman and began to ready a large-scale uprising against the Polish oppression. The garrison of the registered Cossacks in the *Sitch* soon joined his cause. Secret messengers were sent throughout Ukraine to prepare the masses of population for the coming developments; an agreement was negotiated with the Tartars to militarily assist in Khmelnytsky's uprising. The Tartars came under the command of Tuhai-bei.

The military operations of the insurgents began in the early spring of 1648. The Polish government having received the news, was undertaking precautionary measures, but did not take the uprising too seriously. Young regimentarian, Stephan Potocki, did not have proper military experience, and was followed up by the main body of the Polish armed forces under the command of Mikolaj Potocki, his father, and Marcin Kalinowski, the hetmans of the Polish Crown. The registered Cossacks, who moved on boats down the Dnieper River to join the main Polish forces, suddenly arose against the Poles, killed all officers that were still loyal to Poland, and under the leadership of Colonel Mykhailo Krychevsky associated themselves with the uprising and the National Rovolution. It was a bad omen for the Poles. Near Zhovti Vody, Khmelnytsky attacked Stephan Potocki's detachments and, joined by additional registered Cossack troops, completely routed the Poles. Potocki himself was wounded, taken prisoner of war, and died shortly afterwards.

Two Polish hetmans, Mikolaj Potocki and Kalinowski, after having received the sad news, began a retreat, but Khmelnytsky caught up with them and again fully defeated them in the Battle of Korsun on the 26th of May. Both hetmans were taken prisoners of war by the Tartars; the Polish military force became nonexistent. Khmelnytsky continued his march westward.

Meanwhile all Ukraine was erupting in a magnificent, all-encompassing and spontaneous revolutionary uprising. The Polish noblemen were on the run; their palaces and manors were burning; the old Polish socio-political structure was completely collapsing. All Poland was in a panic; meanwhile, King Wladyslaw, the only friend of the Cossacks who might have pacified the situation, died. The hetmans, the top military commanders were gone; the army was gone; all Ukraine, a wealthy country which enriched the Polish nobility, went out of Polish control and became a free land. The roof was falling in upon Poland and the earlier prognosis of some foreigners was being fulfilled. Ukraine was becoming a Commonwealth of her own.

One of the classic developments of that revolutionary time was the hasty retreat from Ukraine of Prince Yarema Vyshnyvetsky, a Polonized renegade of one of the ancient Ukrainian noble families. One of his ancestors, Prince Dmytro Baida-Vyshnyvetsky, was the founder of the Zaporozhe Sitch. Yarema, however, after having established himself Left-bank Ukraine as one of the most potent noble grandees, turned into one of the major exploiters, torturers and haters of the Ukrainian Cossacks and common people, who knew no mercy but only contempt for his own blood, nationality and the Orthodox Church. He was cruel and inhuman in dealing with Ukrainians as long as he was in power. The revolutionary tide immediately turned against individuals like him. Hence, he was forced to leave Ukraine hastily, yet he was followed by Colonel Maksym Kryvonis, the leader of the common folk. Finally, Kryvonis caught up with Yarema near Starokonstantyniv, near the borders of Western Ukraine and beat him soundly. The Prince barely escaped alive.

Meanwhile, Poland readied the election of a new king. But, in order to oppose the victorious march of Khmelnytsky's armies, three new military leaders of highly limited abilities were chosen: Dominik Zaslawski, Mikolaj Ostrorog and Aleksander Koniecpolski; one too old, the other too young, and the third, a scholar rather than a military man. Seventy thousand mercenaries were to be hired to defend Poland against the Cossack onslaught. All that did not spell success for Poland in future encounters with Khmelnytsky.

Without yet knowing that the friendly king Wladyslaw had died, Khmelnytsky stopped his main forces at the city of Bila Tserkva, and from there he sent his demands to Warsaw: to raise the number of the registered Cossacks to 12,000 men; to return to the Orthodox their church buildings; and to pay the Cossacks wages in default for five years. These moderate demands were accepted by the Polish *seim*. At that time Bohdan Khmelnytsky was not aware that his grand scheme had started the construction of a new Ukrainian state. He thought he was not fighting with the king or the Polish-Lithuanian Commonwealth, the *Rzeczpospolita*; he thought he was getting even with the arrogant and cruel Polish aristocracy, the *krolewieta*. He was even a little afraid of the huge revolutionary tide, which included the masses of peasants and commoners. He was a gentry man at heart and believed in class distinctions. Around him the outstanding nobles of Ukrainian descent and the upper crest of the Cossack class continued to assemble, having gradually built the very foundation of a well educated and experienced administrative staff of the central and provincial government machine, with men like Ivan Vyhovsky, Stanyslav Mrozovytsky-Morozenko, Ivan and Danylo Nechai, Ivan Bohun, Mykhailo Krychevsky, and top Cossack military men, such as Dzhedzhalii, Burlii, Nesterenko and others.

The threatening growth of the revolutionary tide of peasants and other common people and the drastic terror of the Polish nobility urged Khmelnytsky to resume his war operations. It dawned on him, perhaps already, that the struggle he started was not in defense of the Cossack rights only, but a large-scale National Revolution for the liberation of the Ukrainian nation. His civilian and ecclesiastic advisors might have suggested just this to him. The Cossack armed forces, the Tartars and peasant insurgents were approximately of the same combat power as that of the Poles, when they met near Pylavtsi, on the Volhinian-Podillian border. The peasant insurgents were poorly armed and poorly disciplined, while the Polish striking force was greatly weakened by its enormous supplies. Khmelnytsky attacked the Polish military camp, causing an immediate panic. The incompetent Polish commanders could not control the situation. The Polish army was beaten and annihilated. The remnants hastily retreated, followed immediately by Khmelnytsky's forces, which occupied the towns of Zbarazh, Vyshnyvets, Brody, and speedily approached the capital of West Ukraine, the city of Lviv. The Hetman did not want to destroy the capital, and after accepting 200,000 red guldens ransom, he proceeded with his huge armed forces toward Warsaw, where the election of the new king was supposed to take place. He wanted to influence the election in such a way as to have a new king elected who would be favorably inclined towards the Ukrainian-Cossack cause. He sent word to Warsaw, indicating that the Ukrainians would prefer

Jan-Casimir, the brother of the deceased King Wladyslaw, to be on the Polish throne.

In leading his huge armed forces across West Ukraine, Khmelnytsky inspired spontaneous and massive uprisings of the Ukrainian population all over Galicia and Volhinia against the Polish oppressors. As in all other parts of Ukraine, this was aimed against the nobility, the Catholics and the Uniats. The nobles and other representatives of Polish rule were killed and their properties pillaged, destroyed or burned.

Since it was late autumn and because he was approaching unfriendly Polish ethnic territory, Khmelnytsky stopped at the city of Zamost, awaiting the results of the election. Jan-Casimir was elected king, and immediately confirmed all Cossack demands. Colonel Sulian Muzhylovsky asserted that prior to his election, Jan-Casimir promised Bohdan Khmelnytsky to agree to his becoming "a king of Rus' " and that the Cossacks "should retain whatever their sabres got for them."[9]

The first phase of the National Revolution was over. Khmelnytsky trusted the new king and began his retreat. On Christmas day 1649, he triumphantly entered Kiev, the ancient capital of Ukraine-Rus', greeted by all the strata of the Ukrainian society as a new ruler of Ukraine, as a Moses who delivered his people from the oppressive hands of foreign tyranny. The uprising, the magnificent victories at Zhovti Vody, Korsun and Pylavtsi, the triumphant entrance into Kiev, were the most glorious days of modern Ukraine, reminiscent of the victories of Prince Sviatoslav, and the "golden age" of Volodymyr the Great and Yaroslav the Wise several centuries beforehand. Polonska-Vasylenko rightly asserted that Khmelnytsky's stay in Kiev was a very important time during the revolutionary war. In Kiev, as a result of numerous debates with the Ukrainian intellectual elite, civilian as well as ecclesiastic, Khmelnytsky's political ideology was formed. From that time on, he no longer fought for the class rights of one social stratum but for the liberation of the entire nation. When in February 1649 he received Polish envoys in Pereyaslav, he did not address them as a chieftain of insurgents, but as the sovereign of the state of Ukraine. He outlined to these envoys his plan to build a huge Ukrainian nation on the whole Ukrainian ethnographic territory, including the cities of Lviv, Halych and Kholm, and warned the Polish government not to hinder him in any way in the realization of his plan.[10] Among the envoys, there was Adam Kysil, a senator and a Ukrainian patriot, who, however, still represented the pro-Polish faction in Ukrainian politics, because he still thought that Poland was still too strong and that the whole war might end in a *fiasco*.

It soon became apparent that neither the king nor the Polish nobility intended to keep the promises given to Khmelnytsky. The Poles marshalled a huge army of 200,000 men and in the summer of 1649 moved it against Ukraine. At the same time the uncertainty of the situation only intensified the insurrections and warlike motions throughout Ukraine. Khmelnytsky ordered his armed forces to march westward and soon he beleaguered a large Polish garrison in Zbarazh, after besieging it for a month and a half. The Lithuanian army, under the command of Prince Radziwil, was also approaching from the north to aid the king and the Poles. Colonel Krychevsky defeated Radziwil at Loyevo, but was killed in the battle.

Meanwhile the king led the main Polish military force to free the Polish units, besieged Zbarazh, and eventually tried to defeat Khmelnytsky. However, Khmelnytsky, by means of a skillful maneuver almost captured Jan-Casimir. The Polish army would have been annihilated, except for the Tartars who were bribed by the Polish chancellor, Ossolinski, to force Khmelnytsky to negotiate a peace. Otherwise, the Tartars threatened to ally themselves with Jan-Casimir.

On August 18, 1649, the Peace Treaty of Zboriv was signed between the Polish and the new Ukrainian governments, according to which the Kievan, Bratslav and Chernihiv regions, and parts of Volhinia and Podillia formed an autonomous Ukrainian-Cossack state, ruled by a Hetman, with 40,000 registered Cossack armed forces. The peasantry was supposed to return to its villages and resume its servitude under bondage. The Orthodox Church acquired an equal position with that of the Roman Catholic Church in Poland. The act of the Union of Berest was annulled and invalidated. The Jesuit schools were closed. Polish noblemen were allowed to return to their estates. Thus, Ukraine actually remained in the framework of the Polish-Lithuanian Commonwealth. The so-called Treaty of Zboriv was certainly a minimum achievement for Khmelnytsky, which did not make the Ukrainians happy. Instead of creating an independent and sovereign nation, the Treaty was expressed as a "Declaration of royal good-will towards the Cossacks," and granted only autonomy for the Cossack class. The peasants became outraged and opposed the paragraph on bondage, and upon being called to return to serfdom, they started an uprising against Khmelnytsky. The Polish government, on the other hand, did not live up to its promises, since discrimination against the Orthodox Church continued.

A new war between Ukraine and Poland was inevitable. Khmelnytsky looked for allies and approached Moscow again, having been persuaded to do so by the Patriarch of Jerusalem, Passii, already before the Treaty of Zboriv.

Yet, Moscow was reluctant to ally herself with Ukraine against Poland, although a war which weakened Poland would have brought considerable territorial advantages for the Muscovites. The negotiations with the Ottoman Empire and the Tartars continued. Then, in order to strengthen his international position, Khmelnytsky resumed the Moldavian project, in which Nalyvaiko and other hetmans were once involved. He compelled Vasyl Lupul, the Moldavian *hospodar*, or prince, to agree to the marriage of Khmelnystky's son, Tymish, and Lupul's daughter, Roxanda. Subsequently, a treaty alliance between Ukraine and Moldavia was concluded. By the end of 1650, a treaty was finalized with the Sultan of the Ottoman Empire and the military assistance of the Tartars for Ukraine, in her renewed struggle with Poland, was assured. Khmelnytsky, like a soverign monarch, maintained diplomatic relations and negotiations with foreign powers. The Poles did not like it at all.

On the domestic front, the Hetman proceeded with the organization of his state. The governing authority rested with the Cossack class; the whole country was divided into sixteen colonelcies or regions, administered by the Cossack colonels. Khmelnytsky's government also assumed the entire fiscal authority.

Political Developments and the Agreement of Pereyaslav. Having no intention of respecting Ukrainian autonomy, the Poles began war operations in the spring of 1651. In the Battle of Krasne, Danylo Nechai, an outstanding military man and Khmelnytsky's close associate, was killed. In the late June of 1651 the main Polish and Ukrainian forces met near the township of Berestechko, in the marshy region of Volhinia. Khmelnytsky's army, together with the Tartars, was about 150,000 men; the Polish one, about 160,000. The Tartars, probably bribed by the Polish government, began to retreat hastily at the very start of the battle. While Khmelnytsky and Vyhovsky went to bring more troops, Colonel Ivan Bohun took command and tried to save the Cossack and peasant insurgent forces under heavy Polish attacks among the marshes. An unexpected panic among the insurgents brought a catastrophe. The Ukrainians were forced to retreat, having suffered grave losses. In August, Radziwil, the Lithuanian *hetman*, chief military commander, captured Chernihiv and Kiev. However, Khmelnytsky, having gathered new troops, stopped the Polish advances at Bila Tserkva, and there a new peace treaty was signed, but much more unfavorable than that of Zboriv. The territory of the Ukrainian autonomous state was substantially reduced and Ukraine's military force was lowered to only 20,000 men. New military encounters were again in sight.

The Hetman renewed his negotiations with Moscow, Moldavia, Crimea and the Turks. Lupul of Moldavia was unfaithful, hence Khmelnytsky sent Tymish, his son, with a considerable military force to persuade the prince to meet the points of the previous agreement. Near the township of Batih, Tymish encountered a Polish army of 20,000 men under the command of Hetman Kalinowski, and defeated it. Kalinowski himself was killed. The Battle of Berestechko was revenged. Tymish then invaded Moldavia and married Roxanda Lupul, but in 1653 he lost his life during the siege of the city of Suchava, taken by Mathew Basarab, prince of Wallachia. It was an unfortunate blow for Bohdan Khmelnytsky, since the event meant the failure of his Moldavian policy, and was also related to his plans of a hereditary monarchy for Ukraine.

At the end of 1653, the Cossacks beleaguered a considerable Polish force in Zhvanets, together with King Jan-Casimir. The Poles were about to surrender, when in the last minute they persuaded the Tartars to conclude a separate treaty. That separate agreement was fatal for Ukrainians, because the Poles granted to the Tartars the right to plunder and to take slaves in the southern parts of Ukraine.

The overall plight of Ukraine was difficult at this time. In addition to the Tartar raids, droughts, plagues, poor crops, military mobilization of manpower and its removal from the fields, war destruction totally impoverished the population, while the prospects of new wars only aggravated the situation. This forced Khmelnytsky to renew his attempts to get Muscovy as an ally.

On the other hand, Moscow badly wanted to strengthen her position in the Black Sea basin. She did not want either Poland or the Ottoman Empire to be permanently established there, but she did not desire any other power, such as a newly established Ukrainian-Cossack State, to have political hegemony or predominance either. Hence, Moscow hesitated with the alliance with Khmelnytsky. She did not want a strong ally in the basin. Kluchevskii characterized Moscow's policy in this respect very well, by asserting the following: Moscow "observed with quiet interest for six years how Khmelnytsky's cause, damaged by the Tartars at Zboriv and Berestechko, was nearing a downfall; how Ukraine was being devastated by the Tartar ally and the terrible internal war; and then, after Ukraine was completely ruined, she was graciously accepted under Moscow's protection."[1]Then, Hrushevsky commented: "The entire course of East European history would have taken a completely different direction if Ukraine had allied herself with Moscow at the very beginnings of her struggle against Poland, having been then still powerful... ."[12] Thus, in 1649, it was definitely not in the Muscovite interest to be allied with Ukraine, as far as Moscow's imperialist plans were concerned.

After prolonged negotiations, the Muscovite Landed Council, the *zemskii sobor*, finally resolved to "accept Ukraine under the Tsar's protection," and a delegation was immediately dispatched to Ukraine. It was headed by *boyar* Basyl Buturlin and accompanied by many civilian and ecclesiastic dignitaries. Khmelnytsky was apparently suspicious from the very beginning. Although the Muscovites wanted to conclude the negotiations in Kiev, the ancient capital, Khmelnytsky refused and brought the delegation to Pereyaslav. He received the delegates coldly; the negotiations were conducted dryly; there were no celebrations, no formal dinners or banquets; Khmelnytsky never invited the Muscovites to his residence. The Muscovites demanded that Khmelnytsky and other top Cossacks take an oath of allegiance to the Tsar; the Cossack leadership demanded that the Muscovite delegates take an oath of allegiance in the name of the Tsar. Buturlin refused. The talks dragged on. Finally, Buturlin twice solemnly promised, that the Tsar "would honor all rights of Ukraine," and assured that the Tsar would not change his word.

On the Ukrainian side not everyone was willing to take an oath of allegiance to the Tsar. Colonel Ivan Bohun, Metropolitan Sylvester Kossiv, and some others were among the prominent opponents to the so-called Agreement of Pereyaslav. Many townspeople refused to take the oath, too. The Agreement was offically concluded in January of 1654, having been approved by the *rada starshyn*, the Council of Seniors, and at a meeting of the people of Pereyaslav. Subsequently, the Muscovite delegation attempted to travel throughout Ukraine to bring as many people as possible to take the oath of allegiance. However, the matter proved to be very difficult to carry out. Metropolitan Kossiv, Colonel Ivan Bohun and other colonels and local administrators not only refused to take it, but they even prohibited the people under their authority to do likewise. In March of the same year a Ukrainian delegation left for Moscow with all kinds of documentation to affirm the Agreement. Though the Muscovites demanded that Khmelnytsky himself go to their capital to pay homage to the Tsar, the Hetman refused to comply.

Since the original text of the Pereyaslav Agreement was lost, perhaps even suppressed purposely by St. Petersburg later on, and the only documents that were preserved were Buturlin's personal report to the throne, which as a subjective paper could not be trusted, and later "documents," were subject to official Muscovite forgery, the true contents of the Agreement may be somewhat reconstructed only on the basis of later developments and statements. It seemed, first of all, that the Agreement established a military alliance between Ukraine and Muscovy. Secondly, the Tsar guaranteed his protection to Ukraine. Thirdly, a guarantee was given by the Tsar to fully respect all sovereign rights and liberties of the Ukrainian-Cossack state. Fourthly, small Muscovite military detachments would be stationed in Kiev to manifest the Ukrainian-Muscovite political alliance and the complete severance of any political dependence of Ukraine upon the Polish Crown. Fifthly, it was an international treaty between two nations which preserved the internal and external political sovereignty of the Cossack state. Sixthly, some limitations were introduced with respect to the diplomatic relations of Ukraine with Poland and the Ottoman Empire, of which Moscow was particularly afraid.[13]

The language of later historical source materials which referred to the Pereyaslav Agreement was not always clear cut, giving rise to all kinds of interpretations as far as the nature and real meaning of the Agreement was concerned. The whole debate has definitely been blown out of proportion, because immediately after Khmelnytsky's death a break came between Ukraine and Muscovy, a war followed, and the Agreement of Hadiach with Poland completely abrogated the Treaty of Pereyaslav. It was Muscovy which insisted on the reenactment of Pereyaslav, and forced a new agreement upon Ukraine in 1659 under the Hetmanate of Yurii Khmelnytsky, again in Pereyaslav. This agreement was supposedly the "original" *Statutes of Bohdan Khmelnytsky*, an arrogant forgery of the original act, substantially limiting the sovereign rights and liberties of Ukraine and subjecting her to the increased political interference and domination of Muscovy. Yurii Khmelnytsky did not see nor have any conception of the original document of the Pereyaslav Treaty of 1654. The said forgery was then submitted to all later hetmans for their signatures and obedience. The forgery was introduced in the *Polnoie Sobranie Zakonov Rossiiskoi Imperii, The Complete Collection of the Laws of the Russian Empire*, and became the legal justification of Russian-Muscovite imperialism in Ukraine and its unquestionable authorization for future references.[14]

The Russian interpretation of the original Agreement of Pereyaslav was as a voluntary submission of Ukraine to the sovereignty of the Muscovite Tsar, the resignation of her own sovereignty, the establishment of a Muscovite protectorate over Ukraine, and with the belief that taking an oath of allegiance by the Ukrainians to the Tsar was the visible sign of that political submission. Some held the Agreement for a personal union. Still others held it for either a real union, protectorate or vassalage. Most of the Ukrainian historians considered the Agreement to be a military alliance of an international nature or a pseudo-protectorate. Thus, M. Diakonov, V. Kluchevskii, O. Popov, V. Sergeievich, M. Hrushevsky, V. Lypynsky, O. Ohloblyn, A. Yakovliv, L. Okinshevych, D. Doroshenko were all attempting to acquire a correct perspective of the notorious Treaty of Pereyaslav.[15]

Doubtlessly, the Muscovite government held that the agreement was a temporary arrangement only, and binding on Bohdan Khmelnytsky only. Consequently, with every new hetman, they insisted upon a solemn renewal of the Treaty, which was forged and made more favorable for Muscovite political plans and interests by text and contents, every time.

Contemporary Ukrainians, according to their assertions and statements, held the Treaty of Pereyaslav of 1654 for a political and military alliance, which by no means limited the sovereignty of the Ukrainian nation. Bohdan Khmelnytsky himself stated to a Polish envoy in 1655, that he already "became the lord of all Rus' and would not submit her to anybody." Carl-Gustav, king of Sweden, also asserted the continuing sovereignty of the Ukrainian-Cossack state. The French government held the Agreement for only a temporary arrangement to assist Ukraine in the war with Poland, while Hryhor Orlyk, a Ukrainian statesman in France from the early eighteenth century, wrote the following: "Khmelnytsky accepted the protection of the Muscovite Tsar for his land and nation with all the rights of a sovereign nation. Yet, the perfidy of the Muscovite Tsar was the very cause that immediately after Khmelnytsky's death the rights of the Cossack nation began to be disturbed by the Muscovites."[16]

Hetman Bohdan Khmelnytsky reigned after the Pereyaslav Agreement as a sovereign monarch and by his moves did not ever indicate his dependence upon the Tsar as his sovereign. The terminology of his letters to the Muscovite government was vague at this point, but the terminology of his relations with other governments was very clear. He called himself "Hetman by the grace of God," "Supreme ruler," or *"Clementia divina Generalis Dux Exercitum Zaporoviensi"* and to Muscovite envoys he pointed out that, "as the Tsar in his land, so the Hetman in his, is the prince and king." But, friction between the two governments developed right away. Moscow dominated certain parts of Byeloruthenia, which gravitated to Ukraine. Then, the Ukrainian-Muscovite alliance induced an alliance between the Poles and the Crimean Tartars and their invasion of Ukraine, attempting to turn all of Ukraine into a desert. The battle of Dryzhypole in January of 1655 was extremely bloody, but it did not bring any decisive victory to either side, Ukrainian or Polish. Meanwhile, Khmelnytsky, aided by the Muscovite general, *voyevoda,* Sheremietiev, invaded Galicia, Volhinia, Polissia and western Podillia, and was thus able to extend the political boundaries of Hetman Ukraine far to the West, and annex western Ukrainian ethnic territories. The Ukrainian population enthusiastically recognized the Ukrainian government. Then, Poland was completely overrun by the Swedes, led by King Carl-Gustav. However, out of that seemingly hopeless situation Poland was saved by her skillful diplomacy. The Poles persuaded the Muscovites to negotiate among themselves a separate peace treaty. The treaty was signed in Vilna in 1656, while Ukraine was ignored and not included in the negotiation.

Khmelnytsky and his Cossack leaders were furious, but the Treaty of Vilna freed them from any political and military ties with Moscow.[17] Moscow breached the Treaty of Pereyaslav by violating its military alliance with Ukraine. From now on, the Ukrainian nation stood alone and fully sovereign, and could freely build its own future. Khmelnytsky negotiated a coalition with Sweden, Brandenburg, Transylvania, Moldavia, Wallachia and Lithuania, aiming at a complete partition of Poland, while Ukraine was supposed to annex all Ukrainian ethnic territories in the West. In addition he kept in touch by correspondence with Cromwell's England. Denmark, however, destroyed the coalition by starting a war with Sweden.

Khmelnytsky built a strong and authoritative state, and in order to make it last, he planned to establish a hereditary monarchy in Ukraine. Initially, he planned to make Tymish his successor. The entire Moldavian project of allying Ukraine with that country, and marrying Tymish with Princess Roxanda and relating in this way the Khmelnytsky family with the ruling dynasty, was supposed to pave the way to establishing a hereditary monarchy in the Cossack-Hetman state of Ukraine. The untimely death of Tymish at Suchava was certainly a blow against this plan. But Bohdan Khmelnytsky did not give up the project, and began to prepare his younger son, Yurii to succeed him. However, Yurii, a man of limited abilities, was a bad choice for the turbulent times ahead. On the other hand, many Cossack grandees and leaders, such as Ivan Vyhovsky, Khmelnytsky's Secretary-General and his faithful collaborator, Colonel Lesnytsky, and some others, opposed the Hetman's plans. Khmelnytsky dealt harshly with the opposition. In 1657, the *rada starshyn* proclaimed Yurii the next hetman without any official election being held. The internal opposition to Yurii's succession and the collapse of the anti-Polish coalition caused Hetman Khmelnytsky's death on July 27, 1657 in his capital of Chyhyryn.[18]

Hetman Bohdan Khmelnytsky was one of the most outstanding political personalities in Ukrainian history. An ingenious strategist and statesman, he built the Ukrainian state and laid its foundations in the course of some nine years for its existence of some one hundred and fifty years, though with a changeable fortune. He changed a nation of "serfs" into a nation with political awareness and ambitions and led it from revolutionary turmoil to constructive statehood.

From Khemelnytsky to Mazepa. Yurii Khmelnytsky or Khmelnychenko was a mediocre son of an ingenious father, who was not talented enough to assume the high and demanding office in demanding times. He realized this, and after one month he abdicated. The *heneralna rada*, the General Council, elected Ivan Vyhovsky, Bohdan's close associate, the new hetman in August of 1657. Vyhovsky was well educated and proved to be an able statesman and diplomat during Khmelnytsky's time. He had worked for the Ukrainian cause since the Battle of Zhovti Vody. Having been disappointed with the alliance with Muscovy, Vyhovsky immediately concluded a treaty with Sweden, which recognized the Ukrainian western borders on the Vistula River. He also annexed the Berest and Novhorod districts, formerly Lithuanian territory, to Ukraine.

However, internal problems beset Vyhovsky's government. At first the Zaporozhe Cossacks opposed him, and then, Yakiv Barabash and Martyn Pushkar plotted a conspiracy against him and denounced him in Moscow. After he was upheld by the *heneralna rada*, Moscow sent its agent, Khitrovo, to Pushkar to persuade him to start an anti-Vyhovsky rebellion. In the final encounter, Pushkar and his associate, Barabash, were defeated by Vyhovsky's forces. Pushkar was killed in the encounter and Barabash punished by execution. The rebellion resulted in very heavy human losses. Meanwhile the Muscovites increased their military garrison in Ukrainian territory.

Anti-Muscovite feelings were on the rise and a pro-Polish orientation among the leading circles in Ukraine was getting an upper hand. Muscovite absolutism and mendacity frightened the Ukrainians, while a strong anti-Polish mood prevailed among the masses. Nevertheless, in September of 1658, the Treaty of Hadiach was signed, by which Ukraine entered into a political union with Poland and Lithuania as the "Grand Principality of Rus' " and as an equal third partner in the federal state of three nations. The Grand Principality of Rus' included the Kievan, Chernihivian and Bratslavian regions, or *voyevidstva*. The legislative power in the new state was supposed to be carried out by the National Council, *natsionalni zbory*, and the executive one, by the hetman. Ukraine had accordingly complete fiscal and military sovereignty and Polish military units were not allowed within her borders. The hetman was elected for life. The Catholic and Orthodox religions were declared equal, while the Uniat Church was nullified. Universities, colleges, other schools and print shops were to be established throughout Ukraine. The Treaty of Hadiach was authored by Yurii Nemyrych, an outstanding personality during Vyhovsky's time, who was thoroughly aristocratic and antagonized the commoners. This added to Vyhovsky's decreasing popularity.[19]

Although the Treaty of Hadiach was not fully realized, it provoked a war between Ukraine and Muscovy in 1659. In response to the said Treaty, a huge Muscovite army under the command of Trubetskoi and Romodanovskii moved against Ukraine. Vyhovsky completely routed the Muscovites in the Battle of Konotop in June of that year. The best *boyar* cavalry of the Muscovites were annihilated. The capital of Moscow was in complete panic. Tsar Aleksei was ready to move to Yaroslavl, afraid of a possible Ukrainian invasion of Muscovy and the capturing of Moscow by Vyhovsky. On the other hand, the Muscovite agents were spreading subversion and chaos in Ukraine, and instigating anti-Vyhovsky rebellions, joined by some of the most respected Cossack leaders for no apparent reason. Probably, the anti-Polish attitude of the masses and the all too aristocratic conduct of Vyhovsky and Nemyrych, coupled with the Muscovite subversion, aggravated the internal situation in Ukraine. To continue the war against Muscovy, which was started so speedily, became impossible. Hence, Vyhovsky abdicated or "gave up the Hetman's mace" during the *heneralna rada*, General Council of the Cossacks in 1659, while Yurii Khmelnytsky was elected for the second time by the pro-Muscovite faction of the Cossacks and under Muscovite instigation. Vyhovsky was made the Kievan *voyevoda*, but was unjustly suspected by the Poles of anti-Polish activity and was shot by them in 1664.[20]

From this time on, Ukrainian foreign policy vacillated between the pro-Polish and pro-Muscovite orientations, making the political situation in Ukraine rather unstable, inconsistent and inconsequential. Yurii Khmelnytsky ruled from 1659 to 1668, and then, he resigned again. He proved this time again what a mediocre person he was. At first he cooperated with the Cossack plan to limit Moscow's interference in Ukrainian affairs. The so- called *Zherdevski statti*, the *Zherdevian Statutes*, which demanded an annexation of some parts of Byeloruthenia and northern regions of the Chernihiv region to Ukraine, the prohibition of Muscovite officials from interfering in the internal matters of Ukraine, and unlimited Ukrainian sovereignty in international affairs, were formulated and presented to the Muscovite representative, Prince Trubetskoi. Trubetskoi rejected the *Stati*. Instead, he invited Yurii to Pereyaslav, and there under threats and pressures, he forced Yurii and the Cossack leaders to accept another forged version of the

Pereyaslav Treaty of 1654, which substantially limited Ukrainian rights and submitted the land to comprehensive Muscovite authority. The Battle of Konotop certainly nullified the Treaty of 1654, and from the Muscovite point of view, it was absolutely necessary to confirm the old "Agreement" in order not to lose control over Ukraine altogether. The bringing of Ukraine under more stringent Muscovite supervision was also desired in Moscow.[21]

The forged text of the Pereyaslav Treaty presented to Yurii Khmelnytsky for acceptance under duress in 1659, contained the following provisions: a newly elected hetman must pay homage to the Tsar; the hetman could not be removed by the *heneralna rada* without the Tsar's consent; the colonels and top officials of the Ukrainian government need the Tsar's consent for their appointment; Ukrainian armed forces must follow Muscovite command; and the Ukrainian Orthodox Church was subjected to the authority of Moscow's patriarch. The most damaging for Ukrainian autonomy was the provision in the new agreement about eliminating the right of Ukraine to conduct her separate diplomatic relations with foreign powers. Yurii, too weak to resist, accepted the conditions, assuming their analogy with the treaty signed by his father.[22]

After the so-called agreement was signed, the Muscovite administration completely ignored Yurii, and unceremoniously interfered with internal matters of Ukraine and exploited her population. Complaints were ignored. By 1660, the Muscovite armed forces invaded Right-bank Ukraine, nominally under Polish authority, and started a war against Poland. Yurii, with his army, accompanied the Muscovites. In the Battle of Chudniv, in Volhinia, the Muscovites were badly beaten. Yurii, taking advantage of the Muscovite defeat, and being completely disappointed in Moscow's attitude towards Ukraine, negotiated an agreement with Poland in the spirit of the Treaty of Hadiach. Ukraine was supposed to receive a broad political autonomy in the framework of the Polish-Lithuanian federation. But, a hope for the reunification of Ukraine, the joining of her Left-bank and Right-bank areas into one political body, was fading away. The Poles claimed some authority over Right-bank, and the Muscovites over Left-bank Ukraine, reinforcing from that time on a division according to their specific political interests. Yurii, disappointed and discouraged, resigned again in 1663. The era of the *Ruin* continued in Ukrainian history.

After Yurii Khmelnytsky, for some time there were actually two parallel hetmans; one for Right-bank and another one for Left-bank Ukraine. In the Right-bank, Pavlo Teteria was the hetman from 1663 to 1665; Petro Doroshenko, from 1665 to 1676; and Yurii Khmelnytsky, for the third time, from 1677 to 1681. The tenures of Petro Sukhovienko and Mykhailo Khanenko were so short and uneventful, that they scarcely deserve any attention. In the Left-bank, Ivan Brukhovetsky governed from 1663 to 1668; Demian Mnohohrishnyi, from 1669 to 1672; and Ivan Samoilovych, from 1672 to 1687. Petro Doroshenko succeeded in uniting both Ukrainian Hetman states into one nation for a short while in 1668.

Pavlo Teteria was once Bohdan Khmelnytsky's close associate, and represented the pro-Polish political orientation of Ukraine. In order to unite Ukraine, he persuaded the Polish government to wage a war against Muscovy. However, the war was lost and his project did not succeed. Teteria resigned and left for Poland. After a brief period of an *interregnum*, during which Stephan Opara, favored by the Tartars, had the hetman's mace, Petro Doroshenko was elected the hetman by the *heneralna rada*. He was an able man and an ardent Ukrainian patriot, who led to the unification of Ukraine into one nation and the elimination of any Polish and Muscovite interferences in the political affairs of his fatherland, which was the very mission of his life.

At first Doroshenko had to recognize Polish supremacy, since Polish garrisons were stationed in various places in Ukraine. But secretly he conducted negotiations with the Ottoman Empire, and with its assistance, he hoped to restore the full sovereignty of Ukraine. Meanwhile, he had also to wage a domestic war against Colonel Drozdenko, who proclaimed himself hetman. Drozdenko was defeated, but Doroshenko's troubles were far from over.

In 1666, taking advantage of turmoil in Poland, Doroshenko started a war and defeated the Poles soundly in the Battle of Bratslav. His victory at Bratslav could be compared to those at Zhovti Vody, Korsun and Konotop. A year later, assisted by the Tartars, he beleaguered a large Polish army at the town of Pidhaitsi in West Ukraine. However, at the same time the Zaporozhe Cossacks, under the command of Ivan Sirko, assaulted the Tartars at Perekop. In response to Sirko's move, Doroshenko's Tartar ally ceased fighting against Poland, and that alone forced Doroshenko to negotiate an unfavorable agreement with Poland, recognizing her supremacy over Ukraine.

Finally in 1668, Ukraine and the Ottoman Empire concluded a treaty, by which the Polish and Muscovite supremacy over Ukraine was annulled, while the sultan recognized the Ukrainian state "from the River Vistula to the town of Putyvl" and accepted it under his protection. At the same time, in Left-bank Ukraine, due to the abuses of the Muscovites and the prolonged servility of Hetman Ivan Brukhovetsky to the Tsar, an uprising began. Doroshenko invaded Left-bank Ukraine, which also recognized the Sultan's protection, and after uniting both Ukraines, Left-bank and Right-bank, into one nation for a while, he thus became the Hetman of all Ukraine. Brukhovetsky was killed during the turmoil. It was the greatest triumph of Petro Doroshenko and the fulfillment of his political dream and ambition.

Soon, however, Warsaw and Moscow militarily reacted to Doroshenko's agreement with Turkey. The war on two fronts forced him to march quickly back to Right-bank Ukraine, leaving behind in Left-bank his viceroy, the *nakaznyi hetman* Demian Mnohohrishny, to defend the land against the invading Muscovites. Nevertheless, Mnohohrishny's forces were too weak and Doroshenko did not send any fresh troops to assist him in the fight against the approaching Muscovites. Mnohohrishny did not have any other choice but to recognize Muscovite protection again. He was even urged by his advisers to do so in order to avoid a hopeless struggle and unnecessary bloodshed. Thereafter he was elected the new hetman of Left-bank Ukraine. The unhappy division of the country was reintroduced as a result of foreign intervention.

In the meantime, Hetman Doroshenko faced two troubles in his land. The Zaporozhe Cossacks proclaimed Petro Sukhovii to be hetman of Right-bank Ukraine, while sometime later, Mykhailo Khanenko became the pretender for the high office. Doroshenko's struggle against the two pretenders was long and hard. An attempt to negotiate with Poland did not succeed, either. Doroshenko, in his negotiations, demanded a broad autonomy for Ukraine, while Khanenko asked only for privileges for the Cossacks. Minimal demands by Khanenko induced the Polish government to recognize him as the hetman, and not Doroshenko. A prolonged and bloody war against Poland developed as a result. Substantial Turkish forces came to Ukraine to support Doroshenko. Poland was badly defeated and accepted the so-called Treaty of Buchach in 1672, by which Ukraine became an independent state under the protection of the Ottoman Empire, while Podillia became a Turkish province.

Nevertheless, Turkish protection proved to be as disastrous as Polish and Muscovite protection. The Turks pillaged the towns and villages, took the people into slavery by hundreds of thousands, exploited the country and introduced Mohammedanism by force, converting churches into mosques. The people emigrated from Right-bank Ukraine by masses, leaving the country deserted. The popularity and prestige of Doroshenko as hetman and leader declined to a record low.

At that very time, Ivan Samoilovych, the hetman of Left-bank Ukraine persuaded the Muscovites to take advantage of the devastating Polish-

Ukrainian-Turkish war in the Right-bank. Samoilovich, with Ukrainian Cossack and Muscovite troops, invaded the Right-bank in 1674, was proclaimed hetman there, and again succeeded for a short time to unite the nation under one national authority. Yet, he was soon forced to retreat under Doroshenko's military offensive, aided by the Turks and Tartars. It was a pity that Doroshenko was too revengeful towards the right-bank territories, which accepted the short-lasting authority of Samoilovych's hetmanate. Subsequently, King Jan Sobieski of Poland, in his warfare against the Turks, further contributed to the destruction of Right-bank Ukraine, especially of the Bratslav regions. Hence, Doroshenko's and Samoilovych's attempts to unite Ukraine failed. Eventually, after Doroshenko's faithful advisor, Metropolitan Tukalsky, died, the hetman himself was completely disappointed and discouraged, abdicated in 1676 and accepted a voluntary and rather honorable exile in Muscovy. He was given the village of Yaropolche, near Moscow, where he died in 1698.[23]

The Turks, in order to prevent the unification of Ukraine, made Yurii Khmelnytsky the hetman of Right-bank Ukraine for the third time, and gave him the title of "Prince of Sarmatia and Ukraine, and Leader of the Zaporozhe Cossacks." With their assistance, Yurii forced Samoilovych to withdraw fully to the left bank of the Dnieper River, taking many people with himself by force. Right-bank Ukraine was destroyed and depopulated. Yurii, with his suspicious and unstable character, soon disappointed everyone who had initially accepted and followed him, and abdicated again. This time the Turks put the Moldavian *voyevoda*, Ivan Duka in charge, who sincerely attempted to rebuild and recolonize the ruined land, but was largely hindered in his endeavors by the Muscovite-Polish "eternal peace" treaty which intended to preserve parts of the right bank area as a completely vacant buffer land. In the early 1680's Poland undertook an effort to colonize the area again. The Polish government appointed Stephan Kunytsky hetman to encourage the population. But, the project was not a success.[24]

The political fortunes of Left-bank Ukraine were a little more favorable. Yakym Somko, a representative of the Cossack aristocracy, displeased the Cossack commoners as a hetman, and they supported Vasyl Zolotarenko for the office. Against all traditional rules of the Cossack constitution, according to which a hetman was supposed to be elected by the *heneralna rada*, a so-called *chorna rada*, or the black council, consisting of the Cossacks, townspeople and peasants, convened and elected Ivan Brukhovetsky the new hetman, while Somko and Zolotarenko were executed.

Ivan Brukhovetsky, a proletarian and first-class demagogue, the candidate of the Cossack plebians, held the hetman's mace, the *bulava*, from 1663 to 1668. He was an uncritical follower of a pro-Muscovite Ukrainian policy, and accepted the Tsar's authority over Ukraine without any question. In 1665, he went to Moscow and agreed to transfer to the Tsar all powers over Ukraine, while securing class rights only for the Cossacks. For that he was made a *boyar* and was allowed to marry a Muscovite princess. Muscovite garrisons in Ukraine were substantially increased, and all fiscal rights, collecting taxes and non-tax receipts, were transfered to Tsarist representatives with the former's full consent. He even asked the Tsar to send a Muscovite metropolitan to Ukraine. Brukhovetsky's servility provoked a furious opposition in Ukraine to such a point that the Muscovites did not dare touch the ecclesiastic autonomy of the Ukrainian Orthodox Church at that time. However, the Muscovite officials committed all kinds of irregularities and abuses in Ukraine. The popularity of Brukhovetsky among the masses began to decline.

The Treaty of Andrusiv, signed between Poland and Muscovy in 1667, definitely divided Ukraine into two parts; Right-bank Ukraine was surrendered to Polish, and Left-bank to Muscovite supremacy, while the Territory of the Zaporozhe Cossacks was put under Polish-Muscovite *condominium*, joint supremacy, and was negotiated between the two powers without any Ukrainian participation. This was the last drop in the bucket. Ukraine rose up against this international rape. Brukhovetsky was frightened and changed his policy. Negotiations with the Ottoman Empire were undertaken to accept Turkish supremacy, while Ukraine was supposed to become a vassal state, the rights of which would be guaranteed. The sultan agreed to the arrangement. The Crimean Tartars came to assist Brukhovetsky and a revolutionary war against Muscovy began. Meanwhile, Hetman Petro Doroshenko also accepted Turkish supremacy, and, taking advantage of the anti-Brukhovetsky feelings, invaded Left-bank Ukraine, dreaming of the unification of the country under his own hetman's mace. Then the developments which were described above took place and led to the election of Demian Mnohohrishnyi, the new hetman of Left-bank Ukraine.

Demian Mnohohrishnyi ruled for three years, from 1669 to 1672, and after accepting Muscovite supremacy, he succeeded in negotiating with Moscow the so-called *Hlukhivski statti*, the *Hlukhiv Statutes*, relatively favorable for Ukrainian political autonomy. The Statutes limited the number of the Muscovite *voyevody*, governors, and their military garrisons in Ukraine. Also, their competence was restricted to commanding their troops and they were prohibited from interfering with the internal matters of the country, administrative as well as judicial. The hetman retained a complete fiscal autonomy with respect to collecting the taxes and making public expenditures. The Ukrainian military force was established at 30,000 men. The Treaty had all the features of an international agreement between two powers. The political status of Left-bank Hetmanate was established, being solely Mnohohrishnyi's achievement.[25]

Mnohohrishnyi was also successful in other areas. He reached a compromise with Doroshenko, because both were ardent Ukrainian patriots who only tried to reach the same goal, Ukrainian independence, by different ways. He suppressed local uprisings using mercenery troops; he quieted down the Cossack oligarchs and he attempted to restore law and order in the land by being very resolute. It must be admitted that under his government, Left-bank Ukraine became peaceful and prosperous. Like Bohdan Khmelnytsky, he thought that by making the hetman rule hereditary, the future of Ukraine would be secure. Hence, he appointed his brother the hetman in 1671. All these measures were greatly disliked by the Cossack oligarchs, who made him the victim of a conspiracy. Mnohohrishnyi, with his family, was arrested, tortured, and sent to Siberia, where he died amidst poverty many years later. He certainly was one of the most outstanding of the hetmans, though his era has not yet been properly researched.[26]

Ivan Samoilovych was elected hetman in 1672 and governed until 1687. He was an able statesman and diplomat who knew well how to deal with Moscow, and certainly desired the best for Ukraine. However, he relied upon Moscow too much. Samoilovych was rather aristocratic and cooperated with the upper crest of the Cossack class and its *rada starshyn*, the Council of Seniors, rather than with the *heneralna rada*, the General Council, and during his entire tenure the monarchic principle and a monarchic atmosphere prevailed. As it was pointed out above, he attempted to unite all of Ukraine under his *bulava*, mace or scepter, by invading the right bank provinces. However, he apparently had no success. Then he attempted to persuade the Muscovite government to demand from Poland the ethnographical Ukrainian western territories, Galicia, Volhinia, Podillia, Pidlashsha and other provinces, and to annex them to the hetman state. He also suggested to Moscow to unite *Slobidska* Ukraine, on the banks of the Donets River, under Muscovite authority, with the hetman state. He did not succeed with either of these suggestions. Yet, he was able to maneuver the preservation of the automony of his state and the inducement of Moscow to stay away from interfering with the internal affairs of Ukraine, although he fully resigned from any international autonomy to deal directly with foreign powers. A very unfortunate move on the part of Samoilovych was his submission of the Ukrainian Orthodox Church to the authority of the Patriarch of Moscow, which was long desired by the Muscovite government and ecclesiastic circles but sternly opposed by the majority of the Ukrainian circles.

The good relations between Samoilovych and the Tsarist court were spoiled by a discord, concerning the Crimean policy of Moscow. In the early 1680's, the Christian countries, the Vatican, Poland, Austria, Venetia and Muscovy planned an anti-Turk and anti-Tartar coalition. Ukraine was asked to participate, but the Ukrainian ruling circles were definitely against the "crusade" for a few fundamental reasons; first, Samoilovych and his associates were against any close cooperation between Muscovy and Poland since they harbored a threat to Ukrainian political autonomy; second, they were afraid that the destruction of the Crimean Tartars and the Muscovite domination of the Peninsula would bring a complete encirclement of Ukraine by Moscow, leading to the full abolition of the autonomy of Ukraine; and third, any Ukrainian participation in a large-scale war operation was not in the immediate political interest of the country. Samoilovych warned Moscow not to get too friendly with Poland, and refused to join the coalition. Nevertheless, Poland and Muscovy signed an "eternal peace" treaty, which, among other things, once more affirmed the Muscovite supremacy over Left-bank Ukraine and the city of Kiev.

In 1687, the war of the "Holy League" began among the countries mentioned above. Moscow was to assault the Crimean Tartars. The Ukrainian government objected, pointing out the enormous difficulties in moving a huge army through the steppes during hot weather. Yet, the war expedition was started. Samoilovych's forces joined the undertaking. Then, suddenly, before entering the deep steppe regions, the Muscovite commander-in-chief, Prince V. Golitsin, ordered a retreat for no apparent reason. The expedition proved to be a failure, and a scapegoat had to be found. Samoilovych and his son, Hryhorii, were made responsible for a supposed plot with the Tartars. The denunciation of some Ukrainian Cossack grandees, who were hostile towards Samoilovych's plan to make Ukraine a hereditary monarchy and towards his authoritarian measures, was taken as the basis. Hetman Ivan Samoilovych was exiled with his family to Siberia, while his son, Hryhorii, was executed.[27] In July 1687, the *heneralna rada* elected Ivan Mazepa the new hetman and the new, *Kolomatski statti*, The Kolomak Statutes based on The Hlukhiv Statutes, were negotiated with Moscow. The events took place on the banks of the Kolomak River.

Hetman Ivan Mazepa and the War for Liberation. Hetman Ivan Mazepa was of noble descent. In recognition of his political stature, he was granted the dignity of "Prince of the Holy Roman Empire" by Emperor Joseph I in 1707. His mother was a very intellectual woman, eventually becoming an abess of a monastery in Kiev and the Hetman's advisor in state matters until her death in 1707. Mazepa was educated in the Kievan-Mohylian Academy and at a Jesuit college in Warsaw. Then for a rather long time, he was in the diplomatic service of the Polish king, Jan-Casimir, and travelled extensively throughout Poland, France, Italy and Germany, substantially adding to his broad education and diplomatic skill. Mazepa was definitely of the pro-Polish political orientation of the Ukrainian aristocracy. Having been in the service of the Polish Crown, he also handled several diplomatic missions to Vyhovsky, Yurii Khmelnytsky and Teteria. In 1669 he joined Doroshenko's court and served the Ukrainian cause there. At that time, when most of the top Ukrainian Cossacks and noblemen became disenchanted with Doroshenko's policies and went over to Samoilovych, Mazepa also joined the court of the left-bank hetman, acquired his full confidence, and in the 1680's became one of the most influential personalities in the left-bank Hetman state. Mazepa was already fifty years old when he became the hetman, and his inborn abilities and enormous political and diplomatic experience enabled him to be the ruler of Ukraine for twenty-two years under the most adverse conditions.

Actually, Ivan Mazepa started his reign in the unfavorable atmosphere of the *Kolomatski statti*, which further limited Ukrainian autonomy and increased Muscovite interference in Ukrainian internal and foreign affairs, even beyond the limitations imposed by the *Hlukhivski statti* of 1669. Ukraine was denied the right to maintain a foreign policy of her own. An obligation was imposed on Ukraine to live in peace and friendship with the Crimean Tartars and to respect to the fullest extent the "eternal peace" between Muscovy and Poland and not to undertake anything that could disturb that peace. The strength and number of Muscovite military garrisons in Ukraine was increased to control the political conduct of the Hetman and his court. Already the *Kolomak Statutes* treated Ukraine as part of the Muscovite Tsardom and not as a separate and autonomous country, as it was intended by the original Agreement of Pereyaslav of 1654. This was unmistakable proof of the Muscovite imperialistic plans with respect to Ukraine. Her complete incorporation was intended at some future date. Ukraine was called "the Little Russian land under Hetman's regime" by the act, while the Ukrainian government was expected to promote a growing accord between the two peoples by all possible means, including intermarriages between

Ukrainians and Muscovites. The *Statutes* were definitely a political success of the Moscow government, and only because of Mazepa's diplomatic skill and patriotism, as Ohloblyn pointed out, was a complete subjugation of Ukraine by Moscow, according to the Act, prevented, and the continuation of the Ukrainian autonomy preserved.[28]

Moscow did not give up its plans in the Black Sea basin in spite of initial misfortunes. The Tartars continued to assault Ukraine and the Don regions, being ultimately repulsed by Colonel Illa Novytsky. Muscovite armed forces, again under the command of Prince V. Golitsin, moved against the Crimeans in the early spring of 1689. Mazepa joined the military expedition. Having reached Perekop in May, Golitsin suddenly retreated. The defeat of the project caused a palace revolution in Moscow. Tsarevna Sophia and her first minister, Prince V. Golitsin, were ousted, and the rule was assumed by Tsar Peter I. Yet, Mazepa, in spite of his cooperation and friendship with Golitsin, politically survived the *coup d'état*, probably because of his tact and diplomacy, and soon acquired the confidence of the new Tsar.

Peter I was obsessed with the project of dominating the Black Sea littorals. Repetitive military expeditions to conquer and annex the area were undertaken by Peter in 1690, 1691, 1692 and 1694, and always participated in by Ukrainian forces. In 1695, Mazepa joined Peter's grand-scale Azov campaign, attacking the Turks from the other side, assaulting Haza-Karmen and other Turkish fortresses, while his relative, Ivan Obydovsky, marched with the main Muscovite forces. Azov was taken by Peter, marking great military and political achievement for the Muscovites. Ukraine, however, gained nothing, except for the sustenance of economic exploitation and the general impoverishment of her population, due to continuous bloody warfare, marches of the military and requisitions. Mazepa participated in eleven Muscovite military expeditions in the course of twelve years. Having gained seemingly nothing for his land, the Hetman was losing popularity among his countrymen who began to call him the "step-father of Ukraine." Nevertheless, he was misunderstood. In order to preserve as much autonomy for Ukraine as was humanly possible under the presumptuous and despotic rule of the tyrant, Tsar Peter I, Mazepa had to use all kinds of measures and tricks to lull his suspicions, imperialist appetites and drives. This included cooperation with his military projects, and awaiting a proper time to break with him to free Ukraine from Moscow's overbearing patronage. This opportunity soon came to Mazepa, but meanwhile serious problems tormented Mazepa and his government. Sporadic Cossack rebellions flared up. The peasants were fleeing to the Zaporozhe and *Slobidska* Ukraine regions to avoid trouble and misery. Mazepa also tried to oppose Moscow's obsessive anti-Turk policies to save a possible ally for Ukraine in the future, but without much success. The top Cossack circles increasingly opposed Mazepa's policies and exposed him at the Moscow court.

In 1691, Petro Ivanenko, popularly called Petryk, began to organize an effective opposition to Mazepa. Arriving at the *Sitch*, he negotiated an alliance with the Crimean Tartars and developed a plan to make Ukraine independent of Moscow with their military assistance, branding Mazepa as a willing tool of Muscovite oppression. Although the Zaporozhe Cossacks did not support Petryk, and this alone prognosticated his failure, he started the uprising with Tartar assistance. He apparently hoped to achieve what Doroshenko could not with the assistance of the Turks. If he had won the contest, he would have become a hero. But, he failed. He started an uprising with a scanty force of insurgents and Tartar allies. Mazepa with Ukrainian and Muscovite regiments defeated him and forced him to retreat. The top Cossack circles, which secretly supported Petryk in his challenge of Mazepa, were silenced, while he himself undertook a few additional abortive military projects as "the Hetman of the Khan Ukraine" between the Dnieper and Boh Rivers. Because his allies, the Tartars, plundered southern borderlands of Ukraine, Petryk's popularity declined. Yet, for a few more years Petro Ivanenko-Petryk worried the Ukrainian Hetman and the Muscovite governments as a representative of the "common people," opposing the official aristocratic element of the contemporary government, although his political significance in fact soon faded away.[29] The contest between Mazepa and Petryk had, doubtlessly, the character of a deep social conflict between the interests of the commoners and the nobles.

Another political complication with deeply rooted social implications developed for Mazepa in Right-bank Ukraine, nominally under Polish sovereignty. There, the Polish king, Jan Sobieski, tried to initiate a large scale re-colonization program. The Cossacks were called to assist to put the program into operation. Colonel Semen Palii (Palyvoda) soon excelled the other Cossack leaders involved in the Polish plan. He established many townships and villages throughout the large territories of the Right-bank, and became a factual ruler. Although the royal decrees reserved all rights to the Polish nobility, Palii ignored these claims, suppressed the noble property rights, and represented and defended the interests of the commoners. The Polish nobles complained against Palii at the royal court and attempted to liquidate him, but he was saved by Cossack intervention.

Palii's domain extended from the Polissia marshes to the Black Sea steppes on the right bank of the Dnieper River. He was aware of the fact that he himself was not able to free Ukraine from Polish oppression. Hence, he negotiated a plan with Mazepa and the Muscovites to defeat Poland by their common forces. Yet, the Muscovites were reluctant to disturb their friendly relations with Poland at this time. They suggested to Palii that he come with his Cossacks to Left-bank Ukraine and accept Muscovite protection. Palii refused; he did not want to leave his people at the mercy of the Poles. Meanwhile, Palii, together with the Zaporozhe and Left-bank Cossacks, participated in many successful war expeditions against the Tartars and Turks, which only underscored the need for the unification of the entire Ukraine in order to effectively defend her against the onslaughts of her rapacious neighbors.

Although the need for unification was desired by all, Mazepa, Palii and the Zaporozhe Cossacks, traditional deep social and political differences made this ideal scarcely possible. The aristocratic attitude of Mazepa and his seemingly pro-Muscovite and pro-Tsarist policies made him unacceptable for Palii and Zaporozhe, who represented democratic principles in the social respect, and national principles in the political respect. The aristocratic Mazepian mind could not accept the democratic attitude of the latter, either. The Polish nobleman, Potocki, asserted in 1701, that Palii wanted to follow Khmelnytsky's path and planned to start the torches of a "peasant war." Mazepa believed in the legitimate government, based on class structure and aristocratism.[30]

The Treaty of Karlowitz in 1699 renewed the Polish drive in Ukraine, and the Polish government demanded Palii to submit to Polish rule. Palii refused to submit. A large-scale war developed. At first Palii and his Cossacks were victorious. Samus, one of the commanders, defeated the Polish forces at Berdychiv. All Podolian and Bratslav regions were dominated by the Ukrainians; the Polish fortress of Bila Tserkva was taken as well. Tidal waves of peasant uprisings covered all of Right-bank Ukraine and threatened to spread to the Left-bank state. The Zaporozhe Cossacks were ready to move militarily against Mazepa's aristocratic and assumingly pro-Muscovite rule.

Already at that time the developments in Ukraine were interwoven with the international complications of the Northern War, in which Muscovy, Ukraine, Poland, Sweden, Denmark and other powers took part. Having been irked by Palii's mob-rule philosophy of solving the problem of Ukrainian independence, and because of the Polish involvement in the Northern War,

Mazepa was not only opposed to any cooperation with Palii, who was then already hard-pressed by the Polish military counter offensive, but moved his armies into right bank regions in 1704 and began war operations against Palii and his forces. Palii was soon defeated, imprisoned, and exiled. Mazepa succeeded in this way in uniting Ukraine into one state under his rule. The dream of many Ukrainian patriots was realized, though they might have had different social and political philosophies.

Of course, as in the case of Petryk, if Semen Palii would have been victorious in his attempts to free Ukraine, he would have become a great historical personality. Since he lost the struggle, he is remembered by history only as an ephemeral adventurous Cossack who left an unpleasant aftertaste with his mob or plebeian political approach. Meanwhile, however, Hetman Mazepa proceeded with the organizational restructuring of the right bank regions of his state and persuaded Tsar Peter that the unified and strong Hetman state would be of interest for Muscovy as an ally against the permanent Polish threat and a worthy ally in the further evolving Northern War. Peter was extremely interested in the Northern War, because if it was victorious for Muscovy it would open up the Baltic Sea, the gate to Western Europe for Muscovy and an important step toward the growth of the Muscovite Empire of which Peter dreamt. Furthermore, Mazepa tried to prevent, by his diplomacy, any Muscovite-Polish reapproachment as a most dangerous combination of anti-Ukrainian forces, such as the Agreement of Andrusiv, the "eternal peace" between Moscow and Warsaw, and similar conventions, proven unfortunate for Ukraine in the past. He certainly succeeded in preserving Ukrainian autonomy in spite of the *Kolomak Statutes*, largely because of his diplomatic skill and personal friendship with Tsar Peter, as pointed out already.

However, Mazepa's aggressive aristocratic approach and his aloofness from the broad masses of the population, in particular, the lower crest of the Cossack class, made him and his policies very unpopular, and he was regarded with suspicion. His very close military cooperation with Moscow and his sending of many troops there to lull down the Muscovite imperialist ambitions, were largely misunderstood. His aloofness from the masses and his belief that only the top social class was called to govern, proved to be disastrous during the subsequent developments of the Northern War and during his political and military association with Sweden for the sake of liberating Ukraine from the Muscovite domination.

Charles XII of Sweden, a military genius, was bringing the coalition of Muscovy, Poland, Denmark and Saxony to its knees in the due course of the

Northern War, having defeated Denmark, badly beaten Peter at Narva in 1700, and having subsequently invaded Poland. Ukrainian forces were participating in the operations in the Baltic regions against the Swedish, but not on a large scale. As a result of the subsequent invasion of Poland by Charles XII, the country was divided into two waring sides with two kings, the pro-Muscovite August and pro-Swedish Stanislaw Leszczynski. Meanwhile Peter I, his wounds sustained at Narva healed, reorganized his armed forces, constructed additional fortresses by using largely slave-labor, including Ukrainians, and attacked anew the Baltic shores of Courland, Ingria and Lithuania. All these war operations and war-related activities, marches, taxes, requisitions and constructions of fortresses heavily exhausted the Ukrainian economy, since Peter demanded more and more from Mazepa. At the same time plans were under consideration in Moscow to abolish the Ukrainian Hetman State and to make it a part of the Muscovite Tsardom under the rule of Prince Aleksander Menshikov, a close associate of the Tsar, or some foreigner, such as the English Prince Marlborough.

At this crucial time, Hetman Mazepa was now faced with a grave decision to make; to stay faithful to Muscovy and then, to surrender Ukraine and be ousted, imprisoned, deported or liquidated, like some Cossack leaders were before; or to negotiate some political deals with Sweden, Turkey, Poland or any other power, in order to preserve Ukraine as a free nation. The idea of a political federation with Poland, based on the former Hadiach Agreement, was most popular among the Ukrainian leading circles. Several secret diplomatic missions were dispatched to King Stanislaw Leszczynski to prepare the grounds for the formation of a Rus' Grand Principality in federation with Poland and Lithuania.[31] The other political conception envisioned an alliance with the Tartars or a Ukrainian autonomy under Turkish protection. The plans were nothing new, so consequently Mazepa did not trust or approve of them, because they had only foretold disillusions for the Ukrainians in the past. Hetman Mazepa wanted a completely sovereign nation of Ukraine, not dependent on or protected by any power. Contemporary sources brought ample evidence of such a political concept of Mazepa.[32]

Mazepa began to proceed secretly and very cautiously with the negotiations with Charles XII of Sweden, a powerful ruler, the terror of Europe, and the most hopeful adversary of Muscovy. Sweden was far away and she could not threaten the sovereignty of Ukraine in any way. Yet, she could be the most effective ally in achieving Ukraine's independence. There was, however, internal Ukrainian opposition to the plan, and Peter's spies were everywhere, even in the most trusted inner circle of the Hetman's advisors and associates. On the other hand, Mazepa had many true friends among the Muscovite aristocracy, who were ready to support his efforts towards the liberation of Ukraine, and who were ready to turn against Peter's brutal tyranny. Charles XII planned to dethrone Peter once his victory in the military contest was assured, of course, with the assistance of those antiregime aristocratic circles, joined by V. Golitsin, B. Sheremietiev, D. Golovkin, and others.[33]

By 1706 the negotiations between Mazepa and Charles XII crystallized into an agreement, the contents of which were reported by Pylyp Orlyk in his work *Vyvid prav Ukrainy, The Derivation of the Rights of Ukraine*, published in 1712. The agreement contained the following provisions: Ukraine would be a sovereign nation, the Principality of Ukraine; Mazepa would be its prince for life; after his death his successor would be elected; the king of Sweden would protect Ukraine militarily.[34] Meanwhile, Mazepa continued his negotiations with Stanislaw Leszczynski of Poland, the Crimean Khan, the Ottoman Empire, Moldavia and other powers, to find a most plausible solution for the political future of his country.

Mazepa, like Khmelnytsky, considered a hereditary monarchy, which was most popular then in the European constitutions, as the best form of government for Ukraine. Yet, many top Cossack leaders disagreed, and disliked Mazepa's favoritism toward his relatives, like Obydovsky and Voynarovsky, and his plan to make them his successors. Furthermore, Mazepa's rather arbitrary conduct irked many. Hence, the Hetman was denounced by some Cossack grandees and even slandered at the Tsarist court in Moscow. Having received the news of the negotiations with Sweden and other powers, Mazepa's archenemy, Vasyl Kochubey, the supreme justice of the Hetman state, conspired with Colonel Ivan Iskra, and informed Moscow's government about Mazepa's move to go over to Peter's enemies, in particular, to join forces with Charles XII of Sweden. Peter pretended not to believe the denouncements, ordered their arrest, torture and execution. In fact, however, Peter did not trust Mazepa at all, and persistently demanded from him evidence of loyalty by constant requirements to steadily send additional Ukrainian troops to Muscovy and more and more workers for the construction of defenses and forts to become ready for the final encounter with King Charles XII. Mazepa complied and even joined the Muscovites to suppress Bulavin's uprising in the Don regions, though Bulavin might have become Ukraine's natural ally.

According to the original plan, Charles XII intended to march on Moscow to dethrone Peter and to arrange matters according to his own liking. But military matters were rather unfavorable for him; his armies were dispersed throughout Eastern Europe, in Livonia, Finland and Poland, and their consolidation for a march on Moscow was not an easy matter. Furthermore, one of his generals, Löwenhaupt, was defeated by the Muscovites in the Battle of Lisna. Hence, Charles decided not to march on Moscow, but to go to Ukraine, where he expected substantial assistance in troops and supplies from Mazepa. The decision was a catastrophic one. Mazepa readied himself to join Charles should all the Muscovite forces be withdrawn from Ukraine to defend Moscow. He had enough supplies to assist the Swedes in their move against Moscow, but he was not ready to receive them in Ukraine. The top Cossack grandees disagreed with respect to the Swedish policies, the masses did not trust the aristocrats and Mazepa's prolonged loyalty to Tsar Peter, and only a fraction of the Ukrainian armed forces were in Ukraine. Most of them were sent to Muscovy to appease suspicious Tsar Peter as long as it was humanly possible in order to join the Swedes at the most opportune time, as was mentioned above.

Mazepa left his capital of Baturyn on October 24, 1708 and joined Charles XII four days later. The war for Ukraine's liberation began. It was supposed to obliterate any traces of the notorious Agreement of Pereyaslav, which opened the road for Muscovite domination of Ukraine. Charles was disappointed with the few troops Mazepa brought to his camp. It explained the hesitation in the first moment. Peter meanwhile moved quickly. First of all, by issuing a few decrees, he tried to confuse the Ukrainian public. He presented Mazepa as a traitor, who wanted to sell out Ukraine to Poland, and he presented himself as a protector of the nation. Meanwhile Aleksander Menshikov was ordered to take Baturyn, the Hetman's capital, to ruin it completely and to massacre the people there in a most unhuman and cruel way, thus terrifying the people and setting an example of punishment for deserting the Muscovites and joining the Swedish camp.

Menshikov ruined, pillaged and massacred Baturyn in a way that shocked not only Ukraine but also foreigners who witnessed or heard about the atrocities. The same atrocities against Mazepa's followers and sympathizers were committed by Menshikov and his aides, as he marched with his troops through Ukraine, without even attempting to ascertain whether someone was guilty or not. Hundreds and thousands of innocent people were tortured and murdered. The Orthodox Church was forced by Peter to anathematize Mazepa. He was ousted as hetman and by order of the Tsar Colonel Ivan Skoropadsky was elected the new one, although Peter did not trust him since he was once Mazepa's loyal associate.

Ukraine was divided into parts. The smaller one was under Mazepa's authority and the Swedish occupation; the larger one was supposedly under Skoropadsky, sustaining terror from Menshikov's military rule. During the difficult winter months of 1709 the Swedish army suffered shortages and sicknesses and was compelled to take food and supplies from the population by force. The broad masses of the Ukrainian people, confused by Peter's propaganda moves and frightened by Menshikov's terror, met the Swedish soldiers with suspicion. They largely misunderstood the political maneuver of their disliked and aristocratic Hetman. The war operation in Ukraine proceeded. Towns, villages and regions were changing masters. A partisan war against the ruthless requisitions of the Swedes began.

Meanwhile Ivan Mazepa intensified his diplomatic action, attempting to organize a broad anti-Muscovite coalition on a global scale, which was supposed to include the Ottoman Empire, the Khanate of Crimea, Moldavia, Wallachia, Transylvania, the Don-Cossacks, the Kuban-Cossacks, the Kalmyks, the Bashkirians and others. Poland attacked Muscovy, but without success. The greatest political success of a nation-wide scope for Mazepa was his alliance with the Zaporozhe Cossacks. The Territory of the Cossack Host, the second Ukrainian political organization, under the leadership of *koshovyi* Kost Hordienko, fully understood the gravity of the situation and joined the Hetman state in the common struggle for the national liberation of all Ukraine from Muscovite domination, in spite of significant differences in their approach to political and social problems of the country.

In response to Hordienko's joining forces with Mazepa in the common struggle, Menshikov sent a Muscovite army against the Zaporozhe. The *Sitch* was taken and destroyed, while the Cossacks who did not go with Hordienko were cruelly tortured and murdered. A similar "pacification" program was carried out by the Muscovites throughout the Territory of the Cossack Host with identical cruelty against the peaceful population, which did not join either Mazepa or Hordienko. It was undertaken simply as a measure of terror against the bastion of Ukrainian national self-assertion "the nest of banditti," according to the Muscovite evaluation.[35] For centuries the Zaporozhe *Sitch* had been the very symbol of the Ukrainian national struggle against the Tartars, the Poles and the Muscovites, who were the traditional enemies of Ukrainian national and political independence, following one after another in an attempt to dominate Ukraine's riches.

When the decisive Battle of Poltava began in the morning hours of June 27, 1709, the armed forces of Charles XII and Mazepa were far smaller than those of Tsar Peter. Charles, however, trusted his personal luck and military genius. Charles was already wounded before the battle and the command of the battle was largely in the hands of his generals. During the battle, the King's horse was killed and Charles fell to the ground unconscious. The Swedes did not have an adequate artillery, while the Muscovite artillery fire decimated the Swedish forces. In eight hours, the Battle of Poltava was lost for Charles and Mazepa. The Agreement of Pereyaslav of 1654 was the beginning of digging the grave for Ukrainian national independence and the Battle of Poltava of 1709 completed it. Muscovy-Russia annihilated the political ambitions of Khmelnytsky, Doroshenko, Mazepa, Hordienko and other patriotic Ukrainians for long decades to come.[36]

The Hetman State After Mazepa. In fact, the Battle of Poltava was one of the most decisive battles in world history. The political fortunes not only of Ukraine, but of entire Eastern Europe, would have been completely different if Charles XII and Mazepa would have won the contest. Muscovy would have probably never achieved the prominence of the Russian Empire of the future. Ukraine would have been a sovereign state. Swedish hegemony would have prevailed in this area for many decades to come. However, Divine Providence ordered things to develop otherwise.

The defeat at Poltava was complete, while the remnants of the Swedish army were lost at the crossing of the Dnieper River. There were not enough boats for the army to reach the other bank, and so General Löwenhaupt surrendered to Menshikov. The famous infantry of Charles XII ceased to exist. Only the king, the hetman, and some of their escorts succeeded in escaping to the other side of the river. Subsequently, Mazepa and Charles with their associates crossed the Moldavian border and were granted political asylum by the Turkish government. Mazepa arrived at the city of Bendery a sick person, and died there in September of 1709. Charles dreamt of a further war against Peter.

After Mazepa's death frictions developed among the Ukrainian political emigrants, but soon Pylyp Orlyk, Mazepa's trusted associate, was elected the hetman in exile. For over thirty years, from 1710 to 1742, he worked for the Ukrainian cause through his broad diplomatic and political activities. An agreement was signed with the Crimean Khan by which he recognized an independent Ukraine. Orlyk conducted negotiations with the Don-Cossacks to get their support for Ukraine. Military undertakings were organized against Muscovy. The Tartars attempted to take Voronizh. A coalition of the Tartars, Orlyk's forces, Hordienko with his Zaporozhe Cossacks and some Polish detachments under Stanislaw Poniatowski reached as far as the city of Bila Tserkva in their anti-Muscovite struggle. But the Tartars betrayed the cause as they usually did, and the allies had to retreat. During Peter's Pruth campaign in 1711, in which he was defeated, Pylyp Orlyk again unfolded considerable diplomatic activity to get the recognition of Ukrainian independence. Yet, Peter succeeded twice, through his maneuvers and the paying of bribes, to avert his own complete defeat and destruction. Orlyk's plans to acquire the Right-bank Ukrainian regions failed, because they were meanwhile occupied by the Polish government.

With the election of Pylyp Orlyk to be the Ukrainian hetman in exile, the constitution of the Cossack state was also adopted, the so-called Bendery Constitution, the official name of which was, *Konstytutsia prav i svobid Zaporozhskoho Viiska*, the *Constitution of the Rights and Liberties of the Zaporozhe Host*. Although the document was never put in practical political life, it continues to have a great significance as a step forward in the development of Ukrainian political thought. It proclaimed the independence of Ukraine from Poland and Muscovy, the establishment of the Cossack parliament, the limitation of the authority of the hetman by the parliament and the institution of a constitutional monarchy in Ukraine, a harmonious relationship among the government agencies of the Hetmanate with the Cossack grandees as the top and leading stratum of the Ukrainian society, and the Zaporozhe Host as the military force. Although some protection was foreseen for the common people, the constitution definitely had an aristocratic character, in accordance with contemporary political theory.[37]

As time went on, it became increasingly difficult for all the Ukrainian armed forces to again unite under Pylyp Orlyk. Recognizing the need for diplomatic activities beyond Eastern Europe, Pylyp's son, Hryhor, began his work in France, which was then considered "the foremost and mightiest kingdom in the Christian world." It is through the French court that Hryhor hoped to reorganize the Ukrainian armed forces under his father and gain a new ally against Muscovy. Eventually, Hryhor became a general in the French army and one of the major advisors of King Louis XV, who bestowed upon Hryhor the Cross of the Order of St. Louis, a very high honor. Throughout his life Hryhor worked towards promoting the interests of Ukraine on the broad international scene and exposing Muscovite-Russian imperialism. Unfortunately, both Orlyks died before their plans were crystallized; however, they both kept alive the Mazepian tradition of Ukrainian self-assertion, which was subsequently continued by others until Ukrainian statehood was finally re-established in the twentieth century.[38]

Political matters in Ukraine, however, were developing in their own ways. Ivan Skoropadsky was elected the hetman through Peter's interference, and he governed from 1708 to 1722, trying his best to protect the interests of his country under the most unfavorable conditions of the ever growing Muscovite-Russian imperialistic pressure. He never referred to Mazepa as a traitor, but as the "Lord-Predecessor," although the memory of the latter was scorned by the Muscovites-Russians. It required skill, tact and diplomacy on Skoropadsky's part to save the last vestiges of the rapidly diminishing political autonomy of the Hetman state and to protect its economic interests as well. It was apparent at that time that the Muscovite-Russian government was determined to liquidate Ukrainian autonomy at an opportune time and to incorporate the land as a province of the Russian Empire. As a matter of fact, by 1713, Peter I by his *ukaz*, decree, declared the Tsardom of Muscovy to be from that time on the Russian Empire, in order to give the finishing touch to all his political successes. The new name surely associated the new Russia with the traditional Rus', the medieval state formation in Ukraine. It insinuated that Russia was the political continuation of Rus' and that the Russians (Muscovites) were of one national stock with the Ukrainians, who began to be officially called by St. Petersburg, the new capital of the Empire, the Little Russians, the younger brothers of the Great Russians. The move certainly prognosticated an intensified imperialist pressure against Ukraine, to make that birth place of medieval Rus' an inseparable component of the indivisible Russian Empire forever after.[39]

The rights and liberties of Ukraine were steadily trampled upon. The repressions against the former *Mazepians*, Mazepa's followers, continued; they were imprisoned and deported by hundreds to Siberia and other distant regions of the new Empire, although amnesty was promised formerly. Cossacks and commoners were sent to Russia to construct fortresses and cities, particularly, the new capital of St. Petersburg, where hundreds of thousands perished. Russians were made colonels in Ukraine and other offices were given to Russians and foreigners by Peter's orders, without even asking Hetman Skoropadsky. Peasant bondage of the Muscovite style was introduced. The Cossacks were sent to fight Russian foreign wars, in particular, the war in Persia, where they were decimated.

After being elected the hetman, Skoropadsky asked Peter I to confirm the traditional rights and liberties of Ukraine. The Tsar, for the most part, ignored or denied the requests. Although he promised that he would order his officials in Ukraine not to interfere with the country's internal matters, this assurance was not taken seriously. Subsequent complaints of the Hetman were thrust aside. These chicaneries were all executed by A. Izmailov, a Tsarist resident sent to Ukraine to watch over the Hetman and his top officials, and to report all their actions to St. Petersburg. Izmailov was soon replaced by a similar court spy, F. Protasiev. In 1722, the so-called Little Russian College was established by the Russians. It was composed of six Muscovite officials, chaired by S. Veliaminov, and was supposedly created to protect the common people of Ukraine from the abuses of the Ukrainian Cossack or noble grandees. In fact, this was another measure to limit the authority of the Hetman and the autonomy of Ukraine. Skoropadsky's protests were ignored. The blow was too vicious. Skoropadsky could not take any more and died a few months later.[40]

After Skoropadsky's death a new hetman was not elected, and instead Pavlo Polubotok, colonel of the Chernihiv region, was authorized by the Cossack leaders, the *starshyna*, to act as a hetman by appointment, the *nakaznyi hetman*. Meanwhile, Veliaminov reorganized the Little Russian College and seriously interfered with the affairs of the Hetman government. Polubotok protested in St. Petersburg against the conduct of Veliaminov and his College. In order not to aggravate the situation, St. Petersburg advised the Little Russian College to cooperate with the General Military Office of the Hetman, the *Generalna Viiskova Kantselaria*. In order to leave the College with no argument of supposedly protecting the lower classes of the people of Ukraine from the abuses of the grandees, Polubotok reorganized the judiciary, established the appellate procedure and suppressed corruption in the judiciary and administration. This made Tsar Peter furious; he ordered Pavlo Polubotok and his top officials to come to St. Petersburg and to explain their actions. When in the Russian capital, Polubotok and his associates presented a petition to the Tsar, demanding the restoration of all the rights and liberties of Ukraine and to allow the election of a new hetman. In response to the petition, Peter ordered the arrest of Pavlo Polubotok and other Cossack leaders. Polubotok and two others died in prison, while others were released after Peter's death in 1725. Ukrainian autonomy was suppressed; the government was in the hands of the Little Russian College.[41]

The Little Russian College continuously increased taxes, and by so doing it antagonized Russian nobles who had latifundia in Ukraine, including Menshikov himself. Hence, after the death of Tsaritsa Catherine I, in order to appease the uncertain situation, the Little Russian College was liquidated and the election of a new hetman was permitted by St. Petersburg. In 1727, Danylo Apostol was solemnly elevated to this dignity and he governed until his death in 1734. Formerly, Danylo Apostol supported Polubotok. For that he was imprisoned, but later released. At the time of his election, Apostol was already 73 years of age. His late age was, perhaps, an important factor in the

Russian decision to allow him to be elected; St. Petersburg assumed that the old man would not cause any problems for Russian imperialist policies, in general, and in Ukraine, in particular.

At the beginning of 1728, a Ukrainian delegation arrived in Moscow for the coronation of the new Tsar, Peter II. The delegation, headed by Danylo, was very graciously received and entertained at the old Muscovite capital. Then, the delegation asked for certain statutes from the Tsarist government, which would confirm Ukraine's rights and liberties. Peter II, however, instead of signing the statutes, which referred to the Agreement of Pereyaslav of 1654 and affirmed Ukraine's autonomous status, issued the so-called *Reshytielnie Punkty*, the *Paragraphs of Decision*. This was in the form of an imperial decree which included a whole series of limitations of Ukrainian political rights, being in itself an annihilating blow against the country's claim to statehood. The Hetman was from now on militarily subject to a field-marshall and not directly to the Tsar; three Russians were introduced to the Ukrainian supreme court of justice, the *Generalnyi Sud*, and its head from now on was the Tsar and not the Hetman; a separate financial administration limited the Hetman's financial prerogatives; the top state officials and colonels were to be appointed by the Tsar and not by the Hetman; the Hetman was limited in his rights to travel domestically and to maintain correspondence abroad. The jurisdictions of the General Military Office were drastically reduced.

Apostol inherited chaos in the government machine, which was caused by the Little Russian College. Main administrative offices were not staffed; some colonelcies were without colonels at all; other colonelcies had foreigners for colonels who did not want to follow the Hetman's instructions, they were instigated by Veliaminov to do so, or otherwise they abused their authority, particularly their property rights. Namely, these properties which were attached to the respective offices as compensation for the administrative work done, and the estates of rank were treated as private landed properties. Apostol tried to fill the offices and to reduce the abuses.

Already under the government of Ivan Skoropadsky work was undertaken to prepare for Ukraine a separate code of laws, which was then heavily based on the *Lithuanian Statute* and the Magdeburg legal system of the previous era. Furthermore, Apostol continued the struggle to retain as much as possible of the dwindling autonomy of Ukraine by arguing various cases with the Russian resident and the Tsarist court in Moscow. He strengthened the administration and streamlined the appellate judiciary, protected Ukrainian commerce and industry, and stabilized the overall way of life in the Hetman state so that some emigrants returned and new colonists came to live there. Of course, he had to pay a price for what he was doing; the Ukrainian armed forces were sent abroad to participate in the Polish war for succession between August II and Stanislaw Leszczynski. Due to his efforts the city of Kiev, the ancient capital of Ukraine-Rus', was also taken from under the authority of the Russian governor-general, and made subject to the Hetman government.[42]

Moscow was only too anxious to eliminate the institution of the Hetmanate, and only some extraordinary developments forced the Tsarist government to tolerate it. With the death of Hetman Danylo Apostol in 1734, Moscow prevented the election of the next Hetman and introduced the so-called Second Little Russian College under the deceptive name of the *Administration of the Hetman Government, Pravlinnia Hetmanskoho Uriadu*. It consisted of three Russians and three Ukrainians, while a Russian, Prince A. Shakhovskii, was in reality the real ruler. At this time, Moscow issued a secret order that all humanly possible measures, including intermarriages, must be undertaken by the College to bring Ukrainians and Russians closer together, and to prevent any closer associations between Ukrainians and Byeloruthenians, on the one hand, and Ukrainians and Poles, on the other. Furthermore, Russian-sponsored propaganda was intensified in Ukraine, making it look like all abuses and evils were coming from the Hetman, and that without him things would be much better.

The willful and abusive action of the College produced opposition and hatred, counterparted by Russian terror. Ukrainian clergy and officials were arrested, tortured and deported. Dissatisfaction was growing. Meanwhile war between Russia and Turkey again broke out in 1735. Ukraine suffered again. The Cossacks had to participate in the war. Ukraine had to supply food, horses, oxen and wagons for the army, while the Tartar excursions ruined the countryside. The war was over by 1739 with a dubious outcome for the Russians, while Ukraine paid a very high price for it with a large number of men being killed, injured, crippled, and by large material losses.

In 1734, the Zaporozhe Cossacks who left the *Sitch* and Ukraine after the Poltava catastrophe, returned to Ukraine and resurrecting the old tradition, established their new *Sitch* on the Pidpilna River, Dnieper's tributary. Hetman Pylyp Orlyk opposed the move, because he maintained that a state of war existed with Muscovy-Russia, and he would rather retain these Cossacks abroad under Turkish protection, to use them in any future war with the Russian Empire.

Probably the only positive work of the Second College, from the Ukrainian point of view, was the completion of the codification of the book of laws, started under Skoropadsky and continued under Apostol. The code was called *Prava, po kotorym sudytsia malorosiiskyi narod, The Laws, according to which justice is done among the Little Rus'ian people.* Because the code would underscore the autonomous status of Ukraine, the Russian government did not permit its ratification.[43]

In 1741 Tsaritsa Elizabeth ascended to the throne of the Russian Empire. Because of her intimate relations with Oleksii Rozum, a Ukrainian, who was subsequently made a count and member of the nobility, and named Rozumovsky, Tsaritsa Elizabeth was favorably inclined towards Ukraine because she was morganatically married to him. While in Ukraine, in 1744 she was approached by the Cossack leaders and asked to restore the Hetmanate. She agreed. Yet, her candidate for the office was Kyrylo Rozumovsky, Oleksii's younger brother, who was not of age and in need of education. So, he was first sent to West European universities. H. Tieplov was his tutor. Upon his return from West Europe, the decree about the election of the new Hetman was announced.

Kyrylo Rozumovsky was elected Hetman in the summer of 1750 by the grace of Tsaritsa Elizabeth, according to all the traditional rituals and in a very solemn way, in the city of Hlukhiv, the capital of Hetman Ukraine. He inherited a very troubled situation. The damages done by the Turkish war were very substantial; the country's business and economy needed to be rebuilt. The Muscovite terror undermined the people's moral standards, which also needed to be restored. Kyrylo Rozumovsky, being a Ukrainian patriot, tried to return to his country some rights and liberties of the previous decades. He partially succeeded because of the friendly attitude of the Tsaritsa, which neutralized, to some extent, the hostility of the Moscow ruling circles towards the Ukrainian self-governing rule. However, the financial autonomy of Ukraine was drastically limited. St. Petersburg demanded financial reports about the public revenues and expenditures of the Hetman government, drastically interfering with its operations. Rozumovsky protested, but to no avail. As a matter of fact, the financial autonomy of Ukraine, secured by the articles of the Agreement of Pereyaslav, were the first to be violated by the Muscovites during the lifetime of Bohdan Khmelnytsky.

During Rozumovsky's time, the class of the Cossack grandees, as a separate and privileged class, was crystallized. The grandees, the *starshyna*, began to be called to attend special conventions, which were gradually developing into a kind of class parliament. Actually, the evolution of the upper stratum of the Cossacks into a separate and dominant class had been initiated already during Khmelnytsky's time, being the reflection of the West European aristocratic pattern of the social structure. Also during Rozumovsky's time a court reform was completed. It was sparked by the scholarly work of Fedir Chuikevych, published in 1750. In 1760 the reform was introduced. The old court system of the Cossack era was replaced by the so-called territorial, cameral and urban courts, and an appellate, general court for the whole land. The new system resembled the court structure from the time before the National Revolution in 1648.

Rozumovsky completely rearranged the military organization. The military training of recruits was introduced, arms and weapons and military uniforms were standardized, and the artillery improved. All was done according to West European patterns.

The Hetman took great care in the development of education. New schools were organized in all colonelcies or districts; the schooling of Cossack sons was made compulsory; also special military schools were established. Rozumovsky also made plans and preparations to establish a university in the city of Baturyn, the Mazepian capital. He cared for the development of culture and arts, constructed buildings, and maintained theaters, choirs and musical bands. Being a well educated man, he would have been an ideal ruler in the well-established and peaceful state of Ukraine.[44]

In 1762, Catherine II (the Great) ascended the Russian imperial throne. Her rule was marked by strong centralization trends in the empire and its tremendous territorial expansion. Along with these developments, she then called Kyrylo Rozumovsky to St. Petersburg and demanded that he "voluntarily" resign from his office. Of course, he had no other choice. In 1764, an imperial decree was promulgated, announcing the "voluntary" resignation of Rozumovsky and the introduction of the so-called Third Little College to govern in Ukraine. A complete incorporation of Ukraine into the Russian Empire was in the making.

The Territory of the Zaporozhe Host. Immediately after the National Revolution of 1648 the majority of the Cossacks left the land beyond the Dnieper rapids for a more civilized life in the Hetman state. The land was largely depopulated. However, the political upheavals and the growing class differentiation in the Ukrainian state resulted in a gradual recolonization of the territories of the lower Dnieper. The common Cossacks and the peasantry, having experienced social equality and democratic freedom during the Revolution, violently opposed the return of the normal times with the customary social stratifications and the limitations imposed on the lower classes. The same social conflicts continued in Hetman Ukraine, starting with

Vyhovsky's Hetmanate, who was a nobleman. The social frictions between the nobility and the Cossack grandees, on the one hand, and the commoners, on the other, were ably supported, instigated and fortified at all times by Muscovite agents throughout Ukraine. It is enough to mention the Little Russian College, created by the Muscovite government supposedly to protect the common people against the assumed abuses committed by the Cossack grandees. Hence, whoever wished to have the old liberties went back beyond the rapids or cataracts. The Territory of the Cossack Host enjoyed political autonomy since the assumed decree of King Stefan Batory; it lived its own life. With foreign powers it conducted its own policies and diplomatic relations which were frequently contradictory to the national interests of all Ukraine.

A typical example of the traditional, extremely libertarian politics of the Zaporozhe Host was represented by Ivan Sirko, the commander-in-chief of the Host, the *koshovyi otaman*, who by his warfares with the Tartars spoiled the Ukrainian-Tartar alliance of Hetman Vyhovsky. Because of Sirko's assault, the Tartars left Vyhovsky after the Battle of Konotop, and did not permit the latter to continue his warfares against Trubetskoi's Muscovites. Later on, the same Sirko damaged, by his obsessive hostilities against the Tartars, Doroshenko's chances to defeat the Poles with the military support of the Tartars and Turks. At the time, Sirko pursued a distinctly pro-Muscovite policy, which spelled doom for Ukraine in the long run. His policies were definitely aimless and destructive.[45]

In the Treaty of Andrusiv of 1667 between Poland and Muscovy, the Territory of the Cossack Host was theoretically made a *condominium* of these two nations. Subsequently, the Cossack Host either severed its political allegiance, or restored its vassal obedience towards the Hetman state. Doubtlessly, Muscovite-Russian diplomatic intrigues helped to extensively confuse and aggrevate relations between these two Ukrainian political entities, to weaken them and to prevent them from uniting into one Ukrainian nation. Of course, there were also deeply rooted social and economic differences between Hetman Ukraine, largely ruled by the aristocratic and semimonarchistic principle, and the Territory of the Cossack Host, where democratic equality prevailed. These factors worked against political unification.

During Mazepa's time, Kost Hordienko was in constant opposition to Mazepa and his policies. He was sympathetic towards Petryk and Palii, the representatives of the common people who were opposing the aristocratism of Ivan Mazepa and his associates. He opposed Mazepa's apparently pro-

Muscovite subservient loyalty. However, after Mazepa joined Charles XII in his struggle for Ukraine's liberation, Hordienko immediately associated himself with Mazepa, with whom he seriously disagreed in other matters. Hordienko, as the commander-in-chief of the Cossack Host, greatly boosted Mazepa's prestige, made his struggle more popular and gained broader support for him, and also strengthened Mazepa's military force in the Swedish camp. The Territory of the Cossack Host paid a heavy toll for Hordienko's patriotism. The *Sitch* was destroyed by Peter's troops in 1709. An enormous number of people were tortured and murdered throughout the Territory, although those who stayed there did not obviously join Hordienko and were not guilty of any anti-Muscovite "crime." The Muscovites simply wanted to exterminate this Ukrainian political organization once and for all under the pretext of Hordienko's "treason." *Koshovyi* Hordienko also shared the fate of the Ukrainian liberation army; he fought at Poltava, went with his Cossacks to Bendery, cooperated with Pylyp Orlyk and participated in the military excursion of the liberation army to Right-bank Ukraine in 1711.

After the war for liberation was clearly lost, there was no return to Ukraine for Hordienko's Cossacks. Hence, they settled "under the Tartar protection" near the town of Oleshi, and then, on the Kamianka River. Otherwise, in the Territory of the Cossack Host not all the people were killed by the revengeful Muscovites after the Poltava catastrophe. Many thousands of people continued to live there in their farmsteads, the *khutory*, under their own administration, regionally organized in the so-called *palanky*, districts, firmly believing in their traditional "Cossack liberties."

The life of the Cossacks under Tartar protection was very hard, since they were economically limited by the Tartars in many respects and were forced to work on Tartar defense projects and participate in their war and booty excursions. Hence, they petitioned the government to allow them to return to their possessions beyond the cataracts and join their own people. By 1731 they received permission, returned to the territory of the Cossack Host, which they considered to be their own for centuries, established a new *Sitch* on the banks of the Pidpilna River, built a town, and placed their central administration there, the *Kish*, with their company organizations, the *kurini*. Their military council was the top legislative authority, with the *Koshovyi otaman*, a secretary, and other officials to administer current matters, as it was before. *Palanky* were the administrative districts.

There were two basic classes in the Territory: the Cossacks and the peasants. The Cossacks were the upper class, living in farmsteads, *khutory*, and they were socially divided into several strata: the senior, the junior, and at a later date, the *insignia* Cossacks or *starshyna*. A separate group were the so-called service men. The political and civil rights, the social prestige, the privileges and obligations of the individual Cossacks were differentiated according to their class status. Although some Cossacks acquired a high social status because of their wealth and office holdings, like the last commander-in-chief, Petro Kalnyshevsky, and the secretary-general, Hloba, whose riches in cattle, horses and money amounted to many thousands of *karbovantsi*, the real Cossack aristocratic stratum did not evolve in the Territory of the Cossack Host, as in Hetman Ukraine. The peasants had no military status and no part in the territories' administration whatsoever. Neither clergy nor townspeople developed as separate social classes.

The social frictions among the commoners and peasants, on the one hand, and the wealthy and influential Cossacks, on the other, led to a few uprisings of the "plebs" against the rich and the Muscovite policies, which aimed at the restriction of the territorial liberties. They were most serious between 1730 and 1770, being related to and influenced by the revolutionary *Haidamaky* movements and uprisings in the right bank regions of Ukraine, which were nationally, religiously, socially, politically and economically motivated. Several times Muscovite troops were sent by the Muscovite government to suppress the uprisings. Tsaritsa Catherine II developed a plan to liquidate the *Sitch* and the autonomy of the Cossack territory, but as long as the threat of the Tartar military and booty onslaughts persisted, the Cossacks were a welcome military deterrent against these onslaughts, and St. Petersburg did not dare to proceed with the plan.

However, as a result of the Russian-Turkish War and the peace treaty of Kuchuk-Kainardji, the Crimean Tartars became a vassal state of the Russian Empire. The Tartar danger was largely suppressed. The autonomous and rebellious Territory of the Cossack Host was definitely an undesirable last bastion of Ukrainian national self-assertion from the point of view of Catherine's centralistic policies. The Hetman state became a victim of the Russian-Muscovite centralist imperialism a few years before, in 1764. Now, the time had come for the Cossack Host. General Tekeley, returning with his army from the Turkish front, received the order to destroy and liquidate the Host. The Sitch was surrendered to the prevailing Russian forces. The fortress was demolished; the leaders, like Petro Kalnyshevsky, Hlobla and others were arrested, tried and deported, although a few years ago they were decorated and rewarded for bravery in the Russian-Turkish War. The Territory of the Cossack Host was then incorporated into the Aziv and the New-Russian gubernatorial districts. The liquidation of the Zaporozhe Cossack

Host by Catherine II took place in June 1775, on the Holy Day of Pentecost. The military-political organization, which for more than four hundred years defended Ukraine against the merciless onslaughts of the Tartars, the Polish imperialist drives, the Muscovite-Russian imperialist domination, was finally defeated by Peter the Great in 1709 and Catherine the Great in 1775, the two Muscovite-Russian Empire builders, and at the same time the executioners of Ukrainian national independence.[46]

The Haidamaky Movement. The political fortunes of West Ukraine and Right-bank Ukraine were quite different from those of the Hetman state and the Territory of the Cossack Host. West Ukraine consisted of the Ukrainian ethnic territories west of the Murakhva and Horyn rivers, and had included Galicia, West Volhinia, the Kholm region, Bukovyna, Carpathian Ukraine, Pidlasha and southern Polissia. These areas were never incorporated into the Hetman state. Except for Carpathian Ukraine and Bukovyna, Polish rule prevailed in all other regions most of the time. There the Polish class system of the nobility, clergy, townspeople and peasantry, with its traditionally enormous power of Polish and Catholic nobility and its unjust discrimination against other classes, and in particular, against the Orthodox Ukrainians, was not affected by the National Revolution, and continued until the partitions of Poland at the end of the eighteenth century.

No Cossack class evolved in West Ukraine to defend the Ukrainian national interest. The national and religious oppression of the Orthodox Ukrainians in West Ukraine was so effective that it resulted in an almost complete denationalization of the gentry and the rapid denationalization of the townspeople as well. In West Ukraine, peasant bondage was made intolerable by giving the nobility the power of life and death over their peasant serfs. Serfs were bought and sold, given as gifts or lost in card play like cattle or other forms of property, by Polish and Polonized nobles.

During Khmelnytsky's uprising, and especially, during the march of his armies through the Galician and Volhinian regions, a spontaneous rise of the Ukrainian population against Polish oppression spread rapidly, as was pointed out beforehand. Yet, these regions were not included in the Hetman state and remained under Polish domination. The revengeful terrorism of the Polish against those guilty and not guilty for the uprising was merciless. Thousands of peasants, townspeople, and some gentry were imprisoned, tortured and executed.[47]

After the wave of post-revolutionary terror subsided and life began to normalize in West Ukraine, national and social conditions for Ukrainians were still progressively worse. The adverse developments and subsequent frequent wars and foreign invasions resulted in the speedy economic decline of West Ukraine as well. In order to relieve the tragic situation at least in part, in the religious aspect, the head of the Orthodox Church in Galicia, Bishop Josyf Shumlansky, accomplished in 1700 a Church union of his diocese with the Holy See in Rome according to the Berest articles, hoping in this way to lessen religious discrimination. The Peremyshl and Lutsk dioceses followed the same path. He hoped in vain. The Polish government did not wish to recognize Ukrainian Uniat Catholics and Polish Roman Catholics as equal.

Although in the second half of the eighteenth century the Polish central government attempted some reforms, they had little success because the almighty nobility of the Polish Crown was not willing to cooperate. The peasants, theoretically, were subject to the jurisdiction of the royal courts, according to the reform, but for all practical purposes the nobles were not restricted from punishing their serfs even by death. Perhaps, the duties of the peasants were more clearly defined. The townspeople finally received the prerogative of *neminem captivabimus*, the privilege of participating in the country's judicial and administrative process, and acquiring the possession of landed estates. Also the burden of city tax was somewhat lowered. More liberal ennoblement processes were introduced to somehow weaken the elevated position of the gentry.

Yet, even these minimal reforms were not much help to the Orthodox Ukrainians, who were still exposed to discrimination, and a worsening social and economic position, giving rise to a large scale "Robin Hoodism," the *oprishkivstvo*. Numerous gangs of "goodhearted" bandits began to operate throughout Galicia and western Podillia, robbing the rich and giving to the poor, trying to solve the social inequities in their own way. It was in some way related to the *Haidamaky* revolutionary movement of Right-bank Ukraine. Naturally, this loosely organized "Robin Hoodism" could not solve the social problems of Galicia, but it at least frightened the manorial lords into lessening, to some extent, the oppression and exploitation of the peasants for a while.[48]

Right-bank Ukraine extended east of the Murakhva and Horyn Rivers to the right bank of the Dnieper River, and southward towards the "wild fields" and the Black Sea possessions, nominally under Tartar or Turk authority. After the Treaty of Andrusiv of 1667, these regions were returned to Poland, and they stayed under that authority most of the time until the partitions of Poland. Polish institutions were reintroduced; peasant and Cossack property rights denied, and the noble *latifundium* system on lands with its intolerable bondage and serfdom reinstated. In the southern border lands the nobility offered temporary freedom to peasant settlers to speed up the colonization process of the empty area. Then, once these new lands were colonized and appropriated, the gentry immediately moved ahead with imposing bondage and serfdom, and economic exploitation on the Ukrainian peasantry, according to the Polish aristocratic patterns. Neither the Polish government nor the Polish noblemen learned anything from the long lasting Polish-Ukrainian wars and their causes and consequences.

Large areas of Right-bank Ukraine again experienced more freedom under Palii's regime, between 1686 and 1704, as discussed before, when Cossack colonization was undertaken to strengthen her defenses against the Tartar onslaughts. Palii attempted to abolish the dominance of the Polish noblemen, provoking Polish retaliatory measures; developments, which were subsequently interrelated with the fortunes of the Northern war. According to the so-called Pruth agreement of 1711, which was accepted by Tsar Peter I under the threat of his complete military annihilation, Right-bank Ukraine was supposed to be given to Hetman Pylyp Orlyk and become an independent Ukrainian state. Yet, Orlyk could scarcely establish himself there, when a new agreement between Poland and Muscovy, signed in 1714, introduced Polish rule in the right-bank again. Thus another partition of Ukraine was accomplished by her two deadly enemies, Muscovy and Poland.[49]

Soon, in the right-bank regions a new breed of the rapacious Polish landed grandees, the *krolewieta*, evolved, such as the families of Lubomirski, Potocki, Jablonski, Sanguszki, Branicki and others, who once more reintroduced bondage and serfdom of the Polish style. Yet, the Ukrainian peasants and Cossack commoners, who had tasted freedom not so long ago, could no longer tolerate serfdom, and already in the 1730's several waves of peasant rebellions erupted. The insurgents or the rebels were generally called the *Haidamaky*. The *Haidamaky* attacked Polish castles, palaces and manors, pillaged and burned them, and ruined Catholic churches and cloisters. An all-out war developed against the Polish aristocracy and clergy, and the Ukrainian Uniats, who were considered by the insurgents as traitors of their faith and nationality. The *Haidamaky* uprisings were certainly nationally, socially and religiously motivated, and were intended to overthrow the discriminatory Polish rule in Ukraine. The West Ukrainian "robinhoodism," the *opryshky*, was deeply affected by the *Haidamaky* uprisings.

The Polish government, having only a small military force at its disposal because of domestic chaos, was not able to deal with the *Haidamaky*. Only small manorial militia troops attemped to check the fury of the *Haidamaky* uprisings. The uprisings in the 1750's spread throughout the Kiev, Bratslav and Podillia regions, and then, the uprisings continued during the 1760's as well, bringing destruction, hatred, and economic devastation. At one time, the struggle also became a real encounter between the Orthodox and the Uniats.

The large-scale *Haidamaky* uprising erupted in 1768. The Polish nobles organized a rebellious and anti-king Confederation in Bar, intending to change the course of political events in Poland. King Stanislaw Poniatowski seemed to patriotic Poles a willing tool of Catherine II, whose lover he was at one time. The king was unable to deal with the revolt. Catherine sent her Russian troops to save Stanislaw Poniatowski. The Ukrainian common Cossacks and peasants thought that the Russians came to aid them in their struggle against Polish oppression. Doubtlessly, numerous Russian undercover agents intensified this false assumption. Maksym Zalizniak became the leader. A massive uprising began. The *Haidamaky* took Polish fortresses and towns, where the nobles and scanty Polish troops took cover. Zhabotyn, Smila, Cherkasy, Korsun, Lysianka, Uman and other towns were conquered. A revengeful slaughter of the Polish nobles, clergy and Uniats, and their servants and fellow-travellers occurred everywhere. The *Haidamaky* dominated the situation. In Uman, the commander of the manorial militia in the landed estates of the Potocki family, Ivan Gonta, joined the insurgents. In the town of Uman the *Haidamaky* achieved their greatest victory against the Poles, when thousands of Polish gentry perished by the wrath of the populace. Then Zalizniak was elected the hetman and Gonta, the colonel of Uman. A statelike organization was established, while the *Haidamaky* war operations extended over a large area of Right-bank Ukraine. This large-scale uprising of 1768 received the name of the *Koliivshchyna*.[50]

Meanwhile, the Russian troops suppressed the Bar Confederation of the Polish nobility, headed by Casimir Pulawski. Initially, the Russians did not interfere with the *Haidamaky* movement, since it was an unwelcome King's ally against the nobles. The *Haidamaky* made a mistake, however. They invaded a part of the territory under Turkish sovereignty. The Turks protested. The incident gave Tsaritsa Catherine a pretext to suppress the uprising, which she actually intended to do from the very beginning. The popular movement of the Ukrainian masses was not to the liking of the aristocratic mind of her majesty. Her general, Krechetnikov, received the order to liquidate the *Koliivshchyna*. Zalizniak and Gonta were treacherously captured with hundreds of their warriors. Gonta and 846 *Haidamaks* were delivered to the Poles, tried, tortured and executed by them, while Zalizniak and 250 of his men were tortured and sent to Siberia. In this way Tsaritsa Catherine finished off still another Ukrainian liberation movement. The *Koliivshchyna* had a political impact on the Territory of the Cossack Host and southern Ukraine, where similar uprisings, as it was mentioned, erupted to lessen the foreign oppression. But the Russian Empire was already too strong to be challenged, and it was decidely against any form of Ukrainian independence or autonomy.

In connection with the discussion of the developments in West and Rightbank Ukraine a few words must be said about Carpathian Ukraine, a small plot of land separated by the Carpathian mountains from the main body of the Ukrainian ethnographic territory, situated south of Galicia. Since the thirteenth century, this land was continually under foreign, predominantly Hungarian, rule. Although subject to intensive national and religious discrimination and oppression by the Hungarian government and the Hungarian nobility, suffering under bondage and serfdom, and having little cultural connections with the centers of the Ukrainian national life, like Lviv and Kiev, the Orthodox Carpathian Ukrainians remained astonishingly patriotic and faithful to their Church and nationality. The Hungarian class system was, in many respects, even worse than that under Polish rule. Consequently, the country, being poorly endowed with natural resources, remained socially and economically retarded. Since the times of Prince Danylo and Prince Lev, in the thirteenth and fourteenth centuries, Carpathian Ukraine was not under any Ukrainian government. Yet, some six centuries later, her national self-assertion was so strong, that when the opportunity rendered itself, the country joined the Ukrainian statehood in the 1920's and then again proclaimed its national independence in March of 1939.

Similar unfavorable conditions also prevailed in Bukovyna, a small plot of Ukrainian land east of Carpathian Ukraine, which was predominantly under Moldavian and Turkish rule for many centuries. There also, national awareness did not fade away. Bukovyna sporadically shared political fortunes with Galicia, yet it joined the Ukrainian National Republic in the 1920's.[51]

The Russian Political Take-Over. After Kyrylo Rozumovsky resigned as Hetman of Ukraine, he was made a Russian field-marshall and induced to live in private in his considerable landed properties. Yet, he remained a Ukrainian patriot although he lived in St. Petersburg far away from his fatherland. His palace continued to be a center of Ukrainian cultural life, frequently visited by Ukrainian patriots, like himself.

A third Little Russian College, composed of four Russians and four Ukrainians, under the chairmanship of Governor-General P. Rumiantsev, was supposed to rule the former Hetman state. Its main goal was to erase any differences between Ukrainians and Russians and to make them feel like one ethnic stock. Rumiantsev was the real ruler of the land. In 1765, he ordered a general census of the country; of all lands, population, live-stock, farms and enterprises, manorial economies and other important details. The work continued for three years, during which an uneasiness prevailed because people were not sure of their holdings. Hundreds of thick volumes of excellent statistical material had been prepared which had enormous scholarly value. In 1767, Catherine established a commission to codify all laws for the Russian Empire. That gave rise to the resurrection of Hetman tendencies in Ukraine, which were subsequently severely suppressed by Rumiantsev. Because of the disagreements among the membership of the said commission, it was dissolved "temporarily," having accomplished nothing and never again was called to reconvene.

At the end of 1780, an imperial decree was proclaimed by which the general Russian administrative system was introduced in Ukraine. The Hetman regime was abolished, including both its Little Russian College and the division into colonelcy districts, and the country was then divided into three gubernatorial areas, Kiev, Chernihiv and Novhorod-Siversky. Similarly, other Ukrainian regions, the Territory of the Cossack Host, *Slobidska Ukraine*, Nova Serbia, and Slavianoserbia were incorporated into the Russian gubernatorial system. Soon, the same fate met Right-bank Ukraine and some parts of West Ukraine as a result of the three partitions of Poland by her three neighboring countries, of Russia, Prussia and Austria. For many decades anarchy was growing in Poland. The aristocratic grandees and the gentry, as a whole, reduced the authority of the king to shambles and made a mockery out of the Polish legislative, administrative and judicial systems. The nobility considered itself to be above the law in Poland. Any due process of government was made impossible there. One delegate of the Polish *seim*, parliament, could by his *liberum veto* paralyze the prolonged works of the body as a whole. Under these chaotic conditions Poland was unable to resist the growing imperialistic pressures of her neighbors. Hence, the said Ukrainian territories, which were within the political borders of the Polish *Rzeczpospolita*, were annexed by the Russian Empire in the second partition of Poland in 1793 and in the third one, in 1795. Only Galicia escaped the fate of becoming a part of the Russian Empire, having been incorporated by Austria in 1772.

1. The grandees, the *magnaty*: N. Polonska-Vasylenko, *Istoria Ukrainy,* Munich,

1972, Vol. I, pp. 455-459; M. Hrushevsky, *Istoria Ukrainy-Rusy,* New York, 1955, Vol. VI, pp. 272-289.

2. M. Andrusiak, *Istoria kozachchyny,* Munich, 1946, pp. 12-15; L. Vynar, "Severyn Nalyvaiko i revolutsyinyi rukh bratslavskoho mishchanstva," *Rozbudova Derzhavy,* 1957, No. 20, pp. 15-20; Polonska-Vasylenko, *op. cit.*, Vol. I, pp. 364-366, 460-463.

3. Hrushevsky, *op. cit.*, Vol. VII, pp. 236-241; I. Kholmsky, *Istoria Ukrainy,* Munich, 1948, pp. 185-186.

4. N. Fr.-Chirovsky, *A History of the Russian Empire,* New York, 1973, Vol. I, pp. 337-350.

5. Petro Sahaidachny: Hrushevsky, *op. cit.*, Vol. VII., pp. 357-387, 426-430; 462-489; Polonska-Vasylenko, *op. cit.*, Vol. I, pp. 440-445.

6. O. Ohloblyn, *Dumky pro Khmelnychchynu,* New York, 1957, p. 21.

7. Kholmsky, *op. cit.*, pp. 191-194; Hrushevsky, *op. cit.*, Vol. VIII, pp. 200-318; Polonska-Vasylenko, *op. cit.*, Vol. I, pp. 445-451; Andrusiak, *op. cit.*, pp. 33-36.

8. Khmelnytsky was at first a rather peaceful citizen: V. Lypynsky, *Ukraina na perelomi,* Vienna, 1920, p. 15; his escape: D. Doroshenko, *Narys istorii Ukrainy,* Munich, 1966, Vol. I, p. 11-12.

9. Lypynsky, *op. cit.*, p. 281; Ohloblyn, *op. cit.*, pp. 55-57: *Vossoiedinenie Ukrainy s Rossieiu,* Moscow, 1954, Vol. II, p. 130.

10. Kholmsky, *op. cit.*, p. 200: "I liberate all Rus'ian people from the Polish yoke ... as far as the cities of Lublin and Cracow ... ."

11. V. Kluchevskii, *Kurs russkoi istorii,* Moscow, 1924, Vol. III, p. 150.

12. Hrushevsky, *op. cit.*, Vol. IX, Part 1, p. 760; Polonska-Vasylenko, *op. cit.*, Vol. II, p. 22-25; the same, "Pereyaslavskyi dohovir v ochakh yoho suchasnykiv", *Vyzvolnyi Shlakh,* London, 1955, Book IV, pp. 40-41.

13. The Treaty of Pereyaslav: O. Ohloblyn, *Ukrainsko-moskovska uhoda 1654 r,* New York, 1954; A. Yakovliv, *Dohovir Bohdana Khmelnytskoho z Moskvoiu,* New York, 1954; Hrushevsky, *op. cit.*, Vol. IX, Part I. pp. 728-869; *Akty, otnosiashchiesia k istorii Yuzhnoi i Zapadnoi Rossii,* St. Petersburg, 1863—1869, Vol. X, pp. 217-228: the interpretation: Doroshenko, *op. cit.*, Vol. II, pp. 37-38.

14. Yakovliv, *op. cit.*, pp. 82-92; *Polnoie sobranie zakonov Rossiiskoi Imperii,* St. Petersburg, Vol. IV, appendix, pp. 111-112.

15. Polonska-Vasylenko, *Istoria Ukrainy*, Vol. II. pp. 26-29.

16. I. Borshchak, *Velykyi Mazepynets Hryhor Orlyk*, New York, 1972, p. 146; Ohloblyn, *op. cit.*, p. 68.

17. *Akty, otnosiashchiesia...*, Vol. III. pp. 551-552; also, Lypynsky, *op. cit.*, pp. 40-45.

18. *Ibid.*, pp. 249-252, 294-297; Polonska-Vasylenko, *op. cit.*, Vol. II, pp. 31-32.

19. M. Holubets, *Velyka istoria Ukrainy*, Lviv, 1935, pp. 483, 485-486; the Treaty of Hadiach: *ibid.*, 487-489; Doroshenko, *op. cit.*, Vol. II, pp. 58-59; Text of the Treaty; Hrushevsky, *op. cit.*, Vol. X, 331-346; Interpretation: *ibid.*, pp. 346-359.

20. A. Vostokov, "Sudba Vyhovskikh i Nechaia", *Kievskaia Starina*, Kiev, 1890, Book I; N. Kostomarov, "Getmanstvo Vygovskavo", *Sobranie sochinenii*, St. Petersburg, 1903, Vol. II, Book 1.

21. Yakovliv, *op. cit.*, pp. 82-90; N. Kostomarov, "Getmanstvo Yuria Khmelnitskavo", *Sobranie sochinenii*, St. Petersburg, 1905, Vol. XII, Book V.

22. Polonska-Vasylenko, *op. cit.*, p. 40; Kholmsky, *op. cit.*, pp. 227-228.

23. Doroshenko's Hetmanate: N. Kostomarov, "Ruina", *Sobranie sochinenii*, St. Petersburg, 1905, Vol. XV, Book VI; O. Ohloblyn, "Do istorii Ruiny", *Zapysky Istorychno-Filolohichnoho Viddilu Ukrainskoii Akademii Nauk*, Kiev, 1928, Vol. XVI; On Doroshenko and Mnohohrishnyi: Doroshenko, *op. cit.*, Vol. II, pp. 73-94; Polonska-Vasylenko, *op. cit.*, Vol. II, pp. 43-45, 49-50.

24. Doroshenko, *op. cit.*, Vol. II, pp. 90-96; Polonska-Vasylenko, *op. cit.*, Vol. II, p. 46.

25. Holubets, *op. cit.*, pp. 506-508.

26. O. Ohloblyn, "Dynastychna ideia v derzhavno-politychnii dumtsi Ukrainy- Hetmanshchyny 17-18 st.", *Derzhavnytska dumka*, Philadelphia, 1951, No. 4, p. 42.

27. M. Hrushevsky, *A History of Ukraine*, New Haven, 1970, pp. 342-346; A. Vostokov, "Sud i kazn Hryhoria Samoilovycha", *Kievskaia Starina*, Kiev, 1889, Book I; O. Ohloblyn, *Hetman Ivan Mazepa ta yoho doba*, New York, 1960, pp. 23-28: The Crimean campaign of 1687 and the plot against Hetman Samoilovych.

28. Ohloblyn, *ibid.*, p. 35.

29. On Petryk: *Ibid.*, pp. 176-195; Polonska-Vasylenko, *op. cit.*, Vol. II, pp. 57-58.

30. Palii and Mazepa: Ohloblyn, *op. cit.*, pp. 196-251; N. Polonska-Vasylenko, "Palii i Mazepa", *Visnyk,* New York, 1959, No. 7-8, pp. 10-11.

31. Mazepa's political plans: Ohloblyn, *op. cit.*, pp. 251-272; Polonska-Vasylenko, *Istoria Ukrainy,* Vol. II, pp. 63-65; M. Andrusiak, "Zviazky Mazepy z Stanislavom Leshchynskym i Karlom XII", *Zapysky Naukovoho Tovarystva im. Shevchenka,* Lviv, 1933. Vol. CL.

32. T. Mackiv, *Mazepa im Lichte der zeitgenossischen deutschen Quellen,* 1956; the same, *Prince Mazepa, Hetman of Ukraine in Contemporary English Publications, 1687—1709,* Chieago, 1967; Doroshenko, *op. cit.*, Vol. II, pp. 102-110, 136-154.

33. Ohloblyn, *op. cit.*, pp. 281-282, 302: a more detailed coverage in his *Studii nad "Istorieiu Rusiv",* essay on "Istoria Rusiv" and Fieldmarshall B. P. Sheremietiev, a manuscript, by O. Ohloblyn.

34. B. Krupnytsky, *Hetman Pylyp Orlyk,* Munich, 1956, pp. 10-14; also O. Ohloblyn, "Vyvid prav Ukrainy", *Visnyk,* New York, 1954, No. 5, pp. 11-14.

35. Ohloblyn, *Hetman Ivan Mazepa...",* as above, p. 352-374; Admiral F. Apraksin called the Sitch "the nest of banditti" in his letter to Tsar Peter congratulating him for the success in 1709.

36. It was prognosticated in the Sitch for a long time, that once the Muscovites annihilate the Zaporozhe, then "... doubtlessly all Ukrainian people would be turned into Moscow's slaves, something... which the Muscovite Tsardom has desired for a long time and had looked for means to achieve it": Ohloblyn, *loc. cit.*

37. The Bendery or Orlyk's Constitution: M. Vasylenko, "The Constitution of Pylyp Orlyk", *The Annals of the Ukrainian Academy of Arts and Sciences in the U.S.",* New York, 1958, Vol. VI, Nos. 3 and 4; the text: *Chtenia v obshchestve istorii i drevnostei Rossii pri Moskovskom Universitetie,* Moscow, 1847, Book 5, pp. 1-17.

38. Borshchak, *op. cit.*, pp. 22, 143, 163, 167.

39. N. Chubaty, "The Meaning of 'Russia' and 'Ukraine,' " *On the Historical Beginnings of Slavic Eastern Europe,* ed. by N. Fr.-Chirovsky, New York, 1976, pp. 131-132 and following.

40. T. Kostruba, *Hetman Ivan Skoropadsky,* Lviv, 1932; Hrushevsky, *op. cit.*, pp. 374-379; Polonska-Vasylenko, *Istoria Ukrainy,* Vol. II, pp. 80-83.

41. M. Vasylenko, "Pavlo Polubotok", *Ukraina,* Kiev, 1925, Book. VI; Doroshenko, *op. cit.*, Vol. II, pp. 176-179.

42. B. Krupnytsky, *Hetman Danylo Apostol i yoho doba,* Augsburg, 1948; Polonska-Vasylenko, *op. cit.*, Vol. II, pp. 86-91.

43. A. Yakovliv, *Ukrainskyi kodeks 1743 roku. Prava, po kotorym sudytsia Malorossiskii narod,* Munich, 1949; Polonska-Vasylenko, *op. cit.,* Vol. II, pp. 220-222.

44. I. Cherkasky, "Chy vplyvav H. Tieplov na Hetmana Rozumovskoho", *Yuvileinyi zbirnyk na poshanu M. Hrushevskoho,* Kiev, 1928, Vol. I; the same, "Sudovi reformy Hetmana Rozumovskoho", *Yuvileinyi zbirnyk na poshanu D. Bahalia,* Kiev, 1927; Polonska-Vasylenko, *op. cit.,* Vol. II, pp. 96-101.

45. *Ibid.,* pp. 120-125.

46. The Sitch: *Ibid.,* pp. 120-138; the same, "Zruinuvannia Zaporozhskoi Sitchi," *Visnyk OOChSU,* New York, 1955, No. 7-; pp. 9-10; the same, "Maino zaporozhskoi starshyny," *Pratsi Komisii dla vyuchuvannia sotsialno-ekonomichnoi istorii Ukrainy,* Kiev, 1932, Vol. I, pp. 77 and following: V. Holobutsky, *Zaporozhska Sitch v ostanni chasy svoho isnuvannia, 1734—1745,* Kiev, 1961; the same, *Zaporozhskoie kozachestvo,* Kiev, 1957.

47. Polonska-Vasylenko, *Istoria Ukrainy,* Vol. II, p. 139; M. Chirovsky, "Chertkamy po istorychnomu mynulomu Zemli Yavorivskoi" (manuscript), pp. 51-56.

48. The Galician "robinhoodism," the *oprishkivstvo:* Holubets, *op. cit.,* pp. 560-562; famous "robinhoods": Drozdenko, 1665, Nestor, 1683; Pysklyvyi 1703—1712; Pynta, 1704; Ivan Panchyshyn, 1712; the most outstanding of them all, Oleksa Dovbush, 1738—1745, and others.

49. Polonska-Vasylenko, *op. cit.,* Vol. II, p. 79.

50. *Ibid.,* pp. 148-151; P. Mirchuk, *Koliivshchyna, Haidamatske povstannia* 1768 r., New York, 1973.

51. Doroshenko, *op. cit.,* Vol. II, 264-266.

CHAPTER NINE

THE POLITICAL STRUCTURE AND THE GOVERNMENT OF THE COSSACK-HETMAN STATE

The constitution and the law — The Hetman — The General Council — The Council of Seniors — The central administration — The local administration — The judiciary — The military

The Constitution and the Law. The state constitution and the legal system and process of the Cossack-Hetman State evolved gradually from the Cossack organization, which slowly evolved for a period of two hundred years prior to the National Revolution. It was shaped as a separate para-military class. Of course, the constitutional and legal system of the Cossack-Hetman State was influenced in its evolution by many important outside social-political forces, such as the general class structure of the European societies at that time, the prevailing monarchistic principle of their political organizations, the social-political structure of the Polish-Lithuanian Commonwealth, of which Ukraine was a part for such a long time, the Polish social and legal institutions, and the spiritual and cultural trends in Europe at the dawn of modern times.

The Zaporozhe Cossacks, the "registered" Cossacks, and the Cossacks living in various towns and settlements outside the official registry, "the *vypyshchyky,*" felt a common social bond among themselves as a separate class, largely democratically organized. Especially in the *Sitch*, the General Council of the Cossacks as the top authority, with all its leaders and commanders elected, clearly indicated that the political principle of the people's sovereignty prevailed. The Polish government, though reluctantly, acknowledged and recognized the Cossacks as a separate class by the institution of their registration. Yet, at first *de facto*, and then, *de jure*, that recognition was extended by certain statements of the *seim* and, later on, by the Agreement of Zboriv and the Agreement of Bila Tserkva to the entire stratum of the Cossacks.

The top military and administrative official, elected by the Cossack Council, the *rada*, was the Commander-in-Chief of the *Sitch*, the *koshovyi otaman*, whose office later on gave rise to the development of the institution of the hetman, who combined in his hands all military, administrative, judicial, representative, and to some extent, legislative authority. He too was elected to office. The name of the office was taken from Poland, where the top field commanders were called *hetmans*, derived probably from the German title, the *Hauptman*, the chief man. The *hetman* was advised by the Council of Seniors, the *rada starshyn*, composed of the top officials of the *Sitch*, which were the Camp Commander, *oboznyi*, the Secretary, *pysar*, the judge, *suddia*, the deputy, *osaul*, a word of Mongol origin, the flag-bearer, *khorunzhyi*, and some other less important officials.

The Council of Cossacks was a self-governing agency, a kind of class parliament which elected the top officers and was involved in the legislative, administrative, military, judicial and financial affairs of the *Sitch* and the surrounding territory. Its deliberations were rather informal and without any elaborate procedural code, concluded by the democratic majority rule.

On the lower level, the Cossacks were organized in the regimental (colonel), *polkovyi*, and centurion, *sotennyi*, system, where the colonels and centurions carried out military and administrative functions in their respective areas. They all were elected and were assisted by respective councils of their regimental or centurion officials, including the secretaries, judges, deputies, and other officers.

With the National Revolution of 1648 and with the creation of an independent Ukrainian state, the organizational system of the Cossack estate or class was immediately, and somehow automatically, since the Cossacks were the standard-bearers of the revolution, extended over the entire political territory of the new state, while subsequent developments contributed to later changes and modifications. The Territory of the Cossack Host at the lower Dnieper River also essentially retained the same organizational scheme, though with lesser elaboration, than that adopted by the Cossack-Hetman State. The system was also copied and introduced in other territories, of Ukraine, such as Right-bank area under Polish supremacy, Village Ukraine,

Slobozhanshchyna or *Slobisdka* Ukraine under Muscovite supremacy, as well as, Nova Serbia and Slovianoserbia for a short while. Of course, each individual territory introduced some modifications and organizational changes of its own, yet, the para-military character of their constitutional structures was always present.[1]

The adoption of the Cossack organizational system by the Cossack-Hetman State was another link in the discontinuous political development of the Ukrainian people, which was briefly discussed in the first volume of this work. The monarchal-princely order of the Kievan and Lithuanian-Rus' periods was not repeated, although there were some strong tendencies under some Hetmans to introduce it. Instead, the para-military and democratic constitutional scheme, with the electoral office of the Hetman, was introduced. Yet, a deep social-political undercurrent was also present, namely, the strict class structure of the society. The class structure was only shortly suspended during the revolutionary turmoil. However, once the orderly organization of the state was under way, already under the rule of Bohdan Khmelnytsky, the class structure was reintroduced by the legislative and administrative acts of the new state, though now without the resistance of the lower classes, the common Cossacks and the peasants in particular.[2]

The constitutional status of the Ukrainian Hetman state was a constantly changing one. From the time of the National Revolution in 1648 Ukraine became a *de facto* sovereign state. In 1649, the Agreement of Zboriv between Jan-Casimir, King of Poland, and Bohdan Khmelnytsky, Hetman of Ukraine, established Ukrainian independence *de jure*, while the Polish Crown retained some shadow of suzerainty over the new political organism. The Agreement of Pereyaslav of 1654 altered the situation completely. With this treaty theoretical Polish supremacy was abolished between the Cossack-Hetman State and the Polish Kingdom, while an unclear form of Muscovite supremacy over Ukraine was introduced. Different interpretations of the Agreement of Pereyaslav have been briefly discussed already. Here it must be asserted that if the original agreement of 1654 had established some kind of Muscovite protectorate, then it was largely an illusory one. Bohdan Khmelnytsky, the Muscovite court, and the other foreign courts considered Ukraine a fully independent nation, which freely ruled itself and freely entertained diplomatic relations and negotiated agreements with other nations. Moscow never objected to or questioned the sovereignty of the Hetman state during Khmelnytsky's lifetime. The supplicatory form of the Agreement on the part of the Cossacks did not indicate a submission of Ukraine, since such a form was conventional in the international relations of those days.[3]

The Agreement of Hadiach of 1658 did not affect the political status of Ukraine because it never materialized. Yet, it was intended to terminate any political relationship of Ukraine with Muscovy, whether it might have been an alliance of the two nations on equal footage or a form of a Muscovite protectorate over Ukraine. Ukraine was supposed to become a member nation of a federation with Poland and Lithuania, as a Rus' Principality. However, the subsequent and second Agreement of Pereyaslav of 1659, which was imposed upon Hetman Yurii Khmelnytsky by Moscow, substantially limited the autonomy of Ukraine, although it still was a form of an international convention between two independent nations. The second version of the Agreement was forged by Moscow's court and presented to Yurii Khmelnytsky under false pretenses. This forged version was then introduced into the *Complete Collection of the Laws of the Russian Empire*, as was pointed out already in the previous chapter.[4]

Subsequent *Statutes*, adopted in particular in Hlukhiv and on the Kolomak River, progressively limited Ukrainian political autonomy and definitely made Ukraine subject to Muscovite-Russian supremacy, while the *Reshytielnie Punkty*, presented to Danylo Apostol in 1728, already treated Ukraine as a province of the Tsardom, with only some self-governing concessions. Doubtlessly, it all happened as a flagrant violation of the political rights of Ukraine, which the Tsar solemnly promised to respect by the Treaty of Pereyaslav of 1654. Such was the state of affairs in the first half of the eighteenth century.

Hetmans Doroshenko and Brukhovetsky were willing to accept a Turkish alliance or protectorate as a way of getting rid of either Polish or Muscovite supremacy and in this manner preserving Ukrainian political autonomy. Thus, for a while Ukraine was really dependent upon the Ottoman Empire as a result of the conventions of the said Hetmans with the Sultan.

The Ukrainian-Muscovite relations in Moscow were at first handled by the so-called Department of Envoys, the *posolskii prikaz*. However, later on, because the above department was overburdened with a great many matters, the Ukrainian affairs were transferred to the newly created Little Russian Department, *malorossiiskii prikaz*, while all the records pertaining to Ukraine were kept in the Ministry of Foreign Affairs.[5]

From 1649 to 1662, the Ukrainian Hetman State territorially extended its political authority over the Left-bank and the Right-bank regions: to the Murakhva and Horyn Rivers in the west; the Byeloruthenian ethnic territory (with an exception to be mentioned later on) in the north; the territory of Village Ukraine, *Slobozhanshchyna*, or *Slobidska Ukraine*, under Muscovite supremacy in the east; to the Territory of the Cossack Host and some regions along the Black Sea littorals, held by the Tartars and Turks in the south; and finally, to the Moldavian borders in the southwest. From 1662 on, Ukraine was divided into two Hetman states: one, Left-bank, east of the Dnieper River, and another, Right-bank, west of that river. As it was discussed in the above chapter, this was one of the political misfortunes of Ukrainian statehood. The Treaty of Andrusiv of 1667 between Poland and Muscovy affirmed that division, and partitioned Ukraine against the will of the Ukrainian people. Left-bank Ukraine was then reserved for Muscovite, and Right-bank Ukraine, for Polish political supremacy. Under Polish supremacy, the autonomous Ukrainian Hetman State did not exist for long, except for the third and short governance of Yurii Khmelnytsky under Turkish protection and some, rather *de facto*, self-governing Cossack communities of brief duration, similar to Palii's administration of certain Right-bank areas from 1686 to 1704. In 1704, Mazepa invaded Right-bank Ukraine, took her away from the Poles, and restored a united Ukrainian Hetman nation until the tragic Battle of Poltava in 1709. From that time on, Polish administration prevailed in the right-bank regions. The Cossack-Hetman State was limited from now on to the left-bank regions. The Territory of the Cossack Host, the *Zaporozhe*, was never really a part of the Hetman State, except, perhaps, during Bohdan Khmelnytsky's rule. Otherwise, the Territory was in some kind of an indirect or vassal relationship to the Hetman State, or a *condominium* of the Hetman State and Muscovite Tsardom. The Andrusiv Treaty attempted to establish a joint, Polish-Muscovite *condominium* over the Territory of the Cossack Host.

The cities of Chyhyryn, Hadiach, Baturyn and Hlukhiv were, in turn, the capitals of the Hetman State. The state never included all Ukrainian ethnographic territory, though Bohdan Khmelnytsky dreamt about it at one time. Yet, it extended over a part of the Byeloruthenian ethnic land for a while. There was no equality of all citizens in the Hetman State, nor was there any direct relationship of an individual to the state and vice-versa, in the modern sense of the term. An individual citizen or subject was first of all a member of a class or estate, and then in the framework of the class his legal status, rights, privileges and responsibilities were defined.

The following social classes existed in the Hetman State: the Cossacks, differentiated into the Cossack grandees, *znatne tovarystvo*, and the Cossack commonors, the country gentry, the townspeople, the peasants and the clergy. The social class structure of the Cossack-Hetman State will be discussed in depth in one of the following chapters. Religion also made a difference in the legal status of a person. The Orthodox religion was dominant in the state; Roman Catholicism was tolerated, while the Uniat Church was outlawed. Thus, the religious affiliation of an individual considerably affected his status in the state. The Muscovite "Old-believers," refugees from the persecution in their homeland, were tolerated and even protected in Ukraine, in spite of the protests of the Muscovite government. Foreigners were numerous in Ukraine and they enjoyed general tolerance and protection.

In order to be effectively organized, the new state needed an efficient legislative process of making laws and rules for the orderly conduct of its public and private affairs. An analysis of the legislative acts of the Cossack-Hetman State indicates clearly how well educated and trained the Ukrainian jurists of that time were.

The leading forms of the legislation of the new state were as follows: the international agreements, the *Hetman Statutes, hetmanski stati*, the universals of the hetman and colonels, the Lithuanian Statute, the compilations of the Magdeburg law, the *Orlyk Constitution* and the *Code of Laws, according to which justice is done among the Little Rus'ian people*. The rules and regulations, issued by various government agencies, including those of the Little Russian Colleges, completed the legal framework of the Hetman State.[6]

The constitutional structure of the new nation was partially established by all kinds of international agreements of the Hetman State, such as the Treaty of Zboriv of 1649, the Treaty of Bila Tserkva of 1651, and the Agreement of Hadiach of 1658 with Poland, the Treaties of Pereyaslav of 1654 and 1659, with Moscow, treaties with the Ottoman Empire in 1668, agreements with Sweden made by Bohdan Khmelnytsky and Ivan Mazepa in 1655 and 1706, respectively, agreements with Moldavia, Transylvania, Wallachia, Lithuania, the Crimean Tartars and other powers. The legal impact of these treaties and agreements upon the constitutional structure of the Hetman State was of varying degrees. The Treaties of Pereyaslav of 1654 and 1659 had the most lasting and deepest impact upon the fortunes of the Hetman state, since they initiated the ruthless drive of Muscovite-Russian imperialism in Ukraine. Whatever the Moscow or St. Petersburg governments did later on was a flagrant violation of the articles of the original act of 1654, since the Tsar most solemnly promised, as it was pointed out before, to respect the political *status quo* of Ukraine, her diplomatic, military, financial, social and otherwise autonomous rights. The Agreement secured a free election of the Hetman by the Cossack Council, a Ukrainian army of 60,000 men, free political and diplomatic relations with foreign powers, of which the Tsar was supposed to be only notified, full fiscal autonomy with respect to collecting taxes and making public expenditures, and the preservation of all rights and liberties of the Ukrainian people, including the social structure of the nation. As previously pointed out, with respect to foreign relations, the limitation was introduced only in regard to negotiations with Poland and the Ottoman Empire, while the fiscal autonomy of Ukraine was actually the very first article of the Treaty, which was violated by the Moscow government.[7] Other foreign agreements of the Hetman State, as listed above, either modified or changed the constitutional status of Ukraine in various directions and to various degrees.

The so-called *Hetman Statutes, hetmanski stati*, developed partially from the international agreements with Muscovy. Each time a new Hetman assumed rule, new *Hetman Statutes* were adoped, by which relations with Muscovy were regulated anew. They certainly had a constitutional aspect, and each time the Muscovite court introduced some modifications which attempted to limit the Ukrainian autonomy. The *Hlukhiv Statutes* were, perhaps, most important in this respect, while the *Paragraphs of Decision, Reshytielnie Punkty*, already had a completely different legal character. They were simply a legal act of the Russian government, referring to Ukraine as a province of the Empire, and no longer the statutes of the Hetman.

The internal legal problems of the Hetman State and the day-to-day businesses of life were regulated by the Hetman's universals or decrees of nationwide coverage, while the legal questions of regional or local importance were regulated by the colonel universals. The advisors and jurists always assisted the respective authorities in the preparation and promulgation of the particular laws and rules. The Hetman's universals followed a certain prescribed form; they were signed by the Hetman and corroborated by the state seal. They regulated public and private life, referring to criminal matters as well, certifying land grants for Cossack grandees, the Church, and monasteries, granting immunities and privileges, and ordering other matters.[8]

The new laws and regulations could not regulate all the detailed problems. Hence, the old laws and legislative acts of the previous historical era, of the Polish-Lithuanian times, were also in force, having been corroborated as binding by the Treaty of Pereyaslav of 1654. These include the *Lithuanian Statute* in its third version of 1588, and various compilations of the Magdeburg law, *Speculum Saxonum, Speculum Saxonum albo Prawo Saske*, and *Porzadek sadow u sprawach miejskich prawa Magdeburskiego, the Judicial Order in the Urban Cases of Magdeburg Law*, traditional in

Ukraine. As a result of this corroboration, the said codes or compilations also became binding in the left-bank regions, though they were not binding there prior to the National Revolution of 1648.

With the progress of time, the conditions in the growing society of the Hetman State made legal matters ever more complicated. The colonel and centurion courts were overburdened with work, and administrative matters were progressively delegated to lower officials who were not properly prepared to handle the cases. Dissatisfaction mounted. Hence, Hetman Skoropadsky, complying with the wish of the Russian government to bring justice to the Ukrainian people, appointed a commission to work on the laws, in particular, to translate the *Lithuanian Statute* and the compilations on the Magdeburg laws. In 1734, the commission was expanded and its competence widened to include the authority to correct and streamline the existing regulations. The new code was entitled the *Laws, according to which justice is done among the Little Rus'ian* people. The code was never ratified, as mentioned above, partially because of the opposition of the Ukrainian upper social crest, and partially because the Russian government did not want any legal particularism to continue in the future. Yet in the practical aspect, the impact of the Code was very considerable. It was a superior codification of binding laws, being much better than many other codifications of laws at that time in Europe, as far as the legal terminology, definition of terms and clarity of presentation were concerned. It was a very good commentary of the *Lithuanian Statute*; hence, it was broadly used.[9] Some fifty people worked on the codification of the *Laws, according to which justice is done among the Little Rus'ian people*. They included F. Chuikevych, V. Stefanovych, and M. Khaneneko. Many other members of the commission were educated either in the Kievan-Mohylian Academy or in foreign universities.

Still another legislative monument must be underscored here, namely, the *Konstytutsia prav i svobid Zaporozhskoho viiska*, the *Constitution of the Rights and Liberties of the Zaporozhe Host*, the so-called Bendery Constitution, adopted and confirmed by Charles XII in 1710. The constitution was a strictly theoretical work of little practical meaning, but an important document of the development of political thought among the Cossack leadership in exile, reflecting the real structure of the Cossack State at home and the dreams of an independent Ukraine in the minds of the Ukrainian patriots. It proclaimed Ukrainian independence from Muscovy and Poland. It formulated the Hetman State as a class (Cossack), electoral, parliamentary monarchy. It reflected the traditional Cossack view, which was never overcome, that Ukraine was actually the country of one class or estate of the

Cossacks, since they got her freedom, while other classes had only a secondary and auxiliary role. Of course, the Cossack government had to protect the other classes, while the constitutional and legal position of the Cossack grandees, aristocrats, was elevated by the said constitutional draft. The Hetman was supposed to govern together with the Council of Seniors, *rada starshyn*, and the General Council, *heneralna rada*, of the Cossacks. Both councils were electoral. The Orthodox Church was supposed to be protected and supported by the government. Towns were guaranteed their traditional legal (Magdeburg) status. The electoral representation of the Zaporozhe Host was embodied into the *heneralna rada*. Some economic affairs were also constitutionally regulated.

Perhaps the most specific detail of the said constitution was its preamble, which underscored the continuity of Rus'ian-Ukrainian statehood from the Kievan Rus' on to modern times.[10]

Of course, the constitutional and legal framework of the Cossack-Hetman State followed the same system as most nations still did at that time. There was no separation of powers in the state, the Hetman, the Council of Seniors, the General Council, the colonels and centurions, largely combined into their own hands the legislative, administrative, judicial, and in addition, military authorities. Other agencies in the governmental structure occasionally did as well. The jurisdictions of individual officers and agencies were not clearly separated, nor were people always entrusted with appropriate authority.

The Hetman. The Hetman was the chief of the state, but the nature and contents of his authority were subject to changes. The question of his authority was directly related to the fundamental constitutional issue of the nature of the state; was it a monarchy or a republic? There is no doubt that at the time of Bohdan Khmelnytsky, Ivan Samoilovych, Ivan Mazepa and some others, the monarchal principle definitely prevailed in Ukraine, while the General Council, *heneralna rada*, had an advisory and auxiliary character only. The mentioned Hetmans even showed a tendency to neglect the Council, and on top of it all, to change their electoral office into a hereditary monarchal one. Bohdan Khmelnytsky made all possible preparations to make his son, Tymish, a hereditary Hetman and head of the Ukrainian nation. For that very reason the marriage between him and the Moldavian Princess Rozanda Lupul was arranged to introduce the Khmelnytsky family to the ruling houses of East Europe. Tymish, however, was killed at the siege of Suchava. Then, Bohdan Khmelnytsky immediately assumed the plan to make his younger son, Yurii, his successor to the Hetman's office. However, Yurii was definitely not the man for the job. The republican and democratic oriented

Cossack grandees, such as Vyhovsky, Zhdanovych and others objected to the plan. Khmelnytsky even resorted to harsh measures to force his will against the opposition. After his death, however, due to Yurii's personal inabilities to handle the situation, the plan failed.

Demian Mnohohrishny was the second Hetman, who planned to establish a hereditary monarchy in Ukraine. The Cossacks opposed him and this brought his downfall. The third attempt in this direction was undertaken by Ivan Samoilovych, who planned at first to leave the Hetman's mace, *bulava*, to his older son, Semen, and after his death, to the other son, Yakiv. He met stiff opposition from the Cossack aristocracy, which also contributed to his downfall and exile. The idea of a hereditary monarchy would have doubtlessly strengthened the Ukrainian statehood. Yet, the Cossack grandees were afraid of losing their power in such cases, while a strong Ukraine was not in the imperialist plans of Muscovy-Russia. Hence, the unholy alliance of the power-hungry Cossack grandees with Muscovite imperial plans killed the chances for the preservation of long-term Ukrainian political independence.

Similarly, Hetman Ivan Mazepa unfolded a plan of a hereditary monarchy (hereditary Hetmanate) in Ukraine. Since he had no son, he planned at first to make his relative, Colonel Ivan Obydovsky, the hetman, and after the latter's death, he designed Andrii Voynarovsky, another relation of his, for the office. Nevertheless, the Poltava catastrophe made the idea unrealizable. When in exile, and after Mazepa's death, Voynarovsky did not demand the office. Pylyp Orlyk was chosen in Bendery to become the Hetman, as it was pointed out above. Yet, a few decades later, when it became apparent during the reign of Catherine the Great that she intended to liquidate the institution of the Hetmanate altogether according to her general centralization drive, some members of the Cossack aristocracy asked the Tsaritsa to make the Hetmanate hereditary in the Rozumovsky family. It was an attempt to save Ukrainian autonomy. Instead, the liquidation of the institution followed in 1764.[11]

The other constitutional trend was the republican one, which insisted on the electoral character of the Hetman office. Essentially, Yurii Khmelnytsky, Ivan Vyhovsky, Pavlo Teteria, Petro Doroshenko and some others resigned from the Hetman office at the Conventions of the General Council, although in principle, they were elected for life. When "putting down the mace," the *bulava*, the Hetman *insignium*, they gave thanks for the dignity and honor bestowed upon them at the convention. By so doing, they were actually acknowledging the Council's constitutional superiority over the Hetman's authority. In fact, the shortage of time of the Hetman era and the growing

Muscovite interference allowed neither the constitutional principle of the Hetmanate, nor the monarchal nor republican, to crystallize into the foundation of the political structure of the Cossack State.

During his tenure, the Hetman had unlimited authority. He was head of the state, the representative in all international political and diplomatic affairs and negotiations, the chief commander of all armed forces, the chief legislator, since the General Council lacked that power, the chief administrator and the supreme justice for the priviliged classes of the people, the Cossack grandees and other important personalities, and for appellate cases, referred to him from the lower courts. At times the senior officers of the state were elected by the General Council; however, they were often appointed by the Hetman. The Hetman made land grants to the grandees, the Church and monasteries, although later on, the Tsar began to progressively assume this authority and compete with the Hetman. In some instances, his authority conflicted or was interlocked with that of the General Council, whenever the republican principle manifested itself more strongly.

Concomitant with the growing interference of the Russian government with Ukrainian affairs, the Hetman's authority was either gradually restricted or at times even replaced. After the Poltava catastrophe, a Russian minister-resident was appointed by the Russian court to watch over the Hetman and the Ukrainian central government. At the end of Skoropadsky's Hetmanate, a *Little Russian College* was established, which substantially reduced the Hetman's authority, and against which Hetman Polubotok strenuously objected. After Polubotok's arrest, the *Little Russian College*, composed of six Russians and Veliaminov as its president, assumed all authority. In 1727 the *College* was abolished, and Hetman Danylo Apostol attempted to regain the powers of his office with little success.

As previously mentioned, Moscow already waited for Apostol's death for another opportunity to eliminate the Hetman's office. A *Second Little Russian College*, under the deceiving name of the *Administration of the Hetman Government*, was introduced. The same performance was repeated by the Tsarist court after Hetman Kyrylo Rozumovsky was forced to resign from his office, and in fact, the *Third Little Russian College* assumed authority. The said colleges were not Ukrainian, but Russian administrative agencies, hence, not much room will be devoted to them in this analysis of the Ukraninian governmental structure. The second College consisted of six members, three Russians and three Ukrainians, where Prince Shakhovsky occupied a leading position; the third one, consisted of eight members, four Russians and four Ukrainians, where Governor-General Rumiantsev was the all-powerful chairman. The Colleges were set up and secretly instructed to suppress the Ukrainian autonomous institutions, notably, in order to prepare for the full annexation of the country into the Russian Empire.[12]

The General Council. The General Council of Cossacks experienced some evolutionary process during the Hetman era. It was the republican element in the governmental structure of the state. Hence, whenever the republican principle took over, the importance of the General Council increased as a government agency, and vice versa, whenever the monarchistic principle prevailed, its significance declined, or it was not called to convene for several years. At first it was only a gathering of the Cossacks for military purposes. Then, its composition changed, including also the representation of the clergy and townspeople. It convened frequently during the first stage of Khmelnytsky's rule, but not after the Pereyaslav Treaty of 1654. Since Vyhovsky and Doroshenko recognized the prime importance of the Council, over the Hetman himself, it convened rather frequently. Hetmans Mnohohrishny, Samoilovych and Mazepa neglected the *heneralna rada* completely. At this time it was only a kind of democratic "ornamentation." These hetmans relied instead, on the advice of the Council of Seniors, *rada starshyn*, according to Okinshevych and other historians. Because of its incidental conventions, unsettled composition, the *ad hoc* character of its deliberations, and the frequent influence of outside forces, such as Russian pressure, the General Council could not become a full-fledged governmental institution, so much more, because of the strong monarchistic tendencies in Ukraine in certain periods.

The General Council, an expression of the people's sovereignty, at the same time constituted a strictly class representation, primarily interested in the preservation of the class rights of the Cossacks. Its character was directly inherited from its predecessor, the Council of the Cossacks in the *Sitch*. The meager representation of the clergy and urban population could not fundamentally change that very nature of the Council, even, when at times the commoners and peasants were also admitted to join the Council. The representation of the Zaporozhe Cossacks was rarely admitted to the deliberations.

The General Council convened in various places, such as Masliv, Pryluky, Kiev, Nizhyn and others. The procedures were very loose. The Hetman normally presided, and deliberations were accompanied with shouting, throwing caps high into the air and brawls. The competence of the *heneralna rada* usually included the election of the Hetman, the acceptance of his resignation, negotiations with foreign powers, Moscow in particular, the election of the top officers of state, and some administrative functions. In many instances its jurisdiction was in conflict with that of the Hetman. Later, in the eighteenth century, the General Council degenerated into a body that rubber-stamped the political and legal impositions of the Russian Tsarist court, inforced by terror, briberies and deceit.[13]

The Council Of Seniors. The *rada starshyn* later developed into a permanent institution, although already in the seventeenth century the Hetmans informally relied more and more upon the advice of the top echelon of the Ukrainian class society. It was a kind of upper class house in the government structure of Hetman Ukraine. Similar institutions existed in other countries of Central and Western Europe, as well, originating in West European feudalism. In the Lithuanian-Rus' Commonwealth, for example, there was the so-called Council of Nobles, along with the parliamentary representation, the *seim*.

According to Okinshevych, the evolution of the Council of Seniors was progressing positively, and was gradually gaining more and more authority, especially, when the significance of the General Council was declining, or when the latter institution was largely neglected by the monarchistically-minded Hetmans. The Hetmans had to consult some advisory body or to share their responsibilities with some other agency. In some instances a competition between the Hetman and the Council developed. The areas where the influence of the Council of Seniors was felt included foreign policies, financial and tax matters, maintenance of the mercenary troops, preparation of legislation like that of the *Laws, according to which justice is done among the Little Rus'ian people*, and groundwork for administrative changes and reforms. During Rozumovsky's time, the Council debated the question of the hereditary Hetmanate in his family.

It seems that the *Bendery constitution* actually gave a full expression of the evolutionary trend in the development of the Council of Seniors. According to the said constitution, the Council was supposed to work in three ways: first, to meet with the Hetman and the top central officers of the state for deliberations and decision making, sometime every day; second, to meet with the colonels and at other times, other regimental officials; and third, to convene with all Cossack officers and grandees, with mayors of the towns at times, with the representation of the clergy, and the delegates of the commoners. In the second and third cases, the *rada starshyn* was expected to convene periodically during Christmas, Easter, Pentecost, and the Day of the Virgin Mary the Protectoress in October. The deliberations continued sometimes for weeks. The conventions were held in the Hetman's residence and under his chairmanship. At times the minutes of the debates were written down. The principle of the majority rule prevailed. The sessions were solemnly initiated and adjourned by the Hetman. Only during Doroshenko's Hetmanate did the Hetman not preside at the deliberations.

The Council of Seniors gained more authority whenever there was no Hetman. Then it actually governed the state, as after the deportation of Demian Mnohohrishny in 1672, after Skoropadsly's death in 1722, or during Rozumovsky's stays in St. Petersburg. During Rozumovsky's time the Council generally received more prestige and acquired more influence.[14]

The General Council of the Cossacks and the Council of Seniors definitely indicated the constitutional trend in the Hetman State in the direction of a bicameral parliamentary representation, although initially featured by a distinctly class bias. No doubt, in the course of a subsequent and democratically-minded evolution, class characteristics would have faded away. It was a tragedy of the Ukrainian people that they fell as one of the first victims of despotic Muscovite-Russian imperialism, which did not allow Ukrainian democracy to mature.

The Central Administration. The central administration of the Hetman State was called, in Ukrainian, the *heneralna starshyna*. It evolved out of the strict military offices, and originated in the Zaporozhe *Sitch* and during the war operations of the National Revolution and subsequent wars, its objective was to sustain Ukrainian national independence. The military organization of the Cossacks as a para-military class, which considered the new state as its property, somewhat automatically developed into the central and regional or local administration of the Hetman State. Although individual officers and agencies of the central and local administration were assigned certain responsibilities, their competence and jurisdiction were not clearly demarcated. This caused some conflicts and confusion in the administrative process, which was not given adequate time to develop fully. Another feature of the central administration, which indicated that it had not yet reached its maturity, was the frequent mixing and compounding of strictly public matters with the Hetman's personal ones.

All the top central officials together constituted an advisory council to the Hetman, while individually they served as administrative agents. Their authority was more comprehensive when the Hetman was absent or during the *interregnum*, when there was no Hetman for whatever reason. The top administrative officials were appointed by the Hetman either at the General Council or the Council of Seniors, and the honors were usually granted for life. These officials were rarely transferred to other duties, but at times colonels were made judges or treasurers or vice-versa. Whenever the republican principle took over in the political process of Ukraine, these top officials were then elected by the respective Councils. At a later date, after Skoropadsky's Hetmanate, the Russian government demanded that three candidates for the offices be presented to it by the Hetman or the Councils, and then it would make the final appointment.

There was definitely a distinction between the higher and lower levels of central officials, and one could be moved to the upper rank. The upper level officials, usually being the wealthy grandees, were called the associates of rank, *rangovi*.

The upper level central offices constituted the camp-commander-general, *heneralnyi oboznyi*, judge-general, *heneralnyi suddia*, treasurer-general, *heneralnyi pudskarbii*, and secretary-general, *heneralnyi sekretar*. The lower level consisted of: two hetman's associates, *osauly*, the flag-bearer, *khorunzhyi*, insignia-bearer, *bunchuzhnyi*, followed up by all kinds of minor clerks and hetman's servants.

The camp-commander-general was first of all a Hetman's deputy, frequently made the appointed Hetman, *nakaznyi hetman*, in case the need arose. He was the commander of the artillery, and in the case of military expeditions he was made the commander-in-chief of the military forces if the Hetman did not participate in the expedition. In many instances the *oboznyi* performed the functions of an ambassador to negotiate important matters in foreign lands. Occasionally, he was entrusted with some other responsibilities. The judge-general attended important court matters and also performed important diplomatic services in the name of the Hetman. For example, S. Bohdanovych worked on the Agreement of Pereyaslav of 1654 in Moscow. At first, there was only one judge-general, but at the end of the seventeenth century there were two of them, working independently, and rather separately from other administrative functions. The office of the treasurer-general was first introduced during Brukhovetsky's time in 1663-1668. Then it disappeared, and was again reintroduced in 1728 with two treasurer-generals being appointed since. They managed the financial matters. One of them had to be Russian in order to protect Russian financial interests in Ukraine, a definite indication of Russian interference with the domestic matters of Ukraine. This was something Tsar Aleksei promised never to do by the Agreement of Pereyaslav of 1654, particularly in respect to the financial affairs of Ukraine, as it was underscored before. The fourth most important office in the Hetman administration was that of the secretary-general. He was the state chancellor, who managed the state chancellory, or office, and maintained the state records and archives. He was the chief diplomatic officer, involved in all kinds of political and diplomatic missions and negotiations of great importance, he centered the foreign relations in his hands, and introduced foreign envoys during the hetman's official state audiences. He also guarded the state seal.

The lower level central offices consisted of two Hetman's associates, *osauly*, the flag-bearer and the insignia-bearer. The Hetman's associates generally carried out special assignments, given to them by the Hetman; at times they were military commanders in the absence of the Hetman, being appointed hetmans, *nakazni*, in particular cases. At times they also handled some diplomatic missions and specific investigations. In addition, they administered the mercenery troops. The flag-bearer protected the state flag, while the insignia-bearer protected the Hetman's insignia or *bunchuk*, of Mongol origin.[15]

In 1720, a new agency was created, the General Military Chancellory, the *heneralna viiskova kantselaria*: an agency of Russian administrative patterns and under Russian influence, headed by the secretary-general of the state. It operated in two ways; as a college of decision-making faculty, *prysutstvie*, constituting a few top officials and soon joined by some Russian members, and the administrative office for carrying out orders. It was mainly involved in central legislative and administrative operations.[16]

The Local Administration. As the central administration, so also the regional and local ones evolved from the military organization, with the similar lack of clear demarcation of jurisdictions and responsibilities among various offices and agencies. From the very beginning the new Hetman state was divided into a number of territorial, so-called regimental, units, the colonelcies or *polky*. Their number was never varied greatly, nor were their territories significantly revised.

The following colonelcies were situated in Right-bank Ukraine with the seats of the colonels who were the chiefs of the administration: Cherkasy, Chyhyryn, Kaniv, Korsun, Bila Tserkva, Vynnytsia, Bratslav, Kropyvna, Uman, Povolotsk, Ovruch and Podillia; in Left-bank Ukraine: Chernihiv, Nizhen, Pryluky, Kiev, Lubni, Myrohorod, Peryaslav, Hadiach, Poltava and Starodub.

Of course, with the changing fortunes of Right-bank Ukraine and her renewed subjection to Polish rule, the colonelcy organization was either eliminated or altered.

The colonel, *polkovnyk*, the head of the given regimental district or colonelcy, was either appointed by the Hetman or elected by the General Council or Council of Seniors. After the Russians got a firm grip over Ukraine, the Russian government began to appoint the colonels. The governmental position of the colonel was a very strong one. Once appointed or elected, he became fully independent of the central administration, and his status was greater than that of the top central officers, like the treasurer-general or secretary-general. The colonel was the military commander, the chief government official and administrator, and the chief judge of his district. The regimental court of justice operated under him. The colonel had complete control over all officials in the colonelcy. He made all the land grants in his district, pending upon the Hetman's confirmations; the making of land grants was the most important source of his power. The *pernach*, a form of mace was the insignia of his authority. The colonel was a member of the Council of Seniors, *rada starshyn*.

The colonel was assisted in his government functions by the regimental council of officers and regimental council of Cossacks, set up according to the central government scheme. The council of officers consisted of the regimental camp-commander, judge, secretary, associate and flag-bearer. Frequently it even competed with the colonel in respect to the administration and responsibilities within the colonelcy. The regimental council of Cossacks was a large and slightly flexible class representation, the importance of which soon declined in northern Ukraine, surviving longer in the south, close to the Territory of the Cossack Host where the particular body was more traditional. The council convened irregularly to resolve organizational, financial and at times, judicial problems.

The regimental office handled administrative functions on a day-to-day basis. In the eighteenth century, however, its significance substantially increased. The above councils on the regimental level faded away, and were replaced by the said office, which under the colonel's chairmanship and with the cooperation of the regimental officers took care of matters of administration, finances and judiciary. The office also assumed the responsibility for the population census, the registration of the *insignia* Cossacks, the *komputy*, property searches, and some other duties.

The regimental districts were divided into centurion districts, the *sotni*. One regimental district might have comprised some ten to fifteen centurion regions. The centurion, the *sotnyk*, was the military, administrative and judicial head of his region, assisted by the regional officers with diversified responsibilities, such as the centurion captain, *sotennyi otaman*, and secretary, *pysar*. There were also the so-called centurion councils, *sotenni rady*. The *sotnyk*, and the other officers could have been elected or appointed by the upper government agencies.

The cities and towns lived a rather separate life from the other classes of the society, because of the Magdeburg legal system that they were endowed with, even prior to the National Revolution. Although the city and town participated indirectly in that revolution, they then remained aloof from the new state, so much more that the Cossacks, who considered that state for an organization of their own, were not very interested in urban affairs, either. For the first time, under Samoilovych and Mazepa, the Hetman government took more interest in the city, and the urban population moved closer to the society as a whole. The cities and towns had a separate local administration. In fact, there were two urban administrative types. The self-governing urban communities of the Magdeburg law system existed in rather larger cities, such as Kiev, Chernihiv, Poltava, Hlukhiv, Oster and some other ones, enjoying the self-governing privilege which they received at various times. Here the Magdeburg law was applied, the urban administration was in the hands of an elected mayor, *burmistr*, and councilmen, *raitsi*. The representation of the cities and towns was then, in the late seventeenth century, invited to join in participation in the Council of Seniors and the General Council of Cossacks, where national affairs were deliberated. Otherwise, the municipal communities administered themselves independently.[17] Small towns did not enjoy the Magdeburg self-government. Though they were administered by elective officials, they were dependent upon the general state administration in particular, being controlled and supervised by the urban captain, *horodovyi otaman*, of the centurion's or *sotenny*, local government. Some small towns might have been owned by Cossack or gentry grandees, thus being placed under their domain, and made exempt from any direct state administration.

The peasants and the village population spontaneously joined the National Revolution to overthrow the sufferings of serfdom and bondage, sustained under Polish rule. They expected complete freedom in the Ukrainian State and subjection to the administration. Yet, matters developed differently and unfavorably for them. According to the class structure of the society of that time, the peasants were supposed to be turned into serfs. The Church, the monasteries, the Cossack grandees and the gentry demanded just that. The process was slow and strongly opposed by the peasantry. Consequently, the village administration evolved in two ways. From the war times on, there were many villages of military status, inhabited by peasants who rendered military services, and were directly included in the Cossack administration scheme of the regiments and centurion district. Under the pressure of the upper classes, the number of villages of military status seemingly declined and their administration gradually went over into the hand of the manorial masters, while their direct relation to the state was lost. Henceforth, the Hetman government gradually allowed a full-fledged serfdom to arise on its territory. Although it was actually the government of the one class of Cossacks, yet it attempted to protect the townspeople and the peasantry to some extent against the abuses of the upper classmen. At times even the representation of the commoners was admitted to the General Council.[18]

The Judiciary. The National Revolution of 1648 also abolished, of course, the old Polish-Lithuanian class oriented court system and replaced it with the new Cossack, equally class-oriented judiciary. The old court system consisted, as previously discussed, of the urban or *grodski*, the territorial or *zemski*, and the cammeral or *pidkomorski* courts for the nobility and gentry; the peasantry being largely subject to the patrimonial, and the townspeople, to the Magdeburg judiciary. The court tribunals in Vilna and Lublin handled the appellate cases of the nobility and gentry. All these courts in their judicial practice used the *Lithuanian Statute* of the third codification of 1588, written down in the Rus'ian language, while the towns and cities mostly applied the codifications or private copies of the Magdeburg law.

With the introduction of the Ukrainian-Cossack government, the Cossack courts were organized as follows: the village or *silski*, the centurion or *sotenni*, and the regimental or *polkovi*, while the General Hetman court served as the appellate institution. The Magdeburg judiciary, on the other hand, continued to be binding in towns, as it was before. Furthermore, the Cossack courts continued to use the old laws, like the *Lithuanian Statute* and those enacted by the Polish Kings and Lithuanian Grand Princes, as well as those established by custom and tradition. This was because during the turbulent revolutionary and war years there was no time left for the Hetman-Cossack government to adopt any new legislation or legal codifications until the third decade of the eighteenth century.

There were two reasons why the upper crest of the Ukrainian society insisted upon keeping the continuing validity of the old laws in its judiciary. First, there was its essential conservativism, which received its full expression some one hundred years later when a new code of laws was under consideration. Second, the Cossack grandees wanted to preserve their country's independence and refused to accept any Muscovite legislation or legal institutions, which could easily threaten and put in doubt that independence, while Moscow's pressure was building up in Ukraine anyway. Hence, the Pereyaslav Treaty of 1654 most expressly included the article by which the Tsar guaranteed the preservation of all previous laws, rights and privileges in

Ukraine. This promise of course, was not kept by Moscow, which was obsessed by its traditional imperialistic drive. Yet, in order to slow down this Muscovite pressure, each subsequent Hetman, negotiating his own *Hetman Statute*, included the repetitive corroboration of the preservation of these old laws in Ukraine.[19]

The situation did substantially change at the beginning of the eighteenth century, as Polonska-Vasylenko, Yakovliv, and other historians and jurists have pointed out. The social and legal developments in the country became more complicated due to the overlapping and interrelated military, administrative and judiciary authorities in the military-styled government of the Cossack-Hetman State. Although more peaceful times came, neither new legislation was enacted to streamline the court system, nor were adequately educated and trained personnel appointed to staff it. The centurions and colonels had no time for judicial matters, and only lower officials handled legal matters. At the lower level, ignorance and incompetence at times made the Cossack judiciary inadequate. Complaints were rather frequent even against the appellate General Court. Only low-ranking officials of the courts knew a little about the law and legal matters. The most tragic consequence of this state of affairs was the very fact that these complaints reached the imperial court in St. Petersburg, and that they were used by Peter I as an excuse for further intervention in Ukrainian internal affairs and for limiting Ukrainian political autonomy. Namely, in 1721, using these complaints as justification, Peter decreed that the *Little Russian College* should from that time on assume jurisdiction over the appellate court for the subjects of the Cossack-Hetman state, and in order to assist the members of the College in their judicial function, it was further decreed to write down and to translate into Muscovite-Russian all the binding laws in Ukraine. Subsequently, Hetman Skoropadsky proceeded with the organization of a respective commission to carry out the said task. At the same time, he also demanded that the "old laws" be respected, as previously done, and that the so-called *Reshytielnie Punkta*, issued by the Russian court, corroborate the demand.

In 1730, Hetman Apostol reformed the judicial system in Ukraine. By his *Instruction for the Courts, Instruktsia sudam*, he decreed that the Hetman's General Court would consist of six judges, three Ukrainians and three Russians, while the Hetman would act as the Court's president. Furthermore, the municipal courts of the Magdeburg law were strictly separated from the Cossack regimental and centurion judiciary. He also suggested a broad codification of the Ukrainian laws. This last suggestion was approved by the Russian court in 1734.[20]

In 1743, the codification work was completed, as it was mentioned already. Yet, the code called *Prava, po kotorym sudytsia malorossiiskyi narod*, did not receive official approval. Nevertheless, its impact on the legal and judicial life of the country was substantial. The reform of the judiciary still remained, therefore, an outstanding issue to be taken care of. Actually, the specific conservativism of the Cossack and noble strata, as indicated, was the reason behind the lack of progress in legislation and the judiciary. The old was cherished and the new abhorred, in particular, because that "new" might be Muscovite. For that reason also, the *Prava, po kotorym...*, the new code, was objected to by upper social crests, while the court reform, which was introduced in 1760, proved this point once more.

The said reform of the court system was carried out according to the wishes of the majority of the Cossack and noble classes. The country was divided into twenty judicial districts. In each district a territorial or *zemskyi*, and a cammeral or *pidkomorskyi* court was established. According to the pre-revolutionary tradition, the first was supposed to handle the civilian, and the second, the land and landmark affairs. Ten *horodski* or urban courts were established for criminal cases in the ten capitals of the regimental districts. A General Court, like the Polish-Lithuanian tribunals, was supposed to serve as the supreme court of justice, and was composed of two judge-generals and ten deputy-judges, elected by the regimental districts, with one from each district. The General Cossack Council approved the above reform in Hlukhiv, in 1763. From the constitutional point of view, the reform was definitely a step in the right direction. It meant a separation of the judiciary from the administrative and military authorities, a welcome division of powers for the protection of the rights of citizens. Some members of the said Council pointed out that the land received the best legal system, which only the most noble and free nation could ever have. However, historically speaking, it was a reactionary move, since after one hundred and twenty years the old structure of the judiciary from the Polish-Lithuanian era was largely reintroduced and the validity of the Lithuanian Statute reaffirmed. The new code of the *Prava, po kotorym sudytsia malorossiiskyi narod* was looked upon unfavorably, as a novelty which could easily endanger class rights and the old style of life.[21]

The Military. In the new Cossack-Hetman State, the military organization of the Cossacks evolved into a para-military community, which inspired and penetrated, by its specific characteristics, the entire political constitution of the new nation, as was explained in the first section of this chapter. The military class of the Cossacks was the elevated stratum of the society.

The Hetman was the commander-in-chief of all the armed forces of the nation, but when necessary he could nominate a so-called appointed hetman, who was put in charge of specific military projects. For example, Demian Mnohohrishny was made an appointed hetman by Petro Doroshenko and was entrusted with the defense of Left-bank Ukraine against Muscovite aggression. Mazepa frequently appointed such deputy hetmans to carry out some special military assignments. The entire armed force consisted of three component military formations: the Cossacks, the common insurgents and the mercenary (hired and voluntary) troops. All formations were divided into regiments, led by the colonels, centuries or *sotni*, led by centurions or *sotnyky*, and decurias or *kureni*, led by decurions or *kurinni*.

The Cossacks were, for a long time, the very core and foundation of the armed force of the Hetman state. Khmelnytsky had, at Lviv, an army of about 200,000 men and at Zboriv some 360,000. It is impossible to say with certainty what its composition was. The Cossacks, the core of the force, and the mercenaries constituted the minority, while the common insurgents outnumbered them substantially. After stability was restored within the state, the Cossack armed forces consisted of 17 regiments or *polky*, as they were listed before. The number of Cossacks in a regiment varied from 5,000 to 20,000 men. By 1723, according to records, the number of Cossacks in a regiment was about 5,000 men. At times, the colonels nominated appointed or deputy colonels for special military tasks.

The regiments were divided into centuries or *sotni*. The number of Cossacks in a sotnia was supposed to be 100 men. Yet, life itself provided differently. During Khmelnytsky's time, the Revolution and the wars with Poland, the *sotnia* consisted of about 200 to 300; around 1723, some 400; and around 1782, some 1,000 men. The number of Cossacks in a *kuren'* was also a changing one, sometimes including a few dozen men.

The Cossack armed forces consisted of infantry, cavalry and artillery, with each branch of weaponry being included in every regiment as a combat unit. Infantrymen composed about one-fourth of the regiment and they were normally assigned to remain in their regimental districts and protect the country. Cavalrymen composed some three-fourths of the regimental force, and they participated in various war expeditions and distant marches. A Cossack was required to report to military service with a rifle, sabre, spear, gunpowder and ammunition and a horse, if he was a cavalryman. He also had to bring his own supplies. During the distant war marches, the supplies were contained in wagon trains.[22]

The artillery branch of arms was a very important one and it received preferable treatment. There was a national artillery, with its headquarters in the city of Baturyn, which consisted of 40 cannons at the time of Menshikov's capture of the city after Mazepa joined Charles XII. The regimental artilleries possessed 10 to 15 cannons each. Artilleries were under the command of special officers. During war expeditions, cannons were drawn by horses or oxen. Cannons were either manufactured in Ukraine, particularly in the town of Hlukhiv, or imported or captured from a defeated enemy. Gun powder was produced throughout Ukraine. The Cossacks had to bear the whole material burden of their military service, and were never paid any wages, except when on prolonged foreign war expeditions; hence, since the notorious Battle of Poltava, in particular, the Cossacks attempted with even greater insistence to drop out of their semi-military class and abandon their additional responsibilities. They did this either by joining the ranks of the commoners, by desertion and resettlement, or by supplying "substitutes." Drafting Cossacks for foreign wars and for the construction of military projects in foreign lands, such as Muscovy, the Don-Volga region or Caspian lands, was especially burdensome. They took the Cossacks away from their homes for long periods of time, while their farms, estates and other businesses declined, contributing to the impoverishment of the class as a whole.

The Tsarist government, which exploited the Cossacks as a military as well as a labor force, tried to prevent the Cossack exodus by special measures and stern prohibitions regarding abandoning class responsibilities. However, this did not help much. The ranks of the Cossacks continued to decline. Kholmsky pointed out that while in 1736 there were some 20,000 Cossacks in Hetman Ukraine, by 1764 their number declined to some 10,000.[23]

In cases of national emergencies, such as uprisings or rebellions, the Cossacks were joined by common insurgents. During the National Revolution and the Revolutionary Wars of Bohdan Khmelnytsky, the common insurgents joined the war effort by hundreds of thousands of men; the force was numerically many times larger than that of the Cossack regiments. Palii and Petryk, as well as the *Koliivshchyna* uprising, were also accompanied by a large force of insurgents. The insurgents were led by their elected or Cossack-appointed leaders or commanders. Col. Maksym Kryvonis was one of those skillful leaders of the common insurgents during Khmelnytsky's time.

The third component of the armed forces of Cossack-Hetman Ukraine was made up of mercenary troops. The Serbs, Wallachians, Germans and Tartars were already hired as mercenaries by Hetman Khmelnytsky. The Hadiach agreement of 1658 provided that the Ukrainian government could hire mercenaries of up to 10,000 men. Doroshenko was using some 1,200 Turkish mercenaries, who subsequently served as infantry troops under Samoilovych.

Volunteers constituted the fourth ingredient of the military of Ukraine at that time. Hetman Mnohohrishnyi organized a regiment of volunteers, the *okhotnyky* or *kompaniiski*, while during Mazepa's time there were already eight voluntary and mercenary regiments, organized according to the traditional Cossack pattern, and subordinated directly under the Hetman himself, who used them as his bodyguard, as a police force, or for border protection and control. The voluntary regiments were not attached to specific territories, like the Cossack regiments were, but were named after their colonels, like the Novitsky or Halahan regiment, as Polonska-Vasylenko points out. The material situation of the mercenaries and volunteers was much more advantageous than that of the common Cossacks, since the former received regular wages from the Hetman's treasury and were kept in quarters, maintained by respective districts or localities, while the latter, as pointed out, bore military duties at their own expense. In order to prevent the Cossacks from deserting their class responsibilities, they were not allowed to join the volunteer troops along with the commoners.[24]

The Muscovite-Russian government, especially since Peter I, began to interfere with the traditional Ukrainian military organization. Individual Cossack regiments were split up and some of their units were incorporated into the Russian military formations in order to defuse Ukrainian "separatism" and to advance the Russification of Ukraine along with St. Peterburg's imperialist plans. The whole project dramatically undermined the military morale of the Cossacks.[25] Financial aspects of the Cossack-Hetman government will be covered in the last chapter of this work, along with the economic matters of the land.

1. D.Doroshenko, *Narys istorii Ukrainy*, Munich 1966, Vol. II. pp. 214-266; N. Polonska-Vasylenko, *Istoria Ukrainy*, Munich, 1976, Vol. II, pp. 107-145.

2. Ye. Stetsiuk, "Sotsialno-ekonomichnyi rozvtok i politychne stanovyshche Ukrainy pisla 'vossoidinennia' z Rosieiu", *Istoria Ukrainskoi RSR*, Kiev, 1953, p. 272; I. Kholmsky, *Istoria Ukrainy*, New York, 1971, pp. 283-284; O. Ohloblyn, *Hetman Ivan Mazepa ta yoho doba*, New York, 1960, pp. 77-100

3. O. Ohloblyn, *Ukrainsko-moskovska uhoda 1654*, New York, 1954; the same, *Treaty of Pereyaslav*, Toronto-New York, 1954; A. Yakovliv, *Dohovir Bohdana*

Khmelnytskoho z Moskvoiu, New York, 1954; Polonska-Vasylenko, *op. cit.,* Vol. II. pp. 26-29; the same, "Pereyaslavskyi dohovir v ochakh yoho suchasnykiv", *Vyzvolnyi Shlakh,* London, 1955, Book IV.

4. Yakovliv, *op. cit.,* pp. 82-92; M. Hrushevsky, *Istoria Ukrainy-Rusy,* New York, 1957, Vol. IX. Pt. I. pp. 728-869: "Instead of the authentic articles, the Muscovite scribes submitted to the Ukrainians their willful revision, a forgery"(p. 866).

5. Polonska-Vasylenko, *Istoria Ukrainy,* Vo. II, p. 153.

6. A. Yakovliv, *Ukrainskyi kodeks 1743 roku, Prava, po kotorym sudytsia Malorossiiskii narod,* Munich, 1949.

7. Ohloblyn, *op. cit.,* also, Doroshenko, *op. cit.,* Vol. II. pp. 32-39.

8. Law in the Cossack-Hetman state: Polonska-Vasylenko, *op. cit.,* Vol. II, pp. 219-222; M. Vasylenko, *Materialy do istorii ukrainskoho prava,* Kiev, 1928, Vol. I, pp. VI-IX and other; Yakovliv, *op. cit.,* the same, "Istoria dzherel ukrainskoho prava,"*Entsyklopedia ukrainoznavstva,*Munich, 1949, Vol. I, pp. 636 and the following; the same (Jakowliw), *Das deutsche Recht in der Ukraine und seine Einflusse auf das ukrainische Recht im 16-18 Jahrhundert,* Leipzig, 1942.

9. Yakovliv, *Ukrainskyi kodeks ...,* pp. 30-34.

10. N. Polonska-Vasylenko, "The Constitution of Pylyp Orlyk", *The Annals of the Ukrainian Academy of Arts and Sciences in the US,* New. York, 1958, Vol. VI, No..3 and 4, New York, 1960.

11. V. Lypynsky, *Ukraina na perelomi,* Kiev-Viena, 1920, pp. 251-297; O. Ohloblyn, "Dynastychna ideia v derzhavnytsko-politychnii dumtsi Ukrainy- Hetmanshchyny", *Derzhavnytska dumka,* Philadelphia, 1951, No. 4, pp. 43-47; the same, *Hetman Ivan Mazepa ...,* pp. 26-28, 46-47; L. Okinshevych, *Lektsii z istorii ukrainskoho prava,* Munich, 1947, p. 130.

12. On the Little Russian Colleges: Okinshevych, *op. cit.,* pp. 130-131; Polonska-Vasylenko, *Istoria Ukrainy,* Vol. I, pp. 156-157.

13. On the General Council: Okinshevych, *op. cit.,* Doroshenko, *op. cit.,* Vol. II. pp. 115-116.

14. Okinshevych, *op. cit.,* pp. 92-109; the same, "Rada Starshynska na Hetmanshchyni", *Ukraina,* Kiev, 1924. Bk. 4.

15. Okinshevych, *Lektsii ...,* pp. 112-113; Polonska-Vasylenko, *op. cit.,* Vol. II. pp. 159-161; L. Okinshevych, "Generalna starshyna na livoberezhnii Ukraini XVII-XVIII vv," *Pratsi komissii dla vyuchuvannia istorii zakhidnio-ruskoho ta ukrainskoho prava,"* UAN, Kiev, 1926, Vol. II

16. Okinshevych, *Lektsii* ..., p. 129; Doroshenko, *op. cit.*, Vol. II. pp. 116-117.

17. On the regional and local administration: Okinshevych, *op. cit.* pp. 50, 76-78, 116-124; On the Magdeburg law: V. Diadychenko, *Narysy suspilno-politychnoho ustroiu Livoberezhnoi Ukrainy kintsia XVII-pochatku XVIII st.*, Kiev, 1959, p. 281.

18. Okinshevych, *op. cit.*, pp. 76-78, 92-99.

19. Yakovliv, *op. cit.*, pp. 17-19, 30-34; Vasylenko, *op. cit.*, pp. VI, XI-XII.

20. Yakovliv, *ibid.*, 18-19.

21. On the judiciary: Polonska-Vasylenko, *op. cit.*, Vol. II. pp. 166-168; Kholmsky, *op. cit.*, p. 289.

22. Kholmsky, *ibid.*, pp. 290-291; Diadychenko, *op. cit.*, pp. 414-429, 439-466; I Krypiakevych and B. Hnatevych, *Istoria ukrainskoho viiska*, Winninpeg, 1953, Vol. II, pp. 258-278: Z. Stefaniv, *Korotka istoria ukrainskoho viiska*, Lviv, 1936—37, Vols. I-III.

23. Kholmsky, *loc. cit.*

24. Krypiakevych, *op. cit.*, Vol. II, pp. 277-278.

25. Polonska-Vasylenko, *op. cit.*, Vol. II, p. 166; also, Doroshenko, *op. cit.*, Vol. pp. 117-118.

CHAPTER TEN

THE SPRITITUAL AND CULTURAL LIFE
OF THE COSSACK-HETMAN ERA

The status of the Churches — Education and the sciences — Literature — Architecture — Painting and carving — Music and theatre — Other arts

The Status of the Churches. There were three Churches in Ukraine at this time with three different legal statuses: the Orthodox, the Uniate and the Roman Catholic. Protestant sects, which initially made some headway in Ukraine, soon lost popularity and had hardly any significance. At first, the Orthodox looked toward the Protestants as a kind of ally in their common resistance against Catholic pressure. Yet, they soon recognized the unacceptability of the Protestant interpretation of the articles of faith and the danger coming from this interpretation, for the purity of Orthodoxy. Thus, they refused to cooperate. Eventually, the Catholic Counter-Reformation fully undercut any growth roots of Protestantism in Ukraine.[1]

In the Cossack-Hetman State, the Orthodox Church enjoyed the status of a privileged and ruling faith, while the Roman Catholic Church was allowed freedom of worship most of the time. The Uniate Church was largely denied any *de jure* recognition; it existed only *de facto*, being exposed to official and unofficial hardships and harassments, since the Ukrainian governing circles, the Orthodox hierarchy, and the Cossacks and the common people held the conviction that the Union of Berest was a Polish intrigue designed to hurt the Ukrainian national interest, and that it was in fact an apostasy from the traditional faith.

Holy Trinity Church, erected by the Cossacks
in Novoselytsia, 1773-1778

Wooden church towers from the 17th and 18th centuries

Wooden church in Matkiv, Boykivshchyna
(1838)

The Union of Berest and the immediate developments thereafter, such as the death of the Orthodox bishop of Peremyshl, Mykhail Kopystensky, prior to the National Revolution of 1648, left the Orthodox Church in Ukraine with practically no upper hierarchy to lead and defend it against the onslaughts of the Roman Catholics and Uniates. As it was pointed out above, the Metropolitan of Kiev and most of the bishops of Ukraine accepted a union with the Apostolic See of Rome and intended to keep things that way. Although some of the lower clergy, many monasteries, the Cossacks in their totality, and some noblemen and the common masses remained Orthodox, the plight of Orthodoxy was confusing and chaotic, and its future seemed to be rather uncertain and gloomy. Hence, the movement for the restoration of the upper hierarchy of the Orthodox Church was under way, aggressively, represented by the Cossack military force, and by its leader, Hetman Petro Konashevych-Sahaidachny, an ardent Orthodox since his youth particularly.

Meanwhile, the conflict between the Orthodox and the Uniates was fiercely growing in all fields: religious, political and cultural, splitting the nation into two warring camps. In 1620 an unexpected opportunity for the restoration of the Orthodox hierarchy developed. In the spring of that year, Theophan, the Patriarch of Jerusalem, was returning from Moscow via Ukraine. He was met in Kiev with great respect and all honors by the leading Orthodox circles, and in particular by Hetman Sahaidachny and his Cossacks, and was asked to consecrate a new Metropolitan and new bishops for their Church in order to successfully resist Uniate pressure. At first, Patriarch Theophan did not dare to undertake anything so drastic or controversial. He simply tried to assist the existing Orthodox organizations, brotherhoods, parishes and monasteries without encountering any Polish opposition. The Polish government officially supported the Church Union. However, a Polish-Turkish war at this time and the Polish attempts to gain Cossack military assistance in the war with the Ottoman Empire made the Poles tolerate what happened in Ukraine in religious matters. This encouraged the Patriarch to undertake an irregular and even revolutionary step, hoping that it would also meet with tolerance and the tacit approval of the Warsaw government, which tried to persuade the Cossacks and their Hetman, an ardent Orthodox, to its side. Theophan yielded to the pleas of the Ukrainian circles and consecrated Yov Boretsky to the Metropolitan's seat in Kiev, Isaia Kopynsky, to the eparchy of Peremyshl, and Meletii Smotrytsky, of Polotsk. The consecration was performed secretly, without any previous consent of the king, the *ktytor* of the Church in the Polish Crown; thus, not in a way that tradition deemed proper. The consecration of three additional bishops was performed by Theophan a little later, on the borders of Ukraine, as he hastily left the country.

The elevation of the new Metropolitan and the new bishops was certainly irregularly accomplished, and for a while the new hierarchs did not have any real ecclesiastic authority, but a new beginning was made under favorable circumstances, when the Polish government, in spite of the protests of the Uniate and Roman Catholic clergy, did not dare to oppose the irregular move and actually gave tacit approval of the restoration of the upper hierarchy of the Orthodox Church, under the pressure of Petro Sahaidachny and other Cossack and noble leaders. In fact, Sahaidachny must be largely credited for the resurrection of the Orthodox ecclesiastic organization from the wreck left by the Union of Berest. The Orthodox Church council of Kiev, in 1621, was another milestone in the recovery of Orthodoxy after the blow, which decided the future course of action, while the Polish government made all kinds of promises to the Orthodox cause in order to gain further assistance from the Cossacks, who practically saved Poland in the war with the Ottoman Empire.[2]

The strengthened position of the Orthodox contributed to the religious conflict between them and the Uniates, culminating in the murder by a Byeloruthenian Orthodox mob of the Uniate archbishop of Polotsk in Byeloruthenia, Josafat Kuncevych, a Ukrainian by birth. The crime angered many, and in reaction many Orthodox began leaving their Church and joined the Union with Rome. Now, the Uniates were making a comeback, the high point of which was the conversion of the Orthodox bishop of Polotsk, another Ukrainian, Meletii Smotrytsky, to the Union. Smotrytsky was condemned by the council of Kiev in 1623, but from that time on he resolutely spoke in favor of the Church Union. In his celebrated work, *Parenethis*, Smotrytsky attempted to prove that Ukraine needs religious unity in the framework of the Union with the Holy See, and that the incipient trend to join the Muscovite Orthodoxy would only hurt Ukrainian Orthodox. He argued that the Union would only bring a rejuvenation in the spiritual and cultural growth of Ukraine.

Later developments apparently brought evidence to the fact that Meletii Smotrytsky might have been right. It was previously discussed that Moscow tried to dominate Ukraine under all kinds of false pretenses. The Orthodox Metropolitan and then, Patriarch of Moscow, were willing tools of the aggressive Muscovite political plans. The Polish discrimination against the Orthodox in Ukraine, on the other hand, produced a favorable atmosphere for Muscovite political and religious propaganda to join the Muscovite Patriarchate and in that way to avoid Polish harassments. Pro-Muscovite feelings, therefore, grew among the naïve, who could not foresee the real Muscovite intentions. One of the leading proponents of rapprochement between the Muscovite and the Ukrainian Orthodox Churches was Isaia Kopynsky, at first a bishop and then a Metropolitan and a highly respected churchman among the "black clergy" and the Cossacks. Luckily, however, his tenure as Metropolitan was too short to hurt the Ukrainian Church immediately. Yet, later on, after the Russians actually succeeded in dominating the Ukrainian Orthodox church, they made the Orthodoxy, *pravoslavia*, a tool of their policies of the Russification of the Ukrainian people and of their complete subjugation to Russian political interests. Smotrytsky might have been correct, suggesting that the Uniate Church, after becoming the Ukrainian National Church, could have prevented this total subjugation by Muscovy-Russia and her subservient Orthodoxy in the future.[3]

The pro-Russian sentiment among some Orthodox circles in Ukraine was greatly weakened, after Kopynsky was ousted from the Metropolitan's seat, and Petro Mohyla became the Kievan Metropolitan in 1633. The great days of the Orthodox Church in Ukraine returned. Mohyla was not only fully sanctioned by King Wladyslaw IV, which meant a full recognition of the restored Orthodox top hierarchy, initiated by Theophan, but he also became one of the greatest personalities and leaders in Ukrainian religious and national life. Petro Mohyla was of Moldavian descent, but he devoted his entire life to the welfare of Ukraine and her Church. He was broad-minded and well-educated in the Netherlands and France, and a man who kept in touch with Rutsky and Smotrytsky, two Uniates, dreaming of religious unity in Ukraine within the framework of the Ukrainian Patriarchate. He was behind the adoption by the *seim* of the so-called *Statutes of Truce, Statti Peremyria*, which were supposed to put the Orthodox Church on an equal legal footing with the Roman Catholic and the Uniate Churches, then under the Polish scepter. He attempted to create a religious peace between the Orthodox and the Uniates by determining their territorial jurisdictions. Yet, neither side was really happy with the solutions suggested. Metropolitan Mohyla organized and protected education, and is credited with founding the so-called Kievan-Mohylian Academy in 1633, the second institution of higher learning in Ukraine. He reformed monastic life, reduced abuses, and increased discipline in the religious orders. He established new monasteries and subsidized the old ones. Mohyla also encouraged the growth of religious brotherhoods, which helped the Orthodox Church greatly at the time of its crisis. He was involved in a grand project of renovating many churches, in particular the St. Sophia Cathedral, and excavating the foundations and ruins of the Church of the Tithe, *Desiatynna*. Already at the time when Mohyla was the abbot of the Pecherska Lavra monastery and also later, he sponsored the publication of many books for ecclesiastic uses. He himself was a renowned theologian and he wrote many works in the field as well, of which his *Confessions of the Orthodox Faith, Ispovid viry pravoslavnoi*, was well known and read throughout the entire Orthodox East.

Ideologically, Metropolitan Petro Mohyla leaned towards the West, and Western educational methods were introduced into those schools sponsored by him. He stayed away from any close contacts with Moscow and its Patriarchate. On the contrary, twice in his discussions with Rutsky, the Uniate Metropolitan, and Smotrytsky, the matter of a Ukrainian Patriarchate, independent from Constantinople or any outside ecclesiastic authority, was raised. Only the strong anti-Uniate feelings of the conservative Orthodox circles and the anti-Orthodox feelings of some Roman Catholics barred the plan from being realized. The Cossack leaders also opposed the plan.[4] Mohyla's death in 1647 brought a decline in the Orthodox Church, which was still exposed to official Polish discrimination.

The National Revolution of 1648 and the formation of the Cossack-Hetman State totally changed the situation of the Orthodox Church. The Cossack leaders and Cossack masses were ardently Orthodox, hence in the Cossack country this Church received a dominant and favored position, as pointed out. Already, the Treaty of Zboriv granted substantial privileges to the Orthodox Church within the framework of the Polish kingdom. But it took a long time before the Poles became reconciled with this fact, and learned to respect the Orthodox hierarchy and clergy.

The Pereyaslav Treaty of 1654 established the dominant position of the Orthodox Church, weakening the Uniate Church in Ukraine on the one hand, and opening a new era of continuously growing Muscovite pressure to subordinate the Ukrainian Church to the Patriarchate of Moscow, on the other. It was a parallel measure, running together with the political pressure of the Muscovite-Russian government to dominate all of Ukraine according to its imperial plans. As long as Metropolitan Sylvester Kossiv, a highly educated man and a close associate of Petro Mohyla, led the Ukrainian Orthodox between 1647 and 1657, the Russian plans made little progress. Kossiv was definitely anti-Muscovite, along with most of the Ukrainian hierarchy at the time, despising Moscow's *ceasaropapism* and religious primitivism. He was definitely an opponent of the Pereyaslav Treaty, as previously discussed. He refused to submit to the Muscovite Tsar and prohibited all the Orthodox under his jurisdiction to take an oath of allegiance to the Tsar as their sovereign. As a true patriot he did not want to submit to foreign dominance.⁵

Yet, after the deaths of Khmelnytsky and Kossiv, Moscow intensified its political and ecclesiastic pressure. The Patriarch of Moscow insisted that the new Metropolitan of Kiev could be installed only with his approval. Yet, Dionisii Balaban of Lutsk was elected and installed in the Metropolitan's seat in Ukraine without any such approval. Moscow protested immediately and received an answer that stated that since the introduction of Christianity in Ukraine, the Kievan Metropolitans accepted approval from Constantinople only, but never from Moscow, and that he, Dionisii, did not need any "blessing" of the Patriarch of Moscow and would not accept any, either.⁶ Meanwhile, however, the Patriarch of Moscow usurped the title of "Patriarch of Great, Little and White Rus'ia" in order to establish a pretense for his future supremacy over the Church of Ukraine, which was called Little Rus'ia according to Moscow's terminology.

The treaty of Hadiach of 1658, between Hetman Vyhovsky and the Polish Crown, brought temporary relief from Muscovite pressure. The Treaty underscored the dominant position of the Orthodox Church and liquidated the Church Union. All the bishops in Ukraine had to be Orthodox, and the Uniates, who did not want to return to Orthodoxy, were subjected to the administration of the Roman Catholic bishops. During the Hetmanate of Yurii Khmelnytsky, who greatly yielded to the Muscovite demands, the Patriarch of Moscow practically dominated the Ukrainian Orthodox Church, while the young Hetman sincerely tried to preserve the traditional allegiance of the Church to Constantinople and to prevent its dependence upon Moscow. Yet, Yurii's personality was too weak to enforce his wish.

Meanwhile, Metropolitan Dionisii Balaban, in order to avoid the Muscovite encroachments, transferred his seat to Right-bank Ukraine where Moscow's influence was much weaker. The Muscovite governors, *voyevody*, took immediate advantage of this move and appointed Lazar Baranovych the administrator of the Kievan Metropolis. Yet, Baranovych did not yield to the Muscovite demands according to their liking; hence Pitirim, a temporary administrator of the Muscovite Patriarchate, consecrated a certain Methodii, a Muscovite, for the Kievan seat. Metropolitan Balaban denounced Methodii, and consecrated Josyf Nelubovych-Tukalsky as the latter's counterpart. Tukalsky became Metropolitan after Balaban's death.

Due to Muscovite interference, confusion in the Ukrainian Orthodox Church was growing. For a number of years, the Kievan Metropolis was practically divided, Right-bank Ukraine being administered by the canonical Metropolitans and the left bank by the Moscow appointees who were preparing for the full dominance of the Patriarch of Moscow over the Orthodox Church in Ukraine. The indignation in Ukraine over the Muscovite machinations was so great that in 1665 Sheremetiev, a Muscovit *voyevoda* in Kiev, asked Moscow not to press the issue any more in order not to provoke any rioting or rebellion.

The Treaty of Andrusiv of 1667 divided Ukraine into two spheres of influence, as previously discussed. Left-bank Ukraine came under the Muscovite-Russian, and the right bank under the Polish dominance, without the Ukrainian government being consulted. This instance greatly weakened the resistance of the left bank clergy against the growing Muscovite encroachments. Bishop Baranovych, who earlier opposed the Patriarch of Moscow, was discouraged and bowed to him. However, Metropolitan Nelubovych-Tukalsky, an ardent supporter of Hetman Petro Doroshenko, continued to resist the Muscovite pressure; he did not recognize the supremacy of Moscow's Patriarch and did not remember the Tsar in the Church services in the right-bank regions under his ecclesiastic authority.[7]

The Patriarch of Moscow finally achieved his end in 1686, during the Hetmanate of Ivan Samoilovych, who tried to appease Muscovy-Russia and in this way preserve as much autonomy for Ukraine as was possible under the circumstances. Samoilovych assisted his relative, once a bishop of Lutsk, Gedeon Sviatopolk-Chetvertynsky, in his bid for the Metropolitan's seat. At the same time, Chetvertynsky declared his complete submissiveness in his letters to the Patriarch of Moscow. On Moscow's advice, Chetvertynsky was elected to the seat by a poorly attended council of Ukrainian Orthodox clergy. He immediately went to Moscow, where he was consecrated by the Patriarch, whose ecclesiastic authority over the Ukrainian Church he recognized. The Tsars acknowledged the move. The Ukrainian Orthodox Church became in this way, at first *de facto*, and soon also *de jure* a part of the Russian Orthodox Church, and fully lost its centuries old tradition of ecclesiastic autonomy under the primacy of Constantinople.

There was, however, another aspect to the submission of the Ukrainian Orthodox to Moscow's Patriarchate. The Patriarchate of Constantinople had to officially agree to the transfer of the ecclesiastic authority over the Kievan Metropolis. Yet, he was in no hurry to do that. Earlier, the Tsar and the Patriarch of Moscow had made attempts to persuade Constantinople to consent to the move. The Tsars even sent bribes to Constantinople. For instance, two hundred rubles in 1684, which was a rather ridiculous price. The Patriarch refused. New gifts were dispatched by Moscow again. Then, the Muscovite envoys tried to persuade Dositeus, Patriarch of Jerusalem, to influence Constantinople. Dositeus refused to back up such an "uncanonical measure." Dionisius, the new Patriarch of Constantinople, continued his opposition as well. Hence, the Muscovite envoys decided on another course of action. They took advantage of the difficult political situation of the Ottoman Empire, which badly wanted to continue friendly relations with the Muscovite Tsardom. The envoys demanded that the Sultan enforce the transfer to the Kievan Metropolis to Moscow's jurisdiction. The Sultan soon called the Patriarch and advised him to meet the Muscovite demand. Having followed the traditional *ceasaropapist* policy of submission of the ecclesiastic authority to the secular sovereignty, Patriarch Dionisius immediately complied. From that time on, Moscow and then St. Petersburg, proceeded with an uninterrupted Russification of the Ukrainian Orthodox Church. Although Hetman Mazepa tried to assist the Church by all possible measures, he could not avert the trend. After Mazepa's alliance with King Charles XII to defend Ukrainian political independence, the Orthodox Church in Ukraine was forced to excommunicate the Hetman disregarding his noble deeds for the Church and for his fatherland. Such was the Muscovite grip. All who assisted Moscow in dominating the Ukrainian Church met a rather miserable end. Samoilovych was imprisoned by the Muscovites and sent to Siberia; he died there in 1687. Bishop Methodii was also imprisoned and died in prison in the Novospasky monastery in 1690; the authority of Metropolitan Gedeon Chetvertynsky was greatly limited by Moscow's Patriarch and he soon died without receiving respect or sorrow. Patriarch Dionisius was soon ousted for his "uncanonical" conduct, being denied any help from Moscow, although he had greatly assisted the Russian cause.[8]

The Uniate-Catholic Church developed rather well during the first decades after the Union of Berest was accomplished. Officially, almost all the top hierarchy and almost the entire country embraced the Union, although the lower clergy, some monasteries, and certain segments of the population remained Orthodox and refused to join this Church. It seemed at first that it would be only a matter of time before the Uniate Church would take over the whole nation. Nevertheless, two developments turned the tide the other way. Above all, the Polish Catholic government, which professed to protect and support the Union, failed to do so. Out of national and political reasons, it continued to treat the Uniate hierarchy unfairly and to discriminate against the Ukrainians. Those Ukrainians who expected to preserve their national interests by way of accepting the Church Union soon became discouraged, and either joined the Orthodox ranks again or became Roman Catholic.

The Ukrainian aristocracy, especially eager to retain its class privileges, embraced Roman Catholicism. The aristocracy included the families of Oginsky, Kysil, Solomyretsky, Puzyna, Stetkevych and many others, and so were totally Polonized. The Poles were disappointed in the Church Union in their own way, since they expected the Union to be the road to the general Polonization of the Ukrainian masses. Yet, this was not the case; it became strictly a Ukrainian faith.

On the other hand, the restoration of the Orthodox hierarchy strengthened the Orthodox resistance and produced an Orthodox renaissance at first with a silent tolerance of the Polish government, and a little later, with its open support which was politically and militarily motivated, as pointed out. This revival greatly weakened the Uniate Church, while the conflict between the two faiths at times erupted into violence. There were great minds on both sides, such as Metropolitans Boretsky, Mohyla, Rutsky, and bishops, such as Smotrytsky, who attempted the reconciliation and unification of the two Churches under one Kievan Patriarch. However, the conservative Orthodox and Catholic circles prevented any such unification.

Metropolitan Ivan Veliamyn Rutsky, a Byelorus'ian by birth and a highly educated man who studied in Prague and Rome, greatly enhanced the Uniate-Catholic Church. Like Metropolitan Mohyla, who reformed the Orthodox Church and led it to new heights, so did Rutsky with the Uniate-Catholic Church. He introduced regular *synods*, councils of bishops to discuss the needs of the Church; he strengthened ecclesiastic discipline and largely eliminated simony, the buying and selling of ecclesiastic offices; and he brought order into the administration of the Church real estate and property matters. In addition, he brought order into the Church records and archives, reformed monastic life by using the Catholic Society of Jesus for that purpose, and raised the educational standards of the clergy by organizing schools and sending young people abroad to further their studies, as Mohyla did, to Rome, Prague, Vienna, Graz and Brownsberg. He courageously defended the Uniate Church against Polish discrimination and Orthodox hostilities, while at the same time seeking reconciliation with the Orthodox and possible religious reunification under one Ukrainian Patriarchate.

In the Cossack-Hetman State the plight of the Union was deplorable. Neither the Agreement of Pereyaslav nor the Agreement of Hadiach granted the Uniates any respectable legal position; Hadiach attempted to abolish the Union altogether. Moscow was always very hostile towards Rome and Rome-related institutions. Hence, it was aggressively anti-Uniate, and it was intriguing and doing everything possible in its power to strengthen the anti-Uniate feelings among the Ukrainians and to facilitate anti-Uniate measures of the Polish government as well. Meanwhile, the Poles still tried to make the Church Union the avenue of the Polonization of the Ukrainian ethnic stock in Western and Right-bank Ukraine, gravely damaging in this way its religious aspect. Thus, Yakiv Susha, the Apostolic administration of the Kholm eparchy went to Rome to see the Pope, asking him to defend the Union against the Polish maneuvers, which included attempts to subject the Uniates to the jurisdiction of the Roman Catholic hierarchy. In response to this move, Rome sent a letter to the Polish king demanding that the Church Union not be used for any political ends and that the discrimination against the Uniates be stopped. Arrangements were made to admit the Uniate Metropolitan to the *senate* of the Polish Crown, though practically the idea scarcely materialized.

With the growing interference of Moscow in Left-bank Ukraine and the Cossack-Hetman State, the Uniate Metropolitan had to leave Kiev and for a number of years had no permanent see of his own. He had to move from one place to another. The Ukrainian Orthodox Church was also suffering from an ever-growing pressure, especially after the Agreement of Andrusiv. In spite of the Polish discrimination, both Ukrainian Churches still enjoyed more freedom in Right-bank Ukraine. Under the leadership of the Uniate Metropolitan Cyprain Zhokhovsky, Orthodox-Uniate dialogue was resumed, and in the 1680, a *synod*, or council, of Lublin was held, participated in by the Ukrainian Orthodox and Uniate hierarchy and clergy. It was held in the spirit of a union of prayer. Further progress in this direction was barred again, however, by the opposition of the papal *nuncio*, some other conservative Catholics, and a lukewarm attitude of some Orthodox, like Bishop Sviatopolk-Chetvertynsky, whose notorious mission was to submit the Ukrainian Orthodox Church to the authority of Moscow only a few years later. Zhokhovsky also resolutely defended the purity of the Eastern Rite in the Ukrainian Church against the introduction of various elements of the Latin rite by the Basilian order and asked the assistance of Rome in this matter.

Meanwhile, the Uniate-Catholic Church established itself in various parts of Western Ukraine. Carpathian Ukraine, under Hungarian authority, became Uniate in 1646, but later on, because of Calvinist intrigues, the religious posture of the area became somewhat blurred. Yet, under the leadership of Bishop Joseph de Camiles, 1690-1704, the Uniate Church was considerably strengthened and its legal position under the Austrian rule improved greatly. The Orthodox religion was, however, retained by a part of the population. After a few years of preparations, the Peremyshl Eparchy, under Bishop Inokentii Vynnytsky, became Uniate, greatly due to the efforts of Metropolitan Zhokhovsky. Then, in 1700, Bishop Joseph Shumlansky, after many years of vacillation and hesitation on his part, led his Lviv eparchy to the official acceptance of Uniate Catholicism. Only the *Stavropigia* brotherhood of Lviv, until 1708, and the Skete of Maniava in the Carpathian mountains, until 1785, remained Orthodox. The Lutsk eparchy became Uniate under Bishop Dionisii Zhabokrytsky in 1702. For having done this, Zhabokrytsky was imprisoned by the Muscovites and sent to Moscow, where he died in 1715. The Uniate Church achieved quite a success in Western and Right-bank Ukraine and would have continued to thrive had it not been for the later intervention of the Russian government.

The consolidation of the Uniate Church was best manifested by the *synod* of Zamost in 1720, under Metropolitan Lev Kyshka, the deliberations of which were promulgated in the form of "Decrees." The *synod* defined certain doctrines of beliefs, regulated some administrative questions, and reserved to the members of the Basilian order exclusively the right to be consecrated for the episcopacy. The *Haidamaky* movement weakened the Uniate Church, because the *Haidamaks*, ideologically closely related to the Cossacks, were ardently Orthodox and hated the Uniates as supposedly national traitors. The Russian emissaries instigated them even more against the Catholics and the Uniates. During the uprisings, Uniate clergy and laity were killed and Uniate churches were destroyed by the *Haidamaks* and the populace.

Russian pressure against the Ukrainian churches was greatly intensified after 1721. At that time, Tsar Peter I reformed the Russian Orthodox Church. He abolished the Moscow Patriarchate as the top authority of the Church, which at least theoretically had a kind of ecclesiastic autonomy, and replaced it by the Holy Synod, or College, in order to completely subordinate the Church to the Tsarist government. The Holy Synod was chaired by a chief-procurator, a lay person, and in reality it became another governmental agency, enforcing the government policies via a pseudo-religious body. The Russification process of the Ukrainian Orthodox Church and the annihilation of the Uniate Church were systematically pursued by the Holy Synod and the government of the Russian Empire. After the partitions of Poland, as it was noted, all of Right-bank and a northern part of Western Ukraine were included in the empire, and the misfortunes of the Ukrainian Churches in Left-bank Ukraine were then shared jointly by almost the entire country. Only a small region of the southern West Ukraine under Austrian rule, Galicia, Carpathian Ukraine, and Bukovyna, enjoyed some religious and national freedom.⁹

The Roman Catholics were thoroughly disliked by the Orthodox in Ukraine, because Catholicism was the dominant religion of the Polish Crown, which discriminated against Orthodoxy. Yet, in the Cossack-Hetman state it was tolerated and enjoyed more freedom than the Uniate Church did. The tolerance for the Roman Catholics was reserved by the Treaty of Zboriv and Bila Tserkva. The Treaty of Haidach granted the Catholics full freedom of worship, while the Uniate Church was supposed to be liquidated. Then again, after the partitions of Poland, by which Russia annexed not only most of Ukraine but also the entire Byelorus'ia and a large portion of Poland, the Roman Catholics enjoyed religious tolerance by the grace of the St. Petersburg government.

As far as the material status of the Churches in Ukraine was concerned, they were in rather good condition. The people of all classes were still deeply religious, and out of their piety they continued to make large land grants, monetary contributions and other gifts, including transfers in testamentary ways, to the Churches. At times they did these things out of penance for their sins and trespasses. Hetmans, such as Samoilovych, Mazepa, Apostol and others, the Cossack grandees, such as Miklashevsky, Kochubey, Mokievsky, Iskra, Horlenko or Myrovych, and the Cossacks of the middle class, the gentry and the commoners, continued to endow the Churches, Orthodox and Uniate, as well.¹⁰ Obviously, in the Hetman state, the Orthodox Church was much wealthier than the Uniate one. There was largely no state intervention in the property matters of the Church, and consequently, this continued to be a very important economic factor in Ukraine. However, with the submission of the Ukrainian Church to the authority of Moscow's Patriarch, and then, with the introduction of the Holy Synod and the progressive Russification of that Church, the Russian interests took over its ecclesiastic wealth and it began to work for the Russian rather than the Ukrainian economy.

Education and the Sciences. It must be asserted that the educational level in Ukraine and the Cossack-Hetman State was very high for the respective time. Even broad classes of the common people were literate, according to Paul of Alepo. He asserted that "they all, almost without exception, even their wives and daughters, know how to read and know the order of the mass and the church songs." Another foreigner, visiting Ukraine in 1711, a Danish envoy, Jul Just, reported that he was greatly surprised to see the Ukrainian peasants in many villages going to Church with prayer books, indicating that they were literate.¹¹ According to historical records, it seemed that almost every village had a school of its own, affiliated with the church, where elementary instruction was given by the *diaky*, the church cantors. In addition, the monasteries, which were quite numerous, also ran their own schools. In the years 1740-1748, in the seven regimental districts of the Hetman Ukraine alone, there were 866 schools for 1,099 larger and smaller settlements. This averaged approximately one school for every 1,000 people. Some twenty years later, in the three regions, Chernihiv, Sosnytsia and Novhorod, there were 134 schools, or one school for every 746 people, where the children of the grandees, Cossacks, clergy and peasants were instructed in the basic skills of writing, reading, arithmetic and religion. In the four regimental districts of Village or *Slobidska* Ukraine, there were, at about the same time, some 124 schools. In those regions, where the population was sparse and lived in a highly scattered way, the so-called travelling cantors, *mandrivni diaky*, travelled from one farmstead, *khutor*, to another, teaching the youngsters. Polonska-Vasylenko underscored, along with other students, that these schools were spontaneously organized by the local population, and were not centrally initiated and organized or imposed upon the people by the central government.[12] In various towns, church brotherhoods maintained schools.

In Right-bank Ukraine, under the Polish domination, the level of education was much lower. Neither the Polish government nor the Polish gentry cared for intelligent and educated Ukrainian masses. They preferred illiterate peasant serfs to work in their manors like draft animals.

Things also turned out the same way in Left-bank Ukraine, after Ukrainian political autonomy was crushed by St. Petersburg and after undisputed Russian domination was established. The Tsarist government and the Russian nobility and gentry favored an illiterate peasant work force. Some one hundred and twenty years later, in 1875, where there used to be many schools, there were only fifty, an average of about one school for every 6,750 people, a dramatic contrast to the situation during the Hetman rule. This was only another dimension of the Russian exploitation of Ukraine, a kind of intellectual suppression.

Metropolitans and bishops, such as Mohyla, Rutsky and Zhokhovsky, paid great attention to the educational process in order to raise the intellectual level of the clergy, who had to lead the masses spiritually and culturally. They subsidized the schools, urged the organization of new ones, and even sent young people abroad to complete their education. Yet, they did not meet with much success, as far as sending the youth abroad was concerned. The young people easily denationalized in a foreign environment, and many of them never came back. Hence, Metropolitan Mohyla conceived an idea of establishing a school of higher learning in Ukraine, since the Academy of Ostroh no longer existed.

In Kiev there had been a brotherhood school of good reputation since 1615. Then, Mohyla organized a new school at Pecherska Lavra according to the Western patterns of advanced teaching techniques. This caused some indignation on the part of the brotherhood, but a year later the matter was reconciled; and both schools were merged, having received public recognition and became a college, *collegium*, in 1633. Since that time the college was known as the Kievan-Mohylian College or Academy, a contemporary of Harvard University. The distinctive feature of the Academy was that it admitted the youth of all classes, and that admissions were not restricted to the sons of the upper class only.

Mohyla took special care that the Academy employed the best teachers, Ukrainian and foreign, in order to secure high scholastic levels in the College. The scholastic method of instruction was adopted by the Academy. It was the method then popular throughout Western Europe. The conservative Orthodox elements were very much opposed to this innovation, while in Muscovy-Russia, the school and its new scholastic approach were deeply hated and scorned for a long time. The instruction extended over a period of six or seven years. Instruction was based upon the Thomistic approach and many textbooks were either brought from the West or were West-oriented, especially in the fields of philosophy and theology.

The following subject matters were within the teaching program of the Academy: grammar, the writing of poetry, rhetoric, philosophy, theology, geography, mathematics and geometry, astronomy and various languages, such as Hebrew, Greek, Latin, Polish, German, French and Old Slavonic. The Academy had a marvelous library for this era, with hundreds of thousands of volumes including rare prints and manuscripts. Mohyla and his successors spent a great deal of money to enlarge it. It was the largest and best library in East Europe. The Academy was also involved in publishing books, written by teachers and former students. It was unfortunate that the library was destroyed by fire in 1780, an enormous loss for the Ukrainian culture. The Academy also became the center of the development of the theatrical arts of the country.

Among the outstanding students of the Kievan-Mohylian Academy were many future ecclesiastic, civilian and cultural leaders. Men such as L. Baranovych, bishop of Chernyhiv, I. Galatovsky, an author, I. Gizel, the author of *Synopsis*, one of the first textbooks on history, T. Prokopovych, archbishop and renegade, who left Ukraine and helped organize the Russian Church, outstanding preachers, D. Tuptalenko, A. Radzyvylovsky and others, who were church dignitaries and authors. I. Samoilovych, a Ukrainian Hetman, O. Bezborodko and O. Myloradovych, statesmen, D. Bortniansky, M. Berezovsky, A. Vedel, composers, O. Maksymovych and M. Bantysh-Kamensky, scholars, H. Skovoroda, a great Ukrainian philosopher, P. Hulak-Artemovsky, a writer, and many others were among the famous students of the Academy which was the first East-European institution of higher learning. Actually, from the very beginning of the Academy, and in particular, after its high scholastic standards were established, many foreigners studied there, such as the Bulgarians, Serbs, Moldavians, Greeks, Arabs, and Muscovites. Among the latter was the outstanding Muscovite-Russian scholar, M. Lomonosov.

For a long time the Polish government did not want to recognize the Academy as an institution of higher learning, since it did not want to acknowledge any Ukrainian cultural center of any substance. At the time of the Hadiach Agreement it was demanded that such a recognition of the Academy would be granted by the Poles. Also, the Muscovite government opposed such recognition until 1701 for the same reason. In addition, the Muscovite government despised the Academy's Western leanings, supposedly dangerous for Orthodoxy.

Although the Academy declined slightly after Mohyla's death, it experienced a new growth during Mazepa's time, since he was a well educated man and fully appreciated the cultural role of the college. He constructed a new building and a new church for the Academy, where its professors delivered their sermons during solemn masses. During his time the Academy had its highest enrollment—2,000 men. After the Poltava defeat, Peter I severely repressed the school, but its new revival came again in 1740-1750, when the number of its students again rose above 1,000. Immediately after the Poltava repressions that number had declined to 161, while foreigners were barred from attending.[13]

The Academy was not only a teaching institution for regular subject matters, but was also the school of morals and piety to raise the ethical and religious standards of the society. During the 150 years of its existence, it educated some 25,000 Ukrainians, many of them children of the most outstanding Cossack and noble families, such as Lomykovsky, Apostol, Lyzohub and Polubotk. However, a dormitory was available for the youth of the poor families of lower classes who were allowed to attend. Its cultural impact upon the Ukrainian society was enormous. Its popularity began to decline in the second half of the eighteenth century, mainly due to Russian oppression. In 1817, the Russian government closed the Academy as the symbol of Ukrainian culture and education. It was turned into an Orthodox seminary for training priests and deacons, strictly supervised by the Metropolitan, a Russian. Later, the Kievan and other universities were established in Ukraine by the Russian authorities within the framework of the Russian educational system only.[14]

The Kievan-Mohylian Academy inspired and served as a pattern to a score of other attempts to organize and run institutions of higher learning. Archbishop L. Baranovych established a College in Novhorod Siversky, which was later transferred to Chernihiv. This college also enjoyed Mazepa's protection and support. Ye. Tykhorsky, bishop of Bilhorod, also organized a college there, which was subsequently transferred to Kharkiv. Bishop A. Berlo established a seminary in Pereyaslav, which was later transferred to Poltava, thus becoming the cultural center for the region for a number of years. Metropolitan Mohyla established schools in Vynnytsia and Kremianets, which, however, did not exist very long as institutions and never reached beyond the elementary or middle educational level.

Once the trend for more secular education developed in the eighteenth century, attempts were made to establish universities in Ukraine. Hetman Mazepa planned to organize a university in Baturyn and to reorganize the Kievan-Mohylian Academy into a university, but the catastrophe of Poltava hindered the realization of his plans. Rumiantsev, the Russian emissary in Ukraine, planned to establish universities in Kiev and Chernihiv. In 1767, the Ukrainian gentry demanded the establishment of universities in Kiev, Baturyn, Chernihiv, Novhorod Siversky and Sumy.[15]

Under Polish domination, the matter of higher and lower education was in much worse shape than in the Left-bank regions.

In 1676, Metropolitan Cyprian Zhokhovsky asked Rome to help him in establishing a seminary for the better training of Uniate priests in Ukraine and Byelorus'ia. Such a school was established in the city of Vilna. The measure did not relieve the situation substantially, since very few Ukrainian students studied there. The Basilian order also started a good school in Uman in 1765, but only for the children of the gentry. However, the school and the monastery were ruined by the *Haidamaks* during the *Koliivshchyna* insurrection. Unfortunately, the schools of the church brotherhoods also began to decline in number and quality, because of the progressive Polonization and Latinization of the Ukrainian gentry and townspeople under Polish discriminatory practices. With the partitions of Poland, the educational matters turned from bad to worse in Right-bank Ukraine, as well as in the whole country, as pointed out above, because of the specific policy of St. Petersburg to keep the masses in its colonies illiterate.

The high cultural level of the Ukrainian upper classes at this time, as Polonska-Vasylenko and Doroshenko asserted, was clearly evident by the large number of libraries throughout the country. There were libraries at the Kievan-Mohylian Academy and other similar institutions, at *Pecherska Lavra* monastery and numerous other monasteries in the land, followed up by many private libraries, such as those of Mazepa, Baranovych, Galatovsky, Tuptalo, Prokopovych, Yavorsky, Kochubei and Rozumovsky. The owners of these libraries imported books, journals and newspapers from abroad in order to be informed about cultural, political and other developments in the world. Jean Baluse, who visited Ukraine at the end of 1704, asserted that he saw French and Dutch newspapers in Mazepa's study. Manuscripts, chronicles and documents were also kept there, including books from various fields of interest ranging from mathematics, astronomy and medicine to philosophy, and in particular, areas of law, history and geography.[16]

Philosophy and theology were still the most important and most respected fields of human knowledge. In the early seventeenth century, Aristotelian philosophical thinking still prevailed in the minds of the Ukrainian intellectual elite, as was indicated when the Kievan Academy and its cultural significance was discussed. Furthermore, the Aristotelian philosophical categories as applied to logic, dialectics, physics, methaphysics and ethics, were understood through the Tomistic interpretation in theology, while the scholastic methods of reasoning were generally used. The conservative Orthodox, and in particular the Moscow oriented ones, did not like the so-called "Latinization" of the Ukrainian Church. Ancient and medieval philosophers and theologians were read and discussed. Subsequently, such thinkers as Thomas Hobbes, Hugo Grotius, S. Pufendorf, and some less important ones were studied. The titles of the philosophical treatises and compendia, written at that time were self-explanatory, as far as their leanings were concerned. For instance, Popovsky published *Universa philosophia commentariis scholasticis illustrata, doctrinam peripateticam complectens ingenuo auditori Roxolano exposita in 1699;* then Rev. Christophor Czarnucki published *Organum Aristotelis seu aurea scientiarum clavis ad universalem rationalis philosophiae portam in 1702;* while Hilarion Jaroshevitsky printed *Cursus philosophicus doctrinam Aristotelis Stagiratae ex methodo quae traditur in scholis complectens inchoatus;* and others like these were written and read. The named publications were connected with the Kievan Academy. Two important and influential works by two people not directly related to the

Academy were also published. *Zertsalo bohoslovia,* the *Mirror of Theology,* by Cyril Stavrovetsky, was published in 1618 and was completely permeated by the Thomistic approach, while *Traktat o dushi,* the *Treatise on the Soul,* was published in 1625 by Kassian Sakovych who was a passionate polemist in favor of Orthodoxy at first, then the Union, and finally Roman Catholicism. Of course, the philosophical and theological issues of both were closely related.

In the eighteenth century a new trend appeared in philosophical thinking. D. Nashchynsky, educated in Leipzig, Germany and prefect of the Kievan Academy, persuaded the Metropolitan to adopt the *Elementa philosophiae recentioris,* written by Baumeister, a follower of Wolffian philosophy. The textbook soon became very popular in Eastern Ukraine, and at the end of the century, due to the efforts of Petro Lodyi, it was also adopted in Lviv, a cultural center in West Ukraine. The Wolffian philosophical system, which was introduced into the training of the Ukrainian youth, was then advanced by other people.[17]

Yet, the first place in Ukrainian philosophy of the eighteenth century belongs to Hryhorii Skovoroda, 1722-1794, who completed his education in the Kievan-Mohylian Academy and in the institutions of higher learning in Munich, Vienna, Breslau and Koenigsberg. Upon his return from the foreign universities, he was a professor of the university in Kharkiv, but only for a short while. Skovoroda liked to be free and did not want to be rigorously tied to any particular responsibilities. He travelled continuously, occasionally instructing the children of aristocrats in their manors and palaces, and then moving on again. He put his own main works in the form of Socratic dialogues, and therefore later writings about Skovoroda rightly compared him to Socrates and sometimes called him the "Ukrainian Socrates."

At the foundation of Skovoroda's philosophical system was a deep belief in God, anthropologism, and self-knowledge. He maintained that the universe consists of two elements: the spiritual and elevated one, and the material or worthless one. It was a form of philosophical dualism. The end purpose of life is happiness, but not a common and material concept of happiness, but the happiness which comes from the conviction of fulfilling the will of God, while self-knowledge derives from learning of God and leads to the forming of one's life according to God's will. He led an ascetic way of life; he did not desire any material comforts or honors. He refused to accept the episcopal dignity offered to him, and severely criticized the contemporary Church for its materialization and secularization. His deep philosophical thought made him one of the greatest philosophers of his time, known all over Ukraine, as well as abroad. Skovoroda's ideas in the field of religion made him, of course, partially a theologian. His personality and his work subsequently gave rise to a considerable amount of writings.[18]

The theology of the seventeenth and eighteenth centuries still bore a substantial feature of the polemical approach, especially in its earlier era. The spiritual and intellectual struggle continued between the Roman Catholics and the Uniates, on the one side, and the Orthodox, on the other.

Treatises were published, presenting and contrasting the postulates of both wings of Christianity. Z. Kopystensky published *Palinodion*; K. Stavrovetsky, *Zertsalo bohoslovia, Mirror of Theology*; I. Gizel, *Myr Bohu z chelovikom, God's Peace to Man*; P. Mohyla, *Ritual* and *Litos*, while H. Skovoroda also wrote several outstanding treatises on theological themes.

Theological treatises were written mostly by people connected with the Kievan-Mohylian Academy in whatever capacity: protectors, teachers or former students. Metropolitan Mohyla, as mentioned, published a very important theological work, *Ispovid viry provoslavnoi*, the *Confessions of the Orthodox Faith*, which made an impact on the entire Orthodox East and is still a respected and influential source material, used even by Uniate churchmen.

Theological questions were also elaborated on in numerous collections of original sermons, written down and published to assist the priests when they delivered their sermons to their flocks, and to be used by the religious and laity as pious readings. The sermons were written with a great deal of literary and artistic ability, where examples were quoted to underline particular points. Quotations from the Latin and Greek literature were introduced, and comparisons, analogies, proverbs and anecdotes were cited to increase the interest of the reader. Among the outstanding books of sermons the following should be named; *Perlo mnohotsinne, Invaluable Pearl*, by Cyril Stavrovetsky: *Kluch rozuminnia, Key to Understanding* and *Nauka albo sposob zlozhennia kazannia, The Theory or Method of Composing a Sermon*; *Nebo novoye, The New Heaven*, and a series of sermons against Uniate Catholicism and the Islamic faith, by I. Galatovsky; *Ohorodok Bohorodytsi, The Garden of Holy Mother*, and *Vinets Khrystov, Christ's Wreath*, by A. Radzyvylovsky; *Mech dukhovnyi*, the *Spiritual Sword*, and *Truby sloves propovidnykh*, the *Trumpets of the Preaching Words*, by Lazar Baranovych, which enjoyed great popularity. Among the outstanding preachers D. Tuptalo, S. Yavorsky, T. Prokopovych and Yu. Konysky should also be mentioned.

Jurisprudence or the science of law was well developed in the Cossack-Hetman state. This field has already been discussed in connection with the law and government in Ukraine at that time. The political revival after the National Revolution facilitated the development of political science thought which was also maturing with the growth of historical studies and history writing. In order to counterpart, consciously or subconsciously, the growth of the Muscovite-Russian political-ecclesiastic idea of Moscow's being the "Third Rome," which was supposedly called upon to save the Orthodox world from the onslaughts of Catholicism and Islam, the theory of Kiev as the "Second Jerusalem" was formed in Ukraine, which required the city to fulfill its mission of leading all Christians to God, *bohospasaiemyi horod Kyiv*. Apparently, the idea was conceived at the time of the consecration of the new bishops for the Ukrainian Orthodox Church by Theophan, Patriarch of Jerusalem, which marked the revival of that Church after the blow it received from the Union of Berest. The idea was then advanced by Metropolitan Y. Boretsky in his letters and sermons, and it was subsequently propagated by I. Kopynsky, P. Mohyla and others. The *Pecherska Lavra* monastery accepted the thought. Of course, the National Revolution and the splendor of Khmelnytsky's state only added to the popularity of the idea of Kiev as the "Second Jerusalem." References to the political-ecclesiastic concept were made by Ukrainian envoys, sent to Moscow on various occasions, and the Ukrainian Church dignitaries later on, such as Metropolitan S. Kossiv.

While the messianic idea of "Kiev being the second Jerusalem" declined during the Era of the Ruin, it recovered with full force again during Samoilovych's and Mazepa's time, especially, after Left-bank and Right-bank Ukraine were unified under Mazepa's rule. At this time, T. Prokopovych was the leading proponent of "Kiev being the second Jerusalem" and the new Sion, and he championed this idea in his sermons and his drama "Volodymyr," in which he praised Hetman Mazepa as a worthy successor of Volodymyr the Great. This same trend of thought was also followed, at first by S. Yavorsky. It was unfortunate that these two men were not strong characters. Later on, they began to serve the Russian cause and the idea of "Moscow being the Third Rome," in exchange for honor and money they received from the hands of the Tsar.[19] Ukrainian political-ecclesiastic thought also rooted the leitmotif of the continuity of Ukrainian history from the Kievan realm on to the Cossack-Hetman state, which was also apparent in the historical writings of that time, such as *Istoria Rusiv, A History of the Rus'ians*, whose authorship has been frequently ascribed to Hryhorii Poletyka, which is not certain at all.

The national revival and political rebirth awakened interests in historical studies, and attempts were made to understand the present in the projection of the past. The religious struggle between the Uniates and the Orthodox also contributed to historical interest, and to searching in the past for the answer of who was right and who was wrong. History writing then developed in four directions: the pragmatic historical works, the so-called Cossack chronicles, the descriptive-analytical works and the memoirs and diaries.

In the Cossack-Hetman State, historical works began to get away from the simple writing of chronicles, which recorded events chronologically, and took the form of pragmatic historiography, although some of them still carried the names of chronicles, such as *Khronika, Chronicle*, by T. Safonovych. The leading work in this respect was the *Synopis*, published in 1674, the authorship of which has been ascribed to I. Gizel. It represents a kind of synthetic text of Ukrainian history used as such for a few decades. The important feature of these works was their insistence on establishing the historical continuity between the Kievan era and the Hetman era of the Ukrainian past, a fact which was persistently denied and confused by Russian historiography as mentioned. The latter, as discussed in the first volume of this work, tried to connect the Kievan era with the Muscovite era to justify the Muscovite-Russian expansionism in Ukraine and Byeloruthenia.

In the eighteenth century the descriptive-analytical works, with the same historiographical leitmotif of the continuity of Ukrainian history, were published. They included *Kratkoie opysanie Malorossii, A Short Description of Little Rus'ia*; then, *Opysanie o Maloi Rossii, A Description of Little Rus'ia*, by H. Pokaz; *Kratkoie opysanie o kozatskom malorossiiskom narode, A Short Description of the Cossack Little Rus'ian people*, by P. Symonovsky; and finally, *Sobranie istoricheskoie, A Collected Historical Work*, by S. Lukomsky.

The so-called Cossack chronicles, *kozatski litopysy*, constituted the third component of the historical writings of that time. It is assumed that R. Rakushka, who participated in the National Revolution, wrote *Samovydets, Eyewitness*, a chronicle account of the insurrection; H. Hrabianka, colonel of Hadiach, published *Diistvia...nebyvaloi brany Bohdana Khmelnytskoho, The Developments... of unbelievable war by Bohdan Khmelnytsky*; S. Velychko, an official of the General Military Chancellory, wrote a similar account *Skazanie o voinie kozatskoi z polakamy chrez Zenivia Bohdana Khmelnytskoho, A Story of the Cossack War against the Poles by Zenovii Bohdan Khmelnytsky*. Velychko utilized many sources to write his story. In addition, all these so-called chronicles had the incipient character of pragmatic historiography as well.

Finally, the memoirs and diaries from that time represent a very important segment of historical source material of the era, its socio-political ideology, the culture of the land, and the world outlook of its leading social elite. Petro Apostol, the Hetman's son, who stayed a long time in St. Petersburg as a Ukrainian "hostage," wrote a *Diary* in French, and a great deal about the Muscovite-Ukrainian relationships. Equally important was the *Diary* of M. Khanenko, who as a member of the *heneralna starshyna*, worked closely with Hetmans I. Skoropadsky, P. Polubotok and D. Apostol. His memoirs throw ample light upon the epoch. Yet, the most important of them all is the *Dnevnyk*, *Diary*, of Yakiv Markovych, treasurer-general, a well-educated man with very broad scholarly interests, who bought foreign language books, journals and newspapers in order to be well informed. His *Diary* very scrupulously related the day-by-day developments of various fields of interests, his health, weather conditions, meetings, conversations, economic affairs and national politics.[20]

In the field of history and political thought, however, the first place had been taken by the *Istoria Rusiv*, *A History of the Rus'ians*, written sometime between 1770 and 1804, and printed and published some thirty-five years later, when it was already well known in certain educated circles of Ukraine, particularly in the Novhorod Siversky circle, where its very idea originated and materialized. The authorship of the *Istoria Rusiv* is actually unknown, although it has often been ascribed to Hyrhorii Poletyka, a Ukrainian nobleman. O. Ohloblyn and other historians searched for establishing its true authorship, but so far with no luck in this respect. Ohloblyn assumed that the work might have even been a product of the collective effort of several people, ideologically connected with Prince A. Bezborodko, a chancellor of the Russian empire, but of Ukrainian descent.

Istoria Rusiv was a true attempt to give the Ukrainian people their historical and political self-assertion and self-assurance. At the end of the eighteenth and the first half of the nineteenth century, the work achieved great popularity and became an inspiration for Ukrainian political thought, historical studies and many literary creations, including the writings of such literary people as Maksymovych, Hrebinka, Hohol (Gogol), Kostomarov, and Taras Shevchenko. *Istoria Rusiv* itself was permeated by the ideas of the Ukrainian struggle for national independence and the right of the Ukrainian people to autonomous statehood, expressed in strong language. Ohloblyn characterizes the *Istoria Rusiv* as follows: It is "not a scholarly history of Ukraine, it is not even a historical work. It is mostly a political treatise, embodied into historiographical form. It is no doubt that the very aim of the treatise was the problem of the Ukrainian-Russian relationship, the deep antithesis between Ukraine and Muscovy."[21]

The natural sciences did not develop at this time in Ukraine, although there existed a vital interest in them, since in various libraries there were books on botany, zoology, meteorology and medicine, widely read by the Ukrainian intellectual elite.

Literature. During this period literary creations still had predominantly religious and moral characteristics for several reasons. First, the writers and authors were largely religious people, priests or monks. Second, the religious conflict between the Orthodox and the Uniates continued to be an important issue during the seventeenth and early part of the eighteenth century, still producing considerable polemical literature of a religious nature. And third, the whole Ukrainian society at that time continued to be deeply religious.

Obviously, Ukrainian folklore in the form of popular songs, legends, stories, folk poetry, proverbs and all kind of rituals, based on customs and related to family, social and religious life, continued to develop and to inspire literary creation in its narrower sense. All these forms of folklore were developed by talented individuals, whose names were soon forgotten, but their cultural creations were soon adopted by the broad circles of the population and became the very component of its culture. The beginnings of the Cossack movement and the struggle against the Turks and Tartars inspired the development of historical songs, which praised either certain remarkable events or some heroic personalities. The *Song about the Holy Mother of Pochaiv*, the *Song about Colonel Nechai*, and the *Song about the Demolition of the Sitch* belong to the group of cultural creations of the Ukrainian people at large.

The *dumy* were another branch of folklore. They were sagas which praised the Cossack heroes and wars or related the dreadful conditions of life of the Ukrainian captives in Turkish and Tartar slavery. Hence, there were two kinds of *dumy*, sagas, the Cossack and the slave ones. The *dumy* were recited by professional bards, *kobzari*, accompanied by music on the folk instrument, the *kobza*. At this point the development of literary and musical creations actually merged together. The sagas frequently contained didactic elements, instructing about the duty of the love of one's country, the sanctity of parental blessings and the power of penance. Some *dumy* were predominantly didactic in character, like the one about a *Storm on the Black Sea*.

Poetry was developing rapidly in Ukraine at that time. At first, it was predominantly religious in its content; the custom of writing and expressing one-self in poetic form came to Ukraine from Western Europe. Religious songs, psalms, religious legends and stories were fashionably transformed and expressed in poetic form. The art of writing poetry became an obligatory subject matter to be instructed in schools, including the Kievan-Mohylian Academy and other similar institutions. Then, themes for poetic writing spread towards more worldly spheres. Panegyrics, epigrams, salutations, valedictions, praising odes and dedications were all delivered in poetic forms during the eras of the Baroque and Rococo styles in Ukraine. Holy days, holidays, anniversaries, birthdays, arrivals of important guests, or any event of some importance could be a theme for writing and delivering poetic verses, composed in very skillful acrostic forms, such as crosses, jugs, eggs, half-moons and other shapes. They were read from left to right and in reverse, which also made some poetic sense. Among the poets who excelled in this kind of poetry were D. Tuptalo, who wrote religious poems and songs, and I. Velychkivsky, C. Zinoviiv, S. Yavorsky and H. Skovoroda.

Epic poetry, the epopee, was not well developed, but there were some examples of such creation, including the poem about the *Battle of Berestechko*, the *Battle of Khotyn*, about the *Defense of Vienna*, and religious epopees by S. Mokrievych and I. Maksymovych.

Prosaic writing was best represented by all kinds of short stories, mostly of religious content, especially about saints and miracles. A collection of such short stories was published by Metropolitan P. Mohyla, while I. Galatovsky published *Nebo novoie, New Heaven*; a similar collection. *Pechersky Pateryk* enjoyed great popularity at this time and was reprinted several times. A very outstanding collection of the lives of saints was arranged by D. Tuptalo at the end of the seventeenth century.

Dramatic writing was well developed at first with religious motives and since the beginning of the eighteenth century with historical motives. This literary creation will be discussed in the next section of this work in connection with the evolution of the theatrical art in Ukraine of this period.

Radzykevych, in his *History of Ukrainian Literature*, pointed out that due to the political pressure of Moscow, relatively few works were published in print in Ukraine and in the spoken Ukrainian language. Hence, he said, a great many of the true Ukrainian literary creations of outstanding value were circulating only in manuscript form at the end of the seventeenth and the early part of the eighteenth century. The Muscovite government and the Patriarch of Moscow officially attempted to suppress the publication and circulation of such works. *Istoria Rusiv*, for instance, was printed some thirty-five to forty years after it was written down and made ready for publication.

Among the early works of poetry the following were printed: *Nativity*, by P. Berynda; *Poetic Eulogies for Sahaidachny's Funeral*, by K. Sakovych; *Invaluable Pearl*, by C. Stavrovetsky, and a few others. Although some of these works were put in poetic form, they also represented important philosophical-theological treatises, such as Stavrovetsky's said work.

In the second half of the eighteenth century, when the Muscovite-Russian imperial pressure became almost intolerable, two important political works in good poetic form were produced. Semen Divovych wrote *Rozhovor Velykorossii z Malorossiieiu, A Conversation between Great Russia and Little Russia*. Divovych was working as an interpreter in the General Military Chancellory and was quite familiar with the dramatic developments of Russian-Ukrainian relations. The *Rozhovor* is presented as a dialogue between the respective countries, by which Ukraine proved her historical rights to political sovereignty. The work is permeated with the sentiment of Ukrainian national pride and a deep understanding of Ukrainian history. Ohloblyn pointed out that the *Rozhovor* was "a powerful literary protest against the Muscovite centralist policies."[22] Another political creation of the literary form was the *Oda na Rabstvo, Ode to Serfdom*, by V. Kapnist. At first it was held for literary protest against the introduction of serfdom in Ukraine by the Russian government. Yet, later on, after a careful analysis of the poem, it has been ascertained that it was also a protest against the Russian centralist domination. An important instance must be underscored here, namely, that both works *Rozhovor* and *Ode*, were not printed in the eighteenth century, because of Russian political pressure and the fear of possible persecutions, and for a long time they circulated throughout Ukraine in hand written manuscript form, copied many times over.

Other areas of literary creations were discussed already above, in particular, scholarly literature such as works in the fields of philosophy, theology, jurisprudence, political thought and history, and all kinds of treatises, books, memoirs, diaries, chronicles and geo-political descriptions.[23]

Architecture. Architecture, the artistic and highly skillful construction of church and secular edifices, was highly developed in Ukraine during the seventeenth and eighteenth centuries, and reached a higher level in Ukraine than in contemporary Poland and Muscovy, according to Sichynsky.[24] Once again, foreign visitors to Ukraine at this time afforded an objective and reliable testimony in this respect. Beauplan supplied descriptions of buildings and city constructions. Alepo, Just and Hildebrandt told about beautiful buildings and strong fortifications. Chojecki noticed impressive stone and wooden buildings in Ukraine, while Zhuiev said that the houses in *Slobidska* or Village Ukraine were "extremely spacious, made of wood and painted with white lime."[25]

Church construction was quite impressive at the time, many artistic monuments of which survived to the twentieth century, especially in some parts of Ukraine, such as the mountainous *Boyko* land. These wooden churches were tripartite edifices, each component of which was under a separate roof but connected with the others. In different territorial regions of the country the composition and ornamentation of these churches was a little different; in particular, the ways of structuring the *copulas*, which consisted of oval tin or shingle tetrahedral roofings of several stories, differed. Only a few private houses have survived from this era. Yet, these remnants, plus the Jewish synagogues, constructed similarly since the second half of the seventeenth century, give adequate illustration of how the private houses of wealthy citizens were built. The houses were spacious, built on various levels, with rich ornamentation and many porches and balconies.

Although in the early seventeenth century the Renaissance architectural style still prevailed in the monuments which one could find all over in Western Ukraine, particularly in the city of Lviv and also in Eastern Ukraine, in the second half of that century the style of Baroque began spreading in Ukraine. The Baroque in Ukraine soon fused together the Ukrainian tripartite church construction with the Western Basilica, becoming richly ornamented with a great many elements of Ukrainian national artistry, inspired by beauty and solemnity.

The formation of an independent Ukraine spurred the development of the country's architecture. First of all, the Hetmans, such as Khmelnytsky, Samoilovych, Mazepa, Apostol and Rozumovsky, and then, the Cossack grandees, such as Miklashevsky, Mokievsky and Myrovych, and the Church dignitaries, spent money lavishly for the construction of churches, convents, palaces and public buildings. Ohloblyn remarked that even those regarded as notorious misers, such as Samoilovych and Borkovsky, spent generously for new churches. Hetman Ivan Mazepa was, of course, the greatest protector and benefactor of the Orthodox Church. A monk from Chernihiv once wrote: "There was nobody before, there is nobody today, and there will be nobody like him in the future" in this respect. Tsar Peter I, Mazepa's deadly enemy after the latter's alliance with Charles XII, could not help but to concede and to call him ... "a great constructor of holy churches."[26] It is almost impossible to give an account of Mazepa's zeal for building. He sponsored and financed the construction of some 22 new churches and reconstructed and renovated many older ones. In every major city of his state, he erected or rebuilt magnificent buildings, either churches or civilian ones.

The construction of palaces, castles and public buildings was impressive. Khmelnytsky built his palaces in Chyhyryn and Subotiv; Mazepa, in Baturyn, Chernihiv and other places; Rozumovsky, in Hlukhiv. From among the Cossack aristocracy many grandees also built palaces: Lyzohub, in Sedniv; Myrovych, in Pereyaslav; and Polubotok, in Lubech. Church dignitaries also constructed splendid palaces.

The Kievan-Mohylian Academy was erected in 1632, and then reconstructed and renovated by Mazepa in 1703-1704. The Kievan city hall, *ratush*, was built in 1697. Buildings were also erected in *Slobidska* Ukraine, as in the cities of Kharkiv, Sumy, Izium, Okhtyrka and Valky, where a number of churches were also constructed as either wooden, stone or brick edifices.

Many of these buildings were constructed in the Ukrainian or Cossack Baroque style, called that way since the architectural style of the West was heavily influenced by Ukrainian architectural elements, as mentioned above, and its great popularity developed exactly at the time of the Cossack-Hetman era, the era of the political and cultural revival of Ukraine.

Cossack Baroque was represented in Ukraine by such outstanding architects as Ivan Baptysta from Lithuania, Adam Zernikau from East Prussia, Josyf and Fedir Startsiv, both Ukrainian, S. Kovnir, also Ukrainian, Gottfried Schädel from Germany, and many others.

Among the numerous examples of Baroque constructions in Ukraine, there were: the Mharsky Monastery in Lubni, erected by Samoilovych and Mazepa; the Church of the Holy Ascension in Pereyaslav, built by Mazepa; St. Michael's Goldroofed Monastery in Kiev, financed and built by M. Vuyakovych, Judge-General and by Hetman Mazepa; St. Sophia Cathedral and the main church of the Kievan *Pecherska Lavra*, reconstucted and enlarged by Metropolitan Petro Mohyla and Hetman Mazepa and a great many others.

In the middle of the eighteenth century the Rococo architectural style, a beautiful elaboration on the Baroque, came to Ukraine, represented by such splendid edifices as St. Andrew's Church in Kiev, the main church of the Pochaiv monastery, and, of course, the beautiful St. Yurii's Cathedral in Lviv. There were also many civilian buildings erected in the Rococo style, while many of them were ruined by subsequent wars and the intentional demolition by the Russian Bolsheviks in order to impoverish the Ukrainian cultural tradition. In Galicia, for example, several municipal buildings were erected in the Rococo style. The names of Schädel, Kovnir and Hryhorovych-Barsky had also been connected with Rococo in Ukraine.

At the end of the eighteenth century, paralleling the progressive subjugation of Ukraine to Russian domination and consequently, the evaporation of the country's political autonomy, the development of the architectural arts declined and the construction of buildings diminished substantially. Soon, under the impact of the imperial ambitions of the Russian court, the Neo-Classical style, a slavish imitation of the ancient architectural patterns, was introduced, and it also penetrated Ukraine, as represented by Rozumovsky's palaces in Baturyn and Pochep, Miklashevsky's buildings in the Starodub region, and others. Both foreign and Ukrainian architects were highly respected and very well paid for their services.[27]

Buildings were chiefly of wood, stone and brick. In the countryside, constructions were primarily of wood, as Zhuiev noticed in *Slobidska* Ukraine. Stones and bricks were extensively used in the cities for the erection of churches, palaces, forts, public buildings, and early factories.

Military construction developed speedily, although less impressively. Mazepa, for example, secretly attempted to fortify the Azov Sea ports and the Ukrainian-Muscovite borders in preparation for a war of liberation against Muscovy-Russia. There is not much information about these fortifications because they were constructed secretly, but Paul Alepo, Hildebrand, Meyerberg and other foreigners referred briefly to this fact, praising the excellence of the works from the strategic point of view and the qualifications of the engineers and builders. The *Sitch*, the capital of the Cossack Territory, seemed to be the most outstanding example of Ukrainian military construction and fortification of the time. Because of a large-scale introduction of firearms and artillery into military operations, a new system of fortifications had to be devised in the seventeenth century based more on earthworks. Deep ditches and high earth walls were built, rather than wood and stone constructions, as in the past. Peasant labor was extensively used for the digging of these ditches and the building of the earth walls.

Painting and Carving. Also in the areas of painting and carving, the artistic evolution proceeded from the Renaissance in the early part of that period, to the Baroque and Rococo, while at the end of the Cossack-Hetman State New-Classicism had already begun to penetrate these forms of artistic creations. Both painting and carving rose to a very high level of artistry. A realistic approach prevailed with a strong leaning towards magnificence, splendor and extravagant beauty of decoration and ornamentation. Church painting developed broad backgrounds with animal and plant decorations.

The images of the saints frequently reflected the faces of the wealthy sponsors and benefectors. National elements of art were widely included. Traditional *icon* painting continued with a heavy imprint of naturalistic portrait painting. The Baroque approach was well manifested in the *iconostasy*, iconostases, multiple partitions with tiers of *icons* in front of the main altars, and the *iconopysy, icon* wall drawings, richly decorating the Baroque church edifices. For instance, the magnificent iconostasis and *icon* wall drawings in the Monastery of Maniavsky Skyt in a Western Ukrainian mountainous region combined the elements of Italian, Flemish and Ukrainian painting patterns. Of course, there were a great many examples of Baroque painting, though not all survived to the present time.

Secular or private painting developed at this time primarily through the portrayal of the members of the Ukrainian nobility and the Cossack and Church elite. The elite was in love with portrait painting; the greater the dignitary, the larger the portrait he had painted of himself. Metropolitans, bishops, hetmans, colonels and others, including the city patricians, hired artists to paint their portraits and portraits of members of their families as well. Rooms, halls and corridors were decorated with all kinds of portraits; small, medium and large ones. Miniature pictures were made for medallions. At times the portraits reflected psychological features of the subjects, while later outer splendor of the clothing, arms and furnishings in the background was underscored by the artists.

Baroque painting was closely associated with the Kievan-Mohylian Academy and the *Pecherska Lavra* Monastery, where artistic painting was taught and books on painting were available. A spiritual connection between the Ukrainian and the Western Baroque was clearly evident; the Western and Ukrainian artists were enriching the country's artistic treasures. Yov Kondzelevych was an artist-painter of great talent and of considerable artistic educational background; apparently mayestro Vasyl was the most outstanding student of the Lviv School.

At the end of the eighteenth century Baroque evolved into the elegant, subtle and very elaborate Rococo. Rococo painting found rich sponsors and benefactors in Ukraine, such as P. Kalnyshevsky, the last *koshovyi* of the Cossack Territory, K. Rozumovsky, the last Hetman, and others. Rococo painting connected beauty, sadness and happiness in *icon* and wall drawing, while later on, portraiture became bright, happy and fair in its expression. In particular, portraitures enable one to easily learn the fashions, customs and even the way of life of the time.[28]

Ukrainian carving also evolved from the Renaissance to Baroque to Rococo artistic style. The Baroque decorative carving developed impressively in the *ikonostasy* or iconostases, and tombstones, where the figures of saints and people showed more life and motions. The *ikonostasy* were carved on several levels, one series of carvings of saints upon another, like those in the Monastery of Maniavsky Skyt in West Ukraine, or in the main church of the *Pecherska Lavra* and the Church of St. Michael in Kiev. In most cases, the carvings included Ukrainian national artistic elements. The iconostases of the wooden village churches in Ukraine of that time were particularly unique and national.

The Rococo era brought in more subtle, elaborate and detailed cuttings. The carving of details on crosses and candlesticks, pulpits, benches, and other furnishings, window and door frames, doors and picture frames were very popular and skillfully done. Rococo carvings were frequently polychromatic, while different colors were always harmoniously combined. Walls and ceilings of rooms, halls, corridors, and churches were ornamented with stucco work with plant motifs, being very ably done by local and foreign artists. In many cases, while close ties between the Ukrainian and Western Baroque and Rococo ages were evident, the local Ukrainian artistry excelled the West European one.

The carving of statues also became popular during the Baroque and Rococo era. In West Ukraine, statues were cut from stones, either single figures or groups of figures, while in East Ukraine they were cut from wood. Statues decorated churches, private buildings, palaces, municipal edifices, parks and gardens, while during the Rococo time, they became less monumental, but showed more motion, expression and inspiration.

Engraving developed magnificently, after its temporary decline during the Pereyaslav Agreement and the Era of Ruin. It was particularly outstanding during Mazepa's time and during the peak of the Baroque style in Ukraine. O. Tarasevych, at the verge of the seventeenth and eighteen centuries, was the most outstanding engraver in all of Eastern Europe, and he attempted to form a Ukrainian school of engraving and graphics. I. Myhura and N. Zubrytsky were two other famous engravers at the time. The Ukrainian engraving of the Baroque era substantially influenced art in other lands of Eastern Europe, such as Poland, Lithuania, Muscovy, Wallachia, Moldavia and Byelorus'ia. After the Poltava catastrophe, engraving again recovered in Ukraine between 1730 and 1740, when in Kiev there were some 50 masters of the art, while in the second half of the eighteenth century the city of Lviv became an important center of engraving.[29]

Music and Theatre. In the previous era of the Ukrainian past, the musical guilds and church brotherhoods in Kiev, Lviv, Lutsk, Chernihiv and other towns sponsored the development of musical art. Church choirs existed everywhere and promoted the art by introducing musical novelties, particularly from the West. Singing in multiple parts was popular for quite a long time. Musical notes were written for five and eight-part singing. The catalogue of the Lviv brotherhood for 1697 listed 267 church songs, composed for three or even twelve-part singing. M. Dyletsky at that time published the first book on musical theory, the *Muzykyiskaia hramatyka*, Musical Grammar, which was later republished over and over again. Foreigners visiting Ukraine, like Paul Alepo, for example, praised the beauty of Ukrainian singing in the urban and rural churches.

Needless to say, the Kievan-Mohylian Academy was for a long time the center of the development of musical art, where music was taught and solo and choir singing promoted. Since 1733, singing, music and musical composition developed at the Kharkiv College. Teachers composed music and taught the students to sing and to play the instruments. Many manuscripts of musical notes circulated. Other schools also taught and fostered musical art.

Hetman Rozumovsky's court in Hlukhiv was another center for the musical and theatrical arts in Ukraine at the end of the Cossack state. Rozumovsky, who *nota bene* lived a long time in St. Petersburg, wanted to make his capital in Ukraine resemble the Russian capital. Hence, in Hlukhiv he maintained a theatre, choirs, musical bands, and fostered the development of other arts as well. Italian music was particularly popular and Italian operas were staged and performed. In Hlukhiv, there was a school of music and a large library of musical texts and books. A. Rachynsky was the conductor of the choir and band at the Hetman's court. His band and choir also travelled to other places to give concerts. Ukrainians, who undertook journeys abroad to West European countries, brought from there a love for new Western music and made it popular in Ukraine by means of staging concerts and other forms of entertainment.

Three early Ukrainian composers, D. Bortniansky, M. Berezovsky, and A. Vedel, from the late eighteenth and early nineteenth centuries, educated in the Kievan Academy, marked the beginning of modern Ukrainian musical art. Two of them, Bortniansky and Berezovsky, worked in the musical band and the choir at Hlukhiv, and from there they were called to St. Petersburg and then sent to Italy, achieving great fame as composers. Bortniansky in particular was famous in the area of church music. Berezovsky composed operas and other music. Not able to resist the court intrigues, he met an early death. Bortniansky wrote four operas, many sonatas for piano, 45 choir concerts and a complete set of music for the Holy Liturgy, and many other works, where Ukrainian musical motifs were quite apparent. However, since he worked in Russia most of the time, the Russians adopted him and still consider him a Russian composer. Vedel was a great talent, but as an ardent Ukrainian patriot he opposed Russian terror and was murdered by the Russian authorities after being imprisoned. His music was essentially Ukrainian in character.[30]

The theatrical arts continued to develop on the foundations of the sixteenth and early seventeenth centuries, generated by the religious conflict between the Catholics and Protestants. Polish influence was apparent, while at a later period these arts acquired strictly Ukrainian national characteristics. Again the Kievan-Mohylian Academy was a standard bearer and a champion of the art. Professors of the Academy wrote dramatic works and the students staged and acted them out. Other schools followed the pattern of staging dramatic plays. At first, the plays had a largely religious content and referred to Christmas and Easter. Only a few have survived to the present time. One of these, written by D. Tuptalo, presents the Christmas miracle, accompanied by shepards, kings, Herod's court, and ritual dances. Other plays, also available to us, reflect Eastern developments and bring to the stage real people and symbolic figures, such as "human nature," "God's wrath," "charity" and "love of neighbor." Still other plays depicted the lives of saints, while those with moralistic ends, the morality plays, were accompanied by allegoric figures.

The historical drama was a later development, associated with the growth of Ukrainian statehood. The themes for historical dramas were taken either from Ukrainian, Roman or other histories. The play *Volodymyr*, by T. Prokopovych, praised the Ukrainian past and compared Hetman Mazepa with Prince Volodymyr the Great. The play *Bozha mylist, God's Kindness*, of an unknown author, presents developments during Khmelnytsky's time. The dramatic plays, either of a religious or historical nature, were interwoven with the traditional *intermedia* of comic and satiric content to entertain the viewers, mostly in the spoken people's dialect or vernacular language.

Puppet theatres were very popular, too, and frequently presented Christ's Nativity with a standardized background and content. They were introduced in Ukraine at the beginning of the seventeenth century and reached their peak in the second half of the eighteenth century, but were still popular during the nineteenth and twentieth centuries, as well.

The theatrical technique was amazingly good, leaving an unforgettable impression upon the audience. The plays also had a great impact upon the society, since all social segments, from the grandees and gentry to the laborers and peasants, attended the plays, receiving entertainment and moral instruction from them.

Hetman Rozumovsky, as pointed out, was an ardent promoter of the theatrical art, and maintained in his capital of Hlukhiv a theatre, a band, a choir, and singers and dancers. Italian operas were performed there. The Cossack and noble grandees imitated the Hetman, and so at the end of the eighteenth century they began to sponsor and finance the so-called *kripatsky teater*, the serf's theatre, where, for the most part, the serfs were the actors and performers, while at times even the members of the noble families participated.[31]

Other Arts. The other arts included artistic weaving, embroidery, rug-making, ceramics, heraldry and some others as well. Artistic weaving of many kinds of materials for the decorating of private homes, palaces and public places proceeded in the Cossack-Hetman state. Some decorative materials were imported, but a great deal of them were produced domestically by skillful masters of the art. Rugs in particular, *kylymy* in Ukrainian, were used to decorate floors and walls, and became very popular during the seventeenth century in the noble households. Embroidering became an inseparable part of decorating clothing, living quarters and churches. New techniques of embroidery developed, which became the favored occupation of women, noble and common alike, and a truly Ukrainian national art, though the patterns of embroidery and use of colors of thread differed in different parts of the country, as before. Towels, tablecloths, shirts, blouses, belts, church vestments and altar cloths were all beautifully embroidered. Village wood cutting, especially in the mountainous regions of Western Ukraine, began to imitate the embroidery patterns. Also the coloring or "writing" of Easter eggs, *pysanky*, according to the Ukrainian custom, also followed the patterns, frequently achieving an unprecedented, high level of artistry.

Ceramics experienced great progress and improvement of techniques and artistry in the seventeenth and eighteenth centuries. The Baroque and Rococo styles affected the patterns and motifs of ceramics substantially, making them uniquely rich and decorative. Multicolor glazed tiles were manufactured to increase the beauty of the interiors of rooms, halls and corridors. Ceramics developed in particular, in the Chernihiv and Poltava regions. The painting and decorating of glass became especially popular in Volhinia and in the northern Kiev region.

Of course, heraldry also continued to develop at this time, showing the impact of the Baroque and Rococo trends toward exaggerated decorativeness and richness.[32]

1. Yu. Fedoriv, *Istoria tserkvy v Ukraini*, Toronto, 1967, pp. 151-152.

2. *Ibid.*, pp. 172-174; H. Luzhnytsky, *Ukrainska tserkva mizh Skhodom i Zakhodom*, Philadelphia, 1954, pp. 329-330; I. Vlasovsky, *Narys istorii ukrainskoi pravoslavnoi tserkvy*, New York, 1956, Vol. II, pp. 33-36; also, N. Polonska-Vasylenko, *Istoria Ukrainy*, Munich, 1972, Vol. I, pp. 472-474; I. Kholmsky, *Istoria Ukrainy*, New York, 1971, p. 169.

3. M. Smotrytsky, *Parenethis*, as quoted by Fedoriv, *op. cit.*, p. 177; also Luzhnytsky, *op. cit.*, pp. 288 and following; O. Halecki, *From Florence to Berest*, New York, 1968, pp. 287-419: generally, on the Union of Berest and the Moscow threat.

4. Luzhnytsky, *ibid.*, pp. 155-165; Fedoriv, *op. cit.*, pp. 183 and 186; Vlasovsky, *op. cit.*, Vol. II, 178 and following; Polonska-Vasylenko, *op. cit.*, Vol. I, pp. 493-495.

5. Mytropolyt Ilarion, *Ukrainska tserkva za Bohdana Khmelnytskoho*, Winnipeg, 1956, pp. 30-38; Vlasovsky, *op. cit.*, Vol II, pp. 299-302.

6. Fedoriv, *op. cit.*, pp. 201-202: on the beginnings of the Moscow pressure against the independence of the Ukrainian Church.

7. Mytropolyt Ilarion, *Ukrainska tserkva za chas Ruiny*, Winnipeg, 1956, pp. 156-161; Polonska-Vasylenko, *op. cit.*, Vol. II, p. 196; also, Fedoriv, *op. cit.*, p. 204.

8. On the Russian-Muscovite intrigue in Church matters; Fedoriv, *op. cit.*, p. 218: "In December 1684, ..., the Tsars sent to the Patriarch of Constantinople a generous gift of two hundred rubles, and asked him to transfer the Ukrainian Church into the authority of Moscow's Patriarchate, ... About the bargaining for three years: *Ibid.*, pp. 217-220; The act was fully against canonical laws: Vlasovsky, *op. cit.*, Vol. II, pp. 340-343; also, Mytropolyt Ilarion, *ibid.*, pp. 461-462.

9. Polonska-Vasylenko, *op. cit.*, Vol. II, pp. 198-205; The Ukrainian Catholic Church: *Ibid.*, Vol. II, pp. 205-211; Luzhnytsky, *op. cit.*, pp. 375-414.

10. O. Ohloblyn, *Hetman Ivan Mazepa ta yoho doba*, New York, 1960, pp. 129-133; V. Lypynsky, *Ukraina na perelomi*, Kiev-Vienna, 1920, pp. 272 and other. Because of all those grants, the Orthodox Church became an important economic factor of the land: Polonska-Vasylenko, *op. cit.*, Vol. II, p. 192.

11. V. Sichynsky, *Ukraine in Foreign Comments and Descriptions from the VIth to XXth Century*, New York, 1953, pp. 95 and 132.

12. Polonska-Vasylenko, *op. cit.*, Vol. II, p. 211; also D. Doroshenko, *Narys istorii*

Ukrainy, Munich, 1966, Vol. II, pp. 227-228; B. Krupnytsky, *Hetman Danylo Apostol i yoho doba*, 1948, p. 163.

13. On the Kievan-Mohylian Academy: Fedoriv, *op. cit.*, pp. 190-196; Polonska-Vasylenko, *op. cit.*, Vol. II, pp. 212-216; Ohloblyn, *op. cit.*, pp. 135-137; N. Petrov, "Kievska Akademia," *Zapysky Istorychno-Filologichnoho Viddilu Ukrainskoi Akademii Nauk*, Kiev, 1919, Vol. I.

14. F. Titov, *Stara vyshcha osvita v Kyivskii Ukraini v XVI-XVII st.*, Kiev, 1924: on the Academy.

15. Polonska-Vasylenko, *op. cit.*, Vol. II, p. 217.

16. Sichynsky, *Ibid.*, pp. 113-114; Kholmsky, *op. cit.*, 291-294; D. Doroshenko "Biblioteky," *Entsyklopedia ukrainoznavstva*, Munich, 1949, Vol. I, p. 1008; Polonska-Vasylenko, *op. cit.*, Vol. II, p. 217: "Among other things, a large number of libraries in Ukraine testified about the high intellectual level of the Ukrainian elite, the Cossack grandees, Church hierachy and townpeople."

17. I. Mirtschuk, *Geschichte der Ukrainischen Kultur*, Munich, 1957, pp. 120-126: Philosophy; the same, "Istoria ukrainskoi filosofii," *Entsyklopedia ukrainoznavstva*, Munich, 1949, Vol. I, pp. 720-721; also, I. Ohienko, *Istoria ukrainskoi kultury*, Kiev, 1918; on philosophy.

18. On Skovoroda: D. Chyzhevsky, *Narys z istorii filosofii na Ukraini*, Prague 1931, pp. 35-62; the same, *Filosofia Skovorody*, Vienna, 1918; Mirtschuk, *loc. cit.*; *H. Skovoroda:* M. Holubets, ed., *Velyka istoria Ukrainy*, Lviv, 1935, pp. 595-597.

19. Ohloblyn, *op. cit.*, pp. 142-147; History writing: D. Chyzhevsky, *Istoria ukrainskoi literatury*, New York, 1956, pp. 301-306; also, V. Radzykevych *Istoria ukrainskoi literatury*, Detroit, 1955, Vol. I, pp. 117-119; O. Ohloblyn, *Ludy staroi Ukrainy*, Munich, 1959, pp. 270-273 and other.

20. Ohloblyn, *ibid.*; Polonska-Vasylenko, *op. cit.*, Vol. I, p. 219.

21. O. Ohloblyn, ed., *Istoria Rusiv*, New York, 1956; its evaluation in the introduction by O. Ohloblyn, pp. V-XXV; quotation above from p. XXIII.

22. Ohloblyn, *Ludy staroi ...*, pp. 14-18.

23. On the literature of the seventeenth and eighteenth centuries: Chyzhevsky, *op. cit.*, pp. 248-321; Radzykevych, *op. cit.*, Vol. I, pp. 97-122.

24. V. Sichynsky, "Arkhitektura," *Entsyklopedia ukrainoznavstva*, Munich, 1949, Vol. I, pp. 806-815; V. Yaniv, *Narys ukrainskoi kultury*, New York, 1961, pp. 44-45; Mirtschuk, *Geschichte der Ukrainischen Kultur*, pp. 199-200.

25. Sichynsky, *Ukraine in Foreign Comments* ..., as quoted above, pp. 94, 132, 171 and other.

26. Ohloblyn, *Hetman Ivan Mazepa* ..., as quoted, p. 130.

27. Yaniv, *op. cit.*, p. 45: "From the middle of the eighteenth century architectural endeavours declined."

28. Yaniv, *ibid.*, pp. 57-58; Mirtschuk, *op. cit.*, pp. 212-214; Polonska-Vasylenko, *op. cit.*, Vol. II, pp. 229-230.

29. On carving and engraving: Yaniv, *ibid.*, pp. 49-50; Mirtschuk, *ibid.*, pp. 205 and 221; V. Sichynsky, "Hrafika-hraverstvo," *Entsyklopedia ukrainoznavstva*, Vol. I, pp. 835-836.

30. Mirtschuk, *ibid.*, p. 174; Yaniv, *ibid.*, p. 72.

31. On music and theatre: Z. Lysko, "Istoria muzyky," *Entsyklopedia ukrainoznavstva*, Munich, 1949, Vol. I, p. 869; V. Vytvytsky, "Istoria muzyky XVIII-XIX st.," *ibid.*, pp. 869-870; Yaniv, *op. cit.*. pp. 71-72, 77-78; Mirtschuk, *op. cit.*, pp. 172-174, 184-186; Polonska-Vasylenko, *op. cit.*, Vol. II, pp. 224-225.

32. Other arts: Yaniv, *op. cit.*. pp. 16-20; *Ukraine, A Concise Encyclopedia*, Toronto, 1963, Vol. I, pp. 383-418.

CHAPTER ELEVEN

THE SOCIAL STRUCTURE OF THE UKRAINIAN COSSACK-HETMAN SOCIETY

Ethnic and social changes — The Cossacks — Nobility and clergy — Peasantry — Townspeople — Foreigners — Eastern and southern frontiers — The colonization of the borderlands

Ethnic and Social Changes. After 1648, the year of the National Revolution, significant and fundamental changes took place in the ethnic and social composition of Ukraine. The abolition of Polish rule in most of the Ukrainian territories, the creation of the Ukrainian national state, and subsequently, the growing influence of the Muscovite-Russians in the course of the seventeenth and eighteenth centuries altered the ethnic and social structure of the nation. It has already been indicated that the new political organism, the Cossack-Hetman State, did not extend over the entire ethnographical area of the Ukrainian people. Thus, the ethnic and social process developed somewhat differently in various parts of that area. As a matter of fact, four distinct areas could be differentiated: the Cossack-Hetman State, the territory of the Cossack host, West Ukraine, and the so-called *Slobidska* (Village) Ukraine.

The Cossack-Hetman State, including the vassal area of the Cossack Host, extended over approximately two-thirds of the Ukrainian ethnic territory. There the essentially Ukrainian cultural patterns predominated, although Russian influences increased constantly, especially following the Poltava defeat. Right-bank Ukraine, where Cossack rule did not last as long and where Polish rule was soon restored, had a slightly different historical development which included greater Polish influences. West Ukraine,

Galicia, Volhinia, Pidlasha and Kholm, westward from the Murakhava and Horyn rivers, were constantly under Polish rule from 1349 to 1793-1795, the time of the Second and Third Partitions of Poland. Old Polish social and legal traits prevailed there, and the Ukrainian western frontiers shrank under the pressure of Polish discrimination and colonial policies. Polish and foreign ethnic elements increased in numbers and continued to be the privileged segment of the population. The Ukrainians, as before, both Orthodox and Uniate Catholic, were socially, economically and above all politically discriminated against. The denationalization of the upper class of the Ukrainian gentry progressed speedily.

In *Slobidska* Ukraine, a province on the banks of the rivers Donets and Don, which remained under the political supremacy of the Muscovite Grand Principality, ethnical and social processes were again quite different. First of all, it was a colonization of a virtual vacuum, of the "wild fields," under the close care of the Grand Princess and, later, the Tsars, who required their officials, *voyevody*, not only to avoid harming but also to protect the incoming *Cherkasy*, Ukrainians. The settlers enjoyed extensive freedom and autonomy until these were curbed by Peter I.[1] Although the Russian government planned, by this settlement policy, to make its rule in these areas more profitable and more effective, after about a century and a half the Ukrainian character of that territory was established and the Ukrainian ethnic area was thereby greatly increased. Village Ukraine was never under the rule of the Hetmans, although plans for its incorporation were nursed by Khmelnytsky, Samoilovych and Mazepa.

In the Cossack-Hetman State of this era, some basic ethnic changes took place. First of all, the National Revolution wiped out the Polish element. Most of the Polish, the Polonized gentry and the Polish colonists left Ukraine, were liquidated, or accepted the Orthodox religion and declared themselves to be Ukrainians. Numerous old Ukrainian noble families, especially those who were Polonized, remembered their national heritage, sometimes even to the point of giving up Catholicism and returning to the nationality and faith of their ancestors. Also, a part of the foreign colonists, still loyal to the Polish regime, left Ukraine to avoid the hostility of the Ukrainians.

Consequently, in its first years the Cossack-Hetman State was almost exclusively Ukrainian, except for its northern provinces and parts of the Starodub and Chernihiv regimental districts, which were populated partially by Byeloruthenians. Later on, however, the foreign element increased considerably in Ukraine because of an intensive colonization of the devastated areas during the wars. The program of internal colonization was sponsored by various hetmans, especially Samoilovych, Mazepa and Apostol. The settlers, however, were not only Ukrainians, but also Russians, Poles, Serbs, Lithuanians, Wallachians, Tartars, Czechs and Germans. Some Polish nobles returned, offering their loyalty and services to the Ukrainian government. Ukrainian officials welcomed this development, but the lower strata of the population viewed it with distaste. The issue of Polish resettlement was the cause of the defeat of the political plans of Hetman Vyhovsky and his Union of Hadiach.

German settlers were recruited from mercenaries, at first in the Polish, then later in the Ukrainian service. The Tartars were settled largely as war prisoners. With the progress of time, these foreign colonial elements denationalized, and they were either Ukrainianized, like the Tartars, Wallachians and Serbs, or Russianized like the Poles and Germans. Foreigners were absorbed into various classes of Ukrainian society: the gentry, the lower and upper strata of the Cossacks, and the peasants and the townspeople. Numerous foreign names among the Ukrainians indicated this process of assimilation. The Jewish population was also subject to a gradual Ukrainization. The families of Moskowitz, Markowitz, Herzig, and Krizhanivsky were Jewish, and the family of Hetman Apostol, for example, was of Wallachian descent, and that of General Orlik, of Byeloruthenian descent.

After the Poltava defeat, the influx of the Russian ethnic element increased rapidly. The Russian government, systematically preparing a final incorporation of its Ukrainian satellite, enthusiastically sponsored Russian settlements all over the country. On the other hand, the Hetmans, and in particular, Apostol, made every effort possible to retard the growing colonization.[2] Muscovite settlers invaded Ukrainian towns and villages; they slowly penetrated the aristocracy, especially after the Samoilovych era. Russian officals and nobles were granted large landed estates all over Ukraine as a reward for military or administrative services rendered to the Tsars and the Russian cause.

This trend was most energetically supported by Tsar Peter the Great, even prior to the decisive Poltava battle. These Russian newcomers soon began to abuse their social position, attempting to increase the burden of bondage of the peasants, and later to transform the common Cossacks into serfs. Only the "Old-believers" among the Russian settlers in Ukraine were really welcomed. These were religious refugees who emigrated to northern Ukraine rather than submit to certain Russian Orthodox Church reforms. Accordingly, they were very loyal to the Ukrainian government and never supported the penetration of the Tsarist regime in Ukraine. In 1781, a vigorous attempt to Russify the Ukrainian upper classes was initiated.

The National Revolution of 1648-1649 and the creation of the Ukrainian national state deeply affected the social processes of the Ukrainian people, but these events cannot be considered a real social revolution. It is true that the majority of the older Ukrainian historians, like Hrushevsky, Efimenko, Slabchenko and others, more or less influenced by socialistic doctrines, were inclined to see in the events of the seventeenth century in Ukraine a prologue to the social-democratic developments of the end of the nineteenth and the beginning of the twentieth centuries. They interpreted these as a resolute trend toward wiping out the class structure of Ukrainian society, abolishing the old aristocratic principle, and introducing social equality. The later process toward the restoration of the class system in the Hetman state was interpreted by the older historians as treason committed by the Cossack hierarchy against the people's interest. This view is erroneous since Ukraine of the seventeenth century certainly did not outstrip the overall social evolution of the European countries of that time; it did not evolve faster than that of its neighbors.

At the time of the National Revolution some social changes favoring the proletarian strata were made. The return of normal political and economic conditions, however, resulted in an immediate reconstruction of the class system and a suppression of the premature egalitarian tendencies. But these tendencies continued to exist and to express themselves in the Cossack-Hetman State, and not infrequently in revolts and civil strifes. The Cossack Host, Hetman Ivan Brukhovetsky, and two revolutionary leaders, Petro Ivanenko-Petryk and Semen Palii, represented the social-democratic trend, while Hetmans like Bohdan Khmelnytsky, Ivan Vyhovsky and Ivan Mazepa championed the old order. The democratic striving for equality and freedom was definitely crushed by the reactionary Russian government after its absorption of Ukraine.

However, the National Revolution of 1648-1649 did bring many social changes. First of all, a new leading class of Cossacks assumed an equal or superior status to the political elite. The upper stratum of the Cossacks took over the entire government.

The position of the peasant-serfs improved somewhat. Nevertheless, the Ukrainian society of that period remained essentially organized into classes headed by an elite group, as maintained by the younger generation of Ukrainian historians, Lypynsky, Hryshko and Ohloblyn, and the Byeloruthenian historian of legal institutions, Okinshevych.[3] It must be stressed, however, that the Ukrainian class structure was comparatively liberal, influenced by traditions inherited from the Kievan era. Upward social mobility was relatively easy. Peasants could be elevated to the rank of common Cossacks. A common Cossack could rise to the Cossack aristocracy. The transition from the Cossack aristocracy to the rank of gentry and vice versa was possible.

On the other hand, a common Cossack could be reduced to the level of a peasant-serf. Wealth, occupation, intellect, services and merits decided the issue of class membership and resulted in numerous changes in the social status of individual families.

Cossack political leadership was in close cooperation with the gentry, while two other strata, the peasants and the townspeople, did not have much voice in the political and social development of the nation. The social structure of Ukraine of the Cossack-Hetman era was therefore based on five major strata, the nobility, the Cossacks, the clergy, the peasants and the townspeople. In this order, the social background of the Ukrainian economic evolution will be briefly discussed.

Throughout the entire Cossack-Hetman period an intense social struggle raged. The upper class continuously tried to increase its prerogatives at the expense of the peasants and townspeople. The latter not only resisted this pressure, but also tried to reverse it. The fluctuation of class barriers and the social mobility constituted one segment of the social dynamism of the times. The other was the open conflicts and clashes, resulting in peasant revolts, mass flights of serfs, mass emigration of the peasants and townspeople and political conflicts among various Cossack leaders, representing different points of view. The conflicts between Doroshenko and Brukhovetsky, Vyhovsky and Pushkar, Mazepa and Palii, which resulted in civil wars, can also be explained in this context.

At times, when they could no longer endure oppression, serious revolts of the peasant proletariat and Cossack commoners blazed into flames. Among these were the revolts of 1687, 1688, 1691-92 and 1693 in the Hetman state, or 1701-1702 in the Cossack Territory. These social upheavals certainly affected the country's overall growth in a negative way, but they should not be exaggerated in their socio-economic significance since they were usually local and short-lasting. Marxist students of East European economic history, such as Lyashchenko, Nesterenko and Vyrnyk, naturally overemphasized the role of conflicts in their interpretation of the history of the seventeenth and eighteenth century Ukraine. Actually, mass emigration and the abandonment of villages and towns hurt the economy more than these isolated and sporadic revolts.

The Cossacks, as the traditional defenders of Ukrainian independence, occupied a leading position in Ukrainian society immediately after the National Revolution. Their rights, privileges and obligations were already sanctioned by historical developments in the Polish kingdom. Naturally, these were increased in the new state but their final crystallization was never achieved, not even at the end of the Hetman period. Their status changed constantly, all the more so because of far reaching internal differentiations and numerous social frictions among them.

A primary differentiation was their division into two strata, the Cossack aristocracy and the common Cossacks. The former was in turn divided into various segments and groups, the outstanding associates, the banner associates and the regimental insignia associates. The stratum of the common Cossacks consisted of a variety of groups, such as the auxiliaries, the voluntaries, the vassal and electorial Cossacks, and the associates and the assisting and soldierly Cossacks. This detailed differentiation, which included under the term "Cossack" some elements without real Cossack social status, such as the assisting and soldierly Cossacks, facilitated continuous social fluctuations and unending transitions in class association.

The Cossack aristocracy was recruited from the old, pre-revolutionary "registered" Cossacks, numerous newcomers from the class of nobility and gentry, and the really "new men" whose extraordinary services for the national cause during and after the Revolution elevated them to the top of the social ladder. The outstanding associates and banner Cossacks were exempt from the competence of the ordinary land, regimental, judicial and administrative authorities, and were subordinated to the authority of the "honorable" Hetman. The regimental insignia Cossacks enjoyed special privileges in their respective regimental districts. The common Cossacks were differentiated largely according to their material status and service obligation, whether they had full or restricted private property rights in real estate. The vassal and assisting Cossacks were socially dependent upon the Cossack aristocrats, and rendered them diversified and specified services, such as hunting, catching beavers and guarding property.[4] There was undoubtedly a persistent trend among the Cossack aristocrats and the wealthier and more intellectual Cossacks to merge fully and completely with the old class of the nobility in order to gain its well established and privileged position, and eventually to disappear as a separate social stratum of indefinite status. On the other hand, the lower and poorer strata of Cossacks also exhibited a clear-cut tendency to disappear as a separate class by merging with the peasants. They wanted to avoid their class burden of military and government services, which proved costly and time-consuming, and which took them away from their homes on distant military and service expeditions.

In the later stage of the Hetman era, for example, the Tsars, in accordance with alliance agreements, called upon the Cossacks to participate in various Russian foreign wars, to work on the construction of new cities and fortresses and to guard new settlements. The Hetman, and later also the Tsarist decrees of 1669, 1723, 1728, 1729, 1772 and 1782, attempted to stop this flight of the common Cossacks from their class obligations. However, these legal measures did not have much apparent success. The Hetman and the Tsar, each for his own reason, was interested in preserving the military class of the Cossacks. Nevertheless, the Cossack stratum, even before it was legally crystallized as a separate class, began to disintegrate and to merge with the other old and well-established classes of the nobility, peasantry and townspeople.

Because of internal differentiation, the class rights and privileges of the Cossacks were neither equal nor uniform for all members of the stratum. The upper aristocratic element was the bearer of political and military authority, exempt from the competence of the ordinary judicial and administrative systems of the land and regimental local governments, legally favored with larger court compensation for losses and damages, and endowed with far reaching exemptions for such taxes and financial burdens as excises, some direct taxes and court fees. Theoretically speaking, the common Cossacks were eligible to participate in politics; practically speaking, they seldom did. They generally bore the obligation of military service, and were subject to the ordinary judicial and administrative authorities of the regimental district, and later also partially of the land provincial systems.

The most precious class privilege of the Cossacks was their right to private property, in particular the right to own land. This right established their importance in the country's economy, agriculture, manufacturing and trading. Above all, the Cossack aristocracy, being more educated and more cultured, knew how to make good use of its property rights. Immediately after the National Revolution, the real property rights of the Cossack class throughout the entire country were officially recognized by the new government. These rights were affirmed by the Pereyaslav Agreement of 1654, and certain other legal documents of a later date. Since prior to the Revolution Cossack property rights in real estate were somewhat questionable in the Polish state, and since the "registered" Cossacks vehemently pressed for its recognition, the issue was one of the leading motives for the Revolution.

Thus in the new Cossack-Hetman State the real property rights of the Cossacks were accepted as a distinctive feature of their class. Even where some communal properties in land had developed among them before the revolution, they soon began to divide them up into private estates. This action was successful, and before long the banner and the insignia associates acquired individual ownership rights in what had originally been public estates given to them on a temporary basis. The Hetmans resolutely opposed any Tsarist attempts to question or to restrict this class privilege of the Cossacks.

The principle of individual ownership in real estate established the economic significance of the Cossack class in the production and distribution processes and promoted an impressive growth of the Cossack class and the nation. According to Slabchenko, these years of national freedom enormously increased the productive potential of Ukraine.[5] Actually, two classes were in charge of the economic process of the country, the Cossacks and the gentry, and both enjoyed full freedom of property and initiative. This freedom was highly important.

The Nobility and Clergy. The old interpretation of the events of 1648-1649 as simply a sweeping social revolution bent on the overthrow of the rule of the nobility has no basis in fact. The changes brought about by this event were not fundamental and deep enough to justify such a view. From the very beginning, the Ukrainian nobility joined the National Revolution in large numbers along with the clergy, the townspeople and the peasantry. This proves the basically national character of the Revolution.

The fidelity of the majority of the Ukrainian gentry to the national cause soon brought the recognition and confirmation of its class rights and privileges by the new government. Subsequently, the Ukrainian gentry associated closely with the upper segment of the Cossack stratum. Many nobles became banner and insignia Cossacks, while numerous Cossack grandees joined the ranks of the country gentry. These nobles soon became an integral component of the Ukrainian government. Hetman Vyhovsky, Hetman Teteria, Colonels Krychevsky, Nechai and Morozenko-Mrozovytsky, the judge-general of Ukraine, Bohdanovych, and many other noblemen, rendered great and unforgettable services to their nation. No wonder, therefore, that Hetman Damian Mnohohrishny referred to the services of the Ukrainian gentry when he confirmed its ancient privileges by the decree of 1670.[6]

Having retained their ancient and traditional individual property rights in land after the Revolution, the country nobles temporarily lost their right to the use of serf labor because the peasants were freed. But later, with the restoration of peasant bondage, serf labor was again made available to the nobles and the Cossack aristocracy. Serf labor was also always a privilege of the Orthodox Church in the Ukrainian state. Thus in 1650, Khmelnytsky, by a decree, restored the patrimonial jurisdiction of the gentry nobles over the peasants in their landed possessions, and made it obligatory for the peasants to render services and to pay certain tributes, mostly in kind. The separate and privileged position of the gentry in the Ukrainian Cossack-Hetman State was confirmed several times.

During the time of Hetman Mazepa, however, the privileges of the old gentry partially faded away, eclipsed by the prevailing position of the upper class Cossack. At the same time, nevertheless, a new nobility began to develop because the Tsars made land grants and distributed titles of nobility among those who actively contributed to the Russification of Ukraine.

The Orthodox clergy suffered heavy discrimination from the Polish government for its role in the Ukrainian national movement. Consequently, a majority joined the National Revolution. The hierarchy of the Orthodox Church not only gave its ecclesiastical blessing to the Revolution and its leaders, but also actively supported Bohdan Khmelnytsky, strengthened him in his plans, sanctioned them, and above all, preached national independence. Such loyalty and patriotism on the part of the Church and its clergy, both secular and cloistered, were fully rewarded by the Ukrainian national government in its acknowledging of the property rights of the Church and the clergy, sanctioning their huge land holdings, leaving them the right to own serfs and to exploit their labor, and in admitting them to participate broadly in the country's administration along with the class of the Cossacks and the nobles.[7]

This permanent privilege of the Church to use serf labor and to keep jurisdiction over the peasants in its possession gave rise to a general restoration of bondage which, as pointed out, was temporarily abolished in the noble landed estates. In the proposed code of laws of 1743, *The Laws, according to which justice is done among the Little Russian people*, it was suggested that the Orthodox clergy be given all the rights and privileges of the nobility. Later on, however, under the impact of Russian institutions, the social position of the clergy was reduced almost to the legal level of the townspeople. The social status of the clergy was subject to intensive fluctuations, perhaps more than that of any other social class, since the infiltration of the nobles, Cossacks, commoners and foreigners into its ranks was steady and considerable. On the other hand, numerous male descendants of the Orthodox clergy joined the Cossack and noble classes, and the female descendants were married to the members of other groups. Of course, the Roman Catholic clergy was denied all these privileges in the Ukrainian state.

From the economic point of view, the role of the nobility and of the Church did not change much in comparison to the previous Lithuanian-Polish period except that the Orthodox Church took the place of the Catholic Church. Having extensive property rights and freedom of initiative and action, the nobles, the Cossacks and the Church sponsored the majority of production, exchange and distribution. In their hands was the larger portion of all entrepreneurial and managerial activities, primarily in agriculture and manufacturing, but also in commerce.

The Peasantry. Peasants were severely oppressed by the Polish agricultural system based upon the principle of large noble land holdings, serfdom and commercial farming. Under these conditions the individual freedom and land ownership of the peasants disappeared completely, and the social position of the peasantry became the lowest and most degraded in the Polish-Lithuanian Commonwealth.

Consequently and most naturally, when the National Revolution broke out, the peasants, believing that "they cannot lose anything any more, but gain everything," joined the revolutionary tide spontaneously. Actually, the first year or two brought to them in most cases a revolutionary change, personal freedom and real property rights, at least technically. Legally, the hated serfdom and bondage were never completely abolished, neither by the Treaty of Bila Tserkva (1651), nor the Treaty of Pereyaslav (1654).

The cloistered (monastic) clergy, the noblemen and the Cossack aristocrats were eager to retain and to preserve the institution of serfdom as a source of cheap labor. Thus, with the establishment of the sovereign Ukrainian nation, where the upper social strata held all the power, the peasants soon lost most of their illusions and hopes of freedom, equality and first-class citizenship. The peasants had no political influence; since they were not even directly subordinated to state authority, as in the Polish kingdom, they could not defend their cause.

Nevertheless, the Revolution improved the social position of the peasantry to some extent. First of all, in the central and southern districts of the country, many villages which had joined the revolution acquired the status of free military communities where bondage was abolished and peasant individual or communal property in land was introduced. Futhermore, the peasants in the new settlements enjoyed freedom and property rights as well. The colonization process was constant in Hetman Ukraine. It was sponsored by the government, the nobility and the Cossack hierarchy in order to populate the areas devastated by the war. In order to attract peasant settlers, all kinds of freedoms—from bondage, from serf labor and from contributions—were granted. But in some northern districts, such as Starodub and Chernihiv, the nobility succeeded in retaining a ruling position as compensation for loyalty to the Ukrainian state and were allowed to use serf labor. Thus the development of free villages of military status was prevented. Serfdom and bondage continued in the Church possessions and the public domains, in the latter, in their most intolerable form.

At first, free villages of military status were numerous. Under the pressure of the upper classes, however, the burdens of serfdom were gradually restored and spread over ever wider areas. Therefore, the free peasant communities of military and autonomous status (even those recently established) progressively lost their social privileges. At first they were obliged by law to render certain services called "usual obediences" to the high Cossack officials who held landed estates in the allodial capacity, as compensation for their services to the state. These "usual obediences" gradually accumulated in the manorial noble economies, also. Later the allodial estates were partially transferred to the individual ownership of Cossack aristocrats with an immediate restoration of serfdom. The soil bondage of the peasants was first reintroduced in the second half of the eighteenth century. It was a normal course of things that paralleled the restoration of bondage in the Cossack possessions. The nobility received the same rights, and acquired more and more power over the peasants.

Despite all these unfavorable developments, the social position of the peasants in the seventeenth and eighteenth centuries was much better than that of the peasantry of Western Europe, Poland or Muscovy at the same time. First of all, the peasant class in Ukraine was not so tightly closed that it constituted a caste. There were many possibilities for able, lucky and intelligent peasants to improve themselves by joining the ranks of the townspeople, the clergy and the Cossacks, or even by obtaining the status of the nobility.

For the first time, during the time of Hetman Apostol, the peasantry became a relatively closed class, and upward social mobility became more difficult but still not impossible. Eventually, with the end of the Cossack-Hetman era, the impact of Russian influence caused the position of the peasant to deteriorate greatly, down to the level of his Russian counterpart.

In addition, the peasant had *de facto* limited property rights in land. Although numerous Hetman edicts and decrees denied the peasant the right to acquire or to dispose of landed estates, the peasants freely bought, used and sold land. And the nearer they were to the eastern and southern frontiers where flight to the "wild fields" was possible, the greater was their freedom in this and other respects.[8] The Hetmans, the Cossack grandees and the nobles, interested in peasant labor, had to be less demanding and conform with the trend in East Ukraine, if they desired to have village population develop colonization in their domains and possessions. Nevertheless, the general albeit gradual growth of bondage produced several waves of emigration of peasants to the Donets and Don regions, where they could enjoy full freedom. The Hetman opposition to emigration was ineffective. The trend toward obtaining individual ownership rights in land was so strong among the peasants that communally owned property, instances of which had appeared in Ukraine after the Revolution, was soon redistributed by the peasants themselves. And whenever any Hetman or Cossack leader was in favor of the institution of private property, he at once received the general support of the peasant class. At that time there were four main social strata of the village peasant population, each with its distinct status. The Ukrainian village populus was the highest social group, *de facto*, with limited individual, personal and real property rights, and limited inheritance rights. This group was not bound to the soil, but it rendered some services and bore some financial obligations to the lords.

The second group consisted of poor, landless peasants, who were either sharecroppers or were hired by the privileged classes as day laborers at meager pay. They frequently shared the dwellings of the wealthy peasants or the Cossack commons, and until Mazepa's time, they were free of the usual taxes and other state burdens.

The third category embraced the peasants on Russian-owned estates which grew in number in Ukraine after the catastrophe of Poltava. They were soil-bound serfs without any rights, serving their masters according to the harsh Muscovite tradition.

The peasants of the fourth strata were actually slaves, called "serfs." These were originally prisoners of war, mainly Turks and Tartars. They could be bought, sold, inherited or given away as gifts. They had no rights whatsoever. Although the institution was popular among the Cossack grandees, comparatively speaking there were very few slaves in Ukraine.

As far as the so-called "usual obediences" were concerned, they were not the same throughout the country, nor for all segments of the peasant class. "Usual obediences" normally included some kind of rental payments, and some forest a melioration and pasture work as well as field work performed for the nobles, the Cossacks, the Orthodox Church or the state. Some other peasant contributions within bondage included the so-called "carol" services and tribute during Christmas, wedding tributes, and road, bridge and building construction and maintenance services. Moreover, the peasants, as subjects of the state, bore the main burden of taxes and non-tax collections. These heavy material responsibilities, placed upon the rural population, greatly hampered the economic development of the village, but the enormous fertility of the soil and the relative freedom of the peasants made progress possible.[9]

From the point of view of the country's economy of this period, the peasantry, as in the previous Kievan and Polish-Lithuanina periods, was the main labor force and the most important production force in Ukrainian society. Furthermore, the surplus of the village population migrated to the towns to supply the necessary labor for the slowly growing manufacturing industries.

The Townspeople. The National Revolution and the creation of the independent Ukrainian state had the least effect on the social and legal status of the townspeople. Like all other segments of Ukrainian society, the townspeople also took an active part in the Revolution, but there was a fundamental difference in the manner of their participation. While other classes served the Revolution as separate entities, the city people joined the peasant insurgents (commoners, *chern'*) or the Cossack commons, and hence did not constitute a separate fighting entity.

The townspeople were characterized by a more rigid class structure resulting from the Magdeburg system of city organization introduced by their Polish rulers, but long since recognized by the Ukrainian government. Some Hetmans, like Khmelnytsky, Samoilovych, Mazepa and Apostol, were friendly toward the townspeople, protecting them as a worthwhile segment of society. Their class rights and privileges, in particular, their Magdeburg self-government and autonomy, were confirmed several times by Hetman edicts and decrees, by international agreements, such as the Pereyaslav Treaty of 1654, and by the proposed code of laws of 1743, the so-called *Laws, by which justice is done among the Little Russian People*.

Subsequently, new towns such as Poltava and Lubni also received Magdeburg autonomy from the Ukrainian or Russian governments. The craft and merchant guilds, enjoying considerable freedom, continued at this time to form the basis of the organization of urban economic and social life. The city and town mayors had a limited authority over guild matters. The more enlightened Hetmans, like Khmelnytsky, Polubotok, Samoilovych, Mazepa and Apostol, tried to preserve municipal self-government at all costs, and objected to the attempts of the Cossack hierarchy to overpower the cities and to subordinate them to the general regimental administrative system. Hetmans Apostol and Rozumovsky did everything possible to protect the townspeople from the frequent abusive acts of the upper classes, which were directed against urban economic interests.

As far as the social and legal status of the town was concerned, however, there was no uniformity during the Cossack-Hetman era. This had a negative effect on its commercial development. The ancient towns as well as the large towns in the northern and central provinces had a clear and established legal municipal status as autonomous communities, only partially subject to the jurisdiction of the Cossack courts and administration. Their population constituted a separate social class.

The administrative authorities of the regimental district system merely exercised a legal supervision over the cities and towns, without any direct governmental authority. The municipal governments of these ancient and large towns were strongly opposed to the Cossacks and their permanent residence in the city, and prohibited any Cossack-owned or operated mercantile establishment—particularly taverns—in their jurisdictions.

The small towns, being of later origin, especially in the eastern and steppe areas, did not have the same clear-cut legal and social status. First of all, they were frequently included in the general administration of the regimental districts, and thus were overpowered by the Cossacks. Sometimes the Cossack aristocrats managed to be elected as mayors or other municipal officials of considerable competence. At other times the towns sought an election of the outstanding Cossacks for their officials in order to gain more freedom and to protect themselves against the prevailing interest of the upper classes.[10] In most cases, however, the townspeople enjoyed the freedom of the Magdeburg law, and centralized the trade and mercantile activities in their own hands, although they received considerable competition from the Cossacks, the nobles and the peasants.

On the other hand, the town population, according to the traditional patterns of the medieval class system, was not allowed to own any landed estates or to engage in farming. But municipal governments could acquire and possess such landed estates. This prohibition was not strictly followed by small towns, especially those of later colonist origin in the east and south. There the rural and urban population, as well as the mercantile and agricultural business, were mixed and performed as parallel functions. Being relatively free, the cities and towns of Hetman Ukraine developed fairly well economically. The older historians who wrote of a general economic decline of the towns during this era were mistaken. Of course, the towns were seriously hampered, along with the countryside, by a great tax and by non-tax burdens imposed by the government. These included not only monetary payments of direct and indirect taxes but also the city obligation of sheltering and feeding the army. The burden was sometimes so intolerable that it drove the towns to despair. Sometimes the townspeople even sought Polish or Russian intervention in an effort to improve their lot. Meanwhile, towns all over Europe were also exploited during this era.

Politically, the town and the townspeople fared slightly better in the Hetman state than in the Lithuanian-Polish Commonwealth. The representation of the urban population was admitted to the country's General Council, along with the Cossacks and the hierarchy of the Orthodox Church. There, the city deputies could speak in the interest of their communities and their class.

Unfortunately, however, there was neither legal nor political equality among the cities and towns. Kiev was the most privileged among the cities, while the city of Chernihiv, for example, did not enjoy all those benefits, and the small towns were frequently overrun by the Cossacks. As a matter of fact, the character of the era, as prevailingly dominated by the Cossack class, resulted in the gradual decline of the town in its legal and political position. With the growth of the power of the Cossack aristocracy, the town was subjected to more and more discrimination, and, foregoing its patriotism, it began to look more and more toward the Russian protector for relief.[11]

Foreigners. There was no discrimination against foreigners because of their national or racial ancestry in Cossack-Hetman Ukraine. This was in direct contrast to Muscovy where foreigners were mistrusted and denied equality with the native population.[12] However, there was no religious tolerance; the Orthodox faith held an official and dominant position. But religious intolerance was part and parcel of all European society during this period. This attitude could also be explained in the light of Polish domination. The Poles and the Polish government greatly and grossly discriminated against the Orthodox religion and the Orthodox Church. The Cossack wars and the National Revolution of 1648, aiming above all at the liberation of the Ukrainian people from foreign oppression, were in part instigated and waged in defense of the Orthodox Church.

Hence, when independence was achieved, the Orthodox religion was immediately proclaimed the established religion of the Cossack-Hetman State. Uniate Catholics, originally Orthodox Ukrainians who acknowledged the spiritual supremacy of the Pope of Rome, were suppressed. The Polish-Ukrainian Treaty of Hadiach of 1658 expressly forbade the Church Union in the Ukrainian Grand Duchy.

The Hebrews and Mohammedans had a right to temporary residence and limited rights to own property and to do business. They could acquire the privilege of permanent residence and status of nobles and townspeople only by accepting Orthodoxy. The Mohammedans, Tartars and Turks were usually slaves, having no legal rights. Protestantism was also not favored, but it suffered less discrimination than Catholicism or Mohammedanism.

Other predominantly Orthodox foreigners, such as Armenians, Byeloruthenians, Czechs, Russians, Serbs, Croatians, Wallachians, Greeks and others enjoyed freedom and government protection. Those living in cities were in many cases exempt from municipal jurisdiction and directly subordinated to the authority of the Cossack regimental administration and Cossack judicial system. This protected them from possible discrimination on the part of jealous municipal officials.

Later Hetmans, like Mazepa and Apostol, initiated a policy of limiting the Russian colonists on political grounds, since they had begun to form a kind of "fifth column" in Ukrainian towns and countryside. Consequently, edicts were issued to prohibit Russians from acquiring real estate, especially in urban areas, and from participating in mercantile activities. Nevertheless, growing Tsarist pressure after the Poltava catastrophe soon overcame the Hetmanic measures. Only the "Old-believers," refugees from Tsarist religious persecution, were welcome in Ukraine.

The northern frontiers of the Hetman state, the parts of the Starodub and Chernihiv regimental districts, were almost exclusively populated by Byeloruthenians. These, being Orthodox, enjoyed all the freedoms of the country according to their class associations, preserving their national identity, culture, customs and institutions. For about four years (1655-1659) the Byeloruthenians formed their own Cossack regimental district which remained in a vassalage relationship to the Hetmans. This autonomous unit was liquidated by the Russians in consequence of the Ukrainian-Russian War of 1658-1659.[13]

Eastern and Southern Frontiers. Unfortunately, Ukraine did not develop uniformly, either politically, culturally, socially or economically. Because of moving frontiers, various territories simultaneously existed at different stages of the socio-economic evolution. Actually, the colonization and conquest of the Black Sea and the Don-Donets steppes by Ukrainians in the seventeenth century was a recapture of ancient Ukrainian lands. The Cuman and Mongol invasion and rule had turned these steppes into a vacuum.

With the decline of the power of the Golden Horde, the Muscovites established their nominal supremacy over the Don-Donets basin.[14] In the fifteenth century, they had already begun to erect a series of fortresses on the southern borders of the Don-Donets basin, continuously moving farther toward the south and east in an attempt to protect the sparcely populated country from Mongol raids. For a long time, however, few dared to settle in these dangerous frontier lands. A few fortresses, defended by Muscovite troops, were the only inhabited places in this vast, empty steppe country until the sixteenth century. Then a feeble attempt at colonization was initiated. A few villages were established close to the forts.

The real colonization of the Donets steppe country began in 1638, when Jatsko Ostrianyn, the leader of one of the Cossack wars against the Poles, after being defeated by the Polish army, left Ukraine with nine hundred colonists, Cossacks and their families, and settled in the Donets basin with the permission and under the protection of the Muscovite Tsar. Although this venture ended in failure, a beginning was made. From that time on, new waves of Ukrainian emigrants, first Cossacks and later peasants also, steadily settled the Donets steppes in ever growing numbers. These waves of emigration from Hetman Ukraine, the largest in the years 1651, 1652, 1654, 1657-67, 1681, 1700-1702, and 1783, were primarily caused by the numerous Ukrainian wars with Poland and Russia, domestic wars among the Cossack leaders, like Palii, and Hetmans, the wars with Turkey, the growing class differentiation and discrimination, and other social and natural disturbances.

The Russian government was very friendly, particularly towards the Cossack immigration into these territories under its domination, since the Cossacks, as experienced soldiers, provided an excellent buffer zone between Moscow and her enemies. Therefore, the Tsars left complete freedom and organizational autonomy to the Cossacks, under the supervisory authority of Tsarist officials, *voyevody*. The Cossack settlers were all the more appreciated because they usually came with all their belongings, tools, cattle and seed, and being self-sustaining, they did not require any financial or material assistance from the Russians.

Soon numerous villages, *slobody*, and towns were built throughout the area, giving it the name "Village Ukraine," *Sloboda Ukraine*, *Slobitshchyna*, or *Slobozhanshchyna*. Official Russian records supply abundant data concerning the colonization process, and the organization and economy of this new Ukraine. A very important role was played by the Orthodox religious orders which established cloisters and schools throughout the area.[15]

The country was organized into a number of regimental districts with colonels elected for life as their heads. The organization was similar to that of the Hetman state, but these colonels had a much wider authority than their prototypes in the old country, and their office usually remained within the fami-

Sahaidachny captures Kaffa

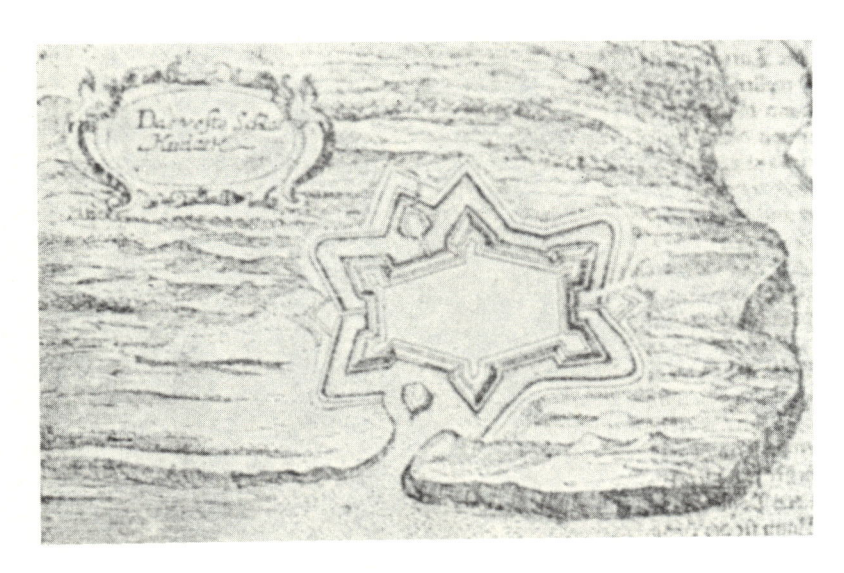

Fortress of Kodak

Cossacks at sea

A Cossack chayka

ly. Each regimental district operated as an autonomous administrative unit directly subordinated to the Tsar and his *voyevoda* official.

Initially, there were only two classes of people in Village Ukraine, the Cossacks and the peasants. With the growth of the towns, however, a third class evolved based on the Magdeburg law system and guild organization of crafts and trades. Urban Church brotherhoods also evolved with their religious and philanthropic activities. Class differentials were also brought from the old country. The records of immigrants distinguished Cossacks, peasants and urban colonists, and their different statuses, positions and occupations.[16]

The Cossacks, the only class considered really important, were free, endowed with full property rights, and honored with the obligation of military services. They were guardians of the political autonomy of the country. Soon two Cossack segments appeared, the wealthy and important electorals, *vyborni*, and the poor but influential associates.

In the beginning the peasants were free. They only had to pay a tax to the Tsar's treasury. With the growth of Russian penetration, "usual obediences" were introduced, and later serfdom. However, bondage in Village Ukraine was not as heavy as in the Hetman State, Western Europe or Muscovy. The fertility of the soil did not require it.

The emigration to the Don-Donets basin produced continuous conflicts between the Hetman government and the Russian Tsar. The Hetmans wanted to prevent the emigration of their people, preferring to retain their labor powers for their own economic growth. The Tsars encouraged these mass movements. Hence, Hetman decrees and edicts prohibiting the emigration had little effect. Finally, Hetman Samoilovych requested that the Russian government give up its domination over Village Ukraine, and agree to its incorporation into the Cossack-Hetman State. The Tsar did not agree. In 1765, the Russian government began to proceed with the gradual abolition of the autonomy of the colonelcies or regimental districts of *Slobozhanshchyna*, Village Ukraine, and the elimination of the Cossack freedoms. The incorporation of the land into the Russian empire was clearly intended from the beginning. Soon the introduction of Russian social and legal institutions followed, including bondage, serfdom and the discriminatory class system, so gravely abhorred by the freedom loving Cossacks and borderland settlers.[17]

The Colonization of the Borderlands. With their growing political influence on Ukrainian developments, both governments, the Polish and the Muscovite-Russian, were increasingly interested in the settlement of the vast

Ukrainian border territories in the South and East. The Polish experiment with settling the southern parts of Right-bank regions by the Cossacks, who were also supposed to defend the land against the Tartar onslaughts, was not a success for the Polish policy, as was the case with Semen Palii. Palii wanted to make Ukraine independent from Poland. Having been unable to suppress the Ukrainian independence movements, the so-called "eternal peace" of 1681, between Poland and Muscovy, later on joined by Turkey, established that the parts of Right-bank Ukraine between the rivers Dnieper and Boh were supposed to be left unpopulated and deserted. The arrangement was soon abandoned and forgotten, as it was referred to earlier, because of the permanent Tartar threat. Then, the Polish government experimented with the Cossack settlements, as it was just mentioned, and failed.[18]

The Moscow government adopted another approach as its authority in Ukraine was growing. Without having any real or theoretical authority over the right bank regions, it authorized a Serbian colonization between the rivers Kaharlyk and Tura. The colonization had a para-military character, since its intended purpose was to build a bulwark against the Tartar threat. The whole area received the name of *Nova Serbia*, New Serbia, and it was under the authority of the Kievan Governor-General. Territorially *Nova Serbia* was divided into a number of administrative-military districts, the *roty*, each with a fortified town. The chief administration was centered in the fortress of St. Elizabeth. The Serbian settlers received certain liberties from the Muscovite government which were supposed to make the whole colonization project more popular.

In 1753, a new wave of Serbian colonization came to Ukraine. This time the settlers were granted a territory in Left-bank Ukraine, from the Siversky Donets to Loza River and the towns of Bakhmut and Luhansk, and the area received the name of Slovianoserbia. The foreign ethnic elements in the above two settlement regions enjoyed a privileged position as compared with the Ukrainian population. Some Ukrainian colonists in these regions were even evicted; the Serbs received larger land grants and the Serbian officials were better paid than the Ukrainian or Cossack ones. The Ukrainians from other provinces were forced to go to *Nova Serbia* and Slovianoserbia to help to construct towns and fortresses there. Then, the Ukrainian population in these regions was even forced to render some services to the foreign settlers. The resentment was intense, so much so that Ukrainians began to leave the area and to seek homes somewhere else: in the Hetman state, the Territory of the Zaporozhe Cossacks, or far east, beyond the Don regions. Subsequently, the Russian government began to bring new settlers from Poland to give the colonization a more established foundation.

In the wake of the centralization drive of Empress Catherine II, and as a result of the incredible administrative abuses and malversations in the said regions, the colonists' self-government was abolished, including the *Slobidsky* colonelcy. Afterwards, the so-called New Russian governership, *Novorossiiska gubernia*, province, a part of the standardized imperial administration, was introduced for all those territories. It was a logical outcome of Russian imperialism, which under Catherine II reflected a most aggressive expression. An administrative reform was introduced in 1764, while at the same time a comprehensive "Plan for the Settlement of the New Russian Governorship" was announced. It was an aggressive manifestation of the government's attempt to regiment in detail all the life in the new province of the Russian Empire. Accordingly, a military man who settled there received full inheritance rights on the land given to him, being obligated to military service. The peasant settlers were not obliged to military service, but had to pay a tax. Also, the nobles received large landed properties, which they were supposed to colonize in the course of three years. The Russian landed grandees were thus given a privileged position.[19]

Although the new governorship was gravely plundered by a Tartar assault in 1769, ruining some 50 settlements, *slobody*, the colonization process, which substantially altered the ethnic composition of the territory, was a success. Of course, the *Haidamaky* uprisings also had their effect on the developments in the so-called New Russian Governorship.

In 1770, a large-scale uprising of the regular military formations, the Ukrainian and Don Cossacks and the peasants erupted everywhere in protest against Russian oppression. Yet, the Russian forces soon cruelly suppressed the uprising by executing, torturing or exiling the leaders, and terrorizing the population.[20] After the Treaty of Kuchuk-Kainardzhi, the regions of southern and eastern Ukraine were subject to another territorial-administrative division to fit the Russian imperial plans.[21]

---

1. P. Lyashchenko, *History of the National Economy of Russia*, New York, 1949, pp. 342-343; Also, the history of colonization: D. Bahalii, *Ocherki iz istorii kolonizatsii i byta stepnoi okrainy Moskovskavo gosudarstva*, Moscow, 1887; D, Doroshenko, *Narys istorii Ukrainy*, Munich, 1966, Vol. II, pp. 230-245.

2. B. Krupnytsky, *Hetman Danylo Apostol i yoho doba* Augsburg, 1948, pp. 111, 113, 123, and other pages; N. Polonska-Vasylenko, *Istoria Ukrainy,* Munich, 1976, Vol. II, pp. 86-91.

3. V. Hryshko, "Do problemy providnoi verstvy za hetmana Bohdana Khmelnytskoho", *Ameryka,* Ukrainian Catholic Daily, Philadelphia, August 2, 3, 6 and 7, 1957; the same, "300 littia Khmelnychchyny", *Zapysky Naukovoho Tovarystva im. Shevchenka,* Munich, 1948, Vol. CLVI, pp. 7-60; O. Okinshevych, *Lektsii z istorii ukrainskoho prava,* Munich, 1947, pp. 28-30 and 59-67; the same, "Hetmanska Derzhava", *Entsyklopedia ukrainoznavstva,* Munich, 1949, Vol. I Part II, pp. 643-647; W. Lipinski, *Z Dziejow Ukrainy,* Cracow, 1912, chapters on the role of the Ukrainian gentry in the National Revolution.

4. Krupnytsky, *op. cit.*, p. 112; degradation of the Cossack class; some Cossacks were reduced to the level of the peasants, others were elevated to the status of the nobility.

5. M. Slabchenko, *Orhanizatsia hospodarstva Ukrainy,* Part I, *Hospodarstvo Hetmanshchyny,* Odessa, 1923, pp. 41-46; Individual land ownership was a leading principle in Ukraine; the landed collectives, the *obshchina,* were artificially championed by Russian historiography: *ibid.*, pp. 56-59. Slabchenko said that no collectives existed in Ukrainian agriculture. To prove his point, he quoted Shymansky, from *Kievskaia Starina,* Kiev, 1883, Vol. I, p. 83, who asserted that individual property was a generally accepted institution in Ukraine, although its extent was flexible. Slabchenko pointed out that Hetman Brukhovetsky was defeated, mainly because he attempted to introduce collectivism: *ibid.*, p. 62 K. Kononenko, *Ukraine and Russia, A History of the Economic Relations between Ukraine and Russia, 1654-1917,* Milwaukee, 1958, pp. 1-33.

6. The decree referred to the gentry of the Lubech region, having stated that since the "beginning of the war (the National Revolution) it defended the public interest". The reference affirmed the noble duty of military service: Okinshevych, *Lektsii...,* as above, pp. 57-58.

7. Doroshenko, *op. cit.*, Vol. II, p. 122; Hryshko, *op. cit.*, pp. 44-46; Kononenko, *op. cit.*, p. 6.

8. Okinshevych, *op. cit.*, p. 82: "the social position of the peasantry in Hetman Ukraine was doublessly a better one than that of the analogous social groups in other countries at that time." The situation resembled developments in North America, where under the impact of the expanding Western frontiers, like the Ukrainian steppes, labor conditions were more tolerable than in West Europe: C. Daugherty, *Labor Problems in American Industry,* Boston-New York, 1948-49, pp. 37-39.

9. Slabchenko, *op. cit.*, Part I, p. 1: "Ukraine was held for a golden country, a country of fabulous riches, where it was enough to kick slightly the earth to open the

golden deposits"; also, G. de Beauplan, *Description d'Ukraine*, New York, 1959, p. 448; V. Sichnysky, *Ukraine in Foreign Comments and Descriptions, from the VIth to XXth century*, New York, 1953, pp. 49: Michael the Lithuanian; p. 74: de Beauplan; p. 96: Paul of Aleppo.

10. Okinshevych, *op. cit.*, p. 78.

11. *Ibid.*, p. 77.

12. *Ibid.*, p. 54: "... any legal discrimination on the grounds of national descent was unknown in the Ukrainian Hetman state".

13. About the Byeloruthenian regiment in a vassal relationship to Ukraine: *ibid.*, pp. 132-136; also, Polonska-Vasylenko, *op. cit.*, Vol. II, p. 30: "The Byeloruthenian population gladly acknowledged the authority of the Hetman and accepted the Cossack organization."

14. The year 1380 witnessed the first strong indication of the disintegrating power of the Mongols-Tartars. It was established by the Muscovite victory on the Kulikovo plain in that year: M. Florinsky, *Russia, A. History and an Interpretation*, New York, 1953, Vol. I, p. 94; N. Fr.-Chirovsky, *A History of the Russian Empire*, New York, 1973, Vol. I, p. 215.

15. Bahalii, *op. cit.*, pp. 174-179 (Ostrianyn), 184-186 (Chuhaii), 504-524 (the role of the monasteries and religious orders); the same, *Materialy dla istorii kolonizatsii i byta stepnoi okrainy Moskovskavo gosudarstva*, Moscow, 1886, pp. 13-17, 42-50, 187, and other pages; about the colonization: Lyashchenko, *op cit.*, pp. 342-343; Doroshenko, *op. cit.*, Vol. II, pp. 214-230.

16. Bahalii, *ibid.*, p. 187; the same *Ocherki ...*, pp. 246-247, 378-569, including the records of cattle, horses and sheep; I. Miklashevskii, *Iz istorii khaziaistvennavo byta Moskovskavo gosudarstva*, Part I, *Zaselenie i selskoie khaziaistvo yuzhnoi okrainy XVII v.*, Moscow, 1894, pp. 77, 168-169, 308, and other pages.

17. On *Slobidska* Ukraine: Polonska-Vasylenko, *op cit.*, Vol. II., pp. 106-110; the same, *Zaselennia pivdennoi Ukrainy v polovyni XVIII st.*, Munich, 1960, Part I; Doroshenko, *loc. cit.*

18. Polonska-Vasylenko, *op cit.*; the same, *Istoria*, Vol. II, pp. 110-120; A. Skalkovskii, *Opyt statisticheskavo opisania Novorossiiskavo kraia*, Odessa, 1853, Vols. I-II; the same, *Khronologicheskoie obozrenie istorii Novorossiiskavo kraia*, Odessa, 1836, Vol. I, pp. 84-85 and other.

19. Polonska-Vasylenko, *Zaselennia pivdennoi Ukrainy ...*, Part II, pp. 46-69, 120-122.

20. K. Huslystyi, *Z istorii klasovoi borotby v Stepovii Ukraini v 60-70-tykh rr XVIII st.*, Kharkiv, 1933, pp. 32, 38-39, 43-44, 85; Polonska-Vasylenko, *op. cit.*, Vol. II, pp. 129-132.

21. On the social structure of the Ukrainian society: Doroshenko, *op. cit.*, Vol. II, pp. 122-128; Polonska-Vasylenko, *Istoria Ukrainy*, Vol. II, pp. 168-178; N. Fr.- Chirovsky, *Old Ukraine, Its Socio-Economic History prior to 1781*, Madison, N.J., 1963, pp. 221-249; V Miakotin, *Ocherky sotsialnoi istorii Ukrainy v 17-18 vv.*, Prague, 1924.

CHAPTER TWELVE
GROWTH OF THE NATIONAL ECONOMY
EXTRACTIVE INDUSTRIES

The national economy of Ukraine — Agriculture — Hunting, fishing and cattle-raising — Mining

The National Economy of Ukraine. The National Revolution of 1648 changed the fundamental character of the Ukrainian economy. In the first place, it ceased to be a mere part of the large economy of the Polish-Lithuanian Commonwealth, and was gradually becoming a Ukrainian national economy in the modern sense of the term. But the birth pangs were enormous, and the process was not completed.

Prior to the Revolution, the so-called "golden peace" prevailed in Ukraine, and the country was economically prosperous for a number of years, as Ohloblyn indicates.[1] After the Revolution, the economy was in many instances non-existent and had to be built from the ground up. For the third time in their history the borderlands experienced this tragedy. In some areas it was necessary to colonize completely vacant lands. At first, primitive hunting and fishing were resorted to, followed by cattle and horse breeding, and then agriculture. However, a new atmosphere prevailed. National freedom, essentially Ukrainian individualism, the absence of foreign oppression and many other factors promoted a speedy economic recovery and reconstruction. Nevertheless, the recovery was neither smooth nor miraculous.

The abolition of Polish domination brought an immediate collapse of the Polish economic system based on large-scale latifundium holdings and serf labor and a contempt for other industries. For a short while, at least, the traditionally Ukrainian, small-scale peasant landholding, based on the principle of individual ownership, agressively took over. This was the third great change produced by the Revolution.

The idea of individual land ownership was so strong in Ukraine, that whoever supported collectivism was doomed to fail. The most striking example of that trend was the known political conflict between the Left-bank Hetman Brukhovetsky and the Right-bank Hetman Doroshenko, as Slabchenko indicated.[2]

Brukhovetsky failed, largely because of his collectivistic tendencies. Although Russian historians have vigorously insisted on the presence of communes in Cossack-Hetman Ukraine, there is no objective historical support for this theory.

A communal economy no doubt existed in the territory of the Cossack Host until the end of the sixteenth century, or perhaps even during the first half of the seventeenth, being induced by the demands of pioneer life in the steppes. Land, both fields and pasture, and fisheries and forests were considered collective property by the Cossacks. At that time, individual Cossacks received land allotments from the communal area for their own use for one or two years. Capital, cattle, draft animals and equipment were also collective to a great extent. After a year or two, land allotments were returned to the collectives, and reallotted on a temporary basis.

However, the communal principle soon gave way under an increase in the number of agricultural settlers. Capital, cattle, draft animals and, finally, the arable land became subject to individual ownership, and only the use of forests, fisheries and hunting grounds retained certain collective characteristics.

But even there the basic approach changed. The collective use of the forests, fishery rights and hunting grounds was considered a voluntary and contractual pooling of common interests. Moreover, at the end of the Cossack-Hetman era these remnants of the commune also disappeared.

Early historiography was largely confused, as far as the problem of collectivism in Ukraine was concerned, by the existence at that time of three semi-cooperative, semi-collective institutions, namely, the brotherhood, the *spriah* and the *siabr* associations. A brotherhood was an association based on an agreement among male individuals for life, to work together and to share everything, at times even wives and children.

A *spriah* was a cooperative association founded on a terminable agreement among a few villages to accomplish jointly certain major projects of mutual interest, such as melioration, digging stumps, establishing settlements or constructing roads. A *siabr* association was also a contractual institution, concluded for a certain time, to pool the monetary funds, implements, tools and work of the interested people either in a colonization project or in the acquisition of land, forests, pastures, lakes or mills.[3]

Being contractual, and, in most cases, terminable, all three forms progressively disintegrated under the impact of Ukrainian individualism.

In a comparatively short time, however, the restoration of class society in Ukraine brought a sweeping return of large landed estates throughout the nation and a parallel liquidation of peasant land ownership and the reintroduction of serfdom. Numerous nobles, like Nemyrych, loyal to the new government, were returned their vast possessions, while the religious orders continued, without any interruption by war, to own and to exploit their latifundia, as explained above.

Soon such Cossack families as Mazepa, Apostol, Skoropadsky, Miklashevsky, Horlenko and Kochubei also acquired enormous landed estates, together with peasant serfs. During the time of Skoropadsky's Hetmanate, Russian nobles also began to acquire land grants at the expense of small-scale peasant farmholdings. It is enough to mention the names of Prince Menshikov, Vorontsov, Fein and Kornis.[4] In particular, the Russian grandees enlarged their latifundia through the usurpation of peasant land and even tried to seize small Cossack farms and attempted to turn the common Cossacks into serfs, contrary to the wishes of both Hetman and Tsar, who wanted to preserve the integrity of this military class.

In discussing the socio-economic processes of the time of Hetman Mazepa, Ohloblin stressed the trend toward a concentration of the ownership of land by inheritance, usurpation and occupation.[5] In the Territory of the Cossack Host, small-scale Cossack and peasant land possession was also gradually suppressed by the growing manorial estates of the Cossack chieftains and the incoming nobles. Vast estates and comparably large fortunes were accumulated by Cossack leaders like Kalnyshevsky, the last Commander-in-Chief, and Hloba, Secretary of Office of the Cossack Host.[6]

In Village Ukraine, all the land belonged to the Tsar, theoretically speaking. However, he made land grants to settlers for their life-time use. The size of the allotment fluctuated during the colonization process. In the Chuhaiv settlement the allotment was 81 acres, and in Okhtirka, 113.3 acres per family plus the use of forests and pasture areas. From 1668, the Tsarist decrees began to minutely regulate the land possessions of the newly established colonies, where the property rights of the Cossacks, peasants and townspeople were fully secured. Government officials were forbidden to violate these ownership rights.

Nevertheless, in Village Ukraine, too, the large manorial landholdings began to progressively replace the small peasant landholdings. The upper strata of the Cossacks and the Russian nobles, equipped with capital, implements and draft animals, could easily take care of more land. Hence, they enlarged their possessions through usurpation and abuse, as well as through legal occupation. This led to sharp class differentiations, a manorial economy and serfdom.

In Right-bank Ukraine, the latifundium land possession abolished the principle of peasant landholding immediately after the reinstatement of Polish domination in this area. Polish noblemen, such as Koniecpolski, Zamojski and Kalinowski, invested large amounts of money in land and in the financing of large-scale colonization projects aimed at an increasingly profitable commercial agriculture. Simultaneously, they reintroduced the bondage of the serf to the soil.

In the over-all picture of the prolonged struggle between peasant landholding and the manorial economy, the concept of individual property rights of the lower strata of society was not completely abolished. The forms of the newly established class order were less cruel, and the peasants retained a degree of personal freedom until this was crushed by the introduction of the Russian legal system after the annexation of Ukraine by the Russian Empire.

The atmosphere of relative freedom in Ukraine during the Cossack-Hetman period produced an impressive growth of the economy in all its segments. Village, manor and city grew in wealth, despite many obstacles to be mentioned later. Farmland increased enormously as a result of continuous and large-scale colonization and the cultivation of increasing areas of steppe land. Commercial activities developed in an atmosphere of private initiative and fading contempt for commerce. "The powerful enterprising skill which dominated everyone, females not excluded, from the Cossack aristocracy, down to a common craftsman, created new workshops, new settlements, and new material wealth," wrote Ohloblin enthusiastically.[7] However, this vital interest of Cossack nobles and Cossack commons in trade and manufacturing developed into dangerous competition for the Hetman town and its people.

During Mazepa's time, the mercantilist doctrine began to find a clear application in Ukrainian economic life. The result was the promotion of manufacturing, textile, linen and tobacco industries. Hetmans Mazepa and Apostol especially, made broad use of mercantilist protectionism in order to sponsor the economic development of their nation in accordance with the prevailing economic theory. At the end of the eighteenth century this system of early capitalism became dominant.

However, there were a few factors which considerably slowed down the impressive industrial growth of the seventeenth and eighteenth centuries. First, the Ukrainian national economy was still agricultural; other industries were merely supplementary. Hence, land ownership and exploitation were the main sources of national income. The peasants and common Cossacks were, therefore, the foundation of the country's productive processes, while their degraded social status had an adverse influence insofar as economic growth was concerned. Secondly, in consequence of many foreign wars, Tartar raids and a few civil wars, the normal evolution of the country's economy was frequently interrupted. Out of the twenty-two years of Mazepa's rule, a little more than one month was really peaceful, as Ohloblin notes. These interruptions and destructive wars, as well as epidemics, plagues, droughts, and locusts, were the leading causes of the serious economic fluctuations, particularly the recurring depressions.

Recurring depressions and disastrous wars produced strong and numerous waves of migration flowing out of Right-bank and Left-bank Ukraine, largely reducing the country's population and its labor force, and increasing serfdom.

The colonial policy of the Tsarist government, pursued agressively in Ukraine since the Battle of Poltava, may be considered the third significant factor which greatly retarded Ukrainian economic development. St. Petersburg desired to keep the country as a source of food and raw materials for Russian imperial markets, and consequently, was opposed to any attempt at industrialization on her part. According to Slabchenko, Volobuyev, Ohloblin and other students of Ukrainian economic history, after the incorporation of Ukraine into Russia, Ukrainian industries were completely suppressed by the Tsars.[8]

Literally, throughout the entire Cossack-Hetman period of Ukrainian history until the last quarter of the eighteenth century, Ukraine continued to be *ukraina,* borderland of Europe, the eastern and southern frontiers of which were in perpetual flux. New areas were continually colonized and added to the Ukrainian ethnic territory. With the exception of West Ukraine, colonization was also carried on throughout the ethnographic area and far beyond in the Don-Volga area and the Kuban basin.

In Right-bank Ukraine the settlement process was resumed immediately within the framework of the independent Ukrainian state. The West Ukrainians, Poles, Germans, Wallachians, Czechs, Lithuanians, Serbs, Bulgarians,

Byeloruthenians and others came as colonists to build a better future for themselves. A new impetus was given to the settlement of the right-bank areas by the reestablishment of Polish rule there. History repeated itself. First, the Polish nobility regained possession of their enormous landed estates to resume their own form of commercial agriculture. This time instead of Polonized names, such as, Ostrozhsky, Vyshnyvetsky or Zaslavsky, the names of a new Polish nobility like Potocki, Branicki, Jablonowski and Zamojski prevailed. At first, in order to obtain more laborers, they offered such advantages to prospective settlers as freedom from bondage and from other obligations to the lords for a number of years. As a result, the population of Right-bank Ukraine increased rapidly. But after a few years when the labor force was adequate, these freedoms were progressively suppressed and the peasant colonists eventually turned into serfs.

The Polish form of serfdom was almost intolerable for the Ukrainian peasant, releasing a series of migrations from the right-bank districts in the direction of the Black Sea steppes, or left-bank Hetman Ukraine, or in the same direction farther eastward to Village Ukraine and the Kuban territory, between the Azov Sea and the Caucasian mountains. This adventurous colonization process, known since time immemorial as *ukhody*, continued with only short interruption due to war. Hundreds of new villages and towns were founded or old ones rebuilt during this period, including such towns as Hlukhiv, Putivl, Sumy, Korolovets, Lebedin, Kharkiv and Okhtyrka, in both Left-bank and Village Ukraine. Hundreds of thousands of people of all social classes were involved. The population movement was partially induced by the Ukrainian, Polish and Russian governments, but for the most part it was a spontaneous, voluntary and privately motivated drive by a people in quest of their national destiny.

The Russian sponsored colonization of the Territory of the Cossack Host by the Serbians after 1751, undertaken without the consent of the Cossacks, resulted in a serious political conflict. The Cossacks went so far as attempting to destroy these Serbian colonies in the Elizabeth and Bakhmut areas. This antagonized the Russians, caused an assault on the *Sitch*, and the liquidation of the Host in 1775.[9]

The quantity of land which could be taken into cultivation in each individual case depended greatly upon the density of the population and the increasing scarcity of land. The settlers sought more and more court action and legal documentation for their rights of land ownership.

In Village Ukraine, a Tsarist grant usually allotted land to the settlers as a group; they divided the arable soil among themselves, keeping forest, hunt-

Ostrozhsky's castle at Stare Selo
(16th Century)

Fortress of Bilhorod
(15th Century)

ing, fishery and pasture areas for common use at least for the time being. However, land was so abundant in Village Ukraine and in the Black Sea steppes that colonists were actually free to possess much additional land and to establish their ownership by *ius primi occupantionis* or *ius traditionis*. This abundance contributed to the emergence of large landed estates. In Hetman Ukraine, and later in other territories as well, the cultivation of the soil, the construction of fences, and the employment of markers were visible signs of the occupation and ownership honored by the courts and administrative authorities.

Agriculture. During the time of the National Revolution, Ukraine was unquestionably an agricultural nation. Agriculture was the foundation of economic growth. Its progress brought prosperity and wealth. Farming was also the most loved and respected occupation during the Hetman times. Slabchenko asserts that the physiocratic philosophy prevailed in Ukraine before it became popular in the West. Then Ukrainian farming quickly recovered from the ravages of war, while cultivated areas were enlarged enormously in successive decades, increasing farm output and thus strengthening the nation's economy. The sowing areas expanded when Tartar raids gradually decreased, permitting greater safety in the steppes and in southern and eastern Ukraine. The power of the Turks also diminished in the Black Sea and Azov Sea shore territories. Large-scale colonization automatically enlarged the arable areas of East Europe. On the other hand, the development of grain production was further encouraged by continuously expanding needs for food and other agricultural raw materials in the West.

The soil and climatic conditions of Ukraine soon made wheat her leading crop and main export item, widely grown in the southern and central parts of Ukraine because of the ideal climatic conditions and fertile black soil. This was noted by such foreigners as Beauplan, Marshall and Weihe, who visited Ukraine in the sixteenth and seventeenth centuries.[10]

In the northern sections of the country, where the climate was harsh and the soil was poorer, rye was by far the leading crop. Yet wheat was the main product of the country. All other traditional crops were grown during the Cossack-Hetman period with acreage and output per acre steadily increasing. Among these were barley, buckwheat, oats, millet, hemp, flax, and hops.

Marshall indicated that nine-tenths of English hemp and flax importation from East Europe came from Ukraine, and that these products were better than those received from her American colonies.[11] These two crops were grown particularly in the northern parts of Hetman Ukraine, the Chernihiv district, and throughout Village Ukraine.

Mulberry trees were grown in Ukraine to provide for the small-scale silk industry. According to Hueldenstaedt's report, mulberry trees grew in Kiev. Silk production was also attempted in Village Ukraine.

Numerous new plants were introduced into the Ukrainian farm economy. Maize was brought in by Bulgarian and Wallachian settlers. It quickly became popular, and soon a considerable area was planted with it. Clover and tobacco were introduced by the Tartars. The cultivation of tobacco grew most rapidly because of government sponsorship. Tobacco plantations were numerous and large in Left-bank Ukraine, Lubni, Hadiach, and Nizhin districts, and Village Ukraine, Okhtyra and Kharkiv areas. On the large plantations of the priviliged classes, tobacco was raised in a system of long belts, and under the supervision of foreign specialists. Tobacco leaves were packed in bales, and delivered to local markets or processing factories in cartloads. The surplus was exported.

Potatoes were introduced into Ukraine, according to Krypiakevych, in the second half of the eighteenth century on a very limited scale, and were used for the most part in feeding animals. In the nineteenth century, during years of excessively poor crops, potatoes became popular as food for humans.

Vegetable and fruit raising was also rapidly developing. In the seventeenth century there existed few orchards and only a small amount of fruit production in Ukraine. Nevertheless, according to foreign visitors, by the eighteenth century orchards had developed all over the country. Hueldenstaedt, an academician who devoted much time to the study of the Ukrainian economy, reported considerable fruit growing in the towns and cities during the period of 1771-1774. He said that in the city of Kiev "fruit trees could be found near almost every home."[12] This certainly was not an isolated case, for fruit trees were also grown extensively in other towns and in the countryside.

Eventually special varieties of fruit trees were imported, sometimes as a hobby of the upper classes. Vice-treasurer Markovych, for example, developed numerous orchards of apple, pear, plum, cherry and walnut trees. In one spring he purchased over a thousand plum trees of various kinds.[13]

The cultivation of grapes for wine was also continued, particularly in the cloisters, but still without much success, since Ukrainian wine was poor and unpopular.

Among the most popular fruits in the Ukrainian orchards were apples, pears, plums, sweet and sour cherries, and walnuts. The expansion of orchard and fruit tree growing became very rapid later on.

Gardening and vegetable production were not very well developed in the seventeenth century, according to Slabchenko, but they expanded later.

Vegetable growing in the towns and manors was intensified to meet an increased demand, while the villages lagged in this respect. Since gardens require more intensive cultivation, they flourished in West Ukraine (Galicia and Podillia) where living conditions were less stormy.

Truck farming was a novelty during the Lithuanian-Polish era, but grew and expanded during the following period. Crops included traditional beans, lettuce, kohlrabi, cabbage, turnips and onions. In all cases the manorial economy pioneered, and induced imitation by the peasants. The variety increased to include carrots, cauliflower, asparagus, beets, cucumbers, peas, watermelons, radishes, horseradish, parsley, celery and pumpkins. Cabbage, onion, radish and cucumber were among the most popular crops.

Agricultural technology and organization progressed rapidly along a recognizable pattern. From western Ukraine it gradually spread over the central, eastern and southern areas. It was at first adopted by the manor and eventually imitated by the peasant. Agricultural technology was initiated in West Ukraine for two reasons. First, because this area suffered less from the devastations of war and conditions were somewhat less turbulent. And, second, because this part of Ukraine was closer to the West, which was at that time the center of civilization. The latter was probably the most important reason.

Hence, first in West Ukraine, and on its larger estates, the three field system was replaced by an intensive crop rotation which wasted no arable land. An extensive application of animal manure was adopted. Initially, only small amounts of manure were used. Then experience recommended ever more amounts of animal fertilizer until maximum fertility was achieved. However, the natural fertility of the soil in East Ukraine rendered the use of manure less important, therefore delaying the adoption of fertilizer.

Better implements and tools were also gradually introduced. Wooden plow shares, wooden plows and other wooden tools, like rakes, harrows and hoes, which were largely used by the peasants in the second half of the seventeenth century, were gradually replaced by iron implements.

In the eighteenth century, however, the so-called Ukrainian plow, a heavy iron implement, came into general use all over the country. In the second half of the eighteenth century, iron implements were used on all estates while wooden tools were still used by the peasants.[14] Oxen remained the leading type of draft animal throughout the country. Horses were raised extensively, not for farmwork but rather for harnessing to coaches, for riding, hunting, and racing.

In order to obtain more arable land, deforestation and melioration and irrigation works were continuously undertaken, primarily on the large landed estates. But these practices were not entirely unknown among the peasants, particularly deforestation. The estates of the religious orders were model farms. Not only was farmland highly fertilized, but also pastures as well. The land was deep-plowed and tilled two or three times a year. Meliorations and irrigations were extensive. Field labor and administration were minutely organized according to an elaborate schedule, as, for example, on the Vydubytsky estates, where a schedule was written down. Many officials and supervisors were assigned to specific duties. In some noble and Cossack possessions farm work was extremely well administered by large staffs. Each manorial economy was managed by an administrator, who had to be a member of the gentry, and directed the work of various officials. A number of the manorial economies in certain areas constituted the so-called "key of estates," the *kluchi,* administered and managed by a noble official, called the economist, who had authority over all manors and administrators, and their farms, mills, distilleries, breweries, sawing mills and other establishments. A number of the key estates were under the management, control and supervision of a "commissioner-general of goods," always a nobleman. Individual establishment of the manorial estates, such as mills, breweries, potash and tar workshops and others, were operated on a rent-lease basis by professional millers, brewers or potash manufacturers, or sometimes directly by the nobles.

Peasant landholding was ordinarily individual and private, contingent upon "usual obediences" toward the master. The concept of a peasant farm always included, according to contemporary criteria, farmland, pastures, forests, stables, barns, implements and servants; while the home dwelling, cattle and horses were not essential components of a farmstead unit — so defined for taxation purposes. Of course, there were numerous poor, landless peasants, *bezzemelni,* who were largely hired as day laborers. Their numbers grew proportionately with the turbulent war years and the inflationary trends of the sixteenth century. Because of inflation their monetary wages were comparatively high, and were usually supplemented by compensation in kind. There was also a group of very poor peasants, called *pidsusidki,* who had no living quarters of their own and shared the homes of those who had.[15]

Miakotin and Slabchenko maintain that these landless peasants paved the way for the return of serfdom throughout the country in conjunction with two other factors, the increasing burdens and the rising indebtedness of both landowning and landless peasants.

The indebtedness of the village population was considerable, in the form of both short-term and long-term credit necessary to buy cattle, horses and farm implements. In general, however, the peasants managed to escape such pitfalls; their social status worsened while economically they slowly improved.

Right-bank and West Ukraine were in a less favorable economic position at this time, being under Polish domination and thus exposed to economic exploitation and national discrimination. The reintroduction of Polish rule in the later seventeenth century quickly aggravated the burdens of bondage and serfdom. As much as four to six days of compulsory manorial labor each week were required of the peasants compared to about half that much in Hetman Ukraine. In addition, compulsory payments, contributions and services, and the unlimited patrimonial power of the Polish gentry over the peasant serfs made life intolerable for the village population. Hence, hundreds of thousands of them took refuge either in the left-bank provinces or in the Territory of the Cossack Host. The fear of heavy penalties, including capital punishment, failed to halt the emigration. Ohloblin supplies some data on this subject. He says that in certain areas of Volhinia and in other parts of Right-bank Ukraine, only four to twelve per cent of the population remained from 1648 to 1690.[16]

Hunting, Fishing and Cattle Raising. These industries, including sheep, hog and poultry production had lost much of their importance by this time. With the growth of agriculture they were reduced to a secondary rank. However, the farther and deeper that the frontiers penetrated into the steppes, the more important these industries became since they always came as the first stages of the economic evolution in any territory or society. Therefore, in the territory of the Cossack Host and Village Ukraine they remained highly significant, as the exports of that time indicated.

Horse and cattle breeding was even more important as a way of making a living in the frontier lands. At the time of the liquidation of the Cossack Host in 1775, the possession of large herds of cattle, horses and sheep was still an indication of individual wealth and opulence in these steppe areas. Hence, the economic significance of the extractive industries varied with the sections of the country.

On the banks of large rivers and the shores of the Black and Azov Seas, fishing was always a leading occupation, even in the nineteenth century, while the significance of hunting was even greater in the forest areas. The technologies of hunting, fishing and cattle raising naturally progressed along with other industries. However, in hunting, some traditional techniques, such as the construction and installation of traps for game, the use of nets, and the training of hunting hounds, falcons and hawks still persisted. The most radical innovation was the general use of rifles and shotguns instead of bows and arrows. In those sections of the country where excellent and abundant hunting opportunities existed, there were trained and experienced hunters among the peasants and other manorial personnel, not to mention the Cossacks and the nobles.

According to available records, memoirs, official documents and codes of law, among the animals hunted were bears, wolves, foxes, wild boars, deer, martens, beavers, rabbits and squirrels, and fowl such as wild geese, ducks, blackcocks, moorhens and peahens. Buffalos, white hares and wildcats were to be found in the northern-most frontiers near the Muscovite borders; bears were found in the mountains and forests, but in steadily decreasing numbers. Beavers were progressively exterminated although they were still available in small numbers in Galicia and Hetman Ukraine as late as the early eighteenth century. According to contemporaries, they were of a nomadic type, up to five feet in length and approaching sixty pounds in weight, living in inaccessible cleavages and clefts along the rivers. Despite legal protection, beavers were soon completely exterminated for their valuable skins. Likewise, bulls and ureoxes of the Ukrainian steppes also became extinct.

Hunting grounds and hunting rights were strictly protected and regulated by the *Lithuanian Statutes*, which were still in force, by *The Laws by which justice was done among the Little Rus'ian People*, the unofficial but popular codification of laws in Hetman Ukraine since 1743, by numerous Hetman decrees, and various other regulations. In the newer laws and decrees, however, the monetary value of the game was doubled or tripled to correspond with rising prices, and it was expressed in rubles instead of guldens.

Punishments were also imposed for demolishing traps and nets, for hunting in somebody else's forests and for stealing or destroying beehives. The traditionally great attention paid by law and administration to hunting rights indicated the relatively great economic significance of hunting in the Cossack-Hetman era.[17]

Beehives were developed in the fields and forests, where the proper plants grew. Nobles, Cossacks and peasants were engaged in beekeeping and honey production. Baranovich says that, for example, in the middle of the eighteenth century, in the latifundium of Vyshnyvets (Volhinia) alone, there were 8,967 peasant, and 2,245 manorial beehives.

Fish production and fishing continued to be significant, and their relative importance even increased in some instances, such as with the fishing businesses on the Azov Sea shores. Artificial pools were constructed and maintained, as before, by the nobles and Cossack aristocrats, and in the possessions of the religious orders, while fishing in the rivers and natural lakes was mainly an occupation of the village population. Sturgeons, carps, tenches, roaches and gordons were the principal kinds of fish, caught by netting and angling. In the manorial economies, artificial pools were emptied of water to catch the fish in large quantities, which were then exported.

At this time, fishing in East Ukraine was no longer merely a way of providing for a meager subsistence of a primitive colonization stage, as in the sixteenth century, but a progressive and commercialized business conducted for profit, similar to that in West Ukraine in the previous period.

Most certainly, cattle and horse raising was the most important business of these three extractive industries. Raising oxen, cows, sheep, hogs, goats, and then also chickens, capons, pullets, geese, ducks, turkeys and other breeds of animals and birds, must be included in the discussion of this economic sector. Horses and mules were raised partially as draft animals, particularly by the peasants. But horses were bred mostly for horseback riding, harnessing, hunting and racing. The nobles and the Cossack aristocrats continued to maintain large horse breeding stations of a thousand or more horses for those purposes, and for commercial speculation as well. Several breeds of horses were known.

The peasants raised horses mainly for hard field work, but they could not always afford to keep them. Sometimes one horse was held for every second or third farmstead. Presumably, the village population preferred in some instances weak breeds of horses, cattle and sheep, since these secured them against frequent requisitions by the government and the military, which looked primarily for outstanding qualities of strength, endurance and fertility in these animals.

Oxen were raised first of all as draft animals for field work in the peasant farmsteads and manorial economies.

Cows, goats and certain sheep were reared for milk and milk products. Dairy production was fairly well developed in the manorial economies of the religious orders, while the peasants and townspeople indulged in this business on a smaller scale, since it was more expensive and required more intensive management. Serfdom certainly did not facilitate the trend. Nevertheless, the output of the peasant dairy production was considerable, as contemporaries related. In both manorial and peasant dairies, production was both for use and for the market. Products included milk, buttermilk, sour milk, sour cream, butter and various kinds of cheese. Naturally, the manorial dairy business was more commercialized.

Dairy production flourished, particularly in the mountainous areas: the Carpathian mountains, Bukovyna, and some parts of Galicia and Podillia, where the traditional Wallachian type of farming still prevailed.[18]

Cattle and horse breeding was especially important in the territory of the Cossack Host and in Village Ukraine because of their vast stretches of land. Here, pasture lands were inexhaustable for years to come. After the remnants of communal ownership disappeared, considerable individual fortunes accumulated among the Cossacks.

At the end of the political autonomy of the territory of the Host, Cossack chieftains owned large herds and flocks, hundreds and thousands of horses, oxen, bulls, cows, sheep and goats.[19] The common Cossack also possessed large herds. During the Tartar raid in 1769, for example, the Tartars took from one Cossack 600 horses; from another, 127 horses, 300 oxen and bulls and 1200 sheep; and from a third, 250 horses and 5000 sheep. According to records, similar growth of cattle breeding also prevailed in Village Ukraine.

In the latter Hetman era, after Samoilovych, sheep raising began to experience a rapid growth, which, however, was followed by an abrupt decline in 1830. Its speedy expansion was motivated by the increased demand for wool in Russia. The modern Russian armies required standard uniforms, as Krupnysky says, and this greatly increased the demand for wool.[20]

Sheep raising was officially encouraged in Ukraine, both by the Hetman government and the Russian resident protectors. The Ukrainian Hetmans, Apostol in particular, following the traditional Ukrainian free enterprise system and agricultural preference, wanted to leave sheep raising to the local population, Cossacks and peasants, and in this way preserve a balance between the interests of grain production and the normal growth of the sheep raising economy.

The Ukrainian Hetman government willingly gave its support to a justifiable sheep production. Germans and German-trained Ukrainian specialists were hired to advance the idea of progressive and scientific sheep raising in the country as a result of which Ukrainian wool exports might have increased greatly.[21] Hence good breeds of long-haired sheep were observed in Ukraine by foreigners.

Hog raising developed very successfully throughout all of Ukraine, because pork was a popular meat. Beauplan and other visitors in Ukraine mentioned hog breeding and pork consumption. It was apparently greater in the forest sections of the country. In the descriptions of the royal economies of the seventeenth century, references were made to the fact that the peasants kept their hogs in a wild state in the birch and oak woods, where the animals could easily find food.

All kinds of fowl, such as chickens, ducks, goslings, geese, capons, pullets, moorhens and turkeys, were raised for meat, eggs, and feathers. Poultry was widely consumed by all social classes; by the wealthier, of course, more often than by the poor. According to records, poultry was also indispensible at official receptions and dinners, along with beef, pork, mutton, veal and all kinds of game meats, prepared in various ways.

Mining. Iron ore mining and processing, saltpetre exploitation, salt extraction and petroleum production constituted the main branches of the extractive mining industries in Ukraine in the seventeenth and eighteenth centuries. The extraction of iron ores from the marshes of northern Ukraine was an ancient industry, originating in prehistoric times. Its growth was very rapid immediately prior to the National Revolution. Ohloblyn says that at the end of the sixteenth century there were scarcely more than ten iron ore pits and iron works in the northern right-bank districts, mainly a small-scale peasant exploitation of the muddy pits. On the eve of the Revolution, there were already over a hundred, usually large-scale and commercialized enterprises, owned, sponsored and operated by the nobles and monasteries.[22]

Of course, no iron production took place in Left-bank Ukraine during the pre-revolutionary era. The war and the revolutionary transitions of 1648-1650 greatly reduced the operation of the iron ore pits and iron workshops, and consequently lowered the iron output for a number of reasons. The shortage of iron, therefore, induced an eager search for iron ore deposits in Left-bank and Village Ukraine in the last quarter of the seventeenth and the beginning of the eighteenth centuries. The Ukrainian government in the Hetman state and the Russian government in Village Ukraine supported any initiative in iron mining and processing. The Cossack aristocrats, common Cossacks, religious orders, city patricians, peasants and professional industrialists increasingly engaged in the search for iron ore, its extraction and processing.

At the time of Hetmans Samoilovych and Mazepa, and later Apostol as well, the output of iron ranged up to several hundred thousand pounds per year, fluctuating up and down according to the political and economic situation of the country. It was extracted in Galicia, Volhinia, the Kholm district, Chernihiv, Mizhin, Starodub and Hlukhiv regimental districts, along the rivers Vorskla, Orel and Samara, and in some sections of Village Ukraine — according to Bahalii.[23]

The exploitation of iron pits and iron smelting became more and more concentrated in the hands of the government, the Hetmans themselves, the Cossack aristocrats and the religious orders, and to a much lesser degree by the commoners and townspeople. Since the iron output was not large, and the demand for the product was steadily rising, particularly in the Hetman state, the Ukrainian government indulged ever more in intensively protecting and supporting the industry, the extraction, the processing and usage of the ore, in order to make the country less dependent upon the import of Russian iron. Of course, this policy was in conformity with the mercantilistic doctrine then in vogue throughout Europe, including Ukraine.

The demand for iron was continuously growing due to the growing population, progressing civilization and technology of production, and the modernization of the armies. Moreover, the Cossack Host, having no iron ore, desired to purchase ever increasing quantities of iron for the use of its semi-military population. This fact affected the iron market of Hetman Ukraine as well. This intensity of demand often induced ruthless practices, primarily on the part of the Cossack hierarchy and the monasteries, to which the iron pits and smelting shops, operated by the commoners, were exposed. The shortage of iron was also aggravated by the Swedish wars. There were even indications that the Swedes were interested in Ukraine as a potential market for their iron and metallurgical products. This might have favorably influenced Swedish-Ukrainian relations which had been friendly ever since Khmelnytsky's time.[24]

Of course, there were many well-trained and experienced mine and iron workers in Hetman Ukraine. They were greatly sought and invited as colonists from the West (Poland and Germany), as well as from Muscovy. There were also skilled ironworkers among the local Ukrainian population.

Saltpetre exploitation originated in the late Polish-Lithuanian era and continued to grow in the southern districts of Ukraine. Foreign visitors such as Beauplan and Gmelin — the former at the time of the National Revolution and the latter at the end of the Hetman period (1770-1784) — reported the existence of this industry in Ukraine. Unquestionably, the war also increased the demand for saltpetre and gunpowder production, and induced an ever growing output of these two products. The industry was extensively supported by the Ukrainian government, too, since it was very anxious to have its own gunpowder supplies for defense purposes, in order to be independent of foreign importation. Hetmans, such as Samoilovych, Mazepa and Apostol, when making land grants to Cossack aristocrats or religious orders, usually either mentioned in the grants or confirmed later by decree, the rights of the owners of real estate to make full use of the saltpetre exploitation privilege. At the end of the seventeenth century, because of the gathering clouds of the Turkish and Northern Wars, a new and very intense interest in saltpetre extraction developed.

At the beginning of the eighteenth century, there were numerous saltpetre establishments on the right and left banks of the river Dnieper, on the banks of the river Orel and in many other places. The entrepreneurship of the Ukrainian people was evident also in this industry in which monks and townspeople were extremely interested. They not only met domestic needs for this product, but also exported the surplus to Russia in considerable quantities.

Salt extraction was another traditionally important mining industry in Ukraine in the seventeenth and eighteenth centuries. In particular, the sub-Carpathian district of Galicia continued to produce salt in large quantities, and supplied it to the West and East Ukrainian regions. Since the previous period, the main centers of West Ukrainian salt production were in the districts of Stara Sil, Drohobych, Peremyshl, Dolyna, Zhydachiv, Kalush, Sianik, Kolomyia, Sniatyn and Kosiv. In those areas so-called "windows" were drilled, from which salt water was hauled by primitive mechanisms powered by horses. Then the water was evaporated in large tin pans to a residue of fine powder and a crude and stony salt. In some places, such as in Drohobych, the salt water was considered "thick" (i.e., good) while in other places like Dolyna and Kosiv, it was of a lesser quality.

There were royal, noble, monastic and municipal salt works, the organization and management of which was diversified. Some salt works, like those in the Peremyshl region, were very large establishments producing several hundred thousand pounds yearly, while others, like those in the Kolomyia and Dolyna districts, were small. The royal salt works were run either by royal administration, or were leased against annual rental payments in salt deliveries to the royal treasury and the fisc. The salt works owned privately by the nobles, religious orders and municipalities were also frequently operated on a lease system.[25]

Already in the sixteenth century petroleum was mentioned in West Ukrainian (Galician) records. In 1591 the noblemen of the Buchach district negotiated a multilateral contract providing for a combined search for oil, gold and other valuable minerals. Toward the end of the eighteenth century, some foreign visitors related that the Ukrainian peasants used oil, called "nepht," for greasing their carriages, and as a drug to combat serious diseases. The peasants dug deeper pits from which they withdrew the "nepht" by means of primitive buckets tied to long wooden poles. Nepht was described as a very odiferous grease, sold in the local markets, and easier to get than tar, although it required some processing.

The Ukrainian Cossacks, while on a military expedition in the Trans-caucasia in 1740, also learned of some of the qualitites of oil, and used it to lubricate their wagons and carriages. Furthermore, Krypiakevych mentioned that in the chambers of the Cossack grandee, Khanenko, there were petroleum (nepht) lamps. Of course, it was an extremely rare and isolated case. The oil lamp was not yet widely known in Ukraine during the Hetman period.[26]

Among other minerals, the extraction of clay for the production of bricks and ceramics gained economic importance. It was used in the manufacture of chalices, jars, pots, candlesticks and other utensils. The industry developed all over Ukraine, wherever clay deposits were available. Dishes and household appliances made of clay were generally used by the people, along with wooden appliances, plates, spoons and jars. Only the upper classes could afford such things as china, silver and gold.

Moreover, the demand for clay also increased greatly in connection with the large-scale building construction projects of some Hetmans, such as Mazepa and Rozumovsky, some Cossack grandees and some monasteries. Bricks were needed in ever increasing numbers for the construction of churches, palaces and public buildings.

Sand was mined for various purposes, primarily for the construction and glass industries. Large lime grounds in the district of Novhorod Siverskii were famous for their output of lime for the building industries. Lime grounds were also available in West and Village Ukraine, and they were intensively exploited in order to meet the growing demands of industry. Outside the construction industry, lime was already used for scientific gardening and orchard care.

1. O. Ohloblyn, *Dumky pro Khmelnychchynu,* New York, 1957, pp. 12-15.

2. M. Slabchenko, *Orhanizatsia hospodarstva Ukrainy,* Part I, *Hospodarstvo Hetmanshchyny,* Odessa, 1923, pp. 19-20.

3. *Ibid.*, pp. 75-77.

4. K. Kononenko, *Ukraine and Russia, A History of the Economic Relations between Ukraine and Russia, 1654-1917,* Milwaukee, 1958, pp. 8-9; A. Nesterenko, I. Romanenko, and D. Vyrnyk, *Ocherki rozvitia narodnavo khaziaistva Ukrainskoi SSR,* Moscow, 1954, pp. 23-27; also V. Miakotin, *Ocherky sotsialnoi istorii Ukrainy v 17-18 vv.* Prague, 1924, Part II, p. 6.

5. O. Ohloblyn, *Hetman Ivan Mazepa ta yoho doba,* New York, 1960, pp. 77-78; Nesterenko, *op. cit.*, p. 19.

6. D. Doroshenko, *Narys istorii Ukrainy,* Munich, 1966, Vol. II, pp. 234-235; P Yefymenko, "Posledniei koshevoi ataman Zaporozhskoi Sichi", *Russkaia starina,* Kiev, 1875, Book XI; the same, "Posledniei pisar Voiska Zaporozhskavo Hloba", *Kievskaia starina,* Kiev, 1882, Book VIII.

7. Ohloblyn, *op cit.*, pp. 67-68; on the over-all economic situation at the time of Samoilovych and Mazepa, *ibid.*, pp. 65-77.

8. I. Dzhydzhora, "Ekonomichna polityka rosiiskoho pravytelstva suproty Ukrainy v 1710-1730 rokakh", *Zapysky Naukovoho Tov. im. Shevchenka,* Lviv 1910-1911, Vols. 98, 101, 103 and 105; I. Vytanovych, "Suspilno-ekonomichni tendentsii v derzhavnomu budivnytstvi Ivana Mazepy", *Papers,* Shevchenko Scientific Society, Chicago, 1959, pp. 11-16; M. Volobuyev, "Do problemy ukrainskoi ekonomiky", *Bilshovyk Ukrainy,* Jan. and Feb. 1928, Nos. 2-3; B. Vynar, *Rozyvtok ukrainskoi lehkoi promyslovosty,* Denver, 1955.

9. Doroshenko, *op. cit.*, Vol. II, pp. 236-238.

10. V. Sichynsky, *Ukraine in Foreign Comments and Descriptions from the VIth to XXth Century,* New York, 1953, pp. 125, 146-149; G. de Beauplan, *Description d'Ukraine,* New York, 1959, p. 448 and other.

11. J. Marshall, *Travels through Holland, Flanders, Germany, Denmark, Sweden, Lapland, Russia, Ukraine and Poland in the Years 1768, 1769 and 1770,* London, 1773, pp. 165-166, 175-182; also, Sichynsky, *op cit.*, pp. 152-155.

12. *Ibid.*, p. 162; other authors: pp,. 96, 124 and other pages.

13. I. Krypiakevych, "Pobut", *Istoria ukrainskoi kultury,* Winnipeg, 1964, pp. 110.

14. Marshall, *op cit.*, 172-174.

15. D. Bahalii, "Generalnaia opis Malorossii", *Kievskaia starina,* 1883; the same, *Istoria Slobidskoi Ukrainy,* Kharkiv, 1918; the same, *Materialy dla istorii kolonizatsii i bita stepnoi okrainy Moskovskavo gosudarstva,* Kharkiv, 1886. Bahalii published considerable materials on the history of the Ukrainian borderlands, in particular, in its social and economic projection.

16. Ohloblyn, *op cit.*, pp. 196-204, 241-244.

17. R. Kobrynsky, "Lis i myslyvstvo v davnim ukrainskim pravi," *Ukrainskyi lisnytskyi almanakh,* New York, 1958, pp. 73-76; A. Kostiakovsky, *Prava, po kotorym sudytsia malorossiiskii narod,* Kiev, 1879, articles 15/4, 17/8, 19/1, 2, 3, 4, 5, 7, 8, 12, 22/9; also, the *Lithuanian Statute* from 1588; A Yakovliv, "Ukrainskyi kodeks 1743," *Zapysky Naukovoho Tov. im.* Shevchenka, Munich, 1949, Vol. 159.

18. A. Stadnicki, "O wsiach t.zw. woloskich", *Biblioteka Ossolinskich*, Lviv, 1848; N. Freischyn-Czyrowski, *Geschichtlicher Abriss der staatsrechtlichen Einrichtungen in Galizien*, doctoral dissertation, Graz, 1943, pp. 99-100; M. Hrushevsky, *Istoria Ukrainy-Rusy*, New York, 1955, Vol. VI, pp. 156-158.

19. Doroshenko, *op. cit.*, Vol. II, pp. 234-235; N. Fr.-Chirovsky, *Old Ukraine, Its Socio-Economic History prior to 1781*, Madison, N.J., 1963, p. 273; On the over-all economic development of Ukraine during the Cossack-Hetman era: N. Polonska-Vasylenko, *Istoria Ukrainy*, Munich, 1976, Vol. II, pp. 179-191.

20. B. Krupnytsky, *Hetman Danylo Apostol*, Augsburg, 1948, pp. 139-140.

21. *Ibid.*

22. O. Ohloblyn, *Dumky pro Khmelnychchynu*, p. 13.

23. Bahalii, *Istoria Slobidskoi Ukrainy*, p. 166; the same, *Materialy*, p. 37; Ohloblyn, *Hetman Ivan Mazepa*, pp. 74-75.

24. O. Ohloblyn, "Khmelnychchyna i zaliznorudna promyslovist pravoberezhnoi Ukrainy," *Zapysky Naukovoho Tov. im. Shevchenka*, Munich, 1948, Vol. 156, p. 136, in particular.

25. Hrushevsky, *op. cit.*, Vol. VI, pp. 212-217; Weihe asserted that the Ukrainians had salt and iron mines: Sichynsky, *op. cit.*, p. 125; Doroshenko, *op. cit.*, Vol. II, p. 235; the Cossacks exported annually over one thousand carloads of salt to Poland alone.

26. Krypiakevych, *op. cit.*, pp. 109, and 170-171.

CHAPTER THIRTEEN

TRADES AND INDUSTRIES

Mercantilism in Ukraine — The city and its economy — Trades and crafts — Textile and leather production — Metallurgy and arms — Chemical industries — Glass and ceramics — Paper industry

Mercantilism in Ukraine. The creation of the Ukrainian national state advanced the popularity of the mercantilistic doctrine in the country, especially in the areas under Hetman domination. Great Hetmans, such as Khmelnytsky, Mazepa and Apostol, understood well that a country's wealth can substantially facilitate its political aspirations.

The mercantilist doctrine in the economic and business affairs of Ukraine first became clearly evident, however, during Mazepa's Hetmanate. Mazepa was not only educated along West European patterns, but he also traveled extensively throughout France, Poland, the Netherlands and Muscovy, where he acquired a direct and comprehensive knowledge of mercantilism. Jean Baluse, a French diplomat who visited the Ukrainian capital city of Baturyn in 1704, wrote: "...I myself saw French and Dutch newspapers in his (Mazepa's) study."[1] Mazepa kept himself well informed about cultural, political and economic developments in West Europe.

Mazepa's interest in the economic affairs of his nation was comprehensive. He sought the harmonious growth of the Ukrainian economy. First of all, he wanted to reduce the social tensions in the Hetman state. He endeavored to protect the lower classes, both townspeople and peasants, from discrimination and exploitation by the upper classes. In his numerous decrees and universals he referred to the social and economic problems of the Ukrainian people. The best known are his decrees of 1687, 1688, 1696 and 1698, the intention of which was a protection of the town, and those of 1692, 1701 and 1708, which were designed to defend and protect the village population from the abuses of the privileged social strata.

Mazepa most extensively assisted, protected and supported commerce and manufacturing through the legal confirmation of the property and operational rights of the Cossacks, merchants and industrialists to mine, process, produce and distribute their products. He sponsored the colonization of depopulated areas. He also tried by all means available to him, to alleviate Russian economic pressure, and to preserve Ukrainian economic autonomy.[2]

The later Hetmans, Skoropadsky, Apostol and Rozumovsky were also mercantilistically minded in their economic policies. Skoropadsky and Apostol had to concentrate all their efforts on the protection of Ukrainian commercial interests against the discriminatory policies of the Russian government, designed to build a great imperial market. Decrees were issued to prohibit the abuses of local administrative authorities. Skoropadsky attemped to regulate commercial credit, which was endangered by Muscovite trade restrictions.

Hetman Apostol seriously undertook the job of regulating land ownership to facilitate agricultural efficiency, assisted capitalist circles, reserved certain industries for Ukrainians only and prohibited aliens from engaging in such industrial activities as the exploitation and processing of iron ore and saltpetre. Furthermore, he attempted to discourage the Russian colonization of Ukraine and to neutralize Russian discrimination. Moreover, Apostol assisted the country's financial and credit market, and tried to introduce a state budget of 144,000 rubles.[3]

Rozumovsky, the last Hetman of Ukraine, was also familiar with mercantilistic ideas. Like other great rulers of the Mercantilist era, he nursed dreams of splendor, of building the magnificent capital city of Ukraine, the city of Hlukhiv, with marvelous palaces, parks, theaters and an opera house, and of reconstructing other Ukrainian towns according to West European patterns. He was only partially successful. Since Russian pressure was already too powerful to resist, Rozumovsky tried in vain to preserve the economic autonomy of Ukraine.

Mercantilism actually had a twofold influence on Ukrainian economic development. In the first place, it had a favorable impact on the national economy of the Hetman State. In the second place, the mercantilistic policies of the Russian Tsars affected Ukrainian national economic interests most unfavorably. The Tsars desired to build an empire and an imperial market and, in the framework of these plans, they decided to turn Ukraine into a Russian province, making her an agricultural colony of the Russian national economy, where food and raw material could be cheaply bought and Russian finished products sold by Russian businessmen. The plan eventually succeeded.

Since the end of Hetman Vyhovsky's rule, and particularly since the tragedy of Poltava, St. Petersburg steadily and consistently proceeded to reduce Ukrainian economic autonomy and to bind her ever more closely to the imperial markets. All possible measures were used: political pressure and extortion, legislative acts, distorted interpretation of these acts, bribery, intrigues, plots, treason and direct physical violence.

First of all, the Russians desired to suppress certain highly competitive industries, such as textile, chemical, armament, saltpetre and tobacco production.

Secondly, the Russian government frequently insisted that certain Ukrainian goods be sold only in Russia, or only through Russia by the use of Russian ports. Hence the Tsars ordered heavy troop concentrations to tightly close the Ukrainian-Polish-Lithuanian borders, and to channel the entire Ukrainian foreign trade with the West through the ports of St. Petersburg, Riga and Arkhangelsk.

Thirdly, Russian merchants and industrialists who settled in Ukraine were protected and subsidized by the Tsarist government. Fourthly, financial measures were also used by the Russians to damage Ukrainian economic interest. In order to reduce the volume of Ukrainian manufacturing and trade, St. Petersburg tried to withdraw all gold and silver money from Ukraine by means of customs, tariffs and tax policies. Fifthly and finally, the large-scale colonization of Russians and foreigners in Ukraine wholeheartedly supported by the Russian government, was, no doubt, meant to keep Ukraine a Tsarist agricultural colony. Enormous land grants were given to numerous Russian and foreign nobles and merchants, such as the Dolgorukiis, Shermietievs, Weissbachs, Menshikovs, Golovkins, Stronganovs, Felz-Feins, Kornises, Filbers, Viazemskiis, Potiomkins and Vorontsovs. Russian and other foreign ethnic elements settled in all parts of greater Ukraine for the purpose of strengthening Russian political and economic interests in the country. Ukrainian economic interests were always and everywhere progressively disregarded by the Tsarist mercantilist and nationalistic policy. Village Ukraine, the Territory of the Cossack Host, as well as Hetman Ukraine, and later the right-bank provinces at the end of the eighteenth century after the partition of Poland, shared the same destiny of being opposed to ruthless contiguous colonization.

The City And Its Economy. The National Revolution and the decades which followed witnessed the accelerated growth of the Ukrainian city and town. Immediately after the Revolution, as Krypiakevich indicated, numerous new towns were established by spontaneous colonization, particularly in the southern borderlands. The old cities grew in size and wealth. In 1650, the typical town was still small. Among the hundred leading towns at that time, the population averaged from 600 to 3,000 people living in 200 to 500 houses, compared to a population of 120 to 180 people in 20 to 30 houses, ten years earlier.[4]

Hetmans Khmelnytsky, Samoilovych, Mazepa, Skoropadsky and Apostol understood the role of the city in the economic life of the nation. Consequently, they attempted to protect the townspeople against the abuses of the upper classes by making land grants of arable soil, pastures and forests to outstanding merchants and municipalities. They either confirmed the municipal autonomy of the Magdeburg order of the older cities, such as Kiev and Chernihiv, or granted the same right to new towns, such as Oster and Poltava, in order to enhance their commercial and industrial development. Within half a century the Ukrainian town had fully recovered from the economic consequences of Polish oppression and the destruction of war.

The commercial and financial standing of the cities must have been relatively high, since their appearance favorably impressed foreign visitors, who talked about their beauty, prosperity and cleanliness. In numerous tourist and travel guides, various Ukrainian fortresses, like Kamianets Podilsky, Bar, and Ochakiv, were described with distinction.

Foreign visitors and Ukrainian official records give a fair conception of commercial progress in the towns of independent Ukraine.[5] Some foreigners also described the ruins, destruction and decline of towns as a result of the Russian invasion of 1709.

During the entire Hetman period, Ukrainian towns were still defended by strong stone walls, frequently referred to by foreign travelers. The stone city walls began to disappear during the first decade of the nineteenth century, in the course of which the appearance and the nature of the East European city fundamentally changed. The old town of merchants and craftsmen became at that time a modern city of businessmen, capitalists and industrialists.

The Ukrainian cities and towns of the seventeenth and eighteenth centuries did represent heterogeneous structures of unequal economic significance. The small towns were still like big villages, where the population was largely mixed, the peasant and merchant classes living side by side. Agricultural and commercial activities took place concurrently. The townspeople owned horses, oxen, ploughs, and other equipment required for agriculture, but they were also merchants and craftsmen. The commercial and industrial elements progressively grew in the towns throughout the Hetman era, and the differentiation between village and town became more and more pronounced. The small towns, particularly in southern Ukraine, were subordinated to Cossack administration, which discouraged urban economies. In the towns the population universally consisted of merchants, craftsmen, Cossacks and peasants. The proportionate size of these social segments differed in various places. Some cities, such as Cherkasy, Kaniv, Korsun and other southern towns, were populated predominantly by Cossacks. In large cities, such as Kiev, Pereyaslav, Nizhyn, Chernihiv and Starodub, the most numerous class was the townspeople, and the Cossacks constituted but a small minority. Where Cossacks were in the majority, the townspeople suffered. Municipal autonomy was violated and the traditional rights of the merchants and artisans ruthlessly disregarded.

In every case, however, fluidity was maintained. Some Cossacks were gradually turned into merchants, and some wealthy merchants became Cossacks. On the other hand, there were cities with a predominantly mercantile and commercial population, such as Baturin and Novi Mlyny. Still other towns, like Pereyaslav, Kiev, and Nizhyn, being industrial in character, were populated primarily by craftsmen and artisans. But merchants usually constituted approximately 25-30 per cent of the townspeople and craftsmen and artisans 70-75 percent.[6]

Such large cities as Kiev, Novhorod Siversky, Starodub, Pereyaslav, Poltava, Nizhyn, Baturyn and Chernihiv were the real commercial and industrial centers of the country. Some of them — Kiev, Chernihiv, Pochep, Novhorod, Pohor and Starodub — had the municipal autonomy of the Magdeburg law from the Polish-Lithuanian period; other towns, like Oster, Poltava and Kozel, were granted that privilege by the Hetman courts, as mentioned above.

Taking advantage of their Magdeburg constitution, a number of cities occupied an outstanding place in the Ukrainian economy. The city of Kiev, so often referred to by foreign visitors, continued to be the spiritual, cultural, ecclesiastical and political focal point of the Ukrainian nation, and at the same time it was also an important market, the center of the silk, glass and paper industries. It not only possessed a Magdeburg constitution since the Polish era (1625), but it also enjoyed other privileges partially or completely denied to other towns. Among these were exemption from state taxes and tolls at certain times, exemption from compulsory military services, the absolute stapel right, unrestricted and free trading and manufacturing, and the full right of its urban population to acquire and own landed estates.

Although some other cities, such as Nizhyn, Pereyaslav and Chernihiv, had similar privileges, the abuses of the Cossack grandees and monasteries were more frequent there. The city of Starodub developed into a central market for the northern part of Left-bank Ukraine, and a center of the textile and metallurgical industries. The city of Hlukhiv grew commercially, along with Starodub, as a result of the rapidly expanding Ukrainian-Russian trade.

The city of Poltava became the center of the southern trade, especially for Hetman Ukraine and the Cossack Territory, and for trade with the Crimean Tartars. Korolovets and Nizhyn were the greatest international markets at that time. The city of Chernihiv was the outstanding center of glass, potash and metallurgical manufacturing. The city of Baturin was for a long time the capital of the Hetman State, and by serving in this capacity it also attained economic prominence.

In Right-bank and West Ukraine, the cities of Zhytomyr, Lviv, Lutsk, Uman, Kholm, Brody and a few others succeeded in attaining some commercial and industrial significance despite the discriminatory and oppressive policies of the Polish Crown. Lviv was an important market; Brody housed textile mills, particularly silk mills. In Village Ukraine there were also economically important towns, such as Chuhaiv, famous for furriers, Okhtyrka, a textile and glass manufacturing center and Vodolaki, the producer of rugs and carpets.

The rise of a strong mercantile stratum in the town began, according to Ohloblin, during Samoilovych's Hetmanate. During this era, it gradually took over commerce, crafts and manufacturing. By Mazepa's time, the city patricians were in complete control of the urban economy.

The mercantile families of the Dereviankos, Tomaris, Herzigs, Skorupis, Shyrais and Maksymovyches were among the most prominent patricians, enjoying prestige, political favoritism and material comfort. The rapidity of their rise is illustrated by two outstanding families, Maksymovych and Shyrai. Maksymovych was still poor in the 1650's. Thirty years later, his family was one of the wealthiest in the country. Spiridon Shyrai, on the other hand, started his mercantile career by trading hemp with Riga and Arkhangelsk. In the course of thirty years, he acquired considerable wealth.

During his life time he was regarded as a "prominent member of the Starodub city patriciate."

Many other representatives of the mercantile class became famous Cossacks, such as Ivan Zolotarenko, colonel of Nizhyn, Martin Nebaba, colonel of Chernihiv, and Michael Tisha, colonel of Volhinia.[7]

The masses, however, were relatively poor. They were city commoners, small merchants and commercial people, craftsmen, artisans and such professionals as painters, musicians and barber-surgeons. Normally, craftsmen and artisans were economically and socially lower than merchants. At the bottom of the town's social pyramid were the artisans who either had no formal professional training or, for some reason, were not admitted into the guilds. They were not allowed to practice their trades openly, and if caught doing so, they were severely prosecuted by guild and municipal authorities. Their workshops were demolished and they themselves were beaten and imprisoned.

The intensely growing conflict between guild craftsmen and non-guild artisans developed in close connection with the increasing Cossack pressure upon the town. The Cossacks (grandees and commoners) and the religious orders progressively increased their commercial and industrial activities, producing serious competition for the townspeople, especially in the non-Magdeburg cities. This competition was characterized by unfair trade practices, discrimination and open abuses on the part of the Cossacks and the monasteries, which took full advantage of their privileged social status.

Records indicate such abuses even in cities which possessed the freedoms of the Magdeburg constitution, like Pereyaslav and Nizhyn. Cossack grandees, such as Myrovych, Miklashevsky and Mokievsky, were among the most notorious offenders. In some instances, the Cossacks usurped municipal offices, but the city population usually did not mind this too much, since in this way they received some protection from abuses.

The mercantilistic minded Hetmans — Samoilovych, Mazepa, Skoropadsky and Apostol — did everything possible to protect the justified interests of the town by reaffirming the Magdeburg privileges, reserving trade exclusively for the cities, rebuking and punishing guilty Cossack grandees, and giving some additional benefits to the townspeople in order to compensate them for the violations of their interests.

On the whole, the social, political and economic position of the town was not uniform during the Cossack-Hetman period. In the first years of national independence, the city played a minor role due to the war and to class discrimination. Its growth began during Samoilovych's Hetmanate, and it flourished during Mazepa's time. Immediately after the catastrophe of Poltava, the city's economic situation worsened because of Russian commercial and industrial discrimination. But under the protective care of Hetmans Skoropadsky and Apostol, it somewhat recovered. In the 1760's, however, the town again began to deteriorate socially and economically. Rigid regimentation of trade by the resident Russian authorities, abuses of military requisitions, and discriminatory policies and illegal and exorbitant taxes had become intolerable.

The economic position of the town in the Polish dominated Right-bank and West Ukraine had also deteriorated. Municipal autonomy was completely suppressed by the Polish nobility, even in the cities where the Magdeburg constitution was theoretically binding. In the process, trade was destroyed by inequitable and discriminatory taxation, economic exploitation and national and religious oppression. If the townspeople tried to oppose this lawlessness, they were beaten, killed and robbed by the hirelings of the nobles. At the beginning of the eighteenth century, conditions became so desperate that in some instances the entire urban population planned to move to the country or to emigrate. In 1719, the townspeople of the city of Starokonstantiniv, for example, decided to leave.[8] Individual flights of city people were very numerous. The country became impoverished; its economy decayed.

The cities of Village Ukraine were in a slightly more favorable position. There, the Magdeburg townspeople had an opportunity to engage in trade and manufacturing on a large scale. Even there, Cossack pressures retarded these developments, but not nearly so much as in the Hetman state. As mentioned above, a few cities such as Kharkiv, Okhtyrka, Putyvl, Summy, Chuhaiv and Vodolaky attained economic prominence.

Trades and Crafts. During the Lithuanian-Polish period, there was a definite trend in the manufacturing industries. Some of these, such as metal processing, textile manufacturing, arms production, and jewelry manufacturing, were largely concentrated in the cities. Others, like forest exploitation, tar and potash production, milling and distilling, were located in the countryside where they complemented the manorial economies. At that time, however, the bulk of manufacturing was still done by city craftsmen and artisans, sponsored and regulated by the guild system.

In the second half of the seventeenth century, a new development appeared. Industrial entrepreneurship was progressively taken over by the Cossack grandees, by capitalistic merchant employers such as Shyrai, Maksymovy and Derevianko, and by monastic orders. The economic role of the small-scale handicraft master and his professional guild organization gradually declined.⁹ The modern factory system was thus born, although its growth was stunted for many years. At the same time, new forms of industrial production developed a consistent tendency to move away from the countryside, and to concentrate in cities where labor and market outlets were more readily available.

The artisans constituted the bulk of the city population; the proletarians outnumbered the wealthy segment of the merchants. Moreover, there were actually two strata among craftsmen and artisans, guild members and those who were not members of guilds. The growing conflict between these two groups was one of the social problems of the town. Although the guilds ruthlessly tried to preserve their position in the town's economy, they did not succeed for many reasons. First of all, their organization was antiquated, selfish and rigid, and did not meet the requirements of new developments. Secondly, the National Revolution fostered the spirit of freedom and considerably weakened the restrictive policies of the guilds. Thirdly, the growing population needed more industrial goods, while the guilds insisted on a *numerus clasus,* limited membership, and restricted production in order to secure a maximum volume of business and revenue for their members. Because the market was expanding, informally trained townspeople and Cossack commoners flourished as illegal craftsmen. The influx of the Cossack element in some urban communities was considerable, upsetting traditional social and economic patterns. Around 1770, in the Poltava regimental district, there were about 167 Cossack artisans who, without any compulsion to join the guilds, practiced various trades. Fourthly, the capitalistic merchant employers and Cossack grandees frequently preferred to hire for their industrial establishments artisans who were not formally trained since they were usually cheaper than guild members. Fifthly, the Hetman government, supporting the large-scale manufacturing of the upper classes, showed no particular preference for the guild organizations. Finally, some craftsmen were exempt from the authority of the guilds by law, and were directly subordinated to the Hetman court. Therefore, the traditional guild system was unable to survive so many disadvantages and gradually faded away, yielding to new forms of industrial manufacturing. Municipal records, the census and other documents listed many trades; butchers, millers, general bakers, bread bakers, roll bakers, grout makers, brewers, wax processors, candle makers, tanners, tailors, shoemakers, builders, turners, wheelers, kettlers, metal cutters, cannon and gun makers, sword makers, spinners, weavers, saddlers, rug and carpet makers, barrel makers, blacksmiths, key makers, goldsmiths, fishermen, barbers and many other specialized trades, many more than in the previous era.[10] In 1781, in Novhorod Siversky, there were thirty-six guilds with a total membership of about 1600. There was no recognizable uniformity or pattern in various towns, as far as the number and type of guilds and their membership were concerned.

Yet, in the eighteenth century, the guilds served as economic units in organizing production and distribution for the craftsmen, as charitable and quasi-religious organizations in protecting the morals of their members and in taking care of the needy, the orphans, and the ancient traditions. They also existed, as in the past, as military units, obliging their members to participate in defending the city in case of emergency.

In the village and countryside, a petty household craftsmanship developed to meet local needs as it had in the Kievan and Polish-Lithuanian eras. The peasants produced their own wool, linen, leather, boots, clothing, appliances, worktools (from clay, wood or metal), and processed their own food. These petty village artisans did not join any guilds. They were still serfs, subject to the authority of the nobles, Cossack grandees, the Church and the religious orders. In the middle-sized "kustar" establishments, they produced not to order but for a market, while in the large-sized factory-like manufacturing establishments of the upper classes and merchant employers, the peasant artisans occupied the position of hired skilled workers.

The processing of agricultural raw materials was unquestionably the leading industrial branch of the predominantly agricultural economy. This industry embraced dairy production, meat and fish processing, flour and grout manufacturing, distilleries and breweries, wine and drinking honey (mead) production, textile and leather manufacturing and tobacco processing. In many instances, the composition, organization and methods of production were similar to those of the previous Lithuanian-Polish era.

In leather processing and shoe manufacturing, fur and tobacco processing, some change was noticeable. Here, business was either done in the traditional form of craftshops working on order, or it had progressed to the stage of "kustar" enterprises, of production for a free market in anticipation of demand. The "kustar" manufacturer usually employed a few workers in his cottage industry establishment, produced goods currently and sold them in the market through jobbers and distributors. The "kustar" enterprise, as a transitional step from handicraft shop to factory, also developed in linen, silk and woolen manufactures and in tobacco, candle and soap production. The real technological and organizational change was under way, however, in flour milling, textile manufacturing, and distilling and brewing, where modern, large-scale factory enterprises emerged and initiated modern industrial growth.

At this point it is important to indicate briefly the specific rent-lease system of business enterprise, widespread in Ukraine, and broadly applied, in particular, to the processing of agricultural raw materials, where the original owners reserved certain monopolistic rights such as the exploitation of forest resources (potash and tar manufacturing), alcohol production and distribution, milling and tobacco processing, or the renting of lakes, ponds and fishing rights. The nobility, Cossack grandees, religious orders, municipalities or the national government were the owners of the rights and properties and the lessors, while the gentry, Cossacks, rich merchants and foreigners and skilled craftsmen, like millers, brewers and distillers, were the lessees. Cossack grandees, such as Lomykovsky, Sylenko and Orlyk, leased state establishments and monopoly rights. Hetmans, like Mazepa and Apostol, often leased public property (distilleries and facilities for potash extraction and tobacco processing) to Cossacks, wealthy merchants and craftsmen, in order to secure better management and a higher revenue for the state. The lessees had to accumulate considerable capital to initiate their commercial ventures since they had to satisfy money-hungry lessors, to finance the acquisition of necessary building and equipment, and to provide for the risk of possible land expansion."Through the system of rent-lease," Yaroshevych says, "the early capitalists penetrated the Ukrainian national economy."[11]

The rent-lease agreements, usually signed for long periods of time, imposed obligations upon the lessors and lessees and gave them rights enforceable in the courts of law. For example, among other things, the lessee had to take good care of the establishment, be honest, pay an annual monetary rent, and supply the lessor with the produce of the business.

Within the peasant, Cossack, manorial and monastic farm economies, butter, buttermilk, sour milk, sour cream and various kinds of cheese were produced. Particularly in the Wallachian villages, special kinds of tasty cheeses were made from cow, goat and sheep milk. Much in demand, these cheeses were shipped as far as northern Galicia, Volhinia, Podillia and even southern Poland. Methods of production were traditional and primitive.

Meat and fish were processed either in the manorial economies or by special craftsmen, such as butchers, sausage makers and fishmongers, or raw meat and fish were purchased by dealers and processed in their "kustar" establishments. A guild of butchers existed in various cities, indicating a developed meat processing industry.

Fish was dried, canned, smoked and exported in great quantities. In other parts of Ukraine, meat was processed in a similar manner, and various meat products, such as sausages, ham, salt pork, fillets, black puddings and other specialties were salted, dried, smoked and sold in the local markets or at the fairs and also exported.

Large-scale manufacturing in flour milling, distilling, brewing and textile production was initiated during the second half of the seventeenth century. The upper levels of Ukrainian society did not initially show much interest and enthusiasm for manufacturing until that time. Social prejudices, regulations, wars, a shortage of capital and a poorly developed credit system seriously hampered the growth of industries.

Only when the Cossack grandees were able to acquire considerable capital through skillful and thrifty management of their large landed estates and the sale of their produce, and when the merchants accumulated some wealth as a result of their trading activities, could large-scale manufacturing, requiring considerable capital investments and risks, successfully emerge. Of course, the rapidly growing population and the consequent increased demand were the primary reasons for the great industrial change. In the eighteenth century, Ukraine was already fairly industrialized, more so than such neighbors as Poland, Lithuania and Wallachia, and in some respects, Muscovy.

Mills were the prototype of big manufacturing since the sixteenth century. As in pre-revolutionary times, various kinds of mills continued to exist during the Cossack-Hetman period, with a definite trend, however, toward a factory-like establishment. Water, wind, horse and hand mills, small, medium and large mills, with one, two or three wheels, operated throughout the country, while water mills became a large-scale enterprise of predominant economic importance. The capacity of the mills was measured by the number of wheels, ranging from one to twelve or more. Nesterenko said that the peasants and common Cossacks ran the small, one, two, or three-wheel mills, while mills of the upper classes had many wheels. Cossack grandees and merchant employers frequently owned a number of milling establishments.[12] Large mills served the national market and the export market as well. Traditionally, the mills not only ground flour and grouts, but they also operated adjunct saw mills, paper mills, wool pulling mills and gunpowder production.

Because of their many uses, water mills became larger and more numerous during the Hetman era, and very profitable, too. Not infrequently, water mills were established in convenient, although not yet settled areas. New villages soon sprang up around them. The type and volume of business varied from one area to another. According to the census of 1666, the city of Oster with its 21 establishments represented the greatest concentration of mills. The mills were owned primarily by wealthy merchants.

Similar ratios of ownership prevailed in other sections of the country. The census of 1666 registered 173 mills in 118 towns. Mills were numerous in Volhinia, Podillia, Poltava and Village Ukraine. Later the Chernihiv region was added to the list. In 1779-1781, there were already 597 mills in this area.

The industry also grew in other sections of the country. In West Ukraine they were largely owned by the Polish gentry and rented by professional millers. The manorial economies derived considerable revenues from their milling monopolies.

Flour was exported to Byeloruthenia, Muscovy, Lithuania and, in particular, the Cossack Host. It was also consumed in great quantities at home, being processed in every household, as well as by numerous general bakers, bread bakers and roll bakers.

Another important sector of the industry, the large-scale processing of agricultural raw material, was the traditional manufacture of alcoholic beverages of all kinds: brandy, rye, whiskey, vodka, beer, wine and drinking honey. All segments of the population were deeply involved in the industry which included household distilling and brewing by almost every family for domestic and local consumption, from the "kustar" type of wine and drinking-honey production, up to the factory-like processing for nationwide distribution and export done by the Cossack grandees, capitalistic merchants, municipalities, and monasteries. At the end of the seventeenth and the beginning of the eighteenth centuries, distilleries and breweries developed into large enterprises, producing mainly for a profitable export business.[13]

Production of strong drinks (whiskey, rye, brandy, vodka and beer) took place prior to the Revolution largely on a monopolistic basis. Alcohol was distilled by the village and town population, either illegally or with permission for special occasions, Holy days, holidays, weddings, baptisms, funerals, in return for payment to the lords. The National Revolution broke down the monopolistic principle to a great extent, and made alcohol processing a relatively free business. In the Chernihiv regimental district for example, a large segment of all the social classes made a living from making and selling alcoholic drinks, such as vodka and beer. Large distilleries and breweries were to be found throughout the country, in the Chernihiv, Kiev, Poltava, Volhinia, Galicia, Podillia and Village Ukraine regions.

Wine and drinking-honey production was also widespread, but it took place on a small scale within the household or "kustar" establishment. There were no large enterprises in this field. Manufacturing of drinking honey developed extensively in connection with the widespread occupation of agriculture, which was quite extensive in the Chernihiv and Poltava regimental districts, the Territory of the Cossack Host and Village Ukraine.

Wine was made not only from grapes, but also from all kinds of fruit— apples, cherries, pears and plums — as well as from bread. The wineries were small establishments, often located on rivers to secure water for the processing.

There are some statistics available, especially for the second half of the eighteenth century, which may serve as a quantitative sampling of the production volume of alcoholic drinks. In 1722, there were some 235 distilleries in the Poltava regimental district. In 1779-1781, some 392 distilleries operated in the Novhorod Siversk districts; and some 87 breweries and 201 malt-houses in the Chernihiv district. In West Ukraine (Volhinia, in particular), distillery was widespread. Alcohol was made from rye, barley, buckwheat and other grains. Three types of "vodka," *horilka*, were produced, simple, ordinary and double, also called "Danzig brand."

Breweries were usually larger establishments than distilleries, employing a large number of workers. They produced two kinds of beer, ordinary and extra-strong. Lease-rent operation was also the customary way of business for breweries.

Distribution of alcoholic beverages was achieved through fairs, taverns, dealers and market places. As in the previous period, there were taverns that specialized, selling only vodka, whiskey, brandy and rye; others sold wine and drinking-honey; still others, wine and beer, or beer exclusively. Taverns were operated mainly as manufacturers' outlets and were leased to tavern keepers. There were also dealers who bought beverages from the manufacturers, delivered them to fairs throughout the country, and also shipped them to Muscovy, Lithuania, Byeloruthenia, Poland and the Cossack Territory. Drinking-honey was exported in quantity to Muscovy and Byeloruthenia. Vodka and whiskey were also important export items.

Along with the business of apiculture and honey production, still other derivative industries developed in the eighteenth century, namely the manufacturing of candles and soap. Wax candles were produced throughout the country, at first as a petty household industry in the manors to supply lighting for their household needs. Then small "kustar" establishments emerged to produce candles in the cities. Gradually these developed into large-scale enterprises. As supplementary to candle and soap production, two other types of manufacturing entered the market: wax pressing and fat melting, supplying raw materials to the candle and soap industries.

At the end of the eighteenth century, soap manufacturing took place in all parts of Ukraine. It was limited to small-scale enterprises, and suffered from an inadequate supply of skilled workers.[14]

Tobacco manufacturing was another important industry processing agricultural materials. The growing of tobacco, like the cultivation of mulberry trees, was discussed previously. Raised all over Ukraine, tobacco was processed mainly on a petty household scale. The Tsarist government insisted on semi-fiscal tobacco processing, and did not allow any competitive, large-scale, factory tobacco manufacturing in the Hetman State. Raising tobacco leaves was encouraged but raw material had to be delivered to the monopolistic state tobacco factories for processing. In the Okhtyrka factory, skilled foreigners, principally from the Netherlands, and students and soldiers were employed.

Otherwise, peasants, townspeople, Cossacks and religious orders raised and processed their own tobacco, particularly in the Lubni, Hadiach, Nizhyn, Romni, Ivanhorod, Oster and Uman regions. It was sold domestically in large quantities at the fairs and market places, and was greatly sought after because of its good quality.[15]

Textile and Leather Production. Textile manufacturing, including linen, wool, silk and cotton goods, was one of the oldest and most important industries of the national economy of Hetman Ukraine. In the Kievan Empire and the Lithuanian-Rus' Commonwealth, various materials, crude and fine, bleached and unbleached, were manufactured for clothing, sails, nets, rugs and carpets. With the progress of civilization and the increasing density of population, the industry naturally had to grow. Hence, a great variety of textiles was produced in the household, craftsman's workshop, "kustar" establishment and textile factory during the Cossack-Hetman period, and sold domestically and abroad. Looms were found literally in every household and home, said Ohloblyn, and Aksakov added that whatever the peasants wore as clothing was exclusively the product of their own land.[16]

Of course, the extensive hemp and flax growing and sheep breeding were closely connected with textile manufacturing and processing. Large-scale, factory-like textile enterprises began to develop in Mazepa's time, as a consequence of the clothing requirements of the modernized Ukrainian and Russian armies. In the seventeenth century, large textile establishments manufacturing linen and woolen yardgoods existed in various locations.

Immediately after the Poltava defeat, Ukrainian linen and woolen production declined, as did other industries, as a result of the Russian invasion and the Russian economic measures in occupied Ukraine; but in Apostol's and Rozumovsky's time production recovered. Sichynsky noted that in the second half of the seventeenth and in the eighteenth centuries, the textile industry experienced continuous fluctuations, reflecting the unstable political Ukrainian autonomy resulting from the changing policies of St. Petersburg.

Concurrently, the linen industry also expanded, to supply shirts, underwear, sails, nets, ropes, cordage and other appliances that were demanded in connection with the development of the Russian navy on the Black and Azov Seas, the growth of armed forces and the emergence of commercialized fishing.

The volume of output of the woolen and linen factories can be estimated on the basis of the fractional statistical data, so far available. Probably the oldest textile factory, a woolen mill, was erected in Putyvl, Village Ukraine, in 1719. In 1722, it already had 455 workers, Russians, Ukrainians and foreigners. Colonel Horlenko established a factory in the village of Riashkiv, in the Chernihiv regimental district. Pay scales differed according to the type of work and skill. A skilled material worker received 24 rubles per year; an apprentice, 10 rubles; a carpenter, 8 rubles; a wool-master, 36 rubles. Hetman Kyrylo Rozumovsky erected a textile factory in the city of Baturyn in 1756, at first operating only 12 machines. The largest linen manufacturing establishment was in Pochep. Established in 1726, it employed 221 workers at 63 benches. Such enterprises were relatively large for the time.

The production of rugs, carpets and embroidery, also one of the ancient Ukrainian industries, developed as a separate branch of textile manufacturing during the Cossack-Hetman era.

In the seventeenth and eighteenth centuries, rugs and carpets were manufactured in individual households by all segments of the population. However, there were also establishments of skilled craftsmen and "kustar" enterprisers who produced them on order or for the market. Cossack grandees, merchant employers and monasteries penetrated the field in an attempt to mass produce rugs, carpets and embroideries. Such factories were established in Nemyriv, Tulchyn, Zalozhtsi, and other towns. These carpets and rugs were distinguished for good quality, artistic design and the use of excellent dye stuffs. Embroidery became a cherished hobby of women as well as an important industry. Woolen, linen and silk materials were artistically embroidered in various colors, including gold and silver threads. Each region of the country began to develop its own style of the art.[17]

Production of silk was a growing industry in Cossack-Hetman Ukraine. Thus, mulberry trees were raised in gardens and plantations in Pereyaslav, Nizhyn, and Kharkiv and Okhtyrka in Village Ukraine. In the city of Brody in Galicia, a silk mill existed since 1641, which produced silk materials, well dyed and with golden and silver embroideries in clearly oriental patterns. In 1724, similar silk establishments were founded in Kiev, Korsun, Sokal, Nemyriv, Kremenchuk, Kharkiv and Okhtyrka. Okhtyrka was especially famous for its silk shawls.

The Poltava event also unfavorably affected this industry, and it was not until the 1720's that silk manufacturing really recovered.

It must be stressed again that the development, growth and decline of the Ukrainian textile industries were conditioned by the economic policies of the Tsarist government. The Russian policy of keeping Ukraine as a source of raw material and an outlet for Russian finished goods prevailed. Hence, the Russians opposed in every way possible the industrialization of textile manufacturing. But this policy was not consistent. Urgent needs sometimes forced the Russian government to favor manufacturing in Ukraine, particularly, that of those textiles including garments, sails, nets, tents and similar items of military importance.

Yet, Ukrainian manufacturers were discriminated against by means of tolls, tariffs, exorbitant taxes and downright chicaneries. The most prosperous linen establishment in Pochep was dismantled in 1754 and shipped to Russia.

Nesterenko stressed the great interest on the part of the Russian government in developing raw silk production in Ukraine. For 75 years the experiment was continued. Peasants and Cossacks, raising the mulberry trees, were offered various benefits, like exemption from military service and from certain taxes and tolls, and guaranteed the purchase of all raw silk by the state.

Leather manufacturing evolved along with large-scale craftshops of "kustar" establishments, although the extent and volume of its production were tremendous; for only leather shoes and boots were worn in Ukraine, according to foreign travelers. The artisans who processed leather and manufactured leather goods — the tanners, shoemakers, and saddlemakers, the belt, glove and leather cap manufacturers — were generally poor, and their shops were usually located in their homes. Each province had its center for the leather industry: the towns of Korop and Olishivka in the Chernihiv region; Okhtyrka, Sumy, Valky and Nova Vodolaka in Village Ukraine; the cities of Zhytomyr, Berdychiv and Porytsk in Volhinia. The annual income of the small leather "kustar" establishments did not generally exceed 100-300 rubles. By the end of the eighteenth century, some large-scale leather establishments had been started in the regions of Novhorod Siversk, Volhinia and Tavria.

Furriery was another segment of the animal skin processing business, fairly developed, but with a lesser economic significance than it had in the earlier periods of Ukrainian history. As before, furs were processed for winter clothing, for decorating living chambers, and for export.[18] In Hetman Ukraine, the city of Oster was an important center of fur and fur garment production.

Metallurgy and Arms. Metallurgical, chemical, wood and construction industries developed under less favorable conditions than the processing of agricultural raw materials. As long as Ukraine preserved its sovereignty or at least an extensive autonomy, they prospered; but when in the eighteenth century Russian pressure was intensified, St. Petersburg, while still tolerant of the processing of agricultural produce because of its strategic importance, ruthlessly tried to liquidate other industries. Of course, this was a violation of Ukrainian autonomy and of the original articles of the Pereyaslav Treaty (1654), but the Muscovites thought it essential to eliminate the competition of Ukrainian manufacturers from the East and Central European markets.[19] Thus, metallurgy, the armament industry in particular, chemical industries, paper manufacturing and printing were reduced or eliminated by the end of the eighteenth century. These industries, however, grew impressively during the first decades of Ukrainian statehood, at least, until the defeat at Poltava.

It is interesting that the Ukrainian Hetmans, Apostol particularly, by not importing Russian iron and other metals, avoided dependence upon Russian supplies. This is a good example of Ukrainian mercantilistic thinking.

In the Hetman times, specialized metallurgical trades existed, such as smelters, smiths, sword makers, kettlers, gun and cannon makers, key and locksmiths, bell founders, zinc processors, watch makers, goldsmiths and many others. Metallurgical manufacturing was done extensively throughout the country, usually in workshops of "kustar" establishments. Metal processing in large factories was rare, except in armament and bell production, which was usually sponsored by the government, or by the Hetmans, Cossack grandees and monasteries.

The production of arms and weapons was certainly the most important sector of metallurgy. In the years of frequent wars, there was a great demand for all kinds of weapons. In all cities and manorial possessions, skilled craftsmen manufactured arms in the seventeenth and eighteenth centuries. Some of these were Ukrainian, of whom three were outstanding; Andrew, Luke, and Matthew; some were German, like Weisse, Froehlich, and Herle; and some were Czech, e.g., Krahl. Their craftsmanship was excellent, known at home and abroad and frequently associated with artistry.[20] Shields, swords, cannons and guns were ornamented with artistic metal carvings and engravings.

During the Revolution, the demand for arms increased greatly. In the Hetman state, armament establishment-craftshops, "kustar" enterprises, and small factories developed throughout the nation, yet were concentrated in the city of Starodub, followed by the cities of Nizhyn, Pochep, Novhorod Siversky, Hlukhiv, Pereyaslav and Kiev.

Cannons were made from iron and copper. Hetman Mazepa established a state arms factory, managed by Friedrich Koenigseck, a German born, Commander-in-Chief of Hetman artillery. Mazepa himself intensively studied the problems of artillery. He was very much interested in the production of arms and weapons, and supported the industry in every way possible, in view of his long-range plans for a war against Muscovy-Russia. After the Poltava defeat, however, Peter the Great ordered the liquidation of all Ukrainian arms and weapons manufacturing. All supplies of firearms and cannons were confiscated and taken to Russia. Later on, Hetman Apostol tried to re-establish the manufacture of cannons, guns and other weapons in Ukraine, but he was not very successful.

The same fate overtook the production of saltpeter and gunpowder. Saltpeter mining and processing and gunpowder manufacturing developed in Ukraine for many decades. The Cossacks were very proficient at producing gunpowder in their own territory. Nobles also made their own gunpowder, by mining saltpeter and making gunpowder production a supplement to their flourmills and sawmills. Even peasants manufactured gunpowder for their own limited use.

During the Revolution, Hetman Khmelnytsky temporarily made saltpeter extraction and gunpowder manufacturing a state monopoly. But immediately after the Revolution, individual initiative and free enterprise took over in the Hetman state. Cossack grandees, nobles, monasteries and capitalistic merchants indulged in the business extensively.

In 1713-1720, however, Peter the Great made the distribution of saltpeter an imperial monopoly. He ordered all saltpeter extracted in Ukraine to be sold exclusively through the state artillery stores in Moscow and St. Petersburg. In 1764, a decree prohibited gunpowder manufacturing in the Hetman state on the flimsy grounds that Ukrainian gunpowder was of inferior quality.[21]

As important as the manufacture of weapons was the manufacture of all kinds of tools and appliances for household, agriculture, trades and transportation. These tools were produced entirely or partially from metals such as iron, copper, tin and so forth.

Because of the deep religious devotion of the Ukrainian people, the manufacture of church bells continued to be an important and growing branch of metallurgy in Cossack-Hetman times. The city of Lviv was a traditional center of bell manufacturing since the fourteenth century. In Hetman Ukraine, bells were produced in left and right bank cities, such as Nizhyn, Starodub, Kiev, Pereyaslav and elsewhere. Iron, copper, bronze and brass were used in their manufacture. The bell-producing industry enjoyed particular protection from Hetman Mazepa, the great protector of the Church, culture, the arts and the economy. The industrialist, Karp Balashevich, engaged extensively in the manufacture of bells along with the large-scale production of huge pots and kettles for the distillery and brewery industries. He manufactured the famous "Pigeon" bell, with Mazepa's portrait and coat of arms, and rich ornamentation.

Jewelry manufacturing, with artistic ornaments and engravings, flourished in Hetman Ukraine. Goldsmiths' establishments, working with gold, silver and other valuable metals, manufactured watches and clocks in all major cities. Craftsmen were largely of Ukrainian descent, and ornamentations and engravings on the jewelry predominantly bore Ukrainian artistic motifs and patterns, as discussed above.

In West Ukraine, the Polish government continued to suppress jewelry manufacturing in Lviv, Zhovkva, Sianik and other cities, where it bore a strictly Ukrainian national character.

Chemical Industries. Gmelin, a German doctor and scientist, gave in his book a favorable picture of Ukraine, and expressed amazement at finding well developed chemical industries, saltpetre manufacturing, chemical and pharmaceutical plants, inoculation against smallpox, and other progressive manifestations of the country's economy and culture.[22] The saltpetre industry and lime processing have been discussed already. Both were considerable. Lime extraction took place in various parts of Ukraine and it was used extensively in construction and for painting dwellings. Lime was largely made in the household economy.

Potash and tar production was doubtlessly leading among the chemical industries, although its extent and output probably declined in Polish times. It was pointed out before that forests were greatly devastated and their reserves depleted as a result of ruthless exploitation. The government had to intervene in order to prevent a catastrophe. In numerous decrees, granting or reserving rights of tar and potash manufacturing to the Cossack grandees, monasteries, merchants and professional potash and tar producers, *budnyky*, the Hetmans attempted to regulate this business in which all classes of people were so greatly interested.

Some Hetmans owned and operated potash works. Among these was Mazepa whose works were in Pochep, Ropsk, Sheptakiv and Yampil. These plants were entirely administered by a Custodian of the Hetman Potash Establishments, and locally managed by special officials. Cossack grandees and noblemen manufactured potash and tar in connection with their enormous forest economies. Merchants, on the other hand, frequently organized companies and partnerships for the purpose of forest exploitation and potash and tar production. In many instances, potash and tar manufacturing was a family prerogative, either by tradition or by an affirmation of the Hetman office. At least ten villages today are called *Buda*, which means in Ukrainian "potash and tar works," thus indicating their historical significance as locations of that particular industry.

Then St. Petersburg attempted to suppress and even destroy this industry. Therefore, in 1718, Peter the Great issued an ordinance prohibiting the establishment of any new potash works in Ukraine. One year later, the Russians began to ship their potash extensively to Ukraine, trying to stifle Ukrainian production by fair and unfair competition.

Glass and Ceramics. In the Lithuanian-Polish era, glass manufacturing in Ukraine was a very modest one, as pointed out. It began to prosper in West Ukraine in the sixteenth century. The records made a reference to the glass works in Belz, Kalush and Horodenka districts in the 1560's, while the use of window glass was supposedly widely popular. In Right-bank Ukraine, glass works began to operate on a larger scale, first in the seventeenth century, in the towns on a guild and craft basis. Glass artisans were of foreign as well as Ukrainian descent. In the eighteenth century, glass manufacturing moved to the suburbs and countryside, and then, it was sponsored by the grandees and wealthy merchant employers, while being localized largely in the northern districts.

According to the eyewitnesses of that time such as Paul Alepo and Weihe, glass was widely used in Ukraine. Slabchenko indicated that even peasants produced glass for their household needs.[23] In the second half of the eighteenth century, glass was manufactured also in *Slobidska* Ukraine, for example, in the *sloboda*, village of Huta, Okhtyrka county. As a matter of fact, the term "huta" means "glass work" in Ukrainian, and it was generally used to identify the villages and towns where glass was produced. There are many villages today in Ukraine called "huta," the name being reminiscent of the days of glass manufacturing in those places, just as with the names of villages called "Ruda" (iron pit) and "Buda" (potash work). Sichinsky said that in Podillia there were 13 villages called Huta, in Volhinia, 9, and in the Kiev area,8.[24]

In Hetman times, glass manufacturing occurred on a large scale, in factory-like establishments owned by Hetmans, Cossack grandees, capitalistic merchants, the Church and monasteries as well. These glass works were operated on a rent-lease basis by professional masters of the trade. Artisans were primarily of Ukrainian descent, coming largely from Galicia and Volhninia, where the glass industry was traditional. The wages of the craftsmen and workers in the glass industry were flexible and depended upon the profitability of the business. The incentive system prevailed.

Window glass, special drinking vessels for wine, beer, whiskey and honey, cups, pots, bowls, plates, jars and vases were manufactured in these establishments. Window glass was at first only slightly transparent, but later beautiful glass, including stained glass mosaics, was produced. Other glass articles were usually ornamented with all kinds of patterns and figures, and with the identification marks of the manufacturing glass works. Glass and glassware were sold at market places, fairs and special glass stores and warehouses throughout Ukraine. In 1781, for instance, there were specialty glass stores in Starodub and Novhorod Siversky. Glass was also exported in large quantities to Muscovy, Lithuania and Byeloruthenia.

Among the owners of the large glass works were Hetmans Mazepa and Rozumovsky, the Cossack grandees and capitalistic merchants, known already because of their extensive business activities, such as Kochubey, Lomykovsky and Orlyk.

Along with glass production, the ceramics and pottery industries developed steadily because good raw material — caoline clay — was available in such parts of Ukraine as Kiev, Chernihiv, Poltava, and Volhinia provinces; they exhibited strong Greek and Roman influences in the Kievan era. After a decline, following the Mongol invasion, when output and quality decreased, a recovery followed at the end of the fifteenth century. This time the industry showed strong Western European influences.

In Hetman Ukraine, the ceramic and pottery industries grew impressively, especially in Right-bank Ukraine. Craftsmen were loosely organized into guilds. They manufactured a variety of appliances in almost all towns and in most of the countryside of Left-bank and Right-bank Ukraine. The production of tile was especially well developed; manufacturing technology was advanced; the produce was of good quality and beautifully ornamented. It was used for building stoves, hearths, and for beautifying walls.

The skill of the Ukrainian pottery artisans was so great that the Russians frequently bribed them by offering very high wages to bring them to Muscovy. The production of ceramics and pottery articles was frequently family business, especially in the countryside, and the trade was passed on from father to son.

China production was started in Ukraine in the 1760's in the village of Poloshky, Chernihiv colonelcy, where an excellent domestic clay was available for that purpose. The Russians, for example, imported hundreds of tons of Poloshky clay for their own domestic china manufacturing.

In connection with clay processing, brick manufacturing must be mentioned as growing in importance with the brick and stone construction industries. Initially, bricks were produced by traveling artisans who moved from one place to another, utilizing temporary brick works to meet existing demands. Later on, the Cossack grandees and religious orders began to establish permanent brick works on their landed possessions, to supply bricks for building walls, towers, churches, palaces, chimneys, stoves and hearths. Thus, in the eighteenth century, there were brick works in Kiev, Poltava, Kharkiv and other places in Ukraine.

The Paper Industry was not only economically significant, but served as an indicator of the society's intellectual life. The paper and printing industries were well developed in Hetman Ukraine. In the first half of the seventeenth century, paper production was a rather small-scale operation in the cities, and in the framework of the guild organization. In the second half of that century, the paper works were usually in the countryside, in noble, Cossack and Church possessions, where labor was cheap and raw materials readily available.

In early Hetman times, paper mills operated in the Kiev, Chernihiv, and Podillia districts producing several kinds of paper. Then, Hetman Mazepa directly established or indirectly sponsored several paper mills in the left-bank areas, mentioned in the records under the years 1748, 1779, and 1781. Paper from these establishments was always furnished with elaborate water marks, not infrequently bearing the image of Mazepa himself. Each individual paper mill used its own special marks to identify the origin of the product.

Northern Ukraine was the major site of the paper industry. The records mentioned 12 paper works in Chernihiv, 8 in Galicia and a number in Kiev. Large religious orders and the bishops of eparchies operated paper mills and print shops; some of these manufactured various kinds and qualities of paper annually.

The artisans in these works were initially of foreign (primarily German) descent, but in the eighteenth century they were predominately Ukrainian. Ukrainian youth were especially trained for jobs in the industry. The Ukrainian character of the industry was also indicated by the well developed Ukrainian technical terminology used in the paper mills.[25]

Production of paper grew rapidly in Hetman times. Paper was used primarily for printing ecclesiastical books and school textbooks, and for keeping records of the central and provincial governments' large private estates. As a matter of fact, paper production in Ukraine during that era was greater than that of the whole Russian Empire. Because of the increased output, paper prices declined steadily in the course of the eighteenth century.

1. V. Sichynsky, *Ukraine in Foreign Comments and Descriptions from the VI to XXth Century,* New York, 1953, p. 113.

2. M. Slabchenko, *Orhanizatsia hospodarstva Ukrainy,* Part I, *Hospodarstva Hetmanshchynyt, Odessa,* 1923, pp. 161-164; O. Ohloblyn, *Hetman Ivan Mazepa ta yoho doba,* New York, 1960, pp. 67-68, 244; about Mazepa's rule and his defense of Ukraine's economic interests: I. Vytanovych, "Suspilno-Ekonomichni tendentsii v derzhavnomu budivnytstvi Ivana Mazepay", *Papers,* Naukove Tov. im. Shevchenka, Chicago, 1959; N. Polonska-Vasylenko, *Istoria Ukrainy,* Munich, 1976, Vol. II, pp. 180-191.

3. B. Krupnytsky, *Hetman Danylo Apostol,* Augsburg, 1948, pp. 124-233; D. Doroshenko, *Narys istorii Ukrainy,* Munich, 1966, Vol. II, p. 184; also, E. Radakova, "Hetman D. Apostol v roli kolonizatora", *Kievskaia starina,* Kiev, 1891, Book VI.

4. I. Krypiakevych, *Bohdan Khmelnytsky,* Kiev, 1954, pp. 34-35, 294-295.

5. Sichynsky, *op. cit.*, excerpts from the relations of various foreign travelers and visitors in Ukraine in the seventeenth and eighteenth centuries, pp. 89-173.

6. Krypiakevych, *op. cit.*, pp. 35-42, 301 and other.

7. L. Okinshevych, *Lektsii z istorii ukrainskoho prava*, Munich, 1947, pp. 53-54; Ohloblyn, *op. cit.*, 102-105, and the reference notes, pp. 154-156; Krypiakevych, *op. cit.*, pp. 307-309.

8. Ohloblyn, *op. cit.*, pp. 200-201.

9. V. Sichynsky, *Narys istorii ukrainskoi promyslovosty*, Lviv, 1936, pp. 95, 101 and other: The decline of the guild organization adversely affected metal and wood processing.

10. Krypiakevych, *op. cit.*, 35-36, 300-309; A Nesterenko, *Rozvytok promyslovosty na Ukraini*, Part I, *Remeslo i manufaktura*, Kiev, 1959, pp. 93-94; P. Klymenko, *Tsekhy na Ukraini*, Kiev, 1929, Vol. I.

11. A. Yaroshevych, "Kapitalistychna orenda na Ukraini za Polskoi doby," *Zbirnyk Sotsialno-Ekonomichnoho Viddilu*, Ukrainska Akademia Nauk, Kiev, 1927, Vol. I, pp. 116-259; I. Baranovich, *Magnatskoie khaziaistvo na yuge Volini v XVIII v.*, Moscow, 1955, pp. 117-137; Ohloblyn, *op. cit.*, pp. 82-83.

12. Nesterenko, *op. cit.*, p. 183; Ohloblyn, *op. cit.*, p. 71; the same, "Hetman I. Mazepa i ukrainska promyslovist," *Kalendar Svobody na mazepynskyi rik*, 1959, Jersey City, N.J., 1959, p. 105; Krypiakevych, *op. cit.*, pp. 301-303; Baranovich, *op. cit.*, pp. 68-71.

13. Sichynsky, *Ukraine in Foreign Comments*, pp. 100 and 125.

14. N. Fr.-Chirovsky, *Old Ukraine, Its Socio-Economic History prior to 1781*, Madison, N.J., 1963, p. 307; on the economy of Ukraine at the Cossack-Hetman era more comprehensively and with considerable bibliographical material: *ibid.*, pp. 250-363.

15. Nesterenko, *op. cit.*, 325-326; in Village Ukraine, A. Nesterenko, I. Romanenko, and D. Vyrnyk, *Ocherky Rozvitia Narodnavo Khaziastva Ukrainskoi S.S.R.*, Moscow, 1954, p. 21; also Krupnytsky, *op. cit.*, pp. 143-144; Sichynsky, *op. cit.*, pp. 162-163: Hueldenstaedt's report of 1774.

16. I. Aksakov, *Issledovanie o torgovle na ukrainskikh yarmarkakh*, St. Petersburg, 1858; Sichynsky, *op. cit.*, pp. 99-100, 106-107, 158-159: the reports of Hildebrandt, Werdum and Gmelin from the seventeenth and eighteenth centuries. In most households looms were a standard equipment: O. Ohloblyn, *Ocherky istorii ukrainskoi fabryky, manufaktura v Hetmanshchyni*, Kiev, 1925, p. 87.

17. Ukrainian textile industry: Nesterenko, *op. cit.*, pp. 150-152, 158-160, 235-236, 287-288; P. Lyashchenko, *History of the National Economy of Russia*, New York, 1949, pp. 287-292; K. Kononenko, *Ukraine and Russia, A History of the Economic Relations between Ukraine and Russia, 1654-1917*, Milwaukee, 1958, pp. 23; S. Szuman, *Dawne kilimy w Polsce i na Ukrainie*, Poznan, 1929.

18. Nesterenko, *op. cit.*, pp. 172-173; Sichynsky, *op cit.*, pp. 162 and other.

19. Ukrainian commerce under the Russian presesure: I. Dzhydzhora, *Ukraina v pershii polovyni XVIII viku, Ekonomichna polityka rossiiskoho pravytelstva suproty Ukrainy v 1710-1730 rokakh*, Kiev, 1930, pp. 8-9, 20-21, 28 and many other; Kononeneko, *op. cit.*, pp. 22-28.

20. Sichynsky, *op. cit.*, pp. 87-90; I. Krypiakevych and B. Hnatevych, eds., *Istoria ukrainskoho viiska*, Winnipeg, 1953, pp. 74, 259-262, 272-274.

21. A. Nesterenko, *Rozvytok promyslovosty na Ukraini*, Part I, *Remeslo i manufactura*, Kiev, 1959, pp. 315-316; Krupnytsky, *op. cit.*, p. 147.

22. Sichynsky, *op. cit.*, p. 159: O. Ohloblyn, "Do istorii budnytskoi promyslovosty Ukrainy za chasiv Khmelnychchyny", *Zapysky Istorychno-Filolohichnoho Viddilu*, Ukrainska Akademia Nauk, Kiev, 1927, Bool. X, pp. 303-310.

23. Slabchenko, *op. cit.*, Part II, pp. 147-149.

24. Ohloblyn, *loc. cit.*; Sichynsky, *Narys istorii* ..., pp. 23-24; O. Ohloblyn, *Dumky pro Khmelnychchynu*, New York, 157, pp. 12-13; Slabchenko, *op. cit.*, Part II, 146-153.

25. On the paper industry and book printing: Chirovsky, *op. cit.*, pp. 323-326; J. Ptasnik, *Papiernie w Polsce w XVI w.* Cracow, 1920, pp. 15, 17, 20, 34-35; I. Ohienko, *Istoria ukrainskoho drukarstva*, Lviv, 1925: Sichynsky, *Ukraine in Foreign Comments* ..., p. 95, 132.

CHAPTER FOURTEEN

COMMERCE AND FINANCE

Transportation and communication — Domestic commerce — Foreign trade, its development and composition — Foreign trade policies — Money and credit — Public finance

Transportation and Communication. With the overall growth of the Ukrainian economy and particularly with the growth of regional specialization, the need for more efficient transportation and communication became more pronounced. On the other hand, traveling was an integral and important part of the social life of that time. People traveled a great deal. Travel was also a demanding venture, because of such inconveniences as great distances and poor roads.

Most travel was by land rather than by water. Such trips were made along the *hostinets*, highway, broad dusty roads with no marks of identification. Traditional routes connected various regions of the country. In West Ukraine this network of highways was better developed, enabling more efficient commerce with Western Europe. As a matter of fact, all commercial interests of Ukraine were closely associated with Western markets. Only under the pressure of Russian economic policies was this traditional current distorted and Ukrainian commerce artificially channeled toward Russian markets.

Only city streets were paved, and probably only those of large cities. For example, Marshall said that "the streets in Kiev were wide and straight and well paved."[1] That foreign visitors did not complain about poor transportation facilities can be explained by the fact that similar conditions existed throughout Europe at that time. People were used to poor roads and the hardships of travel.

Nonetheless, a great deal of commercial and social travel took place on those poorly maintained highways. Only in their worst parts, where swamps and incredible mud made transportation literally impossible, were either plank roads built, or stones, wood, sand or bricks used to fill in the holes. Merchandise was so skillfully packed that even glass and china could be shipped hundreds of miles along rough roads and still arrive safely at distant markets.

Since the Lithuanian-Polish era, main highways were traditional. They ran westward from the city of Lviv to the cities of Yaroslav, Peremyshl, Cracow and Breslau; northward to the cities of Rava Ruska, Zamost, Lublin, Warsaw, Thorn and Danzig; southward to the city of Kolomyia and the Wallachian country; and eastward to the cities of Lutsk, Zhytomyr and Kiev; from the city of Kiev northwards, one highway ran up the left bank of the Dnieper river to Byeloruthenia and another to the cities of Nizhyn and Putivl, and up to Moscow and other Russian cities. Southwards from Kiev a highway ran down along the left bank of the Dnieper toward the Cossack Territory and to the Crimean peninsula.

Different from the highways were the "trails," broad thoroughfares running through the steppes and deserted areas, detouring around all rivers, lakes and streams. These were used for purposes of commerce and strategy. The *Black trail* ran between the rivers Dnieper and Boh, far into the "wild fields" of the Black sea area. The *Kuchman trail* ran between the rivers Dniester and Pruth. Since the Tartars liked to use these trails for their raids, castles and forts were erected along them to protect Ukrainian interests.[2]

Main water routes, although of less importance than highways, and never used to their full capacity, were the rivers Sian and Buh in West Ukraine, the Dnieper in East Ukraine, and their larger tributaries. Water transportation employed various kinds of boats for fishing, commercial shipments, passenger transportation, military use and pleasure, on either long or short trips. Most famous were the *baidaky*, used by the Zaporozhe Cossacks for their military excursions against the Tartars and the Turks. Beauplan and others referred to Ukrainian water transportation.

With the growth of trade the need for better communication became more apparent. At first letters and other communications were sent through "occasion," such as traveling merchants, *chumaks* or friends. In 1629, however, a mail service was organized by Roberto Bandinelli, an Italian, in the city of Lviv connecting Galicia and the western parts of the Polish Kingdom.

In the Hetman State, Hetman Khmelnytsky organized special mail services for the military and the government. His advisor in this matter was Ostap Astamatenko, the Treasurer-General of the state. In 1669, Hetman Demian Mnohohrishny organized regular mail service for Left-bank Ukraine, connecting the cities Kiev, Nizhyn and Baturyn and carrying the mail to Moscow as well. Other hetmans later extended the service to other towns.[3]

Hetman Vyhovsky's printed ordinances, which were sent to the entire Cossack hierarchy and included not only orders and regulations but current news and information as well, are regarded as the beginning of the Ukrainian press. These ordinances had considerable circulation. Under Russian pressure, however, this service which had operated for two years, 1667-69, was discontinued. Ukraine's first real newspaper was published in 1776 in Lviv. It was called *Gazatte de Leopol.*

Domestic Commerce. The basic organizational structure of Ukrainian domestic commerce during Hetman times continued much the same as in the latter part of the Polish-Lithuanian era. Local markets, periodic fairs, a specialized merchant class, the gradual growth of specialty stores, the traveling traders, *chumaks*, commercial class discrimination, and governmental attempts to preserve the social balance of the domestic market, were as previously the chief characteristics of the country's distribution process. However, the composition of the merchant class changed, for, as the volume of domestic trade increased, wider social circles indulged in commercial activities. Practically speaking, every social class was involved in commercial operations to a great extent, while the cities and the townspeople continued to be the center of those operations.

There was a considerable trend toward specialization among the merchants, primarily according to the merchandise they handled. For example, there were sellers of bread, tobacco, cattle, textiles, glass, grain, leather, furs, Oriental spices and Oriental materials, etc. At that time the distinction was already developing between the retailers, dealing with the final consumer and in small quantities, and the wholesalers maintaining large warehouses of costly merchandise.

Considerable trading was done by traveling merchants residing in various cities who were called *korobiinyky*. Substantial salt, grain and leather trade was carried on by a distinctly different group of *chumaky*, Cossack-like traveling traders, recruited largely from the population of villages and small towns. There was also a differentiation between the "merchants" and the "commercial people," according to the volume of capital invested in commercial ventures and the kind of merchandise they sold. The merchants were wealthier, invested more capital in their business and traded domestically as well as internationally. The commercial people covered local markets and nearby areas.

Some merchants were very rich, such as Ivan Teterivsky, Petro Kotovych and Vasyl Mezensky, from Khmelnytsky's time, or Spiridon Shyrai, Isak Derevianko, and Maksymovych, from Samoilovych's and Mazepa's era, who practically dominated financial and marketing matters in their towns and regions, and also enjoyed special consideration from and the protection of the hetmans.[4]

Similarly, urban commerce suffered greatly because of discriminatory practices of the upper classes and of privileged foreigners, which were also common prior to the National Revolution. But whereas the gentry and the Armenian and German merchants had created unfair competition for the local townspeople during the Polish rule, in the Hetman state the Cossack grandees and the Orthodox religious orders, on the one hand, and the Greek and Russian merchants, on the other, were responsible for the abuses and unfair competition.

Hetman Apostol attempted to put an end to such unfair competition which constituted a violation of the original articles of the Pereyaslav Treaty of 1654. Hetman Apostol therefore forbade foreign merchants, especially Russians, to engage in certain industries such as saltpeter extraction, and local trading.

Various cities complained of the discriminatory and illegal levies imposed on them arbitrarily by the Cossack grandees and the monasteries, such as additional and unjustified road and bridge tolls and sales taxes and competitive production and distribution of whiskey and beer in the cities, where actually the municipalities and townspeople had an alcohol monopoly.

Although the Hetman government tried hard to prevent those abuses the Cossack hierarchy and the monasteries through numerous ordinances and administrative measures of such Hetmans as Samoilovych, Mazepa, Skoropadsky and Apostol, and in particular, by Mazepa's edicts of 1687, 1688, 1691, 1696, and 1698, and Apostol's numerous regulations, not much was achieved. The commercial interests of the town in Hetman Ukraine were actually overrun by the predominance of the Cossack class which thought that the state existed chiefly for their benefit.[5]

In some cases, the Hetmans gave privileged treatment to cities, such as Khmelnytsky's preferential protection of the trading activities of Lviv and Mazepa's over those of Kiev, Starodub, Chernihiv and Nizhyn. This unequal treatment and legal status for various cities, some having Magdeburg autonomy and others not, served only to worsen the country's economic situation.

Local markets and local, provincial and nationwide fairs and stores were the centers of mercantile exchange. Markets and fairs continued to be important in the distribution process, just as in the previous period. In every city and town regular market days were held, attended by the peasants from the vicinity, local merchants and outside traders, Cossacks, *chumaks*, artisans, monks who sold for account of their monasteries, and many other people, both men and women. Such market days were held, for instance, on Mondays and Fridays in Pereyaslav, and on other days in other towns. Oxen, cattle, hogs, wool, textiles, honey, alcohol, wax, food, glass, books, potash, tar, leather, footwear, metal utensils, poultry, salt, spices, luxury goods and a great variety of other things were exchanged, bought and sold in these markets. These were also important social events. Imported articles were also available.

Traditionally, fairs were held annually and seasonally in various towns and cities, such as Kiev, Baturyn, Krolevets, Nizhyn, Kharkiv, Sumy, Broznia, Pereyaslav, and Lviv. They also started on specific days, and continued for several weeks. In Kiev and Kharkiv, they were held in the late spring after the roads cleared.

Nesterenko pointed out that during Hetman times the Ukrainian fairs were bigger and more numerous than those of Russia. A few figures may substantiate this statement. In 1648, for example, the merchants from Norinsk sold (in the local markets and fairs) grain for 5,470 guldens. In Putivl, 20 to 30 carloads of whiskey were traded. The merchants from Starodub sold in the city of Briansk alone, hundreds of carloads of potash annually. Aksakov related that annually 100,000 carloads of merchandise were sold by Russian merchants in the Ukrainian fairs. The *chumaks* sold 50 to 60 carloads of salt, fish, leather and grain.[6]

Since the end of the seventeenth century, fairs in the city of Lviv on St. George's day, under the protection of the Ukrainian Catholic Metropolitan, became especially famous. They were held until the first quarter of the twentieth century.

Although trading in the markets and fairs was relatively free of all kinds of guild and monopoly restictions, it was still burdened with various levies, duties, road and bridge tolls, weight and measure charges, sales tax, and a general levy to provide market protection, all of which tended to reduce the volume of trade and to raise prices.

In the seventeenth and eighteenth centuries, trading in the stores acquired an ever growing importance in Ukraine. New kinds of specialty stores developed for a number of articles, including textiles, footwear, glass and ceramics, weapons, hardware, jewelry and clocks. In addition, there were stores adjunct to the craft and "kustar" establishments, like bakeries, butcher and meat stores, fish stores, taverns selling various kinds of alcoholic drinks, stores trading costly Oriental merchandise, and the so-called Nuerenberg stores — selling all kinds of cheap and small items, somewhat like the recent five-and-ten-cent stores. There were also large wholesale warehouses for such goods as woolen materials, Oriental textiles, furs, wines, drugs and arms.

Traveling merchant caravans were known to exist in Ukraine in the early Middle Ages. Later on, in 1352, Rubricus (Rubrik) related that those caravans brought to the city of Theodosia, in Crimea, martens, sables and other furs, in large, strongly built wagons, covered by a roof and drawn by oxen. In the early fifteenth century, a specifically Ukrainian phenomenon of itinerant merchant, half-peasant and half-Cossack, called *chumak*, developed from that very old tradition of merchant caravans. In the next century, and until the second half of the nineteenth century, in every village in Ukraine there were a few *chumak* families, the members of which traveled and traded over a large territory all their lives. In 1499, *chumaky* were mentioned in the city ordinance of Kiev. They evolved into a special caste of people with very rigid customs and traditions of behavior. As Lypa said, everything in their lives was strictly regulated by that unwritten code, the route to travel, when and how to leave home for a mercantile journey, in what manner to travel, where to make stops for rest, how to share the risks and the income.

The *chumaky* had their own commercial routes. In the seventeenth and eighteenth centuries, there were two highly important *chumak* trails. The first, the Shpak trail, named after the famous *chumak* chief, ran from Volhinia, through the city of Uman, and to the river Dnieper at its Syniukha tributary. It was a part of the ancient *Iron Route*. The second one, the *Muravsky trail*, the ancient *Salt Route* from Kievan times, ran in Left-bank Ukraine, bypassing the springs of the rivers Vorskla and Samara, then, through the Territory of the Cossack Host by the Dnieper cataracts, and down to Perekop and the Crimean cities. The *chumak* caravans also traveled westward to Poland and Prussia, and eastward to Astrakhan and Asia Minor.

A considerable portion of the rural population, and later, also, the urban population, were *chumaky*, doing a great deal of mercantile and shipping business, mainly with salt, leather, textiles and grain. At the time of the National Revolution, for example, there were 39 *chumak* families in the Pereyaslav area, 34 in Berizna, 24 in Nizhyn, 20 in Kiev, and 10 in the Oster area, according to Krypiakevych.[7]

Foreign Trade, Its Development and Composition. The National Revolution of 1648 and subsequent wars had an unfavorable impact on Ukrainian foreign trade, which, at the end of the Lithuanian-Polish period, had been favorable. Now its extent was reduced and its composition changed. Grain, the leading export commodity prior to 1648 and amounting to 100,000 guldens annually, declined for years. It was replaced by alcohol, oxen, potash, tar, wood, and later tobacco. Imports were also limited. Mostly necessities were imported: textiles, metal goods, needles, thread, furs and a few other articles. The directions of import-export trade also changed, since the Revolution had blocked the traditional channels to the Polish and Western markets. Hetman Khmelnytsky realized some 200,000 guldens for the country's treasury from the sale of potash to western businessmen. As early as 1649, Russian merchants also became interested in Ukrainian potash, which they bought in the cities on the Ukrainian-Muscovite border. The river Desna was for a long time the main northern water route for potash exportation.

Following the Pereyaslav Treaty of 1654, the volume of Ukrainian-Russian trade slowly began to rise. The Russians purchased Ukrainian cattle, horses, hemp, flax, tobacco, alcohol, wax, saltpetre, textiles and potash, and these items were delivered to markets in Moscow, Kaluga, Briansk, Bielgorod and other places in the Muscovite Tsardom. The main imports from Russia were furs, such as sables, beavers, martens, white foxes and others, some textiles and linen, and leather. Khmelnytsky himself sent his agents to Muscovy in 1652, ordering them to purchase a large quantity of furs. On the whole, however, the volume of Ukrainian-Russian trade was very small for the next two or three decades. At times, when salt from West Ukraine (under Polish domination) and from the shores of the Black and Azov Seas (under Turkish domination) was not available for Left-bank Ukraine, Ukrainian merchants and *chumaky* traveled to the Don region and bought it there. Russian officials even let them do their own salt boiling. This, of course, occasionally increased Ukrainian imports from the territories under the rule of the Russian Tsar.[8]

Salt was also imported from Wallachia in considerable quantities when Galician deposits were not available to the eastern provinces of the country. This happened in 1652 when hundreds of carloads of salt arrived from Wallachia. Trade with Bohemia and Hungary continued at a reduced rate. Most significant was Khmelnytsky's interest in commercial relations with Turkey. More and more numerous caravans rolled to and from the Ottoman Empire through the cities of Bendery and Chechelnyk, shipping great varieties of goods. Oriental merchandise came from Turkey either for direct Ukrainian consumption or as transit goods for Muscovy, Byeloruthenia and

Lithuania. These imports included silk, Oriental rugs and carpets, velvet, belts, handkerchiefs, Persian textiles, cotton materials, rice, tobacco, and such Oriental fruits as figs, almonds, and citrus fruits. Among Ukrainian exports to Turkish markets were meat, furs, grain, wax and a few articles of minor importance. Turkish, Armenian, Jewish, Greek and Ukrainian merchants carried out the growing Oriental-Ukrainian trade which had been, during and before the Kievan period, the most important sector of Ukrainian foreign commerce. In the seventeenth century its revival in the newly independent Ukrainian state was due to a turn of geo-political events favorable to Oriental-Occidental trade. Trading with the Tartars, like earlier trade with the Cumans, was a subsidiary of that large-scale commercial project. Tartars sold horses, cattle and sheep, and for the most part bought grain in the Ukrainian markets.

The new prospects for large-scale Ukrainian-Turkish trade were closely connected to political developments. Khmelnytsky sought to strengthen his political position by intensive and free economic cooperation with all neighboring lands. On this basis he planned to make Ukraine the very center of East European politics. In 1650, he started to work on a commercial treaty with the Ottoman Empire, substantiated by preceding developments in the field of commerce. The treaty was intended to enrich the Ukrainian national economy. It was supposed to include several important provisions, which, practically speaking, reserved the Black Sea and Azov Sea areas exclusively for Ukrainian and Turkish economic interests. It provided, among other things, for abolition of all tariffs and favorable credit terms for the merchants of both nations.

The treaty did not materialize, however, because of subsequent political developments. The Pereyaslav Treaty of alliance with Muscovy dampened the hope for a close Ukrainian-Turkish commercial relationship. Moscow attempted to draw the economic interest of the Ukrainians more closely into dependence upon Muscovite markets and it insisted on severing their friendship with the Ottoman Empire.[9]

The later decades of the seventeenth century brought a splendid recovery and further expansion of Ukrainian foreign trade. The direct and indirect (via Polish markets) mercantile connections with West European countries were restored, and this time the Ukrainian Cossack grandees and nobles and the Ukrainian national economy reaped all the gains from the business, instead of the Polish or polonized gentry and the Polish national economy as before the Revolution. Commercial connections were reintroduced and developed between the Ukrainian cities and Danzig, Koenigsberg, Breslau,

Nuremburg and Riga, and those cities became largely middlemen for Ukrainian trade with Germany (Prussia, Silesia), Austria, Holland, France and Scandinavia. Through these places a great variety of produce and merchandise came from and went to Ukraine in the form of exports, imports and transit business.

Actually, Ukrainian foreign trade was primarily west-bound and west-oriented. As long as the Russians did not have the deciding influence on the political destiny of Ukraine, it always gravitated towards the West culturally, politically and economically. During Samoilovych's Hetmanate, Ukrainian international commerce was already large-scale and multilateral, and was carried out fully automatically in the interest of the Ukrainian people. It continued on this basis during Mazepa's time and until the fateful Poltava battle of 1709.

Commercial relations with the West were supplemented by extensive trading with the Crimean Tartars, the Balkan countries, Ottoman Empire, the Caucasian lands and Iran-Persia. Mercantile ties with the Don-Volga basin were constantly growing.

As far as export was concerned, it included mainly the following produce and merchandise, raised or manufactured in Ukraine: oxen, flax and hemp, wool and rough linen, lumber, potash and tar, fish, salt pork, vegetable oil, fur, saltpetre, alcohol, wax and tobacco. For a few post-revolutionary decades, oxen were the major Ukrainian export. The Hetmans, Cossack grandees, nobles and townspeople were very busy selling oxen and cattle abroad. It was a very profitable business in Polish-Lithuanian times as well. For example, Hetman Apostol himself was vitally interested in cattle export and derived considerable revenue from it. The export of oxen was a brisk and well organized business. Cattle trails were traditionally established, safety measures were relatively good, cattle drives were handled by experienced herdsmen and sales were made by experienced merchants. Financial aspects of the trade in oxen were based on numerous commercial agreements between the Polish and Ukrainian governments. It was definitely west-bound. The cities of Breslau and Leipzig and the ports of Danzig and Koenigsberg were the leading markets for these oxen and cattle, raised mainly in southern Hetman Ukraine and in the Territory of the Cossack Host. Records indicate hundreds of thousands of rubles in revenue from the oxen trade. This aroused the envy of the Russians who attempted to take it over for themselves. At first they discriminated against Ukrainian cattle traders and created difficulties for them; then they resorted to governmental regimentation. As a result of these measures the volume of business and its attractive profits declined at about the middle of the eighteenth century.[10]

The export of flax and hemp was considerable. Ukrainian flax and hemp were better quality-wise than that raised in any other part of Europe. The port of Riga on the Baltic shores was the main route for Ukrainian flax and hemp destined for western markets. Tobacco was shipped mainly to Koenigsberg, Poland and Byeloruthenia, again bringing hundreds of thousands of rubles of income for the Ukrainian exporter before this trade was also suppressed by the Russians.

Grain exportation, ranking first in importance prior to the National Revolution, never reached pre-revolutionary levels during the Cossack-Hetman period. Grain was sold cheaply, and exported to Byeloruthenia, Poland, Lithuania and Muscovy. Very little went to Western markets. The Russians were essentially interested in Ukrainian grain imports, since that produce was scarce in the north, and they left that part of Ukrainian foreign trade relatively free from regimentation and protectionistic restrictions, except for one or two minor attempts to establish a Russian controlling interest.

The chief import articles were manufactured goods, such as Silesian, Dutch and English materials; woolen materials, fine linen and silks; German tools and appliances, such as Nuremburg saws, scythes, sickles, knives, axes and hammers; Steinmark metal; silver and crystal articles, mainly dishes, needles, and again, knives. From the West European markets, via Danzig and Koenigsberg, came copper and iron, mainly for the production of church bells, cannons and other arms, and kettles for the brewery and distillery industries. Hetman Polubotok, for example, was involved in the copper trade, as Dzhydzhora pointed out.

Fine furniture and fine garments were brought from England. Books in foreign languages and all kinds of paper were brought from the cities of Breslau (Wroclaw), in Silesia, and Liepzig, in Prussia, and also from other places in West Europe, via the ports of Danzig and Koenigsberg. From West Europe luxury goods were also imported, such as fine garments, musical instruments, jewelry, fine wines, watches and spices, which were handled through those important markets and then traveled across Polish and Lithuanian territories until they reached the centers of Ukrainian foreign trade; the cities of Starodub, Chernihiv, Nizhyn, Poltava, Kiev, and Lviv.

Imports from the Ottoman Empire, such as velvet, silk and silk materials, rugs, carpets, incense, raisins, almonds, coffee, tea, rice, tobacco and lemons, continued to arrive at Ukrainian markets at a steadily decreasing rate, while imports from Russia, such as furs of all kinds, including sables, martens and white foxes, linen, sugar, paper and books, flooded Ukraine at an ever increasing rate. Imports from other neighboring lands, such as glass and crystal from Bohemia, salt and tobacco from Poland, were less important.

Dubrovsky attempted to give an approximate quantitative description of the overall extent of Ukrainian foreign trade in those times on the basis of official Russian registers and documents for the years 1715 to 1729, compiled by Russian commercial agents in the cities of Nizhyn, Kiev, Pereyaslav, Romni, Starodub and Chernihiv, the most important mercantile centers in Hetman Ukraine. He said that in these years, Ukraine imported over a hundred thousand yards of various textiles from Germany and Turkey, some very costly, all destined for domestic consumption. Millions of furs were imported but millions were also exported. According to Dubrovsky, during that time Ukraine exported 3,776 oxen, 6,047 sheep, 18,049 heads of cattle, 554 carloads of wool, 2,368 carloads of hemp, 8,528 hundredweights of leather, 160 barrels of potash, 150 hundredweights of wax, 351 carloads of tobacco, and about 520 gallons of vegetable oil.[11]

In order to complete the analysis of the composition of the Ukrainian export-import business in those times, a few words must be added about the role of the Territory of the Cossack Host and Village Ukraine. Agriculture was the predominant occupation in these two areas, hence they exported agricultural products. The Cossack Host traded with Hetman Ukraine, Muscovy, Crimea, Turkey, Poland and Wallachia, and exported mainly furs, leather, wool, horses, cattle, butter, vegetable oil, fish, meat and grain. Its imports consisted mainly of manufactured goods, including beer and whiskey, bread, lumber, incense and spices, arms, gunpowder, linen, woolen, cotton and silk textiles, boots and garments.

The foreign trade of Village Ukraine was initially much like that of the Cossack Host from beyond the cataracts, including even the importance of salt exports. At a later date, however, Village Ukraine also began to export some manufactured goods. Its agricultural and manufactured products reached not only the Hetman State and Muscovy, but also West Ukraine, Silesia, Prussia and Crimea. Because of the splendid economic growth in this area, foreign merchants, Polish, German, Armenian, Turkish and Muscovite began to visit the cities of Kharkiv, Izium, Okhtyrka and others. The major export articles of Village Ukraine were cattle, silk, furs from Chuhaiiv, tobacco, rugs from Okhtyrka and many items of minor importance. Of course the scope, extent, composition and growth of Ukrainian trade were decisively influenced by the policies of the Ukrainian government, at first sovereign, then autonomous, and finally foreign dominated. These influences were growing steadily.

Foreign Trade Policies. Two opposite political trends prevailed in Ukrainian foreign trade. The Hetman government tried in every way possible to facilitate Ukrainian commercial interests, and to protect them against foreign discrimination and injustice. The Muscovite government, however, pursued a quite different end, that of turning Ukraine into an economic service area for the Empire. In order to understand properly the trends in the development of Ukrainian foreign trade, it is necessary to examine the commercial policies of both the Ukrainian and the Russian governments.

All Ukrainian Hetmans understood the importance of international trade, and assisted the merchants, the Cossack grandees and the nobles who were engaged in that business. Of course, some Hetmans had a greater appreciation for foreign trade issues than others. It was pointed out that Khmelnytsky was greatly interested in the status of Ukraine in the international market. He urged the merchants to trade internationally. He himself sent merchants abroad to purchase necessary products (furs, salt) and to sell potash for the account of the fisc.

Hetman Doroshenko was also interested in tariffs as a source of government revenue and undertook certain measures to assure that income. Similarly, Hetmans Samoilovych and Mazepa paid much attention to the problems of foreign trade as an important segment of the still sovereign Ukrainian national economy. Their edicts and ordinances aimed to secure the interests of Ukrainian import-export merchants, and to bring order into the fiscal projection of international commerce. Not infrequently they had to intervene in individual cases involving merchants whose commercial interests were violated by foreign governments, particularly by the Polish and Muscovite ones, which discriminated against these merchants by excessive tariffs, and by customs offficials who robbed and beat them and confiscated their merchandise.

Later on, during Skoropadsky's and Apostol's time, these conditions became intolerable. Although Ukrainian merchants still had the opportunity to seek protection and compensation for damages in the usual court and legal procedures, practically speaking, they were ineffective because of the costs and the long delays involved. Consequently, Ukrainian merchants decided that the best way to protect themselves and to even the score was to rob Polish merchants and merchant caravans. As a consequence, Ukrainian trade with the West began to decline.

After the Poltava battle, Ukrainian foreign policy became primarily a defense of Ukrainian economic autonomy against the increasing encroachment of Russia. Skoropadsky complained several times to St. Petersburg of the discriminatory and criminal actions of Russian residents, officials and merchants in Ukraine and Russia, committed against Ukrainian merchants and businessmen and their commercial interests.

As Dzhydzhora said, Hetman Danylo Apostol also fully understood the importance of economic development and its needs and difficulties. In his letters to St. Petersburg he always referred to the "old rights and privileges" of his people, demanding the abolition of unjust and abusive tariffs, discriminatory policies, and abusive actions of Russian officials and military commanders. He asked for equal treatment of Ukrainian and Russian merchants, freedom of trade and a reduction of Russian protectionistic measures.

Apostol had a special concern for the merchants trading with Danzig and Breslau. He also decidedly prohibited the Ukrainian administration from discriminating against, abusing or making difficulties for those merchants who engaged in foreign commerce. Later, however, the *Second Little Russian College* abandoned its fight to protect the rights and interests of the Ukrainian economy in general and its large-scale mercantile operations in particular.[12]

Muscovite political and economic influences in Ukraine increased in strength and intensity by the end of the seventeenth century. However, prior to the Poltava battle, the Russian government used indirect methods to channel Ukrainian foreign trade according to Moscow's designs. In 1701, Peter the Great initiated the first open regulations designed to weaken Ukrainian economic autonomy in international commerce, ordered the Ukrainian merchants to export hemp, flax, potash, leather, wax, and salt pork solely through the port of Archangelsk, and to give up the traditional routes through Danzig, Koenigsberg and Breslau.

Such policies were part of a master plan designed to gradually liquidate the autonomous Ukrainian state. St. Petersburg sought to tighten the commercial ties between Russia and Ukraine and in particular to crush the Ukrainian-Western trade in order to consolidate its hold on Ukraine, a prerequisite to its eventual absorption by the Russian Empire.[13]

The policy of Peter the Great toward Ukrainian foreign trade was inconsistent. At first he wanted to develop the Azov Sea ports and bases for launching an attack on the Ottoman Empire. Therefore he directed Ukrainian merchants to export and import through these ports. Later he changed his mind and gave preference to the Baltic Sea ports, according to his master plan to bring Russia closer to West Europe and its culture and economy.

As a result, the volume of Ukrainian trade with the West was drastically reduced; the financial and commercial interests of the Ukrainian merchants were seriously impaired. Subsequently, the Muscovites established over forty additional toll and customs stations along the western Ukrainian border, and plagued Ukrainian merchants with excessive and discriminatory duties on goods which were not headed for the north-bound route via Russian territory.

The Muscovites then proceeded with other restrictions. Ukrainian merchants were prohibited from importing Muscovite money. Additional measures were undertaken to withdraw gold and silver coins from Ukraine, allowing only copper and nickle money to circulate. Between 1718 and 1721, St. Petersburg prohibited the importation into Ukraine from Western markets of such merchandise as stockings, gold and silver thread, fine textiles, silk materials, woolen materials, linen, tablecloths, sugar, dyestuffs and tobacco. The Russians had begun to develop industries which produced these goods, hence this policy was designed to shut off the competition of Western countries in Ukraine, according to their mercantilist designs.

St. Petersburg was especially anxious to suppress trade with Breslau. In 1714 it was outright prohibited. The Silesian merchants were horrified. The imperial government of Austria officially complained on their behalf, but initially to no avail. In 1720, St. Petersburg promised a liberalization of its policy, and in 1722 under continuous pressure from abroad and numerous petitions from Hetman Skoropadsky, the promise was kept. In 1723, the prohibition on Western exports from Ukraine of cattle, salt pork, bristles, wax and glue was lifted. But Russian maneuvers continued. Austrian agents conferred many times with Apostol and the Polish royal government in order to coordinate their actions, aimed at inducing Russia to give up its extreme protectionism, which hurt Austrian, Polish and Ukrainian commercial interests.[14]

The abuses were frequent, and the Russian government appeared to approve of them. As long as the office of the Hetman was preserved in Ukraine, at least the Ukrainian merchant had someone to appeal to. Rozumovsky was the last Hetman with any power. After 1764, there was nobody to defend the commercial rights of the Ukrainian people. The *Second Little Russian College* failed to champion the Ukrainian cause. The complete subjugation of Ukraine was now an accomplished fact.

Money and Credit. In the early capitalistic economy of Ukraine of the seventeenth and eighteenth centuries, characterized by the specialization of production, growing manufacturing industries and the rise of big business and extensive commerce, money and capital were vitally involved. Throughout that period Ukraine suffered more or less acutely from a shortage of money which hampered economic growth. Russian mercantilistic policies aggravated this condition.

Immediately after the Revolution of 1648 the Ukrainian economy began to suffer an acute currency shortage. Polish guldens became scarce and the circulation of foreign currencies declined sharply because of a drastic and rapid reduction in foreign trade. Consequently, their value increased substantially.

As a matter of fact, foreign coins did not circulate in Ukraine at their face value, either prior to or after the Revolution. They had a highly elastic exchange rate dependent upon the pattern of balance of trade. This, in turn, had an adverse effect on the Ukrainian national economy in the first decade of national independence.[15] With the gradual recovery of foreign trade, more and more foreign coins of gold and silver flowed into the country. Lithuanian, Polish, German, Russian and other coins circulated freely, relieving somewhat the pressing currency shortage. Their exchange rates were determined by the issuing country's economic status. German currency fluctuated considerably, since trade with Danzig, Breslau, Nuremberg and Koenigsberg was extremely important, but its flow was irregular due to Polish and Russian intrigues. Polish currency was relatively stable in value, in particular the Polish red gulden. For example, from 1712 to 1725, the rate of exchange of red guldens increased only from 2 rubles and 10 kopeieks to 2 rubles and 20 kopeieks.

The Russian ruble also fluctuated in value, although Moscow was anxious to maintain its stability of value as an incentive to a growing Russian-Ukrainian trade. A stable ruble would facilitate this growth substantially. However, in the long run the ruble appreciated in value in the Ukrainian market in direct proportion to the increase of Russian political and economic influence in Ukraine.

To relieve the serious money problem in Ukraine some Hetmans, such as Doroshenko and Samoilovych, initiated their own coinage. Doroshenko began to coin money in 1672 in the form of *chechs* valued at one and a half *grosh*. When in 1674 the mint was captured by Hetman Samoilovych, he continued for some time with the consent of Moscow to coin the same *chechs*. Soon, however, he was forced to abandon coinage under pressure from Moscow.[16]

Perhaps it was Brukhovetsky who coined the *karbovanets*. Various authors, such as Kunov and Pototsky, expressed the view that Hetman Khmelnytsky coined his own money too. Doubtlessly, he planned to do so.

Veselaho indicates that in 1654, at the time of the Pereyaslav Treaty, the Muscovites coined new rubles designed for circulation in the Hetman State and the Territory of the Cossack Host. These bore the Czar's image and the inscription "Great and Little Russia." The old ruble, he said carried only the inscription "All-Russia" with no reference to "Little Russia," namely Ukraine.

In spite of Russian pressures, however, the Russian ruble did not have wide circulation in Ukraine. The people preferred West European and Polish money, red guldens, guldens, half and quarter guldens, florins, ducats and other gold and silver coins, and Ukrainian *chechs*. According to Bidnov, they used the Russian ruble reluctantly.[17]

In 1719, a money crisis took place in Ukraine because of the discriminatory money policy of the Tsarist regime. St. Petersburg, following the idea of accumulating its own gold and silver reserves, prohibited the exportation of gold and silver rubles to Ukraine, and attempted to withdraw those already in the hands of the Ukrainian population. Cheaper moneys were designated for use in Russian-Ukrainian trade.

This shortage of money also increased the use of credit. Leading sources of credit were Cossack grandees, monasteries, nobles, rich merchants, municipalities, merchant and craft guilds and the treasuries of local administratives units, colonelcies and *sotnias* (counties). Relatively speaking, the interest rates were not excessive. In 1651, 7 percent interest on loans was common. Later the rate rose to 10 and 20 percent. In periods of acute shortages of loanable funds, the rate sometimes rose to the level of 50 percent per annum.

It was pointed out in connection with the topic of foreign trade that Hetman Skoropadsky and Hetman Apostol had tried very hard, and with considerable success, to regulate credit. Apostol, in particular, provided a base for sound credit in foreign commercial relations. He arranged for a one to three years' credit moratorium in financial hardships developing out of the Ukrainian-Western trade and threatening serious losses and bankruptcies. A debt moratorium had to be handled through the Hetman office. Preference was given to merchants dealing with Danzig and Breslau, since they were exposed to Polish and Russian discriminatory practices.

The Hetman tried to put the credit system on a sound basis by direct negotiations with Poland, Prussia and Austria. In addition, Apostol placed a legal ceiling of 11 percent on interest rates. His government constantly tried to lower interest rates, while money lenders fought to increase them.

Foreign capital also began to reach Ukraine, primarily for forest exploitation and potash and tar production. It was supplied by merchants from Danzig and Koenigsberg. During Samoilovych's and Mazepa's time a class of wealthy merchants entered the economy, accumulating capital through golden opportunities and profitable commercial operations in a free enterprise system. Soon hundreds of thousands of guldens or rubles were available to finance new projects, new ideas, new and larger industrial and commercial operations, pyramiding the accumulated capital. Paralleling these developments were the ruthless tactics of some grandees, nobles and merchants who usurped peasant farmsteads, forced peasants to perform excessive serf labor, turned peasants into serfs for defaulted debts, forced city craftsmen to produce without due compensation, usurped monopolies, charged unlawful and excessive tolls and other fees, arbitrarily confiscated merchandise shipments, and cheated the government.

All these abuses facilitated the accumulation of individual fortunes which, in turn, were reinvested in various business projects, to expand the farm economies, to establish industrial enterprises, and to engage in trade, particularly foreign trade. These excesses were overemphasised by Marxist economists, such as Nesterenko, Vyrnyk and Lyashchenko, who maintained that all private capital accumulated in Hetman Ukraine had come from ill gotten wealth. This is not even a half-truth. Hard work, honest enterprise and saving were the fundamental and primary sources of capital creation in Ukraine.

Public Finance. This area experienced fundamental changes in the Hetman State. It evolved literally from a vacuum to a fairly well developed sytem based on a budget and a thorough accounting of receipts and disbursements. The Revolution had abolished the old and very imperfect Polish system of public finance in Ukraine. The new Ukrainian financial system of public economy had to be organized from the beginning. In the first days of national independence, there was no separation of the private funds of the Hetman and the state treasury, the fisc. Khmelnytsky freely disposed of all funds, through a bursar who took care of the routine administrative work.

In 1654, the office of the Treasurer-General of Hetman Finances already existed. The treasurer was in charge of the collection of public revenues and the managing of public expenditures. Under his authority special officials called "executors" collected taxes, duties, rents, tolls and other levies. Then this office simply disappeared.

In 1663, during the reign of Hetman Brukhovetsky, it was reactivated, and a very able man, Roman Rakushka, was appointed to it. The office continued to operate during Mnohohrishny's Hetmanate. Rakushka himself remained in office until 1669. He succeeded in reorganizing Ukraine's fiscal policies and considerably increasing the revenues collected.

The office was again abolished in 1669, and it was not reestablished until 1728. Mazepa did not have a Treasurer-General; he either administered state finances himself or he appointed able men to do so on a temporary basis. Among these were the Hetman's Commander-in-Chief, I. Lomykovsky, and the successful businessmen, D. Maksymovych and I. Lysytsia.

In 1728, the office of the Treasurer-General was reinstituted as a cabinet post. First of all, a separation of the private treasury of the Hetman and the state fisc was accomplished. Two treasurers were appointed to manage finances, one of whom had to be a Muscovite. The Muscovite treasurer assured the Tsarist government of taxes from Ukraine. Apostol was greatly disturbed by this new violation of Ukrainian autonomy, but could do little about it.

In 1729, the role of the treasurers was spelled out. They had to collect taxes and non-tax receipts, in money and in kind. They were in charge of all expenditures of the central government. They had to supervise local financial matters of individual colonelcies, *sotnias* and municipalities; they were in charge of a new agency called the State Accounts Commission. Regional officers for financial matters were also established during Apostol's Hetmanate.[18]

Apostol improved financial administration considerably. What was formerly chaotic, incidental and sporadic, he organized into a state budget called "the military treasury" for ordinary collections and disbursements. The budget was estimated at 144,000 rubles; it was collected from regular revenues in the form of "induction" (import) and "eviction" (export) duties. Ordinary expenditures were foreseen for central administration, such as the hiring of foreign troops, the maintenance of the state artillery, and diplomatic relations. Extraordinary expenditures for court physicians, painters, poets, libraries and the like were left to the discretion of the Hetman. They would be paid from extraordinary revenues.

Regular account books were introduced, and monthly reports were required. Other top dignitaries of the Hetman's cabinet were forbidden to interfere with the Treasurer-General, whose job soon developed into the third-ranking office in the central administration, being outranked only by the Chancellor and the Chief Justice. Of course, frequently conflicts developed between the Hetman treasurer and the fiscal treasurer, since the latter looked more for the protection of Muscovite rather than Ukrainian interest.

On the lower, local level, fiscal matters were also well organized. Individual colonelcies had their own treasurers and treasuries, well staffed with collectors and clerks. A similar pattern was followed by the municipalities which collected various levies and paid the costs of city government.

Public revenues in Hetman Ukraine were derived principally from government ownership of productive property, and only secondarily from indirect taxes. Direct taxation was new and relatively unimportant. Public property consisted of the pre-revolutionary "royalties" and "economies" of the Polish king and government, which at the time of the creation of the sovereign Ukrainian state automatically became the property of the new Hetmanic government as estates of rank. The estates of the Roman Catholic Church and the Polish nobles who left Ukraine with no intention of returning also became state domains.

The war retarded the effective operation of manorial economies of rank. After a few years, however, they began again to produce considerable public revenues. Krypiakevych estimated that the State derived up to 1,000,000 guldens annually from the precious "royalties" and "economies" alone. An additional 50,000 guldens could come from the confiscated Church and nobles' properties.

Manorial farm economies, mills, sawmills, breweries, distilleries, gun powder, potash and tar works, glass works, iron mines and iron works were examples of state-owned businesses managed on a rental-lease basis by Cossack grandees, common Cossacks, colonists, nobles, foreigners, merchants, craftsmen, monasteries, municipalities, local colonelcy governments, and specialists-manufacturers, who channeled to the state treasury rental payment in honey, flour, wax, fish, whiskey, potash, and even money.

In many cases the state insisted on monopoly rights, in which case the business was very profitable both for the government and for the private lessees. In 1699, during Mnohohrishny's Hetmanate, as a result of the recommendations of the General Cossack Council, monopolies were generally established in industries producing whiskey, tobacco, potash and tar, both in manufacturing and in sale. Whiskey, for example, could be sold in wholesale only by a monopoly and in minimum quantities of a hundred quarts. On the other hand, drinking honey and beer could be sold freely in any quantity.

The rent-lease system proved unpopular and Mazepa abolished it in 1693. He planned to replace it with an excise tax on whiskey, tobacco, potash and several other items. The reform failed. Public revenues declined excessively, necessitating a return to the rent-lease system a year later.

Indirect taxes were many and varied. Among them were customs collections, excise taxes, consumption taxes, sales taxes, and tolls. Customs were of the two major types previously mentioned. They amounted to about 2 percent *ad valorem*. Already in Khmelnytsky's time Ostap Astamatenko was advised to reorganize the collection of duties in order to increase efficiency. Special attention was paid to the Russian and Turkish borders.

The bad feature of tariffs and tolls was their abuse by assessors and collectors, who sometimes charged arbitrary and unlawful rates, cheated the taxpayer or collected twice on the same bill, keeping part of the collection for themselves. Hetmans such as Samoilovych, Mazepa, Skoropadsky and Apostol made every possible effort to stop these criminal practices, but matters grew even worse after Russian officials began to interfere in Ukraine's collection of internal revenue.

Internal commodity taxes, on such items as whiskey, beer, wax, honey, tobacco and tar were important sources of revenue. They were usually associated with the business and sales taxes, levied against the right to run a business, to manufacture or to sell such goods or to purchase and consume them. In 1663-69, under Rakushka's administration, iron mining and smelting were also taxed.

Tolls were also levied on goods crossing bridges, or using ferries or public roads. Tolls were charged not only by the Cossack and local governments, but also by private individuals who sometimes transformed these public revenues into a racket.

The municipalities collected tolls, along with such taxes as those on "all breads," drinks, market places, counters, selling shelves, weights and measures, and transportation. Similar levies were also raised by the colonelcy and *sotnia* governments. Later the Russian authorities established additional toll stations, and introduced new taxes and tolls which soon became almost unbearable.

Direct taxation was poorly developed at this time. Khmelnytsky planned in 1654 a general levy, a "capitation" or head tax on peasants and townspeople, four rubles on each chimney (hut). The Cossacks, nobles and clergy were supposed to be exempted from this levy according to the tradition of the Polish crown. The plan failed and a direct general levy was not effectively established although sporadically a direct tax was imposed especially during Mazepa's time and later.

Among other direct fiscal burdens were service obligations of the peasants and townspeople to work on roads, bridges, toll stations, shoveling snow and constructing forts and castles and other defense projects, and to fulfill the station obligation of maintaining and transporting the Hetman court *en route*. This obligation, originating in the days of the Kievan Empire, also fell upon the nobles and the monasteries. It eventually disappeared.[19]

Because of the limited scope of government activities in those times, public expenditures were few but relatively costly. Defense, administration, administration of justice and the maintenance of diplomatic relations, constituted the ordinary expenditures of the Hetmanic government. Of course, defense and administration were the largest expenditure items, followed by the costs of foreign relations. At that time foreign diplomats were housed, fed and maintained by their hosts. The procurement and maintenance of artillery was the largest single defense item.

Extraordinary expenditures included donations to the Church and its monasteries, paying the court physicians, hiring writers and poets to glorify certain persons, court and national events, and the like. These were covered by the Hetman treasury more often than by the fisc. By 1678, ordinary expenditures of the fisc amounted to 40,181 guldens, while during Apostol's time they rose to exceed the sum of 140,000 rubles or about 120,000 guldens.

Meanwhile, the burden of Russian taxes increased, retarding Ukrainian economic development, particularly in the eighteenth century. According to the original Pereyaslav Agreement of 1654, the Tsar solemnly promised not to invade the financial sovereignty of Ukraine, as it was pointed out above. This promise was repeatedly broken. Russian officials and military commanders soon began to extract from the Ukrainian people contributions of money, oxen, cattle, grain, hemp, flax and other produce. The Hetman government protested, initially with some successes. At the time of Hetman Brukhovetsky, who was at first a willing tool of Muscovite interests, St. Petersburg tried to make further inroads into Ukraine's financial autonomy by claiming the capitation tax, whiskey levy and import duties. In 1666, Russian tax collectors arrived in Ukraine and began collecting money, honey and grain for the Russian fisc. Their behavior was so abusive and insulting that it contributed substantially to another Ukrainian-Russian war.[20]

Things changed considerably for the worse at the time of Peter the Great. This Tsar was most ruthless in extracting taxes from the Ukrainian people in order to finance his numerous wars. In an attempt to free Ukraine, Mazepa joined the anti-Russian coalition during the Northern War, but the fateful outcome of the Poltava battle delivered Ukraine into the hands of the Russians, who since that time have so much more intensely exploited the country.

---

1. V. Sichynsky, *Ukraine in Foreign Comments and Discriptions from the VIth to XXth century*, New York, 1953, p. 149.

2. I. Krypiakevych, "Pobut", *Istoria ukrainskoi kultury*, Lviv, 1937, pp. 120-121, Yu. Lypa, *Pryznachennia Ukrainy*, New York, 1953, pp. 109-110.

3. Krypiakevych, *op. cit.*, p. 122.

4. O. Ohloblyn, *Hetman Ivan Mazepa ta yoho doba*, New York, 1960, pp. 101-107; A Nesterenko, *Rozvytok promyslovosty na Ukraini*, Part I, *Remeslo i manufactura*, Kiev, 1959, pp. 206-215.

5. L. Okinshevych, *Lektsii z istorii ukrainskoho prava*, Munich, 1947, pp. 76-77.

6. Nesterenko, *loc. cit.*

7. I. Krypiakevych, *Bohdan Khmelnytsky*, Kiev, 1954, pp. 310-312.

8. *Ibid.*, pp. 315-317.

9. V. Dubrovsky, "Do pytannia pro mizhnarodniu torhivlu Ukrainy v pershii polovyni XVIII st.," *Zapysky Istorychno-Filolohichnoho Viddilu*, Ukrainska Akademia Nauk, Kiev, 1931, Vol. 26; also, Doroshenko, *Narys istorii Ukrainy*, Munich, 1966, Vol. II, pp. 167-174; N. Polonska-Vasylenko, *Istoria Ukrainy*, Munich, 1973, Vol. II, pp. 188-189.

10. I. Dzhydzhora, *Ukraina v pershii polovyni XVIII viku, Ekonomichna polityka rossiiskoho pravytelstva suproty Ukrainy v 1710-1730 rokakh*, Kiev, 1930, pp. 8 and other; Doroshenko, *op. cit.*, Vol. II, p. 166, 170-174.

11. Dubrovsky, *loc. cit.*; Dzhydzhora, *op. cit.*, pp. 13-14; D. Olanchyn, "Torhovelni zviazky Ukrainy z Breslavom u XVIII st.," *Nasha kultura*, Warsaw, 1935, Book 8; the same, "Torhovelni zviazky Ukrainy z Leipzigom u XVIII st.," *ibid.*, Warsaw, 1936, Book 6.

12. B. Krupnytsky, *Hetman Danylo Apostoly ta yoho doba*, Augsburg, 1948, pp. 150-154: The Poles removed their "stapel right" on produce and merchandise brought by the Ukrainian merchants in 1727; Dzhydzhora, *op. cit.*, 18-60; K. Kononenko, *Ukraine and Russia, A History of Economic Relations between Ukraine and Russia,1654-1917*, Milwaukee, 1958, pp. 23-25; O. Ohloblyn, *Ocherky istorii ukrainskoi fabryky, Manufaktura v Hetmanshchyni*, Kiev, 1925, p. 38 and other; M. Slabchenko, *Orhanizatsia khaziaistva Ukrainy*, Kharkiv, 1925, Part II, p. 92.

13. Doroshenko, *loc. cit.*

14. *Ibid.*; Dzhydzhora, *op. cit.*, pp. 18, 58-60.

15. Slabchenko, *op. cit.*, Odessa, 1923, Part I, pp. 102-103.

16. V. Bidnov, "Hroshi", *Ukrainska zahalna entsyklopedia*, Lviv 1936, Vol. III, p. 995; A. Shuhaievskii, *Moniety i denezhniei shchot na levo-berezhniei Ukrainie*, Cher-

nihiv, 1917; the same, "Moneta na Ukraini" *Entsyklopedia ukrainoznavstva*, New York-Paris, 1955-1957, Vol. I, 447-450.

17. Bidnov, *loc. cit.*

18. V. Modzelevsky, "Pershyi viiskovyi pidskarbii Roman Rakushka", *Zapysky Istorychno-Filolohichnoho Viddilu*, Ukrainska Akademia Nauk, Kiev, 1919, Vol. I; V. Rudniev, "Finansovyi stan Hetmanshchyny za Petra I," *Naukovyi zbirnyk*, Istorychna Sektsia Ukrainskoi Akademii Nauk, Kiev, 1926; Okinshevych, *op. cit.*, pp. 113-14; Doroshenko, *op. cit.*, Vol. II, pp. 125-128.

19. V. Veselaho, "Pryntsypy ekonomichnoi polityky Bohdana Khmelnytskoho," *Narysy z istorii ekonomichnoi dumky na Ukraini*, ed. by D. Vyrnyk, Kiev, 1956, pp. 96-102.

20. On the Russian measures to exploit the Ukrainian economy; in general: S. Balzak, V. Vasiutin, and Ya. Feigin, edts., *Economic Geograpy of the USSR*, New York, 1952, pp. 122-133; R. Dyminsky, "Economic Life," *Ukraine and Its People*, ed. by I. Mirchuk, Munich, 1949, pp. 127-128; N. Fr.-Chirovsky, *The Economic Factors in the Growth of Russia*, New York, 1957, p. 59; the same, *Old Ukraine, Its Socio-Economic History prior to 1781*, Madison, N.J., 1963, pp. 364-366.

BIBLIOGRAPHY

I. *General works on history.*
Andrusiak, M., *Istoria Ukrainy*, Prague, 1941.
Bestuzhev-Riumin, K., *Russkaia istoria*, St. Petersburg, 1872.
Bobrzynski, M., *Dzieje Polski w zarysie*, Warsaw, 1927-1931, 3 volms.
Caro, J., *Geschichte Polens*, Gotha, 1863.
Chase, T., *The Story of Lithuania*, New York, 1946.
Chirovsky, Fr.-, N., *An Introduction to Russian History*, New York, 1967.
Chirovsky, Fr.-, N., *A History of the Russian Empire*, New York, 1973, Vol. I.
Doroshenko, D., *Narys istorii Ukrainy*, Munich, 1966, 2 volms.
Doroshenko, D., and Gerus, O., *A Survey of Ukrainian History*, Winnipeg, 1975.
Halecki, O., *History of Poland*, New York, 1942.
Holubets, M., ed., *Velyka istoria Ukrainy*, Lviv, 1935.
Hrushevsky, M., *Istoria Ukrainy-Rusy*, New York, 1954-1958, 10 volms.
Hrushevsky, *A History of Ukraine*, New Haven, 1970.
Istoria Ukrainskoi RSR, Artymenko, I., ed.-in-chief, Kiev, 1977, 2 volms.
Kholmsky, I., *Istoria Ukrainy*, New York 1971.
Kluchevsky, (Kluchevskii), V., *A History of Russia*, London-New York, 1911-1914, 4 volms.
Krupnytsky, B., *Die Geschichte der Ukraine*, Berlin, 1943.
Krypiakevych, I., and Dolnytsky, M., *Istoria Ukrainy*, New York, 1966.
Manning, C., *The Story of Ukraine*, New York, 1947.
Nahayevsky, I., Rev., *History of Ukraine*, Philadelphia, 1975.
Polonska-Vasylenko, N., *Istoria Ukrainy*, Munich, 1972, 2 volms.
Tomashivsky, S., *Istoria Ukrainy, starynni viky i seredni viky*, Munich 1948.
Vernadsky, G., and Karpovich, M., *A History of Russia*, Vol. III, *The Mongols and Russia*, New Haven, 1953.

II. *Monographic works and special subject matters.*
Aksakov, I., *Issledovanie o torgovle na ukrainskikh yarmarkakh*, St. Petersburg, 1858.
Andrusiak, M., *Istoria kozachchyny*, Munich, 1946, 6 volms.
Bahalii (Bagaley), D., *Orcherk iz istorii kolonizatsii i byta stepnoi okrainy Moskovskavo gosudarstva*, Moscow, 1887.
Bahalii (Bagaley), D., *Materialy dla istorii kolonizatsii i byta stepnoi okrainy Moskovskavo gosudarstva*, Moscow, 1886-1890, 2 volms.
Bahalii, D., *Narys istorii Ukrainy na sotsialno-ekonomichnomu grunti*, Kharkiv, 1928.
Bahalii, D., *Istoria Slobidskoi Ukrainy*, Kharkiv, 1923.
Bahalii (Bagaley), D., *Ukrainskii mandrivnyi filosof H. S. Skovoroda*, Kharkiv, 1926.
Balzer, O., *Historia ustorju Polski: Przeglad wykladow uniwersteckich*, Lviv, 1913.
Balzer, O., *Sadownictwo ormianskie w sredniowiecznym Lwowie.*, Lviv, 1909.
Balzer, O., *Skartabelat w ustroju szlachectwa polskiego*, Cracow, 1911.
Baranovich, I., *Magnatskoie khaziaistvo na yuge Volini v XVIII v.*, Moscow, 1955.

Beauplan, de, G., *A. Description of Ukraine*, New York, 1959.
Borshchak, I., *Velykyi Mazepynets Hryhor Orlyk*, New York, 1972.
Chirovsky, Fr.-, N., *Old Ukraine, Its Socio-Ecomonic History prior to 1781*, Madison, N.J., 1963.
Chirovsky, Fr.-, N., *The Economic Factors in the Growth of Russia*, New York, 1957.
Chodynicki, K., *Kosciol prawoslawny a Rzeczypoospolita Polska 1370-1632*, Warsaw, 1934.
Chubaty, N., *Ohlad istorii ukrainskoho prava, istoria dzerel i derzhavnoho prava*, Munich, 1947, Pt. I-II.
Chubaty, N., *Istoria Khrystianstva na Rusy-Ukraini*, Rome, 1976, Vol. II, Part one.
Chyzhevsky, D., *Narys z istorii filocofii na Ukraini*, Prague, 1931.
Chyzhevsky, D., *Istoria ukrainskoi literatury*, New York, 1956.
Chyzhevsky, D., *Filosofia H. Skovorody*, Vienna, 1918.
Diadychenko, V., *Narys suspilno-politychnoho ustroiu Livoberezhnoi Ukrainy kintsia XVII i pochatku XVIII st.*, Kiev, 1959.
Fedoriv, Yu., *Istoria tserkvy v Ukraini*, Toronto, 1967.
Freischyn-Czyrowski (Chirovsky), N.,*Geschichtlicher Abriss der staatsrechtlichen Einrichtungen in Galizien bis zum Wiener-Kongress 1815*, Graz, 1943, doctor-thesis, manuscript.
Golubinskii, E., *Istoria russkoi tserkvy*, Moscow, 1901-1904, 2 volms.
Halecki, O., *From Florence to Brest*, Rome, 1958.
Holobutsky, V., *Zaporozhskoie kozachestvo*, Kiev, 1957.
Holobutsky, V., *Zaporozhska Sitch v ostanni chasy svoioho isnuvannia, 1734-1745*, Kiev, 1961.
Holubets, M., *Nacherk istorii ukrainskoho mystetstva*, Lviv, 1902.
Holubets, M., *Za ukrainskyi Lviv*, Lviv, 1927.
Hryshko, V., *Istorychne pidgruntia teorii III Rymu*, Munich, 1953.
Huslystyi, K., *Z istorii klasovoi borotby v stepovii Ukraini v 60-70 tykh rokakh XVIII st.*, Kharkiv, 1933.
Ilarion, Metropolitan, see Ohienko.
Kononenko, K., *Ukraine and Russia, A History of the Economic Relations between Ukraine and Russia, 1654-1917*, Milwaukee, 1958.
Korzun, T., *Dzieje wojen i wojskowosci w Polsce*, Cracow, 1912.
Kostiakovsky, A., *Prava, po kotorym sudytsia malorossiiskyi narod*, Kiev, 1879.
Kostruba, T., *Hetman Ivan Skoropadskyi*, Lviv, 1932.
Krupnytsky, B., *Hetman Danylo Apostol i yoho doba*, Augsburg, 1948.
Krupnytsky, B., *Hetman Pylyp Orlyk*, Munich, 1956.
Krypiakevych, I., *Bohdan Khmelnytskyi*, Monografia, Kiev, 1954.
Krypiakevych, I., Hnatevych, B., *Istoria ukrainskoho viiska*, Winnipeg, 1953.
Kutrzeba, S., *Historya ustroju Polski*, Vol. I, *Korona*; Vol. II, *Litwa*, Lviv, 1914-1917.
Kutrzeba, S., *Historja zrodel dawnwgo prava polskiego*, Lviv-Warsaw, 1925, Vol. II, *Metryka litewska*.
Kutrzeba, S., *Sprawa zydowska w Polsce*, Lviv, 1911.
Levkovych, I., *Narys istorii Volynskoi zemli*, Winnipeg., 1953.

Lototsky, O., *Avtokefalia*, Warsaw, 1938, Vol. II.
Lozinski, W., *Patrycyat i mieszczanstwo lwowskie*, Lviv, 1892.
Lubavskii, M. *Oblasnoie dielenie i miestnoie upravlenie Velikavo Kniazhestva Litovskavo*, Moscow, 1893.
Lubomirski, T., *Trzy rozdialy z histoyi skarbowosci w Polsce, 1507-1532*, Cracow, 1868.
Lutsiv, V., *Anty-polske povstannia otamana Mukhy v 1490-1492 rr*, State College, Pennsylvania, 1979 (manuscript).
Lutsiv, V., *Tserkovni bratstva v Ukraini*, State College, Pennsylvania, 1976.
Luzhnytsky, H., *Ukrainska tserkva mizh Skhodom i Zakhodom*, Philadelphia, 1954.
Lyashchenko, P., *History of the National Economy of Russia*, New York, 1949.
Lypa, Yu., *Pryznachennia Ukrainy*, New York, 1953.
Lypynsky (Lipinski), V., *Z dziejow Ukrainy*, Cracow, 1912.
Lypynsky, V., *Ukraina na perelomi*, Kiev-Vienna, 1920.
Lypynsky, V., *Religia i tserkva v istorii Ukrainy*, Philadelphia, 1925.
Maciejowski, A., *Historya rzemiosl i rzemieslniczych wyrobow w Polsce od czasow najdawniejszych az do konca XVIII w.*, Warsaw, 1877.
Mackiv, T., *Prince Mazepa, Hetman of Ukraine in Contemporary English Publications, 1687-1709*, Chicago, 1967.
Mackiv, T., *Mazepa im Lichte der zitgenossischen deutschen Quellen*, Munich, 1936.
Malinovskii, I., *Rada Velikavo Kniazhestva Litovskavo v sviazi s boiarskoiu dumoiu Rossii*, Tomsk, 1904, Part 2, Copy 1, Tomsk, 1912, Part 2, Copy 2.
Miakotin, V., *Ocherky sotsialnoi istorii Ukrainy v 17 i 18 vv.*, Prague, 1924.
Miklashevskii, I., *Iz istrorii khaziastvennovo byta Moskovskavo gosudarstva*, Part. I. *Zaselenie i selskoie khaziaistvo yuzhnoi okrainy XVII v.*, Moscow, 1894.
Mirchuk, P. *Koliivshchyna, Haidamatske povstannia, 1768*, New York, 1973.
Mirtschuk (Mirchuk), I., *Geschichte der ukrainischen Kultur*, Munich, 1957.
Mirtchuk, I., *Ukraine and Its People*, Munich, 1949.
Nesterenko, O., *Rozvytok promyslovosty na Ukraini*, Part I, *Remeslo i manufaktura*, Kiev, 1959.
Nesterenko, O., Romanenko, I., and Vyrnyk, D., *Ocherki rozvitia narodnavo khaziaistva Ukrainskoi SSR.*, Moscow, 1954.
Ohienko, I., (Metropolitan Ilarion), *Istoria ukrainskoi kultury*, Kiev, 1918.
Ohienko, I., *Ukrainska tserkva*, Prague, 1942, Vol. I.
Ohienko, I., *Kniaz Konstantyn Ostrozhsky i yoho kulturna pratsia*, Winnipeg, 1958.
Ohienko, I., *Ukrainska tserkva za Bohdana Khmelnytskoho*, Winnipeg, 1956.
Ohienko, I., *Ukrainska tserkva za chasiv Ruiny*, Winnipeg, 1956.
Ohloblyn, O., *Ocherky istorii ukrainskoi fabryky, manufaktura v Hetmanshchyni*, Kiev, 1925.
Ohloblyn, O., *Moskovska teoria tretioho Rymu v XVI-XVIII st.*, Munich, 1951.
Ohloblyn, O., *Ukrainsko-moskovska uhoda 1654 roku*, New York, 1954.
Ohloblyn, O., *Treaty of Pereyaslav*, Toronto-New York, 1954.
Ohloblyn, O., *Dumky pro Khmelnychchynu*, New York, 1957.
Ohloblyn, O., *Ludy staroi Ukrainy*, Munich, 1959.
Ohloblyn, O., *Hetman Ivan Mazepa ta yogo doba*, New york, 1960.

Okinshevych, L., *Lektsii z istorii ukrainskoho prava*, Munich, 1947.
Polonska-Vasylenko, N., *Zaselennia pivdennoi Ukrainy v polovyni XVIII st.*, Munich, 1960, 2 parts.
Polonska-Vasylenko, N., *Bradstva na Ukraini v mynulomu i suchasnomu*, Munich, 1947.
Ptasnik, J., *Miasta i mieszczanstwo w dawnej Polsce*, Cracow, 1934.
Ptasnik, J., *Papiernie w Polsce*, Cracow, 1920.
Radzykevych, V., *Istoria ukrainskoi literatury*, Detroit, 1955, 2 volms.
Rutkowski, J., *Skup solectw w Polsce w wieku XVI*, Poznan, 1921.
Rutkowksi, J., *Poddanstwo wloscian w XVIII wieku w Polsce i w niektorych krajach Europy*, Poznan, 1921.
Shuhaievskii, A., *Monieta i denezhniei shchot na levo-berezhniei Ukrainie*, Chernihiv, 1917.
Sichynsky, V., *Narys z istorii ukrainskoi promyslovosty*, Lviv, 1936.
Sichynsky, V., *Ukraine in Foreign Comments and Descriptions, from the VIth to the XXth century*, New York, 1953.
Skalkovskii, A., *Opyt statesticheskavo opysania Novorossiiskavo kraia*, Odessa, 1853, 2 volms.
Skalkovskii, A., *Khronologicheskoie obozrenie Novorossiiskavo kraia*, Odessa, 1836.
Slabchenko, M. *Orhanizatsia hospodarstva na Ukraini*, Part I, *Hospodarstvo Hetmanshchyny*, Odessa, 1923.
Smirnov, V., *Krimskoie Khanstvo pod vierkhovenstvom Ottomanskoi Porty*, St. Petersburg, 1887.
Stockel, G., *Die Enstehung des Kozakentums*, Munich, 1953.
Stukas, J., *Awakening Lithuania*, Madison, N.J., 1966.
Szelagowski, A., *Pieniadz i przewrot cen w XVI i XVIII wiekach w Polsce*, Cracow, 1902.
Tytov, F., *Stara vyshcha osvita v Kyivskii Ukraini v XVI-XVII st*, Kiev, 1924.
Vasylenko, M., *Materialy do istorii ukrainskoho prava*, Kiev, 1928.
Vlasovsky, I., *Narys istorii ukrainskoi pravoslavnoi tserkvy*, New York, 1955-1956, 2 volms.
Vozniak, M., *Istoria ukrainskoi literatury*, Lviv, 1921, 2 volms.
Vynar, B., *Rozvytok ukrainskoi lehkoi promyslovosti*, Denver, 1955.
Vyrnyk, D., *Ukrainskaia SSR, Kratkoi istorichesko-ekonomicheskii obzor*, Moscow, 1954.
Vytanovych, I., *Suspilno-ekonomichni tendentsii v derzhavnomu budivnytstvi Ivana Mazepy*, Papers, Chicago, 1959.
Winter, E., *Byzanz und Rom im Kampf um die Ukraine*, Leipzig, 1942.
Wolf, J., *Rod Gedyminow*, Cracow, 1886.
Wolf, J., *Kniaziowie litewsko-ruscy*, Warsaw, 1895.
Yakovliv, A., *Dohovir Bohdana Khmelnytskoho z Moskvoiu*, New York, 1954.
Yakovliv, A., *Ukrainskyi kodeks 1743 roku; Prava, po kotorym sudytsia malorossiiskyi narod*, Munich, 1949.
Yakovliv(Jakowliw), A., *Das deutsche Recht in der Ukraine und seine Einflusse auf das ukrainische Recht im 16-18 Jahrhundert*, Leipzig, 1942.
Yaniv, V., *Narys ukrainskoi kultury*, New York, 1961.

Yatsymirskii, A., *Gigorii Tsamblak, Ocherk yevo zhyzni i deiatelnosti*, St. Petersburg, 1904.
Yevarnitskii, D., *Istoria Zaporozhskikh kozakov*, St. Petersburg, 1895.

III. Articles, chronicles and documents.

Akta grodzkie i ziemskie, Lviv, 1863-1935, Vol. II, III, V, VI and VII.
Akty otnosiashchiesia k istorii yuzhnoi i zapadnoi Rossii, St. Petersburg, 1881.
Akty yugo-zapadnoi Rossii, St. Petersburg, 1861-1869, Volms. II, III, VII, X, XI.
Andrusiak, M., "Zviazky Mazepy z Stanislavom Leshchynskym i Karlom XII," *Zapysky Naukovoho Tovarystva im. Shevchenka*, Lviv, 1933. Vol. CLII.
Antonovych, V., "Proiskhozhdenie Zaporoskavo kozachestva," *Kievskaia Starina*, Kiev, 1884.
Bahalii, D., "Generalnaia opis Malorossii,"*Kievskaia Starina*,Kiev, 1883.
Balzer, O., "Verfassungsgeschichte Polens," *Anzeiger der Akademie der Wissenschft*, Cracow, 1906.
Barvinsky, E., "Prychynky do istorii znosyn tsisaria Rudolfa i papy Klymentia VIII z kozakamy v 1593-94 rokakh," *Zapysky Naukovoho Tovarystva im. Shevchenka*, Lviv, 1895, Vol. X.
Bidnov, V., "Hroshi," *Ukrainska Zahalna Entsyklopedia*, Lviv, 1936, Vol. III.
Cherkasky, I., "Sudovi reformy Hetmana Rozumovskoho," *Yuvileinyi zbirnyk na poshanu D. Bahalia*, Kiev, 1927.
Cherkasky, I., "Chy vplyvav Tieplov na Hetmana Rozumovskoho," *Yuvileinyi zbirnyk na poshanu M. Hrushevskoho*, Kiev, 1928.
Chubaty, M., "The Meaning of "Russia" and "Ukraine," *On the Historical Beginnings of Slavic Eastern Europe*, ed. by N. Fr.-Chirovsky, New York, 1976.
Domanytsky, V., "Chy bula reforma Batoria?," *Yuvileinyi zbirnyk v poshanu M. Hrushevskoho*, Lviv, 1906.
Doroshenko, D., "Biblioteky," *Entsyklopedia Ukrainoznavstva*, Munich, 1949, Vol. I.
Dovnar-Zapolsky, M., "Polsko-litovskaia unija na seimakh do 1569 goda," *Trudy slavianskoi kommisiji*,Moscow, 1897, Vol. II.
Durbrosky, V., "Do pytannia pro mizhnarodniu torhivlu Ukrainy v pershii polovyni XVIII st.," *Zapysky Istor-Fil. Viddilu, Ukrainska Akademia Nauk*, Kiev, 1931.
Dyminsky, R., "Ecomonic Life," *Ukraine and Its People*, ed. by I. Mirchuk, Munich, 1949.
Dzydzhora, I., "Ekonomichna polityka rossiisskoho pravytelstva suproty Ukrainy v 1710-1730 rokakh," *Zapysky Naukovoho Tovarystva im. Shevchenka*, Lviv, 1910-1911, Vols. IIIC, CI, CIII, and CV.
Entsyclopedia Ukrainoznavstva, Munich, 1949, Volms. I-III.
Hrushevsky, M., "Baida Vyshnyvetskyi v poezii i istorii," *Zapysky Ukrainskoho Naukovoho Tovarystva*, Kiev, 1909, Vol. III.
Hryshko, V., "300 littia Khmelnychchyny," *Zapysky Naukovoho Tovarystva im. Shevchenka*, Munich, 1948, Vol. CLVI.
Hryshko, V., "Do problemy providnoi verstvy za Hetmana Bohdana Khmelnytskoho," *Ameryka*, Philadelphia, Aug. 2, 3, 6 and 7, 1957.

Istoria Rusiv, ed. by O. Ohloblyn, New York, 1956.
Jablonowski, A., "Kozaczyzna a legitymizm, dwie legendy polityczno-historyczne Ukrainy — batoryanska i baturynska," *Ateneum*, Warsaw, 1895, Vol. II.
Jablonowski, A., "Ukraina," *Zrodla dziejowe*, Warsaw, 1894-97, Vol. XX-XXI.
Jablonowski, A., "Ziemie ruskie, Wolyn i Podole," *Zrodla dziejowe*, Warsaw, 1889, Vol. XIX.
Jablonowski, A., "Rus Czerwona," *Zrodla dziejowe*, Warsaw, 1903, Vol. XVIII.
Jablonowski, A., "Najanowsze teorye heraldyczne," *Pisma*, Warsaw, 1913, Vol. 7.
Kniga posolskaia, Metryka Velikaho Kniazhestva Litowskaho, St. Petersburg, 1843.
Kobrynsky, R., "Lis i myslvystvo v davnim ukrainskim pravi," *Ukrainskyi lisnytskyi almanakh*, New York, 1958.
Korzon, T., "Organizacia wojskowa Litwy w okresia Jagiellonskim," *Rocznik Towarzystwa Przyjaciol Nauki w Wilnie*, Vilna, 1909, Vol. II.
Kostomarov, N., "Ruina, Getmanstvo Brukhvetskavo," *Sobranie sochinenii*, St. Petersburg, 1905, Vol. XV, Bk. VI.
Kostomarov, N., "Getmanstvo Yuria Khmelnytskavo," *Sobranie sochinenii*, St. Petersburg, 1905, Vol. XII, Bk. V.
Kostomarov, N., "Getmanstvo Vyhovskavo," *Sobranie sochinenii*, St. Petersburg, 1903, Vol. II. Bk. I.
Kravtsiv, B., "Mitolohia ukrainskoi zemli," *Istoria ukrainskoi kultury*, pub. by I. Tyktor, Winnipeg, 1964.
Krypiakevych, I., "Pobut," *Istoria ukainskoi kultury*, ibid.
Krypiakevych, I., "Kozachchyna i Batievi volnosti," *Zherela do istorii Ukrainy- Rusy*, Lviv, 1908, Vol. VIII.
Kurinnyi, P., "Der Rynok von Lemberg," *Ukraine in Vergangenheit und Gegenwart*, Munich, 1954, Nos. 1-2.
Kurinnyi, P., "Arkhitektura Desiatynnoi tserkvy," *Ukrainskyi samostiinyk*, 1953, No. 16.
Kutrzeba, S., "Handel Polski ze Wschodem," *Przeglad Polski*, Cracow, 1903, Vols. 148-150.
Kutrzeba, S., "Handel Krakowa w wiekach srednich," *Rozprawy wydzialu hist.-filoz.* Akademija Umjejetnosci, Cracow, 1902, Vol. 44.
Kutrzeba, S., "Datastanagirk Mechitara Gosza i statut ormianski z roku 1519," *Kwartalnik historyczny*, Lviv, 1908, Vol. 22.
Kutrzeba, S., "Unia Litwy z Polska," *Polska i Litwa w rozwoju dziejowym*, Cracow, 1913.
Lappo, I., "Zemskii sud v Velikomu Kniazhestvi Litovskom v kontse XVI v," *Zhurnal ministerstva narodnavo prosveshchenia*, St. Petersburg, 1897, Bk. 6.
Lappo, I., "Grodskii sud v Velikom Kniazhestvi Litovskom," *Zhurnal ministerstva narodnavo prosveshchenia*, St. Petersburg, 1908, Bk. 1.
Lappo, I., "Podkomorskii sud v Velikom Kniazhestvi Litovskom v kontse XVI i nachale XVII vieka," *ibid.*, 1899, Bk. 8.
Lashchenko, R., "Lytovskyi Statut yak pamiatnyk ukrainskoho prava," *Naukovyi zbirnyk*, Ukrainian Free University, Prague, 1923.
Lashchenko, R., "Kopni sudy na Ukraini, ikh pokhodzhennia, kompetentsia i ustrii," *Zbirnyk pravnychoi komisii*, Naukove Tovarystvo im Shevchenka, Lviv, 1926, Vol. I-II.

Leontovych, T., "Rada velikikh kniazei litovskikh," *Zhurnal ministerstva narodnavo prosveshchenia*, St. Petersburg, 1907, Bk. 9-10.
Leontovych, T., "Viecha, seimiki i seimy v Velikom Kniazhestvi Litovskom," *ibid*, 1910, Bk. 2-3.
Lewicki, A., "Nieco o uniji Litwy z Polska," *Przeglad Polski*, Cracow, 1893, Vol. 110.
Lubavskii, M., "Nachalnaia istoria maloruskavo kozachestva," *Zhurnal ministerstva narodnavo prosveshchenia*, St. Petersburg, 1895, Vol. III.
Lysko, Z., "Istoria muzyky," *Entsyklopedia ukrainoznavstva*, Munich, 1949, Vol. I.
Miller, M. "Heraldyka," *Entsyklopedia ukrainoznavstva*, Munich, 1949, Vol. II.
Mirchuk, I., "Istoria ukrainskoi filosofii," *ibid.*, Vol. I.
Modzalevsky, V., "Pershyi viiskovyi pidskarbii Roman Rakushka," *Zapysky Istor.-Fil. Viddilu*, Ukrainska Akademia Nauk, Kiev, 1919-1923, Vol. I.
Ohloblyn, O., "Hetman Ivan Mazepa i ukrainska promyslovist," *Kalendar Svobody na Mazepynskyi rik 1959*, Jersey City, 1959.
Ohloblyn, O., "Do istorii Ruiny," *Zapysky, Istor. Fil. Viddil*, Ukrainska Akademia Nauk, Kiev, 1928, Bk. XVI.
Ohloblyn, O., "Khmelnychchyna i zaliznorudna promyslovist pravoberezhnoi Ukrainy,"*Zapysky Naukovoho Tovarystva im. Shevchenka*, Munich, 1948, Vol. CLVI.
Ohloblyn, O., "Vyvid prav Ukrainy," *Visnyk*, New York, 1954, No. 5.
Ohloblyn, O., "Dynastychna ideia v derzhavno-politychnii dumtsi Ukrainy- Hetmanshchyny XVII-XVIII st.," *Derzhavnytska dumka*, Philadelphia, 1951, No. 4.
Ohloblyn, O., "Do istorii budnytskoi promyslovosty Ukrainy za chasiv Khmelnychchyny," *Zapysky, Istor. Fil. Viddil Ukrainskoi Akademii Nauk*, Kiev, 1927. Bk. X.
Ohloblyn, O., "Do istorii povstannia Petra Ivanenka (Petryka)," *Zapysky, Istor. Fil. Viddil Vseukrainskoi Akademii Nauk*, Kiev, 1928, Bk. XIX.
Ohloblyn, O., "Problema derzhavnoi vlady na Ukraini za Khemlnychchyny i Pereyaslavska uhoda," *Ukrainskyi istoryk*, 1965, No. 1-4.
Okinshevych, L., "Rada Starshynska na Hetmanshchyni XVII-XVIII vv., *Pratsi, Komisii dla vyuchuvannia istorii zakhidnio-ruskoho ta ukrainskoho prava,"* Ukrainska Akademia Nauk, Kiev, 1929, Vols. VII-VIII.
Okinshevych, L. "Heneralna rada na Ukraini-Hetmanshchyni XVII-XVIII st.," *ibid*, Kiev, 1929, Vol. VI.
Okinshevych, L., "Znachne viiskove tovarystvo v Ukraini-Hetmanshchyni XVII-XVIII st., *Zapysky Naukovoho Tovarystva im. Shevchenka*, Munich, 1948, Vol. CLVII.
Okinshevych, L., "Derzhavne pravo, Lytovsko-Ruska doba," *Entsyklopedia ukrainoznavstva*, Munich 1949, Vol. I.
Okinshevych, L., "Hetmanska derzhava," *ibid*, Vol. I.
Olanchyn, D., "Torhovelni znosyny Ukrainy a Breslavom v XVIII st.," *Nasha kultura*, Warsaw, 1935, Bk. 8.
Olanchyn, D., "Torhovelni znosyny Ukrainy z Leiptsigom v XVIII st.," *ibid.*, Warsaw, 1936, Bk. 6.
Padokh, Ya., "Miski sudy na Ukraini-Hetmanshchyni," *Do 300 littia Khmelnychchyny*, Munich, 1948.

Petrov, N., "Kyivska Akademia," *Zapysky Istor.-Fil. Viddilu*, Ukrainska Akademia Nauk, Kiev, 1919, Vol. I.
Polonska-Vasylenko, N., "Maino Zaporozhskoi starshyny, yak dzherelo sotsialnoekonomichnoho doslidzhennia istorii Zaporizhzhia," *Narysy z sotsialnoekonomichnoi istorii Ukrainy*, Kiev, 1932, Vol. I.
Polonska-Vasylenko, N., "Zruinuvannia Zaporozhskoi Sichi," *Visnyk*, OOCHSU, New York, 1955, No. 7-8.
Polonska-Vasylenko, N., "The Constitution of Pylyp Orlyk," *The Annals of the Ukrainian Akdemy of Arts and Sciences in the US*, New York, 1960, Vol. VI.
Polonska-Vasylenko, N., "Palii i Mazepa," *Visnyk*, OOCHSU, New York, 1959, Nos. 7-8.
Polonska-Vasylenko, N., "The Kozaks," *Ukraine, A Concise Encyclopedia*, Toronto, 1963, Vol. I.
Polonska-Vasylenko, N., "Pereyaslavkyi dohovir v ochakh yoho suchasnykiv," *Vyzvolnyi Shlakh*, London, 1955, Bk. IV.
Rudniv, V., "Finansovyi stan Hetmanshchyny za Petra I," *Naukovyi Zbirnyk*, Istorychna sektsia Ukrainskoi Akademii Nauk, za rik 1925, Kiev, 1926.
Rulikowski, E., "Dawne drogi i szlaki na prawym brzegu Dniepru," *Ateneum*, Warsaw, 1878, Vols. III-IV.
Seniutovych-Berezhnyi, V., "Do dzherel staroruskoi heraldyky," *Litopys Volyni*, New York, 1955, Nos. 2, 12-23.
Shuhaievsky, A., "Moneta na Ukraini," *Entsyklopedia ukrainoznavstva*, Munich, 1955-57, Vol. I.
Sichynsky, V., "Gotyk i renesans," *Entsyklopedia ukrainoznavstva*, Munich, 1949, Vol. I.
Sichynsky, V., "Arkhitektura," *ibid.*, Vol. I.
Sichynsky, V., "Hrafika-heraldyka," *ibid.*, Vol. I.
Sichynsky, V., "Malarstvo," *ibid.*, Vol. I.
Sichynsky, V., "Rizba," *ibid.*, Vol. I.
Sichynsky, V., "Das kunstlerische Schaffen in Lemberg," *Ukraine in Vergangenheit und Gegenwart*, Munich, 1954, Nos. 1-2.
Stadnicki, A., "O wsiach t.z. woloskich," *Bibljoteka Ossolinskich*, Lviv, 1848.
Stetsiuk, K., "Sotsialno-ekonomichnyi rozvytok i politychne stanovyshche Ukrainy pisla 'Vossoiedinenia' z Rosiieiu", *Istoria Ukrainskoi RSR*, Kiev, 1953.
The Union of Berest, the document, *The Way*, Philadelphia, June 10-17, 1979.
Ukraine, A Concise Encyclopedia, ed. by V. Kubiovych, New York, 1963-1971, Vol. I-II.
Ukrainska zahalna entsyklopedia, ed. by I. Rakovsky, Lviv, 1930-1935, Vols. I-II.
Entsyklopedia ukrainoznavstva, ed. by V. Kubiovych, Munich, 1949-1952, Vols. I-II- III.
Ulianov, N., "Kompleks Filofeia," *Novii Zhurnal*, New York, 1956, No. XLV.
Vasylenko, M., "Pavlo Polubotok," *Ukraina*, Kiev, 1926, Vol. VI.
Veselaho, V., "Pryntsypy ekonomichnoi polityky Bohdana Khmelnytskoho," *Narysy z istorii ekonomichnoi dumky na Ukraini*, ed. by D. Vyrnyk, Kiev, 1956.
Volobuiev, M., "Do problemy ukrainskoi ekonomiky," *Bilshovyk Ukrainy*, Jan.-Feb., 1928, Nos. 2-3.

Vossoiedinenie Ukrainy c Rossieiu, documenty i materially, Moscow, 1954, Vols. I-III.
Vostokov, A., "Sud i kazn Hryhoria Samoilovycha," *Kievskaia Starina"*, Kiev, *1889, Bk. I.*
Vostokov, A., *"Sudba Vyhovskavo i Nechaia,"* Kievskaia Starina, Kiev, 1890, Bk. I.
Vynar, L., "Severyn Nalyvaiko i revolutsyinyi rukh bratslavskoho mishchanstva," *Rozbudova derzhavy*, Toronto, 1957, No. 20.
Vytvytsky, V., "Istoria muzyky XVIII-XIX st.," *Entsyklopedia ukrainoznavstva, Munich, 1949, Vol. I.*
Yakovliv, A., *"Istoria dzherel ukrainskoho prave,"* Entsyklopedia ukrainoznavstva, *Munich 1949, Vol. I.*
Yakovliv, A., *"Ukrainskyi kodeks 1743 r,"* Zapysky Naukovoho Tovarystva im. Schevchenka, *Munich, 1949, Vol. CLIX.*
Yaroshevych, A., *"Kapitalistychna orenda na Ukraini za polskoi doby,"* Zbirnyk, Sotsialno-ekonomichnyi Viddil, Ukrainska Akademia Nauk, Kiev, 1927, Vol. V-VI.
Yefymenko, P., "Poslednei pisar Voiska Zaporoskavo Hloba," *Kievskaia Starina,* Kiev, 1882, Bk. VIII.
Yefymenko, P., "Poslednei koshevoi ataman Zaporozhskoi Sichi," *Russkaia Starina,* Kiev, 1875, Bk. XI.
Zrodla dziejowe, Warsaw, Vols. II, III, IV, V, VI, VII, VIII, IX, XII, XVI, XVIII, and XIX.

INDEX OF NAMES

A

Aksakov, I., 345, 355, 361
Aleksei, Metropolitan, 59
Aleksei, Tsar, XIII, 188
Alepo, P., 263, 276, 279, 282, 309, 351
Andrei, of Polotsk, 12
Andrew, craftsman, 349
Andrii, artist, 81
Andrusiak, M., 35-36, 222, 224
Antonovych, V., 15, 34, 110, 112
Apostol, D., Hetman, 208-211, 224, 229, 236, 263, 266, 273, 277, 285, 289-290, 300, 303, 308-309, 313-314, 324-326, 331-332, 334, 337-338, 341, 346, 349, 360, 365, 368-370, 372, 374, 376-377
Apostol, P., diary writer, 273
Apraksin, F., 224
Arik-Buka, Khan, 4
Astamatenko, O., 359, 375
August, king of Poland, 201
Avraam, bishop, 61

B

Bahalii (Bagalei), D., 225, 307, 309, 325, 329-330
Balaban, G., bishop, 69-70
Balaban, D., Metropolitan, 257
Balashevich, K., industrialist, 350
Baluse, J., 331
Balzer, O., 110, 163, 165
Bandinelli, R., 358
Bantysh-Kamensky, M., 266
Baptysta, I., architect, 278
Barabash, Ya., 187
Baranovich, I., 129
Baranovych, L., bishop, 257-258, 265, 267-268, 270

Barvinsky, E., 35
Batory, Stefan, king of Poland, 32, 64, 108
Batu, Khan, 4, 8
Baumeister, C., philosopher, 269
Beauplan, de, G., 120-122, 127, 129, 133, 135, 141, 143-144, 276, 309, 317, 324, 326
Berdibeg, Khan, 6
Berezovsky, M., 266, 282
Berk, Khan, 4-5
Berlo, A., bishop, 267
Berynda, P., 276
Bezborodko, O., statesman, 266, 273
Bidnov, V., 372, 378-379
Bielskii, family, 26
Bilsky, F., 22
Bobrzynski, M., XIII
Bogart, E., 110
Bohdanovych, S., judge, 240, 295
Bohun, I, colonel, 181, 183
Boretsky, Y., Metropolitan, 253, 260, 271
Borkovsky, V., Cossack, 277
Borshchak, I., 223-224
Bortniansky, D., 266, 282
Branicki, family, 316
Bronsky, K., 77
Brukhovetsky, I., Hetman, 190-193, 229, 291-292, 308, 312, 371, 373, 377
Brunn, G., 35
Bulavin, K., 202
Buturlin, V., 183
Bykhovets, A., 76

C

Camiles, de, J., 261
Carl-Gustav, of Sweden, 185-186

Caro, J., 109
Casimir, Jagiellonczyk, of Poland, 20, 28-29, 41, 44, 50, 62
Casimir, of Poland, 3-4, 10, 66, 91-92, 103, 151
Catherine I, Tsaritsa, 208
Catherine II, Tsaritsa, 212, 215-216, 219, 221, 307
Cerularius, 61
Charles XII, of Sweden, 200-205, 214, 224, 233, 248, 259, 277
Chase, T., 34
Cherkasky, I., 225
Chetvertynsky, family, 16
Chirovsky, N., 34-35, 86, 109, 129, 144, 163, 225, 309-310, 330, 355-356, 379
Chojecki, K., 276
Chortoryisky, family, 16, 124
Chortoryisky-Hornostai, H., 71
Chubaty, N., 43-44, 55-56, 101, 105, 110, 164, 224
Chyzhevsky, D., 87, 286
Chuikevych, F., 212, 233
Clement VIII, pope, 35
Cromwell, Oliver, 186
Cyprian, metropolitan, 59-60, 74
Cyryl, metropolitan, 58
Czaplinski, T., 176
Czarnucki, Ch., 268

D

Danilovich, edt., 164
Danylo, of Galicia, 2, 9, 59, 220
Dashkevych, O., 30, 63, 107
Derevianko, family, 336
Derevianko, I., 338, 360
Diadychenko, V., 251
Diakonov, M., 185
Dimitrii, Pretender, the, 171
Dimitrii, of Moscow, 6
Dionisius, patriarch, 259
Dionizii, bishop, 69
Divochka, O., bishop, 64

Divovych, S. 276
Dolgorukii, family, 333
Domanytsky, V., 111
Doroshenko, D., historian, XIII, 34-36, 55, 109, 111-112, 128, 144, 185, 222-225, 229, 249-251, 268, 285-286, 292, 307-310, 329-330, 378
Doroshenko, M., 173
Doroshenko, P., Hetman, 190-194, 196, 205, 213, 223, 229, 235, 237, 239, 247, 249, 258, 292, 312, 371
Dositeus, Patriarch, 259
Dostoyevsky, S., landowner, 64
Dovbush, O., 225
Dovnar-Zapolsky, M., 35
Dovsprunk, prince, 2
Drozdenko, colonel, 190
Drozdenko, "robinhood", 225
Dubrovsky, V., 367, 378
Duka, I., voyevoda, 192
Dyletsky, M., 282
Dyminsky, R., 379
Dymitrii, of Briansk, 12
Dzhydzhora, I., 329, 356, 366, 369, 378

E

Edigey, Khan, 7, 16
Efimenko, P., 291
Elizabeth, Tsaritsa, 211

F

Fedir, prince, 8-9
Fedoriv, Y., 86-87, 285
Fedorovich, I., 75, 142-143
Felz-Feins, family, 313, 333
Ferguson, W., 35
Filbers, family, 333
Filofei, monk, 35
Fiodor, Tsar, 171
Florinsky, M., 309

Freischyn-Czyrowski, see Chirovsky
Froehlich, craftsman, 349
Fylypovych, L., 84

G

Gabor, B., prince, 173
Galatovsky, I., 265, 268, 270, 275
Gedymin, 3, 6, 9, 10, 34, 37-38, 46, 48, 76
Gizel, I., 265, 270, 272
Gmelin, S., 326, 350, 355
Godunov, B., Tsar, 68, 171
Golitsin V., prince, 195, 197, 202
Golovkin, D., 202
Golovkins, family, 333
Gonta, I., 219
Gregory XIII, Pope, 78
Grotius, H., 268

H

Halecki, O., 34, 285
Helena, Hlynsky, princess, 23
Herle, craftsman, 349
Herzigs, family, 290, 336
Hildebrandt, K., 276, 279, 355
Hlikas, J., Patriarch, 59
Hloba, Cossack secretary, 215, 313
Hlynsky, M., prince, 23-24, 28, 35
Hnatevych, B., 57, 251, 356
Hobbes, T., 268
Hohol (Gogol), M., 273
Hoiska, A., 71
Holobutsky, V., 225
Holshansky, family, 63
Holshansky, I., 22
Holub, O., hetman, 173
Holubets, M., 35, 110, 163, 223, 286
Hordienko, K., 204-205, 213-214
Horlenko, D., 263, 313, 346
Hrabianka, H., 272
Hrebinka, Ye., writer, 273

Hrushevsky, M., XIII, 25, 34-36, 55-56, 76, 82, 86-87, 109-111, 121-122, 128-129, 143-144, 147, 163-164, 182, 185, 222-225, 250, 291, 330
Hryhorovych-Barsky, architect, 278
Hryhorii, Metropolitan, 62
Hryshko, V., 35, 291, 308
Hueldenstaedt, J., 318, 355
Hulagu, Khan, 4
Hulak-Artemovsky, P., 266
Hunia, D., 175
Huslystyi, K., 310
Huss, J., 67

I

Ilarion, Metropolitan, Ohienko, 87, 285-286
Iskra, I., 202, 263
Isydor, Metropolitan, 19, 61-62
Ivanenko, P. see Petryk
Ivan III, Tsar, 22, 28
Izmailov, A., 207-208

J

Jablonowski, A., 36, 85, 88, 111-112, 129
Jablonowski, family, 316
Jadwiga, of Poland, 12, 14
Jan-Casimir, of Poland, 179-180, 182, 196, 228
Janibeg, Khan, 6
Jan, of Targowiska, 35
Jan-Olbracht, of Poland, 20
Jaroshevitsky, H., 268
John III, Jan, Sobieski, of Poland, 91, 192, 198
Joseph I., Emperor, 196
Juchi, Khan, 6
Just, J., 263, 276

K

Kalinowski, M., hetman, 176, 182
Kalinowski, family, 314
Kalnyshevsky, P., Cossac, chief, 215, 280, 313
Kapnist, V., 276
Karaimovych, I., 175
Karpovich, M., 34
Kavechynsky, printer, 75
Kemmerer, D., 110
Khadji-Gerey, Khan, 16, 28
Khanenko, M., 190-191, 233, 273
Khitrovo, Russian agent, 187
Khmelnytsky, B., Hetman, XI, 169, 175-187, 190, 199, 202, 205, 211-212, 216, 228-231, 234, 248-249, 271-272, 277-278, 283, 291, 295-296, 300, 326, 331, 334, 349, 358, 360, 363-364, 368, 371, 373, 375-376, 379
Khmelnytsky, Tymish, 181-182, 186, 234
Khmelnytsky, Yurii, 186-189, 190, 192, 196, 223, 229-230, 234-235, 257
Khodkevych family, 63
Kholmsky, I., 35, 222, 248, 251, 285-286 (see also, Krypiakevych)
Kiestut, prince, 3, 10, 12
Kishka, S., 171
Kluchevskii, V., XIII, 182, 185, 222
Klymenko, P., 355
Kobrynsky, R., 329
Kochubey, V., 202, 263, 268, 313, 352
Koenigseck, F., 349
Konashevych-Sahaidachny, P., Hetman, 65, 73, 172-175, 222, 253-254, 276
Koniecpolski, A., command, 177
Koniecpolski, family, 27, 314

Koniecpolski, S., Hetman, 174, 176.
Kononenko, K., 308, 328, 355, 378
Konysky, Yu., 270
Konrad, of Masovia, 2
Konstantyn, prince, 9
Kopynsky, I., bishop, 253, 255
Kopystensky, M., bishop, 70, 253
Kopystensky, Z., abbot, 77, 270
Koriat, prince, 9
Koriatovych, F., 79
Kornis, family, 313
Korybut, prince, 12
Korzon, T., 57
Kossiv, S., metropolitan, 183, 256, 271
Kostomarov, M., 223, 273
Kostruba, T., 224
Kosynsky, K., 170
Kotovych, P., 360
Kovnir, architect, 278
Krahl, craftsman, 349
Krechetnikov, M., general, 219
Krizhanivsky, 290
Krupnytsky, B., 224, 285, 308, 324, 330, 354, 356, 378
Krychevsky, M., colonel, 176, 180, 295
Krypiakevych, I., 36, 57, 111, 129, 134, 143-144, 251, 318, 328-330, 334, 354-356, 362, 375, 377-378
Kryshkovsky, printer, 75
Kryvonis, M., colonel, 177, 248
Kublay, Khan, 4-5
Kucha, I., 64
Kulish, P., 112
Kulpa, Khan, 6
Kunov, author, 371
Kuntsevych, J., bishop, 77, 254
Kunytsky, S., Cossack, 192
Kutrzeba, S., 34, 37, 55-57, 110-111, 163-164
Kyshka, L., bishop, 262
Kysil, A., nobleman, 179, 260

L

Lappo, I., 56
Lashchenko, R., 55-56
Lassota, E., 32, 143
Latos, J., 78
Leontii, bishop, 69
Leontovych, T., 56
Lesnytsky, H., colonel, 186
Leszczynski, Stanislaw, king of Poland, 201-202, 210, 224
Lev, prince, 2, 220
Levkovych, I., 34
Litvin, M., 120, 131, 143, 164, 309
Loboda, H., Cossack chief, 32
Lodyi, P., 269
Lomonosov, M., 266
Lomykovsky, I., 266, 341, 352, 374
Louis XV, of France, 206
Löwenhaupt, Swedish general, 203, 205
Lozinski, W., 163-164
Lubart, prince, 3, 10, 12, 63
Lubavskii, M., 34-35, 112, 114, 128
Lubomirski, T., 165
Ludvig, of Hungary, 10, 12
Luke, craftsman, 349
Lukomsky, S., 272
Lupul, of Moldavia, 181-182
Lupul, R., princess, 181-182, 186, 234
Lutsiv, V., 35-36, 87
Luzhnytsky, H., 64, 86-87, 285
Lyashchenko, P., 105, 111, 129, 144, 292, 307, 309, 355, 373
Lypa, Yu., 109, 362, 377
Lypynsky, V., 185, 223, 250, 285, 291, 308
Lysytsia, I., businessman, 374
Lyzohub, Ya., 266

M

Maciej, bishop, 62
Mackiv, T., 224
Makarii, bishop, 64
Maksymovych, family, 336, 338, 360
Maksymovych, H., historian, 273
Maksymovych, I., 275
Malinin, V., 35
Malinovskii, I., 56
Mamai, Khan, 6, 7
Mangu-Temir, 5
Maria of Hungary, 12
Maria, of Vitebsk, 10
Markovych, Ya., treasurer, 273, 290, 318
Marlborough, prince, 201
Marshall, J., 317, 329, 357
Martin IV, Pope, 60
Mathew, Basarab, prince, 182
Mathew, craftsman, 349
Mauricius, Emperor, 125
Mazarin, Cardinal, 175
Mazepa, I., Hetman, 195-199, 201-203, 205, 207, 213-214, 223-224, 230-235, 237, 243, 247-248, 259, 263, 267-269, 271, 277, 279-283, 289, 291-292, 296, 299-300, 303, 313-315, 325-326, 328, 331-332, 336-338, 341, 345, 349-354, 360, 365, 368, 373-377
Meletii, Patriarch, 78
Mendog, prince, 2, 37, 44-45
Mengli-Gerey, 16, 28, 153
Menshikov, A., 201, 203-205, 208, 313, 333
Methodii, 257, 259
Meyrberg, A., 279
Mezensky, V., merchant, 360
Miakotin, V., 310, 320
Miklashevskii, I., 309
Miklashevsky, M., 263, 277, 313, 337

Miller, M., 88
Mirchuk, P., 225
Mirtchuk, I., 80, 88, 286-287
Mnohohrishny, D., Hetman, 190-191, 193-194, 223, 235, 237, 247, 249, 295, 359, 373
Modzelevsky, V., 379
Mohyla, P., Metropolitan, 74, 255-256, 260, 264-267, 270-271, 275
Mokievsky, K., 263, 337
Mokrievych, S., 275
Mongka, khan, 4
Morozenko-Mrozovytsky, S., 295
Moskowitz, 290
Mueller, J., 131, 143
Mukha, otaman, 23-24, 35
Myhura, I., engraver, 281
Mykhail, Olelkovych, prince, 22
Mykhail Romanov, of Muscovy, 28, 171
Myloradovych, O., 266
Myrovych, F., 263, 277, 337
Mysail, Metropolitan, 75

N

Nalyvaiko, S., 32, 181
Narymunt, prince, 12
Nashchynsky, D., 269
Nebaba, M., colonel, 337
Nechai, D., 181, 223, 295
Nelubovych-Tukalsky, J., Metropolitan, 192, 257-258
Nemyrych, Yu., 188, 313
Nerodych-Borodavka, Ya., 172
Nesterenko, O., 127, 292, 347, 355-356, 361, 373
Nestor, 225
Nevruz, Mongol chieftain, 6
Nicephor, clergyman, 69
Nogay, Mongol chieftain, 5
Novytsky, I., colonel, 197

O

Obolenskii, edt., 163
Obydovsky, I., 197, 202, 235
Oderbron, pastor, 72
Odoievskii, family, 26
Oginsky, family 260
Ohloblyn, O., 35, 185, 223-224, 249-250, 273, 276-277, 285-286, 291, 308-309, 313, 315, 325, 328-330, 345, 355-356, 378
Okinshevych, L., 185, 237-238, 250-251, 291, 355
Oleksander, of Poland, 20, 23, 29, 104
Oleksander, prince, 9-10
Olelko, prince, 19
Olgierd, Grand Prince, 4, 6-12, 22, 38, 45, 59
Opara, S., Hetman, 190
Opilsky, V., prince, 66
Orlyk, H., 185, 202, 206
Orlyk, P., 205-206, 210, 214, 218, 235, 290, 341, 352
Ostrianyn, Y., 175, 304, 309
Ostrozhsky, C., prince, 18, 28, 69-70, 73, 75-76, 78, 83, 117, 124, 142-143, 175
Ostrozhsky, family, 316
Ostrozhsky, J., 170

P

Palii, S., (Palyvoda), 198-200, 213, 218, 230, 291-292, 304, 306
Panchyshyn, I., 225
Passii, Patriarch, 180
Paul, of Alepo, 263, 282
Pavluk, P.,-But, 174-175
Peter I, tsar, 197, 200-204, 206-208, 214, 216, 218, 249, 266, 277, 289, 290, 349, 351, 377
Peter II, of Russia, 209
Petrov, N., 286

Petryk, Ivanenko, P., 198, 200, 213, 223, 291
Philalet, Ch., 77
Photii, Metropolitan, 17, 60-61
Piasecki, bishop, 148, 163
Pidkova, I., Cossack leader, 30, 32
Pitirim, clergyman, 257
Pogodin, M., historian, 128
Pokaz, H., 272
Polonska-Vaylenko, N., XIII, 8, 10, 25, 34-36, 55-56, 68, 86-88, 129, 143-144, 163-164, 221-225, 245, 249-251, 264, 268, 285-287, 308-310, 354, 378
Poloz, S., Cossack leader, 30-31
Polubotok, P., Hetman, 208, 224, 266, 273, 300, 366
Poniatowski, Stanislaw, King of Poland, 205, 219
Popov, O., 185
Popovsky, writer, 268
Potii, I., Metropolitan, 69, 78
Potiomkins, family, 333
Potocki, family, 124, 316
Potocki, M., Hetman, 174, 176
Potocki, P., nobleman, 199
Pototsky, economist, 371
Prokopovych, T., Archbishop, 265, 268, 270, 283
Protasiev, F., Russian agent, 208
Ptasnik, J., 102, 109, 143-144, 163, 356
Pufendorf, S., 268
Pulawski, C., 219
Pushkar, M., Cossack, 187, 292
Putuver, King, 3
Puzyna, family, 260
Pynta, 225
Pysklyvyi, 225

Q

R

Rachynsky, A., conductor, 282

Radivil, family, 104-105
Radziwil, M., prince, 180-181
Radzykevych, V., 87-88, 286
Radzyvylovsky, A., 266, 270
Rakushka, R., 272, 373, 376
Rohoza, M., Metropolitan, 70
Romodanovskii, M., 188
Rozum, O., 211
Rozumovsky, K., Hetman, 211-212, 220, 225, 235, 238, 268, 277, 279-280, 282, 284, 328, 332, 346, 352, 370
Rubricus, of Braband, 362
Rudniev, V., 379
Rudolf II, Emperor, 35
Rulikowski, E., 164
Rumiantsev, P., 221, 236, 267
Ruryk, dynasty, 8-9, 11, 22
Rutkowski, J., 110
Rutsky, V., metropolitan, 255-256, 260, 264
Ruzhynsky, B., Cossack leader, 30

S

Safanovych, T., 272
Sakovych, K., 269, 276
Samoilovych, H., 195, 223
Samoilovych, I., Hetman, 190-192, 194-196, 233-235, 237, 243, 258-259, 263, 266, 271, 277-278, 289, 300, 305, 325-326, 334, 336-337, 360, 368, 371, 373, 376
Samoilovych, S., 235
Samoilovych, Ya., 235
Samus, S., colonel, 199
Sartak, Khan, 4
Schädel, G., 278
Sergeievich, V., 185
Shakh, otaman, 32
Shakhovskii, A., 210, 236
Sheremieitiev, family, 333
Sheremietiev, B., field-marshall, 202, 224

Sheremietiev, P., *voyevoda*, 186, 258
Shevchenko, T., 273
Shuhaievsky, A., 378-379
Shuiskii, V., Tsar, 171
Shuman, S., 355
Shumlansky, J., bishop, 217, 262
Shvarno, prince, 2
Shymansky, 308
Shyrai, family, 336, 338, 360
Sichynsky, V., 87-88, 128-129, 143-144, 276, 285-287, 308-309, 329, 346, 352, 354-356, 377
Sigismund, Emperor, 16
Sigismund, of Lithuania, 18-21, 62
Sigismund, of Poland, 23-25, 103
Sigismund, prince, 12
Sigismund-August, of Poland, 25, 108
Sigismund III, Vasa, 27, 91-92, 174
Sirko, I., Cossack leader, 190, 213
Sixtus IV, pope, 75
Skoropadsky, I., Hetman, 203-204, 206-209, 211, 224, 233, 240, 245, 273, 313, 332, 334, 337-338, 360, 368-370, 372, 376
Skorupis, family, 336
Skoryna, F., 75
Skovoroda, H., 266, 269, 275, 286
Skydan, colonel, 175
Slabchenko, M., 111, 116, 128, 143, 295, 308, 312-313, 315, 317-318, 320, 328, 351, 354, 356, 378
Slozka, M., 143
Smirnov, V., 34
Smolatych, K., Metropolitan, 60
Smotrytsky, H., 73, 78
Smotrytsky, M., 73, 77, 253-256, 260
Solomyretsky, family, 260
Somko, Ya., Cossack leader, 192
Stadnicki, A., 330

Startsiv, F., 278
Startsiv, J., 278
Stavrovetsky, C., 269-270, 276
Stefanovych, V., 233
Stefan-Silvester, clergyman, 64
Stephan, the Great, of Moldavia, 23
Stetkevych, family, 260
Stockl, G., 35
Strassburger, Swedish envoy, 173
Stroganovs, family, 333
Stukas, J., 34
Sukhovienko, or Sukhovii, P. Cossack leader, 190-191
Sulyma, I., Cossack leader, 174
Susha, Ya., clergyman, 261
Sviatopolk-Chetvertynsky, G., 258-259, 261
Svidrigiello, prince, 17-21, 24, 35, 62
Sylenko, family, 341
Symonovsky, P., 272
Szelagowski, A., 129, 158, 164

T

Tamerlane, 6-7
Tarasevych, O., 281
Tarnawski, family, 27
Tekeley, P., general, 215
Tele-Buga, Khan, 5
Temudzhin, Khan, 6
Teodoryt, Metropolitan, 59
Terletsky, C., bishop, 69
Teteria, P., Hetman, 189-190, 196, 235, 295
Teterivsky, I., 360
Theognost, Metropolitan, 59
Theophan, Patriarch, 253, 255, 271
Tieplov, H., 211, 225
Timur-Melik, Khan, 7
Tinibeg, Khan, 6
Tisha, M., colonel, 337
Titov, F., 286

Tokhmatish, 6-7, 16
Tokhta, Khan, 5
Tomaris, family, 336
Tovtovil, prince, 2
Triasylo, T., Cossack leader, 174
Troiden, prince, 2
Trubetskoi, family, 26
Trubetskoi, S., 188
Tsamblak, H., Metropolitan, 17, 60, 75
Tuda-Mangu, Khan, 5
Tuptalo, D., 266, 268, 270, 275, 283
Tyapinsky, V., 75
Tykhorsky, Ye., bishop, 267
Tyshkevich, family, 116

U

Ulagchi, Khan, 4
Ulianov, N., 35
Urus, Khan, 7
Uzbek, Khan, 5-6

V

Vasilii I, of Muscovy, 14
Vasilii III, of Muscovy, 23
Vasylenko, M., 224
Vasylovich, M., 75
Vedel, A., 282-283
Veliaminov, S., 208, 236
Velychkivsky, I., 275
Velychko, S., 272
Vernadsky, G., XIII, 34
Veselaho, V., 372, 379
Viazemskii, family, 333
Viginere, de, B., 122, 129
Vitovt, grand prince, 12-18, 21-22, 28, 39, 45-46, 49, 60-61, 76, 91, 104-105
Vladimirskii-Budanov, M., 112
Vlasovsky, I., 285
Voishelk, prince, 2
Volobuyev, M., 315
Volodymyr, the Great, 1, 179, 271, 283
Volodymyr, Olgierd's son, prince, 8, 9, 12, 63
Vorontsov, family, 313, 333
Vorotynskii, family, 26
Vostokov, A., 223
Voynarovsky, A., 202, 235
Vyhovsky, I., Hetman, 181, 186-188, 196, 213, 233-235, 237, 257, 290-292, 295, 333, 359
Vynnytsky, I., bishop, 262
Vyrnyk, D., 144, 292, 355, 373, 379
Vyshensky, I., 77
Vyshnyvetsky, family, 27, 124, 316
Vyshnyvetsky, Ya., prince, 177
Vyshnyvetsky-Baida, D., Cossack leader, 30-31, 177
Vytvytsky, V., 287

W

Weihe, a Swedish officer, 317, 351
Weissbach, family, 333
Weisse, craftsman, 349
Werdum, U., 120, 124-125, 355
Wisniowiecki, see Vyshnyvetsky
Wladyslaw IV, of Poland, 27, 171, 177, 179, 255
Wladyslaw, Warnenczyk, of Poland, 20, 29
Wolf, J., 34

X

Y

Yagiello, Jagiello, of Poland, 11-18, 45-46, 60, 66, 76, 91
Yakim, yerodiakon, 34
Yakovliv, A., 55, 185, 223, 225, 245, 250-251
Yaniv, V., 88, 287

Yarmolynska, R., 71
Yaroshevych, A., 341, 355
Yaroslav, I., the Wise, 38, 179
Yavorsky, S., 268, 270-271, 275
Yazlovetsky, Yu., 108
Yelizarov, monk, 35
Yeremiah, Patriarch, 68
Yevarnitskii, D., 35
Yona, Metropolitan, 62, 64
Yosyf, Metropolitan, 64
Yov, Metropolitan, 68
Yurii, prince, 9
Yurii-Boleslav, of Galicia, 3, 10, 138
Yurii, Narymuntovych, prince, 10

Z

Zahorovsky, V., 72, 75
Zalizniak, M., Haidamaky leader, 219
Zamoiski, family, 27, 116, 124, 314, 316
Zaslavsky, family, 16, 316
Zaslawski, D., 177
Zazanii, L., 78
Zborovsky, S., 30
Zernikau, A., 278
Zhdanovych, A., colonel, 234
Zhokhovsky, C., Metropolitan, 261-262, 264, 267
Zhmailo, M., Cossack leader, 173
Zhuiev, V., 276, 279
Zinoviiv, C., 275
Zolkiewski, S., Hetman, 170-171
Zolotarenko, I., colonel, 337
Zolotarenko, V., 192
Zubrytsky, N., engraver, 281